Creating Immersive Learning Experiences Through Virtual Reality (VR)

Shaik Mazhar Hussain
Middle East College, Oman

Ahmed Nawaz Hakro
Middle East College, Oman

A volume in the Advances in Educational Technologies and Instructional Design (AETID) Book Series

IGI Global
Publishing Tomorrow's Research Today

Published in the United States of America by
IGI Global
Information Science Reference (an imprint of IGI Global)
701 E. Chocolate Avenue
Hershey PA, USA 17033
Tel: 717-533-8845
Fax: 717-533-8661
E-mail: cust@igi-global.com
Web site: http://www.igi-global.com

Library of Congress Cataloging-in-Publication Data

CIP PENDING

ISBN13: 9798369364079
Isbn13Softcover: 9798369364086
EISBN13: 9798369364093

British Cataloguing in Publication Data
A Cataloguing in Publication record for this book is available from the British Library.

For electronic access to this publication, please contact: eresources@igi-global.com.

Table of Contents

Detailed Table of Contents

The recent decades have been characterised by significant technological advancements, resulting in the creation of innovative products and services. These developments have sparked numerous new inventions and discoveries that were previously unimaginable. Virtual reality has emerged as a promising technology in the field of education, offering immersive and interactive experiences that can enhance learning outcomes. However, several challenges and limitations need to be addressed for its effective integration into educational environments. The purpose of this chapter is to investigate the challenges and limitations associated with the integration of virtual reality technology in educational settings by examining the existing literature and conducting a systematic literature review. Additionally, it seeks to propose viable solutions to address these challenges and enhance the effectiveness of virtual reality applications in education. A systematic literature approach was employed to identify, analyse, and synthesise thirteen studies on its challenges and limitations in education. The initial learning barriers, lack of virtual reality-specific pedagogy, financial costs, technical skills and resources, the effectiveness of virtual reality technology and applications, as well as computer quality, reduced human interaction and communication, users' readiness and attitude towards virtual reality technology and teaching in virtual environments were identified as educational challenges. The limitations consisted of design, health issues, technological and accessibility, cognitive demand and unfulfilled promises. Based on the findings, recommendations were provided for educators, developers, and policymakers to be equipped with the necessary knowledge to make informed decisions and tools to effectively integrate virtual reality into educational settings. By addressing these challenges and limitations, virtual reality has the potential to effectively revolutionise education and enhance learning experiences for students.

This chapter will address the challenges and ethical considerations of integrating technology into education for all educators. It will highlight limited access and support, the shift to emergency remote teaching, challenges in developing countries, obstacles to technology integration, and ethical concerns in using virtual reality. The chapter will conclude by discussing future trends in technology for education. By addressing these challenges and ethical considerations, technology will effectively enhance learning outcomes and promote equitable access to education for all educators.

Virtual reality simulation has revolutionized the healthcare sector by fusing human skills with cutting-edge technology to promote patient-centered care, clinical efficacy, and a compassionate digital healthcare ecosystem. In order to enhance nursing education by providing dynamic and engaging learning settings, the goal of this research is to assess the transformative potential of virtual reality. Through familiarization with state-of-the-art technology through the use of immersive pedagogy and technology framework, the paper proposed a fresh way to nursing education and clinical practice. Student nurses can fully immerse themselves in a personalized virtual reality as if they were actually there, interact with their surroundings, and learn in a dynamic and pedagogically informative digital ecosystem by donning VR headgear or goggles. Virtual reality can be used to create incredibly lifelike simulations that allow trainee nurses to practice problem-solving skills without really putting themselves in danger as clinical simulation offers deep understanding of real-world situations.

Virtual reality (VR) technology has emerged as a promising tool in education, offering immersive and interactive learning experiences that transcend the limitations of traditional teaching methods. There is a gap in leveraging technology to enhance learning experiences beyond traditional methods. The research aims to design VR learning environments by synthesizing insights from existing literature to identify key strategies and principles for creating impactful educational experiences. The study delves into both technical and pedagogical aspects of VR design, highlighting the importance of immersion, interactivity, alignment with learning objectives, and inclusivity. Furthermore, the research discusses future trends and implications for educators, instructional designers, researchers, policymakers, and educational leaders. Overall, this study contributes to advancing the understanding of how VR technology can revolutionize education and empower learners in the digital age.

Virtual reality (VR) is an immersive technology that simulates three-dimensional environments, allowing users to interact with virtual worlds through specialized hardware and software. This chapter explores the evolution of VR, its applications in education, and the integration of artificial intelligence (AI) to enhance user experience. VR's immersive capabilities foster active learning by enabling students to engage with content in ways that traditional methods cannot replicate. Theoretical foundations such as constructivism and experiential learning support the use of VR in educational settings, while practical applications include virtual field trips, simulations, and language learning environments. However, challenges such as high costs and potential accessibility issues must be addressed. This chapter concludes by emphasizing the need for ongoing research and collaboration to fully harness VR's potential in future education and other sectors.

This chapter delves into the comparative effectiveness of virtual reality (VR) against the traditional educational methods, underscoring not only the initial financial outlays associated with VR—such as hardware acquisition and content development—but also evaluating these against the recurrent costs inherent in conventional education systems. The intent is to provide comprehensive long-term economic and educational benefits of investment in VR. The chapter offers VR's ability to enhance learning outcomes through immersive, interactive experiences that traditional methods alternatively might not offer. This includes a detailed examination of VR's scalability and its capacity to reach diverse learners across geographical boundaries without the recurring costs associated with physical infrastructures. Moreover, the economic evaluation may provide the extended assessment of VR's potential for reducing costs associated with learning delays, educational disparities, and the provision of customized learning experiences, which are often more logistically and financially demanding within traditional frameworks. In addition to this, the chapter is likely going to address the broader societal and educational benefits, such as increased accessibility for disadvantaged and differently abled students, and the potential for global classrooms that offer unified learning experiences to students from varying socio-economic backgrounds. Through these discussions, the chapter will argue that VR does not merely replace traditional learning methods but significantly enhances educational value, thereby justifying its adoption as a forward-thinking educational technology.

This chapter investigates the potentially transformative implications of integrating virtual reality technology into the field of electrical and instrumentation engineering to enhance the educational experience and change the traditional way that students study and experiment with electronic instrumentation by utilizing the future possibilities of virtual reality. Electronics and instrumentation have consistently been at the center of modern technological development, powering industry, health care, and scientific study. However, considering its important function in developing this world of teaching, taking complicated topics related to instrumentation remains a difficulty. As a student in this specialization, the author has personally faced and encountered the restrictions of the traditional laboratory environments in universities, where most physical components are frequently in short supply, costly, or even unreachable.

Virtual reality (VR) can completely transform traditional teaching techniques, as this chapter explores its long-term effects in education. It draws attention to the short-term advantages, such as increased engagement and better retention of knowledge, but it also draws attention to the knowledge vacuum about its long-term effects. Pedagogical alignment, curricular integration, professional development, access and equity, and assessment and evaluation are important components that lead to effective integration. The study provides evidence-based suggestions on how to maximize virtual reality's potential to improve learning outcomes for educators, legislators, and stakeholders. Investing in professional development, encouraging teamwork, putting fairness and access first, coordinating VR experiences with curricular standards, carrying out continuous assessment and research, and promoting interdisciplinary and project-based learning are some of the main suggestions.

This study explores how postgraduate students utilize Microsoft Copilot in a virtual reality (VR) environment. From January to February 2024, 125 students participated in the experiment, tasked with crafting assignments directly within Copilot. Using three scales for data collection, including the technology readiness index, extended reality presence scale, and AI technology adoption, the study found positive correlations between technology readiness and both extended reality presence and AI technology adoption. Linear regression analysis showed technology readiness as a significant predictor for both extended reality presence and AI technology adoption, explaining approximately 20.6% and 42.1% of the variability, respectively. These findings emphasize the crucial role of technology readiness in shaping student engagement with emerging technologies.

With the advancement of technology, digital gadgets have progressively become tools for educational pedagogy, enabling the widespread application of virtual reality (VR) and augmented reality (AR) in healthcare education. Neurological rehabilitation, telemedicine, psychotherapy, medical education, and surgical simulation are among the fields in which VR and AR are used. Studies have shown that VR and AR can reduce medical errors resulting from incompetent medical personnel, lessen the inconvenience of traditional medical care, and save medical education and training costs. The application has improved the quality of diagnosis and treatment, raised the bar for medical education and training, and strengthened the bond between clinicians and patients. In an effort to assist clinical professionals in enhancing the standard of care they provide, this study integrates VR and AR technologies into medical-clinical practice, utilizing Actor Network(ANT) model to develop a conceptual framework for the implementation of AR/VR pedagogy simulation on artificial intelligence training platform.

Smart learning in virtual worlds refers to the use of virtual reality (VR) and other immersive technologies to enhance the learning experience. Smart learning in virtual worlds has the potential to revolutionize education and training by providing engaging, adaptive, and immersive experiences in various domains. For this study, the literature on smart learning in distance education has been mapped through Vosviewer. In this research, bibliometric visualizing methods are used with the help of Vosviewer to analyze the different outcomes. Co-occurrences of author keywords and bibliographic couplings of the countries, authors, journals, and institutions are depicted via the software. The initial search on Scopus was performed with "smart learning or virtual learning" and "distance education" which fetched 645 documents. Based on the language of the article, the authors found 587 articles which were published in English. The second basis was the source type that included Journal articles, conference proceedings and book chapters and the authors found 440 articles for the study.

This chapter will delve into the world of virtual reality (VR) and its profound impact on kindergarten education. By offering young students immersive experiences that pique their curiosity, encourage exploration, and improve learning outcomes, VR-based teaching strategies present a novel way to engage students. In addition to discussing the many advantages of virtual reality in kindergarten classrooms, this chapter offers educators helpful advice on how to incorporate VR technology into their lesson plans. Furthermore, this chapter contains several sections of VR-based teaching strategies for kindergarten classes.

Virtual reality (VR) has transitioned from a futuristic concept to a practical tool with wide-ranging applications in engineering. By immersing users in interactive digital environments, VR enhances spatial understanding, improves design accuracy, and facilitates comprehensive testing. This chapter explores the transformative potential of VR across various engineering fields, emphasizing its impact on design, simulation, training, and maintenance processes. This chapter covers the integration of VR in mechanical, civil, and biomedical engineering, highlighting its benefits in prototyping, fluid dynamics, architectural visualization, safety training, surgical simulation, and more. The future of VR in engineering looks promising, with advancements in AI and sensor technology poised to further revolutionize the field. Through detailed exploration, this chapter provides insights into the multifaceted applications of VR, showcasing its ability to drive innovation and improve outcomes across the engineering industry.

The learning technique that involves the learners in facilitating training in a virtual environment hence extends traditional mode of training that was considered new, is known as virtual reality learning. In this chapter, the author examines experiences of technology use in schools specifically in the classroom and then evaluates implications of the use of virtual reality. This study endeavours to expose the specified literature review approach, the definition and guidelines of the integration of VR in education, a systematic approach and case studies in an endeavour of analysing how this technological innovation could contribute to the students' interest, understanding, and recall of issues, matters, and concepts, regardless of discipline and academic year. Therefore, considering the standpoint of the virtual reality integration as one of the effective learning strategies in education, the issues, including high costs, the technical issue, and the lack of professional development concerning VR for educators, must be addressed for this technology to meet its potential. Besides, the guidelines are given for obtaining the optimal results from VR in context of education and for making sure that the opportunities which are derived out from it are reasonable, reachable, and sustainable in nature, which have also been enclosed in the conclusion part of the chapter.

Preface

In the evolving landscape of education, the quest for engaging and effective learning experiences has led educators and researchers to explore the latest technologies. Among these innovations, virtual reality (VR) stands out as a transformative tool with the potential to redefine how we transmit and absorb information. *Creating Immersive Learning Experiences Through Virtual Reality (VR)* embarks on a journey to unlock the full potential of VR in education. This book serves as a comprehensive guide for educators, technologists, and enthusiasts, aiming to create learning environments that are not only informative but truly transformative.

Integrating VR into education is not merely a technical innovation; it is a pedagogical revolution. It marks a shift from passive learning to active learning, where students are not just observers but active participants in their educational journey. The purpose of this book is to illuminate the path to integrating VR into educational environments and highlight its potential to make learning more immersive, accessible, and effective.

VR's ability to simulate real-world scenarios and immerse students in environments otherwise inaccessible or impractical for traditional education opens new horizons for learning. Whether studying the complex functions of the human body or traveling through space, VR makes the impossible possible, transforming abstract concepts into concrete experiences. This book delves into the science behind why immersive learning is so effective, exploring concepts such as presence, embodiment, and the cognitive mechanisms that support learning in virtual environments.

Creating Immersive Learning Experiences Through Virtual Reality (VR) also offers practical guidance for educators and institutions looking to implement VR in their educational practices. This includes technical aspects, from choosing the right hardware and software to designing pedagogically sound and engaging VR content. We address challenges of accessibility and inclusion, ensuring that all students benefit from VR in education, regardless of background or ability.

Beyond the technical and pedagogical aspects, this book also addresses the ethical considerations of using VR in education. We explore the responsibilities of those who create and implement VR experiences, ensuring that they promote positive learning outcomes without unintended consequences.

As we enter a new era in education, *Creating Immersive Learning Experiences Through Virtual Reality (VR)* serves as both a beacon and a guide. It challenges educators, developers, and policymakers to look beyond the novelty of VR technology and embrace its potential to transform learning. Through a combination of theoretical insights and practical advice, this book paves the way for a future where education is not just about imparting knowledge but creating meaningful and memorable learning experiences that inspire and empower students.

The primary objective of this book is twofold: to provide educators, developers, and policymakers with the knowledge and tools needed to effectively integrate VR into educational environments and to stimulate discussion about the pedagogical implications and possibilities of VR in learning. By achieving these goals, the book aims to significantly advance the practical and theoretical dimensions of both educational technology and pedagogy.

One of the main goals of this book is to bridge the gap between theoretical research in learning science and the practical application of VR in teaching. We bring together a wide range of research findings from cognitive psychology, educational theory, and digital learning environments, presenting them in an accessible and usable way for practitioners. This not only helps frame VR education practices in sound pedagogical principles but also provides a foundation for further research.

With detailed case studies, practical guides, and examples of successful VR implementation, this book empowers teachers to use VR creatively and effectively in teaching. By doing so, it expands the tools available to teachers, enabling more personalized, engaging, and effective learning. These guidelines are supported by extensive research to ensure that recommended approaches are both innovative and evidence-based.

The book also promotes ongoing research by providing a comprehensive analysis of current research, identifying gaps in the literature, and suggesting new directions for future research. We examine the effectiveness of VR for different learning goals and populations, the psychological effects of VR learning environments, and pedagogical strategies that optimize learning outcomes. By critiquing existing research and pushing the boundaries of what we currently understand, this book serves as a catalyst for further research and experimentation in the field.

Addressing ethical aspects and promoting inclusive practices adds an important dimension to the educational technology debate. We encourage educators, developers, and policymakers to consider the broader implications of VR technology, including privacy issues, accessibility challenges, and potential biases. At the forefront of these discussions, this book ensures that the integration of VR into education is fair, responsible, and beneficial for all learners.

Creating Immersive Learning Experiences Through Virtual Reality (VR) is carefully crafted to serve a broad readership with a shared interest in harnessing the transformative potential of VR in education. The content and structure have been developed to provide valuable knowledge and practical advice to the following target groups:

Educators and Teachers: This book is an essential resource for teachers and educators at various education levels, from primary to higher education. They will discover in-depth pedagogical strategies, practical examples, and case studies that illuminate how to integrate VR into their teaching practices, enhancing student engagement, understanding, and retention.

Instructional Designers and Curriculum Developers: Instructional designers and curriculum developers tasked with creating innovative and effective learning experiences will benefit from exploring the pedagogical implications of VR and guidelines for designing VR content. The book provides a framework and principles for integrating VR technologies in ways that complement and enhance existing curricula.

Educational Technologists and IT Professionals: For those interested in educational technology, including educational technicians and IT specialists, the book offers a comprehensive overview of the hardware, software, and technical aspects needed to implement VR in educational environments. It serves as a guide for making informed decisions about technology selection and infrastructure development.

Researchers and Academics: Academics and researchers in educational technology, cognitive psychology, and learning sciences will find the book's critical analysis of current research and its suggestions for future directions of study particularly valuable. It not only summarizes existing findings but also identifies gaps in the literature and explores the potential of VR to address long-standing educational challenges.

Education Policymakers and Administrators: Educational policymakers and administrators will benefit from exploring the book's broader implications for VR integration, including policy considerations, ethical issues, and accessibility challenges. The book provides a roadmap for the complex stages of implementing new technologies in educational institutions, ensuring VR implementations are fair and effective.

Technology Developers and Entrepreneurs: Finally, technology developers and entrepreneurs in educational technology will find a comprehensive understanding of the needs of the education sector, the pedagogical aspects of VR, and the market opportunities for VR applications in education. It provides a window into the future of educational experiences and the role technology can play in shaping that future.

Essentially, *Creating Immersive Learning Experiences Through Virtual Reality (VR)* is designed to serve diverse audiences, all of whom play a central role in the educational ecosystem. Offering a multidimensional perspective on VR in education, the book aims to inspire, inform, and empower its readers to create meaningful and transformative learning experiences.

Chapter 1 delves into the multifaceted challenges and limitations associated with integrating virtual reality (VR) technology within educational environments. Utilizing the diffusion of innovation theory as a theoretical framework, this chapter explores initial learning barriers, the absence of VR-specific pedagogy, financial constraints, technical resource limitations, VR's effectiveness, computer quality concerns, reduced human interaction, and users' readiness and attitudes towards VR. Additionally, the chapter identifies limitations related to design, health issues, technological accessibility, and cognitive demands. It concludes by offering recommendations for educators, developers, and policymakers to make informed decisions about VR's integration into education.

Chapter 2 examines the ethical considerations and challenges faced by educators in integrating technology into educational settings. It highlights issues such as limited access and support, the shift to emergency remote teaching, challenges in developing countries, and obstacles in technology integration. Ethical concerns related to VR usage are also discussed, concluding with future trends in educational technology. By addressing these challenges, this chapter aims to enhance learning outcomes and promote equitable access to education through effective technology integration.

Chapter 3 explores the transformative potential of virtual reality (VR) in healthcare education, particularly nursing. By integrating immersive pedagogy and technology frameworks, VR simulation is presented as a revolutionary tool that enhances patient-centered care and clinical efficacy. Nursing students can engage in dynamic, realistic simulations that foster problem-solving skills without real-world risks. This chapter underscores VR's ability to create engaging learning environments that contribute to a compassionate and efficient digital healthcare ecosystem.

Focusing on designing VR learning environments, chapter 4 synthesizes insights from existing literature to outline key strategies and principles for effective educational experiences. It emphasizes the importance of immersion, interactivity, alignment with learning objectives, and inclusivity in VR design. The chapter also explores future trends and implications for educators, instructional designers, researchers, policymakers, and educational leaders, highlighting VR technology's revolutionary potential in empowering learners in the digital age.

Chapter 5 explores the evolution of virtual reality (VR) and its integration with artificial intelligence (AI) to enhance educational experiences. By enabling immersive and interactive learning, VR fosters active engagement that traditional methods cannot replicate. The chapter examines VR's theoretical foundations, practical applications, challenges, and the need for ongoing research to fully harness VR's potential in education. It also highlights VR's capabilities in virtual field trips, simulations, and language learning, underscoring the importance of addressing cost and accessibility issues.

Chapter 6 investigates the comparative effectiveness and economic implications of virtual reality (VR) against traditional educational methods. It evaluates initial financial outlays associated with VR, such as hardware acquisition and content development, and assesses these against the recurring costs inherent in conventional education systems. The chapter highlights VR's ability to enhance learning outcomes through immersive experiences, scalability, and its potential for reducing educational disparities, offering a comprehensive analysis of VR's long-term economic and educational benefits.

Chapter 7 explores the transformative implications of integrating virtual reality (VR) into electrical and instrumentation engineering education. By leveraging VR technology, students can engage with complex topics related to instrumentation in innovative ways. The chapter addresses traditional laboratory environment limitations, such as costly or inaccessible physical components, and demonstrates how VR can revolutionize the study and experimentation of electronic instrumentation, ultimately enhancing the educational experience.

Chapter 8 reviews the long-term effects of virtual reality (VR) in education, highlighting its potential to transform traditional teaching methods. While acknowledging short-term advantages like increased engagement and knowledge retention, the chapter emphasizes the need for evidence-based suggestions to maximize VR's potential. Key components for effective integration include pedagogical alignment, curricular integration, professional development, access, equity, and assessment. By addressing these components, the chapter aims to improve learning outcomes and promote sustainable VR integration in education.

Chapter 9 examines how postgraduate students utilize Microsoft Copilot in a virtual reality (VR) environment. By analyzing data from 125 students using scales such as the Technology Readiness Index and AI Technology Adoption, the study highlights positive correlations between technology readiness, extended reality presence, and AI adoption. The chapter emphasizes the significance of technology readiness in shaping student engagement with emerging technologies, offering insights into the potential of VR and AI in education.

Chapter 10 explores the integration of virtual reality (VR) and augmented reality (AR) in healthcare education, highlighting their impact on fields such as neurological rehabilitation, telemedicine, psychotherapy, and surgical simulation. By reducing medical errors, lowering education costs, and improving diagnosis and treatment quality, VR and AR enhance medical education and training. The chapter introduces a conceptual framework for implementing AR/VR pedagogy simulation in medical practice, aiming to improve clinical professionals' standard of care.

Chapter 11 examines the potential of smart learning in virtual worlds, utilizing VR and immersive technologies to revolutionize education. Through bibliometric visualizing methods, the study maps the literature on smart learning in distance education, analyzing outcomes through Vosviewer. By exploring co-occurrences of author keywords and bibliographic couplings, the chapter provides insights into smart learning's potential to enhance engagement, adaptability, and immersive experiences, ultimately transforming education and training.

Chapter 12 explores the profound impact of virtual reality (VR) on kindergarten education, offering immersive experiences that engage young students and improve learning outcomes. By incorporating VR technology into lesson plans, educators can foster curiosity, exploration, and creativity. The chapter provides practical advice for integrating VR into kindergarten classrooms, highlighting VR-based teaching strategies that enhance student engagement and offer innovative approaches to early childhood education.

Chapter 13 examines virtual reality's (VR) transformative potential across various engineering fields, emphasizing its impact on design, simulation, training, and maintenance processes. By enhancing spatial understanding, design accuracy, and comprehensive testing, VR drives innovation in mechanical, civil, and biomedical engineering. The chapter explores VR's applications in prototyping, fluid dynamics, architectural visualization, safety training, and surgical simulation, showcasing its ability to revolutionize the engineering industry.

Chapter 14 focuses on the effectiveness of virtual reality (VR) as an instructional method, examining its impact on learners' attention, understanding, and recall across various subjects. Through a literature review and case studies, the chapter highlights VR's potential to revolutionize education by increasing motivation and offering personalized learning experiences. Despite challenges related to costs and technical complexity, the chapter emphasizes VR's ability to enhance learner engagement and understanding.

Chapter 15 introduces the MEB-VR model, developed for the Turkish education sector, particularly for applied and laboratory courses. By addressing challenges in selecting the best VR headsets for educational use, the study utilizes the Combinative Distance-based Assessment (CODAS) method with circular Pythagorean fuzzy sets. The chapter demonstrates VR's potential to transform traditional education methods, offering innovative solutions for VR-based education approaches.

Chapter 16 investigates the use of immersive virtual reality (VR) as a tool to aid students in selecting their academic specializations. By enhancing experiential learning, VR provides insights into the factors influencing students' choices and satisfaction levels. The chapter offers valuable guidance for educators, career counselors, and students, highlighting the potential of VR to support informed decision-making and foster personal fulfillment in academic pursuits.

Covering a wide range of topics, this book provides readers with a comprehensive understanding of VR in education, its applications, benefits, challenges, and future directions. A few topics include:

- Introduction to Virtual Reality in Education
- Theoretical Foundations of VR Learning
- Practical Applications of VR in Education
- Accessibility and Inclusivity in VR Learning
- Psychological and Social Considerations
- Implementing VR in Educational Institutions
- The Future of VR in Education

We invite you to join us on this journey of exploration and discovery, as we uncover the potential of VR to transform education and create immersive learning experiences that are impactful and lasting.

Acknowledgment

We thank everyone for their valuable contributions to this edited book titled *Creating Immersive Learning Experiences Through Virtual Reality (VR)*. Our profound thanks extend to IGI Global Book Publishers for their continuous support and guidance throughout the completion of this project. We appreciate all the insightful *reviewers* who have dedicated their time and expertise to reviewing the chapters promptly, ensuring the quality and rigor of the content, and their valuable suggestions and suggested improvements to the content. We are also immensely grateful to all the contributing authors and their contributions, as well as their insightful discussions, diverse perspectives, and expertise in their respective areas of interest.

We thank all of you for being a part of this journey.

Regards,

Shaik Mazhar Hussain

Middle East College, Oman

Ahmed Nawaz Hakro

Middle East College, Oman

Chapter 1
A Systematic Review of the Challenges and Limitations of VR in Education

Joelle Danielle J. D. Ngo Ndjama
https://orcid.org/0000-0002-2472-2329
Vaal University of Technology, South Africa

Johan Van Der Westhuizen
Vaal University of Technology, South Africa

ABSTRACT

The recent decades have been characterised by significant technological advancements, resulting in the creation of innovative products and services. These developments have sparked numerous new inventions and discoveries that were previously unimaginable. Virtual reality has emerged as a promising technology in the field of education, offering immersive and interactive experiences that can enhance learning outcomes. However, several challenges and limitations need to be addressed for its effective integration into educational environments. The purpose of this chapter is to investigate the challenges and limitations associated with the integration of virtual reality technology in educational settings by examining the existing literature and conducting a systematic literature review. Additionally, it seeks to propose viable solutions to address these challenges and enhance the effectiveness of virtual reality applications in education. A systematic literature approach was employed to identify, analyse, and synthesise thirteen studies on its challenges and limitations in education. The initial learning barriers, lack of virtual reality-specific pedagogy, financial costs, technical skills and resources, the

DOI: 10.4018/979-8-3693-6407-9.ch001

effectiveness of virtual reality technology and applications, as well as computer quality, reduced human interaction and communication, users' readiness and attitude towards virtual reality technology and teaching in virtual environments were identified as educational challenges. The limitations consisted of design, health issues, technological and accessibility, cognitive demand and unfulfilled promises. Based on the findings, recommendations were provided for educators, developers, and policymakers to be equipped with the necessary knowledge to make informed decisions and tools to effectively integrate virtual reality into educational settings. By addressing these challenges and limitations, virtual reality has the potential to effectively revolutionise education and enhance learning experiences for students.

1. INTRODUCTION

Recent decades have been characterised by significant technological advancements, resulting in the creation of innovative products and services. These developments have sparked numerous new inventions and discoveries that were previously unimaginable (Wani & Ali, 2015). Among these remarkable innovations, virtual reality (VR) stands out as a significant achievement. LaValle (2023) posits that VR is a powerful technology that promises to change people's lives, unlike any other. It is like a waking dream that could take place in a magical cartoon-like world or could transport people to another part of the earth or universe (LaValle, 2023). The VR technology market has been expanding in tandem with its rapid advancement, with a projected global market size surge from US$ 7.3 billion in 2018 to US$ 120.5 billion in 2026 (Fortune Business Insights, 2019). Compared to 2019 statistics, the analysis of the VR market 5 years later reveals that it is projected to grow significantly in the coming years (Mordor Intelligence, 2024). With an estimated market size of USD 67.66 billion in 2024, it is expected to reach USD 204.35 billion by 2029. This growth is attributed to a compound annual growth rate (CAGR) of 24.74% during the forecast period of 2024-2029 (Mordor Intelligence, 2024). VR is being increasingly utilised in the field of education, not just for gaming and entertainment purposes (Wohlgenannt, Simons & Stieglitz, 2020). The authors argue that it is commonly used for corporate training as well as for university students and in schools and various companies, such as VR Immersive Education and Google Expeditions, which have introduced VR applications specifically designed for classroom use. These applications cover a wide range of subjects, including anatomy, geography, history, physics, and chemistry (Wohlgenannt et al., 2020). Hence, Lege and Bonner (2020) point out that educators have witnessed the progression of VR as a practical tool in classrooms worldwide through various innovations. These computer-generated spaces, known for their immersive and interactive features, present a different approach to conventional educational settings, offering a space where learning can be both stimulating and efficient (Damaševicius & Sidekerskiene, 2024). The study of innovation, specifically VR, is crucial in today's globalised and competitive world where technological advancements, rapidly changing markets, and high customer expectations for quality services are prevalent. It is widely recognised as a key driver of competitive advantage and economic growth (Damanpour & Schneider, 2006).

VR has become a captivating and auspicious area of interest; however, its utilisation within different settings introduces distinct opportunities and obstacles (Damaševicius & Sidekerskiene, 2024). Scavarelli, Arya, and Teather (2020) emphasise that the main hurdle in integrating VR into education lies in the necessity to skilfully harness this technology to enhance student learning without merely duplicating or replacing the conventional classroom setting. This delves into the limitations and challenges faced by educators in effectively harnessing the potential of VR to enrich the educational experience of students, while also ensuring that it does not merely serve as a superficial substitute for traditional teaching methods. As noted by Lege and Bonner (2020), educators have long pondered the potential of VR as a beneficial tool in their teaching practices. However, they have not yet understood how to leverage VR to its fullest extent, ensuring that it enhances the learning process and fosters student engagement, rather than simply acting as a flashy add-on that fails to deliver meaningful educational benefits. Moreover, the continuous evolution of VR technology, characterised by its rapidly changing attributes, applications, and educational advantages, poses limitations for teachers to grasp its true essence and its possible contributions to their instructional settings (Lege & Bonner, 2020). Thus, this chapter aims to identify the challenges and limitations that hinder the adoption and effective implementation of VR technology in educational settings. Moreover, the study seeks to (1) analyse the various challenges faced by educators, students, and institutions when utilising VR technology for educational purposes, such as technical limitations, cost constraints, and the need for specialised training. (2) Comprehend the limitations of the implementation of VR in educational settings such as the lack of VR-specific pedagogy, cognitive demand and immersion breaking. 3) Shed light on the areas that require further research. 4) Recommend potential solutions to enhance the integration of VR into educational practices.

2. BACKGROUND AND SIGNIFICANCE OF THE STUDY

Farsi et al. (2021) note that VR applications enable users to immerse themselves in a 3D environment where they can interact with virtual objects and explore different virtual settings. These applications have significantly impacted various sectors such as learning, teaching, attitude, marketing, engineering and robotics, entertainment, clinical treatments and health, heritage and archaeology, industrial protection, and community skills. Since the start of the new millennium, display technologies have made significant advancements, transitioning from the large cathode ray tube to more compact designs like liquid crystal display (LCD) and organic light-emitting diode (OLED) (Chen et al., 2018). However, Shorey and Ng (2021) comment that the latest developments in display technology go beyond flat panel designs and are focused on transforming the way users interact with their surroundings. VR displays represent one end of this spectrum, offering immersive experiences that revolutionise user interactions. Liao (2024) posits that VR technology nowadays consists of several systems namely the virtual environment system, the processing system of the computer used, display equipment. The application method mainly consist of utilising computer programming as a basis, combined with three-dimensional graphics and multimedia display technologies to create an immersive space, providing users with a realistic three-dimensional experience including immersion, interaction, and imagination, and even simulating various senses such as touch and smell (Liao, 2024). Likewise, Yang, Cheng, Liu & Shih (2022) point out that a fully immersive VR environment involves all five senses. For instance, the Geological Crystallography Learning System developed by China University of Geosciences realises the structural physical characteristics of crystals through VR technology allowing learners to acquire knowledge more efficiently (Liao, 2024). Jiawei and Mokmin (2023) comment that VR typically involves footage presented using desktop computers, head-mounted displays (HMDs), or automated virtual environments in caves. However, HMD have been challenging to use in the past because of the high price and limited system stability and imaging quality (Yang et al., 2022). Nowadays, with VR device products such as HTC VIVE and Oculus, it is relatively easier to build an immersive virtual reality environment.

The education sector has witnessed a transformative impact through the introduction of VR, fostering innovation in various aspects. VR technology has revolutionised the way students learn and engage with educational content by providing immersive and interactive experiences. Moreover, the business world demands that workers possess a distinct set of skills, including critical thinking, creativity, problem-solving, and virtual collaboration skills, which differ from the skills that individuals have (Yildirim, Sahin-Topalcengiz, Arikan & Timur, 2020). Damaševicius and Sidekerskiene (2024) note that VR technologies utilised in education, including collaborative platforms, simulation environments, and game-based learning spaces, have demonstrated significant promise in improving student involvement, drive, and educational achievements. These digital domains provide a platform for innovative exploration, critical thinking, and hands-on learning, rendering education more inclusive, captivating, and customised to unique learning preferences, and present a compelling field for further investigation. (Damaševicius & Sidekerskiene, 2024).

This innovative approach to education has opened up new possibilities for personalised learning, remote education, and collaborative learning environments. The link between VR and the education sector lies in its ability to revolutionise traditional teaching methods and create a more engaging and effective learning experience for students. Hence, this research contributes to the broader Sustainable Development Goals (SDGs) set by the United Nations, particularly in terms of promoting quality education and fostering innovation in the field of education. This study will guide policy and decision-makers to develop practical strategies and policies that would help in improving educational outcomes. Addressing these challenges and limitations and leveraging the relevant theory, it is possible to enhance the integration of VR in education, even in poor educational settings.

3. LITERATURE REVIEW

3.1 Theoretical Framework

The diffusion of innovations (DOI) theory is relevant, as it explains how new technologies spread and are adopted over time. Rogers (1995) refined the DOI theory, first introduced in 1962, which aims to comprehend the process, reasons, and speed at which innovative ideas and technologies disseminate within a social system (Rogers, 1962). Diffusion encompasses the spread and adoption of innovations or ideas (Kolsi, 2023). However, numerous organisations encounter a shared challenge in expediting the acceptance of a new idea (Kolsi, 2023) as the process of adoption can span several years from the moment it becomes accessible, even after significant advancements, and may take decades for the true impact of the innovation to materialise (Satell, 2017). Diffusion refers to the transmission of innovation among members of a social system through specific channels over a period. It is considered a unique form of communication where individuals exchange information to achieve a common understanding (García-Avilés, 2020). For Kolsi (2023), it is the process of acquiring knowledge and exchanging information, whereby various elements influence the acceptance of a new idea or practice. Diffusion, according to Wani and Ali (2015) and Rogers (2006), includes key elements, namely innovation, communication channels, time, and the social system. An innovation refers to a concept, method, or item that is considered novel by an individual or another adopting entity (García-Avilés, 2020). Wani and Ali (2015) explain that innovation is the perception of an idea, practice, or object as new by an individual or adopting unit. The communication system serves as a conduit for users to exchange information among themselves, which acts as a medium that facilitates the back-and-forth flow of information between users (Wani & Ali, 2015). A social system comprises interconnected members or units, such as individuals, organisations, informal groups, or subsystems; however, these units are distinct from one another and collaborate to solve problems to achieve a shared objective (Kolsi, 2023). Time measures the lifespan of an innovation, starting from its creation until it is no longer considered innovative (Wani & Ali, 2015). Reducing the diffusion time of an innovation poses a significant obstacle for companies. Consequently, innovation diffusion happens when a social system embraces innovation and subsequently communicates information about it within the system and to other systems (Wani & Ali, 2015). The majority of the innovations explored in this section pertain to VR technologies in education.

The adoption of innovations has been extensively researched for more than three decades. Rogers' book (2003), DOI, presents one of the most widely recognised adoption models that has been utilised in numerous fields, including political science, public health, communications, history, economics, technology, and education. Rogers (2003) introduced a model for examining the stages of adoption called the innovation-decision process (García-Avilés, 2020). This process involves seeking and processing information to reduce uncertainty about the benefits and drawbacks of a particular innovation, which consists of five sequential steps: knowledge; persuasion; decision; implementation; and confirmation (Rogers, 2006). Figure 1 illustrates the chronological order of these stages.

Figure 1. A model of five stages in the innovation-decision process

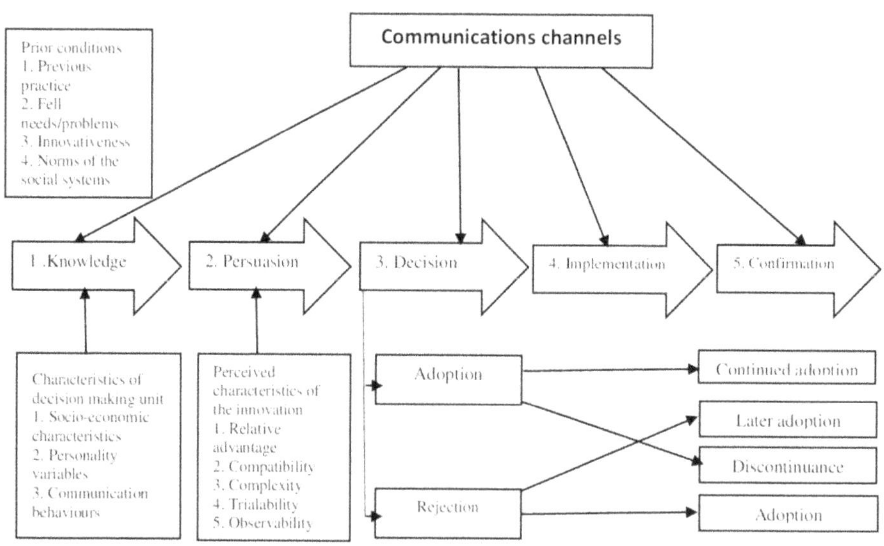

(Wani & Ali, 2015)

Based on Figure 1, the knowledge stage marks the beginning of the innovation-decision process, where individuals focus on gathering information about the innovation. It encompasses various tasks related to identifying a requirement, exploring potential solutions, familiarising oneself with existing advancements, selecting appropriate innovations, and suggesting potential options for implementation (Damanpour & Schneider, 2006). Sahin (2006) explains that this involves developing awareness-knowledge and gaining principles-knowledge to comprehend the underlying mechanisms that make it successful (Sahin, 2006). Wani and Ali (2015) argue that how-to-knowledge contains information about how to use an innovation correctly; while principles-knowledge encompasses the operational principles that explain the mechanisms behind the functionality of an innovation.

The implementation phase marks the time when the technology is use. The implementer may seek technical aid from change agents to mitigate uncertainty surrounding the consequences. Kihlström and Vahlgren (2022) observe that innovations either partially or entirely, falter during this phase. This suggests that a poor implementation is often the primary reason for failure.

During the confirmation stage, adopters evaluate and decide whether to maintain the adoption or reject it (Miranda, Miranda, Schwartz & Almeida, 2016). Individuals subsequently seek validation and support for the decision they have already made.

The persuasion stage involves individuals developing either a positive or negative attitude towards the innovation. LaMorte (2022) explains that it is influenced by five key factors, which vary in their impact across the five adopter categories: (1) the first factor is a relative advantage, which refers to the extent to which the innovation is perceived as superior to the existing programme; (2) compatibility indicates how well the innovation aligns with the needs of potential adopters; (3) complexity determines the level of difficulty in using the innovation; (4) trialability, assesses the extent to which the innovation can be tested before committing to adopt it; (5) lastly, observability measures the degree to which the innovation provides tangible results, influencing its adoption. This attributes give users a sense of confidence in embracing innovations. The summary of the attributes of innovations as outlined by Rogers can be found in Table 1.

Table 1. Summary of Rogers' definition of the attributes of innovations

Attributes	**Definitions**
Relative Advantage	Innovation superiority perception
Compatibility	Alignment with values, experiences, and needs
Complexity	Complexity of understanding and use
Trialability	Limited experimentation feasibility
Observability	Visibility of innovation results

Among the five attributes of innovation complexity presented in Table 1, complexity has a reverse effect on the speed at which an innovation is adopted. Adoption rate means the pace at which the public acquires and utilises new technology, which is measured by the number of individuals who begin using the new technology within a specific timeframe. The rate of adoption of innovations is determined by five variables, which are presented in Figure 2.

Figure 2. Variables determining the rate of adoption of innovations

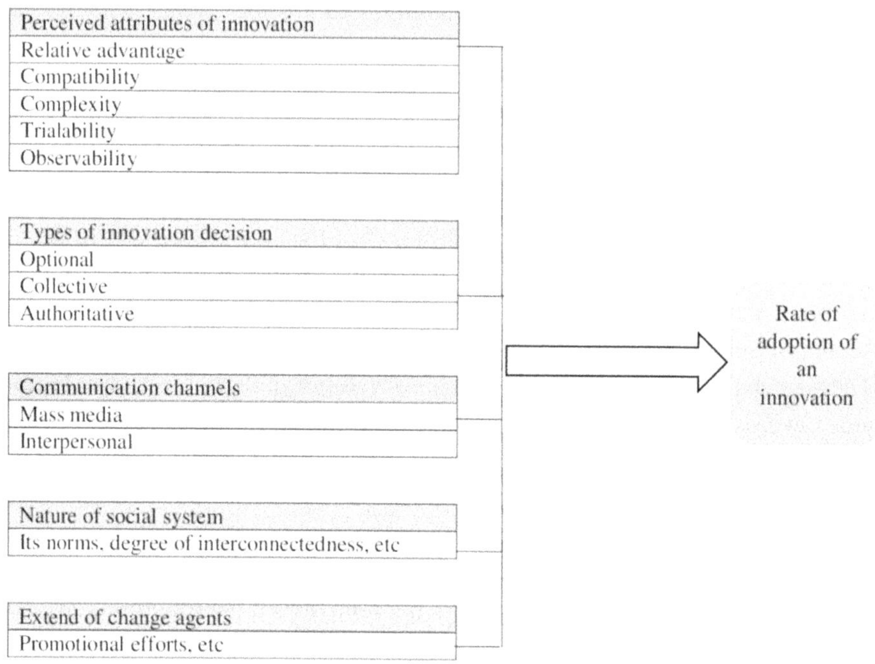

(Rogers, 1983)

Based on Figure 2, three primary categories of innovation-decisions exist', namely optional, collective, and authority. In an optional innovation-decision, individuals independently determine whether to accept or reject the innovation, regardless of others' choices; in a collective innovation-decision, system members reach a consensus on whether to accept or reject it; and in an authority innovation-decision, a small group of individuals with high social status, power, or technical expertise decide to accept or reject it (Kolsi, 2023). The examination of various communication channels is necessary to determine the most effective ones for participants to create and share information.

Rogers' (1962) theory of DOI, as a widely recognised framework, remains pertinent in the context of education, particularly as new technologies are being explored for implementation (Botha, Smuts & De Villiers, 2018). This theory is crucial in comprehending the challenges and limitations of VR in educational settings due to its ability to shed light on the adoption and acceptance of new technologies by educators, students and institutions.

3.2 Virtual Reality Applications in Education

VR is an interactive computer simulation that detects the user's actions and environment and then provides sensory feedback to one or more senses to create a feeling of immersion in a simulated or virtual environment (Sholihin, Sari, Yuniarti & Ilyana, 2020). For Alalwan et al. (2020), VR refers to an environment, whether real or simulated, where a person can experience telepresence. According to Farsi, Yusof, Fauzi, Rusli, Malik, Tawafak, Mathew and Jabbar (2021), it is the utilisation of computer technology to simulate real-world environments and situations artificially. It is a developing innovation that provides a computer-generated representation of an environment that can be interacted within what appears to be real-time, which has found applications in various sectors such as medical training, engineering, and entertainment, and it also holds great promise in the field of education (Marougkas, Troussas, Krouska & Sgouropoulou, 2023). LaValle (2023) posits that VR involves manipulating an organism's behaviour through the use of artificial sensory stimulation without the organism being fully aware of the external influence. This definition encompasses four essential elements: 1) the targeted behaviour, where the organism engages in experiences designed by the creator, such as flying, walking, or socialising; 2) the organism itself, which can be an individual or even a different life form; 3) the utilisation of artificial sensory stimulation, which partially replaces or enhances the organism's natural sensory inputs through engineering techniques; and 4) the organism's lack of awareness, as it becomes immersed in the virtual world without realising the interference. This phenomenon is widely accepted as a natural occurrence (LaValle, 2023).

Within the realm of education, numerous institutions are incorporating VR, often within collaborative networks and other intricate structures, to offer students practical learning experiences (Priatna, Maylawati, Sugilar & Ramdhani, 2020). Alalwan, Cheng, Al-Samarraie, Yousef, Alzahrani and Sarsam (2020) argue that the education sector also has witnessed a significant integration of VR, which has proven to be highly effective in facilitating the learning process across various subjects. These innovative technologies offer unique opportunities to enhance lifelong learning experiences (Alalwan et al., 2020). Wohlgenannt et al. (2020) note that VR technology has been the subject of research for many years by researchers from various fields such as computer science, engineering, and the social sciences as it creates a virtual environment that fully engages users, giving them a sense of actually being present in that environment. Chen Huang and Chou (2019) elucidate that the utilisation of computer-simulated environments can enhance the effectiveness of science learning. By integrating real and virtual environments, a mixed reality is created, offering learners numerous opportunities for exploration. The integration of VR in education offers numerous advantages, with one of the key benefits being the provision of immersive and engaging learning experiences (Marougkas et al., 2023). By utilising VR technology, students have the opportunity to engage with both their classmates and the simulated setting, enhancing the level of interactivity during the learning process. Priatna et al. (2020) conclude that experiential learning offers various benefits by combining multiple approaches, including the utilisation of VR applications to enhance students' learning experiences.

4. METHODS AND MATERIALS

Given the rapid pace of technological advancements, innovations, and the emergence of VR, it is imperative to conduct a comprehensive analysis. Therefore, this systematic review exclusively encompassed publications from the period spanning 2020 to 2024, encompassing the time during and after the COVID-19 pandemic. By focusing on this specific timeframe, this study ensured that the review captures the most up-to-date and relevant research in this dynamic field.

4.1. Search Strategy

The study's objectives were supported by the literature sourced from the Google Scholar database. Manual searches was conducted with Boolean operators like "AND" and "OR" in conjunction with specific keywords, various publications, abstracts, and titles were examined. The search pertained to the following keywords: VR in education; VR systems in education; innovative technologies; VR implementation challenges; VR adoption barriers; and VR technical, financial and social limitations. The search focused on articles written in English that employed qualitative, quantitative, mixed methods, and systematic literature reviews.

This systematic method proved successful in identifying relevant studies in the field of education. In total, in 17 900 studies related to VR, 16 440 were not related to education or academia and were therefore excluded. All studies on extended reality (ER or XR), mixed reality (MR), augmented reality (AR) and metaverse (although VR is a metaverse tool), were excluded from this study. Furthermore, the papers presenting the challenges and limitations of VR in other sectors (other than education), although providing valuable insights about VR challenges and limitations in general, were not included in this review as they did not align with the study's objectives. Overall, only 13 studies were integrated in the systematic review to address the research objectives, as shown in Figure 3.

4.2. Inclusion and Exclusion Criteria

To guarantee the selection of suitable studies for examination in this research, a thorough procedure was carried out to define a set of inclusion and exclusion criteria. This method was put into practice to ensure that the selected studies are in line with the particular requirements and goals of the current investigation. Data presented in Figure 3 were sourced from research studies retrieved from the Google Scholar database, a comprehensive platform that indexes scholarly literature across various disciplines.

Figure 3. Evaluation and selection processes of the sources included to ensure the study's relevance and credibility

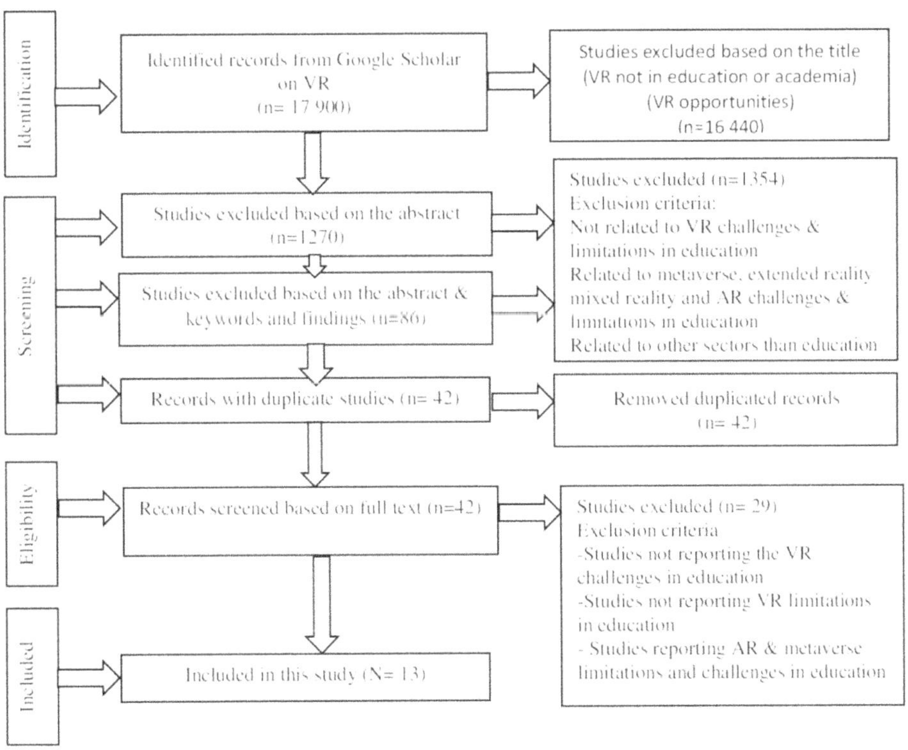

5. KEY FINDINGS RELATED TO THE

Table 2 provides an overview of the findings from the 13 papers discussing VR challenges and/or limitations in Education.

Table 2. Challenges and limitations

Author, year & industry	Methodology	Key findings	Conclusions & Recommendations
1. Lege & Bonner (2020) in education	Through a review of literature published from 2017–2020	**Challenges to applying VR in an educational context:** 1. Lack of VR-specific pedagogy 2. Cognitive demand **Limitation to VR** 1. Immersion breaking	1. Teachers should adopt a cautious approach when incorporating VR into their classrooms, considering the novelty factor. 2. It is advisable for educators to keep up with technological advancements and not overlook VR as merely a tool for teaching technology. 3. Educators must progress beyond the initial excitement and concentrate on the instructional methods and opportunities that VR enables.
2. Paszkiewicz, Salach, Dymora, Bolanowski, Budzik & Kubiak (2021) in in Education for Industry 4.0	Teaching methodology	1. Investment costs 2. The need for highly qualified specialists	It is of utmost importance during the initial phase of project assumptions to explicitly specify the essential skills that need to be acquired throughout the course.
3. Baniasadi, Ayyoubzadeh & Mohammadzadeh (2020) in Medical Education and Treatment	A systematic literature review Science Direct, Google Scholar, and PubMed databases	The main challenges of using VR are categorised as general and specific. 1. General challenges include: a) Reduced face-to-face communications, b) Education, c) Cost challenges, d) Users' attitudes. 2. Specific challenges include: a) Designing b) Health issues	1. Real settings are crucial for evaluating the effectiveness of VR-based educational programs, given the lack of face-to-face interaction with 'real patients'. 2. Integrating AR technology with VR can create immersive and interactive experiences that are both educational and engaging for users. 3. Revise laws, standards, and protocols that contribute to enhancing the successful implementation of VR on a national scale.

continued on following page

Table 2. Continued

Author, year & industry	Methodology	Key findings	Conclusions & Recommendations
4. Alalwan, Cheng, Al-Samarraie, Yousef, Alzahrani, & Sarsam (2020) in Primary School	Qualitative methods using semi-structured interviews Sample: primary school teachers	1. lack of competency, 2. limited instructional design, 3. Lack of attention, 4. lack of time, 5. Limited environmental resources 6. Absence of clear guidelines 7. Lack of practice in utilising VR skills 8. Health concerns related to prolonged VR use were common challenges in VR and AR utilisation.	1. To maximise VR potential in educational settings, decision-makers in the field of education should take into account the commonalities between VR and AR technologies. 2. Educators should enhance their skills and knowledge in educational technology applications through continuous training and updates.
5. Farsi, Yusof, Fauzi, Rusli, Malik, Tawafak, Mathew & Jabbar (2021)	A review of the literature based on 17 papers published between 2010-2020 taken from databases such as Science Direct, Ebscohost, and Scopus	The limitations are: 1. VR is costly 2. The effectiveness of VR technology and applications, as well as computer quality 3. Instructors' reluctance to utilise VR technology due to a lack of confidence.	1. As the cost of certain tools decreases, HEIs can advise students to purchase their own VR tools, guided by the university or instructors' recommendations. This strategy allows HEIs to save on expenses. 2. HEIs should consider strategic investments in VR technology, such as the utilisation of 3D Lab applications within their academic settings. 3. HEIs need to offer VR training for instructors as a solution to the low intention to use VR, which is primarily attributed to ignorance.

continued on following page

Table 2. Continued

Author, year & industry	Methodology	Key findings	Conclusions & Recommendations
6. Alnagrat, Ismail, & Idrus (2022) in academic Laboratories	A successful instructional design process in the field of education, including virtual laboratories	1. Cost, 2. Device, 3. Teacher Readiness, and 4. Sickness.	1. VR became accessible to the public in the early 1960s, and the current equipment offers user-friendly technical features, enhanced comfort, and a significantly more immersive experience than its predecessors in the past. 2. Proper utilisation of VR technology is essential for achieving positive educational outcomes, emphasising the importance of aligning its use with intended objectives. 3. To integrate VR into educational settings, educators need to receive training to enable them to convert traditional classrooms and laboratories into VR-enabled learning environments.
7. Shorey & Ng (2021) For Nursing students and registered nurses	The narrative summary included 18 studies, consisting of both randomised controlled trials and quasi-experimental studies, which were systematically reviewed.	The two primary disadvantages identified: 1. Technological challenges 2. A deficiency in authenticity	Virtual worlds are highly effective in enhancing cognitive outcomes, particularly in terms of theoretical knowledge. This indicates that virtual worlds can serve as a valuable tool in nursing education, either as a substitute or a supplementary approach to teaching theoretical concepts.
8. Chi, ZaffwanIdris & Nugrahan (2021) in Education	Literature review	1. Skills 2. Teaching in virtual environments comes with a range of difficulties 3. Human interaction and communication	1. Implementing a pedagogy that leverages VR's distinct characteristics is essential for enhancing education. 2. Modernising education through the integration of VR could be a beneficial endeavour.

continued on following page

Table 2. Continued

Author, year & industry	Methodology	Key findings	Conclusions & Recommendations
9. Fransson, Holmberg & Westelius (2020) in K-12 schools	Interviews, informal conversations and observations of teachers testing HMD VR and different VR applications in a Digital Learning Lab (DLL) and data from a project involving upper secondary school history teachers discussing the planned implementation of HMD VR in their teaching and being in the DLL	Organisational, institutional, contextual, and practical challenges of utilising VR technology and apps: 1. Economy and technology, 2. Initial learning barriers, 3. Organisation and practical enactment for teaching and learning, 4. Curricula, syllabuses and expected learning outcomes and 5. Teachers' competences, professional development and trust.	1. Teachers should have the autonomy to decide on the integration of VR in education. 2. Educational settings should not be exploited as a market for unproven digital tools pushed by EdTech companies. 3. Collaboration between teachers and EdTech businesses can lead to the development of more effective technology and teaching strategies. 4. Customising content and refining teaching methods through cooperation can enhance the overall learning experience. 5. The focus should be on ensuring that VR adds value to teaching and learning, rather than being used for experimental purposes.
10. Sipilä (2020) In Primary education	A literature review	Limitations pose a significant challenge: 1. Economic and technological 2. Language-related issues 3. The initial learning barriers 4. Health issues	1. VR has made significant progress in recent years, evolving from basic concepts and optical illusions. 2. Careful planning is crucial for the effective implementation of VR in teaching. 3. The value of VR in education lies in the simulations and teaching methods used, not just the devices themselves.

continued on following page

Table 2. Continued

Author, year & industry	Methodology	Key findings	Conclusions & Recommendations
11. Ravichandran & Mahapatra (2023) in vocational education in schools	Literature review	1. Initial cost 2. High level of technical expertise 3. Disorientation or motion sickness in learners 4. VR simulations may not accurately replicate real-world vocational environments 5. Developing high-quality VR content can be time-consuming and resource-intensive	1. The use of VR can lead to more effective assessment and targeted feedback for learners. 2. Increased adoption of VR in vocational training can result in a more skilled and competent workforce. 3. Despite the existing challenges and limitations in incorporating VR technology in schools, educators can benefit from best practices and successful case studies to facilitate the effective integration of VR in vocational education.
12. Fakahani, Aljehani, Baghdadi & El-Shorbagy (2022) In Architecture	Case Studies	System developers encounter three primary obstacles: 1. Acquiring industrial domain expertise, 2. Creating realistic models, and 3. Dealing with technical constraints. In the realm of education, various obstacles impede the progress of VR technology, such as 1. The Uniqueness effect, 2. Cybersickness and danger, 3. Technological and accessibility issues, 4. Architectural and social limitations	1. Achieving the implementation of VR in architecture involves addressing challenges such as the application and prospects of this technology, as well as its significance and utilisation in the field. 2. Case studies can provide valuable insights into the practical use of VR within architectural contexts.

continued on following page

Table 2. Continued

Author, year & industry	Methodology	Key findings	Conclusions & Recommendations
13. Kumar, Carberry, Beenfeldt, Andersson, Mansouri & Gallucci (2021) In chemical and biochemical engineering education	Literature review	1. VR technology is in the early stages of adoption in chemical engineering education 2. Development of VR-based learning environments requires additional technical skills and resources 3. Long-term utilisation of VR tools for education requires regular maintenance and software support	1. Virtual technologies have shown increased promise during the COVID-19 pandemic. 2. VR is considered a valuable tool for remote learning in chemical engineering education.

6. VR CHALLENGES AND LIMITATIONS IN EDUCATION SETTINGS

The discussion derived from the analysis of 13 papers included in the study and presented in Table 2.

6.1 Challenges of VR in Education

This study uncovers a range of challenges associated with the utilisation of VR technology and apps in educational settings, including primary, tertiary, architecture, vocational, chemical and engineering, K-12, medical schools, and academic laboratories.

6.1.1 The Initial Learning Barriers

VR technology is in the early stages of adoption in many educational fields (Ravichandran & Mahapatra, 2023). Kumar et al. (2021) underscore that VR technology is currently in the early stages of being adopted in chemical engineering education. According to Sipilä (2020), the introduction of new technology always brings about initial obstacles in learning. Both students and teachers would need time to grasp the concept of VR and become familiar with the various VR applications. The differences in VR devices and applications can pose challenges when switching between them. Consequently, teachers would need technical expertise to operate the devices and effectively incorporate them into their teaching practices. They would therefore need to receive professional assistance and invest time in learning VR applications and equipment before integrating them into their teaching methods (Sipilä, 2020).

Baniasadi et al. (2020) point out that the integration of VR and contemporary technologies into the practices of patients, therapists, and students for educational purposes is a crucial principle that warrants attention. Insufficient education and guidance for clinicians on how to effectively employ this technology in treating patients may lead to harmful repercussions. However, a thorough guide outlining the suitable applications of VR technology in medical education and psychiatric treatments is essential, detailing the specific circumstances under which this technology is most effective and appropriate for use (Baniasadi et al., 2020).

6.1.2 Lack of VR-Specific Pedagogy

VR can be integrated into current educational frameworks with moderate success; however, scholars concur that to fully harness its educational benefits, a strong pedagogical foundation must be established alongside VR implementation (Lege & Bonner, 2020). Alalwan et al. (2020) opine that the absence of clear guidelines on VR usage negatively impacts students' willingness to engage with the technology, highlighting the importance of comprehensive instructions for successful integration. The absence of a pedagogy specifically designed for VR is a significant issue. While VR can be integrated into current educational methods with some effectiveness, scholars emphasise the necessity of a well-developed pedagogical framework to fully utilise its learning potential (Lege & Bonner, 2020). Hu-Au and Lee (2018) contend that attempting to mimic traditional face-to-face teaching experiences in a VR environment will lead to challenges in implementation.

6.1.3 Financial Costs Associated With the Adoption and Implementation of VR Technology

6.1.3.1 Adoption and Implementation Costs

One of the main challenges is the cost of implementing VR technology in schools, as it requires expensive equipment and software. The perfect experience of VR technology depends on the appropriate VR equipment, and the current price of VR equipment is generally expensive; common VR glasses are generally located in the price of more than three thousand Yen, and one VR equipment can only be used by one user at a time (Liao, 2024). Additionally, there may be challenges in terms of access to VR technology, especially in schools with limited resources. Likewise, Baniasadi et al. (2020) explain that the integration of VR technology comes with a significant cost factor that poses a challenge to its widespread adoption. In addition, Alnagrat et al. (2022) argue that VR technology is hindered by cost constraints, as the full VR hardware setup remains out of reach for many individuals and institutions due to its high price. These requirements contribute to the overall expense associated with setting up VR systems for various industries and applications (Baniasadi et al., 2020). There is a need to provide a dedicated working environment, which is associated with investment costs to develop ready virtual environments. In the same way, Sipilä (2020) notes that the cost of acquiring all the necessary hardware and software for VR is substantial.

6.1.3.2 Maintenance Costs

VR technology requires regular maintenance and software support. Kumar et al. (2021) add that long-term use of VR tools for education requires regular hardware maintenance and software support, which may necessitate collaboration between chemical engineering educators and computer scientists or outsourced service providers. Furthermore, the effectiveness of education using VR technology is dependent on advanced hardware and computer systems, as the unavailability or failure of such devices can impact the intended learning experience (Kumar et al., 2021). Baniasadi et al. (2020) note that there are concerns about the cost of maintaining this technology.

6.1.4 VR-Based Learning Environments Require Additional Technical Skills and Resources

To setup a VR-based learning environment in schools requires a high level of technical expertise (Ravichandran & Mahapatra, 2023). Likewise, Kumar et al. (2021) state that some of the challenges associated with VR technology include the need for technical skills in game design and development, as well as a background in chemical engineering for creating VR-based learning environments. Skills like technical literacy, innovation, empathy, and critical thinking are challenging to impart and often overlooked in educational settings (Chi et al., 2021). However, when considering the utilisation of VR in education, these skills become intricately intertwined with its implementation and effectiveness. Technical literacy, for instance, becomes essential as educators and students navigate the VR platforms, requiring a solid understanding of the technology and its functionalities. Innovation is fostered through the exploration of new ways to incorporate VR into the curriculum, allowing for creative and engaging learning experiences. Empathy, on the other hand, is enhanced through the immersive nature of VR, enabling students to step into the shoes of others and gain a deeper understanding of different perspectives and experiences. This promotes a more inclusive and empathetic society. Alalwan et al. (2020) conclude that the lack of these skills poses a challenge for teachers in creating engaging learning experiences, as infrequent use of VR tools may hinder their ability to effectively incorporate them into lessons.

6.1.5 The Effectiveness of VR Technology and Applications, As Well As Computer Quality

Stakeholders are required to make significant financial investments to convert an educational laboratory into a VR laboratory; however, the substantial capital infusion does not guarantee that the VR lab can be effectively managed by experts possessing advanced technical expertise (Sipilä, 2020). The effectiveness of VR technology and applications, as well as computer quality, have been highlighted in the literature review. Farsi et al. (2021) note that the use of VR applications may not always be beneficial, especially when the immersion experience is compromised by factors like outdated hardware, computers, and less sophisticated brand names in VR technology.

Another effectiveness issue can be related to inadequate competency. Alalwan et al. (2020) indicate that inadequate competency in VR refers to the lack of functionalities to ensure students' competency, with a platform that may not cater to diverse learning needs. For instance, VR is often seen as more suitable for computer-literate, mature, or self-motivated learners, and upper-primary students, while immature students may not engage as effectively (Alalwan et al., 2020). Despite the costliness of VR, its effectiveness is not guaranteed (Farsi et al., 2021). HEIs have the potential to reduce costs by incorporating VR tools that are widely utilised across various disciplines and courses (Farsi et al., 2021).

6.1.6 Reduced Human Interaction and Communication

VR has the potential to greatly enhance various learning domains, yet it also poses significant drawbacks. One of the key challenges in using VR applications and telemedicine in the health sector is its effects on face-to-face communications and medical relationships between physicians and patients (Baniasadi et al., 2020). For example, in telerehabilitation, the use of VR to perform rehabilitation exercises at home or out of the healthcare organisation without direct supervision or physical presence of the healthcare provider could have undesirable outcomes (Baniasadi et al., 2020).

Another problem is the potential for overreliance on technology, which could lead to a decrease in human interaction and personalised care (Baniasadi et al., 2020). Sipilä (2020) states that traditional education relies on personal interactions and interpersonal relationships, whereas VR primarily involves interaction between the individual and software, potentially hindering human connections and communication among students. Therefore, VR should be viewed as a tool to support learning rather than a substitute for traditional educational methods (Chi et al., 2021).

6.1.7 Users' Readiness and Attitude Towards VR Technology Due to a Lack of Confidence

One of the main issues is the resistance to change from traditional methods of treatment and learning. In the academic literature, it has been observed that instructors often lack the necessary confidence to utilise VR due to their unfamiliarity with the technology (Alnagrat et al., 2022; Farsi et al., 2021; Baniasadi et al., 2020). Similarly, certain students may also exhibit reluctance to engage with VR due to their discomfort or lack of familiarity with the technology (Farsi et al., 2021). Moreover, Alnagrat et al. (2022) posit that training teachers without IT backgrounds and lacking prior IT experience poses a significant challenge. Baniasadi et al. (2020) also comment that some patients and therapists may be hesitant to adopt these new technologies due to unfamiliarity or scepticism about their effectiveness. The acceptance and utilisation of modern technology by individuals rely heavily on their attitude towards it. Users' attitudes play a crucial role in determining the success or failure of technological tools. It is important to understand that the key factor in the adoption of technology is not solely based on its technical aspects, but rather on how users perceive and embrace it (Baniasadi et al., 2020).

6.2 Limitations of VR

This section explores the various limitations of VR technology.

6.2.1 Design limitations

6.2.1.1 Non-User-Friendly Apps

Creating engaging and visually appealing content is crucial when developing VR applications for medical education. To enhance user efficiency, it is essential to involve end-users in the design process and consider their feedback and preferences. Baniasadi et al. (2020) corroborated and stated that disregarding users' comments and feedback in system design can cause user dissatisfaction, decreased performance, and render the system useless, leading to the wastage of human and economic resources. Thus, it is essential to prioritise the development of usable and user-friendly applications.

6.2.1.2 Limited Instructional Design

This pertains to the scarcity of materials that align with students' learning objectives. Teachers note that current VR offerings do not always match local syllabi and lack in-depth explanations and assessments, leading to a broad but less meaningful learning experience (Alalwan et al., 2020).

6.2.1.3 Language-Related Issues

According to Sipilä (2020), language-related issues can pose a challenge, particularly when implementing VR technology in educational settings for younger individuals. This is primarily due to the limited availability of content in languages other than English. Mistranslations and even minor spelling errors can further hinder the learning experience (Sipilä, 2020).

6.2.1.4 Immersion Breaking

The level of immersion in a VR experience is influenced by a combination of factors from VR hardware and software (Lege & Bonner, 2020). Failure to address these factors effectively can reduce the immersive quality of VR due to issues like visual distortions or poor 3D graphics (Lege & Bonner, 2020). Ravichandran and Mahapatra (2023) suggest that VR simulations may not accurately replicate real-world vocational environments, limiting skill transferability. The authors add that failure to achieve this effectively can reduce the immersive advantages of VR due to factors like visual distortions or poor-quality 3D elements. Kavanagh, Luxton-Reilly, Wuensche and Plimmer (2017) highlighted in their examination of VR in educational settings that insufficient realism in VR experiences could negatively impact the learning process.

6.2.1.5 Creating Realistic Models

To incorporate digital information into the physical world, VR systems must acquire a precise representation of the real environment, known as a real model. A crucial aspect in the advancement of VR systems for architecture and design lies in the implementation of reliable systems and precise techniques to generate these reality models (Fakahani et al., 2022).

6.2.1.4 Architectural and Social Limitations

VR has yet to fully replicate real-life experiences in various aspects (Fakahani et al., 2022). This holds particularly true when attempting to incorporate the "social dimension" into the virtual world. Nevertheless, the creation of believable virtual characters and the portrayal of meaningful and appropriate social behaviours remains a significant hurdle for VR to overcome in the future. This challenge encompasses both technical considerations, such as the system's real-time capabilities, and psychological factors, such as human communication mechanisms (Fakahani et al., 2022). Ravichandran and Mahapatra (2023) observe that developing high-quality VR content can be time-consuming and resource-intensive, potentially leading to overreliance on simulations.

6.2.1.5 A Deficiency in Authenticity

Another limitation identified in the research was a deficiency in authenticity. This deficiency refers to a lack of genuineness, credibility, or originality in the context of the study or the data being analysed (Shorey & Ng, 2021). It may suggest that the information or findings presented may not be entirely reliable, accurate, or representative of the true nature of the subject matter, raising concerns about the validity and trustworthiness of the research results (Shorey & Ng, 2021).

6.2.1.6 Numerous Devices

Numerous VR gadgets are available for purchase, making it difficult to select the most suitable one for individualised learning settings. Alnagrat et al. (2022) argue that the constraints of both hardware and software pose challenges, as they may not fully cater to the diverse needs of a classroom. The ongoing evolution of VR technology, with frequent updates in hardware and software, adds to the complexity for educators in adjusting to a particular device and software (Alnagrat et al., 2022).

6.2.2 Health Issues

Health concerns related to prolonged VR use are noted as potential negative impacts of VR on students' well-being and learning outcomes (Alalwan et al., 2020).

6.2.2.1 Visual Fatigue, Motion Sickness and Discomfort

Visual fatigue is a significant disadvantage of VR devices, leading to motion sickness and discomfort for students and learners during and after virtual learning (Alalwan et al., 2020). The disparity between the visual representation of the real world and the virtual world contributes to this issue, causing problems with focusing, far vision, and near vision (Baniasadi et al., 2020). Additionally, motion sickness can result in feelings of sleepiness, nausea, and dizziness among individuals (Alnagrat et al., 2022).

6.2.2.2 Cybersickness

Ravichandran and Mahapatra (2023) posit that VR may cause disorientation or motion sickness in learners due to its high level of immersion. Liao (2024) observes that some users may get dizziness, vomiting and other uncomfortable feelings when using VR equipment. Sufficient refresh rates of displays and updates in the virtual world are key factors to consider when using VR, as the user will be otherwise likely prone to motion sickness on longer exposure (Liao, 2024). Sipilä (2020) explains that the extent and occurrence of this phenomenon, known as cybersickness, differ from person to person, resulting in a negative perception of VR and reduced learning effectiveness. Cybersickness, akin to motion sickness, can occur before or after engaging in a VR session, hindering the overall experience (Fakahani et al. 2022). It is commonly triggered by sensory inconsistencies, such as when a virtual avatar moves while the user's physical body remains stationary in the real world (Sipilä, 2020). This issue is particularly concerning in educational settings, as individuals experiencing discomfort are less likely to effectively absorb and retain information, impeding their learning progress (Fakahani et al., 2022).

6.2.3 Technological and Accessibility Limitations

Shorey and Ng (2021) highlighted issues related to technological challenges, which could encompass a range of obstacles such as software limitations, hardware constraints, or connectivity issues that hinder the effectiveness of a particular system or process. Chi et al. (2021) comment that virtual worlds necessitate robust broadband internet connectivity and high-performance computing devices, prompting students to adapt to engage as users (Alismail & McGuire, 2015). However, this technology is frequently unavailable to students outside of educational settings, where computer labs or classrooms may lack the necessary specifications for optimal virtual world utilisation (Chi et al., 2021). Fakahani et al. (2022) state that the use of a highly precise monitor is essential in VR to prevent noticeable mis-registrations between real and virtual entities, as even small faults can have a significant impact. These challenges can impede the smooth operation of a technology-dependent task or project, leading to delays, errors, or even failures in achieving desired outcomes.

6.2.4 Cognitive Demand

Lege and Bonner (2020) highlighted that the use of immersive VR technology can lead to excessive cognitive processing, which in turn can impede the learner's ability to effectively grasp the key content of a lesson. This suggests that while VR offers a unique and engaging learning experience, it may also present cognitive challenges that need to be carefully managed in educational settings. In a study conducted by

Makransky, Terkildsen, and Mayer (2017), it was discovered that participants using VR faced heightened demands on their working memory, which ultimately resulted in a decrease in knowledge acquisition. This finding underscores the importance of understanding the cognitive demands imposed by VR technology on learners, as it can impact the overall effectiveness of using VR in educational contexts. Furthermore, Pollard et al. (2020) noted that simply increasing the level of immersion in VR may not always lead to improved learning outcomes. This suggests that while immersion is a key feature of VR technology, educators and instructional designers need to consider how to balance the immersive experience with the cognitive demands it places on learners to optimise learning outcomes effectively.

6.2.5 Limitations Related to Teaching in Virtual Environments

6.2.5.1 Limited Environmental Resources

These encompass issues such as inadequate computers, poor internet connectivity, small classrooms, lack of technical support, restricted internet access, and low-spec computers, hindering the effective use of VR technology (Alalwan et al. 2020).

6.2.5.2 Lack of Attention

The lack of attention occurs when students struggle to maintain concentration on a task without distractions, especially when exploring virtual environments and engaging with peers simultaneously (Alalwan et al., 2020).

c) Insufficient time for students to fully grasp VR materials

Time is a concern, as mastering VR concepts may require more time than allotted in traditional learning settings (Alalwan et al. 2020).

6.2.6. Unfulfilled Promises

The perception of VR has been marred by the disappointment of unmet expectations, as the excitement and anticipation surrounding it often outweigh the actual experiences it offers. This is especially true for those who do not have the means to afford expensive laboratory equipment, as they are unable to fully access the immersive virtual reality experiences that have been promised (LaValle, 2023).

7. LIMITATIONS AND FUTURE RESEARCH STUDIES

The results showed that VR presents certain constraints and obstacles, which have been deliberated upon in this chapter. However, it is important to note that there were some limitations associated with the study.

Primarily, the majority of studies incorporated in this comprehensive literature review employed a systematic literature review as a research methodology. This indicates a trend in the academic community towards utilising systematic literature reviews to explore the challenges and limitations of VR technology in academic settings. Future studies may use quantitative, qualitative or both research methods.

Furthermore, based on the literature examined, researchers often use the terms "challenges" and "limitations" interchangeably when discussing the drawbacks of VR technology in education. This interchangeable usage may lead to a lack of clarity in understanding the specific issues faced in the implementation and development of VR applications in education. Future studies may aim to establish a clear distinction between these terms to enhance comprehension and facilitate more effective problem-solving in the field of education.

Lastly, a significant portion of the scholarly articles addressing the challenges and limitations of VR in education were published in 2020, a year marked by the global COVID-19 pandemic. This temporal context may have influenced the nature of the challenges identified and the strategies proposed to overcome them in the realm of VR research. Moving forward, it is recommended that future studies continue to examine the challenges and limitations related to the adoption and utilisation of VR technologies in educational settings, as well as explore novel strategies to enhance the effectiveness and accessibility of VR applications in various domains.

8. CONCLUSION

The findings of this study highlight several challenges and limitations associated with the use of VR in education. The challenges include initial learning barriers, the absence of VR-specific pedagogy, financial costs, technical skills and resources, the effectiveness of VR technology and applications, computer quality, reduced human interaction and communication, and users' readiness and attitude towards VR technology and teaching in virtual environments. On the other hand, the limitations of VR encompass design issues, health concerns, technological and accessibility barriers, cognitive demand, and unfulfilled promises. This study prompts a deeper exploration of how VR can be effectively integrated into teaching practices to create authentic, immersive learning experiences that transcend the limitations of traditional classroom settings, thereby paving the way for a more dynamic and interactive educational environment. Hence, efforts should be made to develop appropriate pedagogical approaches, improve affordability and accessibility, address health and design concerns, and enhance user readiness and acceptance of VR technology in educational settings.

9. RECOMMENDATIONS

Based on the challenges and limitations identified in this study, educators, technology developers, and policy-makers can successfully integrate VR in educational settings.

Firstly, the government should invest in professional development programmes for educators to enhance their understanding of VR technology and its potential applications in the classroom. This can include workshops, training sessions, and online courses that provide educators with the necessary knowledge and skills to effectively integrate VR into their teaching practices.

Additionally, technology developers should focus on creating user-friendly VR platforms and applications that are specifically designed for educational purposes. This involves developing VR tools that are easy to navigate, customisable, and aligned with curriculum standards. Moreover, developers should prioritise addressing health concerns associated with VR, such as motion sickness, eye strain, and fatigue, by implementing safety features and guidelines.

Due to the high cost of VR technology, many institutions may struggle to afford its adoption and implementation. To overcome this financial barrier, policy-makers can play a crucial role in supporting the integration of VR in educational settings by allocating resources and funding to ensure that schools have access to VR technology and necessary infrastructure. Moreover, there is a need for collaboration between technology companies, non-profit organisations, and/or government agencies that can offer financial support or resources to facilitate VR initiatives. This partnerships can give access to institutions to necessary funding to successfully integrate VR technology into their programs, ultimately enhancing the overall learning experience of their learners.

REFERENCES

Alalwan, N., Cheng, L., Al-Samarraie, H., Yousef, R., Alzahrani, A. M., & Sarsam, S. M. (2020). Challenges and prospects of virtual reality and augmented reality utilization among primary school teachers: A developing country perspective. *Studies in Educational Evaluation*, 66, 66. DOI:10.1016/j.stueduc.2020.100876

Alnagrat, A., Ismail, R. C., & Idrus, S. Z. S. (2022). The opportunities and challenges in virtual reality for virtual laboratories. *Innovative Teaching and Learning Journal*, 6(2), 73–89. DOI:10.11113/itlj.v6.91

Baniasadi, T., Ayyoubzadeh, S. M., & Mohammadzadeh, N. (2020). Challenges and practical considerations in applying virtual reality in medical education and treatment. *Oman Medical Journal*, 35(3), 1–10. DOI:10.5001/omj.2020.43 PMID:32489677

Botha, A., Smuts, H., & De Villiers, C. (2018). *Emerging technologies for education*. Springer Nature.

Chen, C.-H., Huang, C.-Y., & Chou, Y.-Y. (2019). Effects of augmented reality-based multidimensional concept maps on students' learning achievement, motivation and acceptance. *Universal Access in the Information Society*, 18(4), 257–268. DOI:10.1007/s10209-017-0595-z

Chi, P.G., ZaffwanIdris, M.Z. & Nugrahan, R. (2021). Virtual Reality (VR) in 21st: century education: the opportunities and challenges of digital learning in classroom. *Asian Pendidikan*, 1(2), 105–110.

Damanpour, F., & Schneider, M. (2006). Phases of the adoption of innovation in organizations: Effects of environment, organization and top managers. *British Journal of Management*, 17(3), 215–236. DOI:10.1111/j.1467-8551.2006.00498.x

Damaševicius, R., & Sidekerskiene, T. (2024). Virtual worlds for learning in metaverse: A narrative review. *Sustainability*, 16(5), 1–41. DOI:10.3390/su16052032 PMID:38510213

Fakahani, L., Aljehani, S., Baghdadi, R., & El-Shorbagy, A.-M. (2022). The use and challenges of virtual reality in architecture. *Civil Engineering and Architecture*, 10(6), 2754–2763. DOI:10.13189/cea.2022.100638

Farsi, G. A., Yusof, A. B. M., Fauzi, W. J. B., Rusli, M. E. B., Malik, S. I., Tawafak, R. M., Mathew, R., & Jabbar, J. (2021). The practicality of virtual reality applications in education: Limitations and recommendations. *Hunan Daxue Xuebao. Shehui Kexue Ban*, 48(7), 142–155.

Fortune Business Insights. (2019). Virtual reality market size, share & industry analysis. *Fortune Business Insights.* https://www.fortunebusinessinsights.com/industry-reports/virtual-reality-market-101378

Fransson, G., Holmberg, J., & Westelius, C. (2020). The challenges of using head mounted virtual reality in K-12 schools from a teacher perspective. *Education and Information Technologies*, 25(4), 3383–3404. DOI:10.1007/s10639-020-10119-1

García-Avilés, J. A. (2020). *The international encyclopedia of media psychology*. Wiley.

Hu-Au, E., & Lee, J. J. (2018). Virtual reality in education: A tool for learning in the experience age. *International Journal of Innovation in Education*, 4(4), 215–226. DOI:10.1504/IJIIE.2017.091481

Kihlström, K., & Vahlgren, A. (2022). *Innovation implementation as a dynamic process with multiple outcomes: A single case study at Saab. MSc Business Administration*. Linköping University.

Kolsi, T. (2023). *Accelerating the innovation adoption rate of laggards in B2B context*. Master's Programme in International Marketing Management. Lahti University of Technology

Kumar, V. V., Carberry, D., Beenfeldt, C., Andersson, M. P., Mansouri, S. S., & Gallucci, F. (2021). Virtual reality in chemical and biochemical engineering education and training. *Education for Chemical Engineers*, 36, 143–153. DOI:10.1016/j.ece.2021.05.002

LaMorte, W. W. (2022). *Diffusion of innovation theory*. Boston University School of Public Health.

LaValle, S. M. (2023). *Virtual Reality*. Cambridge University Press. DOI:10.1017/9781108182874

Lege, R., & Bonner, E. (2020). Virtual reality in education: The promise, progress, and challenge. *The JALT CALL Journal*, 16(3), 167–180. DOI:10.29140/jaltcall.v16n3.388

Liao, R. (2024). *Virtual reality technology in art education system*. China Academic of Art. DOI:10.3233/FAIA231425

Makransky, G., Terkildsen, T. S., & Mayer, R. E. (2019). Adding immersive virtual reality to a science lab simulation causes more presence but less learning. *Learning and Instruction*, 60, 225–236. DOI:10.1016/j.learninstruc.2017.12.007

Marougkas, A., Troussas, C., Krouska, A., & Sgouropoulou, C. (2023). Virtual Reality in education: A review of learning theories, approaches and methodologies for the last decade. *Electronics (Basel)*, 12(13), 2832. DOI:10.3390/electronics12132832

Miranda, M.Q., Miranda, J.S., Schwartz, C.A. & Almeida, J.P.L. (2016). Technology adoption in diffusion of innovations perspective: introduction of an ERP system in a non-profit organization. *Scientific Information System*, 103-124.

Mordor Intelligence. (2024). Virtual Reality (VR) Market Size. https://www.mordorintelligence.com/industry-reports/virtual-reality-market/market-size

Paszkiewicz, A., Salach, M., Dymora, P., Bolanowski, M., Budzik, G., & Kubiak, P. (2021). Methodology of implementing virtual reality in education for industry 4.0. *Sustainability (Basel)*, 13(9), 5049. DOI:10.3390/su13095049

Pollard, K. A., Oiknine, A. H., Files, B. T., Sinatra, A. M., Patton, D., Ericson, M., Thomas, J., & Khooshabeh, P. (2020). Level of immersion affects spatial learning in virtual environments: Results of a three-condition within-subjects study with long intersession intervals. *Virtual Reality (Waltham Cross)*, 24(2), 783–796. DOI:10.1007/s10055-019-00411-y

Priatna, T., Maylawati, D., Sugilar, H., & Ramdhani, M. (2020). The key success factors for implementing e-learning in higher education. *International Journal of Emerging Learning Technologies*, 15(17), 101–114. DOI:10.3991/ijet.v15i17.14293

Ravichandran, R., & Mahapatra, J. (2023). Virtual Reality in vocational education and training: Challenges and possibilities. *Journal of Digital Learning and Education*, 3(1), 25–31. DOI:10.52562/jdle.v3i1.602

Rogers, E. M. (1962). *Diffusion of innovations*. Free Press.

Rogers, E. M. (1983). *Diffusion of innovations* (3rd ed.). Free Press.

Sahin, I. (2006). Detailed review of Rogers' diffusion of innovations theory and educational technology-related studies based on Rogers' theory. *The Turkish Online Journal of Educational Technology*, 5(2), 1–10.

Satell, G. (2017). *Mapping innovation: a playbook for navigating a disruptive age*. McGraw-Hill.

Scavarelli, A., Arya, A., & Teather, R. J. (2020). Virtual reality and augmented reality in social learning spaces: A literature review. *Virtual Reality (Waltham Cross)*, 25(1), 257–277. DOI:10.1007/s10055-020-00444-8

Sholihin, M., Sari, R. C., Yuniarti, N., & Ilyana, S. (2020). A new way of teaching business ethics: The evaluation of virtual reality-based learning media. *International Journal of Management Education*, 18(3), 1–13. DOI:10.1016/j.ijme.2020.100428

Shorey, S., & Ng, E. D. (2021). The use of virtual reality simulation among nursing students and registered nurses: A systematic review. *Nurse Education Today*, 98, 98. DOI:10.1016/j.nedt.2020.104662 PMID:33203545

Sipilä, J. (2020). *Benefits and challenges of adopting virtual reality in primary education*. [Bachelor's Thesis in Information Processing Science, University of Oulu].

Wani, T. A., & Ali, S. W. (2015). Innovation Diffusion Theory: Review & Scope in the Study of Adoption of Smartphones in India. *Journal of General Management Research*, 2(2), 98–115.

Wohlgenannt, I., Simons, A., & Stieglitz, S. (2020). Virtual Reality. *Business & Information Systems Engineering*, 62(5), 455–461. DOI:10.1007/s12599-020-00658-9

Yang, X., Cheng, P.-Y., Liu, X., & Shih, S.-P. (2022). The impact of immersive virtual reality on art education: A study of flow state, cognitive load, brain state, and motivation. *Education and Information Technologies*, 29(5), 6087–6106. DOI:10.1007/s10639-023-12041-8

Yildirim, B., Sahin-Topalcengiz, E., Arikan, G., & Timur, S. (2020). Using virtual reality in the classroom: Reflections of STEM teachers on the use of teaching and learning tools. *Journal of Education in Science, Environment and Health*, 6(3), 231–245. DOI:10.21891/jeseh.711779

Chapter 2

Challenges, Ethical Considerations, and Future Trends in Integrating Technologies for Education

Hamida AL Maamari
https://orcid.org/0009-0000-7303-228X
Universiti Tenaga Nasional, Malaysia

Abbas Al-Ghaili
Universiti Tenaga Nasional, Malaysia

Manjit Singh Sidhu
Universiti Tenaga Nasional, Malaysia

Kirandeep Kaur Sidhu
Universiti Tunku Abdul Rahman, Malaysia

ABSTRACT

This chapter will address the challenges and ethical considerations of integrating technology into education for all educators. It will highlight limited access and support, the shift to emergency remote teaching, challenges in developing countries, obstacles to technology integration, and ethical concerns in using virtual reality. The chapter will conclude by discussing future trends in technology for education. By addressing these challenges and ethical considerations, technology will effectively enhance learning outcomes and promote equitable access to education for

DOI: 10.4018/979-8-3693-6407-9.ch002

all educators.

INTRODUCTION

Learners often face challenges in accessing and using technology in today's information-driven society. However, the use of technology in education for these learners aims to ensure equal opportunities and promote fairness in their educational experiences. The implementation of technology in inclusive education for students faces various challenges. Johnson et al. (2023) highlights these challenges faced by educators when using technology in the classroom and provides solutions to overcome them. They identify external challenges such as limited access to equipment, inadequate training, and insufficient support. The authors emphasize the importance of widespread access to computers and the Internet, improved teacher training, and better technical and administrative support. They suggest making incremental changes at the institutional level and highlighting funding options like crowdfunding and grants. The article also addresses internal challenges related to teachers' attitudes, beliefs, resistance, and skills, emphasizing the significance of addressing these factors through training and support (Johnson et al., 2023).

Additionally, the sudden shift from traditional learning to Emergency Remote Teaching (ERT) presents significant problems and challenges. Even before the pandemic, issues of accessibility and affordability were already widespread across the nation. Therefore, combining the transition to remote learning with concerns about affordability, accessibility, skills and knowledge, curriculum integration, evaluation and assessment, the digital divide, and technical issues creates a complex set of challenges. These challenges arise due to financial constraints, limited physical access, insufficient knowledge and skills of educators, the need for careful planning to integrate technology into the curriculum, difficulties in assessing student learning, the gap between those with and without technology access, and technical problems that disrupt the learning process (Alvarez, 2020).

Although learning technologies are becoming part of instructional integration in a face-to-face classroom, it is also no doubt that in developing countries. In the Philippines, challenges related to technology access and digital citizenship include limited internet access, digital inequalities, oversimplified understanding of connectivity, neglect of non-users' perspectives, lack of a structured analysis framework, and gender disparities. To address these challenges, it is important to understand technology access nuances, prioritize non-users' perspectives, identify socioeconomic factors, and implement strategies for equitable and inclusive digital citizenship (Roberts & Hernandez, 2019).

In addition to the challenges mentioned earlier, there are several obstacles that teachers and learners face when it comes to integrating technology effectively into education (Liu et al., 2020). The technological challenges include integrating ICTs effectively, addressing perceptions and attitudes, acquiring digital skills, transforming pedagogical approaches, and promoting sustainable education through technology. Professors need to embrace technology, overcome resistance, and develop the necessary skills to enhance teaching and learning in the digital age. They must adapt their teaching methods, promote active learning and collaboration, and ensure equal access to education through ICTs. Ultimately, professors play a key role in leveraging technology to develop 21st-century skills in students and prepare them for the challenges of the future (LiesaOrús et al., 2020).

Additionally, the article by Alexander Skulmowski discusses ethical concerns in using VR for education. The issues include reduced learner autonomy, health risks like cybersickness and mental health effects, privacy concerns regarding data collection and manipulation, and the impact of realism on comprehension based on spatial abilities. The article proposes guidelines like spatial ability testing, providing alternative paths in VR experiences, and using privacy-protecting algorithms to address these ethical challenges and promote the ethical use of VR in education (Skulmowski, 2023).

In short, integrating VR, AR, and AI technologies in education has transformative potential. However, their adoption in education faces challenges. Figure 1 presents a summary of the key challenges posed by VR, AR, and AI technologies in education.

The key challenges include:

1. High cost and technical requirements: Technical equipment and software can be expensive, making it difficult for schools and institutions with limited budgets to afford and maintain the necessary technology. Additionally, technical systems often require powerful hardware and reliable internet connectivity, which may not be readily available in all educational environments.
2. Lack of standardized guidelines and best practices: The development and delivery of technologies such as VR, AR, and AI content for educational purposes lack standardized guidelines and evidence-based best practices. This can make it difficult for educators to ensure the quality, effectiveness, and alignment of VR, AR, and AI experiences with educational objectives.
3. Ethical and legal considerations: The use of technologies such as VR, AR, and AI in education raises ethical and legal concerns, particularly regarding data privacy and security. Technologies experience collecting and storing personal data, which must be handled responsibly to protect student privacy and comply with regulations and policies.

4. Potential negative effects on health and well-being: Extended use of VR, AI, and AR technologies can lead to health-related issues such as motion sickness, eye strain, and fatigue. Prolonged exposure to virtual environments may also result in social isolation if not balanced with real-world interactions and collaborative learning experiences.
5. Barriers to adoption: Some educators and learners may face barriers to using technologies such as VR, AR, and AI in education. These barriers can include inadequate training, insufficient support, a lack of skills or confidence in using the technology, limited interest, or motivation to explore VR, AR, and AI as a learning tool, or resistance to change in traditional teaching methods.

Figure 1. Challenges and ethical considerations in adopting AR, AI, and VR in education

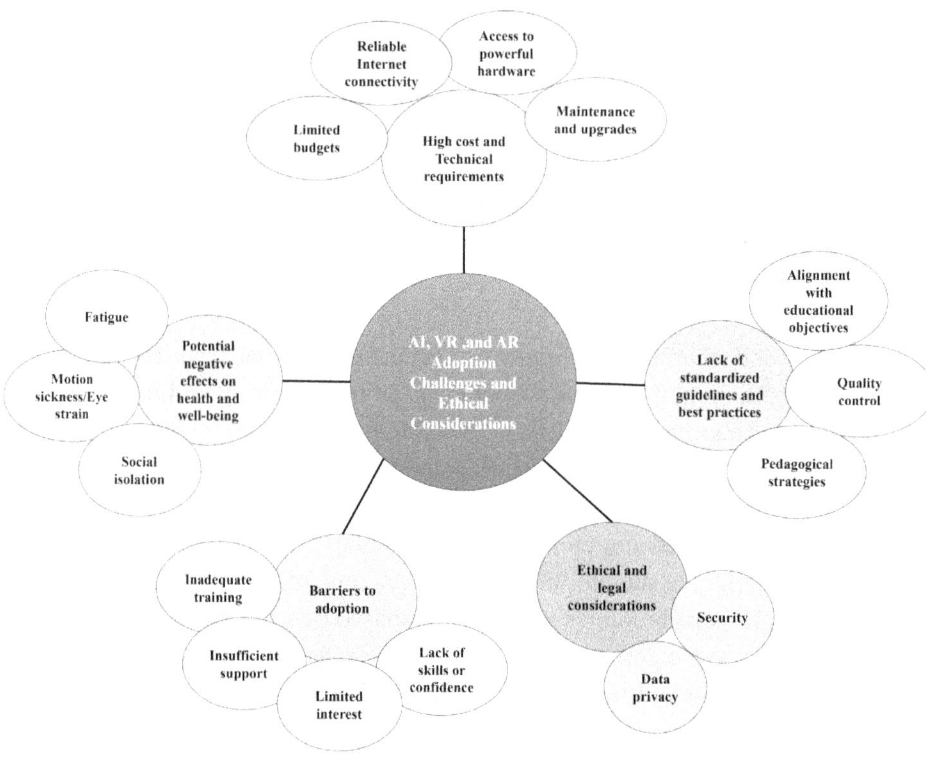

Implementing technologies in education can face challenges on a larger scale. However, when it comes to a specific aspect like using technology for a specific reason such as SENSs during examinations, the financial cost is not expected to be high. The equipment will be used exclusively in the examination hall for a specific group of students, resulting in limited expenses for its preparation. Furthermore, the challenge of a lack of standardized guidelines and best practices for technologies like VR, AR, and AI is less pronounced during the examination. Educators can depend on established examination protocols to ensure these technologies meet quality standards, are effective, and align with educational objectives.

Additionally, ethical, and legal concerns related to the use of technologies like VR, AR, and AI in education, particularly regarding data privacy and security, are expected to be less prominent. Since the focus is on the examination process, the collection and storage of personal data may be minimized or limited to essential information required for the assessment. However, it remains essential to handle data responsibly, safeguard student privacy, and comply with regulations and policies.

Furthermore, the potential negative effects on health and well-being from the extended use of technologies are less pronounced. Since the focus is on the assessment process, the duration of technology usage may be relatively shorter, reducing the likelihood of health-related issues such as motion sickness, eye strain, and fatigue. Additionally, the examination setting typically involves limited exposure to virtual environments, minimizing the risk of social isolation. However, balancing virtual and real-world interactions is important to support students' well-being and foster collaborative learning beyond the exam.

The barriers to adopting technologies in education are expected to be fewer. Since the focus is on the assessment process, educators and learners may be more motivated to embrace these technologies as valuable tools specifically for the examination context. The need for extensive training or skills development may be reduced, and resistance to change in traditional teaching methods may be minimized. However, it is important to provide support and resources to ensure the effective use of technology during the examination.

To ensure the quality, effectiveness, and sustainability of advanced technologies for education, it is important to follow some best practices. These best practices include aligning activities with learning objectives and standards, selecting or developing accurate and engaging content, providing adequate training and support, evaluating the impact on student learning, balancing with other learning methods, establishing guidelines, prioritizing ethics, and promoting well-being. All these best practices can help guarantee the successful integration of immersive technologies into existing curricula and assessment systems.

FUTURE TRENDS OF TECHNOLOGY FOR EDUCATION

The development of technology has revolutionized the world of education, especially special education, by providing various solutions to meet SENS needs (Cumming & Rose, 2022; Starks & Reich, 2023; Timotheou et al., 2023). These technologies create a conducive learning environment that promotes independence and academic success (Feng & Xia, 2023; Starks & Reich, 2023). The future of technology in education aims to achieve inclusive and equitable quality education for all, aligning with the United Nations' 2030 Agenda for Sustainable Development (Burbules et al., 2020).

The metaverse is poised to become a significant trend in the future of education. It has the potential to transform higher education by providing flexible and accessible virtual learning environments enriched with analytics, immersive virtual learning, 3D technologies, virtual collaboration, personalized avatars, AI-customized content, school buildings, supportive technologies, and wearable devices (Mozumder et al., 2022; Tlili et al., 2022; Zhang et al., 2022). It is projected that by 2027, a significant portion of the population will spend time in the metaverse for various purposes, including education. The metaverse presents new opportunities and innovations for education, overcoming the limitations of current educational technologies (Tlili et al., 2022).

Additionally, Digital games and simulations will be important in the future of education, particularly in engineering. The COVID-19 pandemic has made virtual learning popular. It leads to more interest in virtual labs and digital games for learning. Institutions will use digital labs as a cost-effective and accessible alternative to physical labs. Students' interest in digital games will drive the adoption of game-based learning, especially during social distancing(Udeozor et al., 2023).

Furthermore, Digital technologies are transforming education by shifting goals towards critical thinking and digital literacy. It allows for flexible learning beyond traditional classrooms and creates interactive and engaging learning experiences. Furthermore, they empower educators with new tools and resources and influence educational policies (Burbules et al., 2020).

Integrating technology in education improves teaching practices and overall quality. The rising interest in digitalization makes it essential to integrate digital games and virtual reality as educational tools. Research confirms their success and value in improved outcomes and student engagement. These trends lead to better teaching and learning outcomes due to their benefits and students' enthusiasm for using them(Alghamdi, 2020).

The report, prepared by the Joint Research Centre of the European Commission, identifies key technology trends that can greatly impact education. These include faster connectivity with 6G networks, immersive technologies like extended reality and virtual worlds for better learning, big data, blockchain, and the use of digital credentials and identifiers in education. The report also explores how artificial intelligence and learning analytics can improve personalized learning and assessment. Additionally, The European Union aims to drive a safe and secure digital transformation during the "Digital Decade" and recognizes the need for the education sector to adapt to the changing information and media environment. These trends have the potential to reshape education(Tuomi et al., 2023).

These trends highlight technology's potential, requiring a revaluation of educational aims, methods, and institutions while considering associated risks. Figure 2 illustrates a range of trends that are currently shaping and will continue to shape the field of education.

Figure 2. Examples of current and future education technologies

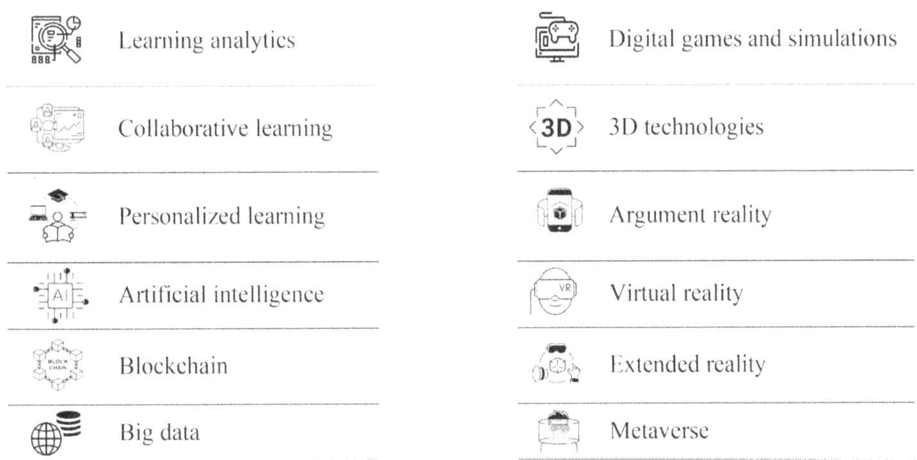

REFERENCES

Alghamdi, F. (2020). Trends in Educational Technology. In *JAAR* (*Vol. 8*, Issue 3). https://www.american-journals.com

Alvarez, A. V. (2020). The phenomenon of learning at a distance through emergency remote teaching amidst the pandemic crisis. *Asian Journal of Distance Education*, 15(1). https://files.eric.ed.gov/fulltext/EJ1289949.pdf

Burbules, N. C., Fan, G., & Repp, P. (2020). Five trends of education and technology in a sustainable future. *Geography and Sustainability*, 1(2), 93–97. DOI:10.1016/j.geosus.2020.05.001

Cumming, T. M., & Rose, M. C. (2022). Exploring universal design for learning as an accessibility tool in higher education: A review of the current literature. *Australian Educational Researcher*, 49(5), 1025–1043. DOI:10.1007/s13384-021-00471-7

Feng, M., & Xia, X. (2023). Discussing the Effect of Computer-Based Instruction on College Students' Learning Outcomes in Statistics. *2023 IEEE 12th International Conference on Educational and Information Technology, ICEIT 2023*, (pp. 59–62). IEEE. DOI:10.1109/ICEIT57125.2023.10107772

Johnson, A. M., Jacovina, M. E., Russell, D. G., & Soto, C. M. (2023). *Challenges and solutions when using technologies in the classroom*. Taylor & Francis. https://www.taylorfrancis.com/chapters/edit/10.4324/9781315647500-2/challenges-solutions-using-technologies-classroom-amy-johnson-matthew-jacovina-devin-russell-christian-soto

Liesa-Orús, M., Latorre-Cosculluela, C., Vázquez-Toledo, S., & Sierra-Sánchez, V.LiesaOrús. (2020). The technological challenge facing higher education professors: Perceptions of ICT tools for developing 21st Century skills. *Sustainability (Basel)*, 12(13), 5339. DOI:10.3390/su12135339

Liu, Q., Geertshuis, S., & Grainger, R. (2020). Understanding academics' adoption of learning technologies: A systematic review. *Science Direct, 151*. https://www.sciencedirect.com/science/article/abs/pii/S0360131520300579

Mozumder, I., Athar, A., & Sheeraz, M. (2022). *Technological Roadmap of the Future Trend of Metaverse based on IoT, Blockchain, and AI Techniques in Metaverse Education*. IEEE. https://ieeexplore.ieee.org/document/9728808

Roberts, T., & Hernandez, K. (2019). Digital Access is not Binary: The 5'A's of Technology Access in the Philippines. *The Electronic Journal on Information Systems in Developing Countries*, 85(4), e12084. Advance online publication. DOI:10.1002/isd2.12084

Skulmowski, A. (2023). Ethical issues of educational virtual reality. *Computers & Education: X Reality, 2*, 100023. DOI:10.1016/j.cexr.2023.100023

Starks, A. C., & Reich, S. M. (2023). *"What about special ed?":* Barriers and enablers for teaching with technology in special education. *Computers and Education, 193*. DOI:10.1016/j.compedu.2022.104665

Timotheou, S., Miliou, O., Dimitriadis, Y., Sobrino, S. V., Giannoutsou, N., Cachia, R., Monés, A. M., & Ioannou, A. (2023). Impacts of digital technologies on education and factors influencing schools' digital capacity and transformation: A literature review. *Education and Information Technologies*, 28(6), 6695–6726. DOI:10.1007/s10639-022-11431-8 PMID:36465416

Tlili, A., Huang, R., Shehata, B., Liu, D., Zhao, J., Metwally, A. H. S., Wang, H., Denden, M., Bozkurt, A., Lee, L. H., Beyoglu, D., Altinay, F., Sharma, R. C., Altinay, Z., Li, Z., Liu, J., Ahmad, F., Hu, Y., Salha, S., . . . Burgos, D. (2022). Is Metaverse in education a blessing or a curse: a combined content and bibliometric analysis. In *Smart Learning Environments* (*Vol. 9*, Issue 1). Springer. DOI:10.1186/s40561-022-00205-x

Tuomi, I. Cachia, Romina., Villar-Onrubia, Daniel. & European Commission. Joint Research Centre. (2023). *On the futures of technology in education : emerging trends and policy implications.* Research Gate. https://www.researchgate.net/publication/374163715_On_the_futures_of_technology_in_education_Emerging_trends_and_policy_challenges

Udeozor, C., Toyoda, R., Russo Abegão, F., & Glassey, J. (2023). Digital games in engineering education: systematic review and future trends. In *European Journal of Engineering Education* (Vol. 48, Issue 2, pp. 321–339). Taylor and Francis Ltd. DOI:10.1080/03043797.2022.2093168

Zhang, X., Chen, Y., Hu, L., & Wang, Y. (2022). The metaverse in education: Definition, framework, features, potential applications, challenges, and future research topics. In *Frontiers in Psychology* (Vol. 13). Frontiers Media S.A., DOI:10.3389/fpsyg.2022.1016300

Chapter 3
Clinical Simulation in Nursing Education:
Immersive Educational Tech for Nurses and Midwives

Ajibola Olaosebikan Waliu
https://orcid.org/0009-0002-6857-3035
Southampton Solent University, UK

Esther Emarobebh Muojekwu
https://orcid.org/0000-0002-5671-3603
Niger Delta University, Nigeria

Ugochukwu Okwudili Matthew
https://orcid.org/0000-0003-0828-9710
Hussaini Adamu Federal Polytechnic, Nigeria

Jazuli Sanusi Kazaure
https://orcid.org/0000-0001-7681-2177
Hussaini Adamu Federal Polytechnic, Nigeria

Victoria Enemona Oseni
University of Salford, UK

Chamberlyn Chisom Ononiwu
Imo State Polytechnic, Nigeria

Khalid Haruna
Bayero University, Kano, Nigeria

ABSTRACT

Virtual reality simulation has revolutionized the healthcare sector by fusing human skills with cutting-edge technology to promote patient-centered care, clinical efficacy, and a compassionate digital healthcare ecosystem. In order to enhance nursing education by providing dynamic and engaging learning settings, the goal of this research is to assess the transformative potential of virtual reality. Through familiarization with state-of-the-art technology through the use of immersive pedagogy and technology framework, the paper proposed a fresh way to nursing education and clinical practice. Student nurses can fully immerse themselves in a personalized

DOI: 10.4018/979-8-3693-6407-9.ch003

virtual reality as if they were actually there, interact with their surroundings, and learn in a dynamic and pedagogically informative digital ecosystem by donning VR headgear or goggles. Virtual reality can be used to create incredibly lifelike simulations that allow trainee nurses to practice problem-solving skills without really putting themselves in danger as clinical simulation offers deep understanding of real-world situations.

INTRODUCTION

The global healthcare initiative that propelled the integration of nursing education into higher education institutions have resulted in a rise in the enrollment of nurses and midwives in the career training programs(Oyekunle, Ugochukwu, Rosa, Rodriguez, & Fatai, 2024). The clinical practice situation is already complicated and inadequate, and the amount of nursing students vying for the limited occupational and career progressive available space simply makes it worse(Lowman & Harms, 2022). There is a focus on clinical knowledge and dexterity, and entry-level competencies are expected of nurses and midwifery students(Ryder et al., 2024). Nurse educators are bringing back old techniques for student skill development in response to the problems with clinical space and practice adequacy(Rodríguez, de Cortez, Gómez, Pérez, & Huuskonen, 2024). The need for proactive and contemporary methods to be incorporated into the teaching curriculum is required to be updated as the health industry debates how much high fidelity simulation can be situated within the clinical experiences, ushering in 3D computer simulation model into the mainstream educational syllabus(Jagatheesaperumal, Ahmad, Al-Fuqaha, & Qadir, 2024). In order to prepare students for clinical practice, 3D computer simulation model is designed to enhance teaching, learning and understanding of anatomical systems and its responses to environmental and chemical stimulus. This aligned with the viewpoint of active pedagogic stimulations and is used in the context of health and nursing education. It is linked to the growth of the clinical judgment, decision-making, and problem-solving abilities required by nurses and midwives in the health services, as well as the emotional competencies essential to the work process and all-encompassing care(Malekzadeh, 2017). It is also mentioned that the simulation is acknowledged for encouraging a secure learning environment where a mistake does not endanger the patient.

Given that the architecture of the simulation can influence improved learning results, figuring out what makes it up can help fund the development of more assertive simulation-based experiences (SBE) in nursing and health sector(Cant, Cooper, & Ryan, 2022). Furthermore, SBE formulators can create trustworthy simulation scenarios for clinical practice by using the components of simulation design that have been identified in this paper. In order to contribute to the body of knowledge by encouraging methodological rigor in the development and application of simulation scenarios, this research was proposed with the aim of aiding in the synthesis and establishment of standards for the elaboration of SBE in the pedagogical and research context(Birkheim, Calogiuri, & Martinsen, 2023). Thus, from the standpoint of instructional design, structured simulation comprises the application of the pedagogical strategy in accordance with the most appropriate guiding theory that will support the learning process, the best structure that is currently available, and the appropriate methodology in accordance with the previously established educational goals(Domingueti, Barbosa Feres Carvalho, Colombo Dias, & Oliveira, 2022). Understanding the basic elements that will make up the simulation and its conduct is crucial to explaining SBE from the perspective of instructional design. These constructs were defined in the current study as elements of the simulation design, which the authors regarded to be the essential qualities required for the development of SBE.

In the future, nurses and midwives will play multifaceted important roles in promoting healthcare equity worldwide by taking on additional duties, cooperating with various communities and sectors, and experimenting with new ideas when working in cutting-edge digital settings. But only if the obstacles preventing nurses from using their education and training to the fullest be adjusted, then the promise to improve the healthcare of individuals and communities can't be achieved(Wakefield, Williams, & Le Menestrel, 2021). In order to do this, it will be essential to amend statutes pertaining to the scope of practice, public health and health system guidelines, state laws governing the use of standing orders, and Medicare and other guidelines surrounding nursing education(Haney, 2023). The setting that the future generation of nurses will practice and lead will change significantly as a result of impressive changes taking place in both the healthcare system and society at large. Nursing programs must prioritize training all nurses to be able to address socio-economic determinants of health and meet patients where they are and being able to navigate technology environment, if healthcare equity is to be accomplished in its entirety(Garber et al., 2023). In this paper, a thorough virtual reality (VR) and simulation training program that gives nurses access to an advanced academic health sciences and clinic environment that promotes a deeper comprehension of the human body and modern digital settings used in healthcare occupations is presented. Nurse Dr. Amber Santos, Director of Innovation and Immersive Learning at Jacksonville University and Assistant Professor of Nursing, agreed that a new generation of nurses will need to be prepared through immersive clinical training and be familiar with VR clinical simulations(Oyekunle et al., 2024). In terms of how the brain and nervous system work in the actual world, the clinical VR simulation will offer an experience that is quite similar to that through the use of an immersive virtual environment.

A greater understanding of the human body and the current healthcare environment will be available to nurses thanks to the significant VR and simulation training options provided by the new academic health sciences curriculum(Shorey & Ng, 2021). In order to succeed in healthcare occupations that demand knowledge of cutting-edge technology and medical procedures, clinical worker's education should make use of extensive simulation-based learning, including VR and augmented reality (AR) techniques that have seen significant expansion in the recent years(Mathew & Pillai, 2020). One of the well-known and frequently used technique in nursing education is simulation-based learning(Weeks, Herron, & Buchanan, 2024). In recent years, skills laboratories have emerged as a mode of instruction that, without the need for clinical placements, may teach psychomotor skills and implicit contextual information by repeated practice. Nurses with varying levels of expertise might benefit from simulations that mimic a wide range of scenarios that teach new skills on digital and electronic settings(Matthew & Kazaure, 2020). Their simulations range from basic low-fidelity to high-fidelity and employ a wide range of technologies to replicate real-life situations. Nurse decision-making and clinical skills are enhanced through the use of cardiopulmonary resuscitation(CPR) manikin and simulated patients to help students hone their clinical and conversational skills for a real patient interactions as widely utilized in medical and nursing education(L'her et al., 2020). An intimate examination can be taught to aspiring medical professionals through the use of a specially trained simulated patient. The use of virtual worlds in clinical practice and nursing education is growing in popularity because of technology improvements and the heightened tech-savvy nature of the current generation(Kutzin, Kipper, & Dahl, 2021). Virtual reality technology, such as augmented reality and virtual simulation, is becoming more and more popular in nursing education as a way to engage students in the curriculum. Because simulations can mimic elements of reality, they offer students secure learning settings in which they can practice until they master a skill by giving them feedback and allowing them to make corrections on their own. Nursing curriculum now include simulations as a core component, including trained individuals, lifelike virtual settings, patient simulators, and role-playing to augment human competence that necessitate occupational efficiency(Matthew, Kazaure, & Haruna, 2020).

In order to optimize patientcare delivery and improve healthcare outcomes, person-centered treatment must be combined with immersive technological support and greater patient health literacy. When clinical occupational environments incorporate creative health literacy, nurses will undoubtedly perform better(Duffy, 2022). The use of clinical simulation in nursing education has become essential in the current day, revolutionizing the training of future medical professionals(Matthew et al., 2021). This study explores the realm of simulation-based learning, illuminating its importance, difficulties, and endless potential in the field of nursing education. However, there are unique difficulties associated with the successful application of simulation-based learning in nursing education. Creating and incorporating realistic scenarios that reflect clinical practice is a major task(Sox, Higgins, Owens, & Schmidler, 2024). These simulations have to include a variety of patient demographics and ailments, as well as a wide range of healthcare settings, from emergency rooms to long-term care facilities. Keeping simulations current with the most recent developments in technology and health also adds a level of complication(Fiani et al., 2020). The implementation of simulation-based learning is made more difficult by time, faculty training, and budgetary limitations. With the implementation of universal health coverage (UHC), Sustainable Development Goal 3 (SDG3) consists of 13 goals and 26 indicators that seek to enhance health outcomes by lowering mortality, putting an end to epidemics, and avoiding diseases(Takian, Raoofi, & Haghighi, 2022). SDG 3 is fundamentally people-centered and encompasses universal coverage and good health for all citizens. The dynamic global health landscape and the shortage of health workers impede SDG 3's progress, especially when it comes to achieving UHC(Walton-Roberts, 2023). In the current era of technological automation and digital supremacy, nursing education institutions need to be more robust and durable than ever in order to support clinical students achievement and fulfill occupational requirements(Stoumpos, Kitsios, & Talias, 2023). Enough infrastructure, funding, and resources for healthcare will help to enhance patient outcomes and experiences even in the face of low clinical manpower distribution in the health system. A sufficient supply of highly motivated healthcare professionals with immersive technology capacity is essential to delivering high-quality treatment to patients(Ramos, 2024). This research is organized thematically into introduction, research objective, research question, literature review, research design, research methodology, implementation, future research focus and conclusion.

Research Objective

Given their expertise and skills, nurses are vital in the ever changing healthcare sector because they can perform well in a fast-paced digital work environment. Nurses need to be able to prioritize and assess treatment in order to fulfill the complex and varied requirements of their patients, provide safe and high-quality results. Nursing students might benefit from simulation as a teaching and readiness tool for real-world scenarios. Through realistic, secure, and effective learning environments, virtual reality simulations improve nursing education. The integration of VR into nursing curricula can be highly advantageous for patients and nursing students as technology advances. The following are study's objectives.

i. To fashion VR simulation approaches to nurses preparing for uncommon, difficult, expensive, and complex procedures to rehearse in virtual reality environments without putting actual patients at risk. This keeps patients safe while giving student nurse practical experience in handling a range of clinical scenarios.
ii. To enable VR improves remote learning by creating dynamic, realistic learning environments. It is still possible for students to engage in safe practice, standardized scenarios, and active learning even in circumstances when there is restricted physical access to clinical environments
iii. To establish VR simulations as more affordable approaches to immersive learning in place of traditional SBE. Because of their enhanced scalability, more students are able to actively engage in real-world work-based learning opportunities.
iv. To create virtual reality that helps students develop critical thinking abilities by putting them in challenging clinical scenarios. Preparing them for practical nursing practices, it pushes them to think critically, decide, and act appropriately.

Research Question

Virtual reality simulations have grown in popularity in nursing education due to its effectiveness and unique advantages. Let us investigate some research questions concerning virtual reality applications in nursing education.

i. What is the efficacy of using virtual reality simulation as a teaching technique among student nurses and professionally registered nurses, in comparison to other teaching methods?
ii. What pedagogical results were found in the research that used virtual reality simulation as a tool for curricular engagement?
iii. What benefits and drawbacks come with adopting virtual reality simulation in clinical practice and nursing education?

LITERATURE REVIEW

The adoption of 5G spectrum infrastructure has enabled advancement in innovation along digital extreme automation, promoting Internet of Health Things (IoHT) dominance(Matthew et al., 2021), which has considerably improved extended reality(XR) technology in healthcare simulation. The deployment of a private 5G network can provide low latency, high dependability, and high bandwidth connectivity to makers of medical and clinical equipment and accessories (Matthew, Kazaure, & Okochi,

2022). This will allow them to link and control many devices in real-time, for better decision-making and process optimization, as well as safer and more effective operations. All immersive technologies that extend the traditional learning experience through immersive interaction are grouped together under the umbrella term of XR(Baxter & Hainey, 2023). Under the umbrella of XR, mixed reality (MX), VR, and AR simulations have brought forth fresh and inventive ways for professionals and learners to become fully immersed in training scenarios and thereby expand their knowledge and abilities(Yadav, 2024). Numerous technological tools, including software, headsets, online scenarios, and more, enable XR healthcare teaching. MR, VR, AR and XR devices are all compatible with a range of instructional software and methodologies(Simon-Liedtke & Baraas, 2022). These technological learning aids offer learners realistic training environments to enhance real-world or manikin-based clinical simulation. XR platforms have the power to transform the way that medical students are taught to comprehend difficult ideas and activities, such as surgery and procedures. More businesses are beginning to develop XR solutions, and the costs of XR-based technology are set to decline. The opportunities for academic institutions, healthcare facilities, and other organizations that rely on clinical simulation to deliver healthcare education are growing significantly.

For the reason that XR technologies may be used anywhere at any time with the right hardware and software, they are advantageous to learners for a variety of reasons(Newton & Annetta, 2024). This has the potential to improve equity in healthcare simulation-based education initiatives worldwide. Since the equipment is frequently reusable, it lowers the expenses associated with teaching a large number of students over time. The simulation with AR is a subset of XR in which digital overlays are utilized to change the learner's actual environment(Levy & Liu, 2022). The AR has the potential to improve the realism and moulage of physical-based healthcare simulations by providing visual clues, such rashes, that manikins might not be able to convey. VR simulations in other hand is a subset of XR-based healthcare simulations in which participants interact with a virtual environment by donning a VR headset(Qayyum et al., 2024), creating a full virtual reality and immersive world. Even though learners frequently interact with VR as avatars in virtual environments, the healthcare simulation setting can provide incredibly transforming learning opportunities. Numerous research investigations indicate that virtual reality medical simulations enhance the capacity for learning and augment precision in real-world medical applications. According to(Rauschnabel, Felix, Hinsch, Shahab, & Alt, 2022), Virtual and physical elements are combined in MR simulation, which is a subset of XR. A real manikin or in-person clinical simulation can be used in conjunction with a headset-based XR medium in MR. Many new groups and associations are forming around XR in healthcare simulation settings that focus on ergonomics and human safety(Kaplan et al., 2021). A group that distribute information about virtual reality in healthcare sector has emerged to ensure proper blending of the technology within the occupational setting as International Virtual Reality Healthcare Association (IVHA). The IVRHA is a membership-driven association made up of organizations from all around the healthcare ecosystem, including insurance companies, teaching hospitals, universities, and technology businesses. The purpose of IVRHA is to promote and assist the expansion of the virtual reality and healthcare sectors, as these two fields are increasingly impacted by the same new computing platform. In addition to having membership subscriptions worldwide and across occupational boundaries, IVRHA organizes international conferences. An organization dedicated to furthering the study and application of medical extended reality is the American Medical Extended Reality Association (AMXRA) (Zhang & Spiegel, 2024). By advancing clinical care delivery, scientific research, innovation, education, advocacy, and community, AMXRA hopes to improve the field of medical extended reality.

Through the use of immersive, three-dimensional VR simulation, clinical nurses can rehearse techniques and procedures in a secure yet authentic setting(Clarke, 2021). Since it enables students to acquire the necessary skills in a setting that does not jeopardize patient safety, simulation is an indispensable part of medical education. In order to provide context explanations, simulation is the imitation of a system or process that could be found in the actual world(Carr & England, 2023). In a variety of settings, including educational training and health video gamifications, simulation is employed to better understand how human or natural systems function in optimizing or tuning its performance(Arif, Ayunda, Diah, & Garcia, 2024). A variety of clinical simulations that captured reality of the state of art nursing practices were created through innovative simulated pedagogy for academic development especially for nurses and clinical workforce(Jeffries, 2022). Technology advancements and the need to find safety and diversified practice for nurses in obtaining clinical experiences is driving the ongoing nursing education and teaching methodologies(Hassmiller & Wakefield, 2022). The health researchers are also devising approaches in replicating those novel finding for opportunity in the emerging new world that advance clinical professionalism. These innovations are helping students prepare for the extreme digital automation of healthcare system connecting pertinent theories with practical reality in the twenty-first century. Even though simulation-based teaching methods have been around for a while, it's still difficult to create engaging and pedagogical linkages. For clinical students to learn, a simulation must be credible and realistic in serving its purpose within the educational context(Theobald, Tutticci, Ramsbotham, & Johnston, 2021).

Simulation is recognized as a helpful teaching technique in nursing education, creating market for healthcare gamification, which includes fitness games, serious games, and leisure games, based on application in education, treatments and diseases prevention(Jibril et al., 2022),(Mishra, Kulshreshtha, Srivastava, Gandhi, & Rastogi, 2019). In situations including decision-making, role-playing, recognizing and motivating clinical students who are decreasing, and delivering end-of-life care, its efficacy and influence on learning have been demonstrated(Barger, 2018). Simulation is becoming an increasingly popular tool in nursing education to enhance practical outcomes by fostering and practicing clinical thinking. While most researches have evaluated specific clinical reasoning frameworks, differences in clinical reasoning terminology have broaden the usefulness of simulation for clinical reasoning acquisition(Heitzman et al., 2019). Due to the overwhelming potential indicated by the literature on its application in nursing, it is also becoming more and more beneficial in educational settings. However, cost, space, accessibility, and the ability to accommodate larger student groups are the disadvantages these emerging technology is facing. As a key component of the curriculum in nursing education, simulation was formerly the purview of professors who appreciated the technical elements of working with computerized mannequins(Foster, Moroney, Phillips, & Lilienthal, 2024). These days, virtual simulation, digital mannequins, role play, and standardized patients are all forms of simulation available for nursing students. Today, simulation must be included into every aspect of the nursing curriculum, as students can acquire skills, hone their clinical reasoning abilities, and gain competency in providing safe patient/family care through simulation(Englar, 2017). In order to address the socioeconomic determinants of health and promote healthcare fairness, the nursing organizations are expected to work together to find opportunities for education, practice, and policy. In addition to accompanying data and criteria for assessing impact, the agenda should include clear priorities across nursing practice, education, leadership, and involvement in health policy(Schwingrouber, Bryant-Lukosius, Kilpatrick, Mayen, & Colson, 2024).

With the development in federated learning, the exponential rise of AR-enabling technology increases support for Industry 5.0 and Healthcare 5.0 service enhancement(Peterson, Charles, Yeung, & Coyle, 2021). Since its inception in 2020, Healthcare 5.0 has placed a strong emphasis on customer-centric models and personalization with the goal of fostering lasting relationships and enhancing well-being for the sustainability of global digital health. It advances healthcare sustainability, lowers costs, and improves patient outcomes by integrating Industry 5. 0 technologies like IoT, AI, big data and immersive technologies(Alahi et al., 2023). Meanwhile, the practical challenges of AR and VR play a major role in developing cognitive tools and analytics in many industry-wide advancements and real-time applications. Artificial intelligence (AI) and immersive technologies seem to be influencing clinical precisions in a way that is a major model for the growth of society(Matthew, Onumaku, et al., 2024). The upcoming wave of AR/VR devices will offer experiences that are personalized, easily accessed, and beautifully made in a manner that advance pedagogic constructivism. Instead of lecturing students on abstract ideas, constructivist education encourages them to create their own knowledge via experiences and activities(Matthew, Kazaure, et al., 2024). Teachers that employ constructivist pedagogy encourage students to master skills and subjects by utilizing practical instruction and self-directed learning opportunities. Students are expected to do their own research to draw their own judgments about a subject. Constructivist pedagogy is an instructional paradigm that emphasizes rich investigation as a means of helping students learn and comprehend course content(Matthew, Kazaure, Kazaure, Nwamouh, & Chinonso, 2022). Students learn via doing when using constructivist education, which encourages experiential learning. When a non-constructivist technique is used, students could read a chapter from a textbook and respond to discussion questions. For more student engagement, a constructivist instructor can assign students to finish a simulation that illustrates the processes involving clinical practice. Constructivist school of thought, ultimately upholds the notion that information is constructed and that it altered through personal experiences rather than passively absorbed(Haker, 2024).

In general, education is a type of intellectual exchange in which habits, knowledge, and abilities of a community are imparted through study, teaching, training, and autodidactism(Ugochukwu Okwudili Matthew, Ado Saleh Kazaure, et al., 2022),(Matthew, Kazaure, Kazaure, Onyedibe, & Okafor, 2022). It has been a way for people to pass along their cultures from generation to generation. It involves altering human behavior in a way that is largely permanent. Technically speaking, education is the confined, formal process through which society consciously passes along its acquired information, skills, customs, and values from one generation to the next, such as through instruction in schools. Since education is the oldest sector of the economy, it serves as society's primary tool for preserving and improving its social equilibrium(Okwudili & Kazaure, 2020). VR refers to a category of computer-based platforms that allow users to experience micro worlds that are somewhat based on reality and are created by hardware and software. A category of computer-controlled multimodal communication technologies known as VR enables more natural interactions with data and novel ways to engage human senses. Virtual reality is essentially a method of recreating or reproducing an environment and providing the user with the impression that they are there, in charge, and directly engaging with it(Nikolić & Whyte, 2021). Virtual reality is a technology that lets a person engage with a computer-simulated world, either real or imaginary. Virtual reality has the potential to be an experience learning tool that enhance interactivity with the virtual world. Immersion is a perceptual and psychological sensation of being in the digital world that is delivered to the senses in virtual reality.

Research Motivation

One important characteristic that sets virtual reality apart from other kinds of computer applications is the feeling of presence or immersion(Caldas, Sanchez, Mauledoux, Avilés, & Rodriguez-Guerrero, 2022). A computer-generated artificial intelligence environment that is at least partially formed and controlled by the user is called virtual reality(Sharma, Khera, & Singh, 2020). With the use of a virtual reality system, a user can leave the real world and enter one where artificial intelligence is used to produce the sights, sounds, smells, and other senses instead of real objects(Bibbò & Morabito, 2022). The user can then control the virtual world's items and processes to a great extent. The creation of educational apps using virtual reality techniques opens up new avenues for subject matter instruction, very essential to comprehend the methods and technology. Three main categories exist for virtual reality systems: (a) Immersive (Fully Immersive), (b) Semi-Immersive, and (c) Non-Immersive. The least amount of VR technology is implemented in non-immersive VR systems. Compared to desktop virtual reality systems, it has a higher level of interaction since it allows the user to fully immerse themselves in the virtual world by obstructing out numerous visual components of the surrounding environment and evoking sensations that are consistent with the virtual world. It entails setting up virtual reality on a desktop PC. When using a desktop computer, a typical high-resolution display is used to observe the virtual environment through a portal or window, the conventional methods of interacting with the virtual world include a keyboard, mouse, and trackball, refer to **Figure 1**.

Figure 1. Interactive Simulation Model for Nursing Education Pedagogy

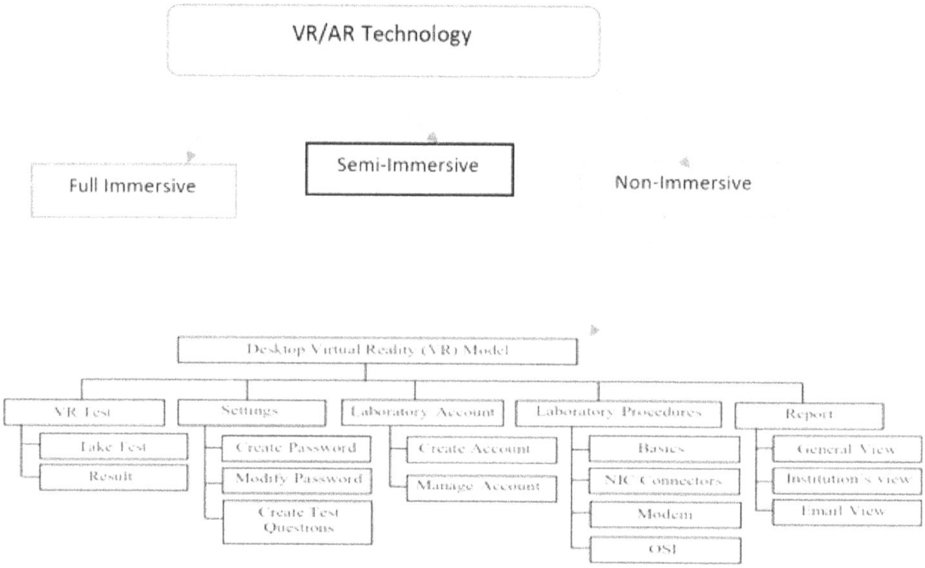

(Onyesolu, Nwasor, Ositanwosu, & Iwegbuna, 2013)

A 3D computer environment called the virtual world sometimes called virtual reality according (Steindorff, Redlich, Paulicke, & Jahn, 2024), gives users interactive experiences of a different reality in which they are avatars with the ability to move, sense, touch, and interact with simulated objects that seem genuine. Two types of virtual worlds exist: immersive virtual reality simulation (iVRS) and desktop virtual reality simulation (dVRS)(Steindorff et al., 2024). The dVRS, or non-iVRS, is a type of virtual reality where users utilize a mouse, keyboard, joystick, or touchscreen to interact with an environment that is projected on a computer monitor. As opposed to this, iVRS offers a fully immersive virtual environment in which the user is outfitted with many sensory output devices, including a haptic, stereoscopic, audio, and head-mounted device(Kooijman, Asadi, Mohamed, & Nahavandi, 2023). A comparatively powerful graphics processing system that can be connected to a large screen monitor, a large screen projection system, or several television projection systems makes up the Semi-Immersive VR Systems. These technologies amplify the user's sense of presence or immersion through a broad field of view, and stereographic imaging can be accomplished with the use of shutter glasses(Kress, 2019). The most direct way to encounter virtual surroundings is through immersive (fully immersive) VR systems(Hazarika & Rahmati, 2023). By allowing users to engage with a computer-simulated environment, virtual reality environments (VREs) create a digital experience that gives users the impression that they are carrying out tasks in the real world. It is an interactive digital scenario that allows the user to react to an abstract idea or simulation in order to learn how to do certain tasks and obtain comprehension. Virtual reality games are one example of a simulated environment that deviates greatly from reality, while pilot or military training simulations can be similar to the real world. Because of severe technical constraints on processing power, image quality, and transmission bandwidth, it is still exceedingly difficult to generate a high-fidelity virtual reality experience. Because of its immersive, highly visual, three-dimensional surroundings, the term virtual reality environment is frequently used to describe a wide range of applications.

Figure 2. Fully immersive VR simulation: Adopted from Jacksonville University simulation lab

In addition to certain tracking and haptic devices, the user views the virtual environment by donning a head mounted display (HMD) or using a head-coupled display like a Binocular Omni-Orientation Monitor (BOOM)(Mukkawar, Netak, & Nikam, 2021). Little monitors that are positioned in front of each eye to offer stereo, binocular, or monocular views are called HMDs or BOOMs. The Automatic Virtual Environment (CAVE) has been more successful and well-liked as the sensors that are normally affixed to the 3D glasses detect the motions of the CAVE user, and the video continuously modifies to maintain the viewer's perspective(Sudharson et al., 2024). Stereo pictures are projected on the walls and floor of a room-sized cube in CAVE environments to give the sensation of immersion. In the CAVE environment, participants can move about freely while donning lightweight stereo glasses. A head-tracking computer system continuously modifies the stereo projection to match the viewer's present position(Schröder-Dering, Zachmann, & Weller, 2022).

Research Design

When AR and VR simulations are properly integrated, nursing education can undergo a revolution that will ensure patient safety while educating students for real- world occupational challenges. For specialists, experts, graduate and under-graduate students alike, a simulation lab is intended to offer a realistic point-of-care learning scenario. With the use of models like manikins or virtual reality, real-world situations are replicated so that students can practice activities and procedures. Through simulation-based training sessions, students in the lab acquire and retain a variety of information, skills, and competencies, including how to communicate, operate specific equipment, follow teamwork protocols, and so forth. In line with the research questions and the research objectives, this paper framed specific objective in nursing education with reference to **Figure 1andFigure 2**.

Table 1. Capturing specific interest in AR and VR simulation in nursing education

Simulation Component	Objective	Why?
Authentic Learning Experiences:	Create realistic scenarios that mirror actual clinical situations.	Authenticity fosters clinical decision-making and critical thinking in students by assisting them in applying theoretical information to real-world situations(Vázquez-Calatayud, García-García, Regaira-Martínez, & Gómez-Urquiza, 2024).
Standardization:	Ensure consistency across simulations.	Standardized situations facilitate consistent skill practice for learners, leading to improved learning results(Quail, Brundage, Spitalnick, Allen, & Beilby, 2016).
Interactivity and Engagement:	Foster active participation	VR and AR simulations engage students through interactive experiences, enhancing their understanding and retention of complex concepts(Familoni & Onyebuchi, 2024).
Safety and Risk-Free Learning:	Provide a safe environment for skill development	Simulations allow students to make mistakes without real-world consequences, promoting confidence and competence(Elendu et al., 2024).
Collaboration and Communication:	Encourage teamwork and effective communication.	Simulations involving multiple learners promote collaboration, vital for healthcare professionals(Stenseth et al., 2022).
Critical Thinking and Problem-Solving:	Develop analytical skills.	Complex scenarios challenge students to think critically, analyze information, and make informed decisions(Patel, Puah, & Kok, 2024).
Cost-Effectiveness:	Optimize resources	VR and AR simulations can be more cost-effective than traditional methods, especially when scaling up to accommodate larger student cohorts(Akdere, Jiang, & Acheson, 2023).

The provision of nursing care depends on people interacting with one another via information and communication technologies (ICTs) platforms(Rouleau et al., 2017). In order to preserve patient safety, satisfaction and technology exchanges in written and spoken interactions are crucial ideas to accurately replicate human responses in a lab setting. The spiral structure of the nursing curriculum implies that current learning from a simple to a complicated trajectory is influenced by prior knowledge and engaging associations(Tahsin et al., 2023). Incorporating increasingly complex scenarios and activities is a tactic for fostering relationships, identifying inferences, contextual considerations, and data processing that results in clinical decision-making abilities and active learning(Nordin et al., 2021). ICT use by nurses can change how they plan, document, and evaluate clinical care, but it can also have an overall impact on the dimensions and indicators of nursing care. Healthcare practitioners can now use electronic medical records (EMR), telemedicine, remote patient monitoring, and other services because to the ever-expanding role of technology in the field. What changes has this brought about for the treatment of patients and the medical staff who give it? Answering that question is the goal of nursing informaticists. A nurse that blends clinical expertise with an understanding of computers, technology, and data is known as a nursing informaticists. Complex jobs are assigned to informaticists, such as teaching nursing staff how to use new patient care technologies or analyzing health data to examine service outcomes.

Table 2. Capturing diversities in nursing education

Nursing Diversity	Specifics
Anaesthetic Nursing	Patients receive anesthetic (pain medication) treatment from a nurse anesthetist prior to, during, and following surgery(Bhatia & Buvanendran, 2019). They continuously monitor all of the patient's bodily functions and give drugs to keep patients pain free or sleeping during surgery.
Informatics (Tech) Nursing	A high-level position in nursing informatics entails a great deal of responsibility in analyzing patient care data and applying the findings to enhance outcomes(Navab, Hoseini Azizi, & Darvish, 2024). Monitoring the effectiveness of patient care initiatives. Investigating or creating cutting-edge technology for medical facility. Experimenting with new technologies like AR, VR, XR, MX and AI application is healthcare technology. Teaching employees how to use new technology and addressing inquiries concerning medical technologies from the personnel. Keeping an eye on the outcomes of applying the new technology and acting as a contact between the departments of technological development and nursing personnel.
Psychiatric(Mental) Nursing	A registered nurse (RN) with specific training who is qualified to provide care and support to people with mental health issues is known as a psychiatric mental health nurse (PMHN)(Gerolamo et al., 2024).

continued on following page

Table 2. Continued

Nursing Diversity	Specifics
Pediatric (Maternal & Child Health) Nursing	Maternal-child nursing is a specialty focused on the care of women throughout their pregnancy and childbirth and the care of their newborn children(Keenan-Lindsay & Leifer, 2023). This specialty includes obstetric nursing, perinatal nursing and pediatric nursing.
Orthopaedics Nursing	Orthopaedics nursing is a nursing specialty focused on the prevention and treatment of musculoskeletal disorders(Klunder-Rosser, 2020). Orthopaedics issues range from acute problems such as fractures or hospitalization for joint replacement to chronic systemic disorders such as loss of bone density or lupus erythematosus.
Ear Nose and Throat(ENT) Nursing	An ENT Nurse is a medical professional that specializes in this field, also called otorhinolaryngology. ENT nurses work with patients to treat injuries to these specific areas and help diagnose illnesses and chronic conditions, such as ear infections, allergies, tonsillitis, laryngitis, and sleep apnea(Leigh et al., 2021).
Occupational Nursing	Occupational health nursing is a specialty nursing practice that provides for and delivers health and safety programs and services to workers, worker populations, and community groups(Daley & Dale, 2024).
Community Midwifery	A Community Midwife is a trained provider specialized in normal pregnancy and birth, who provides comprehensive pregnancy, birth and postpartum care in the community or out-of-hospital setting(Stoll et al., 2020). Community Midwives work with low-risk, healthy individuals.
Preoperative Nursing	Perioperative nursing is a nursing specialty that works with patients who are having operative or other invasive procedures. Perioperative nurses work closely with surgeons, anaesthesiologists, nurse anaesthetists, surgical technologists, and nurse practitioners(Riesen, Hoekman, & Björkelund, 2023).
Nursing Administration	Managing nursing staff, patient care, and facility resources strategically with the help of governing policies is perhaps the best way to characterize nursing administration(Morsiani, Bagnasco, & Sasso, 2017). It is the duty of nurse administrators to make sure that medical facilities, such as hospitals, run safely and economically.
Community/Public Health Nursing	Community health Nursing is the synthesis of nursing and public health practice applied to promote and protect the health of population(Iwamoto, 2023). It combines all the basic elements of professional, clinical nursing with public health and community practice.
Nursing Education	Nurse education consists of the theoretical and practical training provided to nurses with the purpose to prepare them for their duties as nursing care professionals(Steindorff et al., 2024).
Medical-Surgical Nursing	Medical-surgical nursing is a nursing specialty area concerned with the care of adult patients in a broad range of settings(Mahmoud, Finnell, Sereika, Lindsay, & Mitchell, 2024). Traditionally, medical-surgical nursing was an entry-level position that most nurses viewed as a stepping stone to specialty areas.

RESEARCH METHODOLOGY

In addition to offering a consistent means of improving practical abilities over time, VR training helps nurses become more familiar with digital nursing technology and broadens their digital competencies in a real-world context. This method can be applied to sustainability challenges as well. All studies, however, have emphasized that virtually supported teaching-learning scenarios are still not a panacea for instruction; rather, their use should be carefully considered and critically reflected at the points where traditional teaching methods become insufficient to fully prepare students for the role of a professionally acting nurse in the future. With regard to developing and implementing digitally supported scenarios for educational demands in nursing education, this scoping review provides an overview of the implications, considerations, and recommendations. To improve nursing education in compliance with the National Policy on Nursing Education, an evaluation of three nursing schools was conducted with regard to the creation of a virtual reality simulation lab. The National Information and Communication Technology Policy, the National Information Technology Education Framework, and the Ministerial Strategy Plan for the Education Sector (2016–2019) provide important components and infrastructure recommendations that form the basis of the proposed model. Information was obtained from two hundred and fifty (250) nursing students, fifteen (15) nursing teachers, and six (6) ICT center staff in accordance with the study's objectives. Academic staff, ICT Center staff, and students from three nursing and midwifery training schools participated in the quantitative investigation reported in the paper. Three hundred twenty (320) randomly selected stakeholders from the three nursing and midwifery institutions were given the questionnaires to fill out in order to gather data relevant to the study's purpose. 271 of the 320 issued questionnaires were properly filled out and returned, accounting for an 84.7% response rate.

Clinical simulation has the power to transform healthcare delivery and enhance patient outcomes when it is incorporated into nursing education(Hauze, Hoyt, Frazee, Greiner, & Marshall, 2019). This scoping study did, however, draw attention to the fact that nurses must have a variety of competencies (such as knowledge, abilities, and attitudes), as well as behaviors and self-efficacy (which may act as a mediator of the phenomena). Therefore, to guarantee the successful use of new technologies in nursing, it is crucial to develop a thorough conceptual framework that takes into account each of these factors. We suggest using Immersive Pedagogy and the Technological Framework for healthcare professionals as the foundation for developing new clinical simulation evidence, based on the results previously presented, refer to **Figure 3**. Several essential elements that are centered around the use of immersive pedagogical technology make up the framework for the paradigm adoption. The ability to use mobile devices, comprehend electronic medical records, and operate digital health information systems is a prerequisite for nurses. Furthermore, the ability to interpret, evaluate, and make defensible decisions based on digital data requires critical thinking abilities. The ability for nurses to comprehend the clinical and technical aspects of digital and electronic solutions makes knowledge another essential component of the framework.

Nurses need to understand how these solutions function, as well as the advantages and disadvantages of using them to enhance patient care. In addition, nurses must be aware of the ethical and legal dilemmas raised by digital technology, particularly those pertaining to confidentiality and privacy. Another essential component of the framework is attitude, which affects how nurses view technology and clinical simulation. For these ideas to be successfully incorporated into mainstream nursing education, positive attitudes about them are necessary. Positive-thinking nurses see these solutions as useful tools that can boost productivity, lower errors, and improve patient care. On the other hand, unfavorable opinions may prevent these ideas from being adopted or reduce their potential advantages. The foundation of the framework is competence, which is created by adding together knowledge, skill, and attitude. Skilled nurses may improve patient outcomes by integrating digital and technological solutions into their workflow with ease. When applying reasonable competence, knowledge, and attitude to a digital assignment, true competency entails exhibiting stress tolerance and confidence. Conversely, in the event that resources and proper communication are lacking, nurses can find it difficult to fully utilize these technology. Therefore, when creating and implementing digital and technical solutions in nursing, it is crucial to take into account both the work environment and individual characteristics. To sum up, in order to guarantee the successful adoption of digital and technology solutions in nursing education, a thorough conceptual framework covering all of their facets is necessary. Crucial elements of this paradigm include knowledge, abilities, competence, attitudes, self-efficacy, and behaviors alongside skills. Our goal is to give nurses, healthcare professionals, academics, and policymakers a theoretical reference to reinforce and expand upon the body of current evidence by creating and disseminating the immersive pedagogic and technological framework.

Figure 3. Immersive pedagogic and technological framework

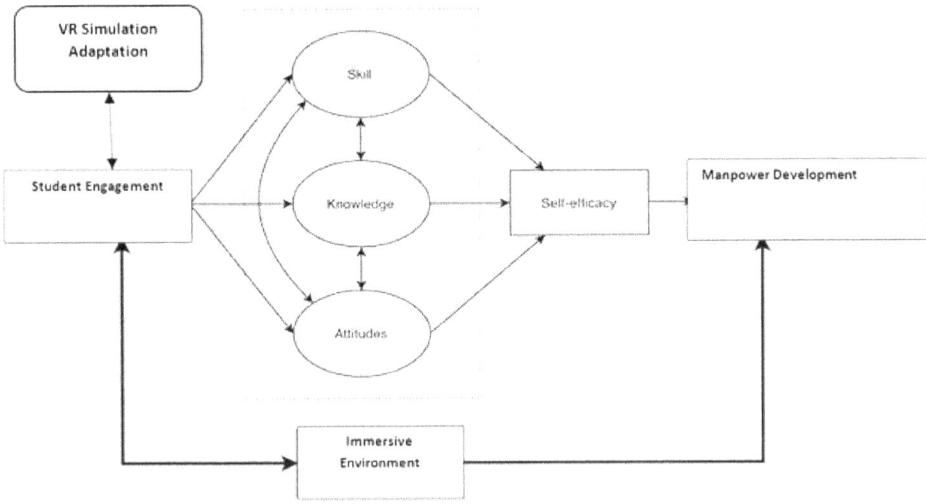

Nurse's confidence in their ability to use digital and technological solutions effectively is referred to as immersive simulation and technological self-efficacy. It is essential for nurses to have high self-efficacy since it helps them to overcome obstacles that may occur when using these solutions. High self-efficacy may also boost nurses' motivation to use these solutions, which could result in their successful adoption. In addition, behaviors describe what nurses do when they use technology and digital solutions in the real world(Conte, Arrigoni, Magon, Stievano, & Caruso, 2023). Effective communication, precise data entry, and prompt documentation are examples of positive behaviors that might enhance patient outcomes. Conversely, negative behaviors that restrict the potential benefits of these solutions and jeopardize patient safety include data input errors and resistance to change. The successful implementation of immersive pedagogic and technological framework in nursing education and practice is contingent upon several factors, including individual qualities and the work environment, in addition to the previously described issues. Nurses' views and behaviors toward these solutions might be influenced by individual factors, including motivation, learning styles, and personality features. Nurses who are receptive to acquiring new competencies and technology, for instance, could be more inclined to embrace and employ the suggested framework. However, professional nurses who struggle with change or poor self-efficacy could be less willing to employ these tools. The way that nurses use technology and digital tools might also be influenced by their work environment. Resources, communication, and organizational support are a few examples of factors that can affect how well these solutions are adopted and used.

DISCUSSION OF RESEARCH FINDINGS

Our goal in doing this research was to develop a thorough framework to direct the adoption of immersive pedagogic and technological frameworks in nursing education by reviewing the literature in the field. Our research demonstrates how an immersive pedagogical and technical framework, which supports nurses in their clinical and organizational practice, has the potential to change the healthcare industry. When it comes to presenting, putting into practice, and utilizing immersive pedagogic and technological framework in clinical practice, nurses are essential. In addition to defining virtual reality simulation (VRS) in nursing education and professional practice, our scholarly contribution offers a comprehensive assessment of the literature currently available on the use of immersive pedagogic and technological frameworks in the nursing field. The synthesis and reworking of data from published literature establishes the foundation for further investigation into the adoption of immersive pedagogic and technological frameworks in nursing, as well as the creation of evidence-based tactics to enhance nursing practice via the use of these frameworks. In spite of this, immersive pedagogical and technical frameworks in nursing education and occupational practice have several drawbacks. Furthermore, there appears to be an excessive focus on how proficient nurses are with technology. Future research should address these limitations by creating measurement tools that are both valid and reliable, investigating the moral implications of technology use in nursing, and giving nurses the support and training they need to acquire the skills they need to use these technologies efficiently.

Future Research Focus and Limitations on Simulation in Nursing Education

In an effort to promote health equity, numerous nursing organizations have created educational resources, backed legislation, interacted with the media, and carried out numerous other tasks(Wakefield et al., 2021). Although, these individual association efforts are significant, the current study urges nursing organizations to pool resources, pool knowledge, and prioritize these emphasis areas more quickly and collaboratively on behalf of the patients they serve(Gustad, Bangstad, Torsvik, & Rise, 2024). The use of evidence-based educational strategies that demonstrated increase and diversity of faculty and students from historically underrepresented and disadvantaged groups should be the main focus of future researches. Other areas of focus should include developing evidence-based education strategies that effectively prepare nurses to eradicate implicit bias and structural racism, as well as improving the use of cutting-edge information technology to improve care coordination without causing more inequality(Saric et al., 2024). In addition to guaranteeing students' wellbeing, educators should have a crucial responsibility to provide them with the knowledge and skills necessary to maintain that wellbeing throughout their careers. It is the responsibility of educators to create and maintain cultures that meaningfully and visibly include well-being into the curriculum

Nursing schools will employ simulation extensively, and this trend is only going to grow because of its many advantages. Nevertheless, there are several drawbacks to using simulation to teach nursing skills; the following are the most important ones: Two distinct elements of nursing courses, holistic nursing care as a concept and simulation as a technique, have been combined in the process of learning the skills and knowledge needed to provide patient care. Using standardized patients, virtual environments, and simulators, simulation offers possibilities to learn and apply new abilities. Providing nurses with training, regardless of the method, particularly through simulation, is an expensive endeavor. The cost of operating and maintaining a modern laboratory is high. A significant amount of money is needed for the purchase of computers, high-fidelity simulation models, and ongoing maintenance. The equipment's amortization will be facilitated by prompt and suitable student training and, subsequently, by the patient care that skilled nurses deliver. A noteworthy constraint that could arise in a simulation is incomplete training. Negative learning could come from a situation that is badly planned. Students might ignore and overlook to examine specific bodily reactions, for instance, if they are absent throughout the simulation process. Often, because of time limits, simulation is unable to evaluate certain crucial aspects of the medical procedure and communication.

Given these drawbacks, research in the future ought to concentrate on creating accurate and valid measuring tools, comprehending the variations in technology use among various populations, and investigating the moral ramifications of using technology in nursing. It is essential to give nurses the right instruction and assistance so they may acquire the skills needed to use these technologies effectively. It is also crucial to take nurses' perspectives and experiences into account when designing and implementing these solutions. To fully utilize digital and technological solutions to raise the standard and efficiency of healthcare, it is imperative to address the shortcomings of the existing literature in the subject of immersive pedagogy and technology framework in nursing. Scholars and professionals can progress the area of nursing technology and improve the standard of care given to patients by concentrating on these constraints. A thorough framework and a sound conceptualization are necessary to steer future research toward a nuanced and sophisticated understanding of the immersive pedagogic and technological setting.

CONCLUSION

The integration of modern technology into nursing education requires not only technical proficiency with immersive digital platforms but also customization to professional requirements in line with the healthcare curriculum. This study focused on the necessity of a shared learning environment with a variety of educational resources to facilitate coordination between learning objectives and activities. The study went on to highlight the situational nature of learning and made the case that, in order to promote awareness of learning needs and enhance teacher-student interaction, educators and students must be involved in the design process. A technique for applying digital gamification to teach knowledge in a real-world setting is VR simulation-based learning. These virtual reality applications can help prepare nurses for potential future professional obstacles. Training participants can effectively engage with simulated real life and experience circumstances that are getting more and more concrete thanks to the ongoing development of VR applications. One way to enhance learning in nursing schools is through virtual reality where information visualization is particularly useful for exploring anatomy-related learning content. High levels of acceptability of the VR application were seen during the trials, emphasizing potential for pedagogy adoption. This demonstrates that the new technologies have a fair probability of being adopted into nursing schools from the perspective of the students. Educational institutions wishing to use portions of this pedagogical curriculum component can replicate several sections either in their whole or in other configurations. A conceptual framework for the implementation of VR simulation through multi-dimensional ICT policy was developed by the study by utilizing the immersive pedagogic and technological framework. Three research questions were identified and thoroughly addressed with the proposed framework and theoretical setting. Most of the objectives and strategies that the authors had previously recommended for the conceptual framework were supported by the findings. Research indicates that employing developmental strategies in combination with top-down policy reinforcement is a more effective way to impact academic ICT use than relying solely on educators and their organizations.

Conflict of Interest

There is no conflict of interest regarding this paper. However, the paper was supported by U&J Digital Consult Limited. An IT and Educational Consulting Firm base in Nigeria.

REFERENCES

Akdere, M., Jiang, Y., & Acheson, K. (2023). To simulate or not to simulate? Comparing the effectiveness of video-based training versus virtual reality-based simulations on interpersonal skills development. *Human Resource Development Quarterly*, 34(4), 437–462. DOI:10.1002/hrdq.21470

Alahi, M. E. E., Sukkuea, A., Tina, F. W., Nag, A., Kurdthongmee, W., Suwannarat, K., & Mukhopadhyay, S. C. (2023). Integration of IoT-enabled technologies and artificial intelligence (AI) for smart city scenario: Recent advancements and future trends. *Sensors (Basel)*, 23(11), 5206. DOI:10.3390/s23115206 PMID:37299934

Arif, Y. M., Ayunda, N., Diah, N. M., & Garcia, M. B. (2024). A Systematic Review of Serious Games for Health Education: Technology, Challenges, and Future Directions. *Transformative Approaches to Patient Literacy and Healthcare Innovation*, 20-45.

Barger, S. (2018). *Vicarious learning and perceived self-efficacy among pre-licensure nursing students during pediatric end-of-life situations*. The University of Alabama.

Baxter, G., & Hainey, T. (2023). Using immersive technologies to enhance the student learning experience. *Interactive Technology and Smart Education.*

Bhatia, A., & Buvanendran, A. (2019). Anesthesia and postoperative pain control—Multimodal anesthesia protocol. *Journal of Spine Surgery*, 5(S2, Suppl 2), S160–S165. DOI:10.21037/jss.2019.09.33 PMID:31656870

Bibbò, L., & Morabito, F. C. (2022). Neural network design using a virtual reality platform. *Global Journal of Computer Science and Technology*, 22(D1), 45–61. DOI:10.34257/GJCSTDVOL22IS1PG45

Birkheim, S. L., Calogiuri, G., & Martinsen, R. (2023). Advancing immersive virtual reality-based simulation practices: Developing an evidence-based and theory-driven pedagogical framework for VR-based simulations of non-technical skills among healthcare professionals. *Interactive Learning Environments*, 1–13. DOI:10.1080/10494820.2023.2186896

Caldas, O. I., Sanchez, N., Mauledoux, M., Avilés, O. F., & Rodriguez-Guerrero, C. (2022). Leading presence-based strategies to manipulate user experience in virtual reality environments. *Virtual Reality (Waltham Cross)*, 26(4), 1507–1518. DOI:10.1007/s10055-022-00645-3

Cant, R., Cooper, S., & Ryan, C. (2022). Using virtual simulation to teach evidence-based practice in nursing curricula: A rapid review. *Worldviews on Evidence-Based Nursing*, 19(5), 415–422. DOI:10.1111/wvn.12572 PMID:35261156

Carr, K., & England, R. (2023). *Simulated and virtual realities: Elements of perception*. CRC Press.

Clarke, E. (2021). Virtual reality simulation—The future of orthopaedic training? A systematic review and narrative analysis. *Advances in Simulation (London, England)*, 6(1), 1–11. DOI:10.1186/s41077-020-00153-x PMID:33441190

Conte, G., Arrigoni, C., Magon, A., Stievano, A., & Caruso, R. (2023). Embracing Digital and Technological Solutions in Nursing: A scoping review and conceptual framework. *International Journal of Medical Informatics*, 177, 105148. DOI:10.1016/j.ijmedinf.2023.105148 PMID:37453178

Daley, D., & Dale, A. M. (2024). *Promoting Occupational Health and Productivity: Adults Interprofessional Perspectives for Community Practice*. Routledge. DOI:10.4324/9781003524649-15

Domingueti, D., Barbosa Feres Carvalho, D., Colombo Dias, D. R., & Oliveira, V. C. (2022). Software-Based Simulation on a 3D Environment for Vaccination Teaching and Learning: Design Science Research. *JMIR Medical Education*, 8(4), e35712. DOI:10.2196/35712 PMID:36459390

Duffy, J. R. (2022). *Quality caring in nursing and health systems: Implications for clinicians, educators, and leaders*. Springer Publishing Company. DOI:10.1891/9780826136961

Elendu, C., Amaechi, D. C., Okatta, A. U., Amaechi, E. C., Elendu, T. C., Ezeh, C. P., & Elendu, I. D. (2024). The impact of simulation-based training in medical education. *Revista de Medicina (São Paulo)*, 103(27), e38813. PMID:38968472

Englar, R. E. (2017). A novel approach to simulation-based education for veterinary medical communication training over eight consecutive pre-clinical quarters. *Journal of Veterinary Medical Education*, 44(3), 502–522. DOI:10.3138/jvme.0716-118R1 PMID:28876987

Familoni, B. T., & Onyebuchi, N. C. (2024). Augmented and virtual reality in us education: a review: analyzing the impact, effectiveness, and future prospects of ar/vr tools in enhancing learning experiences. *International Journal of Applied Research in Social Sciences*, 6(4), 642–663. DOI:10.51594/ijarss.v6i4.1043

Fiani, B., De Stefano, F., Kondilis, A., Covarrubias, C., Reier, L., & Sarhadi, K. (2020). Virtual reality in neurosurgery:"can you see it?"–a review of the current applications and future potential. *World Neurosurgery*, 141, 291–298. DOI:10.1016/j.wneu.2020.06.066 PMID:32561486

Foster, T. C., Moroney, W. F., Phillips, H. L., & Lilienthal, M. G. (2024). Human Factors in Simulation and Training: An Overview. *Human Factors in Simulation and Training*, 1-64.

Garber, K., Chike-Harris, K., Vetter, M. J., Kobeissi, M., Heidesch, T., Arends, R., Teall, A. M., & Rutledge, C. (2023). Telehealth policy and the advanced practice nurse. *The Journal for Nurse Practitioners*, 19(7), 104655. DOI:10.1016/j.nurpra.2023.104655 PMID:37235075

Gerolamo, A. M., Delaney, K. R., Phoenix, B., Black, P., Rushton, A., & Stallings, J. (2024). Psychiatric nursing workforce survey: Results and implications. *Journal of the American Psychiatric Nurses Association*, 30(3), 690–696. DOI:10.1177/10783903221146190 PMID:36582042

Gustad, L. T., Bangstad, I.-L., Torsvik, M., & Rise, M. B. (2024). Nurses' and Physicians' Experiences After Implementation of a Quality Improvement Project to Improve Sepsis Awareness in Hospitals. *Journal of Multidisciplinary Healthcare*, 17, 29–41. DOI:10.2147/JMDH.S439017 PMID:38192738

Haker, L. J. (2024). *A Constructivist Grounded Theory on CPS Social Worker's Conceptualization of the Access Screening Tool in Relation With Their Experiences, Training, and Values*. Saybrook University.

Haney, B. (2023). 35th Annual APRN legislative update: Updates to APRN practice authority in the United States. *The Nurse Practitioner*, 48(1), 20–47. DOI:10.1097/01.NPR.0000903012.03553.a4 PMID:36573856

Hassmiller, S. B., & Wakefield, M. K. (2022). The future of nursing 2020–2030: Charting a path to achieve health equity. *Nursing Outlook*, 70(6), S1–S9. DOI:10.1016/j.outlook.2022.05.013 PMID:36446536

Hauze, S. W., Hoyt, H. H., Frazee, J. P., Greiner, P. A., & Marshall, J. M. (2019). Enhancing nursing education through affordable and realistic holographic mixed reality: The virtual standardized patient for clinical simulation. *Advances in Experimental Medicine and Biology*, 1, 1–13. DOI:10.1007/978-3-030-06070-1_1 PMID:30919290

Hazarika, A., & Rahmati, M. (2023). Towards an evolved immersive experience: Exploring 5G-and beyond-enabled ultra-low-latency communications for augmented and virtual reality. *Sensors (Basel)*, 23(7), 3682. DOI:10.3390/s23073682 PMID:37050742

Heitzman, N., Seidel, T., Opitz, A., Hetmanek, A., Wecker, C., Fischer, M., & Siebeck, M. (2019). Facilitating diagnostic competences in simulations: A conceptual framework and a research agenda for medical and teacher education. *Frontline Learning Research*, 7(4), 1–24. DOI:10.14786/flr.v7i4.384

Iwamoto, S. (2023). *Developing a Theory of Community Caring for Public Health Nursing*. Paper presented at the Healthcare. DOI:10.3390/healthcare11030349

Jagatheesaperumal, S. K., Ahmad, K., Al-Fuqaha, A., & Qadir, J. (2024). Advancing education through extended reality and internet of everything enabled metaverses: Applications, challenges, and open issues. *IEEE Transactions on Learning Technologies*, 17, 1120–1139. DOI:10.1109/TLT.2024.3358859

Jeffries, P. (2022). *Clinical simulations in nursing education: Advanced concepts, trends, and opportunities*. Lippincott Williams & Wilkins.

Jibril, A. U., Abdullahi, N. M., Ali, A. S., Abdulkadir, H., Matthew, U. O., & Haruna, K. (2022). Motivational aspects of digital games in learning process. *Science in Information Technology Letters*, 3(1), 1–9. DOI:10.31763/sitech.v3i1.885

Kaplan, A. D., Cruit, J., Endsley, M., Beers, S. M., Sawyer, B. D., & Hancock, P. A. (2021). The effects of virtual reality, augmented reality, and mixed reality as training enhancement methods: A meta-analysis. *Human Factors*, 63(4), 706–726. DOI:10.1177/0018720820904229 PMID:32091937

Keenan-Lindsay, L., & Leifer, G. (2023). *Leifer's Introduction to Maternity & Pediatric Nursing in Canada-E-Book: Leifer's Introduction to Maternity & Pediatric Nursing in Canada-E-Book*. Elsevier Health Sciences.

Klunder-Rosser, J. (2020). Should the development of orthopaedic trauma nursing be a priority in low to middle income countries? A scoping review. *International Journal of Orthopaedic and Trauma Nursing*, 37, 100749. DOI:10.1016/j.ijotn.2019.100749 PMID:32001191

Kooijman, L., Asadi, H., Mohamed, S., & Nahavandi, S. (2023). A virtual reality study investigating the train illusion. *Royal Society Open Science*, 10(4), 221622. DOI:10.1098/rsos.221622 PMID:37063997

Kress, B. C. (2019). *Digital optical elements and technologies (EDO19): applications to AR/VR/MR*. Paper presented at the Digital Optical Technologies 2019.

Kutzin, J., Kipper, K., & Dahl, W. (2021). Emergency Nursing Continuing Professional Development Using Simulation. *Comprehensive Healthcare Simulation: Emergency Medicine*, 181-188.

L'her, E., Geeraerts, T., Desclefs, J.-P., Benhamou, D., Blanié, A., Cerf, C., & Ouanes, I. (2020). Simulation-based teaching in critical care, anaesthesia and emergency medicine. *Anaesthesia Critical Care & Pain Medicine*, 39(2), 311–326. DOI:10.1016/j.accpm.2020.03.010 PMID:32223994

Leigh, L. Y., Vannelli, P., Crow, H. C., Desai, S., Lepore, M., Anolik, R., & Glick, M. (2021). Diseases of the respiratory tract. *Burket's Oral Medicine*, 469-504.

Levy, J., & Liu, D. (2022). Extended Reality (XR) environments for flood risk management with 3D GIS and open source 3D graphics cross-platform game engines: advances in immersive sea level rise planning technologies for student learning and community engagement. *Paper presented at the International Conference on Intelligent Technologies*. Research Gate.

Lowman, G. H., & Harms, P. D. (2022). Addressing the nurse workforce crisis: A call for greater integration of the organizational behavior, human resource management and nursing literatures. *Journal of Managerial Psychology*, 37(3), 294–303. DOI:10.1108/JMP-04-2022-713

Mahmoud, K. F., Finnell, D. S., Sereika, S. M., Lindsay, D., & Mitchell, A. M. (2024). Comparing Medical-Surgical, Psychiatric–Mental Health, and Addiction Specialty Nurses' Personal Attitudes, Professional Attitudes, and Motivation Toward Working With Individuals With Alcohol and Opioid Use Problems: Implications for the Nursing Workforce Using a Nationwide Sample. *Journal of Nursing Regulation*, 15(2), 17–27. DOI:10.1016/S2155-8256(24)00052-8

Malekzadeh, S. (2017). *Simulation in Otolaryngology, An Issue of Otolaryngologic Clinics of North: Simulation in Otolaryngology, An Issue of Otolaryngologic Clinics of North* (Vol. 50). Elsevier Health Sciences.

Mathew, P. S., & Pillai, A. S. (2020). Role of immersive (XR) technologies in improving healthcare competencies: a review. *Virtual and Augmented Reality in Education, Art, and Museums*, 23-46.

Matthew, U. O., Kazaure, A. S., Kazaure, J. S., Hassan, I. M., Nwanakwaugwu, A. C., & Okafor, N. U. (2022). Educational Technology Adaptation & Implication for Media Technology Adoption in the Period of COVID-19. *Journal of Trends in Computer Science and Smart Technology*, 4(4), 226–245. DOI:10.36548/jtcsst.2022.4.002

Matthew, U. O., & Kazaure, J. S. (2020). Multimedia e-learning education in nigeria and developing countries of Africa for achieving SDG4. [IJICTHD]. *International Journal of Information Communication Technologies and Human Development*, 12(1), 40–62. DOI:10.4018/IJICTHD.2020010103

Matthew, U. O., Kazaure, J. S., Amaonwu, O., Adamu, U. A., Hassan, I. M., Kazaure, A. A., & Ubochi, C. N. (2021). *Role of internet of health things (IoHTs) and innovative internet of 5G medical robotic things (IIo-5GMRTs) in COVID-19 global health risk management and logistics planning Intelligent Data Analysis for COVID-19 Pandemic*. Springer.

Matthew, U. O., Kazaure, J. S., & Haruna, K. (2020). Multimedia Information System (MIS) for Knowledge Generation and ICT Policy Framework in Education: Innovative Sustainable Educational Investment. [IJICTHD]. *International Journal of Information Communication Technologies and Human Development*, 12(3), 28–58. DOI:10.4018/IJICTHD.2020070102

Matthew, U. O., Kazaure, J. S., Kazaure, A. S., Nwamouh, U. C., & Chinonso, A. (2022). ICT Policy Implementation as Correlate for Achieving Educational Sustainability: Approaching Development in Multi ICT Dimensions. *Journal of Information Technology*, 4(4), 250–269.

Matthew, U. O., Kazaure, J. S., Kazaure, A. S., Onyedibe, O. N., & Okafor, A. N. (2022). The twenty first century E-learning education management & implication for media technology adoption in the period of pandemic. *EAI Endorsed Transactions on e-Learning, 8*(1).

Matthew, U. O., Kazaure, J. S., Ndukwu, C. C., Ebong, G. N., Nwanakwaugwu, A. C., & Nwamouh, U. C. (2024). *Artificial Intelligence Educational Pedagogy Development: ICT Pedagogy Development for Education 5.0 Educational Perspectives on Digital Technologies in Modeling and Management*. IGI Global. DOI:10.4018/979-8-3693-2314-4.ch003

Matthew, U. O., Kazaure, J. S., & Okochi, P. I. (2022). 5G Mid-Range Electromagnetic Spectrum Implementation for Critical Infrastructure Development: Electromagnetic Spectrum Sustainability. [IJITN]. *International Journal of Interdisciplinary Telecommunications and Networking*, 14(1), 1–26. DOI:10.4018/IJITN.307103

Matthew, U. O., Onumaku, V. C., Fatai, L. O., Adekunle, T. S., Waliu, A. O., Ndukwu, C. C., & Ebong, G. N. (2024). *E-Healthcare Data Warehouse Design and Data Mining Using ML Approach Reshaping Healthcare with Cutting-Edge Biomedical Advancements*. IGI Global.

Mishra, S. P., Kulshreshtha, D., Srivastava, A. K., Gandhi, A. K., & Rastogi, M. (2019). *Gamification to promote the engagement in healtcare and wellness of patients under therapeutic care: gamification and healthcare Application of Gaming in New Media Marketing*. IGI Global. DOI:10.4018/978-1-5225-6064-7.ch015

Morsiani, G., Bagnasco, A., & Sasso, L. (2017). How staff nurses perceive the impact of nurse managers' leadership style in terms of job satisfaction: A mixed method study. *Journal of Nursing Management*, 25(2), 119–128. DOI:10.1111/jonm.12448 PMID:27917561

Mukkawar, V. V., Netak, L. D., & Nikam, V. B. (2021). Architectural view of non-face-to-face experiential learning through the immersive technologies. *Paper presented at the International Conference on Intelligent Human Computer Interaction*. Research Gate.

Navab, E., Hoseini Azizi, T., & Darvish, A. (2024). Comparative study of master's degree curricula in nursing informatics at Tehran University of Medical Sciences and the University of Maryland. *Journal of Medical Education Development*, 17(53), 91–100.

Newton, M. H., & Annetta, L. A. (2024). The Influence of Extended Reality on Climate Change Education. *Science & Education*, 1–21. DOI:10.1007/s11191-024-00518-y

Nikolić, D., & Whyte, J. (2021). Visualizing a new sustainable world: Toward the next generation of virtual reality in the built environment. *Buildings*, 11(11), 546. DOI:10.3390/buildings11110546

Nordin, S., Sturge, J., Ayoub, M., Jones, A., McKee, K., Dahlberg, L., Meijering, L., & Elf, M. (2021). The role of information and communication technology (ICT) for older adults' decision-making related to health, and health and social care services in daily life—A scoping review. *International Journal of Environmental Research and Public Health*, 19(1), 151. DOI:10.3390/ijerph19010151 PMID:35010408

Okwudili, U. M., & Kazaure, J. S. (2020). Digital activism and digital revolution in objective journalism. [IJICST]. *International Journal of Interactive Communication Systems and Technologies*, 10(2), 39–56. DOI:10.4018/IJICST.2020070104

Onyesolu, M. O., Nwasor, V. C., Ositanwosu, O. E., & Iwegbuna, O. N. (2013). Pedagogy: Instructivism to socio-constructivism through virtual reality. *International Journal of Advanced Computer Science and Applications*, 4(9).

Oyekunle, D., Ugochukwu, O. M., Rosa, R. L., Rodriguez, D. Z., & Fatai, L. O. (2024). Novel Approaches in Clinical Simulation: Immersive Educational Technology to Enhance Nursing Education. *INFOCOMP Journal of Computer Science, 23*(1).

Patel, N. S., Puah, S., & Kok, X.-F. K. (2024). Shaping future-ready graduates with mindset shifts: studying the impact of integrating critical and design thinking in design innovation education. *Paper presented at the Frontiers in Education*. IEEE. DOI:10.3389/feduc.2024.1358431

Peterson, A., Charles, V., Yeung, D., & Coyle, K. (2021). The health equity framework: A science-and justice-based model for public health researchers and practitioners. *Health Promotion Practice*, 22(6), 741–746. DOI:10.1177/1524839920950730 PMID:32814445

Qayyum, A., Butt, M. A., Ali, H., Usman, M., Halabi, O., Al-Fuqaha, A., Abbasi, Q. H., Imran, M. A., & Qadir, J. (2024). Secure and trustworthy artificial intelligence-extended reality (AI-XR) for metaverses. *ACM Computing Surveys*, 56(7), 1–38. DOI:10.1145/3614426

Quail, M., Brundage, S. B., Spitalnick, J., Allen, P. J., & Beilby, J. (2016). Student self-reported communication skills, knowledge and confidence across standardised patient, virtual and traditional clinical learning environments. *BMC Medical Education*, 16(1), 1–12. DOI:10.1186/s12909-016-0577-5 PMID:26919838

Ramos, M. (2024). Emerging Technologies in Radiotherapy: Advances in Health Literacy and Healthcare Practice. *Transformative Approaches to Patient Literacy and Healthcare Innovation*, (pp. 89-110). Research Gate.

Rauschnabel, P. A., Felix, R., Hinsch, C., Shahab, H., & Alt, F. (2022). What is XR? Towards a framework for augmented and virtual reality. *Computers in Human Behavior*, 133, 107289. DOI:10.1016/j.chb.2022.107289

Riesen, M., Hoekman, J., & Björkelund, K. (2023). *Global Development of Nurse Anesthesia Education from Mid-Nineteenth Century into Today's Advanced Nursing Practice Nurse Practitioners and Nurse Anesthetists: The Evolution of the Global Roles*. Springer.

Rodríguez, J. H., de Cortez, M. H., Gómez, J. L., Pérez, J. L., & Huuskonen, A. (2024). *3.4 Professional Growth in Nursing Education*. SmartNurse.

Rouleau, G., Gagnon, M.-P., Côté, J., Payne-Gagnon, J., Hudson, E., & Dubois, C.-A. (2017). Impact of information and communication technologies on nursing care: Results of an overview of systematic reviews. *Journal of Medical Internet Research*, 19(4), e122. DOI:10.2196/jmir.6686 PMID:28442454

Ryder, M., Browne, F., Curtin, M., Furlong, E., Connolly, M., Larkin, J., & Zampiero, N. (2024). *A Report of the Review of Undergraduate Nursing and Midwifery Curriculum leading to Registration in Ireland*. Research Gate.

Saric, J., Aerts, A., Anne, M., Barboza, J., Boch, J., Dashdorj, N., & Rollemberg, S. M. S. (2024). Assessing the contributions of an urban population health initiative to shift political priority towards cardiovascular health: Three case studies from Brazil, Mongolia and Senegal. *BMC Health Services Research*, 24(1), 16. DOI:10.1186/s12913-023-10432-8 PMID:38178108

Schröder-Dering, C., Zachmann, G., & Weller, R. (2022). Dynparity: Dynamic disparity adjustment to avoid stereo window violations on stationary stereoscopic displays. *Computer Animation and Virtual Worlds*, 33(6), e2099. DOI:10.1002/cav.2099

Schwingrouber, J., Bryant-Lukosius, D., Kilpatrick, K., Mayen, S., & Colson, S. (2024). Evaluation of the implementation of advanced practice nursing roles in France: A multiple case study. *Journal of Advanced Nursing*, 80(3), 977–992. DOI:10.1111/jan.15840 PMID:37658619

Sharma, D. K., Khera, A., & Singh, D. (2020). Using Artificial Intelligence to Bring Accurate Real-Time Simulation to Virtual Reality. *Advanced Computational Intelligence Techniques for Virtual Reality in Healthcare*, (pp. 141-163). Research Gate.

Shorey, S., & Ng, E. D. (2021). The use of virtual reality simulation among nursing students and registered nurses: A systematic review. *Nurse Education Today*, 98, 104662. DOI:10.1016/j.nedt.2020.104662 PMID:33203545

Simon-Liedtke, J. T., & Baraas, R. C. (2022). The need for universal design of eXtended Reality (XR) technology in primary and secondary education: identifying opportunities, challenges, and knowledge gaps from the literature.*Paper presented at the International Conference on Human-Computer Interaction*. Springer. DOI:10.1007/978-3-031-06015-1_9

Sox, H. C., Higgins, M. C., Owens, D. K., & Schmidler, G. S. (2024). *Medical decision making*. John Wiley & Sons. DOI:10.1002/9781119627876

Steindorff, J.-V., Redlich, L.-M., Paulicke, D., & Jahn, P. (2024). Use and Design of Virtual Reality–Supported Learning Scenarios in the Vocational Qualification of Nursing Professionals: Scoping Review. *JMIR Serious Games*, 12, e53356. DOI:10.2196/53356 PMID:38976873

Stenseth, H. V., Steindal, S. A., Solberg, M. T., Ølnes, M. A., Mohallem, A., Sørensen, A. L., & Riegel, F. (2022). Simulation-based learning supported by technology to enhance critical thinking in nursing students: Protocol for a scoping review. *JMIR Research Protocols*, 11(4), e36725. DOI:10.2196/36725 PMID:35373777

Stoll, K. H., Downe, S., Edmonds, J., Gross, M. M., Malott, A., McAra-Couper, J., & Team, I. S. (2020). A survey of university students' preferences for midwifery care and community birth options in 8 high-income countries. *Journal of Midwifery & Women's Health*, 65(1), 131–141. DOI:10.1111/jmwh.13069 PMID:31957228

Stoumpos, A. I., Kitsios, F., & Talias, M. A. (2023). Digital transformation in healthcare: Technology acceptance and its applications. *International Journal of Environmental Research and Public Health*, 20(4), 3407. DOI:10.3390/ijerph20043407 PMID:36834105

Sudharson, D., Malik, R., Sathya, R. R., Vaishali, V., Balavedhaa, S., & Gautham, S. (2024). A Novel Adaptive Framework for Immersive Learning Using VR in Education. *Transforming Education with Virtual Reality*, 1-26.

Tahsin, F., Armas, A., Kirakalaprathapan, A., Kadu, M., Sritharan, J., & Steele Gray, C. (2023). Information and communications technologies enabling integrated primary care for patients with complex care needs: Scoping review. *Journal of Medical Internet Research*, 25, e44035. DOI:10.2196/44035 PMID:37074779

Takian, A., Raoofi, A., & Haghighi, H. (2022). *COVID-19 pandemic: The fears and hopes for SDG 3, with focus on prevention and control of noncommunicable diseases (SDG 3.4) and universal health coverage (SDG 3.8) COVID-19 and the Sustainable Development Goals*. Elsevier.

Theobald, K. A., Tutticci, N., Ramsbotham, J., & Johnston, S. (2021). Effectiveness of using simulation in the development of clinical reasoning in undergraduate nursing students: A systematic review. *Nurse Education in Practice*, 57, 103220. DOI:10.1016/j.nepr.2021.103220 PMID:34781195

Vázquez-Calatayud, M., García-García, R., Regaira-Martínez, E., & Gómez-Urquiza, J. (2024). Real-world and game-based learning to enhance decision-making. *Nurse Education Today*, 140, 106276. DOI:10.1016/j.nedt.2024.106276 PMID:38851020

Wakefield, M., Williams, D. R., & Le Menestrel, S. (2021). *The future of nursing 2020-2030: Charting a path to achieve health equity*. National Academy of Sciences. DOI:10.17226/25982

Walton-Roberts, M. (2023). *Global Health Worker Migration: Problems and Solutions*. Cambridge University Press. DOI:10.1017/9781009217781

Weeks, K., Herron, E., & Buchanan, H. (2024). Aligning Simulation-Based Education With Didactic Learning in Prelicensure Baccalaureate Nursing Education. *Nurse Educator*, 49(3), 125–129. PMID:37851404

Yadav, S. (2024). *Empowering Educators With Augmented and Virtual Reality: Integrating AR and VR for Enhanced Interactive Learning Environment Reshaping Learning with Next Generation Educational Technologies*. IGI Global. DOI:10.4018/979-8-3693-1310-7.ch005

Zhang, H., & Spiegel, B. (2024). *Introducing the Journal of Medical Extended Reality* (*Vol. 1*, pp. 1-3): Mary Ann Liebert, Inc.

Chapter 4
Designing Effective VR Learning Environments:
Immersive Strategies and Methods

Biswabhusan Pradhan
https://orcid.org/0000-0001-6011-0605
Central University of Jammu, India

Asit K. Mantry
Central University of Jammu, India

ABSTRACT

Virtual reality (VR) technology has emerged as a promising tool in education, offering immersive and interactive learning experiences that transcend the limitations of traditional teaching methods. There is a gap in leveraging technology to enhance learning experiences beyond traditional methods. The research aims to design VR learning environments by synthesizing insights from existing literature to identify key strategies and principles for creating impactful educational experiences. The study delves into both technical and pedagogical aspects of VR design, highlighting the importance of immersion, interactivity, alignment with learning objectives, and inclusivity. Furthermore, the research discusses future trends and implications for educators, instructional designers, researchers, policymakers, and educational leaders. Overall, this study contributes to advancing the understanding of how VR technology can revolutionize education and empower learners in the digital age.

DOI: 10.4018/979-8-3693-6407-9.ch004

1. INTRODUCTION

Virtual Reality (VR) has indeed revolutionized education by providing immersive and interactive learning experiences (Shaukat, 2023). By creating computer-generated environments, VR transcends traditional teaching methods, allowing students to engage with realistic simulations, historical events, and complex concepts in a three-dimensional space (Marougkas et al., 2023). This experiential learning approach enhances student engagement, curiosity, and critical thinking skills (Piovesan et al., 2012). Whether exploring the human body, ancient civilizations, or chemical reactions, VR enables educators to deliver immersive educational experiences that promote deep learning and conceptual understanding. The impact of VR on education is evident in its ability to captivate learners' attention and facilitate interactive learning experiences that bridge the gap between theory and practice (Predescu et al., 2023).

Moreover, the versatility of VR makes it applicable across various disciplines and educational levels(Martarelli et al., 2023),from elementary classrooms to university lecture halls, VR can be tailored to meet diverse learning objectives and cater to students with different learning styles(Predescu et al., 2023). For example, in science education, VR simulations can provide a safe and controlled environment for conducting experiments that may be too hazardous or impractical to perform in a traditional laboratory setting(Sumardani & Lin, 2023). Similarly, in history or geography classes, VR can take students to different time periods or geographic locations, allowing them to witness historical events or explore distant landscapes firsthand(Alshammari, 2019). This versatility underscores VR's potential to democratize access to high-quality educational experiences, irrespective of geographical location or resource constraints.

Furthermore, VR holds promise for addressing longstanding challenges in education, such as student engagement, retention, and accessibility(Makransky & Lilleholt, 2018), by providing immersive and interactive learning environments, VR captivates students' attention and encourages active participation in the learning process. Moreover, for learners with disabilities or special needs, VR can offer personalized and inclusive educational experiences(Nganji & Brayshaw, 2017). Through customizable settings and adaptive features, VR platforms can accommodate diverse learning preferences and provide individualized support, thus promoting greater equity and inclusivity in education(Uzza et al., 2022). As technology continues to advance and VR becomes more accessible, its potential to revolutionize education and empower learners to explore, create, and innovate will only continue to grow.

The importance of designing immersive VR learning environments cannot be overstated, as these environments hold the key to unlocking the full potential of VR technology in education(Hamilton et al., 2021; Webster, 2016). By immersing learners in rich and realistic virtual worlds, educators can create dynamic and interactive learning experiences that captivate students' attention and foster deep engagement(Allcoat & von Mühlenen, 2018). Unlike traditional classroom settings, where students may passively absorb information, immersive VR environments empower learners to actively participate in their own learning journey(Webster, 2016). Whether it's exploring the human body at the cellular level, navigating through historical landmarks, or conducting virtual experiments in a laboratory, VR offers an unprecedented level of interactivity and hands-on learning opportunities(Serin, 2020).

Furthermore, immersive VR environments have been shown to enhance student motivation and retention of information, by leveraging the power of sensory immersion, VR engages multiple senses simultaneously, creating a more memorable and impactful learning experience(Gomes et al., 2020). Research has demonstrated that learners are more likely to remember information that they have experienced firsthand in a virtual environment compared to traditional instructional methods(E. Ryan & Poole, 2019). This heightened level of engagement and retention can lead to deeper learning outcomes and better academic performance. Additionally, immersive VR environments have the potential to cater to diverse learning styles and preferences, accommodating the individual needs and preferences of each learner(C. J. Chen et al., 2005). Whether visual, auditory, kinesthetic, or tactile, VR can provide customized learning experiences that resonate with students and empower them to achieve their full potential(Hamilton et al., 2021). As such, the design of immersive VR learning environments is not merely a matter of technological innovation, but a fundamental aspect of creating inclusive, engaging, and effective educational experiences for learners of all backgrounds and abilities(Choi et al., 2022).

The objective of this chapter was to delve into the existing body of literature surrounding the design of Virtual Reality (VR) learning environments, with a keen focus on identifying and analyzing strategies that optimized the efficacy and impact of such environments. Through a meticulous review and synthesis of scholarly works, the chapter endeavoured to distill key insights, principles, and best practices that underpinned the creation of immersive and effective VR learning experiences. By elucidating the theoretical underpinnings and practical applications of VR in education, the chapter aimed to contribute substantively to the ongoing discourse on the integration of VR technology within pedagogical frameworks. Moreover, the chapter sought to serve as a valuable resource for educators, instructional designers, and researchers who were grappling with the challenges and opportunities presented by VR in educational settings. By offering a comprehensive overview of the current state of knowledge in this domain.

2. LITERATURE REVIEW

2.1 Role of Virtual Reality in Education

The term Virtual Reality entails employing computer technology to generate an immersive three-dimensional environment where objects possess a feeling of spatial presence, fostering interactivity(Bryson, 2013).Virtual Reality (VR) technology has gained significant attention in the field of education due to its potential to revolutionize traditional learning methods(Martín-Gutiérrez et al., 2017; Onyesolu & Eze, 2011). Researchers have extensively explored the applications and implications of VR in educational settings, investigating its effectiveness in enhancing student engagement, motivation, and learning outcomes. One prominent area of research focuses on the use of VR for immersive learning experiences. According to Fromm et al.(2021)VR provides learners with opportunities to engage in authentic and experiential learning activities that simulate real-world scenarios. By creating immersive environments, educators can facilitate hands-on exploration and experimentation, allowing learners to develop practical skills and apply theoretical knowledge in context(Asad et al., 2021; Oh & Nussli, 2014; Rossoni et al., 2024; Ummihusna et al., 2024).Moreover, studies have examined the role of VR in promoting active learning and knowledge retention. For instance, Chen et al.(2022)conducted a meta-analysis of empirical studies on VR in education and found that VR-based learning experiences led to higher levels of engagement and knowledge retention compared to traditional instructional methods. The interactive and multisensory nature of VR environments engages multiple cognitive processes, resulting in deeper learning experiences(B. Chen et al., 2022). Additionally, researchers have investigated the potential of VR to address diverse learning needs and preferences. According to Jollibekova (2024)VR technology has the unique ability to create customizable learning experiences that cater to individual learning styles and abilities. By providing flexible and adaptive learning environments, VR can accommodate a wide range of learners, including those with special needs or disabilities(Nuguri et al., 2021).Furthermore, studies have explored the psychological and social implications of using VR in education. For example, Slater & Sanchez-Vives(2016)conducted experiments on the use of VR for social interaction and found that immersive virtual environments can elicit strong emotional responses and social presence among users. These findings suggest that VR has the potential to foster empathy, collaboration, and communication skills, which are essential for effective learning and interpersonal relationships. Despite the promising findings, researchers have also identified challenges and limitations associated with the use of VR in education. Technical constraints, such as high costs, limited accessibility, and hardware requirements, remain significant barriers to widespread adoption(Davila Delgado et al., 2020). Moreover, ethical considerations, such as data privacy, content appropriateness, and digital equity, raise important questions about the responsible and ethical use of VR technology in educational settings(Adams et al., 2018; Etambakonga, 2021; Southgate et al., 2019).

2.2 Challenges of Integrating VR in Educational Settings

The significance of VR learning environments in education is immense, as they offer an immersive and engaging platform that transcends the limitations of traditional teaching methods. However, incorporating Virtual Reality (VR) into educational settings faces numerous obstacles, including the high expense of proprietary headsets and content platforms, which limits widespread use. Technical difficulties, the availability of content, and the need for a robust technical infrastructure add to the complexity (Akhtar et al., 2024; Shankar et al., 2023). Additionally, the success of VR integration relies heavily on teachers' readiness and proficiency with the technology, as well as the effective incorporation of VR into educational curricula(Carpenter et al., 2023). The scarcity and inconsistent quality of VR applications for education, such as in music education, highlight the need for collaborative development efforts with stakeholders, including teachers, to overcome current technical and pedagogical challenges(Poutiainen & Krzywacki, 2023). Despite VR's potential to boost student engagement, motivation, and knowledge retention in vocational education, issues like the cost of equipment and the necessity for specialized technical support remain significant hurdles(Ravichandran & Mahapatra, 2023).

3. THEORETICAL FOUNDATIONS

3.1 Constructivist Learning Theory

Constructivist Learning Theory emphasizes the importance of creating a learning environment that promotes active engagement, critical thinking, and knowledge construction(W. Li et al., 2023). Virtual Reality (VR) technology has emerged as a valuable tool to enhance cognitive learning experiences by providing immersive virtual environments that compensate for traditional teaching limitations(Karwasz & Wyborska, 2023). By integrating VR technology into education, educators can design virtual learning environments that stimulate cognitive processes, facilitate knowledge acquisition, and reduce cognitive load, ultimately improving learning outcomes(Chaijaroen et al., 2020). The use of digital technologies, such as VR, in constructivist learning environments has shown positive results in developing students' cognitive and metacognitive abilities, fostering critical thinking, and enhancing collaborative behaviors among learners.

3.2 Experiential Learning Theory

Kolb's Experiential Learning Theory, emphasizing concrete experiences and reflective observation, aligns well with VR learning environments that immerse learners in realistic simulations, facilitating experiential learning(Marougkas et al., 2023). VR technology provides opportunities for learners to engage in the iterative cycle of experiencing, reflecting, and applying knowledge, enhancing the depth and retention of learning, as supported by the Cognitive Theory of Multimedia Learning (Mystakidis & Lympouridis, 2023). By offering immersive and interactive experiences, VR enables learners to practice and apply theoretical concepts in a hands-on manner, promoting active participation and skill development(T.-C. Huang et al., 2023). This integration of experiential learning in VR not only enhances understanding but also increases self-efficacy perceptions, as demonstrated in studies focusing on the effectiveness of VR in improving science learning outcomes (X. Huang et al., 2023).

3.3 Cognitive Load Theory

Sweller's Cognitive Load Theory emphasizes the importance of managing cognitive load to enhance learning outcomes (Lämsä et al., 2023). Virtual Reality (VR) environments can be tailored to decrease extraneous cognitive load by offering user-friendly interfaces, explicit instructions, and helpful feedback mechanisms, thus enabling learners to concentrate on essential learning tasks and improving learning efficiency and effectiveness (Zhang & Liu, 2023). Studies have shown that immersive VR learning environments can lead to higher cognitive loads compared to traditional settings due to increased visual loads, potentially hindering learning outcomes(Brunzini et al., 2023). By incorporating feedback into VR environments, learners can experience reduced extraneous cognitive load, increased engagement, and improved performance in practical hands-on tasks (Kun et al., 2023). Additionally, physiological data, such as heart rate variability, can be utilized to assess cognitive load management performance in VR training, complementing traditional behavioral indicators.

By integrating these theoretical foundations, the proposed model for VR learning environments aims to create immersive, interactive, and effective educational experiences that enhance engagement, motivation, and learning outcomes for diverse learners.

4. PROPOSED MODEL FOR VIRTUAL REALITY (VR) LEARNING ENVIRONMENTS

4.1 Virtual Reality (VR) Learning Environments

Designing VR Learning Environments involves the comprehensive integration of technical and pedagogical elements to create immersive and engaging virtual settings tailored to educational goals. This process entails crafting virtual environments that not only captivate users but also align seamlessly with learning objectives. It necessitates a balance between technical feasibility, ensuring the smooth operation of VR systems, and adherence to pedagogical principles, guaranteeing meaningful learning experiences.

4.2 Technical Aspects

4.2.1 Immersion

Immersion in the context of virtual reality (VR) refers to the extent to which users experience a deep sense of mental and emotional involvement within the virtual environment, it encompasses various strategies aimed at heightening the user's perception of being physically present in the virtual world, thus enhancing the overall engagement and immersion level(Shin, 2018). Key strategies to augment immersion include the integration of realistic graphics, spatial audio, and environmental effects(Naef et al., 2002). Additionally, environmental effects such as dynamic lighting, weather simulations, and interactive objects contribute to the immersive experience by creating a rich and interactive virtual world that users can explore and interact with. By employing these strategies, VR designers strive to create environments that captivate users' senses and evoke a profound sense of immersion, thereby enhancing the overall quality of the VR experience.

4.2.2 Presence

Presence refers to the profound sensation of being physically present in a virtual environment, transcending mere visual and auditory stimuli(Weber et al., 2021). It encompasses the feeling of complete immersion, where users perceive themselves as fully integrated into the simulated world(Sadowski & Stanney, 2002). Achieving presence in virtual reality (VR) involves meticulous attention to detail in design, aiming to create an environment that feels indistinguishable from reality(Pillai et al., 2013). This entails not only crafting visually convincing landscapes but also incorporating natural interactions that seamlessly respond to user input. By imbuing the virtual world with a sense of dynamism and interactivity, designers can enhance the user's feeling of presence(Sundar et al., 2008).

4.2.3 Interactivity

Interactivity within virtual environments represents more than just user input, it embodies the essence of engagement and participation(M.-L. Ryan, 1999). Designing for interactivity entails not only providing users with responsive controls but also creating opportunities for meaningful engagement and manipulation of virtual objects(Roussou, 2004). This involves implementing dynamic simulations that respond to user actions in real-time, fostering a sense of agency and immersion. Moreover, interactive feedback mechanisms play a crucial role in guiding user interactions and facilitating exploration within the virtual space, by prioritizing interactivity in design, developers can create experiences that empower users to actively engage with the virtual environment, enhancing learning outcomes and overall user satisfaction(Roussou et al., 2006).

4.2.4 Realism

Realism in virtual environments encompasses the intricate balance between visual fidelity and experiential authenticity(Slater et al., 2009). Designing for realism entails meticulous attention to detail, striving to replicate real-world phenomena with utmost accuracy, this involves employing high-fidelity graphics and lifelike animations to evoke a sense of visual realism that closely mimics reality(Newman et al., 2022). Additionally, realistic physics simulations play a crucial role in enhancing the believability of interactions within the virtual space. By prioritizing realism in design, developers can create immersive experiences that transport users into lifelike environments, fostering a deep sense of immersion and authenticity(J. Huang et al., 2019; Stachoň et al., 2018). Ultimately, the pursuit of realism in virtual reality enriches user experiences, enabling meaningful engagement and learning opportunities.

4.2.5 Feedback Mechanisms

Feedback mechanisms serve as integral components in virtual environments, offering users vital insights into their interactions and progress(Wang et al., 2023). Beyond mere user input, they provide dynamic cues visual, auditory, and haptic that reinforce learning objectives and guide user behaviour, these mechanisms offer real-time responses to user actions, fostering a sense of agency and accomplishment(Mulders et al., 2020). Visual cues, such as on-screen prompts or changes in object appearance, offer immediate feedback on user actions. Auditory cues, like sound effects or verbal instructions, further enhance user engagement and immersion(Roussou et al., 2006). Additionally, haptic feedback, through tactile sensations or vibrations, adds a tactile dimension to the virtual experience, enriching user interaction and enhancing overall immersion(De Troyer et al., 2010). Through these feedback mechanisms, users receive continuous guidance and reinforcement, facilitating deeper engagement and learning within the virtual environment.

4.3 Pedagogical Aspects

4.3.1 Alignment with Learning Objectives

Alignment with learning objectives is paramount in the design of VR learning environments, requiring meticulous attention to educational goals(Pellas et al., 2021). Designers must closely align VR experiences with specific learning outcomes, ensuring that the content and activities within the virtual environment directly support the intended educational objectives(C. J. Chen, 2006). This entails mapping VR experiences to curriculum standards and pedagogical frameworks, crafting immersive scenarios and interactive simulations that facilitate the acquisition of knowledge and skills outlined in the learning objectives(Pellas et al., 2021). Ultimately, alignment with learning objectives ensures that VR experiences contribute effectively to educational outcomes and student learning.

4.3.2 Accessibility

Accessibility in VR learning environments is about ensuring inclusivity and equal access for users with diverse needs and abilities(Wehrmann & Zender, 2023). It involves designing interfaces that accommodate alternative input methods and are adjustable to cater to individual preferences(Qorbani et al., 2022). Additionally, supporting assistive technologies is crucial to facilitate seamless interaction for users with disabilities(Creed et al., 2024). By prioritizing accessibility, VR designers strive to create environments that are welcoming and usable for all users, fostering an inclusive learning experience where everyone can participate and engage effectively.

4.3.3 Inclusivity

In the realm of Virtual Reality (VR), inclusivity is paramount for fostering a sense of belonging and authenticity among users from diverse backgrounds(Lauring et al., 2023). This involves embracing cultural sensitivity, representing various perspectives, and implementing inclusive design practices to create environments where all users feel valued and represented (Ratnam, 2023). By prioritizing inclusivity, VR designers aim to develop experiences that resonate with a wide range of users, contributing to a more enriching and empathetic learning environment (Fang & Yatani, 2023). Through practices like recognizing neurodivergent strengths and efforts at work, understanding differences, and utilizing VR simulations to communicate diverse experiences, inclusivity in VR can be enhanced to promote a sense of belonging for all users(Lowy et al., 2023).

4.3.4 Engagement

Engagement in VR learning environments is crucial for fostering active participation and sustained interest among users. Design strategies aimed at enhancing engagement may encompass the integration of gamification elements, storytelling techniques, and interactive challenges(Sun et al., 2023). These elements serve to motivate and captivate users, encouraging them to immerse themselves fully in the virtual experience(MacQuarrie & Steed, 2017). By fostering a sense of curiosity and excitement, designers can create VR environments that not only educate but also inspire and empower users to explore and learn(Y. Li et al., 2023).

4.3.5 Adaptability

Adaptability in VR learning environments is essential for catering to the diverse needs and preferences of users. This entails designing environments with customizable settings, adaptive learning pathways, and personalized content recommendations(Lui et al., 2023). By tailoring the experience to individual user profiles and performance data, VR environments can dynamically adjust to meet the unique learning requirements of each user(Singh et al., 2022). This adaptability ensures that users can engage with the content in a manner that is most conducive to their learning styles, enhancing overall effectiveness and user satisfaction(Rishard et al., 2022).

4.3.6 Usability

Usability in VR environments emphasizes the importance of intuitive design and seamless navigation for users(Sun & Li, 2023). This involves crafting user interfaces that are easy to understand, implementing clear navigation pathways, and considering ergonomic factors to enhance comfort during interactions(Alnagrat et al., 2023). By prioritizing usability, designers aim to create VR environments where users can explore and interact with content effortlessly and efficiently(Xie, 2023). This user-centric approach fosters a positive user experience, encouraging continued engagement and facilitating effective learning within the virtual space.

4.3.7 User Experience (UX) Design

User Experience (UX) Design in VR revolves around crafting an intuitive and seamless experience for users(Nacke et al., 2023). This encompasses various considerations, including interface design, navigation flow, and user interaction patterns, all aimed at enhancing usability and maximizing user satisfaction(Xie, 2023). By meticulously designing every aspect of the user's journey within the VR environment, UX designers strive to create an immersive and enjoyable experience that encourages continued engagement and fosters a deep sense of connection with the virtual conten(Sun & Li, 2023)t. Ultimately, prioritizing UX design ensures that users can navigate and interact with VR environments effortlessly, resulting in a positive and fulfilling experience.

4.3.8 Content Development

Content development in VR involves the creation of educational materials and interactive experiences tailored to the virtual environment(Kuna et al., 2023). This includes crafting engaging narratives, developing interactive modules, and curating multimedia resources to align with learning objectives and captivate users(Belani et al., 2023). By designing compelling content that leverages the immersive capabilities of VR, developers can facilitate meaningful learning experiences and foster deep engagement(Díaz et al., 2022). This iterative process of content creation ensures that VR environments offer rich and dynamic educational opportunities, enhancing learning outcomes and user satisfaction.

4.3.9 Assessment and Evaluation

Assessment and evaluation in VR encompass the systematic measurement of learning outcomes and user performance(Udeozor et al., 2023). This involves designing both formative and summative assessment activities within the virtual environment, collecting user data, and analyzing performance metrics to assess the effectiveness of the VR learning experience(Gyll et al., 2023). By continuously monitoring user progress and gathering feedback, educators can identify areas for improvement and tailor instructional strategies to enhance learning outcomes(Paolanti et al., 2023). This iterative process of assessment and evaluation ensures that VR environments are optimized for educational effectiveness and user engagement.

4.3.10 Psychological Considerations

Psychological considerations in VR encompass a deep understanding of the cognitive, emotional, and behavioral factors that influence user engagement(Kay et al., 2023). This entails addressing aspects such as motivation, attention, and emotional resonance to optimize the overall user experience and learning outcomes(Dubovi, 2023). By incorporating psychological principles into VR design, developers can create environments that effectively capture and sustain user interest, fostering deeper levels of engagement and facilitating meaningful learning experiences(Markwell et al., 2023). This holistic approach ensures that VR environments not only deliver educational content but also support the psychological well-being of users, promoting enhanced learning and retention.

4.3.11 Social Interactions

Social interactions within VR learning environments play a crucial role in fostering collaboration, communication, and peer learning among users(Spike et al.,2024). Design strategies aimed at promoting social interactions may involve creating multiplayer experiences, collaborative activities, and communication tools within the virtual environment(Sykownik et al., 2023). By facilitating social engagement and knowledge sharing, VR environments enable users to interact with peers, exchange ideas, and collaborate on learning tasks, thereby enhancing overall engagement and facilitating deeper learning experiences(Galleguillos et al., 2022). These social interactions contribute to a sense of community and camaraderie, enriching the overall educational experience within the virtual space.

4.3.12 Ethical Considerations

Ethical considerations in VR education encompass addressing various concerns related to the responsible use of technology(PenjIšević et al., 2023). This involves prioritizing issues such as data privacy, obtaining informed consent, ensuring user safety, and promoting equity in access and participation(Skulmowski, 2023). By upholding ethical standards, educators and developers can mitigate potential risks and safeguard the well-being of users within VR environments(Piragauta & De Oliveira, 2023). Striving for ethical excellence ensures that VR technology is deployed responsibly, fostering trust, transparency, and accountability in educational settings.

4.3.13 Technological Infrastructure

Technological infrastructure in VR learning encompasses the hardware and software components that underpin the virtual environment(Fasihuddin, 2023). This entails ensuring device compatibility, robust network connectivity, and reliable system performance to deliver a seamless and immersive user experience(C.-H. Li, 2023). By investing in reliable infrastructure, educators can minimize technical disruptions and optimize the functionality of VR systems, thereby enhancing user engagement and facilitating effective learning experiences(Predescu et al., 2023). A robust technological foundation forms the backbone of VR learning environments, enabling educators to harness the full potential of immersive technology for educational purposes.

4.3.14 Implementation Strategies

Implementation strategies in VR education encompass the systematic planning and execution of deploying VR learning environments within educational contexts(Marougkas et al., 2023). This involves providing comprehensive training for educators and administrators to familiarize them with VR technology and its pedagogical implications(Kouijzer et al., 2023). Additionally, ensuring robust technical support and scalability is essential for the successful integration and adoption of VR technology across various educational settings(Zigunovs et al., 2023). By employing effective implementation strategies, institutions can maximize the benefits of VR technology and create impactful learning experiences for students.

4.3.15 Future Trends

Future trends in VR learning environments encompass a proactive approach to anticipate emerging technologies, pedagogical approaches, and educational practices shaping the future of VR in education(Wei & Yuan, 2023). This involves staying abreast of advancements in VR technology, pedagogical research, and industry trends to inform future design and development efforts(Fei et al., 2023). By embracing innovation and adapting to evolving educational needs, educators and developers can harness the full potential of VR technology to create immersive and impactful learning experiences that prepare students for the challenges of tomorrow's world.

Figure 1. Virtual learning (VR) environments

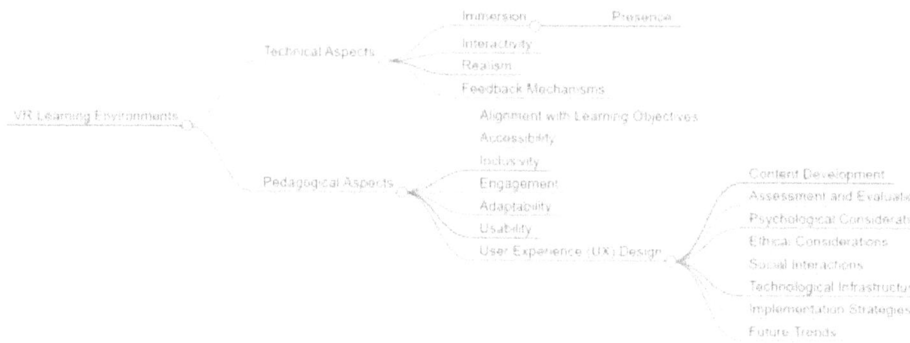

5. DISCUSSION

The importance of VR environments in educational settings cannot be overstated, as they offer a dynamic platform that transcends the limitations of traditional teaching methods. By immersing learners in computer-generated environments, VR facilitates unparalleled levels of engagement and interactivity, allowing students to explore, experiment, and interact with educational content in a three-dimensional space. This experiential approach to learning not only captivates students' attention but also stimulates their curiosity and critical thinking skills, fostering deep learning and conceptual understanding. As a result, VR environments hold the potential to revolutionize education by offering immersive educational experiences that cater to diverse learning styles and preferences.

The results of the study underscore the multifaceted nature of designing VR learning environments, encompassing both technical and pedagogical aspects. From enhancing immersion and interactivity to aligning with learning objectives and promoting inclusivity, effective design strategies are essential for creating immersive and impactful VR learning experiences. By synthesizing insights from existing literature, the study identifies key principles, best practices, and theoretical frameworks that inform the design of VR learning environments. Moreover, the study highlights the importance of continuous assessment and evaluation to measure learning outcomes and refine instructional strategies, ensuring that VR environments remain aligned with educational objectives and contribute effectively to student learning.

Furthermore, the study sheds light on the potential of VR technology to address longstanding challenges in education, such as student engagement, retention, and accessibility. By providing immersive and interactive learning environments, VR captivates students' attention and encourages active participation in the learning process. Additionally, VR environments have the potential to cater to diverse learning needs and preferences, offering personalized and inclusive educational experiences for learners of all backgrounds and abilities. As technology continues to advance and VR becomes more accessible, its potential to empower learners to explore, create, and innovate in education will only continue to grow.

Looking ahead, future trends in VR learning environments offer exciting opportunities for innovation and exploration in education. By anticipating emerging technologies, pedagogical approaches, and educational practices, educators and developers can leverage VR technology to create immersive and impactful learning experiences. Moreover, addressing ethical considerations and investing in robust technological infrastructure are essential for ensuring responsible and effective use of VR technology in education. Overall, the study underscores the transformative potential of VR technology in education and highlights the importance of designing immersive and engaging VR learning environments to unlock its full benefits for learners.

6. IMPLICATIONS

This study advances the theoretical understanding of VR learning environments by synthesizing existing literature and identifying key principles and best practices for integrating VR into educational settings. The research highlights the intricate interplay between technical and pedagogical elements, offering a comprehensive framework that merges immersive technology with educational objectives. It enriches the theoretical discourse on immersion, presence, interactivity, and realism in VR, contributing to a deeper understanding of how these factors influence user engagement and learning outcomes. Additionally, the study underscores the importance of accessibility, inclusivity, and ethical considerations, expanding the theoretical boundaries of inclusive education in the context of emerging technologies. By addressing these multifaceted dimensions, the study lays a foundation for future research to build upon, fostering a nuanced understanding of VR's role in enhancing educational experiences.

The practical implications of this study are significant for educators, instructional designers, policymakers, and educational leaders. Educators can apply the study's insights to effectively integrate VR technology into their teaching practices, creating immersive and engaging learning experiences that cater to diverse student needs. Instructional designers can leverage the recommendations to develop impactful VR content that aligns with educational objectives, enhancing student engagement and learning outcomes. Policymakers and educational leaders can use the findings to advocate for strategic investments in VR technology, ensuring equitable access to high-quality immersive learning experiences. The study also provides a roadmap for implementing robust technological infrastructure and effective teacher training programs, essential for the successful adoption of VR in educational settings. Additionally, by addressing ethical considerations and promoting inclusivity, the study guides stakeholders in fostering responsible and equitable use of VR technology in education.

7. LIMITATIONS AND FUTURE RESEARCH DIRECTIONS

While VR environments offer significant potential for enhancing educational experiences, several limitations must be acknowledged. Technical barriers, such as high costs and substantial infrastructure requirements, pose financial and logistical challenges, particularly for underfunded institutions. Pedagogical challenges include the need for professional development and the effective integration of VR into teaching practices. Limited research and evaluation hinder definitive conclusions about VR's effectiveness, while accessibility concerns affect students with disabilities. Ethical considerations, including data privacy and the psychological impact of immersive experiences, require careful management. The increasing reliance on VR risks overshadowing traditional teaching methods and may exacerbate issues related to screen time. Furthermore, the rapidly evolving nature of technology introduces uncertainties that necessitate continuous adaptation and re-evaluation of strategies.

Future research on VR learning environments should focus on several key areas to fully harness their potential and address existing gaps. Longitudinal studies are needed to assess the long-term impact of VR on learning outcomes, while comparative analyses should explore its efficacy relative to traditional teaching methods across various subjects and educational levels. Personalization and adaptive learning technologies within VR can enhance educational outcomes, particularly for diverse student populations. Accessibility and inclusivity research is crucial for developing assistive technologies that ensure equitable access. Ethical considerations and the psychological impacts of VR, including data privacy and prolonged use effects, require comprehensive examination. The role of social interactions and collaboration in VR learning, along with teacher training and professional development needs, should be explored to facilitate effective VR integration. Investigating the usability of emerging VR technologies, conducting cost-benefit analyses, and considering cross-cultural perspectives will inform more effective, inclusive, and globally relevant VR educational tools.

8. CONCLUSION

This chapter has explored the multifaceted landscape of designing VR learning environments, encompassing both technical and pedagogical considerations. By synthesizing insights from existing literature, the study has identified key strategies and principles for crafting immersive and effective VR experiences in education. From fostering immersion and interactivity to addressing accessibility and ethical considerations, designing VR learning environments requires a holistic approach that integrates technological innovation with pedagogical best practices. While challenges and limitations exist, the potential of VR to revolutionize education and empower learners is undeniable. Moving forward, continued research and innovation are crucial for unlocking the full potential of VR technology in education.

REFERENCES

Adams, D., Bah, A., Barwulor, C., Musaby, N., Pitkin, K., & Redmiles, E. M. (2018). Ethics emerging: The story of privacy and security perceptions in virtual reality. *Fourteenth Symposium on Usable Privacy and Security (SOUPS 2018)*, (pp. 427–442). USENIX. https://www.usenix.org/conference/soups2018/presentation/adams

Akhtar, M. H., Anderson, M., & Cochrane, T. (2024). Implementing Augmented Reality and Virtual Reality for authentic healthcare education. *Pacific Journal of Technology Enhanced Learning*, 6(1), 2–3. DOI:10.24135/pjtel.v6i1.177

Allcoat, D., & von Mühlenen, A. (2018). Learning in virtual reality: Effects on performance, emotion and engagement. *Research in Learning Technology*, 26(0). https://journal.alt.ac.uk/index.php/rlt/article/view/2140. DOI:10.25304/rlt.v26.2140

Alnagrat, A. J. A., Alkhallas, M. I., Mohamed, A. S. I., Ismail, R. C., Idrus, S. Z. S., & Saed, H. S. (2023). Virtual Reality Semiconductor Laboratory: Usability Testing to Improve User Experience (UX) in Virtual Environments. *2023 IEEE 3rd International Maghreb Meeting of the Conference on Sciences and Techniques of Automatic Control and Computer Engineering (MI-STA)*, (pp. 469–473). IEEE. https://ieeexplore.ieee.org/abstract/document/10169788/

Alshammari, S. H. (2019). The role of virtual reality in enhancing students' learning. *International Journal of Educational Technology and Learning*, 7(1), 1–6. DOI:10.20448/2003.71.1.6

Asad, M. M., Naz, A., Churi, P., & Tahanzadeh, M. M. (2021). Virtual reality as pedagogical tool to enhance experiential learning: A systematic literature review. *Education Research International*, 2021, 1–17. DOI:10.1155/2021/7061623

Belani, M., Singh, H. V., Parnami, A., & Singh, P. (2023). Investigating spatial representation of learning content in virtual reality learning environments. *2023 IEEE Conference Virtual Reality and 3D User Interfaces (VR)*, (pp. 33–43). IEEE. https://ieeexplore.ieee.org/abstract/document/10108413/

Brunzini, A., Grandi, F., Peruzzini, M., & Pellicciari, M. (2023). An integrated methodology for the assessment of stress and mental workload applied on virtual training. *International Journal of Computer Integrated Manufacturing*, 1–19. DOI:10.1080/0951192X.2023.2189311

Bryson, S. (2013). *Virtual Reality: A Definition History - A Personal Essay* (arXiv:1312.4322). arXiv. http://arxiv.org/abs/1312.4322

Carpenter, R. E., McWhorter, R., & Stone, K. (2023). *Adopting Virtual Reality for Education: Exploring Teachers' Perspectives on Readiness, Opportunities, and Challenges*. Scholar Works. https://scholarworks.uttyler.edu/hrd_fac/43/

Chaijaroen, N., Jackpeng, S., & Chaijaroen, S. (2020). The Development of Constructivist Web-Based Learning Environments to Enhance Learner's Information Processing and Reduce Cognitive Load. In Huang, T.-C., Wu, T.-T., Barroso, J., Sandnes, F. E., Martins, P., & Huang, Y.-M. (Eds.), *Innovative Technologies and Learning* (Vol. 12555, pp. 475–482). Springer International Publishing. DOI:10.1007/978-3-030-63885-6_52

Chen, B., Wang, Y., & Wang, L. (2022). The effects of virtual reality-assisted language learning: A meta-analysis. *Sustainability (Basel)*, 14(6), 3147. DOI:10.3390/su14063147

Chen, C. J. (2006). The design, development and evaluation of a virtual reality based learning environment. *Australasian Journal of Educational Technology*, 22(1). https://ajet.org.au/index.php/ajet/article/view/1306. DOI:10.14742/ajet.1306

Chen, C. J., Toh, S. C., & Ismail, W. M. F. W. (2005). Are Learning Styles Relevant To Virtual Reality? *Journal of Research on Technology in Education*, 38(2), 123–141. DOI:10.1080/15391523.2005.10782453

Choi, J., Thompson, C. E., Choi, J., Waddill, C. B., & Choi, S. (2022). Effectiveness of immersive virtual reality in nursing education: Systematic review. *Nurse Educator*, 47(3), E57–E61. DOI:10.1097/NNE.0000000000001117 PMID:34657101

Creed, C., Al-Kalbani, M., Theil, A., Sarcar, S., & Williams, I. (2024). Inclusive AR/VR: Accessibility barriers for immersive technologies. *Universal Access in the Information Society*, 23(1), 59 73. DOI:10.1007/s10209-023-00969-0

Davila Delgado, J. M., Oyedele, L., Beach, T., & Demian, P. (2020). Augmented and Virtual Reality in Construction: Drivers and Limitations for Industry Adoption. *Journal of Construction Engineering and Management*, 146(7), 04020079. DOI:10.1061/(ASCE)CO.1943-7862.0001844

De Troyer, O., Kleinermann, F., & Ewais, A. (2010). Enhancing Virtual Reality Learning Environments with Adaptivity: Lessons Learned. In Leitner, G., Hitz, M., & Holzinger, A. (Eds.), *HCI in Work and Learning, Life and Leisure* (Vol. 6389, pp. 244–265). Springer Berlin Heidelberg., DOI:10.1007/978-3-642-16607-5_16

Díaz, M. J., Mantell, C., Caro, I., de Ory, I., Sánchez, J., & Portela, J. R. (2022). Creation of immersive resources based on virtual reality for dissemination and teaching in chemical engineering. *Education Sciences*, 12(8), 572. DOI:10.3390/educsci12080572

Dubovi, I. (2023). Facial expressions capturing emotional engagement while learning with desktop VR: The impact of emotional regulation and personality traits. *Interactive Learning Environments*, 1–17. DOI:10.1080/10494820.2023.2208173

Etambakonga, C. L. (2021). The rise of virtual reality in online courses: Ethical issues and policy recommendations. *Factoring Ethics in Technology, Policy Making, Regulation and AI.* https://books.google.com/books?hl=en&lr=&id=9a5aEAAAQBAJ&oi=fnd&pg=PA131&dq=ethical+considerations+of+virtual+reality,+such+as+data+privacy,+content+appropriateness,+and+digital+equity,+raise+important+questions+about+the+responsible+and+ethical+use+of+VR+technology+in+educational+settings+&ots=gX989_AQmX&sig=GeYFOHMZpKzkTp1PQ4OMCcmJmXk

Fang, S., & Yatani, K. (2023). Towards Understanding Sense of Inclusion in Social VR Onboarding. *Extended Abstracts of the 2023 CHI Conference on Human Factors in Computing Systems*, (pp. 1–8). ACM. DOI:10.1145/3544549.3585751

Fasihuddin, H. (2023). Virtual Reality Technology in Teaching Computer Hardware: A Prototype and Assessment from User Perspectives. *TEM Journal*, 12(2), 899–907. DOI:10.18421/TEM122-36

Fei, T., Mao, Q., Wu, F., & Yu, P. (2023). The Future Prospects of Importance of VR's Impact on Education. *Highlights in Science. Engineering and Technology*, 39, 111–120.

Fromm, J., Radianti, J., Wehking, C., Stieglitz, S., Majchrzak, T. A., & vom Brocke, J. (2021). More than experience?-On the unique opportunities of virtual reality to afford a holistic experiential learning cycle. *The Internet and Higher Education*, 50, 100804. DOI:10.1016/j.iheduc.2021.100804

Galleguillos, M. R., Eloiriachi, A., Serdar, B., & Coşkun, A. (2022). Design Strategies to Promote Intercultural Meaningful Social Interactions. *Proceedings of the Design Society*, 2, 2203–2212. DOI:10.1017/pds.2022.223

Gomes, N., Lou, Y., Patwardhan, V., Moyer, T., Vavala, V., & Barros, C. (2020). The Effects of Virtual Reality Learning Environments on Improving the Retention, Comprehension, and Motivation of Medical School Students. In Ahram, T., Taiar, R., Colson, S., & Choplin, A. (Eds.), *Human Interaction and Emerging Technologies* (Vol. 1018, pp. 289–296). Springer International Publishing. DOI:10.1007/978-3-030-25629-6_45

Gyll, S. P., Shader, K. K., Zikas, P., & Papagiannakis, G. (2023). Design, Technology, and Measurement Considerations in Virtual-Reality Assessment. *Designing Context-Rich Learning by Extending Reality*, 132–160.

Hamilton, D., McKechnie, J., Edgerton, E., & Wilson, C. (2021). Immersive virtual reality as a pedagogical tool in education: A systematic literature review of quantitative learning outcomes and experimental design. *Journal of Computers in Education*, 8(1), 1–32. DOI:10.1007/s40692-020-00169-2

Huang, J., Lucash, M. S., Simpson, M. B., Helgeson, C., & Klippel, A. (2019). Visualizing natural environments from data in virtual reality: Combining realism and uncertainty. *2019 IEEE Conference on Virtual Reality and 3D User Interfaces (VR)*, (pp. 1485–1488). IEEE. https://ieeexplore.ieee.org/abstract/document/8797996/

Huang, T.-C., Limniou, M., & Wu, W.-C. V. (2023). Virtual learning environments in educational institutions. In *Frontiers in Virtual Reality* (*Vol. 4*, p. 1138660). Frontiers Media SA. https://www.frontiersin.org/articles/10.3389/frvir.2023.1138660/full

Huang, X., Huss, J., North, L., Williams, K., & Boyd-Devine, A. (2023). Cognitive and motivational benefits of a theory-based immersive virtual reality design in science learning. *Computers and Education Open*, 4, 100124. DOI:10.1016/j.caeo.2023.100124

Jollibekova, M. (2024). THE USE OF INFORMATION AND COMMUNICATION TECHNOLOGIES IN LEARNING ENGLISH LANGUAGE. *Евразийский Журнал Академических Исследований*, 4(3), 76–80.

Karwasz, G. P., & Wyborska, K. (2023). How constructivist environment changes perception of learning: Physics is fun. *Education Sciences*, 13(2), 195. DOI:10.3390/educsci13020195

Kay, T., Raswan, M., Camarillo-Abad, H. M., Qi, T. D., & Cibrian, F. L. (2023). Using Virtual Reality to Foster Creativity for Co-design a New Self-Expression and Relaxation Virtual Environment for Students. *Creativity and Cognition*, 365–367, 365–367. DOI:10.1145/3591196.3596611

Kouijzer, M. M. T. E., Kip, H., Bouman, Y. H. A., & Kelders, S. M. (2023). Implementation of virtual reality in healthcare: A scoping review on the implementation process of virtual reality in various healthcare settings. *Implementation Science Communications*, 4(1), 67. DOI:10.1186/s43058-023-00442-2 PMID:37328858

Kun, B., Yan, W., & Han, D. (2023). Exploring Interactive Design Strategies of Online Learning Platform Based on Cognitive Load Theory. *Human Factors and Systems Interaction*, 84(84). Advance online publication. DOI:10.54941/ahfe1003585

Kuna, P., Hašková, A., & Borza, L. (2023). Creation of virtual reality for education purposes. *Sustainability (Basel)*, 15(9), 7153. DOI:10.3390/su15097153

Lämsä, J., Mannonen, J., Tuhkala, A., Heilala, V., Helovuo, A., Tynkkynen, I., Lampi, E., Sipiläinen, K., Kärkkäinen, T., & Hämäläinen, R. (2023). Capturing cognitive load management during authentic virtual reality flight training with behavioural and physiological indicators. *Journal of Computer Assisted Learning*, 39(5), 1553–1563. DOI:10.1111/jcal.12817

Lauring, J., Jonasson, C., & Jackowska, M. (2023). Virtuality and inclusiveness in organizations. In *Handbook of Virtual Work* (pp. 384–402). Edward Elgar Publishing. https://www.elgaronline.com/edcollchap/book/9781802200508/book-part-9781802200508-31.xmlDOI:10.4337/9781802200508.00031

Li, C.-H. (2023). Instructional Design, Learning Satisfaction, and Learning Outcome in a Virtual Reality Learning Environment Aimed at Improving the Cognition of Computer Hardware Components. *International Journal of Engineering & Technology Innovation*, 13(2). https://search.ebscohost.com/login.aspx?direct=true&profile=ehost&scope=site&authtype=crawler&jrnl=22235329&AN=162741872&h=DhnNrK88ug4kEmy1matB9PKSQezB1M%2BdbZqYkg0phZsyFgVSAEvB3hgay4GDRf3n1C5M4M%2BDjRhzjtztpSiEnw%3D%3D&crl=c

Li, W., Liu, X., Zhang, Q., Zhou, B., & Wang, B. (2023). VR-Enhanced Cognitive Learning: Method, Framework, and Application. *Applied Sciences (Basel, Switzerland)*, 13(8), 4756. DOI:10.3390/app13084756

Li, Y., Ch'ng, E., & Cobb, S. (2023). Factors Influencing Engagement in Hybrid Virtual and Augmented Reality. *ACM Transactions on Computer-Human Interaction*, 30(4), 1–27. DOI:10.1145/3589952

Lowy, R., Gao, L., Hall, K., & Kim, J. G. (2023). Toward Inclusive Mindsets: Design Opportunities to Represent Neurodivergent Work Experiences to Neurotypical Co-Workers in Virtual Reality. *Proceedings of the 2023 CHI Conference on Human Factors in Computing Systems*, (pp. 1–17). ACM. DOI:10.1145/3544548.3581399

Lui, L. F., Radhakrishnan, U., Chinello, F., & Koumaditis, K. (2023). Adaptive Immersive VR Training Based on Performance and Self-Efficacy. *2023 IEEE Conference on Virtual Reality and 3D User Interfaces Abstracts and Workshops (VRW)*, (pp. 25–29). IEEE. https://ieeexplore.ieee.org/abstract/document/10108645/

MacQuarrie, A., & Steed, A. (2017). Cinematic virtual reality: Evaluating the effect of display type on the viewing experience for panoramic video. *2017 IEEE Virtual Reality (VR)*, (pp. 45–54). IEEE. https://ieeexplore.ieee.org/abstract/document/7892230/

Makransky, G., & Lilleholt, L. (2018). A structural equation modeling investigation of the emotional value of immersive virtual reality in education. *Educational Technology Research and Development*, 66(5), 1141–1164. DOI:10.1007/s11423-018-9581-2

Markwell, L. T., Velten, J. R., Partridge, J. A., & Porter, J. M. (2023). Virtual motivation: The psychological and transfer of learning effects of immersive virtual reality practice. *Journal of Motor Learning and Development, 1*(aop), (pp. 1–15). Research Gate.

Marougkas, A., Troussas, C., Krouska, A., & Sgouropoulou, C. (2023). Virtual reality in education: A review of learning theories, approaches and methodologies for the last decade. *Electronics (Basel)*, 12(13), 2832. DOI:10.3390/electronics12132832

Martarelli, C., Dubach, J., Schelleis, N., Cacchione, T., & Tempelmann, S. (2023). *Virtual reality in primary science education: Improving knowledge of the water cycle*. https://osf.io/preprints/psyarxiv/qj2a5/DOI:10.31234/osf.io/qj2a5

Martín-Gutiérrez, J., Mora, C. E., Añorbe-Díaz, B., & González-Marrero, A. (2017). Virtual technologies trends in education. *Eurasia Journal of Mathematics, Science and Technology Education*, 13(2), 469–486.

Mulders, M., Buchner, J., & Kerres, M. (2020). A framework for the use of immersive virtual reality in learning environments. [iJET]. *International Journal of Emerging Technologies in Learning*, 15(24), 208–224. DOI:10.3991/ijet.v15i24.16615

Mystakidis, S., & Lympouridis, V. (2023). Immersive learning. *Encyclopedia*, 3(2), 396–405. DOI:10.3390/encyclopedia3020026

Nacke, L. E., Mirza-Babaei, P., & Drachen, A. (2023). User Experience Design and Research in Games. *Extended Abstracts of the 2023 CHI Conference on Human Factors in Computing Systems*, (pp. 1–3). ACM. DOI:10.1145/3544549.3574181

Naef, M., Staadt, O., & Gross, M. (2002). Spatialized audio rendering for immersive virtual environments. *Proceedings of the ACM Symposium on Virtual Reality Software and Technology*, (pp. 65–72). ACM. DOI:10.1145/585740.585752

Newman, M., Gatersleben, B., Wyles, K. J., & Ratcliffe, E. (2022). The use of virtual reality in environment experiences and the importance of realism. *Journal of Environmental Psychology*, 79, 101733. DOI:10.1016/j.jenvp.2021.101733

Nganji, J. T., & Brayshaw, M. (2017). Disability-aware adaptive and personalised learning for students with multiple disabilities. *The International Journal of Information and Learning Technology*, 34(4), 307–321. DOI:10.1108/IJILT-08-2016-0027

Nuguri, S. S., Calyam, P., Oruche, R., Gulhane, A., Valluripally, S., Stichter, J., & He, Z. (2021). vSocial: A cloud-based system for social virtual reality learning environment applications in special education. *Multimedia Tools and Applications*, 80(11), 16827–16856. DOI:10.1007/s11042-020-09051-w

Oh, K., & Nussli, N. (2014). Teacher training in the use of a three-dimensional immersive virtual world: Building understanding through first-hand experiences. *Journal of Teaching and Learning with Technology*, 33–58.

Onyesolu, M. O., & Eze, F. U. (2011). Understanding virtual reality technology: Advances and applications. *Advances in Computational Science and Engineering*, 1, 53–70.

Paolanti, M., Puggioni, M., Frontoni, E., Giannandrea, L., & Pierdicca, R. (2023). Evaluating Learning Outcomes of Virtual Reality Applications in Education: A Proposal for Digital Cultural Heritage. *Journal on Computing and Cultural Heritage*, 16(2), 1–25. DOI:10.1145/3593432

Pellas, N., Mystakidis, S., & Kazanidis, I. (2021). Immersive Virtual Reality in K-12 and Higher Education: A systematic review of the last decade scientific literature. *Virtual Reality (Waltham Cross)*, 25(3), 835–861. DOI:10.1007/s10055-020-00489-9

PenjIšević, A., Sančanin, B., & Bogdanova, M. (2023). AN ETHICS CRISIS IN VIRTUAL MEDIA SPACE. *Social Informatics Journal*, 2(1), 7–13. DOI:10.58898/sij.v2i1.07-13

Pillai, J. S., Schmidt, C., & Richir, S. (2013). Achieving presence through evoked reality. *Frontiers in Psychology*, 4, 86. DOI:10.3389/fpsyg.2013.00086 PMID:23550234

Piovesan, S. D., Passerino, L. M., & Pereira, A. S. (2012). Virtual Reality as a Tool in the Education. *International Association for Development of the Information Society*. https://eric.ed.gov/?id=ED542830

Piragauta, J. A. R., & De Oliveira, J. M. (2023). Do Ethics and Values Play a Role in Virtual Education? A Study on the Perception of Students and Teachers. *Journal of Academic Ethics*, 21(2), 343–356. DOI:10.1007/s10805-022-09459-z PMID:36247220

Poutiainen, A., & Krzywacki, H. (2023). Virtual reality in pre-service teacher education: Challenges of realization in music education. *International Conference on Education and New Developments END2023*, (pp. 330–334). Research Portal. https://researchportal.helsinki.fi/files/275544512/Poutiainen_Krzywacki_VR_in_pre_service_teacher_education_2023_END.pdf

Predescu, S.-L., Caramihai, S. I., & Moisescu, M.-A. (2023). Impact of VR application in an academic context. *Applied Sciences (Basel, Switzerland)*, 13(8), 4748. DOI:10.3390/app13084748

Qorbani, H. S., Abdinejad, M., Arya, A., & Joslin, C. (2022). Improving accessibility of elevation control in an immersive virtual environment. *2022 IEEE International Conference on Artificial Intelligence and Virtual Reality (AIVR)*, (pp. 26–35). IEEE. https://ieeexplore.ieee.org/abstract/document/10024457/

Ratnam, T. (2023). Exploring the notion of inclusivity as facilitating students' ontological engagement for personally relevant learning. *European Journal of Education*, 58(2), 277–288. DOI:10.1111/ejed.12552

Ravichandran, R. R., & Mahapatra, J. (2023). Virtual reality in vocational education and training: Challenges and possibilities. *Journal of Digital Learning and Education*, 3(1), 25–31. DOI:10.52562/jdle.v3i1.602

Rishard, M. A. M., Jayasekara, S. L., Ekanayake, E., Wickramathilake, K., Reyal, S., Manathunga, K., & Wickramarathne, J. (2022). Adaptivo: A Personalized Adaptive E-Learning System based on Learning Styles and Prior Knowledge. *2022 Seventh International Conference on Informatics and Computing (ICIC)*, (pp. 1–9). IEEE. https://ieeexplore.ieee.org/abstract/document/10007006/

Rossoni, M., Spadoni, E., Carulli, M., Barone, C., Colombo, G., & Bordegoni, M. (2024). Virtual Reality in Education to Enable Active Learning and Hands-on Experience. *Computer-Aided Design and Applications*, 21(2), 258–269.

Roussou, M. (2004). Learning by doing and learning through play: An exploration of interactivity in virtual environments for children. *Computers in Entertainment*, 2(1), 10–10. DOI:10.1145/973801.973818

Roussou, M., Oliver, M., & Slater, M. (2006). The virtual playground: An educational virtual reality environment for evaluating interactivity and conceptual learning. *Virtual Reality (Waltham Cross)*, 10(3–4), 227–240. DOI:10.1007/s10055-006-0035-5

Ryan, E., & Poole, C. (2019). Impact of virtual learning environment on students' satisfaction, engagement, recall, and retention. *Journal of Medical Imaging and Radiation Sciences*, 50(3), 408–415. DOI:10.1016/j.jmir.2019.04.005 PMID:31229502

Ryan, M.-L. (1999). Immersion vs. interactivity: Virtual reality and literary theory. *SubStance*, 28(2), 110–137. DOI:10.1353/sub.1999.0015

Sadowski, W., & Stanney, K. (2002). Presence in virtual environments. In *Handbook of virtual environments* (pp. 831–846). CRC Press. https://www.taylorfrancis.com/chapters/edit/10.1201/9780585399102-51/presence-virtual-environments-wallace-sadowski-kay-stanney

Serin, H. (2020). Virtual reality in education from the perspective of teachers. *Amazonia Investiga*, 9(26), 291–303. DOI:10.34069/AI/2020.26.02.33

Shankar, A. U., Tewari, V., Rahman, M., Mishra, A., & Bajaj, K. K. (2023). Impact of virtual reality (Vr) and augmented reality (Ar) in education. *Tuijin Jishu/Journal of Propulsion Technology, 44*(4), 1310–1318.

Shaukat, S. M. (2023). Exploring the Potential of Augmented Reality (AR) and Virtual Reality (VR) in Education. *International Journal of Advanced Research in Science. Tongxin Jishu.*

Shin, D. (2018). Empathy and embodied experience in virtual environment: To what extent can virtual reality stimulate empathy and embodied experience? *Computers in Human Behavior*, 78, 64–73. DOI:10.1016/j.chb.2017.09.012

Singh, H., Praveena, K. V. S., Raja, M., Kumar, T., & Tongkachok, K. (2022). Adaptive 3D and VFX Films Virtual Learning Environments. *2022 5th International Conference on Contemporary Computing and Informatics (IC3I)*, (pp. 1129–1134). IEEE. https://ieeexplore.ieee.org/abstract/document/10073177/

Skulmowski, A. (2023). Ethical issues of educational virtual reality. *Computers & Education: X Reality, 2*, 100023.

Slater, M., Khanna, P., Mortensen, J., & Yu, I. (2009). Visual realism enhances realistic response in an immersive virtual environment. *IEEE Computer Graphics and Applications*, 29(3), 76–84. DOI:10.1109/MCG.2009.55 PMID:19642617

Slater, M., & Sanchez-Vives, M. V. (2016). Enhancing our lives with immersive virtual reality. *Frontiers in Robotics and AI*, 3, 74. DOI:10.3389/frobt.2016.00074

Southgate, E., Smith, S. P., Cividino, C., Saxby, S., Kilham, J., Eather, G., Scevak, J., Summerville, D., Buchanan, R., & Bergin, C. (2019). Embedding immersive virtual reality in classrooms: Ethical, organisational and educational lessons in bridging research and practice. *International Journal of Child-Computer Interaction*, 19, 19–29. DOI:10.1016/j.ijcci.2018.10.002

Spike, J., Xie, Y., Spike, J., & Xie, Y. (2025). *Using VR for Collaborative Learning: A Theoretical and Practical Lens.* IGI Global. Https://Services.Igi-Global.Com/Resolvedoi/Resolve.Aspx?Doi=10.4018/978-1-6684-7366-5.Ch040

Stachoň, Z., Kubíček, P., Málek, F., Krejčí, M., & Herman, L. (2018). The role of Hue and realism in virtual reality. *7th International Conference on Cartography and GIS.(Jun. 2018)*, 932–941. https://iccgis2018.cartography-gis.com/7ICCGIS_Proceedings/7_ICCGIS_2018%20(104).pdf

Sumardani, D., & Lin, C.-H. (2023). *Investigating the Factor that Influences the Implementation of Virtual Reality for Science Learning*. Research Square. https://www.researchsquare.com/article/rs-2737402/latest

Sun, Y., & Li, J. (2023). User Interface Design and Interactive Experience Based on Virtual Reality. *Computer-Aided Design and Applications*, 184–195. DOI:10.14733/cadaps.2023.S13.184-195

Sun, Y., Pandita, S., Madden, J., Kim, B., Holmes, N. G., & Won, A. S. (2023). Exploring Interaction, Movement and Video Game Experience in an Educational VR Experience. *Extended Abstracts of the 2023 CHI Conference on Human Factors in Computing Systems*, (pp. 1–6). ACM. DOI:10.1145/3544549.3585882

Sundar, S. S., Oeldorf-Hirsch, A., & Garga, A. (2008). A cognitive-heuristics approach to understanding presence in virtual environments. *PRESENCE 2008: Proceedings of the 11th Annual International Workshop on Presence*, (pp. 219–228). Research Gate.

Sykownik, P., Karaosmanoglu, S., Emmerich, K., Steinicke, F., & Masuch, M. (2023). VR Almost There: Simulating Co-located Multiplayer Experiences in Social Virtual Reality. *Proceedings of the 2023 CHI Conference on Human Factors in Computing Systems*, (pp. 1–19). ACM. DOI:10.1145/3544548.3581230

Udeozor, C., Chan, P., Russo Abegão, F., & Glassey, J. (2023). Game-based assessment framework for virtual reality, augmented reality and digital game-based learning. *International Journal of Educational Technology in Higher Education*, 20(1), 36. DOI:10.1186/s41239-023-00405-6 PMID:36644670

Ummihusna, A., Zairul, M., Ab Jalil, H., & Sulaiman, P. S. (2024). Immersive virtual reality in experiential learning for architecture design education: An action research. *Journal of Applied Research in Higher Education*. https://www.emerald.com/insight/content/doi/10.1108/JARHE-06-2023-0266/full/html

Uzza, A. A., Hamdan, A., & Singh, A. D. (2022). Improving Equity and Inclusion in Education using Virtual and Augmented Reality in Open Distance Learning. *Tenth Pan-Commonwealth Forum Open Learn*. Research Gate. https://www.researchgate.net/profile/Aisyamariam_Abdul_Uzza2/publication/363189882_Improving_Equity_and_Inclusion_in_Education_using_Virtual_and_Augmented_Reality_in_Open_Distance_Learning/links/64490de37b3bca311ca3be3c/Improving-Equity-and-Inclusion-in-Education-using-Virtual-and-Augmented-Reality-in-Open-Distance-Learning.pdf

Wang, W.-S., Lin, C.-J., Lee, H.-Y., Wu, T.-T., & Huang, Y.-M. (2023). Feedback Mechanism in Immersive Virtual Reality Influences Physical Hands-on Task Performance and Cognitive Load. *International Journal of Human-Computer Interaction*, 1–13. DOI:10.1080/10447318.2023.2209837

Weber, S., Weibel, D., & Mast, F. W. (2021). How to get there when you are there already? Defining presence in virtual reality and the importance of perceived realism. *Frontiers in Psychology*, 12, 628298. DOI:10.3389/fpsyg.2021.628298 PMID:34025504

Webster, R. (2016). Declarative knowledge acquisition in immersive virtual learning environments. *Interactive Learning Environments*, 24(6), 1319–1333. DOI:10.1080/10494820.2014.994533

Wehrmann, F., & Zender, R. (2023). Inclusive Virtual Reality Learning: Review and Best-Fit Framework for Universal Learning. *Electronic Journal of E-Learning*, 00–00.

Wei, Z., & Yuan, M. (2023). Research on the current situation and future development trend of immersive virtual reality in the field of education. *Sustainability (Basel)*, 15(9), 7531. DOI:10.3390/su15097531

Xie, H. (2023). The Applications of Interface Design and User Experience in Virtual Reality. *Highlights in Science. Engineering and Technology*, 44, 189–198.

Zhang, L., & Liu, G. (2023). A review of factors affecting cognitive load in immersive virtual learning environment. *2023 IEEE 12th International Conference on Educational and Information Technology (ICEIT)*, (pp. 48–52). IEEE. https://ieeexplore.ieee.org/abstract/document/10107848/

Zigunovs, M., Mamchur, D., & Kolodinskis, A. (2023). The Use of Virtual Reality Solutions to Improve Educational Experience for IT Students. *ENVIRONMENT. TECHNOLOGIES. RESOURCES. Proceedings of the International Scientific and Practical Conference, 2*, 214–218. https://journals23.rta.lv/index.php/ETR/article/view/7219

Chapter 5
Educational Virtual Reality (VR):
Revolutionizing Future Academic Practices

Mohsen Mahmoudi-Dehaki
https://orcid.org/0000-0002-4962-6827
Department of English, Islamic Azad University, Najafabad, Iran

Nasim Nasr-Esfahani
https://orcid.org/0000-0002-2388-6524
Department of English, Islamic Azad University, Isfahan, Iran

ABSTRACT

Virtual reality (VR) is an immersive technology that simulates three-dimensional environments, allowing users to interact with virtual worlds through specialized hardware and software. This chapter explores the evolution of VR, its applications in education, and the integration of artificial intelligence (AI) to enhance user experience. VR's immersive capabilities foster active learning by enabling students to engage with content in ways that traditional methods cannot replicate. Theoretical foundations such as constructivism and experiential learning support the use of VR in educational settings, while practical applications include virtual field trips, simulations, and language learning environments. However, challenges such as high costs and potential accessibility issues must be addressed. This chapter concludes by emphasizing the need for ongoing research and collaboration to fully harness VR's potential in future education and other sectors.

DOI: 10.4018/979-8-3693-6407-9.ch005

1. INTRODUCTION

Virtual reality (VR) is a simulated three-dimensional environment that allows users to interact with and explore a virtual world. This immersive experience is achieved through specialized hardware and software, often requiring the user to wear head-mounted displays (HMDs), motion controllers, and data gloves. VR seeks to immerse users in an authentic computer-generated environment, enhancing the sense of presence and realism (Bailenson, 2018). This immersion is achieved through realistic visuals, spatial audio, and multi-sensory haptic feedback. Users can manipulate and control objects, navigate through virtual space, and engage in activities within the virtual world. The environment can be fully immersive, providing a complete 360-degree spherical field of view, or semi-immersive, blending the real and virtual worlds.

The immersive nature of VR is enhanced by realistic visuals, which include high-resolution monitors and sophisticated graphics rendering techniques to produce vivid, lifelike images. Spatial audio technology provides realistic sound effects positioned physically within the virtual environment, enhancing the user's sensation of presence and immersion. Multi-sensory haptic feedback can provide tactile sensations, such as force feedback, vibrations, or full-body haptic suits, further enhancing the immersive experience (Burdea & Coiffet, 2017). VR enables individuals or groups to work together and communicate in a typical virtual environment, regardless of physical location. This collaborative feature is handy in education, business, and entertainment. Most VR systems offer a whole 360-degree spherical field of view, allowing users to look in any direction and explore the virtual space from different perspectives.

VR is used in various fields, including gaming, education, business, and entertainment. VR has been popular in gaming with titles like Beat Saber, Minecraft VR, and Skyrim VR. VR is used for training, education, and collaboration in education, such as in medical, safety, or military training. In business, VR is used for virtual meetings, product demonstrations, and training simulations. In entertainment, VR is used in social networking, fitness, and leisure activities. The concept of VR dates back to the 1960s, with significant advancements in technology and software. The term “virtual reality” was first used in the 1980s, and widespread adoption began in the 1990s with the development of more sophisticated HMDs and motion-tracking systems. VR continues to evolve, with new applications and technologies emerging, such as mixed reality (MR) and augmented reality (AR), which combine elements of the real and virtual worlds.

The integration of artificial intelligence (AI) and VR has recently led to significant advancements in immersive technologies (Dede et al., 2017). This integration has created more realistic, interactive, and personalized VR experiences. One of the critical aspects of this integration is the use of AI-powered avatars, which can understand and respond to user inputs, recognize emotions, and mimic human-like behavior, enhancing the sense of social presence and immersion within the virtual environment. Furthermore, AI algorithms can generate realistic simulations within VR environments, including the simulation of physics, behaviors, and interactions of objects and characters, making the virtual world feel more lifelike and immersive. Additionally, AI can personalize VR experiences by analyzing user preferences, behavior, and biometric data. By tailoring of VR content to individual users enhances immersion and engagement.

Natural interactions in VR can be facilitated through AI-driven hand-tracking and gesture-recognition technologies, making the experience more intuitive and immersive (Dede, 2018). AI algorithms can also predict user movements, reducing motion sickness in VR by adjusting the virtual environment accordingly. Enhanced graphics in VR environments can be achieved through AI-powered upscaling techniques, making visuals appear crisper and more detailed even with lower-resolution displays. AI can also automatically generate content within virtual environments, such as landscapes, objects, and characters, reducing the manual effort required to create VR content. Real-time data integration is another area where AI can be applied, allowing the virtual environment to dynamically adapt based on real-time data from various sources, such as sensors or user inputs. Dynamic environments can be created using AI, which can respond to user behavior, such as adjusting the difficulty level in a game based on a player's skill and previous performance. AI can also help VR systems recognize real-world objects and integrate them into virtual experiences, enhancing the realism and interactivity of the virtual environment.

2. EDUCATIONAL VR

VR has emerged as a transformative technology in education, offering myriad benefits that enhance students' learning experience. The immersive nature of VR enables learners to engage with educational content in a manner that transcends the limitations of traditional teaching methods. By simulating real-world scenarios or creating entirely novel environments, VR fosters a sense of presence and interactivity that captivates students and promotes active participation in the learning process. VR's applications in education span various disciplines, from Science, Technology, Engineering, and Mathematics (STEM) subjects to language learning, history, and social studies. In STEM education, VR provides a safe and cost-effective platform for conducting virtual experiments, allowing students to explore concepts that may be physically difficult or dangerous to replicate. Language learning benefits from VR's ability to create immersive environments that simulate real-world conversations and cultural experiences, enhancing students' proficiency and confidence in their target language. Furthermore, VR enables students to embark on virtual field trips, transporting them to historical landmarks or distant lands and expanding their understanding of the world and its diverse cultures.

Despite the numerous advantages of VR in education, some challenges must be addressed for its successful implementation (Slater & Wilbur, 2019). The high costs associated with acquiring and maintaining VR hardware and software can be a significant barrier, particularly for schools with limited budgets. Additionally, ensuring equal access to VR technology for all students is crucial to avoid exacerbating educational disparities. Educators must also consider the potential drawbacks of VR usage, such as motion sickness and the need for careful monitoring of usage time, especially for younger children. As the field of educational VR continues to evolve, researchers and practitioners need to collaborate to explore the pedagogical implications of this technology. By conducting rigorous studies and developing evidence-based guidelines for VR implementation, the educational community can harness the full potential of VR to enhance learning outcomes and foster a more engaging and inclusive educational landscape.

2.1. Theoretical Foundation of Educational VR

The theoretical foundations of virtual reality (VR) in education are rooted in various learning theories and approaches that leverage the unique capabilities of VR to enhance learning experiences (Fowler, 2015). These foundations are deeply intertwined and mutually reinforcing, creating a comprehensive framework for effectively using VR in educational settings. Constructivist principles, for instance, emphasize the active construction of knowledge through experiences and interactions. VR's immersive and interactive nature facilitates this process, allowing learners to engage with complex concepts and develop a deeper understanding aligning with experiential learning theory, which posits that learning is most effective based on direct experiences. VR provides a simulated environment for learners to engage in hands-on experiences, such as exploring virtual labs or conducting virtual experiments, which can enhance their understanding of scientific concepts.

The cognitive theory of multimedia learning suggests that multimedia learning is more effective when it includes multiple sensory modalities. VR provides a multi-sensory environment that can enhance learning by engaging multiple senses simultaneously, such as visual, auditory, and tactile inputs. This is further supported by social constructivist principles, emphasizing the importance of social interaction and collaboration in learning. VR can facilitate collaborative learning environments where learners interact and work in virtual spaces, fostering teamwork and communication skills. Scientific discovery learning involves learners actively exploring and discovering scientific principles. VR can provide a simulated environment where learners can conduct experiments and make discoveries, enhancing their understanding of scientific concepts. This aligns with cognitive load theory, which suggests learners have limited working memory capacity. VR can help manage cognitive load by providing interactive, engaging content that reduces cognitive overload and enhances learning.

Design thinking principles involve using design principles to solve complex problems. VR can simulate real-world scenarios and provide learners with the tools to design and test solutions, fostering critical thinking and problem-solving skills. This is further supported by learning through problem-solving, which emphasizes the importance of problem-solving in learning. VR can provide learners with complex problems, allowing them to develop critical thinking and problem-solving skills. The Technological Pedagogical Content Knowledge (TPACK) framework integrates technological, pedagogical, and content knowledge to enhance teaching and learning (Mikropoulos & Natsis, 2016). VR can integrate these elements, providing teachers with tools to create engaging and compelling learning experiences. This framework also considers learning styles and preferences, catering to different modes of interaction and engagement. For example, learners who prefer visual learning can use VR to explore 3D models, while those who prefer auditory learning can use VR to listen to audio explanations. VR can also connect emotionally with learners by immersing them in realistic and engaging scenarios, enhancing motivation and retention. Additionally, VR can be personalized to meet each learner's needs and learning styles, enhancing the learning experience by providing tailored content and interactions. Furthermore, VR can provide an accessible and inclusive learning environment for learners with disabilities, simulating real-world scenarios that are difficult or impossible for learners with mobility impairments to experience in person.

2.2. Applications of Educational VR

The integration of VR in educational settings can revolutionize how students engage with learning materials. By providing immersive and interactive experiences, VR can facilitate the acquisition of knowledge and skills more effectively and engagingly. For instance, virtual field trips can transport students to historical landmarks, cultural sites, and geographic regions, allowing them to explore and learn from these environments without needing physical travel. Similarly, VR can simulate experiments in STEM subjects, enabling students to conduct experiments safely and interactively. Additionally, VR can enhance language learning by providing opportunities for students to practice their target language with native speakers in virtual environments. Furthermore, VR can create immersive and interactive stories, allowing students to engage with narratives more engagingly.

VR can improve accessibility in educational settings by providing accessible learning environments for students with disabilities. For instance, VR can create customizable therapy environments and provide real-time assistance for students with special needs. Moreover, VR can be used to create immersive environments for students with autism, helping them to develop social skills and reduce anxiety. Additionally, VR can be used to create immersive environments for students with dyslexia, helping them to develop reading skills and improve comprehension. VR can enhance teaching methods by providing teachers with tools to create immersive and interactive learning experiences. For instance, VR can create virtual classrooms, allowing students to interact with each other and their teachers in a virtual environment. Furthermore, VR can facilitate distance learning by providing remote students with interactive and immersive learning experiences. Additionally, VR can create virtual conferences and meetings, allowing students to participate in discussions and presentations from anywhere.

Numerous practical examples exist of how VR can be used in educational settings. For instance, VR anatomy labs can allow students to explore the human body in 3D, fostering hands-on learning. Similarly, VR chemistry labs can allow students to conduct experiments safely and interactively. Additionally, VR can create immersive environments for students to explore and create art, allowing them to interact with virtual canvases and tools. Furthermore, VR can create immersive environments for students to explore and create music, allowing them to interact with virtual instruments and environments. The use of VR in educational settings has numerous benefits. For instance, VR can significantly increase student engagement and motivation, leading to better retention and comprehension of concepts. Additionally, VR experiences can make complex facts more memorable and engaging. Furthermore, VR provides safe environments for conducting experiments and practicing skills that might be challenging or unsafe in traditional settings. Moreover, VR can facilitate collaboration among students and teachers, allowing for more interactive and engaging learning experiences.

There are several drawbacks to consider when implementing VR in educational settings (Kirk, 2016). For instance, the initial and ongoing costs of purchasing VR devices and training teachers can significantly challenge schools. Additionally, there is a need for more research to determine the exact impact of VR on learning outcomes and to ensure effective implementation in the curriculum. Furthermore, VR devices can sometimes experience technical issues, such as latency and motion sickness, affecting the learning experience. Moreover, VR must be integrated effectively with traditional teaching methods to ensure a smooth transition and avoid disrupting the learning process. The future of VR in educational settings holds significant promise. For instance, integrating AI with VR can enhance the learning experience by providing personalized feedback and adaptive learning paths. Integrating MR and AR with VR can provide more immersive and interactive learning experiences. Furthermore, VR can provide teachers with professional development opportunities, allowing them to engage in immersive and interactive training. Moreover, VR can create immersive and interactive assessment tools, allowing students to demonstrate their knowledge and skills more engagingly.

3. DESIGNING EDUCATIONAL VR

The design of VR learning experiences requires a structured approach that aligns with learning objectives, ensures user engagement, and balances realism and simplicity. This section will outline critical steps and best practices for designing practical VR learning experiences (Freina & Ott, 2015). It is essential to define clear and specific learning objectives to ensure the VR experience aligns with the planned outcomes. These objectives should be measurable, achievable, relevant, and time-bound (SMART). Additionally, they should be aligned with the curriculum and overall educational goals. The choice of hardware and software is crucial in determining the effectiveness of the VR learning experience. This includes selecting hardware that meets the technical requirements of the intended audience, such as bandwidth, processing power, and display resolution. Software options should support the learning objectives and be user-friendly.

The choice of hardware and software is crucial in determining the effectiveness of the VR learning experience. This includes selecting hardware that meets the technical requirements of the intended audience, such as bandwidth, processing power, and display resolution. Software options should support the learning objectives and be user-friendly. Interactive simulations, branching scenarios, and gamification components can enhance engagement and allow learners to interact with the virtual environment. Interactive elements such as buttons, levers, and virtual tools can be incorporated to facilitate interaction. Gamification elements like points, badges, and leaderboards can be used to make learning more engaging.

User experience is paramount in VR learning design. The user interface should be intuitive and easy to navigate, eliminating unnecessary distractions. Physical comfort, such as measures to reduce motion sickness and provide frequent rest, should be considered. Comfortable viewing distances and angles should also be ensured. User testing is essential to gather feedback and make improvements to the design. Feedback mechanisms such as surveys, focus groups, and analytics can be used to gather user feedback. Based on this feedback, iterative design changes should be made to improve the experience continuously. The VR learning experience should balance realism and simplicity. Realistic visuals and audio can enhance immersion, while simplified interactions and gradual difficulty levels can prevent overwhelming the user.

VR learning experiences can incorporate constructivist, behaviorist, and experiential learning theories. Constructivist approaches can encourage learners to construct knowledge through their experiences. Behaviorist approaches can focus on interaction with the environment to modify behaviors. Experiential learning can allow learners to learn by doing, simulating real-world scenarios safely. VR should be used to complement traditional learning methods, not replace them. Pre- and post-VR activities, discussions, and feedback sessions can reinforce learning and assess understanding. Traditional assessments can be integrated with VR to evaluate learning outcomes comprehensively.

Accessibility is crucial in VR learning design. Features such as voiceovers, subtitles, and alternative navigation options can be included to ensure the experience is accessible to all users, including those with disabilities. User customization options can also be provided to accommodate individual needs. The VR learning experience should be continuously reviewed and updated to stay relevant and practical as the world of VR and learners needs to evolve. Regular content updates, technical updates, and user feedback should be used to identify areas for improvement and make necessary changes. By following the steps and best practices mentioned, educators can create comprehensive and practical VR learning experiences that enhance the learning process for learners of all ages.

The metaverse is conceptualized as an integrated virtual environment that merges augmented physical reality with persistent digital spaces, encompassing various virtual worlds, applications, and the broader internet. Within this expansive framework, VR is pivotal, providing immersive experiences that can potentially transform various domains, including professional environments, educational settings, and social interactions. VR technology enables instantaneous interactions among users worldwide, facilitating effective collaboration and communication within a virtual context. Through VR, individuals can engage in virtual tourism, allowing them to explore realistic reconstructions of actual locations or entirely fictional landscapes. Incorporating VR into the metaverse can revolutionize educational practices by creating immersive classrooms and interactive learning experiences, promoting more profound understanding and knowledge retention. Furthermore, VR expands the realm of entertainment by introducing novel interactive experiences, such as games and simulations, that provide opportunities for engagement beyond the physical world's limitations. The development of the metaverse, fueled by advancements in VR technology, creates new avenues for entrepreneurship and innovation, thereby contributing to economic growth. As the metaverse continues to evolve, the role of virtual reality in shaping digital interactions and experiences is expected to become increasingly significant, influencing how individuals connect, learn, and engage within this dynamic landscape.

4. TECHNOLGOIES IN EDUCATIONAL VR

VR is a rapidly progressing field that generates immersive, computer-simulated environments, enabling users to interact with and realistically navigate virtual worlds. The core components of VR technology encompass a range of hardware and software designed to replicate real or imagined experiences. Foremost among these components are VR headsets essential for delivering immersive experiences. These devices can be categorized into three main types: PC-based VR headsets, which are tethered to a computer and offer the most immersive experiences with high-quality visuals and advanced motion tracking; standalone VR headsets, which are all-in-one devices that do not require a PC or console, integrating processing power within the headset itself; and mobile VR headsets, which utilize smartphones as displays and processing units, providing a more affordable but less immersive experience.

Various input devices are employed to facilitate interaction with the virtual environment. These include motion controllers, which allow users to manipulate virtual objects and navigate through the VR space; haptic feedback devices, which provide tactile sensations to enhance immersion by simulating touch and interactions within the virtual world; and optical tracking sensors, which track the user's movements and position, enabling a more natural interaction with the virtual environment. In addition to these input devices, VR systems often incorporate multiple sensory feedback mechanisms to create a more immersive experience. Spatial audio technology creates an immersive sound environment, placing sounds in 3D space to correspond with visual elements, enhancing the realism of the experience. High-resolution screens with stereoscopic imaging are used to create depth perception and realistic visuals, with some systems utilizing advanced rendering techniques for lifelike graphics. Emerging technologies are further expanding the capabilities of VR. AI is being integrated to enhance user interactions and create more dynamic environments, while 5G connectivity allows for low-latency streaming of high-quality VR content, enabling more users to connect and interact in shared virtual spaces.

The applications of VR technology span various fields, including entertainment, where it is used for video games and immersive experiences in movies; education, where it is employed for training simulations, such as medical procedures or military training, enhancing learning through practical experience; architecture and design, where architects use VR to visualize spaces and designs before construction, allowing for better planning and client presentations; healthcare, where VR is used in therapy and rehabilitation, helping patients manage pain or overcome phobias through controlled exposure in a safe environment; and industry, where virtual simulations are used for training and testing in manufacturing and engineering, allowing for the creation of digital twins of physical objects. As VR technology continues to evolve, advancements in hardware and software promise to enhance user experiences and broaden the scope of applications, further solidifying its position as a transformative technology in various domains.

5. EDUCATIONAL VR AND PERSONALIZED LEARNING

VR facilitates the development of personalized learning environments that can be customized to meet the diverse needs of individual learners (Frehlich, 2020). For instance, VR can incorporate features such as closed captioning for auditory content and provide visual or haptic alerts for sounds, thereby ensuring full participation for individuals who are deaf or hard of hearing in workplace training simulations. Furthermore, VR systems can dynamically adjust tasks' complexity, pacing, and difficulty according to a learner's specific abilities and progress, allowing for a more tailored educational experience. Additionally, alternative interaction modalities, such as voice recognition and eye-tracking technologies, can be integrated to accommodate users with physical disabilities. VR is a powerful tool for dismantling physical obstacles, enabling students with mobility challenges to engage in experiences and activities that would typically be beyond their reach. For example, learners with limited mobility can utilize VR to virtually explore museums, journey through outer space, or ascend mountains, thereby broadening their experiential horizons and fostering a sense of autonomy and empowerment. Moreover, VR can simulate real-world scenarios, such as navigating urban environments or professional settings, allowing students to practice and hone essential skills in a safe, controlled context.

The immersive nature of VR has the potential to enhance empathy and understanding by placing users in virtual situations that allow them to experience life from another person's perspective. In healthcare, VR is increasingly employed to train medical professionals in empathetic patient care by enabling them to inhabit the experiences of individuals with various disabilities or chronic conditions. For instance, a VR simulation might allow healthcare providers to understand the challenges faced by patients with limited mobility or sensory processing disorders, thereby cultivating a deeper appreciation for their experiences and ultimately leading to more compassionate and effective care. VR promotes experiential, simulation-based learning, which is advantageous for all students, including those with disabilities. Instead of relying solely on traditional reading comprehension assessments, VR provides opportunities for learners to engage in realistic scenarios relevant to their lives. This approach is particularly beneficial for individuals who thrive in hands-on learning environments. For example, students on the autism spectrum may utilize VR to practice social interactions and enhance communication skills within a safe, low-pressure setting. Additionally, VR can teach practical skills, such as cooking or personal care, through interactive simulations that offer immediate feedback and opportunities for repeated practice.

Modern VR systems increasingly offer customizable controller configurations and interfaces tailored to users' specific needs and capabilities. This adaptability enables individuals with mobility impairments to engage fully with VR experiences. For example, controllers can be modified for one-handed use, or alternative input methods, such as voice commands and eye-tracking, can be employed. A user with limited dexterity may benefit from a controller with larger buttons or a joystick, while a visually impaired user might rely on auditory cues and haptic feedback. Furthermore, customizable interfaces allow users to adjust virtual elements' size, color, and contrast to align with their personal preferences and requirements. The integration of haptic feedback devices into VR systems enhances accessibility for users with visual impairments by providing tactile sensations that enrich the immersive experience. These devices enable users to perceive virtual textures and shapes, adding a crucial sensory dimension to their interactions. For instance, a user may don a haptic glove that simulates the feel of virtual objects or a haptic vest that conveys tactile feedback when interacting with virtual elements. Haptic feedback can communicate information, such as movement direction or force intensity, through vibrations or pressure sensations. Despite existing challenges in achieving full accessibility in VR, including the financial barriers associated with equipment and the necessity for more diverse and inclusive content, this technology holds significant promise for transforming educational practices and fostering inclusive learning opportunities for individuals across the spectrum of abilities.

5.1 Educational VR and Modern Assessment

Integrating VR technology into contemporary assessment practices represents a transformative approach to enhancing student engagement and improving educational outcomes (Guazzaroni & Pillai, 2020). This extended discussion delves deeper into the methodologies for utilizing VR in assessments, the theoretical frameworks supporting its effectiveness, and the implications for educators and institutions. The effectiveness of VR in enhancing engagement can be explained through several educational theories. Constructivist learning theory posits that learners construct knowledge through experiences. VR provides a platform for experiential learning, allowing students to engage in realistic simulations that promote deeper understanding. Additionally, the Flow Theory, proposed by Mihaly Csikszentmihalyi, suggests that individuals experience optimal engagement when fully immersed in an activity that balances challenge and skill. VR can create such immersive environments, making assessments not only more engaging but also more effective.

VR fosters active learning environments where students are not passive recipients of information but active participants in their education. For instance, in a VR biology assessment, students might explore a virtual human body, interacting with organs and systems, which allows them to apply theoretical knowledge in a practical context. This kind of active participation can lead to higher retention rates and improved critical thinking skills. The design of scenario-based assessments in VR allows for the simulation of real-world challenges relevant to various fields. For example, medical students can practice surgical techniques in a risk-free environment, receiving immediate feedback on their performance. This approach not only enhances skill acquisition but also prepares students for real-life situations by mimicking the complexities they will face in their professional careers. VR can also facilitate collaborative assessments, where students work together in virtual environments to solve problems. This not only assesses individual knowledge but also evaluates teamwork and communication skills, which are essential in many professional contexts. For example, engineering students could collaborate on a virtual construction project, requiring them to apply their knowledge while working effectively as a team.

The integration of real-time analytics in VR assessments allows educators to track student performance dynamically. By collecting data on how students interact with the VR environment, educators can gain insights into their decision-making processes and areas of struggle. This data-driven approach enables personalized feedback, allowing instructors to tailor their teaching strategies to meet individual student needs. VR assessments can also incorporate adaptive learning technologies that modify the assessment experience based on student performance. For instance, if a student struggles with a particular concept, the VR system can present additional resources or alternative scenarios to reinforce learning. This adaptability ensures that assessments are not one-size-fits-all but are customized to enhance each student's learning experience. VR technology caters to various learning styles by providing multisensory engagement. Visual learners benefit from immersive graphics, auditory learners from sound cues, and kinesthetic learners from interactive elements. By appealing to multiple senses, VR can enhance understanding and retention across diverse student populations. Moreover, VR can be designed to accommodate students with disabilities. For example, students with mobility impairments can engage in simulations that allow them to perform tasks they might find challenging in the physical world. This inclusivity ensures that all students have equitable access to assessment opportunities, promoting a more diverse learning environment.

While the potential of VR is significant, several challenges must be addressed. Technical limitations, such as the need for high-quality hardware and software, can pose barriers to implementation. Institutions may need to invest in infrastructure and ensure that all students have access to the necessary technology, which can be a substantial financial commitment. Effective implementation of VR assessments requires educators to be well-trained in technology and the pedagogical strategies that maximize its benefits. Professional development programs should focus on equipping teachers with the skills necessary to create, administer, and assess VR-based assessments effectively. The use of VR in education also raises ethical considerations, particularly regarding data privacy and the psychological impact of immersive experiences. Institutions must establish clear guidelines to protect student data and ensure that VR experiences are designed to promote positive educational outcomes without causing undue stress or anxiety.

The integration of VR technology into modern assessment practices can revolutionize educational evaluation by enhancing student engagement, providing real-time feedback, and accommodating diverse learning needs. By leveraging theoretical frameworks like constructivism and Flow Theory, educators can create immersive, active learning environments that foster more profound understanding and skill acquisition. As educational institutions continue to explore and implement VR solutions, addressing the associated challenges, including technical limitations, educator training, and ethical considerations, is crucial to fully realize the benefits of this innovative approach to assessing student learning outcomes. Through careful planning and implementation, VR can become a powerful tool in the educational landscape, transforming how assessments are conducted and experienced.

6. CONSIDERATIONS IN EDUCATIONAL VR

The integration of virtual reality (VR) in educational settings presents a range of psychological, social, technological, pedagogical, and economic challenges that must be carefully considered (Huang & Liaw, 2021). While VR can potentially enhance learning experiences through immersive and interactive environments, it also raises significant concerns regarding user well-being, accessibility, and effective implementation. Understanding these multifaceted challenges is essential for educators, policymakers, and technology developers to harness the benefits of VR while mitigating its risks. This analysis explores the various dimensions of these challenges, providing insights into how they can be addressed to promote more effective and equitable use of VR in education.

6.1. Psychological Challenges

One of the most pressing psychological issues related to virtual reality (VR) is the phenomenon of reality distortion. This challenge is particularly significant for individuals with pre-existing mental health conditions, such as schizophrenia or severe anxiety disorders, who may already have difficulties distinguishing between real-life events and virtual experiences. Prolonged exposure to immersive VR environments can exacerbate these difficulties, blurring the lines between reality and simulation. Research indicates that this distortion can manifest in various ways, including altered perceptions of time and space, contributing to confusion and disorientation. For vulnerable populations, such as those with psychotic disorders, the risk of exacerbating symptoms is a critical concern that necessitates careful monitoring and intervention.

Cybersickness is a common adverse effect experienced by VR users, characterized by symptoms akin to motion sickness, including dizziness, nausea, headaches, and eye strain. These symptoms arise from a mismatch between visual input and vestibular sensory signals, leading to discomfort and disorientation. Studies have shown that factors such as the quality of VR hardware, the design of virtual environments, and individual susceptibility can influence the severity of cybersickness. For instance, rapid movements within VR or poorly designed user interfaces can heighten the likelihood of these symptoms. As a result, many users may develop negative associations with VR technology, deterring them from future use and limiting the potential benefits of immersive experiences.

The capacity of VR to evoke strong emotional responses is both a strength and a potential drawback. While VR can be an effective tool for therapeutic interventions, such as exposure therapy for phobias or PTSD, it can also provoke intense anxiety or distress if the virtual scenarios are not carefully controlled. For example, a user undergoing exposure therapy for fear of heights may experience overwhelming fear if the VR environment is not calibrated to their comfort level. Therefore, practitioners need to possess a nuanced understanding of individual user profiles, including their emotional triggers and coping mechanisms, to tailor VR experiences that are both safe and effective.

6.2. Social Challenges

While VR has the potential to enhance social interactions, particularly in educational settings, it can paradoxically increase feelings of isolation for some users. Individuals with low self-esteem, social anxiety, or introverted personalities may find social VR environments intimidating, leading to heightened feelings of loneliness rather than fostering connection. Research has indicated that, for these individuals, the immersive nature of VR can amplify feelings of disconnection, as they may struggle to engage meaningfully with others in virtual spaces. Thus, educators and developers must consider the psychological profiles of users when designing social VR experiences to promote genuine interaction and community building.

The immersive qualities of VR can lead to a decline in traditional face-to-face interactions, which are vital for developing social skills, emotional intelligence, and effective communication. Over-reliance on virtual interactions may hinder the development of essential interpersonal skills, particularly among younger users who are still in the formative stages of social development. Studies have shown that prolonged engagement with VR can result in decreased empathy and social awareness, as users become accustomed to interacting in a controlled virtual environment rather than navigating the complexities of real-world relationships. This shift necessitates careful consideration of how VR is integrated into educational curricula to ensure that it complements rather than replaces in-person interactions.

Engagement in social VR can sometimes lead to antisocial behaviors, including cyberbullying, harassment, or gaming addiction. The anonymity and detachment virtual environments provide can embolden negative behaviors that might not occur in face-to-face interactions. For instance, users may feel less accountable for their actions in a virtual space, leading to harmful behaviors that can affect others. These risks underscore the importance of implementing monitoring and guidance mechanisms in educational settings to promote positive interactions and mitigate potential harm. Educators must establish clear guidelines and support systems to ensure that VR is utilized constructively.

6.3. Technological Challenges

The cost and complexity of VR hardware represent significant barriers to widespread adoption in educational settings. Many institutions face challenges affording the necessary equipment, such as high-quality headsets, motion sensors, and compatible computers. Additionally, VR setups' bulkiness and technical requirements can deter usage, particularly in resource-limited environments where space and funding are constrained. To promote the effective use of VR in education, manufacturers and developers must work towards creating more affordable and user-friendly hardware solutions.

A lack of standardized and compatible VR software can lead to fragmentation within the educational technology landscape. This fragmentation complicates educators' efforts to find suitable content that aligns with their curriculum needs and pedagogical goals. The scarcity of high-quality, curriculum-aligned VR content can impede the integration of VR into existing educational frameworks, limiting its potential impact on learning outcomes. Collaborative efforts among developers, educators, and policymakers are needed to create a more cohesive ecosystem of VR educational resources.

Technical challenges such as latency and connectivity issues can significantly disrupt the immersive VR experience, leading to users' frustration. High latency can result in lag between user actions and responses within the virtual environment, diminishing the sense of presence and immersion that VR aims to provide. Ensuring stable internet connectivity is essential for a seamless VR experience, particularly in collaborative settings where real-time interaction is crucial. Educational institutions must invest in robust technological infrastructure to support effective VR implementation.

6.4. Pedagogical Challenges

The absence of pedagogical frameworks for VR complicates its implementation in educational contexts. Educators may struggle to design practical learning experiences that leverage VR's unique capabilities, such as immersion and interactivity. Without clear guidelines, there is a risk that VR will be used in ways that do not enhance learning or may even detract from it. Developing comprehensive pedagogical frameworks that outline best practices for integrating VR into curricula is essential for maximizing its educational potential.

Assessing the effectiveness of VR-based learning experiences presents unique challenges. Traditional evaluation methods may not adequately capture the complexities of learning within a virtual environment, necessitating the development of new metrics and assessment tools. For instance, measuring engagement, collaboration, and critical thinking in VR settings requires innovative approaches beyond standardized testing. Educators must explore diverse assessment strategies that reflect the multifaceted nature of learning in immersive environments.

The immersive nature of VR can lead to cognitive overload for some users, particularly if the content is poorly designed or overly complex. When users are overwhelmed by sensory input or information, their ability to process and retain knowledge diminishes. Striking a balance between engagement and information processing is crucial to prevent overwhelming students. Educators should prioritize designing user-centered VR content, ensuring that it is accessible and aligned with learners' cognitive capacities.

6.5. Economic Challenges

The initial costs of acquiring VR technology and developing content can be prohibitively high for many educational institutions. This financial barrier limits the widespread adoption of VR in classrooms, particularly in underfunded schools.

The hardware, software, and training costs can create significant hurdles, deterring institutions from pursuing VR initiatives. Policymakers and educational leaders must seek funding opportunities and partnerships that can help alleviate these financial constraints and promote equitable access to VR technology.

Creating and maintaining high-quality VR educational content requires ongoing investment and resources. Many institutions may struggle to secure funding for continuous updates and improvements, leading to outdated or irrelevant educational materials. The sustainability of VR content development is crucial for ensuring that educational experiences remain current and effective. Collaborative efforts between educational institutions and content developers can help address these challenges, fostering a dynamic ecosystem of VR resources that evolve with changing educational needs.

The disparity in access to VR technology can exacerbate existing inequalities in education. Students in well-funded schools may benefit from advanced VR experiences, while those in under-resourced environments may be left behind. This inequity highlights the need for equitable solutions that ensure all students have the opportunity to engage with VR technology. Addressing these access issues requires a concerted effort from educators, policymakers, and technology developers to create inclusive strategies that promote equal access to immersive learning experiences.

7. ETHICAL ISSUES IN EDUCATIONAL VR

Incorporating VR technology into educational environments presents exciting opportunities and significant ethical challenges that must be carefully examined (Miller, 2022). This paper delves into the various ethical concerns associated with the use of VR in learning contexts, providing an in-depth analysis of the potential implications and considerations for educators, policymakers, and stakeholders. One primary concern is the potential reduction of learner autonomy within VR-based educational experiences. The immersive nature of VR environments may inadvertently limit students' choices and decision-making abilities, as they are often guided through specific narratives or learning pathways. This reduction in autonomy raises questions about the impact on critical thinking skills and the risk of manipulation, as the emotional intensity of VR experiences may influence students' perceptions and responses.

Another crucial consideration is the health risks associated with prolonged VR use. Extended exposure to VR headsets can lead to physical ailments such as eye strain, headaches, and motion sickness, particularly in younger users whose visual and vestibular systems are still developing. Additionally, concerns exist regarding the long-term cognitive impacts of immersive VR experiences, including potential changes in attention spans, memory retention, and the ability to engage with non-digital learning environments. Privacy concerns are also paramount when integrating VR into educational settings. Many VR platforms collect extensive data on user behavior, preferences, and performance, which can be valuable for tailoring educational experiences but poses significant risks to student privacy. Schools must ensure that data collection practices are transparent and that students' information is safeguarded against unauthorized access or commercialization.

Accessibility and equity issues also arise when considering the integration of VR into education. The high costs of VR equipment can create economic barriers, potentially exacerbating existing disparities in educational opportunities. Furthermore, technological literacy among students and educators may vary, leading to disparities in using VR effectively in learning. Content accuracy and bias are additional concerns that must be addressed. VR experiences can present biased or inaccurate information, propagating misconceptions and limiting students' understanding of diverse cultures and perspectives. Developers and educators must ensure that VR content is factually correct and inclusive and encourage critical thinking about the reliability of the information presented.

Consent and parental approval are essential when implementing VR in educational settings, mainly when working with minors. Obtaining informed consent is crucial, and consent forms should clearly outline the nature of the VR experience, potential risks, and educational objectives. Ongoing communication with parents about using VR in the classroom is necessary to address concerns and foster stakeholders' trust. Finally, psychological and emotional considerations must be taken into account. The emotional intensity of VR experiences can lead to profound learning moments but may also trigger anxiety or distress in some students. Educators must be trained to recognize signs of emotional discomfort and provide appropriate support while also considering the potential for desensitization and its impact on empathy development. Integrating virtual reality into educational settings presents exciting opportunities and significant ethical challenges that require careful consideration. By engaging in ongoing dialogue and establishing clear ethical guidelines, educators can harness the potential of VR to enhance learning while prioritizing the well-being and rights of students. Collaboration among stakeholders, including educators, developers, policymakers, and parents, will be essential in navigating these complex issues and ensuring that VR is a valuable and responsible tool in education.

8. EDUCATIONAL VR IN ALTERNATIVE EDUCATION

VR has emerged as a promising tool in the realm of alternative education, offering immersive and engaging learning experiences that transcend the limitations of traditional teaching methods. This innovative technology enables students to interact with complex concepts and environments in ways that were previously unattainable, thereby enhancing their overall learning outcomes. The implementation of VR in alternative education settings has been shown to yield numerous benefits. Firstly, the immersive nature of VR experiences significantly enhances learning by creating a sense of presence that allows students to engage with the material on a more personal level. For instance, in language education, students can immerse themselves in the culture and daily lives of native speakers through 360-degree videos, which not only aids in language acquisition but also fosters a deeper understanding of cultural contexts. Such immersive experiences lead to a more nuanced understanding of cultural dynamics, which traditional methods often lack.

Furthermore, the active learning facilitated by VR is particularly beneficial in alternative education settings. Students can engage in simulations that replicate real-world scenarios, such as conducting scientific experiments or exploring historical events. This hands-on approach allows learners to apply theoretical knowledge in practical situations, enhancing retention and comprehension. Research indicates that VR can outperform traditional teaching methods in motivating students and improving learning outcomes, particularly in fields like medicine, where empathy and understanding are crucial. Another significant advantage of VR in alternative education is its ability to accommodate diverse learning needs, making education more inclusive. Adaptations can be made for students with visual impairments by providing audio descriptions of VR content, and offering 2D alternatives for those who experience discomfort with VR headsets ensures that all students can participate meaningfully in the learning process. This adaptability is vital in alternative education, where student needs can vary widely.

In practical applications, VR has been utilized to enhance cultural exploration, collaborative learning, and scalable learning experiences. Programs that integrate VR into the curriculum can transport students to different cultural settings, allowing them to engage with local populations and challenge stereotypes. VR also facilitates remote collaboration, enabling students from different locations to work together in virtual environments, which is particularly beneficial in alternative education settings where students may not be able to physically attend classes together. Furthermore, the scalability of VR makes it possible to conduct practical, hands-on learning activities that might be logistically challenging in a traditional classroom, such as virtual field trips to historical sites or experiments in a safe, controlled environment.

Despite the numerous benefits of VR in education, there are challenges to consider. The initial costs of VR technology and the ongoing expenses related to maintenance and software updates can be significant barriers for many educational institutions. Additionally, there is a need for more comprehensive research to understand the long-term impacts of VR on learning outcomes fully and to establish best practices for its integration into curricula. In regard to addressing these challenges and maximizing the potential of VR in alternative education, it is crucial to align VR experiences with learning objectives, utilize existing resources, and focus on inclusivity. Educators should develop a structured approach that includes preview, immersive, and analysis phases to scaffold the learning experience effectively. Additionally, many free or low-cost VR resources, such as educational films and simulations, are available online, which can be leveraged to enhance lessons without incurring significant costs. Finally, considering the diverse needs of students when implementing VR and providing alternatives to ensure that technology is accessible to all learners will maximize the benefits of VR in the classroom. VR presents a unique opportunity to enhance alternative education by providing immersive, engaging, and inclusive learning experiences. By addressing the challenges of implementation and focusing on best practices, educators can harness the full potential of VR to transform the educational landscape and better serve the needs of diverse learners.

9. SUMMARY

VR is an immersive technology simulating three-dimensional environments, enabling users to interact with and navigate virtual worlds using specialized hardware and software. This technology aims to enhance the sense of presence and realism through high-resolution visuals, spatial audio, and multi-sensory feedback. VR has applications across various fields, including gaming, education, business, and entertainment. In the context of education, VR offers transformative potential by providing immersive experiences that promote active participation and engagement. The immersive nature of VR enables learners to engage with educational content in ways that transcend the limitations of traditional teaching methods. VR's applications in education span disciplines such as Science, Technology, Engineering, and Mathematics (STEM), language learning, history, and social studies. For instance, VR provides a safe platform for conducting virtual experiments in STEM subjects, allowing students to explore complex concepts that may be difficult or dangerous to replicate in a traditional classroom setting. Language learning benefits from VR's ability to create immersive environments that simulate real-world conversations and cultural experiences, enhancing students' proficiency and confidence in their target language. The theoretical foundations of VR in education are rooted in various learning theories and approaches, such as constructivism, experiential learning, and cognitive theories. These theories emphasize the importance of active knowledge construction, direct experiences, and multi-sensory engagement in enhancing learning outcomes. VR aligns with these principles by facilitating interactive experiences, simulating real-world scenarios, and engaging multiple senses simultaneously. Despite the numerous advantages of VR in education, challenges such as high costs, accessibility issues, and potential technical problems must be addressed for successful implementation. As the field of educational VR continues to evolve, ongoing research and collaboration among educators, technologists, and researchers will be essential to fully realize its potential and develop evidence-based guidelines for practical integration into curricula.

REFERENCES

Bailenson, J. (2018). *Experience on demand: What virtual reality is, how it works, and what it can do*. Norton & Company.

Burdea, G., & Coiffet, P. (2017). *Virtual reality technology*. Wiley.

Dede, C. (2018). *Immersive interfaces for learning: The future of learning in a digital world*. MIT Press.

Dede, C., Jacobson, J., & Richards, J. (2017). *Virtual, augmented, and mixed realities in education*. Springer.

Fowler, C. (2015). *Virtual reality and augmented reality in education: A new frontier for learning*. Routledge.

Frehlich, C. (2020). *Immersive learning: A practical guide to virtual reality's superpowers in education*. Rowman & Littlefield.

Freina, L., & Ott, M. (2015). *A literature review on immersive virtual reality in education: The State of the art*. Springer.

Guazzaroni, G., & Pillai, A. S. (2020). *Virtual and augmented reality in education, art, and museums*. Springer. DOI:10.4018/978-1-7998-1796-3

Huang, T. C., & Liaw, S. S. (2021). *Virtual reality in education: A new paradigm for learning and teaching*. Springer.

Kirk, D. (2016). *The immersive learning revolution: how virtual reality is transforming education*. Routledge.

Mikropoulos, T. A., & Natsis, A. (2016). *Educational virtual reality: A new era for learning*. Springer.

Miller, D. (2022). *Ethics of virtual reality: A philosophical perspective*. Routledge.

Slater, M., & Wilbur, S. (2019). *A framework for immersive virtual environments (five): Speculations on the future of virtual reality*. Springer.

ADDITIONAL READING

Huggett, C. (2022). *The facilitator's guide to immersive, blended, and hybrid learning. association for talent development*. American Society for Training & Development.

LaValle, S. M. (2023). *Virtual reality*. Cambridge University Press. DOI:10.1017/9781108182874

Tyagi, A. K. (Ed.). (2021). *Multimedia and sensory input for augmented, mixed, and virtual reality*. IGI Global. DOI:10.4018/978-1-7998-4703-8

Verma, J. K., & Paul, S. (Eds.). (2022). *Advances in augmented reality and virtual reality*. Springer. DOI:10.1007/978-981-16-7220-0

Wang, M., Ryoo, J., & Winkelmann, K. (Eds.). (2023). *Cross reality (XR) and immersive learning environments (ILES) in education*. Taylor & Francis. DOI:10.4324/9781003457121

KEY TERMS AND DEFINITIONS

Augmented Reality (AR): AR is a technology that overlays digital information, such as images, videos, or 3D models, onto the natural world in real time. This integration enhances the user's perception of their environment by providing contextual information that can facilitate learning and engagement. In educational settings, AR allows students to interact with virtual objects superimposed on their physical surroundings, promoting hands-on learning experiences and improving knowledge retention.

Educational Virtual Reality (VR): It refers to applying VR technology in learning environments, where immersive, computer-generated simulations create engaging educational experiences. This technology enables learners to explore virtual worlds and scenarios that would be impossible or impractical in the real world, such as historical events or complex scientific phenomena. By immersing students in these environments, VR promotes experiential learning, allowing them to participate in their education rather than passively receiving information.

Extended Reality (XR): It is an umbrella term that encompasses all immersive technologies, including AR, VR, and MR. XR represents a continuum of experiences that blend the physical and digital worlds, offering varying degrees of immersion and interaction. In education, XR technologies can enhance learning by providing diverse and engaging ways for students to interact with content, thereby facilitating deeper understanding and retention of knowledge.

Immersive Platform: An immersive platform is a digital environment that utilizes technologies such as AR and VR to create interactive and engaging learning experiences. These platforms often include a combination of hardware (like VR headsets), software for content delivery, and a library of educational materials. They are designed to facilitate deep engagement and collaboration among learners, enhancing their educational outcomes through immersive experiences that mimic real-world interactions.

Mixed Reality: It is an advanced technology that merges real-world environments with computer-generated elements, allowing for interactive experiences where physical and digital objects coexist and interact in real time. This integration creates a seamless blend of the physical and virtual worlds, enabling users to engage with both types of elements simultaneously, often through the use of specialized headsets or devices that provide visual and sensory feedback.

Non-Immersive Platform: A non-immersive platform refers to a digital learning environment lacking interaction and engagement in immersive platforms. Typically, these platforms may include traditional online learning tools such as videos, slideshows, and text-based materials, which do not provide the same depth of experience as AR or VR. While they can effectively deliver information, they do not engage learners in the same active, participatory manner as immersive platforms do.

Semi-Immersive Platform: A semi-immersive platform combines elements of both immersive and non-immersive environments, offering moderate interaction and engagement. These platforms may utilize 3D simulations or interactive elements that allow learners to engage with content more dynamically than traditional methods. However, they do not fully immerse the learner in a virtual environment as fully immersive platforms do. This approach can enhance learning by bridging conventional e-learning and fully immersive experiences.

Virtual Reality (VR): It is a technology that creates a fully immersive digital environment, allowing users to interact with a simulated world through specialized equipment, such as VR headsets. This technology enables users to experience and manipulate virtual objects and scenarios, fostering experiential learning and engagement. In educational contexts, VR can simulate real-life situations for training purposes, such as medical procedures or historical explorations, thereby providing learners with practical experience in a safe and controlled setting.

Chapter 6
Effective Learning Outcomes Through Virtual Reality

Shaik Mazhar Hussain
Middle East College, Oman

Saadia Mesti
https://orcid.org/0000-0003-0600-7302
Universiti Putra Malaysia, Malaysia

Ahmed Nawaz Hakro
https://orcid.org/0000-0001-8150-8663
Middle East College, Oman

ABSTRACT

This chapter delves into the comparative effectiveness of virtual reality (VR) against the traditional educational methods, underscoring not only the initial financial outlays associated with VR—such as hardware acquisition and content development—but also evaluating these against the recurrent costs inherent in conventional education systems. The intent is to provide comprehensive long-term economic and educational benefits of investment in VR. The chapter offers VR's ability to enhance learning outcomes through immersive, interactive experiences that traditional methods alternatively might not offer. This includes a detailed examination of VR's scalability and its capacity to reach diverse learners across geographical boundaries without the recurring costs associated with physical infrastructures. Moreover, the economic evaluation may provide the extended assessment of VR's potential for reducing costs associated with learning delays, educational disparities, and the provision of customized learning experiences, which are often more logistically and financially

DOI: 10.4018/979-8-3693-6407-9.ch006

demanding within traditional frameworks. In addition to this, the chapter is likely going to address the broader societal and educational benefits, such as increased accessibility for disadvantaged and differently abled students, and the potential for global classrooms that offer unified learning experiences to students from varying socio-economic backgrounds. Through these discussions, the chapter will argue that VR does not merely replace traditional learning methods but significantly enhances educational value, thereby justifying its adoption as a forward-thinking educational technology.

1. INTRODUCTION

VR is an advanced technology that generates a simulated environment, providing users with an immersive experience that can surpass or imitate real-life interactions. In the field of education, VR enables students to participate in interactive and immersive learning experiences that traditional educational approaches may likely not able to offer. By immersing students in a controlled virtual environment, they can explore and engage with content in a manner that improves their comprehension and memory retention (Lopez et al., 2021).

VR can take students on virtual journeys to historical landmarks, allowing them to immerse themselves in the past. It also offers a platform for conducting simulated science experiments and provides a means to explore intricate anatomical structures in three dimensions. This heightened level of immersion and interactivity enhances the learning process, especially for subjects that require visual and hands-on approaches. Additionally, VR can accommodate diverse learning styles and paces, creating a personalized learning experience tailored to individual needs (ALIM et al., 2022).

VR provides the decision-makers ample opportunities to compare the financial impact of adopting VR in education. Contrary to traditional education, the costs incur on ongoing expenses such as textbooks and other materials need to be updated regularly, incurring continuous costs. On the other hand, VR necessitates a substantial initial investment in hardware and software but may lead to lower long-term operational costs. This comparison assists in assessing the cost-effectiveness of VR. The educational outcomes in VR could be influential (Adedoyin Tolulope Oyewole et al., 2024).

VR is crucial for assessing its efficacy (Nasrabadi et al., 2017). Conventional methods, although effective, might not always captivate students or cater to diverse learning preferences. VR presents a distinctive approach that has the potential to improve information retention, expedite the learning process, and offer personalized learning experiences. By comparing these outcomes, we can gain insight into the transformative possibilities of VR in education. One of the disadvantages associated with traditional education may include the limitation of the possibility to attend academic facilities due to multiple physical and geographical factors. Moreover, some disadvantaged or differently abled individuals may find the system to limit their capabilities (Carreon et al., 2023).

VR can eliminate this factor by creating opportunities to learn from any location in the world regardless of physical capacity. Hence, the level of accessibility and inclusivity in VR education can be analyzed through the comparison. The VR also have long term benefits in engagement and motivating the learnings. The two factors are important that might accompany the traditional form of education, as some students may get bored with academic environments. Given that VR is immersive by design, another difference between the two forms of learning can be drawn. The advantages in terms of reducing the disparity in education and enabling learning models tailored to each student's cognitive needs should also be considered. It is necessary to compare long-term costs incurred due to the need to maintain traditional schools and universities with the savings derived from implementing VR. Thus, this is expected to create a nuanced review of VR's potential benefits and limitations in the sphere of education. The goal is to frame VR as an investment in the future that can revolutionize the educational sector, delivering long-term financial and economic advantages.

Figure 1. illustrates a person using VR headset to experience virtual reality. Virtual reality (VR) offers a wide range of benefits to learners across various educational contexts. Here are some of the keyway's VR enhances learning (Ghaznavi et al., 2016).

Figure 1. VR illustration

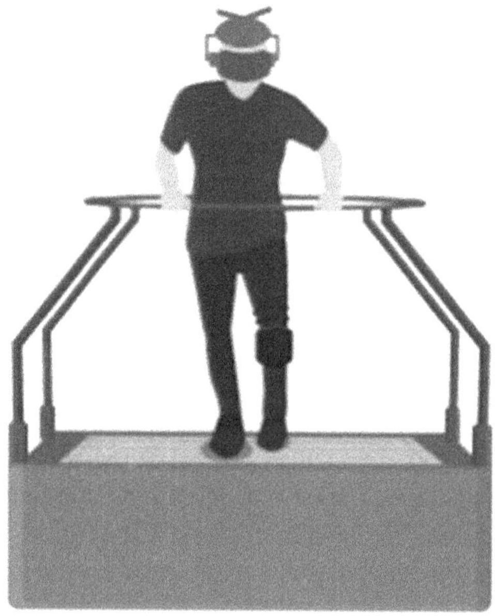

i. Immersive Learning Experiences: VR creates immersive environments that capture learners' attention and make learning more engaging.

By simulating real-life scenarios, VR allows learners to actively participate in their education rather than passively absorbing information.

ii. Enhanced Understanding of Complex Concepts: VR can bring abstract concepts to life, making them easier to understand. For example, students can explore the human body in 3D or visualize complex mathematical structures.

Learners can experiment with variables and see the outcomes in real time, deepening their understanding of scientific and mathematical principles. Some examples of mathematical principles and formulas that can benefit from VR are Geometry and Spatial Reasoning, Calculus, Trigonometry, Linear Algebra, Statistics and Probability, Differential Equations, Complex Numbers, Graph theory. By providing interactive and visual representations of these mathematical principles and formulas, VR can significantly enhance comprehension and retention, making abstract concepts more concrete and accessible.

iii. Safe and Controlled Environment: VR provides a safe for learners to practice skills without real-world consequences. This is particularly beneficial in fields like medicine, aviation, and engineering. Students can learn from their mistakes in a controlled environment, enhancing their skills through trial and error.
iv. Accessibility and Inclusivity: VR can bridge geographical gaps, allowing students from different parts of the world to participate in the same learning experiences. VR can be tailored to meet the needs of diverse learners, including those with disabilities, by providing customized and adaptable learning environments.
v. Collaboration: VR can recreate classroom settings where students and teachers interact in real time, fostering a sense of community and collaboration. Learners can work together on projects in a shared virtual space, developing teamwork and communication skills.
vi. Practical Skills Development: VR can simulate practical tasks, such as surgical procedures, mechanical repairs, or artistic techniques, allowing learners to develop hands-on skills.
vii. Personalized Learning: VR can adapt to the pace and style of individual learners, providing personalized feedback and adjusting difficulty levels accordingly. VR platforms can track progress and performance, offering valuable data to educators for tailoring instruction to meet learners' needs.
viii. VR learning modules can be used by an unlimited number of students, making it a scalable solution for educational institutions.

Figure 2 shows the block diagram of VR technology that illustrates the key stages involved in the creation, transmission, and display of VR content (Ghaznavi et al., 2016).

Here's a detailed explanation of each block:

i. Capturing VR video: This is the initial stage where VR content is created. It involves:
   a) Cameras and Sensors: Specialized VR cameras capture 360-degree video or multiple angles that can be stitched together to create a spherical video.
   b) Audio Capture: Surround sound or spatial audio is also recorded to enhance the immersive experience.
   c) Motion Tracking: Sensors track the movement of the camera and objects within the scene to ensure that the VR content matches the user's perspective.
ii. Pre-processing: In this stage, the raw VR footage is processed to prepare it for encoding. This stage involves stitching, calibration, and correction, compression.
   a) Stitching: If multiple camera feeds are used, the individual video streams are stitched together to create a seamless 360-degree view.

b) Calibration and Correction: Color correction, distortion correction, and other adjustments are made to ensure visual consistency.
c) Compression: The video and audio data may be compressed to reduce file size while maintaining quality.

iii. Encoding: The processed VR content is then encoded into a suitable format for transmission: This stage includes the following:
a) Compression Algorithms: Advanced video codecs like H.265/HEVC are used to compress the video data efficiently without significant loss of quality.
b) Bitrate Adjustments: The bitrate is adjusted based on the network capabilities to ensure smooth streaming.
c) Packaging: The encoded video is packaged into a format that can be transmitted over networks, such as DASH or HLS for streaming.

iv. Network: This stage involves the transmission of the encoded VR content over a network.

v. Decoding: Once the VR content reaches the user's device, it needs to be decoded before it can be displayed:
a) Decompression: The encoded video stream is decompressed using the same codec that was used for encoding.
b) Synchronization: Audio and video streams are synchronized to ensure that they are perfectly in sync.

vi. Rendering/Display: The final stage is rendering the decoded VR content for display on a VR headset or other VR-enabled device:
a) Rendering Engine: The VR application renders the video frames, considering the user's head movements and inputs to adjust the perspective in real-time.
b) Display: The rendered frames are displayed on the VR headset's screens, providing an immersive experience.
c) User Interaction: The VR system tracks the user's movements and inputs, updating the rendered scene accordingly to maintain immersion and interactivity.

Figure 2. Block diagram of VR technology

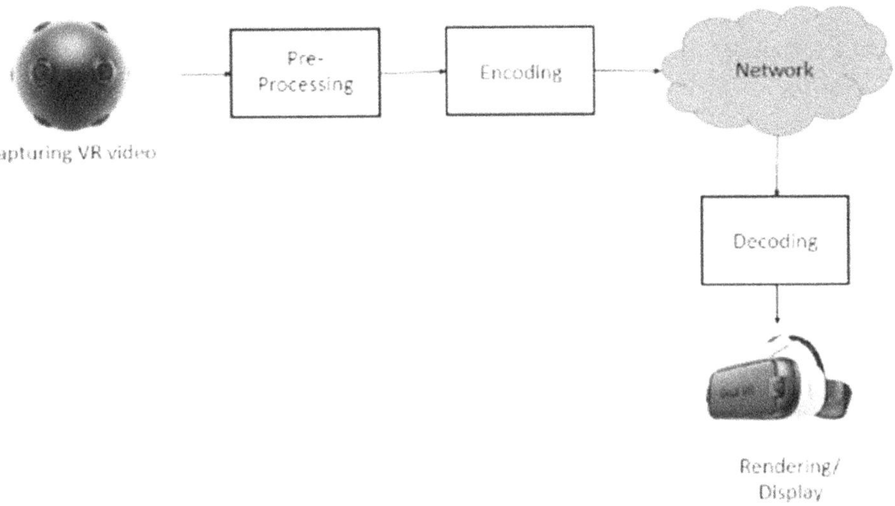

Consequently, the chapter is designed to examine and assess the efficacy of Virtual Reality as a tool for education in comparison to traditional educational approaches. Its goal is to offer a thorough comprehension of the potential advantages and difficulties associated with VR in the field of education, supported by up-to-date research and case studies. Subsequently, the chapter addresses the through comparison between the initial and ongoing costs of VR education systems and traditional education systems. Later, the chapter examine the educational outcomes associated with VR, including factors such as retention rates, learning speed, and student engagement. Subsequently, it will provide the analysis of scalability and accessibility of VR education, particularly in terms of its ability to reach diverse and geographically dispersed learners. The discussion section highlights, the broader societal and educational advantages of VR, such as increased accessibility for disadvantaged and differently abled students. The chapter provides some evaluation of the long-term economic and educational benefits that come from investing in VR technology.

2. EDUCATIONAL TECHNOLOGIES

Educational technologies went through significant transformations for centuries, changing the ways information is presented to the recipient or learners' cognitive process. Among the most remarkable stages in the development of educational technologies are the print, books, and textbooks, which became possible with the emergence of the printing press in the 15th century and became the most widespread educational media. With the help of textbooks, people could receive a standardized and accessible form of knowledge. The invention of the printing press revolutionized the field by making books accessible to most people. Textbooks became the most common method of presenting knowledge and helped standardize education. In 20th century, the development of film, radio, and television opened a new era in the delivery of educational content. These audio-visual aids became an integral part of traditional teaching, allowing a more dynamic and appealing form of content presentation. Recently, in last century, the first modern personal computers and the subsequent emergence of internet technologies were particularly important has emerged. Computers enabled interactive learning through educational software, and the establishment of the internet made it possible to expand students' access to educational resources and enable distance learning and digital collaboration. In the 2000s, many e-learning platforms and Massive Open Online Courses were introduced. They democratized learning and presented cost-free or inexpensive access to millions of students worldwide, frequently from the top universities. smartphones and tablets' dissemination that was ordinary in the 2010s made the above-described technologies accessible to any learner. An opportunity to study on-the-go, e-learning apps brought learning closer to more students than ever. The modern classroom is nothing without its wise technologies: interactive whiteboards, resources to fit them, and other Smart technologies. Moreover, new educational technologies include audio-visual aids, which are possible thanks to the development of the film, radio, and television industry in the early 20th century. Indeed, the audio-visual aids added dynamics and engagement to the traditionally performed materials. The educational technologies are thousands of years old and includes significant changes that have occurred in the way knowledge is delivered and students learn it. Key milestones in their brief history are mentioned below:

Throughout its history, Virtual Reality has developed from a niche concept into an innovative and efficient educational method: Its early beginnings can be traced back to the invention of the first head-mounted system by Ivan Sutherland, the Sword of Damocles, theory that was created to mimic the experience of flight through space. Though technology progressed resulting in the development of more advanced headsets and gloves, it still was characterized by high costs and low computing. Therefore, it was used in military training and flight simulations. In the early 2000s, the world faced an increased computing power and graphics. Companies such as Oculus VR established in 2012 provided affordable VR headsets for the public. The VR industry was revitalized with the assistance of accessible for general consumers such tools as Oculus Rift, HTC Vive and PlayStation VR; they provided high-quality experiences that created the desire for its implementation into various spheres, including education. In the late 2010s, VR found its way into educational environments. Educators experimented with VR in medical schools, as a means of taking students on virtual trips, and in immersive simulations. However, as some early research showed, VR had the potential to improve learning through interactive and immersive experiences. Nowadays, VR keeps improving; the headsets are getting lighter and more comfortable, and the content and platforms for education are becoming more complex and efficient. It is therefore no surprise that VR is used to teach students of all ages and specializations from K-12 to higher education and professional environments. More educational institutions adopt VR technology, allowing its implementation in the education process in science, history, art, and other subjects. VR labs and VR classrooms created specifically to study the possibilities of VR usage are examples. Current VR platforms also enable collaboration and create an opportunity for students to work together in virtual reality classrooms and labs. Virtual reality classes help students to study immersed in locations located hundreds or thousands of kilometers from each other without access barriers in the form of walking. Instructing in VR is largely accompanied by interactive simulations, and not just boring 3D presentations. Virtual reality allows for more accurate simulations that can still provide students with hands-on experience. For example, medical students can perform surgery virtually; students of engineering departments can plan and test structures. With affordable VR technology, schools and universities can use this asset as an additional method of education. Moreover, the cost of headsets dropped dramatically, and the variety of available educational VR platforms increased over time. VR can provide a unique experience for every student as some special educational platforms in VR can adjust the difficulty or the type of material after each task based on the student's performance and response. Teachers and educators are using this technology to explore professional development using VR programs. By allowing teachers to teach using new teaching techniques and student management styles, it can help a teacher apply VR programs to their teaching styles better. This will help students with a proven disability learn better in terms of programs because like in measures class, it will be easier to engage vs traditional classroom. Research done to see the impacts using VR programs has on learning concept for students and development as well. Help with the studying pace to find the fastest and easiest way to keep all educational qualities high.

2.1 Financial Considerations

Initially, introducing Virtual Reality in education demands the following investments into facilities and materials: VR headsets, motion controllers, and powerful computers or mobile devices capable of operating VR applications are the most common elements. The cost of VR headsets such as Oculus Rift, HTC Vive, or PlayStation VR can vary from a few hundred to thousands of dollars based on quality and performance. In some cases, external sensors, haptic feedback devices, or other equipment, and even VR-unique furniture, may be needed. The critical item includes the cost of VR applications themselves, educational platforms, and licenses for using proprietary content. The cost depends on the complexity and scope of the VR content and may range from several thousand dollars to millions. In some cases, software providers may offer subscription models, but a one-time fee is common. Moreover, it is important to remember the expenses related to the customization or development of proprietary VR content according to individual learning needs. Setting up a VR lab or integrating VR into existing classrooms requires infrastructure upgrades. This may include improving the network's ability to handle large data transfers, creating dedicated VR spaces with appropriate security measures, and ensuring that the physical environment is conducive to an immersive experience. Creating quality VR educational content is critical to the success of VR in education. Content development costs include. Developing VR content requires a lot of time and expertise. Content producers must design and program immersive environments, interactive elements, and educational stories. This process often requires collaboration between subject matter experts, instructional designers, and VR developers. The cost of hiring these professionals can be significant, especially in complex simulations and high-fidelity environments. Educational institutions can license existing VR content from third parties. License fees may vary depending on the use, quality, and duration of the content. Some service providers may also charge a usage fee based on the number of users or frequency of use. VR content needs to be updated regularly to stay relevant and effective. This VR content needs to be updated regularly to stay relevant and effective. This VR content needs to be updated regularly to stay relevant and effective. This includes adding new information, improving user interfaces, and solving technical problems. Continues maintenance ensures that VR content is compatible with the latest hardware and software. Teachers must be trained to use VR technology effectively and integrate it into their teaching strategies. This training may incur additional costs, including workshops, professional development courses and support services. Traditional education includes running costs such as textbooks, classroom supplies, maintenance of physical infrastructure and salaries of teachers and support staff. These costs accumulate over time and can be significant, especially at large institutions. Although the initial investment in VR is large, it can lead to long-term savings. For example, VR can reduce the need for physical resources such as laboratory equipment, as virtual laboratories can simulate the same experiments. In addition, VR can minimize the cost of tours by offering virtual tours. VR can be more scalable than traditional methods. Once the initial setup and content development is complete, the marginal cost of adding new students is relatively low. In contrast, traditional education requires a proportional increase in resources (e.g., additional classrooms, teachers) as student numbers increase. VR can potentially reduce the opportunity costs associated with learning delays and educational gaps. By providing a personalized and immersive learning experience, VR can improve student outcomes and reduce the need for remedial training, which can be expensive over time. VR can significantly improve learning outcomes through immersive and interactive experiences. Better educational outcomes can lead to higher graduation rates, better job readiness and increased lifetime income for students. Immersive and effective VR experiences can help keep students motivated and interested in their studies and decrease dropout rates. A lower dropout rate can lead to a higher overall level of education and a skilled workforce. VR can be used for continuous learning and professional development, allowing people to update and relearn throughout their careers. Such adaptability can lead to a more dynamic and flexible workforce, which is essential in an ever-changing labor market. By providing accessible learning environments for disadvantaged and differently abled students, VR can help bridge educational gaps and promote social equity. This inclusion can lead to a more diverse and inclusive workforce, which has been shown to drive innovation and economic growth. VR can facilitate global classrooms, allowing students around the world to learn together and from each other. This global perspective can promote international cooperation and understanding, which is valuable in a globalized economy. In the long run, the use of VR in education can lead to more efficient allocation of educational resources. By optimizing learning processes and outcomes, VR can help educational institutions achieve better results with the same or fewer resources.

2.2 Educational Effectiveness

VR provides students with an immersive and interactive environment where they can deeply engage with educational content. This hands-on experience allows practical application of knowledge, which can improve understanding and make learning more interesting compared to traditional methods. For example, students can hands-on explore historical sites, conduct science experiments, or simulate complex design tasks, providing engagement that is difficult to achieve with standard classroom tools. Research shows that VR can significantly improve retention rates and learning outcomes. The immersive nature of VR helps students retain information better by providing memorable and immersive experiences. Studies have shown that students using VR often have higher retention rates than those learning through traditional methods because the interactive and stimulating environment helps to better understand concepts. VR allows for highly customized and personalized learning experiences tailored to the individual needs of students. Adaptive learning technologies in VR can adjust the difficulty and pace of lessons based on student performance and feedback. This customization helps accommodate different learning styles and paces, ensuring that each student can learn in the way that works best for them, enhancing their overall educational experience. Many comparative studies have highlighted the effectiveness of VR in education. For example, studies comparing VR-based learning with traditional teaching methods often find that VR increases student engagement, understanding, and retention. Meta-analyses and case studies across educational levels and disciplines consistently demonstrate the benefits of VR in providing richer and more effective learning. These findings support the adoption of VR as a complement to traditional educational methods and reinforce its value in modern education.

2.3 Scalability and Accessibility

With VR, educational institutions can reach students around the world, breaking geographical barriers. It supports distance learning by enabling students to engage in immersive educational experiences from anywhere, facilitating global classrooms and collaborative learning among diverse learners. By providing virtual environments for learning, VR reduces the need for physical infrastructure such as classrooms and laboratories. This can result in significant savings in property maintenance and utilities, allowing institutions to allocate resources more efficiently. VR makes education more accessible to disadvantaged and differently abled students by providing tailored learning experiences for different needs. It can provide specialized content and environments that traditional classrooms may not, ensuring inclusion and equal learning opportunities for all students.

2.4 Reducing Educational Disparities

VR can help reduce learning delays by providing interactive and engaging content that boosts comprehension and retention. Students who struggle with traditional methods can benefit from the immersive nature of VR, allowing them to learn concepts faster and more effectively. VR ensures equal access to quality educational resources regardless of the student's socioeconomic background. By providing virtual experiences that would otherwise be out of reach due to cost or location, VR helps create a level playing field for students from different financial backgrounds.

VR enables personalized learning experiences tailored to individual needs according to different learning styles and paces. This personalization ensures that every student receives the support they need to succeed, improving overall educational outcomes. Many case studies illustrate the impact of VR in reducing educational gaps. For example, schools in underserved areas have used VR to provide students with virtual field trips and interactive science labs, significantly improving engagement and learning outcomes. Another example includes VR programs for students with disabilities that offer customized learning modules that meet their specific needs.

2.5 Implementation Challenges and Solutions

Implementing VR in education involves technical hurdles, such as ensuring appropriate hardware, software compatibility and a reliable internet connection. Logistical challenges include setting up VR labs and integrating VR systems into existing infrastructure. Solutions include investing in robust hardware, using scalable software platforms and ensuring strong technical support. Implementation Teachers need training to effectively integrate VR into their teaching methods. This includes understanding VR technology, designing VR-based lessons, and managing VR classroom dynamics. Providing comprehensive professional development programs and ongoing technical support can help educators use VR to support education. Students may initially have challenges adapting to VR technology and understanding how to navigate the virtual environment. Engagement can be improved by designing intuitive and user-friendly VR experiences and organizing orientation sessions.

Continuous feedback and play can further increase student engagement and motivation. To effectively scale VR, educational institutions can deploy cloud-based VR platforms that allow easy access and updates. Collaboration with VR content producers and using open-source resources can reduce costs. Implementing a phased rollout and gathering feedback for iterative improvements can ensure a successful large-scale rollout.

3. PROSPECTS

Future advances in VR technology, such as higher-resolution displays, more comfortable and affordable headsets, and advanced motion tracking, will enhance the immersive experience and make VR easier and more effective for educational purposes. Integrating artificial intelligence and machine learning with VR can create adaptive learning environments that tailor education to individual student performance and learning styles. AI can provide real-time feedback, automate administrative tasks, and provide advanced analytics to improve learning outcomes. The long-term vision for VR in education includes widespread adoption, where VR becomes a standard tool in classrooms around the world. It aims to create global, interconnected learning environments, provide equal opportunities for quality education, and continuously innovate teaching and learning methods to prepare students for the future.

4. CONCLUSION

Virtual reality (VR) provides immersive and interactive learning that improves engagement and retention. VR reduces educational gaps by addressing learning delays, bridging socioeconomic gaps, and providing personalized learning for diverse needs. Implementation challenges include technical barriers, teacher training, student adaptation, and scalability issues. Prospects for VR in education include technology development, integration with artificial intelligence and a long-term vision of global adoption. While traditional educational methods have their advantages, VR offers unique advantages in terms of engagement, accessibility, and personalized learning. It complements traditional teaching methods and can revolutionize education by providing equal access to quality learning experiences. Educational institutions should invest in VR technology and provide comprehensive training for teachers and support for students. Governments and decision makers must allocate resources and create policies to promote the integration of VR in Education.

REFERENCES

Alim, E., Coşkun, Ö., & Peker, T. V. (2022). *Comparison and Evaluation of the Effectiveness of Traditional Neuroanatomy Teaching in Medical Education with Virtual-Reality Application Based on 3D Virtual Neuroanatomical Models, Which Is an Innovative Approach*. Research Square. DOI:10.21203/rs.3.rs-2351422/v1

Carreon, A., Criss, C., & Mosher, M. (2023). Classroom virtual reality for students with disabilities: A PRELIMINARY GUIDE TO AVAILABLE virtual content. *Journal of Special Education Technology*, 39(1), 143–150. DOI:10.1177/01626434231170593

Lopez, M., Arriaga, J. G., Nigenda Álvarez, J. P., González, R. T., Elizondo-Leal, J. A., Valdez-García, J. E., & Carrión, B. (2021). Virtual reality vs traditional education: Is there any advantage in human neuroanatomy teaching? *Computers &amp. Computers & Electrical Engineering*, 93, 107282. DOI:10.1016/j.compeleceng.2021.107282

Nasrabadi, A. T., Mahzari, A., Beshay, J. D., & Prakash, R. (2017). Adaptive 360-degree video streaming using Scalable Video coding. *Proceedings of the 25th ACM International Conference on Multimedia*. DOI:10.1145/3123266.3123414

Oyewole, A. T., Adeoye, O. B., Addy, W. A., Okoye, C. C., Ofodile, O. C., & Ugochukwu, C. E. (2024). Augmented and virtual reality in financial services: A Review of Emerging Applications. *World Journal of Advanced Research and Reviews*, 21(3), 551–567. DOI:10.30574/wjarr.2024.21.3.0623

Youvalari, G. Ramin. (2016). *360-Degree Panoramic Video Coding*. Research Gate. DOI:10.13140/RG.2.2.21662.25921

Chapter 7
Enhancing Electronics Engineering Laboratory With Experimental Learning Using Virtual Reality

Sana Al-Ghawi
Middle East College, Oman

Shaik Asif Hussain
https://orcid.org/0000-0001-5312-4320
Middle East Collage, Oman

ABSTRACT

This chapter investigates the potentially transformative implications of integrating virtual reality technology into the field of electrical and instrumentation engineering to enhance the educational experience and change the traditional way that students study and experiment with electronic instrumentation by utilizing the future possibilities of virtual reality. Electronics and instrumentation have consistently been at the center of modern technological development, powering industry, health care, and scientific study. However, considering its important function in developing this world of teaching, taking complicated topics related to instrumentation remains a difficulty. As a student in this specialization, the author has personally faced and encountered the restrictions of the traditional laboratory environments in universities, where most physical components are frequently in short supply, costly, or even unreachable.

DOI: 10.4018/979-8-3693-6407-9.ch007

1. INTRODUCTION

This title investigates the potentially transformative implications of integrating virtual reality technology into the field of electrical and instrumentation engineering to enhance the educational experience and change the traditional way that student's study and experiment with electronic instrumentation by utilizing the future possibilities of virtual reality. Electronics and instrumentation have consistently been at the center of modern technological development, powering industry, health care, and scientific study. However, considering its important function in developing this world of teaching, taking complicated topics related to instrumentation remains a difficulty. As a student in this specialization, I have personally faced and encountered the restrictions of the traditional laboratory environments in universities, where most physical components are frequently in short supply, costly, or even unreachable.

There is a clear need for new educational solutions that solve this problem, and the introduction of virtual reality gives a transformative possibility. This technology provides an interactive setting that can connect theoretical and practical knowledge gaps. (Kamińska, 2019). Finally, virtual reality technology will assist students and professors in describing and teaching the experiment outside of the educational establishment. Students and teachers may connect with and control technological gadgets while also feeling as if they are communicating with actual educational institutions. The laboratory equipment's and components can be simulated in the VR environment which can provide a safe and cost-effective way to teach and train students to use the laboratory equipment. Furthermore, virtual reality technology can make the laboratory more flexible and accessible to students who may not have a physical laboratory like students who are in remote areas or have disabilities (i3-Technologies, 2023).

In order to address the flaws of conventional teaching methods, the notion aims to revolutionize education by introducing an immersive laboratory augmented by virtual reality. use the Unity platform, it is possible to create a virtual reality laboratory that is interactive with students and can be viewed through an "Oculus Quest 2 Headset," all while improving student engagement, knowledge, and retention through practical, hands-on learning experiences. The strategy entails democratizing access to education enabling remote distance learning and developing an extensible user-friendly platform by using the Unity engine which helps to design virtual reality environments that's suits any program in VR technology. Moreover, the integration will be between 3D Max or SketchUp and Unity software, then to transfer this program to "Oculus Quest 2 Headset" which is the main device to create the laboratory environment. The Unity software has button called C# language which is required to program the design (Program-ace, 2022). Furthermore, the virtual reality environment allows professors and students to live in the same area at the same time and communicate with one another, allowing them to leave and enjoy their lesson. The significance of designing the VR environment is that the virtual reality approach provides students with an immersive and interactive. The expected results at the end of the project are done as planned before. The expected are helping the students to learn about the possibilities to do experiments outside the education institute, so it will extend the reach of education to wherever the teachers imagine they want to take their students. Also, VR technology will help to increase student learning with statistics of 90% and 97% of the students will be attending the VR headset courses.

2. HARDWARE AND SOFTWARE SPECIFICATIONS

2.1. Hardware Specifications

To create the VR environment, one must use components (hardware and software). Examples of hardware like VR helmets or glasses, Oscilloscope, Breadboard, resistors, LED, battery, wires and DC power supply. Examples of software like 3D Max, Unity in C# language, and Oculus VR. Both hardware and software are essential to acting inside the VR environment. Inside the VR environment, it will Simulate the Oscilloscope. The Oscilloscope (scope) is the device that converts Electrical Waves to Mechanical Waves (Fluke Corporation, 2023). Also, will simulate a DC power supply that produces both high (negative) voltage and low (positive) voltage, it will apply to the Cathode Rayes Tube (CRT) screen.

- **Virtual Reality (VR) Headset:**

Figure 1. VR Quest 2

(Kevin Brook, 2020)

Figure 1 depicts Oculus Quest 2 as the successor to Oculus Quest 1, it is a popular Mobile VR Headset. Oculus Quest 2 works with battery power, so can use it anytime and anywhere without the need to connect to the computer. The student must register to the account and can upload the games or designs that were installed before in the library to the headset. The features of the Quest 2 VR headset are a Qualcomm Snapdragon XR2 processor, (1832×1920) per eye resolution, and a refresh rate of 12 per 120 Hz. The Oculus has Wi-Fi,3.5mm headphone socket, USB-C with Oculus link, a stereo speaker, and a Microphone (Kevin Brook, 2020).

2.2. Software Specifications

- **3D Max Software:**

Figure 2. 3D Max logo

(Estaarmax, n.d.).

Figure 2, a, it shows the logo and interface of the 3D Max Software. 3D Max is a Software Program for creating 3D Models, Animations, and Digital Images. In the project, it will be used to design 3D Oscilloscope and DC Power Supply devices. It is Autodesk software and is used for gaming, designing, TV, etc. Also, it can operate on the Windows platform. The interface of the 3D Max software, it is to design the cross-sectional and box collider images for the devices' Oscilloscope and DC power supply (Estaarmax, n.d.).

- **SketchUp Software:**

Figure 3. SketchUp logo

(Bacus, 2020)

SketchUp is an easy-to-use 3D modeling program, SketchUp is utilized for many different drawing applications, including engineering, interior design, landscape architecture, and architecture. It provides tools for texturing, rendering, and building intricate 3D models. The program works nicely with other design and rendering programs like Enscape and enables plugins and extensions to expand its capabilities (Bacus, 2020).

- **Oscilloscope (Scope) in Unity Software:**

Figure 4. Tektronix TDS 220 Oscilloscope

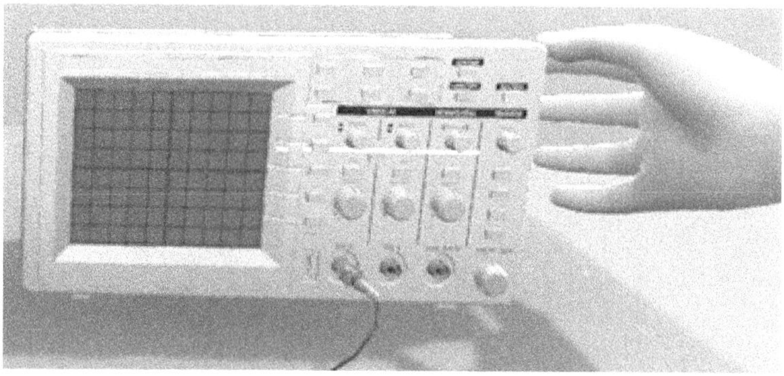

Figure 4 shows the Oscilloscope, which is the device that converts Electrical Waves to Mechanical Waves. To display the Signal one must use an Oscilloscope (Tektronix Digital Storage 220) to show the Voltage Signals in which the vertical axis (Y) represents the Voltage Magnitude, while the horizontal axis (X) represents the time. The results will be shown on the Cathode Rays Tube (CRT) screen, and the students can change the settings of the Oscilloscope by increasing or decreasing the voltage, changing the scale of the waveform, and other settings (Artisantg, 2024).

- **DC Power Supply in Unity Software:**

Figure 5. DC regulated power supply

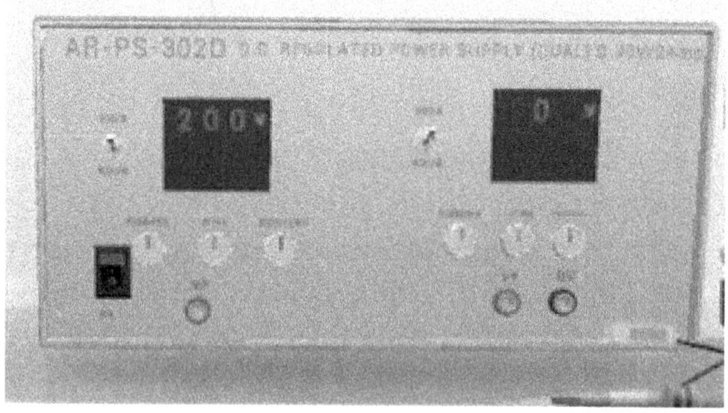

Figure 5 shows the DC Regulated Power Supply (Dual AR-PS-302D) which produces both High (negative) Voltage and Low (Positive) Voltage. Both voltages are applied to the Cathode Rayes Tube (CRT) and other circuits respectively (Series). This device is connected to the Oscilloscope to show the signal inside the screen and can change the setting of the Voltage from the DC Power Supply (Trade India, 2023).

- **Unity Software:**

Figure 6. Unity 2022 logo

(Program-ace, 2022)

Figure 6 shows the Unity 2022 Software. It is a Software to design 2D and 3D models to give designers and developers access to development tools. Nowadays, Unity presents modern techniques, the designers can design with the Metaverse which combines Blockchain and Virtual Reality techniques. In this project, Unity will be used for connecting Oscilloscope and DC Power Supply devices using C# language and operating them in the VR headset. Unity software has a good relationship with VR technology. It can make designs directly from Unity software and operate the design through C# language, then integrate Unity software with Oculus VR type Quest 2 to interact with the devices. Also, the design of two devices together and able to act to show the waves and make changes by sockets (Program-ace, 2022).

After rendering the design it will be transferred to Unity, it is another popular game production platform that offers creators a variety of tools for developing interactive 2D, 3D, VR, and augmented reality experiences. Unity, like Unreal Engine, is well-known for its ease of use and adaptability, making it a popular choice for both independent developers and huge studios. (Zenva, 2023)

- **Oculus VR:**

Figure 7. Oculus VR logo

(Oculus, 2023)

Figure 7 show the Oculus logo. The Oculus helps the VR environment to function like a Digital twin technique that can operate and act inside it like in real life. It operates through the user's senses. Oculus VR is the Software to uploads the design from the Unity Software with the VR environment (Quest 2) into Oculus Software to be operating inside the VR Education environment. The vision inside the VR environment with the Quest 2 headset and can interact with the virtual reality environment (Oculus, 2023).

3. RESULT AND IMPLEMENTATION

Figure 8. Integration of devices together

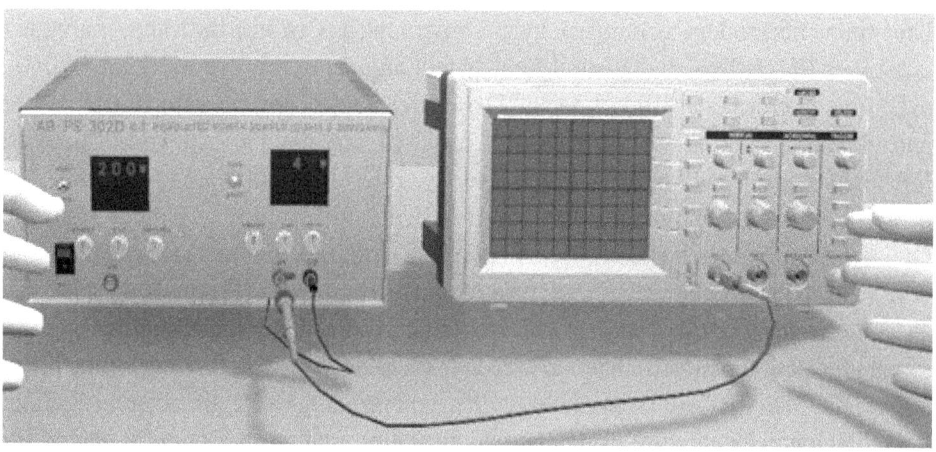

Figure 8 shows the results after connecting DC power supply and Oscilloscope together. The Oscilloscope has four parts, each part has four rows and four columns.

- When DC power supply 3V

Setting the Volt/dev =(1)

Figure 9. Setting DC power supply 3V and adjusting the volt/dev equal to 1.

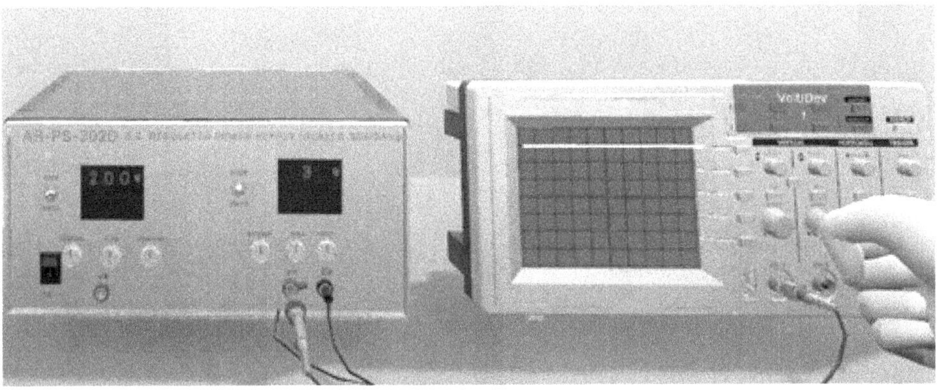

Figure 9 shows the adjusting the volt/dev make the volt/dev equal to (1). So, the number of squares in the CRO is equal to (3) starting line from the center.

$V = 3 \times 1v \Rightarrow \therefore V = 3v.$

Figure 10. (a) Components design for resistor, (b) DC power supply (c) SketchUp components design in breadboard, (d) Battery connection in Unity platform

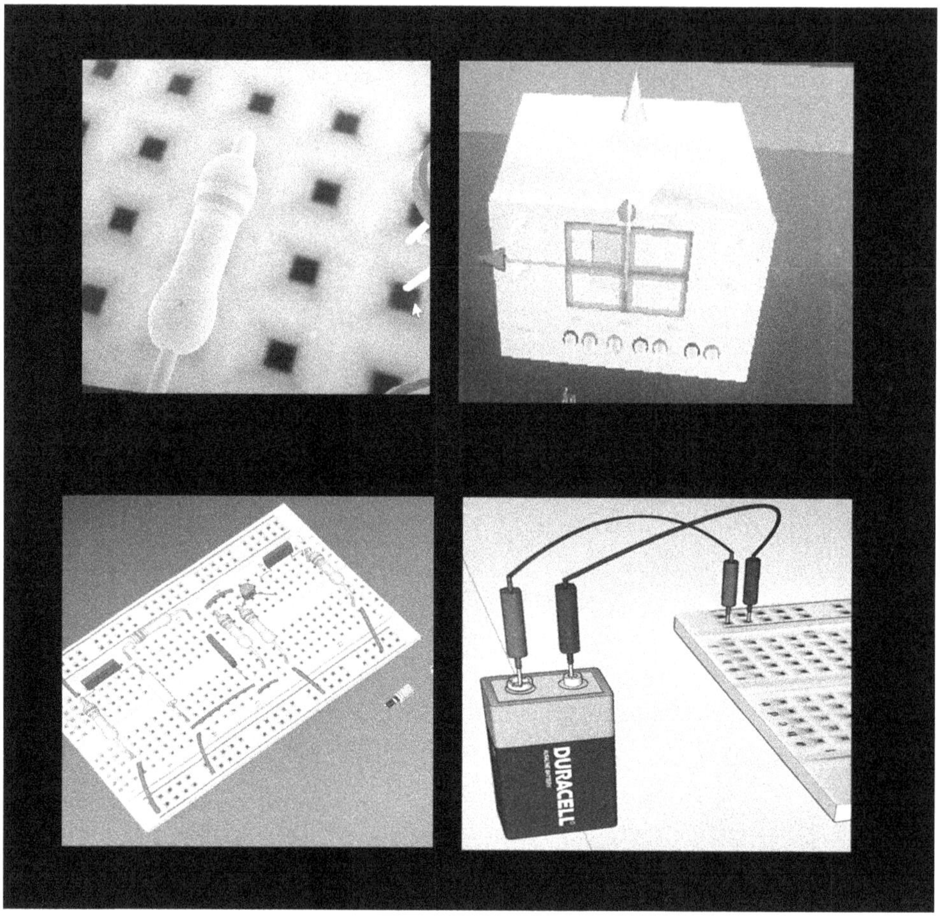

Figure 11. Unity platform- virtual reality laboratory

Figure 11 shows the final step which is transferring the hole design to the Unity platform there will be the simulation configuration of the components design and the program and it will be transferred to the "Oculus Quest 2 headset" which is the VR glasses which contain the virtual reality laboratory that user can interact and see the electrical circuits and components, and this is the final step.

4. CONCLUSION

In conclusion, by utilizing virtual reality's capabilities, enhancing electronics engineering laboratory using Virtual Reality seeks to close a large gap in engineering education. While traditional lab sets frequently have limitations that might impede learning, virtual reality technology provides an innovative and engaging workaround. This initiative intends to expand the students' understanding of electronics and instrumentation in addition to revolutionizing the educational process.

REFERENCES

I3-Technologies. (2023). *VR in the classroom: benefits and drawbacks.* I3 Technologies. https://www.i3-technologies.com/en/blog/stories/education/vr-in-the-classroom-benefits-and-drawbacks/#:~:text=Some%20benefits%20of%20using%20VR,retention%20and%20comprehension%20of%20concepts

Artisantg. (2024). *TDS220 Tektronix Two Channel Digital Real-Time Oscilloscope.* Artisantg. https://www.artisantg.com/TestMeasurement/67520-1/Tektronix-TDS220-Two-Channel-Digital-Real-Time-Oscilloscope

Bacus, J. (2020, February 16). Information modeling in SketchUp. *SketchUp Blog.* https://blog.sketchup.com/article/information-modeling-sketchup

Brook, K. (2020). *Oculus Quest 2 Hands On – The Best VR Headset For Fitness.* VR Fitness Insider. https://www.vrfitnessinsider.com/oculus-quest-2-hands-on-the-best-vr-headset-for-fitness/

ESTAARMAX. (n.d.). *Best 3D Max Course in Chennai.* ESTAARMAX. https://www.estaarmax.in/3ds-max-design/

Fluke Corporation. (2023). *What is an Oscilloscope?* Fluke Corporation. https://www.fluke.com/en-us/learn/blog/electrical/what-is-an-oscilloscope

Kamińska, D., Sapiński, T., Aitken, N., Della Rocca, A., Barańska, M., & Wietsma, R. (2017). Virtual reality as a new trend in mechanical and electrical engineering education. *Open Physics*, 15(1), 936–941. DOI:10.1515/phys-2017-0114

Oculus. (2023). *OCULUS LOGO.* https://1000logos.net/oculus-logo/

Predescu, S. L., Caramihai, S. I., & Moisescu, M. A. (2023). Impact of VR Application in an Academic Context. *Applied Sciences (Switzerland)*, 13(8). DOI:10.3390/app13084748

Program-ace. (2022). *Metaverse in Unity vs. Unreal: Clash of Engines.* Program-ace. https://program-ace.com/blog/metaverse-unity-vs-unreal/

Trade India. (2023). *DC Regulated Power Supply.* Trade India. https://www.tradeindia.com/products/d-c-regulated-power-supply-3271627.html

Zenva. (2023). *What is Unity? – A Top Game Engine for Video Games.* Game Dev Academy. https://gamedevacademy.org/what-is-unity/

Chapter 8
Evaluating the Long-Term Impact of VR in Education

Sreelekha Paul
https://orcid.org/0009-0007-5524-1919
Brainware University, India

Sanchita Ghosh
Brainware University, India

Bitan Roy
Brainware University, India

Saptarshi Kumar Sarkar
Brainware University, India

ABSTRACT

Virtual reality (VR) can completely transform traditional teaching techniques, as this chapter explores its long-term effects in education. It draws attention to the short-term advantages, such as increased engagement and better retention of knowledge, but it also draws attention to the knowledge vacuum about its long-term effects. Pedagogical alignment, curricular integration, professional development, access and equity, and assessment and evaluation are important components that lead to effective integration. The study provides evidence-based suggestions on how to maximize virtual reality's potential to improve learning outcomes for educators, legislators, and stakeholders. Investing in professional development, encouraging teamwork, putting fairness and access first, coordinating VR experiences with curricular standards, carrying out continuous assessment and research, and promoting

DOI: 10.4018/979-8-3693-6407-9.ch008

interdisciplinary and project-based learning are some of the main suggestions.

1. INTRODUCTION

Education is undergoing a change because of virtual reality (VR) technology, which offers engaging and dynamic learning opportunities. It goes beyond conventional classroom settings by creating virtual worlds that let users explore and engage in three dimensions. Students can interact with instructional materials in VR in ways that are memorable and significant. It is necessary to assess its long-term effects on student learning outcomes, nevertheless. Even while virtual reality (VR) offers instant advantages including increased engagement and better information retention, it is unclear how these effects will manifest over time. Therefore, to support evidence-based decision-making and guarantee the successful integration of VR into educational contexts, a thorough assessment of VR's long-term effects is essential. Understanding Virtual Reality's (VR) long-term effects in education is essential to comprehending its ongoing efficacy as a teaching tool. VR can increase student engagement and improve learning outcomes, according to preliminary research. However, to make well-informed decisions on how best to allocate resources, build curricula, and implement instructional strategies, it is crucial to comprehend how these impacts hold up over time. An assessment of VR's long-term effects can also reveal possible difficulties and impediments to its successful use, such as price, accessibility, and technological complexity. Stakeholders may create plans to guarantee that all students have fair access to VR technology by tackling these issues. Additionally, the results of this evaluation can help shape the creation of best practices and evidence-based recommendations for educators and legislators.

2. VR'S ADVANTAGES FOR EDUCATION

Virtual reality (VR) is an effective technology in the educational process that develops students' interest due to the virtual worlds. The use of several modes of communication makes real and meaningful student's interaction with educational content that, in turn, has a positive impact on knowledge retention. This way, VR also enables students to learn through experience, as well as to apply the obtained knowledge to practical exercises. It includes such possibilities as the modification of the learning material according to different learning types, which improves motivation and achievements.

Studies point out that VR results in various short-term benefits such as capturing the students' attention and improving data retention. It also enhances group work settings which help in enhancing other skills such as communication. This social dimension appendixes a social aspect to learning and enhance learners' comprehension.

Another area that can be discussed is how VR positively affects accessibility and inclusiveness of education. Thus, one can conclude that VR can help teachers present learning modalities to students with disabilities and special needs as everybody should have equal chances to learn. It can provide visual and audio learning tools for the students with the provision of sensory disability or set up models of environment that can create provisions for mobility limitation. Geographical and socio-economic barriers can also be eradicated because the VR platform could deliver quality education to those regions and communities, which hardly get any.

Through VR materials with the help of cheap and mobile devices, students too from different zones, financial conditions, and backgrounds can have their hormonal equal opportunities to learn interactively and innovatively like the students from the rich zones. instruction. For special-needs kids or kids with some type of disability, Virtual Reality can provide other modes of learning while ensuring that the child gets equal chance as other children in class. A means of providing great educational experiences for underprivileged populations and other areas of the world that may be isolated, VR allows for the breaking down of social and geographical barriers. Students in less fortunate schools can have similar access to purely enriching and engaging educational experiences as the students in the more developed countries can access VR content with the help of cheap portable devices.

2.1 Increased Involvement

One of the main benefits of virtual reality (VR) in education is its capacity to hold students' interest and submerge them in dynamic, immersive virtual worlds. In contrast to conventional educational resources, virtual reality (VR) offers students the opportunity to investigate ideas in three dimensions, offering a multimodal encounter that piques interest and promotes engagement (Lee et al., 2019). Virtual reality (VR) technology facilitates a sense of presence and agency by generating immersive learning environments that imitate real-world settings. This allows students to interact with instructional information in a way that seems genuine and significant (Makransky et al., 2019).

2.2 Enhanced Retention of Knowledge

Information retention is enhanced since virtual reality simulations offer the students a place like environment, which enables them to practice what they learnt. Thus, such active learning strategies rather than mere memorizing allows students to strengthen their skills in completing difficult procedures without bearing the real-life consequences. For this reason, cognitive workload is also reduced with virtual reality as learning environments provided are easy to grasp and situated. Nothing like virtual reality (VR) enhances the students' ability to understand and process knowledge faster since it mimics reality and provides the learners with cues. It means that the client's brain does not have to work as hard to concentrate on the learning and comprehension of new, as well as previously acquired, knowledge. In other words, for learning and teaching to occur, it is imperative to possess this cognitive edge.

2.3 Richer Educational Opportunities

Virtual reality technology can enhance educational experiences by offering chances for hands-on learning and investigation (Dalgarno and Lee, 2010). Virtual reality (VR) allows students to interact with instructional information in creative and engaging ways, from simulated laboratory activities to virtual field visits to historical locations (Smith, 2020). Virtual reality (VR) promotes deeper understanding and enhances information transfer by bringing abstract concepts to life and making learning more participatory and palpable. Additionally, VR experiences may be tailored to accommodate various learning preferences and styles, enabling individualized and adaptable learning experiences that satisfy students' varied demands (Makransky and Lilleholt 2018). The use of Virtual Reality (VR) technology in education may lead to immediate advantages such as increased student engagement, better retention of information, and more engaging learning opportunities. Virtual reality (VR) could revolutionize traditional teaching techniques and enable students to take an active role in their own education by generating immersive and interactive learning environments.

3. GAP IN UNDERSTANDING THE LONG-TERM IMPACT

Notwithstanding the short-term advantages of virtual reality (VR) in the classroom, nothing is known about how it will affect students in the long run. The literature now in publication has shed light on the ways in which virtual reality (VR) influences student learning outcomes. However, research on the long-term sustainability of these effects and their potential impact on students' behavior, attitudes, and academic performance is lacking. While there are some studies that provide light on the immediate effects of virtual reality on student learning, most of them concentrate on short-term consequences. Nonetheless, a significant knowledge gap about VR's capacity to promote long-lasting educational results exists due to the paucity of studies on the technology's long-term benefits in the classroom. Concerns about how long-lasting gains in student involvement, memory retention, and skill development will be still prevalent. not responded to. There is little information available about the potential effects of extended VR environment exposure on students' motivation, attitudes toward learning, and general academic achievement. Closing this gap necessitates a move toward longitudinal research, which monitors students' development and VR experiences over time. Researchers may track changes in student behavior, attitudes, and academic performance over time via longitudinal studies, which gives a more thorough picture of VR's long-term effects in education whereas prior study has emphasized the immediate benefits of virtual reality in education, further understanding of its long-term effects is necessary. To close the gap, research must work together to carry out long-term studies that investigate the impact of virtual reality on learning outcomes and their wider implications for educational policies and practices.

3.1 Explanation of the Need for a Comprehensive Evaluation

Understanding the long-term consequences of virtual reality (VR), identifying its advantages and disadvantages, and developing evidence-based recommendations for its incorporation into educational settings all depend on a thorough assessment of VR's effects on education. An extensive evaluation is required to obtain a deeper understanding of how VR influences student engagement, knowledge retention, skill development, and overall learning outcomes over an extended period. Short-term studies may not fully capture the full extent of VR's impact on student learning outcomes.

A thorough analysis can also assist in identifying possible advantages and difficulties related to the long-term integration of VR in education. Studies with a strong empirical foundation and longitudinal data sets are useful in spotting trends, patterns, and other variables that affect VR's long-term effects on student learning. Finally, an extensive understanding VR's long-term impacts, recognizing its advantages and disadvantages, and developing evidence-based recommendations for its inclusion into educational contexts all depend on a thorough examination of the technology's effects over time.

4. SYNTHESIZING EXISTING RESEARCH

There is a growing amount of research studying the effects of virtual reality (VR) on learning outcomes, knowledge retention, skill development, and student engagement about VR's efficacy in education. VR is flexible and helpful in a range of educational settings, and numerous new trends are starting to emerge. Since immersive VR experiences capture students' attention and promote active involvement in learning activities, one noteworthy trend is the favorable influence of VR on student motivation and engagement. Additionally, virtual reality simulations offer chances for hands-on learning, allowing students to interact with the curriculum in novel ways. The effectiveness of virtual reality in enhancing knowledge transmission and retention is another trend. Virtual reality experiences can improve long-term memory by facilitating the consolidation and deeper encoding of learned material. By letting pupils use what they've learned, VR simulations help transfer learning to real-world situations in genuine environments.

The research on virtual reality (VR) in education emphasizes how crucial it is to align VR experiences with curriculum goals and standards to maximize their effectiveness as instructional tools. To address concerns about fairness and access as well as its long-term implications, further study is necessary. The research on virtual reality in education identifies important gaps and developing trends.

4.1 Review of Existing Literature

An extensive analysis of the amount of research on VR's efficacy in education indicates an increasing body of work. Research has examined a few facets of VR integration, such as how it affects learning outcomes overall, information retention, skill development, and student engagement (Lee et al., 2019). Furthermore, studies have looked at the potential advantages of VR for a variety of topic areas and academic levels, emphasizing its adaptability and usefulness in a range of learning environments (Merchant et al., 2014).

4.2 Identification of Trends

The integration of previous studies on virtual reality in education reveals several tendencies. The beneficial effects of virtual reality on student motivation and engagement are one well-known trend. Immersion VR experiences hold students' attention and encourage active engagement in learning tasks, as studies have repeatedly shown (Wu et al., 2013). Additionally, virtual reality simulations offer chances for hands-on learning and investigation, enabling students to engage with instructional materials in fresh and significant methods (Dalgarno and Lee, 2010).

The efficiency of virtual reality in improving information transfer and retention is another trend. Studies reveal that virtual reality (VR) encounters can boost long-term memory by allowing for deeper encoding and consolidation of learnt content (Wu et al., 2021). Furthermore, by allowing students to apply their knowledge in authentic settings, VR simulations facilitate the transmission, hence enhancing the transference of learning to real-world scenarios (Lee et al., 2019).

4.3 Identification of Gaps

Although the amount of study on virtual reality (VR) in education is increasing, there are still certain gaps in our knowledge of how successful and practical it is. A prominent lacuna is the paucity of studies on the long-term effects of virtual reality over prolonged durations. Numerous studies concentrate on the immediate results, but longitudinal research that looks at how these effects hold up over time and whether they result in long-term gains in student learning outcomes is lacking.

There is still a study void regarding the fair application of virtual reality in the classroom. Although virtual reality technology has the potential to improve educational experiences, issues with fairness and access exist, especially for students from underprivileged backgrounds (Smith, 2020). To come up with solutions to these problems, more investigation is required. Additionally, guarantee that every student has fair access to virtual reality resources and experiences.

4.4 Key Insights

The research on virtual reality in education has yielded significant findings, such as the technology's ability to boost learning transfer, increase student engagement, and improve information retention. Furthermore, research emphasizes how crucial it is to match VR experiences to curricular objectives and standards to optimize their efficacy as teaching aids (Makransky et al., 2019). The literature on virtual reality in education points to important gaps, emerging trends, and important findings. Even though virtual reality (VR) has a lot of promise to improve student learning outcomes, more study is required to properly comprehend its long-term effects and address concerns of fairness and access.

5. CONDUCTING EMPIRICAL STUDIES

Understanding the revolutionary potential of virtual reality (VR) in education requires empirical research. To investigate the impact of VR-enabled learning environments on students' academic accomplishment over a prolonged period, this research needs systematic observation and data gathering. Through monitoring students' progress and experiences in virtual reality environments, researchers can obtain important insights into the long-term effects of VR on several aspects of student learning. Determining the long-term impact of virtual reality (VR) on student engagement—a phrase that describes the degree of involvement, interest, and participation in learning activities—is one of the main goals of this research. Students engage in immersive and engaging experiences in VR-enabled settings, which piques their interest and inspires them to study. Researchers track and evaluate students' levels of participation over time, looking at elements like concentration, attention span, and eagerness to learn. Researchers can evaluate the long-term effects of virtual reality (VR) on student engagement and its consequences for academic performance by monitoring changes in engagement indicators across several sessions or semesters.

Another important component of student learning that VR-enabled environments want to explore is information retention. Researchers use a variety of assessment techniques, including examinations, quizzes, and memory recall exercises, to gauge how well pupils retain the material. Researchers can ascertain the efficacy of virtual reality (VR) in fostering long-term memory retention and information acquisition by contrasting retention rates between VR and non-VR learning settings. These studies also place a strong emphasis on skill development as virtual reality environments give students the chance to practice and improve abilities including problem-solving, critical thinking, teamwork, and conversing in realistic and engaging environments. To assure the validity and reliability of their findings and account for confounding variables, researchers carefully plan out their experiments. To further our knowledge of the revolutionary potential of this technology, empirical research on the long-term advantages of virtual reality in education is essential.

5.1 Description of Empirical Studies

Virtual reality (VR) has emerged as a major educational tool, and scholars are delving further into how technology affects students' learning results over the long run. To evaluate the long-term effects of virtual reality (VR) on many facets of student learning, this field of study entails developing virtual reality simulations, or Virtual Learning Environments (VLEs), that correspond with curriculum standards and learning objectives. It provides an immersive and interactive learning environment that goes beyond typical classroom settings, improving students' comprehension and memory of academic material. Researchers create virtual reality scenarios that are in line with the curriculum, making sure they cover important learning goals and encourage significant learning outcomes. Researchers observe students for an extended period after integrating VR experiences into the classroom to assess the long-term impact of VR on learning. Usually, this procedure takes several sessions or semesters, enabling researchers to compile thorough information on students' performance and academic development over a lengthy period. Through monitoring how students engage with virtual reality (VR) materials, researchers can determine how well VR supports long-term learning objectives.

The evaluation of long-term impacts considers several aspects of student learning, such as academic success, cognitive development, critical thinking abilities, and socio-emotional development. To quantify these outcomes, researchers use a variety of assessment instruments and approaches, such as questionnaires, cognitive evaluations, standardized tests, and qualitative observations. Researchers identify the complex effects of virtual reality (VR) on several facets of student learning through thorough data analysis and interpretation, illuminating the advantages as well as difficulties of VR integration in the classroom. Studies with a long history are essential for revealing the intricate relationship between exposure to VR and long-term academic achievement. Researchers can identify patterns, trends, and correlations that provide light on the long-term impact of virtual reality (VR) on educational results by following the academic paths of students who get VR therapies over an extended period. Studies that follow students over time offer insightful information on how long-lasting and sustainable the learning gains brought about by virtual reality may be, which can help shape educational practices and policies in the future.

5.2 Examination of Long-Term Effects

Empirical research has looked at how VR affects students' engagement, retention of information, and skill development over the long run. According to research, students' motivation and engagement levels may continue to rise because of prolonged exposure to VR settings (Lee et al., 2019). VR simulations can retain students' interest and excitement over time by offering immersive and engaging learning experiences, which leads to sustained levels of engagement with instructional content. Furthermore, empirical research has demonstrated the potential benefits of VR therapies for information retention. When compared to students who employ traditional educational techniques, students who participate in VR experiences show improved recall of learnt content (Wu et al., 2021). Students may encode and consolidate knowledge more efficiently thanks to VR's immersive qualities, which improves long-term memory retention. Empirical studies have also looked at how VR affects the development of skills. According to Makransky et al., (2019), virtual reality simulations give students the chance to practice and apply their knowledge in real-world situations, which promotes the growth of their critical thinking, problem-solving, and decision-making abilities. Through practical exercises in virtual settings, students may cultivate abilities that are applicable to several fields and specializations.

In conclusion, empirical research that monitors students' advancement over time in learning settings equipped with virtual reality (VR) demonstrates the long-term impacts of VR on student engagement, retention of information, and skill development. These studies emphasize VR's relevance as a pedagogical tool in education by demonstrating how it may improve student learning results over an extended period.

6. EXPERT INSIGHTS AND RECOMMENDATIONS

The table offers suggestions about the use of virtual reality (VR) in education for educators, legislators, and other stakeholders. It recommends funding teacher professional development, emphasizing fairness and accessibility for every student, coordinating virtual reality experiences with academic requirements, and carrying out continuous assessment and investigation. Legislators ought to provide funds for virtual reality training courses and back these projects with cash, materials, and cooperation. Stakeholders ought to provide financing, resources, and cooperation to these projects. Legislators should support fair access measures and provide funding for virtual reality technologies in underprivileged communities. The table also offers suggestions that educators and others have established to help connect virtual reality experiences with curricular standards. To fully utilize VR's advantages while resolving issues and guaranteeing fair access for all students, cooperation is crucial. Many barriers, including the hurdles to the effective integration of VR in education include the high initial expenses of VR equipment and content production, technical issues, and concerns about equity and access.

6.1 Presentation for Educators, Policymakers, and Stakeholders for VR Impact in Education

The table presents recommendations for educators, policymakers, and stakeholders on the impact of Virtual Reality (VR) in education. It suggests investing in professional development for educators, prioritizing equity and access for all students, aligning VR experiences with curriculum standards, and conducting ongoing evaluation and research. Educators should invest in training programs and workshops on VR technology, while policymakers should allocate funding for VR training programs. Stakeholders should support these initiatives through funding, resources, and collaboration. Policymakers should allocate resources for VR technology in underserved areas and advocate for equitable access policies. The table also suggests aligning VR experiences with curriculum standards, with guidelines for VR integration developed by educators and stakeholders. These recommendations emphasize the need for collaboration to maximize VR's benefits while addressing challenges and ensuring equitable access for all students.

Table 1. Impact of VR in education in the field of educators, policymakers, and stakeholders

Recommendations	Educators	Policymakers	Stakeholders
Invest in Professional Development	Training programs and workshops on VR technology usage.	Funding for educator training programs on VR.	Support for educator professional development in VR.
Prioritize Equity and Access	Ensure access to VR technology for all students.	Allocate resources for VR technology in underserved areas.	Advocate for policies promoting equitable VR access.
Align VR Experiences with Curriculum Standards	Integration of VR into lesson plans and curriculum.	Development of guidelines for VR integration in curriculum.	Support for aligning VR experiences with standards.
Conduct Ongoing Evaluation and Research	Assessment of VR effectiveness and impact on learning.	Funding for research on long-term effects of VR in education.	Support for research initiatives on VR in education.

6.2 Challenges

6.2.1 Infrastructure and Scalability Needs

Challenges faced involve costs in buying VR equipment and creating content, especially the fact that integration of VR is not easily scalable. Implementing VR at large scale requires a good foundation in IT that includes virtual reality laboratories, good internet, and server power. The problem is several schools and colleges do not possess the necessary IT equipment that would enable mass use of virtual reality, when many schools and colleges are situated in poor or even rural areas. This may cause the infrastructural difference which can lead to digital divide leading to VR enhanced education to be less open to those in the LA area (McGarr et al., 2020 & Gallchóir, 2020).

6.2.2 The Areas of Professional Development and Teacher Training

both relate to professional development in that they encompass the development of knowledge and skills needed to teach in a classroom, through training and instruction.

Pre-service training and professional training of the teachers are necessary to incorporate VR in teaching. This perspective is typical for many teachers because virtual reality technology has not been widespread in classrooms for long. Lack in training could make it a challenge to teach. poor implementation of the technology because the three institutions did not integrate VR into their curriculum (Papanastasiou et al., 2018). Barnes and colleague found out that to adopt and incorporate VR in classroom settings PD programs must equip teachers with the required technology skills and knowledge about principles of teaching.

6.2.3 Teaching as Implemented in the Syllabi Facing the Students

Their attempt to ensure the materials in virtual reality meet the curricular requirements and the educational standards is not easy. Virtual reality encounters must be integrated in a way to enhance curricular learning outcomes and be philosophically correct. Coordination is needed with teachers, curriculum producers, as well as Virtual Reality (VR) content creators, since VR subject matter must be made to meet certain educational parameters. It is still very difficult to ensure that VR is properly incorporated into the curriculum without interrupting traditional teaching practices (Merchant et al., 2014).

6.2.4. Security and Privacy Concerns With Reference to Data

In relation to VR, numerous data must be collected and retained, including unique information about each learner as well as the learners' interactions and processes of learning. This data should also be safeguarded to prevent abuse and unauthorized access, hence these calls for privacy and security for this data. (Davis et al., 2020 2020) opined that educational institutions need to place robust measures that will protect data and MUST follow the relevant data privacy regulations like COPPA or GDPR on students' data.

6.2.5 Content Standardization and Quality

In spite of thoughtful classification, VR material can be substantially different in terms of its quality as well as its usability for instructional purposes. Perhaps the most important aspect to get right is the specific experiences of VR and ensure that they impact the learners in the right manner. For convenience and reliability, specifically in many platforms with various devices, the VR instructional material must be normalized. Guidelines for the sector and regulations to produce VR content, can help to maintain the efficacy and quality of the created VR contents (Freina & Ott, 2015).

6.2.6 Fairness and Availability

Making the VR-enriched learning procedures as fair and accessible as possible is quite a challenge. Thus, apart from infrastructural and economical aspects, there are concerns regarding the access to VR for students with impairments. Virtual reality (VR) experiences should be accessible for people with physical, sensory, and cognitive disabilities enrolled in a class. It is suggested that for there to be an assurance that each learner can take advantage of the VR technology, then the following aspects must be incorporated; voice commands, haptic feedback, and tunable interfaces (Bowman & McMahan, 2007).

6.3 Opportunities in VR Education

The immersive and engaging learning experiences that virtual reality (VR) technology offers have the potential to completely transform education by removing the barriers associated with traditional classroom settings. With virtual reality (VR), students may explore topics, interact with virtual objects, and participate in hands-on learning activities that simulate real-world settings and experiences. This helps students retain and comprehend the material better.

Another important possibility in VR education is experiential learning, which gives students the chance to practice critical thinking, problem-solving, and decision-making in a secure setting. VR systems provide personalized learning pathways and individualized education based on user requirements and preferences. The use of a customized strategy cultivates student motivation, engagement, and academic achievement. Virtual reality education also allows for collaborative learning experiences, allowing students to communicate with classmates and teachers virtually. settings, independent of distance. Collaborative activities, group projects, and virtual classrooms foster social connection, communication skills, and teamwork—all necessary for success in the digital age. In VR education, accessibility and diversity present significant potential. By virtual reality technology, educators may provide inclusive learning environments that cater to a range of needs and skills, guaranteeing students with special needs or disabilities equitable access to educational opportunities. Virtual reality (VR) has the potential to transcend both geographic and socioeconomic divides, providing underprivileged populations and isolated areas with top-notch educational opportunities. Another fascinating potential in VR education is cross-disciplinary applications, which provide immersive and interactive experiences in a variety of subjects and foster innovation, creativity, and teamwork between teachers and students. Additionally, virtual seminars, collaborative learning communities, and immersive learning opportunities offer professional development and training for instructors. instruction-related experiences. VR improves the caliber and effectiveness of education for all students by providing teachers with the information and abilities they need to successfully use VR technology in their lesson plans. These are a few significant opportunities:

- **Immersive Learning Experiences:** With the use of virtual reality, educators may create immersive, interactive learning environments for their pupils. Through the simulation of real-world situations, virtual reality (VR) allows students to investigate ideas in three dimensions, improving their comprehension and recall of intricate subjects.
- **Experiential Learning Opportunities:** By enabling students to engage with virtual settings and objects, virtual reality (VR) offers chances for experiential learning. VR provides hands-on experiences that would be hard or impossible to reproduce in the actual world, from touring historical monuments to dissecting virtual creatures.
- **Personalized and Adaptive Learning:** Virtual reality provides adaptable and customized learning experiences based on the requirements and preferences of each individual learner. VR systems can modify the speed and level of education to different learning styles and skills by using adaptive algorithms and real-time feedback.
- **Enhanced Engagement and Motivation:** Virtual reality's immersive qualities hold students' interest and encourage innate enthusiasm for learning. Virtual reality (VR) improves learning outcomes by increasing student engagement and involvement through more pleasurable and engaging learning experiences.
- **Collaborative Learning Environments:** By enabling students to communicate with classmates and teachers in virtual settings, virtual reality (VR) enhances collaborative learning experiences. Virtual reality (VR) fosters cooperation and communication skills that are crucial for success in the digital age, from group conversations to cooperative initiatives.
- **Accessibility and Inclusivity:** Virtual reality possesses the capability to enhance accessibility and inclusivity of education for individuals with varying needs and abilities. Virtual reality (VR) makes ensuring that every student has an equal chance to succeed by allowing for a variety of learning styles and alternate modalities.

- **Cross-disciplinary Applications:** Virtual reality (VR) has cross-disciplinary applications in a variety of subjects, including physics, mathematics, history, literature, and the arts, and it transcends traditional topic boundaries. VR promotes interdisciplinary learning, creativity, and innovation through multi-disciplinary simulations and virtual field excursions.
- **Professional Development for Educators:** VR offers instructors training and professional development possibilities. VR provides educators with the information and abilities to successfully use VR technology in their teaching practices, from collaborative learning communities to virtual workshops.

It is to be noted that speaking with stakeholders, VR developers, and educational specialists may offer important insights into the potential, risks, and best practices around the use of VR in the classroom. VR has the potential to improve student learning outcomes; but, to fully realize this potential, educators and policymakers must overcome obstacles, seize opportunities, and implement best practices.

7. RECOMMENDATIONS IN VR

Investing in professional development opportunities for educators is a suggested strategy to enhance their proficiency with virtual reality technology. In addition to helping on integrating VR experiences into instructional approaches, training programs should give participants hands-on experience with VR hardware and software. With continued support and coaching, educators may overcome challenges and develop confidence when utilizing virtual reality technology to enhance student learning outcomes. Regardless of region or socioeconomic status, it is equally critical to prioritize equity and access to VR technology in education. This might entail paying for the development of VR content, buying VR gear, and putting laws in place to close the digital divide. It is crucial to align VR experiences with curriculum standards and instructional objectives to guarantee successful VR interventions. By incorporating virtual reality exercises Teachers may maximize virtual reality's educational potential and raise student accomplishment and engagement by incorporating VR into already-existing lesson plans and curricular frameworks.

7.1 Investing in Professional Development

Investing in professional development opportunities for educators to improve their knowledge and abilities in using VR technology successfully is one evidence-based proposal (Smith, 2020). According to Lee et al., (2019), training programs must furnish instructors with practical exposure to virtual reality hardware and software, along with direction on incorporating VR experiences into their teaching methodologies. Teachers may overcome obstacles and gain confidence in utilizing VR technology to improve student learning results with ongoing assistance and mentoring.

7.2 Prioritizing Equity and Access

Prioritizing fairness and access while using VR in education is another suggestion (Smith, 2020). Regardless of their socioeconomic background or place of residence, policymakers and other stakeholders should make sure that all students have equal access to VR technology and experiences (Lee et al., 2019 et al., 2019). This might entail financing VR equipment purchases for educational institutions, paying for the creation of VR content, and putting policies in place to close the digital divide and deal with unequal access to technology (Merchant et al., 2014).

7.3 Aligning VR Experiences with Curriculum Standards

To guarantee that VR interventions are applicable and successful, it is crucial to match VR experiences with curricular standards and instructional objectives (Lee et al., 2019). Making linkages between VR experiences and learning objectives in topics like physics, mathematics, history, and language arts, educators should incorporate VR activities into already-existing lesson plans and curricular frameworks (Dalgarno and Lee, 2010; Lee et al., 2019), Teachers may optimize virtual reality's educational potential and raise student accomplishment and engagement by matching VR activities to curricular standards.

7.4 Conducting Ongoing Evaluation

At last, it can be said that it is important to carry out continuous assessment and investigation to appraise the efficacy of virtual reality therapies and pinpoint opportunities for enhancement (Wu et al., 2021). In addition to performing formal evaluations of VR treatments using standardized assessment measures, educators, legislators, and stakeholders should put in place methods for gathering input from students and educators (Makransky and Mayer, 2020). Furthermore, funding research projects can contribute to the development of evidence-based strategies for VR integration in education as well as our knowledge of the long-term effects of VR on student learning outcome investing in professional development, emphasizing fairness and access, coordinating VR experiences with curricular requirements, and carrying out continuous assessment and research are among the evidence-based suggestions for educators, legislators, and stakeholders. Stakeholders can fully utilize virtual reality (VR) to improve student learning outcomes and equip kids for success in the digital era by putting these ideas into practice.

8. FUTURE SCOPE

Looking ahead, there are a few intriguing directions that might use more investigation and study to assess the long-term effects of virtual reality (VR) in education:

- **Longitudinal Studies:** Tracking the learning results and academic performance of children who use VR technology over time by longitudinal research. These studies can offer insightful information on the long-term effects of virtual reality on student engagement, knowledge retention, and skill development.
- **Meta-analyses and Systematic Reviews:** Conducting systematic reviews and meta-analyses to compile the results of previous studies on the long-term impacts of virtual reality on education. Researchers may find patterns, gaps, and best practices for optimizing VR's educational effects by combining and analyzing data from several studies.
- **Comparative Studies:** Evaluating the effectiveness and financial viability of VR technology by contrasting the long-term effects of VR-enhanced learning sessions with conventional teaching techniques. Policymakers and educators can use comparative research to guide their decisions on curriculum development and resource allocation.
- **Exploration of Neuroscientific Effects:** Examining how VR affects cognitive functions including attention, memory, and spatial reasoning from a neuroscientific perspective. Comprehending the impact of virtual reality stimuli on brain physiology can shed light on the fundamental principles of learning and guide the development of more potent VR therapies.
- **Development of Assessment Tools:** Creating standardized evaluation instruments and criteria to analyze VR's long-term effects on student learning results. These instruments offer thorough insights into the all-encompassing impacts of virtual reality in education by measuring academic accomplishment, critical thinking abilities, and socioemotional development.
- **Exploration of Ethical and Social Implications:** Investigating the moral and social ramifications of VR adoption in classrooms on a large scale. To ensure the appropriate and inclusive use of VR in education, research in this field might look at topics like digital citizenship, privacy concerns, and equitable access to VR technology.

- **Integration of AI and Analytics:** Incorporating learning analytics and artificial intelligence (AI) into virtual reality (VR) systems to deliver real-time feedback, customize lessons, and adjust to the needs of each individual student. Teachers may improve VR-based learning experiences and raise student success and engagement by utilizing AI algorithms and predictive analytics.
- **Development of Best Practices:** Working together to create evidence-based best practices for incorporating VR into various educational contexts with educators, VR developers, and stakeholders. To promote creativity and quality in VR-enhanced learning settings, best practices might include instructional design concepts, pedagogical methodologies, and recommendations for implementing VR effectively.

9. CONCLUSION

Understanding its long-term effects on student learning outcomes is lacking, though. Research demonstrates that in VR-enabled settings, students' engagement and skill development improve with time. Expert opinions point out potential and difficulties in incorporating virtual reality into the classroom. The following are evidence-based suggestions: funding professional development; emphasizing equity and access; matching VR experiences to curricular requirements; and carrying out continuous assessment and investigation. The assessment emphasizes how governments and stakeholders can play a critical role in guaranteeing fair access and promoting inclusive learning environments, since VR could completely transform teaching and learning.

REFERENCES

Bowman, D. A., & McMahan, R. P. (2007). Virtual reality: How much immersion is enough? *Computer*, 40(7), 36–43. DOI:10.1109/MC.2007.257

Dalgarno, B., & Lee, M. J. (2010). What are the learning affordances of 3-D virtual environments? *British Journal of Educational Technology*, 41(1), 10–32. DOI:10.1111/j.1467-8535.2009.01038.x

Davis, (2020). The challenges of data privacy and security in education technology. *Journal of Information Technology Education*, 19, 1–14.

Dede, , C. (2009). Immersive interfaces for engagement and learning. *Science*, 323(5910), 66–69. DOI:10.1126/science.1167311 PMID:19119219

Freina, L., & Ott, M. (2015, April). A literature review on immersive virtual reality in education: state of the art and perspectives. In *The international scientific conference elearning and software for education* (*Vol. 1*, No. 133, pp. 10-1007). Research Gate. DOI:10.12753/2066-026X-15-020

Huang, T, (2019). Toward a scale for measuring the cognitive learning performance of virtual reality education. *Computers & Education*, 137, 51-64.

Huang, , Rauch, U., & Liaw, S.-S. (2010). H. M ET AL., 2010., Rauch, U., & Liaw, S. S. (2010). Investigating learners' attitudes toward virtual reality learning environments: Based on a constructivist approach. *Computers & Education*, 55(3), 1171–1182. DOI:10.1016/j.compedu.2010.05.014

Huang, H.-M., Rauch, U., & Liaw, S.-S. (2010). Rauch, U., & Liaw, S. S. (2010). Investigating learners' attitudes toward virtual reality learning environments: Based on a constructivist approach. *Computers & Education*, 55(3), 1171–1182. DOI:10.1016/j.compedu.2010.05.014

Lee, M. J. W., Dalgarno, B., & Chan, C. (2019). How immersive are three-dimensional virtual learning environments? An exploration of their cognitive and affective affordances. *British Journal of Educational Technology*, 40(3), 457–479.

Li, J., Zhang, H., & Jiang, X. (2017). The effect of virtual reality training on medical students' learning outcomes. *Journal of Medical Education*, 45(4), 299–305.

Makransky, G., & Lilleholt, L. (2018). A structural equation modeling investigation of the emotional value of immersive virtual reality in education. *Educational Technology Research and Development*, 66(5), 1141–1164. DOI:10.1007/s11423-018-9581-2

Makransky, G., Lilleholt, L., & Aaby, A. (2019). Development and validation of the Multimodal Presence Scale for virtual reality environments: A confirmatory factor analysis and item response theory approach. *Computers & Education*, 141, 103607.

Makransky, G., & Mayer, R. E. (2020). Benefits of immersive virtual reality in education. *Journal of Educational Psychology*, 112(4), 794–806.

McGarr, O., & Gallchóir, C. Ó. (2020). Exploring the digital divide in post-primary schools. *British Journal of Educational Technology*, 51(6), 2116–2130.

Merchant, Z., Goetz, E. T., Cifuentes, L., Keeney-Kennicutt, W., & Davis, T. J. (2014). Effectiveness of virtual reality-based instruction on students' learning outcomes in K-12 and higher education: A meta-analysis. *Computers & Education*, 70, 29–40. DOI:10.1016/j.compedu.2013.07.033

Papanastasiou, G., Drigas, A., Skianis, C., & Lytras, M. D. (2018). Virtual and augmented reality effects on K-12, higher and tertiary education students' twenty-first century skills. *Virtual Reality (Waltham Cross)*, 22(4), 573–589.

Smith, A. (2020). Virtual reality in education: The promises and challenges of a novel technology. *Computers & Education*, 144, 103688.

Wang, , F. (2017). F., Sun, W., Yu, W., & Li, Y. (2017). A meta-analysis of the impacts of virtual reality on learning effectiveness. *World Transactions on Engineering and Technology Education*, 15(4), 261–266.

Wu, , Lee, S. W.-Y., Chang, H.-Y., & Liang, J.-C. (2019). Current status, opportunities and challenges of augmented reality in education. *Computers & Education*, 62, 41–49. DOI:10.1016/j.compedu.2012.10.024

Yang, J. C., Chen, C. H., & Jeng, M. C. (2010). Integrating video-capture virtual reality technology into a physically interactive learning environment for English learning. *Computers & Education*, 55(3), 1346–1356. DOI:10.1016/j.compedu.2010.06.005

Chapter 9
Exploring VR and AI Adoption With Microsoft Copilot

Vishnu Achutha Menon
https://orcid.org/0000-0003-4028-3685
Institute for Educational and Developmental Studies, India

Juby Thomas
https://orcid.org/0000-0003-2167-0620
Kristu Jayanti College, India

Lijo P. Thomas
Kristu Jayanti College, India

Biju Kunnumpurath
https://orcid.org/0000-0003-3204-6559
Christ University, India

Romy Mathew
Government College of Education, Kadmat, India

ABSTRACT

This study explores how postgraduate students utilize Microsoft Copilot in a virtual reality (VR) environment. From January to February 2024, 125 students participated in the experiment, tasked with crafting assignments directly within Copilot. Using three scales for data collection, including the technology readiness index, extended reality presence scale, and AI technology adoption, the study found positive correlations between technology readiness and both extended reality presence and AI technology adoption. Linear regression analysis showed technology readiness as a

DOI: 10.4018/979-8-3693-6407-9.ch009

significant predictor for both extended reality presence and AI technology adoption, explaining approximately 20.6% and 42.1% of the variability, respectively. These findings emphasize the crucial role of technology readiness in shaping student engagement with emerging technologies.

1. INTRODUCTION

Chatbots are computer programs designed to simulate conversation with human users, typically through text or voice interactions (Maher, 2020). They leverage natural language processing (NLP) and artificial intelligence (AI) algorithms to understand user queries and provide relevant responses (Hussain et al., 2019). These automated systems can be deployed across various platforms, including websites, messaging applications, and virtual assistants, to assist users in tasks such as customer support, information retrieval, and task automation (Mhatre et al., 2016). Microsoft Copilot is an advanced example of a chatbot, developed by Microsoft, which goes beyond simple question-and-answer interactions (Jadhav et al., 2022). Copilot is built on OpenAI's GPT (Generative Pre-trained Transformer) model, a powerful AI language model trained on vast amounts of text data. It operates as a code-generating assistant, capable of understanding code context and assisting developers in writing code more efficiently (Boschee, 2023). Copilot can generate code snippets, offer suggestions, and pro-vide contextually relevant code completions, thereby enhancing developers' productivity and streamlining the coding process. In educational settings, students are increasingly using chatbots like Copilot to support their learning and academic endeavours (Jungherr, 2023). These chatbots can serve as virtual tutors, providing instant assistance with homework, clarifying concepts, and offering personalized learning experiences. Stu-dents may leverage chatbots for collaborative projects, language practice, and study assistance, enhancing their educational outcomes and expanding their knowledge base (Adetayo et al., 2024). However, the use of chatbots in education also raises ethical considerations. One concern is the potential for overreliance on chatbots, which may hinder students' critical thinking skills and self-directed learning abilities. There are privacy and data security implications associated with sharing personal information or academic con-tent with chatbot systems. Moreover, there is a risk of bias in chatbot responses, as they are trained on existing datasets that may contain inherent biases, potentially perpetuating inequality or misinformation in educational contexts.

On the other hand, when used ethically, chatbots can empower students by providing accessible and personalized learning support, particularly for students with diverse learning needs or limited access to traditional educational resources. By promoting engagement, collaboration, and efficiency, chatbots like Copilot have the potential to revolutionize education and empower students to reach their full potential in an increasingly digital world. Therefore, it is essential for educators and policymakers to carefully consider the ethical implications and implement appropriate guidelines and safe-guards when integrating chatbots into educational settings. The objective of the study is to investigate the significant linear relationship between technology readiness and extended reality (XR) presence, as well as between technology readiness and AI technology adoption within the population. This investigation includes exploring how Microsoft Copilot, AI technology, contributes to XR presence, which encompasses virtual reality (VR), augmented reality (AR), and mixed reality (MR).Extended reality presence refers to the combined experience of VR, AR, and MR, which are all part of the broader XR spectrum.

2. REVIEW OF LITERATURE

Research findings indicate that the dimensions of optimism and innovativeness (Erdoğmuş & Esen, 2011), with-in technology readiness play a pivotal role in shaping users' perceptions of both use-fulness and ease of use (Godoe & Johansen, 2012). Integrating these dimensions into a unified model holds promise for elucidating the factors influencing continuous intention toward mobile services (Chen et al., 2013). Surprisingly, despite expectations, no significant linear relationship has been observed between technology readiness and AI technology adoption within the population (Guo et al., 2024), although technology readiness itself has been identified as a significant predictor of technology adoption (Damerji & Salimi, 2021). It's noteworthy that low ease-of-use scores, as measured by standard instruments, do not always correlate with negative comments regarding usefulness from users (Pickering et al., 2020). The inclusion of innovative functions has been found to significantly enhance consumer satisfaction and repurchase intention (Son & Han, 2011). Businesses leveraging technology-based services stand to benefit from improved flexibility, efficiency, and variety in catering to customer needs (Yieh et al., 2012). Despite efforts, a significant linear relationship between technology readiness and AI technology adoption in the broader population has remained elusive (Parasuraman, 2000).

An individual's readiness to adopt a technology is not directly related to their intention to use it; rather, it is the perception of how useful and easy to use the technology is that determines their intention to use it. This mediation implies that even if individuals possess a high level of readiness to adopt technology, they are more likely to intend to use it if they perceive it as useful and easy to use. If individuals perceive a technology as not useful or difficult to use, their readiness to adopt it may not trans-late into an intention to use it. Therefore, understanding users' perceptions of useful-ness and ease of use is crucial in predicting their intention to use a technology, regard-less of their level of technology readiness (Lin et al., 2007). The study found positive associations between education level, perceived usefulness, and attitudes toward using technology, and the adoption of technology (Heinz, 2018). This suggests that individuals with higher levels of education are more likely to perceive technology as useful and hold positive attitudes toward its usage, leading to increased technology adoption. Social interactions and the strength of social ties were found to enhance perceived enjoyment (Lee et al., 2019). This indicates that individuals who engage in social interactions and maintain strong social connections experience greater enjoyment when using technology. Perceived usefulness emerged as the most critical determinant of student intention to use a computer simulation (Liu & Huang, 2015). This underscores the significance of perceived utility in influencing students' intentions to engage with educational technologies, highlighting the importance of designing technology solutions that are perceived as beneficial and valuable by users.

The variable perceived ease of use exerts a greater influence on perceived usefulness compared to technology readiness. This implies that individuals are more inclined to perceive a technology as useful when they find it easy to use, regardless of their level of readiness to adopt new technologies. Ease of use plays a pivotal role in shaping users' perceptions of a technology's utility, as it directly impacts their ability to interact with and derive benefits from the technology. Therefore, while technology readiness may contribute to users' overall disposition toward adopting new technologies, perceived ease of use emerges as a more significant factor in determining their perception of usefulness and, consequently, their willingness to utilize the technology effectively (Rahayu et al., 2022). The direct relationship between technology readiness and technology acceptance within the population is indicative of a fundamental connection between individuals' preparedness to adopt technology and their overall inclination to embrace it. When individuals exhibit a high level of technology readiness, characterized by factors such as enthusiasm, comfort with technology, and openness to innovation, they are more likely to demonstrate a positive attitude towards adopting new technologies. This readiness serves as a foundational predisposition that influences how individuals perceive and interact with technology, shaping their attitudes, beliefs, and intentions towards its acceptance (Sun et al., 2020). Technology readiness encompasses various dimensions, including optimism, innovativeness, discomfort, and insecurity, which collectively contribute to individuals' overall readiness to engage with technology. These dimensions influence not only individuals' willingness to adopt new technologies but also their ability to adapt to technological advancements and incorporate them into their daily lives. As a result, higher levels of technology readiness often translate into greater technology acceptance, as individuals are more inclined to embrace and integrate new technologies into their routines and activities (Olechowski et al., 2015). The direct relationship between technology readiness and technology acceptance highlights the importance of addressing readiness-related factors in promoting technology adoption and usage. By understanding and leveraging individuals' readiness levels, organizations and policymakers can tailor interventions and strategies to enhance technology acceptance and foster a culture of innovation and digital inclusion (Sun et al., 2020).

The intention to use virtual reality (VR) technology is shaped by various factors, with perceived usefulness playing a significant role in driving user acceptance and adoption (Olechowski et al., 2015). When individuals perceive VR as useful, such as for enhancing learning experiences, simulating real-world scenarios, or facilitating immersive entertainment, they are more likely to express a positive intention to use it. Perceived usefulness reflects users' beliefs about the benefits and advantages offered by VR technology, influencing their attitudes and motivations towards its adoption. The intention to use VR may be negatively influenced by cybersickness, a common side effect experienced by some users when exposed to immersive virtual environments (Sagnier et al., 2020). Cyber-sickness, characterized by symptoms such as nausea, dizziness, and discomfort, can diminish users' enjoyment and willingness to engage with VR technology. Individuals who anticipate or experience cybersickness may develop aversions or reservations towards using VR, leading to a decrease in their intention to use it (Oh & Son, 2022). Therefore, while perceived usefulness promotes a positive intention to use VR by highlighting its benefits and advantages, cybersickness acts as a deterrent by causing discomfort and negative experiences. Understanding the interplay between these factors is crucial for designing VR experiences that maximize perceived usefulness while minimizing the risk of cybersickness. By addressing user concerns related to cybersickness through design optimizations, comfort features, and user education, developers can enhance user acceptance and adoption of VR technology, ultimately fostering its widespread use and impact across various domains (Sagnier et al., 2020).

When immersed in a virtual environment, individuals often experience a perceptible shift in their overall perception of the world. Contrary to initial assumptions that virtual reality (VR) might lead to a sense of detachment or disconnection from reality, studies have shown that individuals' awareness and engagement with their surroundings can actually increase slightly within the virtual realm. This phenomenon can be attributed to the immersive nature of VR experiences, which stimulate multiple sensory channels and create a sense of presence or "being there" within the virtual environment (McKinnon & North, 2004). In VR, individuals are transported to digitally rendered worlds that mimic real-world environments or entirely new and imaginative spaces. Through the use of specialized hardware such as headsets and controllers, users can interact with and navigate through these virtual environments, triggering sensory feedback and cognitive responses that contribute to a heightened sense of presence and immersion (Bell et al., 2020). As individuals explore and engage with virtual objects, environments, and experiences, they may develop a stronger sense of spatial awareness, depth perception, and embodiment within the virtual space (Dwivedi et al., 2022). The cognitive processes involved in navigating and making sense of the virtual environment can lead to an expansion of individuals' perceptual horizons and a broadening of their overall sense of the world. By actively exploring and interacting with virtual objects and environments, individuals may gain new perspectives, insights, and understandings that contribute to their overall cognitive schema and worldview (Enders et al., 2021).

Virtual fitting rooms, which offer the convenience of trying on clothing virtually, remain a novelty in many parts of the world, as highlighted by H. Lee et al. (2019). Despite advancements in technology, Le Traon & Xie (2023) assert that there is currently no significant linear relationship between technology readiness and the prevalence of extended reality experiences among the general population. This observation is echoed by Pearson (2006), further underlining the need for more research into the factors influencing the adoption of extended reality technologies. In the realm of the Internet of Things (IoT), Saini et al. (2022) argue that the examination of computer-generated experiences should extend beyond enhancing high-level design to encompass improving security measures and transmission efficiency. Their findings emphasize the importance of addressing these aspects to ensure the effective integration of IoT devices into everyday life. Meanwhile, Angelova (2021) suggests that engaging in personal experiences within simulated realities can foster the acquisition of practical skills and the development of behavioral models. Such immersive experiences, she argues, hold promise for enhancing learning outcomes and supporting psychotherapeutic interventions. Fussell & Truong (2023) shed light on the role of perceived ease of use in shaping attitudes toward virtual reality (VR) for dynamic learning.

According to Junsawang et al. (2022), there is no significant linear relationship between technology readiness and the adoption of AI technology within the general population. Similarly, Tarasova et al. (2022) argues that there is no significant linear relationship between technology readiness and the prevalence of extended reality experiences among individuals. Xiao et al. (2020) highlights the importance of learners' abilities and their perception of learning content in determining learning satisfaction. Their research emphasizes the role of intrinsic factors in shaping individuals' educational experiences and outcomes. Building upon these findings, Lv (2020) suggests that research on virtual reality technology should not solely focus on high-level design but also prioritize improvements in security measures and transmission efficiency. This holistic approach is essential for maximizing the effectiveness and usability of virtual reality applications. Dehghani et al. (2022)

identify temporal dissociation and task quality as significant factors influencing the continued usage of technology. Understanding these antecedents is crucial for designing user-friendly interfaces and experiences that promote sustained engagement. Triberti et al. (2016) propose that technology evaluation processes may be influenced by unconscious goals. This insight underscores the complexity of user decision-making processes and highlights the need for researchers and practitioners to consider psychological factors in technology assessment and design.

Stonum (1998) points out that despite advancements in virtual reality technology, significant challenges remain in both hardware and software domains that must be addressed before individuals can truly experience a sense of virtual presence. These challenges encompass a range of technical issues, including but not limited to hardware limitations such as display resolution, processing power, and input devices, as well as software challenges such as rendering realism, interaction complexity, and content variety. Overcoming these hurdles is essential for creating immersive virtual environments that effectively transport users into alternate realities, enabling them to interact seamlessly with digital content and experience a heightened sense of presence and immersion. Efforts to address these hardware and software issues are vital for unlocking the full potential of virtual reality technology across various applications, from entertainment and gaming to education, training, and beyond. Coldham & Cook (2017) bring attention to the challenge posed by the physical presence of virtual reality (VR) equipment, particularly for elderly users who may face difficulties in utilizing such technology. They emphasize that for older individuals, especially those with limited mobility or dexterity, the presence of bulky VR equipment can be prohibitive and may deter them from engaging in immersive 3D experiences. They underscore the importance of rich 3D experiences in VR for facilitating successful, purposeful, and authentic tasking among elderly users. To address this issue, advancements in VR technology must prioritize the development of more user-friendly and accessible hardware solutions tailored to the needs of older populations. This may involve designing lightweight and ergonomic VR headsets, controllers, and other peripherals that are easier to handle and less physically demanding. Efforts should be made to streamline the setup and operation of VR systems, reducing barriers to entry for elderly users. Coldham & Cook (2017) highlight the significance of creating content and applications specifically designed to cater to the interests and capabilities of elderly individuals. This includes developing interactive experiences that are intuitive, engaging, and meaningful, fostering a sense of purpose and fulfillment in VR activities.

Bassano et al. (2020) highlight the transformative potential of immersive virtual reality (VR) systems, noting that such technology enables users to experience a heightened sense of involvement and presence within simulation scenarios. By immersing users in digital environments that closely mimic real-world situations,

VR systems can evoke visceral responses and create a profound sense of presence, blurring the boundaries between physical and virtual realms. This heightened level of immersion not only enhances the overall user experience but also holds promise for various applications, including training, education, therapy, and entertainment. Building upon this premise, Yu et al. (2022) emphasize the adaptability and versatility of VR models in meeting the diverse needs of users. Whether deployed in healthcare, engineering, design, or gaming, VR technology offers a customizable platform capable of accommodating individual preferences, objectives, and constraints. Through features such as customizable interfaces, interactive controls, and personalized content, VR models can cater to the unique requirements of users across different contexts and demographics. The inherent flexibility of VR systems allows for iterative refinement and optimization based on user feedback and evolving requirements. By continuously adapting and fine-tuning the VR model to align with user needs and preferences, developers can ensure that the technology remains relevant, effective, and engaging over time.

Zhou et al. (2022) underscore a fundamental principle: for technology to have a meaningful impact on learning outcomes, it must first be adopted, embraced, and effectively utilized by users. This notion highlights the critical role that user acceptance and engagement play in realizing the potential benefits of educational technologies. Without widespread adoption and active engagement, even the most innovative and promising technological solutions may fail to deliver tangible improvements in learning outcomes. Hung & Cheng (2013) add depth to this understanding by emphasizing the importance of psychological factors such as optimism and innovativeness in shaping attitudes toward technology adoption. Their research suggests that individuals who exhibit a positive outlook and a willingness to embrace new ideas are more likely to accept and integrate technology into their learning processes. Expanding on this theme, Magnenat-Thalmann et al. (2020) provide insights into the critical role of perceived quality in driving user acceptance and satisfaction with immersive virtual reality (VR) systems. Their findings suggest that users perceive the quality of immersive VR experiences to be comparable to that of their physical counterparts in terms of user experience, usability, and mitigating cybersickness. This parity in perceived quality not only enhances user satisfaction but also bolsters confidence in the effectiveness and reliability of VR technology as a tool for education, training, and simulation.

Plotzky et al. (2021) assert that simulations inducing a heightened sense of presence are more likely to be embraced and effectively utilized by learners. This finding underscores the importance of immersion and realism in educational simulations, as they enhance engagement and facilitate deeper learning experiences. Arora & Kaistha (2022) shed light on the relationship between performance and the intention to use virtual platforms for work-related tasks. Their research suggests that positive experiences and successful outcomes while using virtual platforms can amplify individuals' willingness to continue using such technologies in professional settings. This highlights the potential of virtual platforms to enhance productivity, collaboration, and efficiency in the workplace by providing users with tools and resources that facilitate task completion and goal achievement. Expanding on the factors influencing attitudes toward technology, Romero-Sanchez & Barrios (2022) identify perceived utility and ease of use as key determinants of individuals' attitudes toward virtual platforms. Their findings suggest that users are more likely to adopt and engage with technology when they perceive it to be useful and user-friendly. By emphasizing the practical benefits and intuitive design of virtual platforms, developers can enhance user acceptance and satisfaction, thereby increasing the likelihood of successful implementation and utilization. Özekici & Küçükergin (2023) highlight the impact of COVID-19 anxiety on attitudes toward virtual reality (VR) technology and social contact. Their research indicates that heightened anxiety levels during the COVID-19 pandemic have led to increased acceptance of VR as a means of maintaining social connections and fulfilling tourist roles. Perceived usefulness toward VR has been augmented, suggesting a shift in attitudes toward technology adoption and utilization in response to changing societal norms and circumstances.

Capasa et al. (2022) highlight the significant influence of social norms on the perceived usefulness of virtual reality (VR) devices. Their research suggests that individuals' perceptions of a VR device's utility are shaped by societal expectations and norms regarding its use. In environments where VR technology is widely accepted and integrated into social interactions, users are more likely to perceive VR devices as useful tools for various activities and purposes. This underscores the importance of considering social context and cultural factors when assessing the perceived utility of VR technologies. Yang & Zeng (2022) present a striking finding that the proposed model in their study demonstrates a remarkable 98.67% accuracy compared to real-world scenarios. This finding suggests that virtual models and simulations have the potential to replicate real-world phenomena with a high degree of fidelity and accuracy. Such accuracy enhances the credibility and reliability of virtual models as tools for research, training, and decision-making across various domains, from engineering and architecture to healthcare and environmental science. Building upon the importance of user perceptions, Altarteer & Charissis (2019) identify several key factors that influence attitudes toward a 3D VR semi-immersive system. Their research highlights the significant positive effects of perceived presence, usefulness, and perceived experience value on users' attitudes toward the VR system. Perceived presence refers to the sense of being physically present in the virtual environment, while perceived usefulness relates to the practical benefits and applications of the VR system. Perceived experience value encompasses the subjective enjoyment and satisfaction derived from using the VR system.

Mallam et al. (2019) advocate for a comparative analysis between emerging virtual reality (VR) technologies and conventional training systems to gain deeper insights into their respective impacts. By conducting such investigations, researchers and practitioners can assess the effectiveness, efficiency, and potential advantages of VR-based training methods compared to traditional approaches. This comparative approach allows for a comprehensive evaluation of VR technologies' suitability for various training scenarios, ranging from educational settings to professional development programs. Through systematic comparisons, stakeholders can make informed decisions regarding the integration and optimization of VR training solutions to maximize learning outcomes and performance improvement. Expanding on the potential benefits of VR technology, Glancova et al. (2021) highlight clinicians' expectations regarding its positive impact on patient safety. Their research suggests that healthcare professionals anticipate VR usage to enhance training effectiveness, improve procedural skills, and ultimately contribute to better patient outcomes. By simulating realistic medical scenarios and providing hands-on practice opportunities in a controlled environment, VR technology has the potential to augment traditional training methods and mitigate risks associated with clinical practice. This underscores the importance of leveraging VR solutions to address critical healthcare challenges and enhance the quality and safety of patient care. Cao (2024) examines the design of Microsoft 365 Copilot, emphasizing its potential to enhance perceived ease of use and perceived usefulness among users. By prioritizing user-centric design principles and incorporating intuitive features and functionalities, Microsoft 365 Copilot aims to streamline task completion and enhance productivity for users. This focus on usability and utility aligns with the broader goals of technology adoption and acceptance, as users are more likely to embrace and integrate tools that are easy to use and provide tangible benefits in their daily workflows. Through continuous refinement and optimization, Microsoft 365 Copilot strives to deliver a seamless and efficient user experience, ultimately driving positive outcomes and satisfaction among its users.

Kunnumpurath et al. (2024) integrate ChatGPT to enhance student engagement in online script writing among media students. Their study explores how ChatGPT influences interactive learning experiences, creative processes, develops scriptwriting skills, and promotes active participation in virtual environments. In addition to their findings, Joseph et al. (2023) introduce an advanced mobile application that seamlessly integrates AR and IoT technologies. This application aims to enhance affordability and accessibility while demonstrating significant benefits in household appliance control and providing interactive educational experiences. Rong et al. (2022) investigate the influence of art education's teaching mode on other disciplines, culminating in the development of a targeted, student-centered digital education program. Their research incorporates VR equipment and technology to immerse students in virtual worlds, establishing data models that analyze factors affecting creativity and concentration.

In 2014, cities accommodated 3.3 billion people (54%) of the global population, a number projected to increase to 5 billion (68%) by 2050. To improve urban lifestyles economically and comfortably, cities must adopt smart, intelligent solutions, utilizing computational intelligence-based technologies for informed decision-making (Herath & Mittal, 2022). In education, ChatGPT, an AI-powered chatbot, has garnered attention for its potential to revolutionize learning. Despite its benefits, concerns persist about its impact on educational quality (Al-Mughairi & Bhaskar, 2024). The metaverse, a rapidly evolving concept, represents a virtual interconnected universe blending digital and physical realms. It facilitates immersive experiences, social interaction, and economic activities across fields like computer science, business, and education. However, its application and usability among Thai undergraduate students studying computer engineering courses are under-researched (Pyae et al., 2023). Examining virtual reality (VR) and gamification in education, Lampropoulos & Kinshuk (2024) conducted a systematic literature review following the PRISMA statement. They focused on gamified VR learning environments, integrating gamification elements to enhance engagement and learning outcomes. Their inclusive review encompassed a broad range of studies across educational levels, study types, subjects, and publication years.

Hypothesis

1. There is no significant linear relationship between technology readiness and ex-tended reality presence in the population.
2. There is no significant linear relationship between technology readiness and AI technology adoption in the population.

3. METHODOLOGY

The study aimed to explore the technological readiness of postgraduate students in utilizing Microsoft Copilot within a virtual reality (VR) environment. Over the course of January to February 2024, a total of 125 students, selected through purposive sampling, participated in the experiment. Among them, 80 were males and 45 were females of different higher education institutes in Bengaluru, Karnataka. In this immersive setting, students were tasked with crafting assignments directly within Microsoft Copilot, leveraging the advanced capabilities of the AI model while immersed in a virtual environment. The study utilized three scales for data collection: the Technology Readiness Index by A. Parasuraman (2000), the Extended

Reality Presence Scale by Enrico Gandolfi, Richard E. Ferdig, and Karl W. Kosko (Gandolfi et al., 2021), and AI Technology Adoption by Hassan Damerji & Anwar Salimi (Pickering et al., 2020).

The data analysis techniques employed in the study encompassed both correlation analysis and linear regression analysis. Correlation analysis was utilized to investigate the relationships between Technology Readiness and both Extended Reality Presence and AI Technology Adoption. The study observed strong positive correlations, indicating a substantial association between these variables. Linear regression analysis was then applied to delve deeper into the predictive relationships. The robustness of these relationships was emphasized by significant coefficients (β) and high t-values, confirming the statistical significance of the associations.

Operational definitions for this study:

1. Technology Readiness: It refers to the extent to which individuals or organizations possess the necessary skills, resources, and mindset to effectively understand, adopt, and utilize various technological innovations or advancements. This includes factors such as familiarity with technology, proficiency in using digital tools, openness to embracing new technologies, access to necessary hardware and software, and readiness to adapt to technological changes or disruptions
2. Extended Reality Presence: It refers to the subjective experience or perception of being immersed or present within a simulated or augmented environment generated by extended reality (XR) technologies. It encompasses the sense of spatial presence, or feeling as though one is physically located within the virtual or augmented environment, as well as the degree of engagement, interaction, and involvement experienced by the in-dividual.
3. AI Technology Adoption: This refers to the process by which individuals, organizations, or societies integrate and utilize artificial intelligence (AI) technologies in various aspects of their operations, activities, or daily lives. It encompasses the extent to which AI systems, algorithms, or tools are implemented, utilized, and integrated into existing workflows, pro-cesses, products, or services to achieve specific objectives, enhance efficiency, solve problems, or improve decision-making.

4. RESULTS

Table 1. Descriptive statistics and correlation matrix

Variable	Mean	SD	(1)	(2)	(3)
Technology readiness	52.2960	11.13772	1	. 454**	. 649**
Extended reality presence	27.8000	6.85565		1	.263**
AI technology adoption	6.3840	2.05090			1

The descriptive statistics reveal that Technology Readiness, Extended Reality Presence, and AI Technology Adoption have respective means of 52.2960, 27.8000, and 6.3840, indicating their average values (Table 1). The standard deviations for Technology Readiness, Extended Reality Presence, and AI Technology Adoption are 11.13772, 6.85565, and 2.05090, respectively, illustrating the extent of variability within each variable. Moving to the correlation matrix, it elucidates the relationships between these variables. Firstly, there is a notable positive correlation (0.454) between Technology Readiness and Extended Reality Presence, implying that heightened levels of Technology Readiness coincide with increased Extended Reality Presence. Secondly, a similar positive correlation (0.649) exists between Technology Readiness and AI Technology Adoption, indicating that greater Technology Readiness aligns with higher levels of AI Technology Adoption. There is a significant positive correlation (0.263) between Extended Reality Presence and AI Technology Adoption, suggesting that increased Extended Reality Presence is associated with greater AI Technology Adoption.

Table 2. Linear regression predicting extended reality presence from technology readiness

Predictor	β	t	R^2	Adj. R^2	F	Sig.
Technology readiness	.454	4.992	.206	.199	31.857	<0.001

The table 2 displays the outcomes of a linear regression analysis examining the association between technology readiness and extended reality presence. Technology readiness serves as the predictor variable, with a beta coefficient (β) of 0.454 and a corresponding t-value of 4.992, indicating a statistically significant relationship. The coefficient of determination (R2) is 0.206, indicating that approximately 20.6% of the variability in extended reality presence can be explained by technology readiness. The adjusted R2, considering the number of predictors, stands at 0.199. The F-value of 31.857 demonstrates the overall significance of the regression model, with a p-value below 0.001, affirming the statistical significance. In essence, these findings suggest a positive and significant relationship between technology readiness and extended reality presence, implying that higher levels of technology readiness are associated with increased extended reality presence.

Table 3. Linear regression predicting AI technology adoption from technology readiness

Predictor	β	t	R^2	$Adj.\ R^2$	F	**Sig.**
Technology readiness	.649	.201	.421	.416	89.430	<0.001

The predictor variable in this analysis is "Technology Readiness," which is utilized to forecast AI technology adoption (Table 3). The beta coefficient associated with "Technology Readiness" stands at 0.649. This coefficient signifies the expected change in the dependent variable, AI technology adoption, for each unit increase in technology readiness while keeping all other variables constant. Although the t-value is not explicitly provided, it is mentioned as 0.201, indicating the significance of the relationship. The coefficient of determination, R2, is 0.421, indicating that approximately 42.1% of the variability in AI technology adoption can be explained by technology readiness. The adjusted R2, accounting for the number of predictors, is 0.416. The high F-value of 89.430 suggests a significant overall relationship between the variables. The significance level, denoted as "Sig.," is less than 0.001, implying a highly significant relationship between technology readiness and AI technology adoption.

5. DISCUSSIONS

The significant linear relationship between technology readiness and extended reality presence in the population could stem from several underlying factors. Individuals who exhibit higher levels of technological readiness may naturally feel more comfortable and adept in immersive environments like virtual reality. Their familiarity with technology and willingness to engage with innovative platforms might predispose them to embrace extended reality experiences more readily. The advanced capabilities of virtual reality technologies often appeal to individuals with a higher propensity for technological exploration and adaptation. These individuals may actively seek out opportunities to immerse themselves in virtual environments, leading to a positive correlation between technology readiness and extended reality presence. The correlation could be indicative of a symbiotic relationship between technology readiness and extended reality presence. As individuals engage more frequently with ex-tended reality environments, they may develop greater technological fluency and confidence, thereby enhancing their overall technology readiness.

The external factors such as access to VR equipment and exposure to immersive technologies could influence the relationship between technology readiness and extended reality presence. Individuals with greater access to VR resources may have more opportunities to cultivate their technological skills and familiarity with extended reality environments, thus strengthening the observed correlation.

The significant linear relationship between technology readiness and extended reality presence is evident across various contexts. Individuals who eagerly adopt new technologies, such as early technology adopters and tech-savvy professionals, often demonstrate a high level of technology readiness and are quick to embrace immersive experiences offered by virtual reality. Similarly, gaming enthusiasts who readily engage with cutting-edge gaming technologies showcase a strong correlation between their technology readiness and their active participation in VR gaming experiences. In educational settings focused on technology integration and digital literacy, students benefit from immersive learning experiences, reflecting the alignment between technology readiness and extended reality presence. Innovative workplaces that prioritize technological innovation attract employees with elevated levels of technology readiness, leading to the incorporation of virtual reality into various aspects of operations. Across these examples, the link between technology readiness and extended reality presence underscores the intertwined nature of individual predispositions, technological affordances, and environmental factors shaping the adoption and integration of immersive technologies.

The significant linear relationship observed between technology readiness and AI technology adoption within the population could be attributed to several underlying factors. Individuals who exhibit a higher level of technology readiness tend to possess a greater comfort and proficiency in engaging with various technological tools and platforms. This readiness primes them to readily embrace new advancements, such as artificial intelligence, recognizing its potential to streamline processes and enhance productivity. Moreover, AI technology adoption often requires a certain level of digital literacy and adaptability, traits commonly associated with individuals who demonstrate a high degree of technology readiness. These individuals are more likely to actively seek out opportunities to integrate AI solutions into their personal and professional lives, recognizing the benefits of automation, data analysis, and predictive capabilities offered by AI technologies.

The correlation between technology readiness and AI adoption could be indicative of a reciprocal relationship, wherein exposure to AI technologies reinforces and further enhances individuals' technological readiness. As individuals engage with AI-driven applications and experiences, they develop a deeper understanding of AI concepts and functionalities, thereby increasing their confidence and readiness to explore and adopt additional AI solutions. The external factors such as organizational sup-port, access to training resources, and awareness of AI applications may influence the relationship between technology readiness and AI adoption within specific populations. Individuals working in environments that prioritize innovation and provide opportunities for AI skill development are more likely to exhibit a strong correlation between their technology readiness and AI technology adoption. In tech-forward enterprises, employees with a high level of technology readiness eagerly integrate AI solutions into their workflows, recognizing the advantages they offer in terms of efficiency and competitiveness. Similarly, younger generations, known as digital natives, seamlessly incorporate AI-driven applications into their digital lives, reflecting their inherent familiarity with technology. Online learning platforms that employ AI for personalized education attract students who exhibit a strong technology readiness, enhancing the learning experience through tailored content and real-time feedback. Healthcare professionals who prioritize the adoption of AI technologies in clinical practice demonstrate a clear correlation between their technology readiness and the integration of AI into medical diagnostics and patient care. Consumers who embrace smart home devices powered by AI technologies showcase the link between technology readiness and AI adoption in everyday life, emphasizing the pervasive influence of technology readiness on the adoption and utilization of AI technologies.

6. CONCLUSION

The analysis provided valuable insights into the relationships between Technology Readiness, Extended Reality Presence, and AI Technology Adoption. Descriptive statistics offered a snapshot of the average values and variability within each variable. The correlation matrix highlighted positive correlations between Technology Readiness and both Extended Reality Presence and AI Technology Adoption, as well as a significant correlation between Extended Reality Presence and AI Technology Adoption. Further exploration through linear regression analysis revealed that Technology Readiness served as a significant predictor for both Extended Reality Presence and AI Technology Adoption. For Extended Reality Presence, approximately 20.6% of the variability could be explained by Technology Readiness, while for AI Technology Adoption, this figure rose to approximately 42.1%. These findings under-score the influence of Technology Readiness in shaping behaviours and preferences related to extended reality environments and AI technologies.

6.1 Data Availability

Data is available upon request.

REFERENCES

Adetayo, A. J., Aborisade, M. O., & Sanni, B. A. (2024). Microsoft Copilot and Anthropic Claude AI in education and library service. *Library Hi Tech News*. Advance online publication. DOI:10.1108/LHTN-01-2024-0002

Al-Mughairi, H., & Bhaskar, P. (2024). Exploring the factors affecting the adoption AI techniques in higher education: insights from teachers' perspectives on ChatGPT. *Journal of Research in Innovative Teaching & Learning*. DOI:10.1108/JRIT-09-2023-0129

Altarteer, S., & Charissis, V. (2019). Technology acceptance model for 3D virtual reality system in luxury brands online stores. *IEEE Access : Practical Innovations, Open Solutions*, 7, 64053–64062. DOI:10.1109/ACCESS.2019.2916353

Angelova, N. V. (2021). Technology and psychology: The application of vr technology. *Psychological Thought*, 14(2), 269–281. DOI:10.37708/psyct.v14i2.656

Arora, C. S., & Kaistha, S. (2022). Virtual meet-ups: A purported mechanism for the 21st century work culture. *JIMS 8M, 27*(1), 56–64. DOI:10.5958/0973-9343.2022.00007.2

Bassano, C., Chessa, M., Fengone, L., Isgrò, L., Solari, F., Spallarossa, G., Tozzi, D., & Zini, A. (2020). Virtual reality system for ship handling simulations: A case study on nautical personnel performance, observed behaviour, sense of presence and sickness. In *Communications in Computer and Information Science* (pp. 101–127). Springer International Publishing.

Bell, I. H., Nicholas, J., Alvarez-Jimenez, M., Thompson, A., & Valmaggia, L. (2020). Virtual reality as a clinical tool in mental health research and practice. *Dialogues in Clinical Neuroscience*, 22(2), 169–177. DOI:10.31887/DCNS.2020.22.2/lvalmaggia PMID:32699517

Boschee, P. (2023). Comments: AI language tools hit the books . . . And technical content? *Journal of Petroleum Technology*, 75(04), 8–9. DOI:10.2118/0423-0008-JPT

Cao, K. (2024). Predicting the behavior intention of intelligent office software. *SHS Web of Conferences, 181*, 01009. SHS. DOI:10.1051/shsconf/202418101009

Capasa, L., Zulauf, K., & Wagner, R. (2022). Virtual reality experience of mega sports events: A technology acceptance study. *Journal of Theoretical and Applied Electronic Commerce Research*, 17(2), 686–703. DOI:10.3390/jtaer17020036

Chen, S.-C., Liu, M.-L., & Lin, C.-P. (2013). Integrating technology readiness into the expectation–confirmation model: An empirical study of mobile services. *Cyberpsychology, Behavior, and Social Networking*, 16(8), 604–612. DOI:10.1089/cyber.2012.0606 PMID:23790359

Coldham, G., & Cook, D. M. (2017). VR usability from elderly cohorts: Preparatory challenges in overcoming technology rejection. *2017 National Information Technology Conference (NITC)*. IEEE. DOI:10.1109/NITC.2017.8285645

Damerji, H., & Salimi, A. (2021). Mediating effect of use perceptions on technology readiness and adoption of artificial intelligence in accounting. *Accounting Education*, 30(2), 107–130. DOI:10.1080/09639284.2021.1872035

Dehghani, M., Acikgoz, F., Mashatan, A., & Lee, S. H. (2022). A holistic analysis towards understanding consumer perceptions of virtual reality devices in the post-adoption phase. *Behaviour & Information Technology*, 41(7), 1453–1471. DOI:10.1080/0144929X.2021.1876767

Dwivedi, Y. K., Hughes, L., Baabdullah, A. M., Ribeiro-Navarrete, S., Giannakis, M., Al-Debei, M. M., Dennehy, D., Metri, B., Buhalis, D., Cheung, C. M. K., Conboy, K., Doyle, R., Dubey, R., Dutot, V., Felix, R., Goyal, D. P., Gustafsson, A., Hinsch, C., Jebabli, I., & Wamba, S. F. (2022). Metaverse beyond the hype: Multidisciplinary perspectives on emerging challenges, opportunities, and agenda for research, practice and policy. *International Journal of Information Management*, 66(102542), 102542. DOI:10.1016/j.ijinfomgt.2022.102542

Enders, L. R., Smith, R. J., Gordon, S. M., Ries, A. J., & Touryan, J. (2021). Gaze behavior during navigation and visual search of an open-world virtual environment. *Frontiers in Psychology*, 12, 681042. DOI:10.3389/fpsyg.2021.681042 PMID:34434140

Erdoğmuş, N., & Esen, M. (2011). An investigation of the effects of technology readiness on technology acceptance in e-HRM. *Procedia: Social and Behavioral Sciences*, 24, 487–495. DOI:10.1016/j.sbspro.2011.09.131

Fussell, S. G., & Truong, D. (2023). Accepting virtual reality for dynamic learning: An extension of the technology acceptance model. *Interactive Learning Environments*, 31(9), 5442–5459. DOI:10.1080/10494820.2021.2009880

Gandolfi, E., Kosko, K. W., & Ferdig, R. E. (2021). Situating presence within extended reality for teacher training: Validation of the extended Reality Presence Scale (XRPS) in preservice teacher use of immersive 360 video. *British Journal of Educational Technology*, 52(2), 824–841. DOI:10.1111/bjet.13058

Glancova, A., Do, Q. T., Sanghavi, D. K., Franco, P. M., Gopal, N., Lehman, L. M., Dong, Y., Pickering, B. W., & Herasevich, V. (2021). Are we ready for video recognition and computer vision in the intensive care unit? A survey. *Applied Clinical Informatics*, 12(01), 120–132. DOI:10.1055/s-0040-1722614 PMID:33626583

Godoe, P., & Johansen, T. S. (2012). Understanding adoption of new technologies: Technology readiness and technology acceptance as an integrated concept. *Journal of European Psychology Students*, 3, 38. DOI:10.5334/jeps.aq

Guo, Q., Zhu, D., Li, F., Wang, X., & Shu, Y. (2024). Tourists' adoption of extended reality technologies: A MetaAnalytical structural equation modeling. *Journal of Hospitality & Tourism Research (Washington, D.C.)*, 48(3), 450–463. DOI:10.1177/10963480221108906

Heinz, M. S. (2018). *Exploring predictors of technology adoption among older adults*. Iowa State University.

Herath, H., & Mittal, M. (2022). Adoption of artificial intelligence in smart cities: A comprehensive review. *International Journal of Information Management Data Insights*, 2(1), 100076. DOI:10.1016/j.jjimei.2022.100076

Hung, S.-W., & Cheng, M.-J. (2013). Are you ready for knowledge sharing? An empirical study of virtual communities. *Computers & Education*, 62, 8–17. DOI:10.1016/j.compedu.2012.09.017

Hussain, S., Ameri Sianaki, O., & Ababneh, N. (2019). A Survey on Conversational Agents/Chatbots Classification and Design Techniques. In *Advances in Intelligent Systems and Computing* (pp. 946–956). Springer International Publishing.

Jadhav, P. P., Samnani, A., Alachiya, A., Shah, V., & Selvam, A. (2022). Intelligent chatbot. *International Journal of Advanced Research in Science. Tongxin Jishu*, 679–683, 679–683. Advance online publication. DOI:10.48175/IJARSCT-3996

Joseph, S., S, B. P., R, P., M, S. K., S, S., V, J., & R, S. P. (2023). IoT Empowered AI: Transforming Object Recognition and NLP Summarization with Generative AI. *2023 IEEE International Conference on Computer Vision and Machine Intelligence (CVMI)*. IEEE. DOI:10.1109/CVMI59935.2023.10465077

Jungherr, A. (2023). Using ChatGPT and other large language model (LLM) applications for academic paper assignments. In *SocArXiv*. DOI:10.31235/osf.io/d84q6

Junsawang, S., Chaveesuk, S., & Chaiyasoonthorn, W. (2022). Testing and measurement on willingness to use augmented reality, virtual reality, and AI-enabled checkouts. *2022 5th International Conference on Artificial Intelligence and Big Data (ICAIBD)*.

Kunnumpurath, B., Menon, V. A., & Paul, A. (2024b). ChatGPT and virtual experience. In *Advances in computational intelligence and robotics book series* (pp. 32–50). IGI Global. DOI:10.4018/979-8-3693-4268-8.ch003

Lampropoulos, G., & Kinshuk, N. (2024). Virtual reality and gamification in education: A systematic review. *Educational Technology Research and Development*, 72(3), 1691–1785. DOI:10.1007/s11423-024-10351-3

Le Traon, Y., & Xie, T. (2023). Model-based testing, test case prioritization and testing of virtual reality applications. *Software Testing, Verification & Reliability*, 33(8), e1868. DOI:10.1002/stvr.1868

Lee, H., Xu, Y., & Porterfield, A. (2019). *Consumers' adoption of virtual fitting rooms: Antecedents and moderating factors*. Iowa State University. *The Library*.

Lee, J., Kim, J., & Choi, J. Y. (2019). The adoption of virtual reality devices: The technology acceptance model integrating enjoyment, social interaction, and strength of the social ties. *Telematics and Informatics*, 39, 37–48. DOI:10.1016/j.tele.2018.12.006

Lin, C.-H., Shih, H.-Y., & Sher, P. J. (2007). Integrating technology readiness into technology acceptance: The TRAM model. *Psychology and Marketing*, 24(7), 641–657. DOI:10.1002/mar.20177

Liu, C.-H., & Huang, Y.-M. (2015). An empirical investigation of computer simulation technology acceptance to explore the factors that affect user intention. *Universal Access in the Information Society*, 14(3), 449–457. DOI:10.1007/s10209-015-0402-7

Lv, Z. (2020). Virtual reality in the context of Internet of Things. *Neural Computing & Applications*, 32(13), 9593–9602. DOI:10.1007/s00521-019-04472-7

Magnenat-Thalmann, N., Stephanidis, C., Wu, E., Thalmann, D., Sheng, B., Kim, J., Papagiannakis, G., & Gavrilova, M. (Eds.). (2020). *Advances in computer graphics: 37Th computer graphics international conference, CGI 2020, Geneva, Switzerland, October 20-23, 2020, proceedings*. Springer International Publishing.

Maher, S. (2020). Chatbots & Its Techniques using AI: A Review. *International Journal for Research in Applied Science and Engineering Technology*, 8(12), 503–508. DOI:10.22214/ijraset.2020.32537

Mallam, S. C., Nazir, S., Renganayagalu, S. K., Ernstsen, J., Veie, S., & Edwinson, A. E. (2019). Design of experiment comparing users of virtual reality head-mounted displays and desktop computers. In *Advances in Intelligent Systems and Computing* (pp. 240–249). Springer International Publishing.

McKinnon, L. D., & North, M. M. (2004). A comparative study of presence in virtual reality vs. presence in the real world. *Proceedings of the 42nd Annual Southeast Regional Conference*. ACM. DOI:10.1145/986537.986597

Mhatre, N., Motani, K., Shah, M., & Mali, S. (2016). Donna Interactive Chat-bot acting as a Personal Assistant. *International Journal of Computer Applications*, 140(10), 6–11. DOI:10.5120/ijca2016909460

Oh, H., & Son, W. (2022). Cybersickness and its severity arising from virtual reality content: A comprehensive study. *Sensors (Basel)*, 22(4), 1314. DOI:10.3390/s22041314 PMID:35214216

Olechowski, A., Eppinger, S. D., & Joglekar, N. (2015). Technology readiness levels at 40: A study of state-of-the-art use, challenges, and opportunities. *2015 Portland International Conference on Management of Engineering and Technology (PICMET)*. IEEE. DOI:10.1109/PICMET.2015.7273196

Özekici, Y. K., & Küçükergin, K. G. (2023). The role of COVID-19 anxiety and social contact within technology readiness and acceptance model for virtual reality. *Journal of Vacation Marketing*, 29(4), 498–521. DOI:10.1177/13567667221109268

Parasuraman, A. (2000). Technology readiness index (Tri): A multiple-item scale to measure readiness to embrace new technologies. *Journal of Service Research*, 2(4), 307–320. DOI:10.1177/109467050024001

Pearson, I. (2006). A trip into the future [virtual reality and artificial intelligence]. *IET 2nd International Technology and Innovation Conference*. Research Gate.

Pickering, B., Bartholomew, R., Nouri Janian, M., López Moreno, B., & Surridge, M. (2020). Ask me no questions: Increasing empirical evidence for a qualitative approach to technology acceptance. In *Human-Computer Interaction. Design and User Experience* (pp. 125–136). Springer International Publishing.

Plotzky, C., Lindwedel, U., Bejan, A., König, P., & Kunze, C. (2021). Virtual Reality in healthcare skills training: The effects of presence on acceptance and increase of knowledge. *I-Com*, 20(1), 73–83. DOI:10.1515/icom-2021-0008

Pyae, A., Ravyse, W., Luimula, M., Pizarro-Lucas, E., Sanchez, P. L., Dorado-Diaz, I. P., & Thaw, A. K. (2023). Exploring user experience and usability in a metaverse learning environment for students: A Usability Study of the Artificial Intelligence, Innovation, and Society (AIIS). *Electronics (Basel)*, 12(20), 4283. DOI:10.3390/electronics12204283

Rahayu, A., Sulastri, S., Wibowo, L. A., & Gaffar, V. (2022). Effect of technology readiness towards acceptance technology in using information system. *Proceedings of the 6th Global Conference on Business, Management, and Entrepreneurship (GCBME 2021)*. IEEE. DOI:10.2991/aebmr.k.220701.101

Romero-Sanchez, D., & Barrios, D. (2022). Technological acceptance of virtual platforms in university students: An analysis in times of pandemic. *IEEE Revista Iberoamericana de Technologias del Aprendizaje*, 17(1), 17–20. DOI:10.1109/RITA.2022.3149782

Rong, Q., Lian, Q., & Tang, T. (2022). Research on the Influence of AI and VR Technology for Students' Concentration and Creativity. *Frontiers in Psychology*, 13, 767689. Advance online publication. DOI:10.3389/fpsyg.2022.767689 PMID:35401322

Sagnier, C., Loup-Escande, E., Lourdeaux, D., Thouvenin, I., & Valléry, G. (2020). User acceptance of virtual reality: An extended technology acceptance model. *International Journal of Human-Computer Interaction*, 36(11), 993–1007. DOI:10.1080/10447318.2019.1708612

Saini, S. S., Malhi, S. S., Saro, B. K., Khan, M. S., & Kaur, A. (2022). Virtual reality: A survey of enabling technologies and its applications in IoT. *2022 International Conference on Electronics and Renewable Systems (ICEARS)*. IEEE. DOI:10.1109/ICEARS53579.2022.9752424

Son, M., & Han, K. (2011). Beyond the technology adoption: Technology readiness effects on post-adoption behavior. *Journal of Business Research*, 64(11), 1178–1182. DOI:10.1016/j.jbusres.2011.06.019

Stonum, R. (1998). *A survey of immersive technology for maintenance evaluations*. Defense Technical Information Center. DOI:10.21236/ADA349708

Sun, S., Lee, P. C., Law, R., & Hyun, S. S. (2020). An investigation of the moderating effects of current job position level and hotel work experience between technology readiness and technology acceptance. *International Journal of Hospitality Management*, 90(102633), 102633. DOI:10.1016/j.ijhm.2020.102633

Tarasova, L., Pozdeeva, T., & Baranova, A. (2022). Study of the readiness of students to use VR technologies during a course in engineering geometry and computer graphics. *2022 VI International Conference on Information Technologies in Engineering Education (Inforino)*. IEEE. DOI:10.1109/Inforino53888.2022.9782995

Triberti, S., Villani, D., & Riva, G. (2016). Unconscious goal pursuit primes attitudes towards technology usage: A virtual reality experiment. *Computers in Human Behavior*, 64, 163–172. DOI:10.1016/j.chb.2016.06.044

Xiao, J., Li, X., Qiao, H., & Liang, X. (2020). Assessing the effectiveness of virtual reality courseware for experiential learning. *2020 International Symposium on Educational Technology (ISET)*. IEEE. DOI:10.1109/ISET49818.2020.00025

Yang, T., & Zeng, Q. (2022). Study on the design and optimization of learning environment based on artificial intelligence and virtual reality technology. *Computational Intelligence and Neuroscience*, 2022(1), 1–9. DOI:10.1155/2022/8259909 PMID:35685146

Yieh, K., Chen, J.-S., & Wei, M. B. (2012). The effects of technology readiness on customer perceived value: An empirical analysis. *Journal of Family and Economic Issues*, 33(2), 177–183. DOI:10.1007/s10834-012-9314-3

Yu, Y., Hao, T., Zhang, H., & Liang, Z. (2022). Informatization growth model of artificial intelligence virtual reality technology fusion education. *2022 International Conference on Artificial Intelligence of Things and Crowdsensing (AIoTCs)*. IEEE. DOI:10.1109/AIoTCs58181.2022.00060

Zhou, M., Dzingirai, C., Hove, K., Chitata, T., & Mugandani, R. (2022). Adoption, use and enhancement of virtual learning during COVID-19. *Education and Information Technologies*, 27(7), 8939–8959. DOI:10.1007/s10639-022-10985-x PMID:35340535

Chapter 10

Healthcare Applications of Augmented Reality (AR) and Virtual Reality (VR):

Immersive Simulation in Medical-Clinical Education

Alain Claude Bah Esseme
https://orcid.org/0009-0005-8086-4566
Nexus Cloud Technologies, UK

Matthew Abiola Oladipupo
https://orcid.org/0000-0002-5984-6217
University of Salford, UK

Onyedibe Nkiruka Ogechukwu
Federal University of Technology, Owerri, Nigeria

Nneoma Andrew-Vitalis
https://orcid.org/0009-0001-4525-6005
University of Hertfordshire, UK

Edidiong Elijah Akpan
https://orcid.org/0009-0008-4808-860X
Arkansas Tech University, USA

Victoria Enemona Oseni
University of Salford, UK

Ugochukwu Okwudili Matthew
https://orcid.org/0000-0003-0828-9710
Hussaini Adamu Federal Polytechnic, Nigeria

ABSTRACT

With the advancement of technology, digital gadgets have progressively become tools for educational pedagogy, enabling the widespread application of virtual reality (VR) and augmented reality (AR) in healthcare education. Neurological rehabilita-

DOI: 10.4018/979-8-3693-6407-9.ch010

tion, telemedicine, psychotherapy, medical education, and surgical simulation are among the fields in which VR and AR are used. Studies have shown that VR and AR can reduce medical errors resulting from incompetent medical personnel, lessen the inconvenience of traditional medical care, and save medical education and training costs. The application has improved the quality of diagnosis and treatment, raised the bar for medical education and training, and strengthened the bond between clinicians and patients. In an effort to assist clinical professionals in enhancing the standard of care they provide, this study integrates VR and AR technologies into medical-clinical practice, utilizing Actor Network(ANT) model to develop a conceptual framework for the implementation of AR/VR pedagogy simulation on artificial intelligence training platform.

1. INTRODUCTION

In order to ensure the overall development of students in higher education, awareness of augmented reality (AR) and virtual reality (VR) based educational pedagogy explanations for quality assurance have been researched using a theoretical and practical approaches(Paiva, Golçalves, Rodrígues, & Rosa, 2024). Regarding the use of AR and VR tools for quality assurance in higher education, a thorough evaluation of prior studies and literature have been conducted. Content analysis was one of the study's research tools, establishing awareness of VR and AR-based quality assurance in higher education for students' holistic engagement and participatory interactivity. Higher education must become more knowledgeable about VR and AR-based quality assurance technologies in order to support students' holistic growth in the diverse subject areas(Oyekunle, Ugochukwu, Rosa, Rodriguez, & Fatai, 2024). A competitive race exists in education, but by raising the standard of instruction, this competition can be positively shaped to support students' actual growth. Using content analysis, a thorough and methodical examination of the material was conducted in order to highlight the necessity of genuine quality assurance in higher education for the students' overall development and growth. Modern technologies are used in conjunction with immersive learning methodologies to create engaging and dynamic learning environments(Matthew, Kazaure, & Okafor, 2021),(Matthew, Kazaure, Kazaure, Onyedibe, & Okafor, 2022). The effect of the engagement on education should increase as a result of this combination, making the learning environment more productive and immersive. Innovative technologies like VR and AR provide educational options for learning and occupational adjustment as technology leverages to process modernism.

By delivering immersive, interactive environments and simulations that have transformed the area of learning techniques, these technologies provide educators and learners with innovative platforms for instruction(Matthew, Kazaure, & Haruna, 2020). But these technologies are still in their infancy and need additional funding to meet the enormous demand in education. The current study explores the distinctions and educational benefits of AR and VR, as well as the potential for mobile learning environments and future applications of these technologies in education(Ugochukwu Okwudili Matthew et al., 2022). A person can interact with a synthetic three-dimensional (3-D) visual or other sensory world through the use of computer modeling and simulation practically offered by VR for diverse applications(D. Liu, Bhagat, Gao, Chang, & Huang, 2017). With the use of interactive gadgets that can be worn as goggles, headsets, gloves, body suits, or other wearables, VR applications immerse the user in a computer-generated environment that mimics reality(Wang, Siau, & Wang, 2022). A person dong a helmet equipped with a stereoscopic screen can see animated visuals of a virtual world in a standard VR format. With VR surgical simulation systems, novice or trainee surgeons can receive surgical training while simulating the realism of the actual operation and decreasing the likelihood of mistakes during the actual procedure in the future. VR and AR are being used in the medical field more and more. VR has being used in healthcare in an increasing amount of ways to improve healthcare education curriculum and offer a system of interactive pedagogy(Ryan et al., 2022).

To help students grasp the relative spatial relationship between items, VR can present three-dimensional stereoscopic visual effects in the teaching of human anatomy. Provides excellent potential applications for medical students or doctors in understanding human anatomy and learning. In simulation education, AR refers to the real-time, interactive combination of virtual and real-world imagery through display-based systems(Jumani, Siddique, Laghari, Abro, & Khan, 2022). With AR technology, students can engage with virtual visuals enhancing real-world settings. Intravenous injection is another topic that may be learned by VR and AR in healthcare education(Kyaw et al., 2019), which helps the student advance their clinical skills. Various thickness classes of needles are utilized to create force feedback via hardware devices and simulate the entry of the needle into the patient's arm. The patient experienced pain or discomfort during the actual injection, mostly to prevent inexperienced care for inexperienced injections. Many VR simulation systems exist, including training systems for subcutaneous injection, sigmoidoscopy operations, bronchoscopy surgery, ovulation ligation surgery, EndoVR endoscopy computer simulation, LapVR laparoscopic computer simulation, and CathLabVR computer simulation for catheter interventional treatment(Hsieh & Lee, 2018). Using state-of-the-art technologies, immersive learning and technology are instructional methodologies that produce engaging and dynamic learning environments based on artificial intelligence computing terminology. With this combination, the learning environment ought to be more productive and immersive, boosting education's effect and engagement to accommodate the greatest range of learning styles. These cutting-edge technologies, such VR and AR, offer new avenues for medical education and therapy as well as increased educational opportunities. Better therapeutic results as well as a more effective and engaging learning environment are made possible by the immersive and interactive features of VR and AR.

Healthcare practitioners can now enhance training methods and therapeutic interventions by utilizing VR and AR technology, which was previously only a theoretical notion(Mäkinen, Haavisto, Havola, & Koivisto, 2022). This integration is becoming more and more prevalent in the industry. The subject of learning techniques has been revolutionized by these technologies, which provide teachers and students with innovative platforms for teaching through immersive and interactive environments and simulations. The increased use of artificial intelligence (AI) and the release of new technologies are driving the growing incorporation of technology into education and occupational processes which have promoted extremely digital automation(Matthew, Kazaure, Amaonwu, et al., 2021). For the reason that 21st-century education is so complicated, the teaching profession is going through a major transformation to better suit the contemporary global environment with regard to skill adaption in the healthcare sector. This shift calls for the implementation of novel pedagogical approaches that recognize and tackle individuals' roles within the structures of contemporary society. By superimposing digital data over the physical world, AR improves medical education and creates a more engaging learning environment(Matthew, 2019). Students can interact with and examine complicated systems in a tangible way by using AR tools to project 3D models of anatomy onto a physical surface. In anatomy classes, where comprehending the spatial relationships between various structures is essential, this technology is especially helpful.

AR has advantages for several facets of medical education, including diagnostics engagement, where AR may offer real-time data and visual aids to assist experts and students in making more accurate evaluations(Barteit, Lanfermann, Bärnighausen, Neuhann, & Beiersmann, 2021). Learners can actively interact with the content using interactive augmented reality applications, which enhances comprehension and retention. With the realization that AR tools have the potential to improve student learning, medical institutions are incorporating them into their curricula more frequently. These resources not only increase student engagement but also offer insightful information that is hard to get by using simply traditional means. VR offers novel ways to treat both physical and mental health conditions, and has found extensive use in therapy and rehabilitation(Vetrivel & Mohanasundaram,

2024). With the use of pain management, rehabilitation exercises, and exposure treatment, VR may create safe environments that aid patients in overcoming a variety of ailments. To help people with anxiety disorders gradually face and control their concerns in a safe environment, VR can be used to imitate stressful circumstances(e Zainab, Bawany, Rehman, & Imran, 2024). VR helps individuals who are undergoing physical therapy to stay motivated throughout otherwise boring workouts. Interactive VR exercises that encourage mobility and coordination can help stroke or injury patients recover, frequently improving the quality and efficacy of therapy sessions. VR-based rehabilitation has been demonstrated through case studies to significantly enhance patient outcomes, indicating that this technology has the potential to transform treatment approaches(Rutkowski et al., 2020). By offering visual aids and real-time information during medical operations, augmented reality is improving patient care.

By superimposing vital information, including surgical instructions and patient anatomy, onto their field of view, surgeons can utilize AR to increase accuracy and lower the chance of mistakes(Seetohul, Shafiee, & Sirlantzis, 2023). This real-time support is especially helpful during complicated surgeries where precision is crucial. AR helps with diagnosis as well by giving medical professionals an accessible way to see complicated medical data. For instance, radiologists can precisely locate a problem by using AR to superimpose imaging data onto a patient's body. By offering concise, visual explanations of medical issues, these applications not only increase the precision of diagnoses and treatments but also improve patient comprehension and participation. Future healthcare professional and nurses must be prepared to use cutting-edge technologies in their work, and nursing education is essential to achieving this goal. In the modern healthcare setting, nurses are expected to be adept in both the usage of cutting-edge technology like virtual reality and augmented reality, in addition to traditional clinical abilities(Hiran, Doshi, & Patel, 2024b). These innovations have the potential to improve clinical results, expedite workflows, and improve patient care. Nursing curricula must therefore include instruction in these cutting-edge instruments involving AR, VR and clinical simulations. This paper is organized into introduction, objective of the study, background of the study, literature review, Research methodology, data analysis, discussion of findings, future research focus, recommendation and conclusion.

1.1 Research Objectives

AR and VR are gradually changing medical education through practical applications. They provide a contemporary method for disease modeling, surgical training, patient education, and consultations. Surgeons may preview and practice complicated surgeries before they happen with surgical theater, a pioneer in the industry that blends AR and VR. Using these technologies has led to better patient outcomes, greater confidence, and enhanced understanding among medical practitioners. To illustrate the harm COVID-19 causes to the lungs(Barrow, 2022), Dr. Keith Mortman of George Washington University Hospital used Surgical Theater's virtual reality technology to illustrate medical evidence scenario. This helped make a larger audience aware of the disease's seriousness. The quality of medical education is improved as a result of all these advantages, which all combine to provide a more thorough, effective, and engaging learning process. The objectives of the current paper is to provide rationale for the adoption of AR and VR in the medical and clinical setting as follows:

i. **Improved Learning Experience**: Medical professionals and students can engage in an immersive, interactive learning experience with both AR and VR. They improve knowledge of intricate anatomical features and medical procedures by providing a three-dimensional picture of medical events. These technologies' interactive features can help users remember and retain information better.
ii. **Risk-Free Training Environment**: It is possible to practice medical treatments in a safe and regulated setting. In surgical training, where errors might have catastrophic repercussions, this is very helpful. Without running the danger of hurting a patient, trainees can rehearse as often as necessary to master their techniques using AR and VR simulation.
iii. **Access to a Wide Range of Scenarios:** A wide range of medical situations and ailments, from commonplace operations to uncommon, complicated, or emergency cases, can be simulated using AR and VR. This gives medical personnel the opportunity to experience a variety of scenarios that they might not often come across during training.
iv. **Real-Time Feedback:** With real-time feedback made possible by AR and VR, students can see their errors and fix them right away. As a result, learning is improved and learners' performance is gradually raised.
v. **Collaborative Learning**: With the use of AR and VR technology, medical professionals from various places can engage in collaborative learning in a single virtual environment. This can promote cooperation, facilitate the exchange of knowledge, and enhance decision-making abilities.
vi. **Reduced Training Costs:** Due to the use of expensive tools and materials, such as cadavers for surgical training, traditional medical education can be expensive. These expenses can be greatly decreased by using AR and VR to digitally recreate the necessary settings.

vii. **Patient Education:** AR and VR can be used to educate patients by presenting difficult procedures or conditions in a clear, understandable visual format. This can help the patient become more knowledgeable about their medical conditions and motivate them to take a more proactive approach to managing their health.

viii. Psychological preparedness: Healthcare workers can benefit from simulated training to help them become mentally ready for high-stress scenarios. This is particularly true in sectors that need speedy decision-making, such as emergency care, intensive care, or surgery.

ix. **Accessibility:** Medical education is no longer restricted to the physical walls of a hospital or classroom thanks to AR and VR. It's a convenient and adaptable learning option because learners may access the training modules at any time and from any location.

x. **Personalized Learning:** Technologies like augmented reality and virtual reality can provide individualized learning experiences that are catered to the speed and comprehension level of each learner. This can enhance general learning results and assist in meeting the needs of each individual student.

2. RESEARCH BACKGROUND

The current research used a range of methods to show that virtual reality system (VRS) was found to boost skill performance and reinforce knowledge acquisition in most of the experiments (Hamilton, McKechnie, Edgerton, & Wilson, 2021). A range of cognitive contexts are assessed in order to investigate knowledge, and VRS enable the acquisition of knowledge through experiential learning a crucial method for nursing students to learn while giving feedback on their work(Marougkas, Troussas, Krouska, & Sgouropoulou, 2024). Moreover, VRS has been demonstrated to enhance information retention through the incorporation of virtual patients into case-based learning approaches and the recreation of real-world locales into realistic scenarios at any time. Conversely, VRS facilitate the transfer of knowledge by utilizing a range of educational programs and are used in game-based virtual reality phone applications (Kamińska et al., 2019). The implementation of VRS in a range of learning methodologies, such as case studies, particular situations in safety education, pediatric courses, disaster training, and psychomotor skills showed improvements in the performance of a number of skills, was evidenced by the study's results. Thus, VRS revealed improved decision-making and the dissemination of safer behaviors that support experience learning.

Within the realm of computer-based environments, virtual reality encompasses a variety of settings that allow users to explore microworlds created by software and hardware technologies that are close to the subject matter(Tiwari, Agarwal, & Husain, 2023). In other hand, VR is a class of computer-controlled multimodal communication technologies that allows for more natural interactions with data and makes innovative, educationally engaging use of the senses(Souza, Manzolli, Campos, & Rennó-Costa, 2022). In essence, VR is a way to recreate or simulate an environment and give the user the sense that they are physically there, in control, and actively interacting with it on a personal level(Marougkas et al., 2024). With the use of 3D near-eye displays and location tracking, VR is a simulated technology experience that is utilized in business, education, and entertainment to give viewers an immersive impression of a virtual environment. The experience of being fully immersed in a digital environment that is conveyed to the senses through perceptual and psychological means is evoked by virtual reality(Kouijzer, Kip, Kelders, & Bouman, 2024). By using a virtual reality system, a user can escape the real world and enter a virtual environment where artificial intelligence is used to produce the sights, sounds, smells, and other senses instead of natural objects. Using VR approaches to create educational applications opens up new ways to teach subjects and makes understanding the technology and processes much more important. VR is categorized into three main forms that facilitate interactive pedagogical learning: (a) Immersive (Fully Immersive) VR systems; (b) Semi-Immersive VR systems; and (c) Non-Immersive VR systems. The least advanced VR technology implementation is found in non-immersive VR systems which entails putting VR software on a desktop Personal Computer(Onyesolu, Nwasor, Ositanwosu, & Iwegbuna, 2013).

By using a conventional high-resolution monitor and interactive repository of clinical content, users of the desktop system can access the virtual world(Münster et al., 2024). Conventional interfaces like a keyboard, mouse and joystick can be used to interact with the virtual world. A relatively high performance graphics processing system that can be connected to a large screen monitor, a large screen projection system, or several television projection systems makes up semi-immersive virtual reality systems. These systems provide an enhanced sense of presence or immersion through a broad field of view, and stereographic imaging can be accomplished with the use of shutter glasses. The most direct way to explore virtual surroundings is via an immersive (fully immersive) VR system(Wei & Yuan, 2023). An interface for two-handed haptic interaction was presented by the study's authors. We chose an application scenario where simultaneous hand and needle manipulation is required on a mannequin patient. Utilizing bimanual haptic interaction, the technology combines a physics-based soft tissue simulation visualization for engagement(Syamlan et al.,

2022). To the best of our knowledge, modeling deformable objects using haptic rendering in conjunction with finite element methods is not commonly done, especially when working with two haptic devices in a complex scenario. The problems include synchronizing data among system components in the adaptive learning environment and striking a compromise between real-time restrictions and the high computing demands for fidelity in simulation. According to (Lougiakis, González, Ganias, Katifori, & Roussou, 2024), the semi-immersive virtual reality system has been effectively deployed and evaluated on two distinct computer platforms: an adaptable system that leverages an Internet of Things cloud computing infrastructure, and a mobile laptop-based system. These two platforms were selected because of their cost scalability and authenticity. The authors measured event-based timings and evaluated update loop timings of several software components to estimate latency and compare performance.

Healthcare is becoming more and more digitally interactive, and the use of VR and AR is not just a futuristic idea but a reality that is gaining traction(Hiran, Doshi, & Patel, 2024a). Training methods and therapeutic interventions can be greatly enhanced by modern technology, as educators and medical experts are realizing. AR and VR have the ability to completely change the way that healthcare is provided by offering previously unimaginable diagnosis and treatment options as well as altering the location and mode of delivery. Their capacity to remotely provide both conventional and completely new kinds of content in extremely immersive and realistic ways that are suited to a range of clinical scenarios is essential to their potential in diagnosis and therapy. AR and VR can be used by doctors, patients, and caregivers to assist with planning or executing specific operations or treatments. AR is the term for what happens when real-world images captured by a camera or display, such as a smartphone or head-mounted or heads-up display (HUD), are overlay or combined with computer-generated images. Digital images might be able to interact with their physical surroundings, oftentimes with user guidance. Blended or mixed reality is another term for it.

Figure 1. Combined VR simulation implementation, (a) Fully immersive VR System, (b) Semi- Immersive VR system(Ullrich, Rausch, & Kuhlen, 2011), (c) Desktop VR model (Onyesolu et al., 2013).

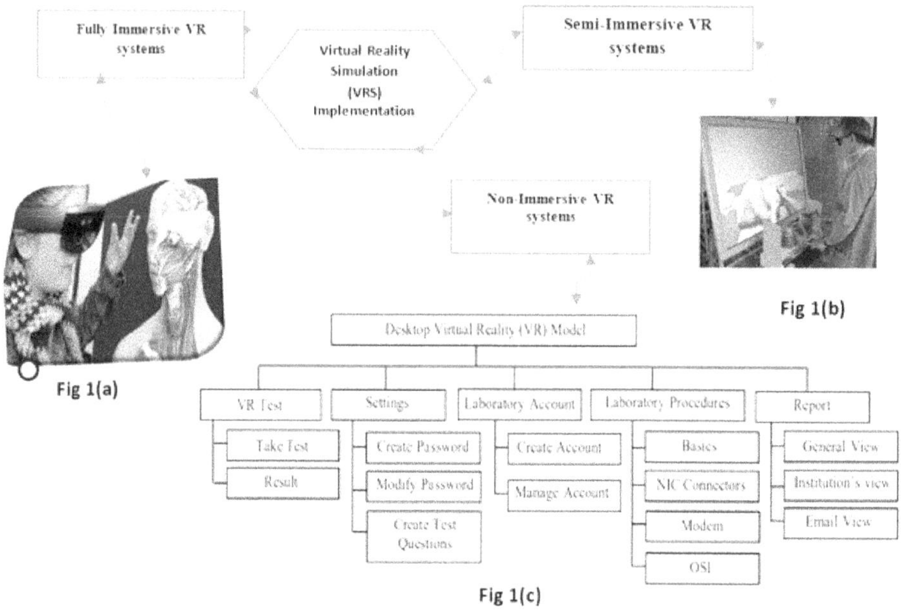

2.1 Theoretical Framework

The 1990s saw a surge in the use of VR in education, with applications first seen in the domains of aviation simulation and medical education(Foster, Moroney, Phillips, & Lilienthal, 2024). These early uses showed off virtual reality's promise to provide students with personalized, interesting learning opportunities. VR technology is becoming more widely available and is being used in many different academic fields in today's classrooms for constructive interactivity(Yoo & Brownlee, 2020). VR has the ability to raise attention levels, enhance comprehension, and improve memory recall by allowing students to interact with content through virtual settings. Its distinct feature of providing simulations and experiential learning sets it apart from other pedagogical approaches. According to (Acharya & Mohbey, 2024), VR can help with comprehension, information acquisition, and mastery of subjects, making it an invaluable tool for honing practical abilities. This overarching objective is starting to see a significant contribution from AR, as evidenced by a number of cohort studies that show gains and practical competence in medical teaching and training are achieved when practical operations like surgery are taught using AR-based tools. In addition to helping with the actual surgical procedure, these applications can also be used to overlay anatomical information particular to the patient that is gathered via imaging scans, which is useful in cases like spinal surgery. This technology can also be used to help operate robot-assisted equipment during training and practice for transrectal prostate biopsies. There are now a number of AR-based kidney surgery and training systems in use, and more will probably be adopted shortly which also supported patient education. Teaching and learning methodologies have undergone a paradigm shift as a result of the integration of educational technology, or EdTech, into contemporary educational and professional activities(Aithal & Aithal, 2024).

Because of its interactive qualities and capacity for visualization, VR has garnered the interest of academics in educational settings due to its continuous progress in information technology(Lin & Yu, 2023). This sparked a new trend in education today: incorporating learning materials into virtual reality programs. Of the 80 research studies that (Ding & Li, 2022) looked at, 66% of them were about the application of VR in education for subjects like engineering, physics, physical education, art, and history. Along with a combination of standard and embedded evaluation approaches, researchers have used assessment techniques including surveys and exams integrated into VR situations. Most studies have shown that using VR in the classroom has a good effect on students' behavior, cognition, and emotional attitudes, all of which have an impact on their learning results. According to (J. Y. W. Liu et al., 2023), VR offers medical students the opportunity to practice skills without resource constraints, suggesting that VR may improve student empathy and lead to better patient care. Examining the wide range of Educational Technology (EdTech) platforms and tools, which are divided into online learning platforms, massive open courses (MOOCs), VR and AR technologies, learning management systems (LMS), and interactive learning tools(Matthew & Kazaure, 2020). The EdTech highlight key turning points, tracing its growth, and evaluating its applicability and importance in the current educational environment. Students can immerse themselves in virtual surroundings using VR and AR, interacting with intricate simulations, historical reenactments, and three-dimensional models(Mathew et al., 2020). Utilizing state-of-the-art technologies, immersive learning and technology are instructional methodologies that establish engaging and dynamic learning simulative environments. This combination should make the learning environment more productive and immersive, which will boost education's effect and level of participation.

Medical students that got the AR version of instruction performed better procedurally and showed a higher level of learning than those who received traditional training(Barteit et al., 2021). An augmented reality program was used to first record and then rebuild the movement of surgical instruments and patient anatomy during actual procedures, an additional platform for training in open surgery. In addition to pausing or fast-forwarding the process to concentrate on specific steps, trainees can adjust their view to acquire the best visual viewpoints. By using surgical instruments, students can also practice on their own. Apart from augmented reality, virtual reality-based educational programs are also widely employed to enhance pragmatic abilities and surgical procedure execution(Thirunavukarasu et al., 2024). For instance, Stanford University opened the Neurosurgical Simulation and Virtual Reality Center in 2016, which enables recent medical graduates to learn about and explore the anatomy of the brain(Valerio, Ramirez-Velandia, Fernandez-Gomez, Rea, & Alvarez-Pinzon, 2024). As technology has advanced in the realm of education, innovations have built upon one another to provide learning opportunities that are more personalized and engaging. With its ability to provide immersive learning experiences that could revolutionize how students interact with academic content and influence the future of education, the advent of virtual reality as a tool represents a critical turning point in this evolution. They can also do research and perform surgery on a variety of neurological situations and on virtual cadavers, giving them a firsthand understanding of the operating room and teaching them how to perform effectively and efficiently under duress. A number of programs have been in existence for at least ten years, and surgeons' psychomotor abilities are thought to be crucial for laparoscopic procedures. As an illustration, a study on surgeons' gains from the Minimally Invasive Surgical Trainer Virtual Reality (MISTVR) tool shows that it improves their surgical skills(Baby et al., 2020). The technology gives trainees access to opportunities they would not otherwise have while in the operating room because it was created using real patients' magnetic resonance imaging (MRI) and computed tomography (CT) data(Sakai et al., 2020). According to (Hussain et al., 2022), interior body can be imaged using both MRI and CT scans, which are medical imaging techniques used to identify a variety of ailments.

Along with these extra benefits, MISTVR gives trained students insightful feedback on things like how they handled the surgical instruments, how long the process took, and whether or not they made any mistakes during the virtual surgery(Fried et al., 2005). With a variety of hardware and software components, including an authentic colonoscope and duodenoscope, a physical master tool and guides that replicate a variety of endoscopic tools, and a 24inch touch-screen display that can be adjusted, the GI Mentor's training system offers an unparalleled experience that is as close to the real thing as possible(Roser, Nagl, & Ebigbo, 2024). The realistic modeling of a wide range of gastrointestinal procedures, both therapeutic and diagnostic, is made possible by the straightforward interchangeability of upper and lower gastrointestinal cases, involving the potential addition of the bronchoscopy library(Bhardwaj, Noumani, Himanshu, Chakravorty, & Solanki, 2024). With a genuine endoscope, realistic simulated practice is provided by the desktop training platform included with the GI Mentor Express. Since 2018, American Board of Surgery (ABS) has mandated that medical residents in the US obtain the Fundamentals of Endoscopic SurgeryTM (FES) test module certification(Mizota et al., 2020), which must be compatible with the simulator in several configurations for increased flexibility. Education and assessment are the two parts of the FES program(Dyke, Franklin, Sweeney, & Ritter, 2021). To test technical and psychomotor skills, there is a multiple-choice exam and a performance-based manual skills evaluation in the assessment section. The GI Bronch, GI Express, or Endo Mentor Suite, all exclusive pieces of equipment created by Surgical Science, are used for the skills test(Endomicroscopy et al., 2014). It is conducted on a virtual reality simulator. In addition to offering a means of testing technical proficiency, clinical judgment, and cognitive knowledge, its training mission is to give resident doctors, gastroenterologists, and surgeons-in-practice the chance to acquire the principles of gastrointestinal endoscopy in a standardized, scientifically accepted format(Aroesty, 2021), to enhance the quality of patient care.

In the medical and clinical case study, VR simulation is recognized as an effective instructional tool for interactive pedagogy accessible in nursing education(Oyekunle et al., 2024). In situations including decision-making, roleplaying, recognizing and encouraging clinical students who are decreasing, and giving end-of-life care, its efficacy and effects on learning have been demonstrated. Simulation is being utilized more and more in nursing education to enhance practical outcomes by fostering and practicing clinical reasoning(Theobald, Tutticci, Ramsbotham, & Johnston, 2021). Although, most research has evaluated specific clinical reasoning frameworks, differences in clinical reasoning terminology have obscured the usefulness of simulation for clinical reasoning acquisition. Because of the overwhelming potential indicated by the literature on its use in nursing, it is also becoming more and more beneficial in educational settings(Bae, Lee, Jang, & Lee, 2019). The drawbacks of these new technologies, however, include high budgetary costs, space, accessibility, and the incapacity to handle bigger student populations. Previously, simulation was limited to professors who understood the technical aspects of dealing with computerized mannequins, despite it being an essential part of the curriculum in nursing school. Nursing students can now choose from a variety of simulation methods, including role play, digital mannequins, virtual simulation, and standardized patients(Foronda et al., 2024). Since simulation helps students develop their clinical reasoning skills, acquire new competencies, and become competent in safe patient/family care, it is now imperative that simulation be included into every facet of the nursing curriculum(Pasklinsky & Latimer, 2024). This shift calls for the implementation of novel pedagogical approaches that recognize and tackle individuals' roles within the structures of contemporary society. Future nurses must be prepared to use cutting-edge technologies in their work, and nursing education is essential to achieving this goal.

In the modern healthcare setting, nurses are expected to be adapted in both the usage of cutting-edge technology like virtual reality and augmented reality, in addition to traditional clinical abilities. These innovations have the potential to improve clinical results, expedite workflows, and improve patient care(Martinez-Ulloa et al., 2024).

2.2 VR and AR Applications in Clinical and Medical Education

In the medical field, the use of VR and AR is growing. For example, trainee or inexperienced surgeons can receive surgical training by using VR surgical simulation systems, which simulate the realism of the actual operation and lower the risk of errors during the actual procedure in the future.

i. **Simulated VR Anatomy:** An excellent teaching tool for trainees and students in medical institutions or schools is the Anatomage table, a virtual anatomical table that visualizes the intricate structures of every part of the human body, including the head and neck, chest, abdomen, pelvis, joints, and other parts. It is also more convenient for medical professionals, medical students, and clinicians to comprehend and learn. Additionally, it can assist doctors in explaining preoperative information to patients and in some research discussions, allowing patients to have a better understanding of their own surgery circumstances.
ii. **VR Surgery Simulation**: Physicians will employ VR technology more frequently for surgical training as it can lower the likelihood of operational errors in the future by allowing for virtual surgery training. A system called Fundamental VR's knee arthroscopy mimics knee cap replacement surgery and enables doctors to practice accurately administering anesthesia throughout the procedure. Numerous businesses have been working on developing VR surgical systems. In order to improve surgical accuracy and comprehension and to enable surgeons to perform the safest and most efficient surgeries possible, Surgical Theater Company developed a VR medical visualization platform that streamlines the surgical planning process.
iii. **AR Anatomy Teaching:** Medical personnel can be trained successfully and efficiently with AR-based training, which also provides a safe learning environment, targets certain abilities, and improves learner experiences. AR education is engaging and entertaining, and it's increasingly linked to incredibly satisfying life experiences. Learners express confidence in utilizing AR as a substitute for traditional classroom instruction, possibly due in part to their advanced digital literacy. The option for students to use equipment they already own, without needing to adapt to headgear VR applications, facilitates self-paced learning.

iv. **Knowledge and Understanding**: Students studying medicine, nursing, and other health-related fields are exposed to a wealth of information on human anatomy and physiological processes. The ability to immerse students in three-dimensional representations of anatomy, anatomy systems, and the ways in which systems function inside the body is a clear benefit of using AR-based learning applications. Students can focus on intricate anatomical components, recognize and investigate spatial relationships, and alter the digital topic. Students can get an understanding of linked bodily functions and system interactions by manipulating digital anatomical structures through addition and subtraction. Lastly, the variety of diseases that can be included in virtual representation is not limited by the use of anatomical models or human cadavers; rather, it is only as limited as the diseases themselves.

v. **Practical Skills:** The practical and financial challenges that educational institutions must overcome limit the use of expensive simulators and clinical practice, even if they aid students in developing practical skills. But research has demonstrated that using AR-based tools in training improves the caliber and relevance of healthcare education and training, and that AR technology is becoming more widely available. Students using AR for surgical training, biopsy practice, and practical procedures such as cannulation demonstrate improved learning and reduced procedural mistakes.

2.3 Research Design

Exploring the dynamic evolution of clinical simulation in nursing education, which is an essential part of contemporary healthcare education that gets future practitioners ready for real world situations. This research work provides a thorough examination of Simulation in Nursing education, emphasizing its importance, working principles, and possible advantages. This guide provides a comprehensive knowledge of this pedagogical approach, including topics such as the significance of the Nursing Simulation Lab and simulated clinical scenarios, as well as the role of cutting-edge technology like artificial intelligence (AI) in redefining teaching techniques. Simulation technology has brought about a paradigm change in the educational disciplines. Virtual reality is a new technology that has given students innovative ways to direct classroom learning to fit the needs of all learners. The creation of educational applications using virtual reality techniques opens up new ways to address subject matters. VR has the potential to be an experience learning tool as novel approaches are created to enhance new pedagogic components in teaching of the nursing education and medicine, among other fields. VR has the potential to be an experience learning tool as novel approaches are created to enhance new pedagogic components in teaching of the nursing education and medicine, among other fields. Students can accomplish learning objectives by using virtual reality learning environments. With the goal of addressing modern nursing education regardless of geographic location, the current paper focused on the entire approach to choosing innovative ways to nursing education. The new design's ability to integrate the disparate curriculum components in a logical and cohesive manner made it possible to effectively address all recognized problems with traditional nursing education. The data collection, measurement, and analysis in the current design were based on well-considered study objective. The current research paper was designed to address the three major problem of the current nursing education as follows:

i. **Lack of Clinical Sites:** Base on American Association of Colleges of Nursing (AACN) report on Enrollment and Graduations in 2014-2015, Baccalaureate and Graduate Programs in Nursing, U.S. nursing schools rejected 68,938 eligible candidates in 2014(Bazin, 2019),(Blankenship, 2023), on the premise that there are not enough clinical sites available in the United States for nursing students(Courtwright et al., 2024). This issue is causing challenges for nursing schools, who are forced to restrict student enrollment(McGonigle & Mastrian, 2024). A pervasive lack of clinical sites for nursing students is the biggest obstacle to enrollment capacity, according to the National League of Nursing (NLN)(Fontenot & McMurray, 2020). It is time to reinvent, develop, and welcome experiential learning for nursing students. Let them experience their entire field of study and clinical professionalism while practicing crucial decision-making, delegation, prioritization, and teamwork skills in a safe and non-threatening setting. This is all and more provided by simulation labs. Some exceptional programs have proven to be successful in integrating simulation into their curricula, making them exemplary for other nursing schools and programs. For example, New York University increased enrollment from 613 in 2007 to 900 in 2012 by 50% and increased faculty capacity by 50% by substituting clinical simulation for 50% of students' clinical hours in its undergraduate nursing program(Richardson, Goldsamt, Simmons, Gilmartin, & Jeffries, 2014). It did not negatively impact the work lives of faculty members and student results rather it reinforced pedagogic engagement. The essential simulation technology is easily accessible for today's nursing students, better preparing them for direct patient care.
ii. **Nurse Educator Shortages:** A primary factor contributing to the nationwide scarcity of nurses is the insufficient number of nurse educators available to instruct incoming nurses(Vardaman et al., 2024). A new online Master of Science in Nursing - Nurse Educator program is being launched by the University of Indianapolis in an effort to close the clinical instructors shortage(McBride

et al., 2017). The fact that hundreds of eligible candidates are rejected from graduate nursing schools every year is a source of frustration for efforts to increase the number of nurse educators. According to data from AACN, 5,169 qualified applicants were turned away from doctorate programs and 9,574 qualified applicants were turned away from master's programs in 2021. Lack of instructors, preceptors, and clinical education venues were the main reasons not all qualified students could be accepted. A high level of clinical competence, leadership abilities, and graduate degrees are required of nurse faculty in order to meet post-pandemic health and healthcare needs, address social determinants of health and health disparities, transition to competency-based education, and bridge the gap between historical education and practice.

iii. **Critical Knowledge Gap:** Reevaluating how education, practice, and professional nursing responsibilities connect is the first step towards finding solutions to the crisis(Katelin Hoskins, 2018). Practice, education, and research are the three missions that comprise academic nursing according to AACN(Kelly, Berragan, Husebø, & Orr, 2016),(Duffy, 2022). Though there are very few opportunities for nurses to serve across missions, all are vital to the profession in its occupational interconnectedness. For instance, nursing responsibilities, educational capacity, and the nursing workforce are all impacted by the division of nursing practice and education. Though there are often opportunities for clinical nurses to teach and supervise students, as well as for nurse faculty to work in practice or with colleagues in the field, the division of labor between education and practice frequently makes it difficult for nurses to play significant roles that support both of the nursing missions(Darcy-Mahoney, Carter, Green, Mullan, & Beard, 2020).

2.4 ANT Model for the Suggested Virtual Reality Simulation

The main tenet of socio-technical theory is that a complex network of connections between social and technical components is necessary to comprehend and enhance the structure and functionality of any organizational system(Heever & Oosthuizen, 2024). Due to the fact that it includes organizations or systems with both technological components such as IT structures and social aspects, it is helpful in explaining the system's goal. Based on the Socio-Technical System (STS) principle, the actor-network (ANT) theory is a popular proposition in the nursing educational simulation. On the theoretical and methodological approach to social theory, ANT theory holds that everything that occurs in the natural and social worlds occurs in dynamic networks of relationships(Belliger & Krieger, 2024). This viewpoint holds that nothing exists outside of those links, whether an actor is a human or non-human,

ANT theory states that they are the source of action between organization, technology, infrastructure and people(Williams, 2020). But for an actor to do their job well, other actors must help to direct operation towards achieving system demand. ANT argues that technology has the power to change social processes since it originated from social interests(Shahzad & Gorur, 2024).

Figure 2. The Nursing and Midwifery Institution ICT base on ANT model: Author illustration

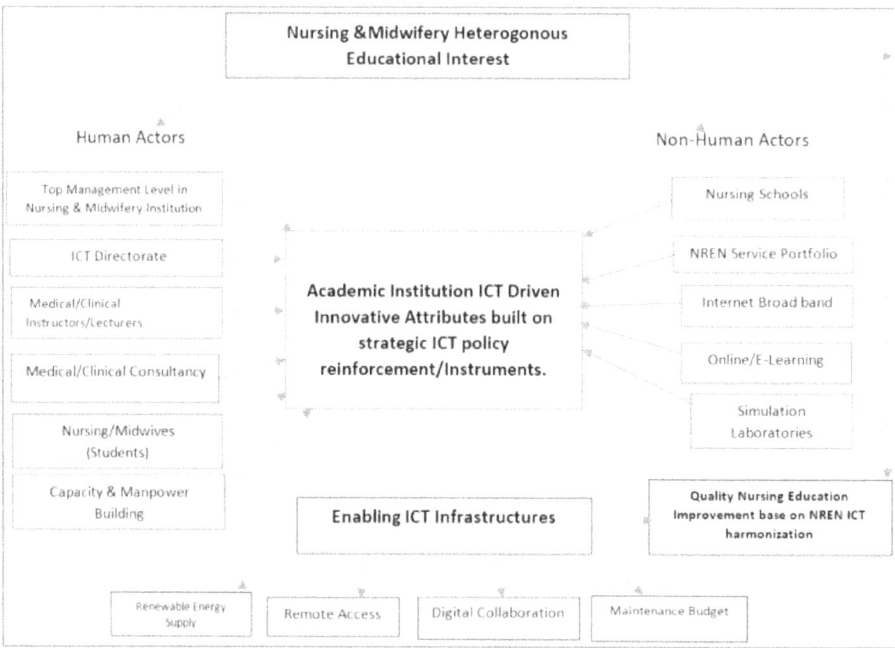

The recommended ANT model is seen in Figure 3. As a matter of fact, the process of developing the nursing education simulation program's service portfolio and roadmap could involve other actors. Whereas social structures and technological issues are linked in the case study, the ANT approach does not give priority to social or technological factors. Insofar as seemingly equivalent technologies provide notably diverse outcomes in different neighborhoods due to specialized network-building and translation processes, the ANT will persistently highlight the interpretative flexibility of IT and systems. Instead of taking technology for granted, ANT's study demonstrated how to recognize the boundaries between technological and social structures, as well as how they are connected and how they are discussed when facts are created. There were two significant additions to the literature in this section:

i. The current paper offered a methodological strategy that may be utilized to direct future national research and education network (NREN) service requirements for nursing education, with the goal of raising the standard of pedagogical teaching and research in the nursing schools.
ii. Improving the use of conventional technology in education as a pedagogical tool for determining end-user demands and offers the chance to incorporate new technological trends for environmentally lifelong learning.

3. RESEARCH METHODOLOGY

A review of the three nursing institutions in our case study, in relationship to the establishment of virtual reality simulation for education in accordance with the National Policy on nursing education. The foundation of the suggested model is to adopt the critical components and infrastructural recommendations from the National Information and Communication Technology Policy, the National Information Technology Education Framework, and the Ministerial Strategy Plan for the Education Sector (2016–2019). In compliance with the study's goals, information was gathered from six (6) ICT center employees, fifteen (15) nursing instructors, and two hundred and fifty (250) nursing students. Participants in the paper's quantitative study included academic personnel, employees of the ICT Center, and students from three nursing and midwifery training institutions. To get information pertinent to the study's goal, three hundred twenty (320) randomly chosen stakeholders from the three nursing and midwifery institutions were given the questionnaires to complete. Out of the 320 distributed questionnaire, 271 where dully completed and returned, representing 84.7% response rate.

3.1 Questionnaire Design

Each of the three segments that made up the questionnaire for this study examined a different aspect of the research issue. In order to determine the intended participants' feelings regarding the integration of the VR Simulation engagement, the initial component is put up. The subsequent portion comprises inquiries regarding the VR simulation ICT infrastructure of the beneficiary institution, which would power the expected enhancements, in order to determine the nursing institutions' willingness to use the VR simulation system. A total of three hundred and twenty (320) questionnaires were distributed to the ICT center staff, nursing educators, and nursing students from various nursing institutions and levels.

Table 1. Research Questionnaire Design

Questionnaire segment	Number of questionnaire item	Description of Questionnaire item
A	5	It is time to reinvent, develop, and welcome experiential learning for nursing students. The purpose of this section is to ascertain how the targeted participants feel about the proposed VR simulation systems and whether they are willing to accept the proposed system as a part of nursing and midwifery pedagogical component.
B	5	This section of the questionnaire focused on the development of the ICT infrastructure at the target institution, specifically whether there is an existing infrastructure systems, organizational information system, management information system, campus inter-networking, centre for information technology, wireless digital access points, internet broadband data communication, electronic learning platforms or digital library automation. This is done to see if the institutions can actually adopt the suggested system.
C	5	Nurse supply and demand in the healthcare system are impacted by the expensive issue of student retention in nursing programs. The social and academic institutional structures must be taken into account while developing effective retention techniques, paying particular emphasis to the integration of students into the program. The racial minority status of the students or different indicators of their academic achievement were used to preselect the strategies' participants. Mentoring, study skills, literacy and language methods, and tutoring are the most frequently mentioned components of the single-program, multifactorial retention solutions that have been documented in studies.

3.2 Implementation

Refer to **Figure 3,Figure 4** and **Figure 5** the aim of the study was to illustrate situations in which the technology actor actively participates in the process of resource integration and service exchange with the user and other relevant actors, leading to interactive and context-aware VR and AR mobile gamification. AI is significantly contributing to the development of VR and AR systems, particularly in the area of clinical and medical education. These interactive, realistic training scenarios are made possible by these immersive technologies, and they can be very similar to actual healthcare operations.

Figure 3. High Speed Connected NRENs Nursing Laboratories: Author Illustration

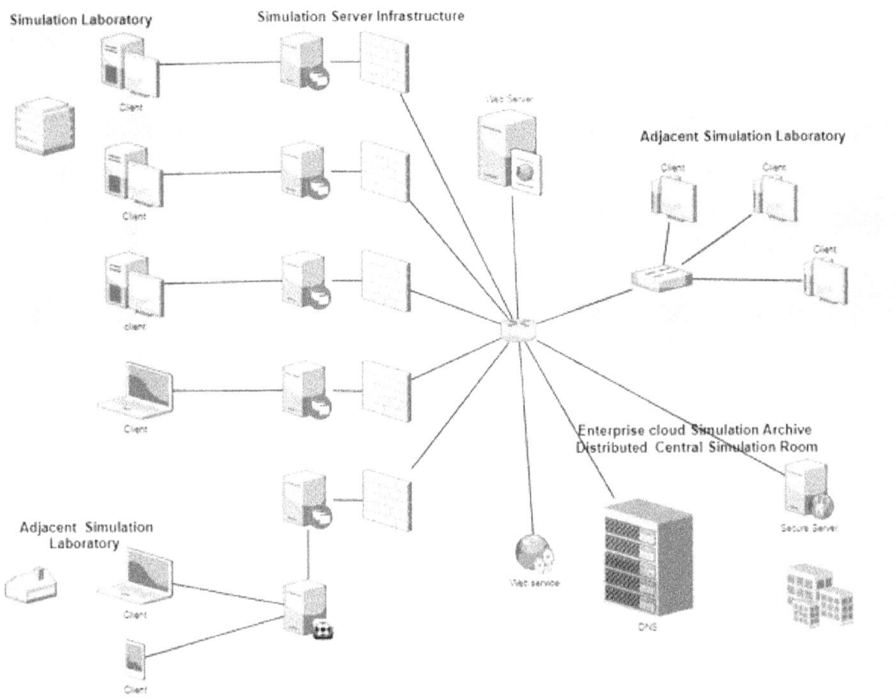

Figure 4. Adaptive Learning Environments with VR and AR: Author illustration.

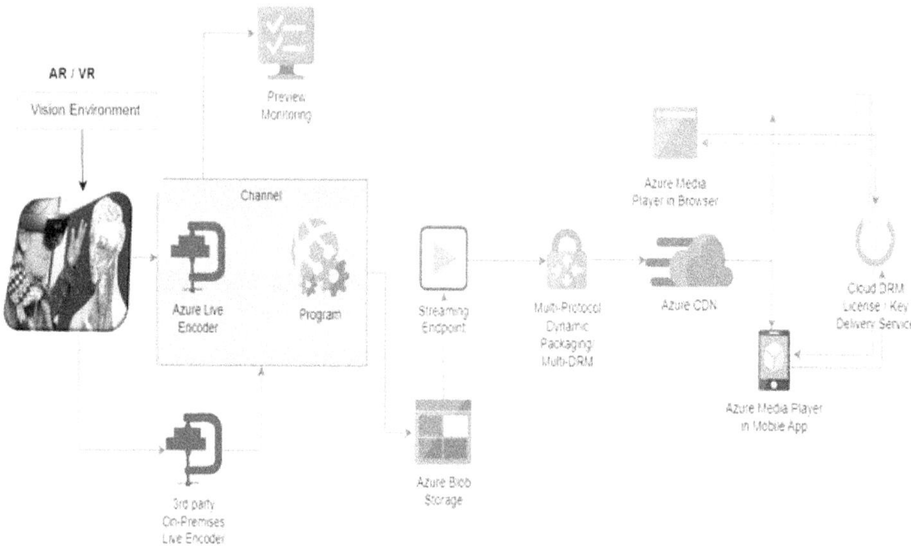

Figure 5. Artificial Intelligence Platform for VR and AR Training: Author illustration.

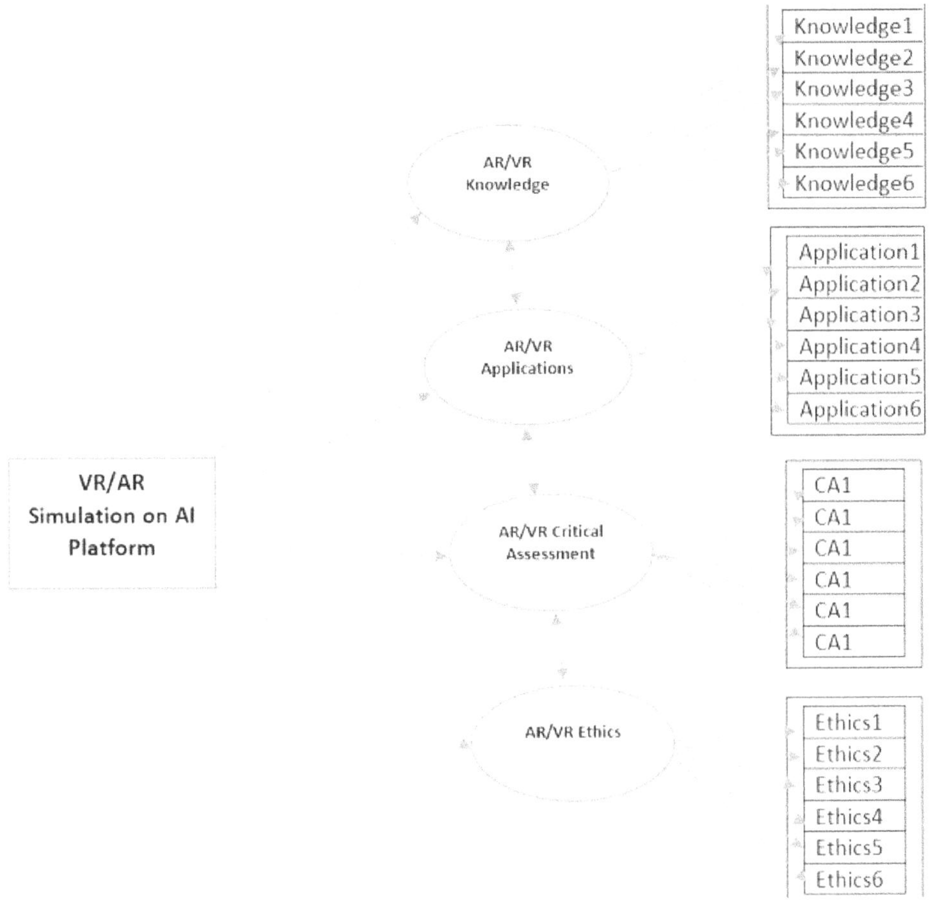

The AI training platform is an adaptable pedagogical training system that gives instructors the ability to oversee classes with a large number of students, regardless of their degree of experience or learning speed. Four modules with expandable course content that was suggested based on the curriculum were included in the bundle. AR/VR Knowledge Base (i), AR/VR Applications (ii), AR/VR Critical Assessment (iii), and AR/VR Ethics (vi) are all included in the package. Our article presents the development of a cutting-edge training system that combines virtual and augmented reality, and is patent-protected. It offers the most realistic welding simulator teaching experience possible. With endless opportunities for practical experience, the most lifelike instruction is offered by a revolutionary augmented reality simulation that is both efficient and effective. Both a tailored AI-based solution and training ranging from novice students to professionals in real-world settings are offered. Artificial intelligence machine learning, specifically artificial neural network techniques, uses learner data sets to build models that can accomplish tasks like information classification and student performance prediction based on simulations. The system's output allowed for each medical student to be evaluated.

3.3 Benefits of NRENs and VR Simulation

Virtual reality simulation is predicted to be a leading feature of all ICT-driven nursing institutions, when implemented and to be at the forefront of efforts to fully integrate NRENs. The ICT center and institutional REN, which will serve as the hub and house the application server, database server, and networking capabilities, will be connected to the various sections of the institutions using a cable or wireless network connection in the proposed system. In order to provide quick and timely access, every classroom, lab, and library will be directly connected to the ICT infrastructure utilizing the recommended network configuration.

i. The initial benefit of having a fully functional VR simulation and NREN in nursing institutes would be that users would have access to all of the resources of all other institutions linked to the network. The VR simulation, digital resources, and multimedia instructional content for interactive pedagogy are all available in each member nursing institution lab.
ii. In case of a network disruption or as a disaster recovery mitigation measure, the electronic resources of the nursing facility can be protected with NREN or multimedia cloud data warehouse storage area network technology.
iii. The nursing program has access to other e-resources through the NREN, the VR Simulation, and may be able to purchase subscriptions at a significantly lower cost if resources are shared by associated institutions. Due to the bulk purchases of subscriptions, expenses are lowered, sustainability is preserved, and additional digital synergy is allowed.
iv. Another significant benefit is the VR simulation and NREN's ability to offer linked institutions and clinical labs long-term, reasonably priced Internet bandwidth made possible by resource pooling. This is due to the benefits of making larger purchases and again pooling resources.

Table 2. AR /VR Simulation Vendor and Product Supplier

Vendor	Services Provided
3B Scientific Smart Anatomy	This function, which blends analog and digital learning, is included with every 3B Scientific Anatomy model. Together with 3D4Medical, 3B Scientific is able to provide educators and students with accurate digital 3D anatomy content. In order to access interactive anatomy classes, quizzes, and virtual models, 3B Smart Anatomy combines human anatomy models with a computer, tablet, or smartphone app.
OculAR SIM	This app was created especially for the Deakin University Faculty of Optometry on smartphones. With AR, educators and students can investigate the visual system and its elements.
SentiAR:	SentiAR creates holographic simulations of patient anatomy using medical augmented reality. The anatomical picture hovers over the patient while interventional treatments are performed. This piece discusses AR and VR.
Elsevier	To help learners be ready for success in a variety of healthcare training situations, Elsevier collaborates with educators in higher education and healthcare simulation programs. The simulation solutions offered by Elsevier are designed with nursing and medical aid programs in mind.
Healthcare Systems Simulation International:	A multinational team of professionals, Healthcare Systems Simulation multinational (HSSI) is committed to providing education and consulting services to individuals and businesses. HSSI employs a team approach using in-situ simulation to address operational and clinical challenges within health sector.
HTC Vive	In order to help healthcare organizations equip the upcoming generation of professionals with the skills they need to meet the needs of 21st-century healthcare education, HTC Vive is building Virtual Reality (VR). Hospitals, colleges, and healthcare organizations have been using simulations for decades to give students access to risk-free, practical settings where they may develop their abilities.
InSimo	With a focus on surgical education and training to lower medical errors and enhance student outcomes, InSimo is a surgical simulation software provider. The goal of their surgical simulator technologies is to accelerate the creation of more advanced, realistic medical patient simulators that may be used for more innovative and widely available applications. Through the use of medical simulation, InSimo recreates complex cases, opening up new possibilities for the rapid training of several surgeons. According to the business, in order for surgeons to learn, replicate, and enhance their procedures, they need to be able to see and feel an accurate replication of every act that takes place during surgery.
KCS Health Sciences Consulting	In order to help health sciences education institutions, nursing programs, emergency medical services programs, and medical schools solve the lack of clinical placements in CTU, KCS Health Sciences Consulting uses our expertise to implement pertinent, evidence-based, and focused simulation-based teaching and learning. Simulation-based teaching and learning has been shown to produce learning outcomes that are equal to those of clinical training while offering significant time and cost savings—a crucial benefit in these times of global physician, nurse, and healthcare worker shortages.
Lucid Reality Labs/ Lumeto	Specializing in immersive XR training and simulations for the healthcare, medtech, pharma, aerospace, and defense industries, Lucid Reality Labs is a top immersive technology consulting, design, and development firm. For training, education, and collaborative settings, the business develops VR simulation solutions with gamification components. In a safe and regulated setting, these scenarios allow users to explore, interact, learn, develop, and master the skills and procedures related to the role.

continued on following page

Table 2. Continued

Vendor	Services Provided
ORamaVR:	A deep technology company founded on science, ORamaVR strives to offer cutting-edge solutions for the medical training and healthcare simulation industries. The company delivers a proprietary, psychomotor, gamified, multi-user virtual reality software platform that is built on cutting-edge research by internationally known scientists. It does this by utilizing state-of-the-art virtual reality clinical simulation tools. By offering practical medical and surgical training, ORamaVR aims to transform the present standards of medical education and enhance health outcomes through the use of virtual reality in medicine.
Surgical Theater	Modern simulation technology is combined with a patient's own anatomy scans by Surgical Theater, a virtual and augmented reality-based healthcare services provider. This is accomplished by reconstructing the patient's anatomy and disease in 360°-3D virtual reality using medical imaging techniques including MRI, CT, and DTI. With cutting-edge surgical planning and navigation capabilities in the operating room, as well as potent tools for medical education and collaboration, the company's precision VR revolutionizes patient interaction prospects in the clinic.

3.4 Future Prospects and Challenges of AR and VR in Healthcare Education

There are obstacles to VR and AR's mainstream acceptance in medical education and therapy, despite their apparent benefits. Accessibility may be hampered by high prices and technical obstacles like the requirement for complex gear and software. Furthermore, a large financial and human resource commitment is needed to integrate new technologies into the current healthcare systems. VR and AR in healthcare, however, have a lot of promising futures. Costs should go down and accessibility should get better as long as technology keeps improving. The goal of research and development is to increase the functionality and realism of VR and AR apps, which will increase their efficacy as teaching and therapeutic aids. With continued development, these technologies have the power to revolutionize healthcare and raise standards of care for patients everywhere. The adoption of AR technologies in medical and healthcare education is beset by challenges such as the high cost of developing interactive platforms, the lack of availability for a growing number of students, and the provision of digital technology in a fair and accessible manner for all students. Despite these challenges, teachers have been successful in providing students with engaging, rewarding, and student-centered experiences in areas where these barriers may be overcome. This article has examined the ways in which these technologies, with their distinct features, are enhancing medical education and opening up a multitude of opportunities for an immersive, interactive learning process. While AR improves learning by superimposing digital information onto the real world, VR with its complete immersion capabilities provides a risk-free environment for healthcare professionals to practice and refine their skills.

Both technologies provide benefits and drawbacks of their own, but they work best together to improve education and give students a more thorough, realistic grasp of difficult medical ideas and procedures. With ongoing technological development and increasingly integrated applications, AR and VR have enormous promise for use in medical education in the future. Healthcare education is expected to enter a new era marked by these technologies, which will make learning more effective, interesting, and tailored to each student's needs. One thing is certain as we explore this intriguing nexus of technology and medical science: AR and VR are actively crafting the future of medical education rather than merely influencing it. Technological advancements in AR and VR are expected to bring about exponential growth in the field of healthcare education. The use of these technologies in medical curriculum appears to be growing, as more medical schools become aware of their advantages, according to current trends. More complex simulations, tailored learning experiences with AI incorporated, and wider application across different medical specialties are anticipated future developments. A new era of experiential learning that integrates technology and medicine to create better-prepared healthcare practitioners is expected to be ushered in by these technologies, which will also likely play a major influence in determining the future of medical education.

4. CONCLUSION

The ANT network model was utilized in the study to develop a conceptual framework for the implementation of VR simulation through multi-dimensional ICT policy. The outcomes mostly confirmed the objectives and strategies that the writers had previously recommended for the conceptual framework. Research has shown that employing developmental strategies along with top-down policy reinforcement is a more effective way to impact academic ICT use than relying solely on educators and their organizations. This problem and the gap it creates served as the inspiration for the current virtual reality simulation method described in this work. The NREN, which links different higher education and nursing establishments over the internet, provides a plethora of chances for collaboration and resource exchange. This collection of invaluable publications from numerous medical facilities, research centers, and other higher education organizations makes access to almost endless resources feasible. To maximize the network's potential, it is advised that the administration, school of nursing, and university library collaborate with those at other universities to find resources that may be utilized in concert and connect them to the network. Establishing the infrastructure required to make use of the NREN's capabilities is also important. The research problems described in the report were adequately handled by utilizing the recommended technology.

The paper, therefore made the following specific recommendations.

i. Curriculum Update and Teaching Methods: The curriculum and teaching strategies urgently need to be updated to reflect the dynamics of AR and VR realization in the nursing education. A calculated move toward developing engaging and comprehensive learning experiences is the curriculum's inclusion of technology. Consequently, it is imperative to create educational modules that use technology as a means of augmenting students' comprehension of the subject matter.
ii. Creative Teaching Approaches for the Digital Age: Assisting students with authentic projects enables them to utilize their acquired knowledge and abilities in authentic settings.
iii. Empowering Teachers as Agents of Change: Developing teacher professionalism is at the center of educational transformation in order to meet the needs of change in the era of AR and VR digital ascendancy.

Therefore, the healthcare industry has paid increasing attention to VR and AR technology. It can enhance the efficacy and efficiency of nursing and medical health care services in addition to lessening the drawbacks of conventional medical practices and education. Nonetheless, a few technical issues still need to be resolved. Examples include the hardware's endurance, the display image's clarity and sharpness, and the integration of the nursing and medical health care information system. Many educational institutions, healthcare facilities, and businesses are currently creating innovative methods to solve connected technical issues. In summary, it is highly anticipated that AR, VR, and MR will become widely used in the nursing and medical fields. The approach shown may be a more cost-effective and practical way to use immersive technologies for improving medical education, especially in cases when it is not feasible for every student to purchase such a device. By offering educational benefits beyond those of conventional simulated learning media, XR technology could assist in preparing graduates who are prepared for the workforce.

By enabling students to express their understanding of phenomena, see the dynamic relationships between variables in a system, see abstract concepts in a 3D format, and experience events that might not be possible due to time, money, safety, or availability constraints, the integration of XR technology into nursing education offers a unique and innovative solution. Training in medicine is changing dramatically thanks to the use of VR and AR. With the use of these technologies, medical personnel can learn more effectively and creatively treat patients while also gaining new perspectives. Benefits of VR and AR in healthcare are evident, even though obstacles still exist. The quality of medical education and patient care can be enhanced by educational institutions and healthcare practitioners exploring and implementing these technologies. A new age in healthcare is expected to be ushered in by the seamless and significant integration of VR and AR technology into medical practices as they develop.

4.1 Conflict of Interest

There is no conflict of interest regarding this paper. However, the paper was supported by U&J Digital Consult Limited. An IT and Educational Consulting Firm base in Nigeria.

REFERENCES

Acharya, M., & Mohbey, K. K. (2024). *Virtual Environment Role in Higher Education Students Learning Enhancement with Intellectual Disabilities Applied Assistive Technologies and Informatics for Students with Disabilities*. Springer.

Aithal, P., & Aithal, S. (2024). Future of Higher Education through Technology Prediction and Forecasting. *Poornaprajna International Journal of Management* [PIJMESS]. *Education & Social Science*, 1(1), 1–50.

Aroesty, S. V. (2021). *Development of a Conceptual Framework for Peer Surgical Coaching Programs*. McGill University.

Baby, B., Singh, R., Suri, A., Dhanakshirur, R. R., Chakraborty, A., Kumar, S., Kalra, P. K., & Banerjee, S. (2020). A review of virtual reality simulators for neuroendoscopy. *Neurosurgical Review*, 43(5), 1255–1272. DOI:10.1007/s10143-019-01164-7 PMID:31444716

Bae, J., Lee, J., Jang, Y., & Lee, Y. (2019). Development of simulation education debriefing protocol with faculty guide for enhancement clinical reasoning. *BMC Medical Education*, 19(1), 1–7. DOI:10.1186/s12909-019-1633-8 PMID:31185972

Barrow, J. (2022). *The Future with Extended Reality, Three-Dimensional, and Advanced Imaging for Molecules, Microscopy, and Anatomy Technologies in Biomedical and Life Sciences Education: Approaches and Evidence of Efficacy for Learning*. Springer.

Barteit, S., Lanfermann, L., Bärnighausen, T., Neuhann, F., & Beiersmann, C. (2021). Augmented, mixed, and virtual reality-based head-mounted devices for medical education: Systematic review. *JMIR Serious Games*, 9(3), e29080. DOI:10.2196/29080 PMID:34255668

Bazin, S. J. (2019). *The Relationship between Reading, Math, Science, and English/Language Usage and National Council Licensure Exam Success for Nursing Students*. Northcentral University.

Belliger, A., & Krieger, D. J. (2024). *From Systems to Actor-Networks: A Paradigm Shift in the Social Sciences*. Ethics International Press Limited.

Bhardwaj, H., Noumani, A., Himanshu, J. K., Chakravorty, S., & Solanki, P. R. (2024). Recent advancement in the detection of potential cancer biomarkers using the nanomaterial integrated electrochemical sensing technique: A detailed review. *Materials Advances*, 5(2), 475–503. DOI:10.1039/D3MA00621B

Blankenship, D. M. (2023). *Simulation as Orientation to Perinatal Clinical Experiences: Effects on Anxiety and Confidence in Prelicensure Nursing Students*. Wilmington University.

Courtwright, S. E., Turi, E., Barr, E. A., Burns, J. C., Gigli, K. H., Bennett, C. R., Sonney, J., Francis, L., & Poghosyan, L. (2024). Facilitators and Barriers to Pediatric Nurse Practitioner Practice in the United States: A Systematic Review. *Journal of Pediatric Health Care*, 38(4), 520–543. DOI:10.1016/j.pedhc.2023.12.003 PMID:38284964

Darcy-Mahoney, A., Carter, B., Green, K., Mullan, F., & Beard, K. V. (2020). Looking backwards to move forward: Using a social mission lens in nursing education. *Journal of Professional Nursing*, 36(5), 412–416. DOI:10.1016/j.profnurs.2020.03.005 PMID:33039077

Ding, X., & Li, Z. (2022). A review of the application of virtual reality technology in higher education based on Web of Science literature data as an example. Paper presented at the *Frontiers in Education*. IEEE. DOI:10.3389/feduc.2022.1048816

Duffy, J. R. (2022). *Quality caring in nursing and health systems: Implications for clinicians, educators, and leaders*. Springer Publishing Company. DOI:10.1891/9780826136961

Dyke, C., Franklin, B. R., Sweeney, W. B., & Ritter, E. M. (2021). Early implementation of Fundamentals of Endoscopic Surgery training using a simulation-based mastery learning curriculum. *Surgery*, 169(5), 1228–1233. DOI:10.1016/j.surg.2020.12.005 PMID:33583604

Endomicroscopy, P.-B. C. L., Diana, M., Dallemagne, B., Chung, H., Nagao, Y., Halvax, P., & Demartines, N. (2014). 2014 Scientific Session of the Society of American Gastrointestinal and Endoscopic Surgeons (SAGES), Salt Lake City, Utah, USA, 2–5 April 2014. *Surgical Endoscopy*, 28(S1), S311–S445. DOI:10.1007/s00464-014-3476-z

Fontenot, J., & McMurray, P. (2020). Decolonizing entry to practice: Reconceptualizing methods to facilitate diversity in nursing programs. *Teaching and Learning in Nursing*, 15(4), 272–279. DOI:10.1016/j.teln.2020.07.002

Foronda, C. L., Gonzalez, L., Meese, M. M., Slamon, N., Baluyot, M., Lee, J., & Aebersold, M. (2024). A comparison of virtual reality to traditional simulation in health professions education: A systematic review. *Simulation in Healthcare*, 10, 1097. PMID:37651101

Foster, T. C., Moroney, W. F., Phillips, H. L., & Lilienthal, M. G. (2024). Human Factors in Simulation and Training: An Overview. *Human Factors in Simulation and Training*, (pp. 1-64). Research Gate.

Fried, M. P., Satava, R., Weghorst, S., Gallagher, A., Sasaki, C., Ross, D., & Zeltsan, M. (2005). The use of surgical simulators to reduce errors. *Advances in patient safety: from research to implementation, 4*, 165-177.

Hamilton, D., McKechnie, J., Edgerton, E., & Wilson, C. (2021). Immersive virtual reality as a pedagogical tool in education: A systematic literature review of quantitative learning outcomes and experimental design. *Journal of Computers in Education*, 8(1), 1–32. DOI:10.1007/s40692-020-00169-2

Heever, H., & Oosthuizen, R. (2024). Application of cognitive work analysis in support of systems engineering of a socio-technical system. *International Journal of Industrial and Systems Engineering*, 46(1), 90–106. DOI:10.1504/IJISE.2024.135830

Hiran, K. K., Doshi, R., & Patel, M. (2024a). *Applications of Virtual and Augmented Reality for Health and Wellbeing*. IGI Global. DOI:10.4018/979-8-3693-1123-3

Hiran, K. K., Doshi, R., & Patel, M. (2024b). Modern Technology in Healthcare and Medical Education: Blockchain, IoT, AR, and VR: Blockchain, IoT, AR, and VR: IGI Global.

Hsieh, M.-C., & Lee, J.-J. (2018). Preliminary study of VR and AR applications in medical and healthcare education. *J Nurs Health Stud*, 3(1), 1. DOI:10.21767/2574-2825.100030

Hussain, S., Mubeen, I., Ullah, N., Shah, S. S. U. D., Khan, B. A., Zahoor, M., Ullah, R., Khan, F. A., & Sultan, M. A. (2022). Modern diagnostic imaging technique applications and risk factors in the medical field: A review. *BioMed Research International*, 2022(1), 5164970. DOI:10.1155/2022/5164970 PMID:35707373

Jumani, A. K., Siddique, W. A., Laghari, A. A., Abro, A., & Khan, A. A. (2022). *Virtual reality and augmented reality for education Multimedia computing systems and virtual reality*. CRC Press.

Kamińska, D., Sapiński, T., Wiak, S., Tikk, T., Haamer, R. E., Avots, E., Helmi, A., Ozcinar, C., & Anbarjafari, G. (2019). Virtual reality and its applications in education: Survey. *Information (Basel)*, 10(10), 318. DOI:10.3390/info10100318

Katelin Hoskins, M. (2018). Ethics education in nursing: Instruction for future generations of nurses. *Online Journal of Issues in Nursing*, 23(1), 1–11.

Kelly, M. A., Berragan, E., Husebø, S. E., & Orr, F. (2016). Simulation in nursing education—International perspectives and contemporary scope of practice. *Journal of Nursing Scholarship*, 48(3), 312–321. DOI:10.1111/jnu.12208 PMID:27061858

Kouijzer, M., Kip, H., Kelders, S. M., & Bouman, Y. (2024). The introduction of virtual reality in forensic mental healthcare–an interview study on the first impressions of patients and healthcare providers regarding VR in treatment. *Frontiers in Psychology*, 15, 1284983. DOI:10.3389/fpsyg.2024.1284983 PMID:38746916

Kyaw, B. M., Saxena, N., Posadzki, P., Vseteckova, J., Nikolaou, C. K., George, P. P., & Zary, N. (2019). Virtual reality for health professions education: Systematic review and meta-analysis by the digital health education collaboration. *Journal of Medical Internet Research*, 21(1), e12959. DOI:10.2196/12959 PMID:30668519

Lin, Y., & Yu, Z. (2023). A meta-analysis of the effects of augmented reality technologies in interactive learning environments (2012–2022). *Computer Applications in Engineering Education*, 31(4), 1111–1131. DOI:10.1002/cae.22628

Liu, D., Bhagat, K. K., Gao, Y., Chang, T.-W., & Huang, R. (2017). The potentials and trends of virtual reality in education: A bibliometric analysis on top research studies in the last two decades. *Virtual, augmented, and mixed realities in education*, 105-130.

Liu, J. Y. W., Yin, Y.-H., Kor, P. P. K., Cheung, D. S. K., Zhao, I. Y., Wang, S., Su, J. J., Christensen, M., Tyrovolas, S., & Leung, A. Y. (2023). The effects of immersive virtual reality applications on enhancing the learning outcomes of undergraduate health care students: Systematic review with meta-synthesis. *Journal of Medical Internet Research*, 25, e39989. DOI:10.2196/39989 PMID:36877550

Lougiakis, C., González, J. J., Ganias, G., Katifori, A., & Roussou, M. (2024). Comparing Physics-based Hand Interaction in Virtual Reality: Custom Soft Body Simulation vs. Off-the-Shelf Integrated Solution.*Paper presented at the 2024 IEEE Conference Virtual Reality and 3D User Interfaces (VR).* IEEE. DOI:10.1109/VR58804.2024.00094

Mäkinen, H., Haavisto, E., Havola, S., & Koivisto, J.-M. (2022). User experiences of virtual reality technologies for healthcare in learning: An integrative review. *Behaviour & Information Technology*, 41(1), 1–17. DOI:10.1080/0144929X.2020.1788162

Marougkas, A., Troussas, C., Krouska, A., & Sgouropoulou, C. (2024). How personalized and effective is immersive virtual reality in education? A systematic literature review for the last decade. *Multimedia Tools and Applications*, 83(6), 18185–18233. DOI:10.1007/s11042-023-15986-7

Martinez-Ulloa, L., Flores, A., Maldonado-Aguayo, Y., Fuentealba-Urra, S., Rubio, A., Guerreo, J., & Ravazzano, C. (2024). Incorporation of a digital health literacy model into the curricula of medical and rehabilitation science courses in higher education. *Salud, Ciencia y Tecnología*, 4, 909–909. DOI:10.56294/saludcyt2024909

Matthew, U. O. (2019). Information System Management & Multimedia Applications in an E-Learning Environment. [IJICTHD]. *International Journal of Information Communication Technologies and Human Development*, 11(3), 21–41. DOI:10.4018/IJICTHD.2019070102

Matthew, U. O., Kazaure, A. S., Kazaure, J. S., Hassan, I. M., Nwanakwaugwu, A. C., & Okafor, N. U. (2022). Educational Technology Adaptation & Implication for Media Technology Adoption in the Period of COVID-19. *Journal of Trends in Computer Science and Smart Technology*, 4(4), 226–245. DOI:10.36548/jtcsst.2022.4.002

Matthew, U. O., & Kazaure, J. S. (2020). Multimedia e-learning education in nigeria and developing countries of Africa for achieving SDG4. [IJICTHD]. *International Journal of Information Communication Technologies and Human Development*, 12(1), 40–62. DOI:10.4018/IJICTHD.2020010103

Matthew, U. O., Kazaure, J. S., Amaonwu, O., Adamu, U. A., Hassan, I. M., Kazaure, A. A., & Ubochi, C. N. (2021). *Role of internet of health things (IoHTs) and innovative internet of 5G medical robotic things (IIo-5GMRTs) in COVID-19 global health risk management and logistics planning Intelligent Data Analysis for COVID-19 Pandemic*. Springer.

Matthew, U. O., Kazaure, J. S., & Haruna, K. (2020). Multimedia information system (MIS) for knowledge generation and ICT policy framework in education: Innovative sustainable educational investment. [IJICTHD]. *International Journal of Information Communication Technologies and Human Development*, 12(3), 28–58. DOI:10.4018/IJICTHD.2020070102

Matthew, U. O., Kazaure, J. S., Kazaure, A. S., Onyedibe, O. N., & Okafor, A. N. (2022). The twenty first century E-learning education management & implication for media technology adoption in the period of pandemic. *EAI Endorsed Transactions on e-Learning, 8*(1).

Matthew, U. O., Kazaure, J. S., & Okafor, N. U. (2021). Contemporary development in E-Learning education, cloud computing technology & internet of things. *EAI Endorsed Transactions on Cloud Systems*, 7(20), e3–e3.

McBride, A. B., Campbell, J., Barr, T., Duffy, J., Haozous, E., Mallow, J., Narsavage, G., Ridenour, N., & Theeke, L. (2017). The impact of the nurse faculty scholars program on schools of nursing. *Nursing Outlook*, 65(3), 327–335. DOI:10.1016/j.outlook.2017.01.013 PMID:28416201

McGonigle, D., & Mastrian, K. (2024). *Nursing informatics and the foundation of knowledge*. Jones & Bartlett Learning.

Mizota, T., Anton, N. E., Huffman, E. M., Guzman, M. J., Lane, F., Choi, J. N., & Stefanidis, D. (2020). Development of a fundamentals of endoscopic surgery proficiency-based skills curriculum for general surgery residents. *Surgical Endoscopy*, 34(2), 771–778. DOI:10.1007/s00464-019-06827-6 PMID:31102077

Münster, S., Maiwald, F., Bruschke, J., Kröber, C., Sun, Y., Dworak, D., Komorowicz, D., Munir, I., Beck, C., & Münster, D. L. (2024). A digital 4D information system on the world scale: Research challenges, approaches, and preliminary results. *Applied Sciences (Basel, Switzerland)*, 14(5), 1992. DOI:10.3390/app14051992

Onyesolu, M. O., Nwasor, V. C., Ositanwosu, O. E., & Iwegbuna, O. N. (2013). Pedagogy: Instructivism to socio-constructivism through virtual reality. *International Journal of Advanced Computer Science and Applications*, 4(9).

Oyekunle, D., Ugochukwu, O. M., Rosa, R. L., Rodriguez, D. Z., & Fatai, L. O. (2024). Novel Approaches in Clinical Simulation: Immersive Educational Technology to Enhance Nursing Education. *INFOCOMP Journal of Computer Science, 23*(1).

Paiva, H. W. A., Golçalves, J. G., Rodrígues, D. Z., & Rosa, R. L. (2024). A Comprehensive Analysis of Virtual Reality Applications in Healthcare. *INFOCOMP Journal of Computer Science, 23*(1).

Pasklinsky, N., & Latimer, B. (2024). Simulation Modalities for Undergraduate Nursing Education *Comprehensive Healthcare SimulationNursing*, 27–33.

Richardson, H., Goldsamt, L. A., Simmons, J., Gilmartin, M., & Jeffries, P. R. (2014). Increasing faculty capacity: Findings from an evaluation of simulation clinical teaching. *Nursing Education Perspectives*, 35(5), 308–314. DOI:10.5480/14-1384 PMID:25291926

Roser, D., Nagl, S., & Ebigbo, A. (2024). Navigating the Learning Landscape: Comprehensive Training in Third Space Endoscopy Training, Techniques, and Practical Recommendations. *Best Practice & Research. Clinical Gastroenterology*, 71, 101918. DOI:10.1016/j.bpg.2024.101918 PMID:39209422

Rutkowski, S., Kiper, P., Cacciante, L., Cieslik, B., Mazurek, J., Turolla, A., & Szczepanska-Gieracha, J. (2020). Use of virtual reality-based training in different fields of rehabilitation: A systematic review and meta-analysis. *Journal of Rehabilitation Medicine*, 52(11), 1–16. DOI:10.2340/16501977-2755 PMID:33073855

Ryan, G. V., Callaghan, S., Rafferty, A., Higgins, M. F., Mangina, E., & McAuliffe, F. (2022). Learning outcomes of immersive technologies in health care student education: Systematic review of the literature. *Journal of Medical Internet Research*, 24(2), e30082. DOI:10.2196/30082 PMID:35103607

Sakai, D., Joyce, K., Sugimoto, M., Horikita, N., Hiyama, A., Sato, M., Devitt, A., & Watanabe, M. (2020). Augmented, virtual and mixed reality in spinal surgery: A real-world experience. *Journal of Orthopaedic Surgery (Hong Kong)*, 28(3), 2309499020952698. DOI:10.1177/2309499020952698 PMID:32909902

Seetohul, J., Shafiee, M., & Sirlantzis, K. (2023). Augmented reality (AR) For surgical robotic and autonomous systems: State of the art, challenges, and solutions. *Sensors (Basel)*, 23(13), 6202. DOI:10.3390/s23136202 PMID:37448050

Shahzad, R., & Gorur, R. (2024). Actor-Network Theory: A material-semiotic approach to policy analysis. *AnalysingEducational Policy*, 157–170. Routledge.

Souza, A. M. C., Manzolli, J., Campos, C. D. S., & Rennó-Costa, C. (2022). Playing the Hypercube–Using Augmented Reality to Enhance a Multimodal Musical Performance. Paper presented at *the Proceedings of the 24th Symposium on Virtual and Augmented Reality*. ACM. DOI:10.1145/3604479.3604530

Syamlan, A., Fathurachman, , Denis, K., Vander Poorten, E., Pramujati, B., & Tjahjowidodo, T. (2022). Haptic/virtual reality orthopedic surgical simulators: A literature review. *Virtual Reality (Waltham Cross)*, 26(4), 1795–1825. DOI:10.1007/s10055-022-00666-y

Theobald, K. A., Tutticci, N., Ramsbotham, J., & Johnston, S. (2021). Effectiveness of using simulation in the development of clinical reasoning in undergraduate nursing students: A systematic review. *Nurse Education in Practice*, 57, 103220. DOI:10.1016/j.nepr.2021.103220 PMID:34781195

Thirunavukarasu, A. J., Hu, M. L., Foster, W. P., Xue, K., Cehajic-Kapetanovic, J., & MacLaren, R. E. (2024). Robot-Assisted Eye Surgery: A Systematic Review of Effectiveness, Safety, and Practicality in Clinical Settings. *Translational Vision Science & Technology*, 13(6), 20–20. DOI:10.1167/tvst.13.6.20 PMID:38916880

Tiwari, R. G., Agarwal, A. K., & Husain, M. (2023). 13 Integration of virtual reality in the e-learning environment. *Augmented and Virtual Reality in Industry, 5*(2), 253.

Ullrich, S., Rausch, D., & Kuhlen, T. W. (2011). *Bimanual Haptic Simulator for Medical Training: System Architecture and Performance Measurements.* Paper presented at the EGVE/EuroVR.

Valerio, J. E., Ramirez-Velandia, F., Fernandez-Gomez, M. P., Rea, N. S., & Alvarez-Pinzon, A. M. (2024). Bridging the Global Technology Gap in Neurosurgery: Disparities in Access to Advanced Tools for Brain Tumor Resection. *Neurosurgery Practice*, 5(2), e00090.

Vardaman, S. A., Logan, L., Davis, S. P., Sciarra, E., Doria, J. B., Baker, J., Feeney, S., Pajarillo, E. J. Y., Seibold-Simpson, S., & Bajwa, M. (2024). Addressing the Shortage of Academic Nurse Educators: Recommendations for Educational Institutions Based on Nominal Group Technique Research. *Nursing Education Perspectives*, 10(4), 1097. DOI:10.1097/01.NEP.0000000000001264 PMID:38602384

Vetrivel, S., & Mohanasundaram, T. (2024). Breaking down walls: The influence of virtual reality on accessible healthcare delivery. *Digital Transformation in Healthcare 5.0: Volume 1: IoT, AI and Digital Twin*, 129.

Wang, Y., Siau, K. L., & Wang, L. (2022). Metaverse and human-computer interaction: A technology framework for 3D virtual worlds. Paper presented at the *International Conference on Human-Computer Interaction*. Springer. DOI:10.1007/978-3-031-21707-4_16

Wei, Z., & Yuan, M. (2023). Research on the current situation and future development trend of immersive virtual reality in the field of education. *Sustainability (Basel)*, 15(9), 7531. DOI:10.3390/su15097531

Williams, I. (2020). Contemporary application of ANT: An introduction. *Contemporary applications of actor network theory*, 1-13.

Yoo, J., & Brownlee, E. A. (2020). *The past, present, and future of virtual reality in higher education Handbook of Research on Adult Learning in Higher Education.* IGI Global.

eZainab, H., Bawany, N. Z., Rehman, W., & Imran, J. (2024). Design and development of virtual reality exposure therapy systems: Requirements, challenges and solutions. *Multimedia Tools and Applications*, 83(2), 6137–6160. DOI:10.1007/s11042-023-15756-5

Chapter 11
Mapping Virtual Learning in Distance Education: Review and Research Agenda

Narendra Kumar
https://orcid.org/0000-0002-3325-3448
Amity University, Noida, India

ABSTRACT

Smart learning in virtual worlds refers to the use of virtual reality (VR) and other immersive technologies to enhance the learning experience. Smart learning in virtual worlds has the potential to revolutionize education and training by providing engaging, adaptive, and immersive experiences in various domains. For this study, the literature on smart learning in distance education has been mapped through Vosviewer. In this research, bibliometric visualizing methods are used with the help of Vosviewer to analyze the different outcomes. Co-occurrences of author keywords and bibliographic couplings of the countries, authors, journals, and institutions are depicted via the software. The initial search on Scopus was performed with "smart learning or virtual learning" and "distance education" which fetched 645 documents. Based on the language of the article, the authors found 587 articles which were published in English. The second basis was the source type that included Journal articles, conference proceedings and book chapters and the authors found 440 articles for the study.

DOI: 10.4018/979-8-3693-6407-9.ch011

1. INTRODUCTION

In the realm of education, the integration of technology has significantly transformed traditional learning paradigms. One of the most groundbreaking advancements in this regard is the emergence of virtual worlds as powerful tools for education. These immersive digital environments offer a unique platform for interactive learning experiences, fostering engagement and enhancing retention. Virtual worlds are computer-simulated environments where users can interact with each other and with computer-generated objects in real-time (Mir, 2016). These environments can range from realistic simulations of physical spaces to fantastical realms limited only by imagination. Users typically navigate through these worlds using avatars, digital representations of themselves that can move, communicate, and interact with objects and other avatars.

The concept of virtual worlds has its roots in gaming, with early examples such as Second Life gaining popularity in the early 2000s. However, in recent years, virtual worlds have found applications beyond entertainment, particularly in education. Institutions and educators are increasingly leveraging virtual worlds to create immersive learning experiences that transcend the limitations of traditional classrooms. Smart learning in virtual worlds refers to the application of intelligent technologies and pedagogical strategies to optimize learning outcomes within these environments. Unlike traditional e-learning platforms, which often rely on passive consumption of content, smart learning in virtual worlds emphasizes active engagement, collaboration, and personalized learning experiences (Arifin, 2018).

One of the key features of smart learning in virtual worlds is its adaptability (Letseka, 2016). Intelligent algorithms can analyze user interactions and performance data in real-time to tailor learning experiences to individual needs and preferences. For example, if a student is struggling with a particular concept, the virtual environment can dynamically adjust the difficulty level or provide additional resources to support learning. Another aspect of smart learning in virtual worlds is its emphasis on collaboration and social interaction. Unlike traditional online courses, which can feel isolated, virtual worlds provide a sense of presence and social presence, allowing learners to interact with instructors and peers in a more natural and immersive manner. This social dimension fosters collaboration, communication, and teamwork, essential skills in today's interconnected world.

Furthermore, smart learning in virtual worlds often incorporates gamification elements to enhance engagement and motivation. By introducing game-like mechanics such as challenges, rewards, and progression systems, educators can create compelling learning experiences that encourage active participation and persistence.

1.1 Applications of Smart Learning in Virtual Worlds

The applications of smart learning in virtual worlds are diverse and span across various fields and disciplines. In the field of Science, Technology, Engineering and Mathematics (STEM) education, for example, virtual laboratories allow students to conduct experiments in a safe and cost-effective manner, gaining hands-on experience without the need for physical equipment.

In medical education, virtual simulations enable students to practice surgical procedures and patient care in a realistic yet risk-free environment (Chattopadhyay, 2014). These simulations can provide valuable opportunities for skill development and decision-making under pressure, ultimately improving patient outcomes in clinical settings.

Virtual worlds also hold promise for language learning, cultural exchange, and cross-cultural communication. By immersing learners in virtual environments that replicate real-world scenarios, educators can facilitate authentic language practice and cultural understanding, transcending the limitations of traditional classroom-based instruction.

Furthermore, virtual worlds have the potential to address the needs of diverse learners, including those with disabilities or learning differences. By offering customizable interfaces, alternative communication modalities, and assistive technologies, virtual environments can accommodate a wide range of learning styles and preferences, promoting inclusivity and accessibility.

1.2 Challenges and Considerations

While the potential benefits of smart learning in virtual worlds are significant, several challenges and considerations must be addressed to realize its full potential. Technical issues such as network latency, hardware compatibility, and system reliability can hinder the effectiveness of virtual learning environments, particularly in resource-constrained settings. Moreover, ensuring the privacy and security of user data within virtual worlds is paramount, given the sensitive nature of educational content and personal information. Educators and institutions must implement robust data protection measures and adhere to ethical guidelines to safeguard the confidentiality and integrity of learner data.

A big challenge is the design and implementation of effective instructional strategies within virtual worlds. Educators must possess the necessary skills and expertise to leverage the unique affordances of these environments and create engaging and pedagogically sound learning experiences. Professional development and training programs can play a crucial role in equipping educators with the knowledge and skills needed to succeed in this rapidly evolving landscape.

Smart learning in virtual worlds represents a paradigm shift in education, offering immersive, interactive, and personalized learning experiences that transcend the limitations of traditional classrooms. By harnessing the power of intelligent technologies, collaboration, and gamification, virtual worlds have the potential to revolutionize education in the digital age, fostering creativity, critical thinking, and lifelong learning skills.

However, realizing this potential requires concerted efforts from educators, institutions, policymakers, and technology developers to address technical, ethical, and pedagogical challenges. With careful planning, investment, and innovation, smart learning in virtual worlds can empower learners of all ages and backgrounds to thrive in the 21st century and beyond.

1.3 Usage and Applications of Virtual Learning in Distance Education

Distance education has undergone a remarkable evolution with the advent of virtual learning technologies. Virtual learning, also known as online learning or e-learning, utilizes digital platforms and tools to deliver educational content remotely, transcending geographical barriers and traditional classroom settings. In this article, the authors delve into the usage and applications of virtual learning in distance education, exploring its transformative potential and implications for learners, educators, and institutions.

1.4 The Evolution of Distance Education

Distance education has a rich history dating back to the 19th century, with correspondence courses being the earliest form of remote learning (Martinez-Garcia et al., 2023a). Over the years, advancements in communication technologies, such as radio, television, and the internet, have revolutionized distance education (Martinez-Garcia et al., 2023b), making it more accessible, interactive, and effective. However, it was the emergence of virtual learning technologies in the late 20th and early 21st centuries that truly transformed distance education (Shtaleva et al., 2021). Virtual learning platforms leverage the power of the internet to deliver multimedia-rich content, facilitate communication and collaboration, and provide interactive learning experiences that rival traditional classroom instruction. Virtual learning encompasses a wide range of technologies and approaches, including online courses, webinars, virtual classrooms, and multimedia resources (Seilkhan et al., 2022). These tools enable learners to access educational content anytime, anywhere, using a variety of devices such as computers, tablets, and smartphones.

One of the key advantages of virtual learning in distance education is its flexibility. Learners have the freedom to study at their own pace and schedule, accommodating work, family, and other commitments (Hietanen & Svedholm-Häkkinen, 2023). This flexibility is particularly beneficial for adult learners, working professionals, and individuals with disabilities who may face challenges attending traditional face-to-face classes (Pei & Wu, 2019). Moreover, virtual learning platforms offer a wealth of resources and multimedia content, including videos, simulations, interactive quizzes, and discussion forums (Singh & Thurman, 2019). These diverse learning materials cater to different learning styles and preferences, enhancing engagement and retention.

1.5 Applications of Virtual Learning in Distance Education

The applications of virtual learning in distance education are vast and diverse, spanning across various fields and disciplines. In higher education, online courses and degree programs have become increasingly popular, offering students access to a wide range of subjects and specialization options from top institutions around the world (Schoech & Helton, 2002).

Virtual learning has also gained traction in vocational and professional education, with online certifications and training programs catering to the needs of learners seeking to acquire new skills or advance their careers. Platforms such as Coursera, Udemy, and LinkedIn Learning offer courses in fields ranging from programming and digital marketing to healthcare and project management. Furthermore, virtual learning has proven to be particularly effective in continuing education and lifelong learning initiatives. Professionals can stay updated with the latest developments in their fields, earn certifications, and acquire new competencies through online courses and webinars, enhancing their employability and career prospects. In addition to formal education, virtual learning has also found applications in informal and non-traditional learning contexts. Massive Open Online Courses (MOOCs) and Open Educational Resources (OERs) provide free or low-cost access to educational content, democratizing learning and expanding access to knowledge for learners around the globe.

1.6 Challenges and Considerations

While virtual learning holds immense promise for distance education, it also presents several challenges and considerations that must be addressed to ensure its effectiveness and sustainability. One of the key challenges is the digital divide, which refers to disparities in access to technology and internet connectivity among different populations. Inadequate infrastructure limited digital literacy, and socio-economic factors can hinder the ability of learners to fully participate in virtual learning initiatives, exacerbating existing inequalities in education. Efforts to bridge the digital divide through initiatives such as community broadband projects, digital skills training programs, and affordable device subsidies are essential to promote equitable access to virtual learning opportunities.

Moreover, ensuring the quality and rigor of online education programs is crucial to maintain credibility and trust among learners, employers, and accrediting bodies. Institutions must adhere to rigorous standards for course design, instructional delivery, assessment, and student support services to uphold academic integrity and meet the diverse needs of learners.

Virtual learning has emerged as a powerful tool for distance education, offering unprecedented opportunities for learners to access high-quality educational content and resources remotely. From online courses and webinars to virtual classrooms and multimedia resources, virtual learning platforms provide flexible, interactive, and engaging learning experiences that transcend the limitations of traditional classroom instruction. However, realizing the full potential of virtual learning in distance education requires addressing challenges such as the digital divide, ensuring quality assurance, and promoting inclusivity and accessibility. By leveraging technology, innovation, and collaboration, educators, policymakers, and stakeholders can harness the transformative power of virtual learning to expand access to education, empower learners, and drive social and economic development in the digital age.

2. REVIEW OF THE LITERATURE

Many researchers have made significant contributions to the field of virtual learning in distance education, shaping the overall understanding of how technology can be effectively utilized to facilitate learning beyond traditional classroom settings. Michael G. Moore is recognized for his work on distance education and the theory of transactional distance, which emphasizes the interplay between the instructor, the learner, and the educational content in distance education settings. His insights have been instrumental in understanding the dynamics of virtual learning environments. Another researcher Terry Anderson has made significant contributions to the theory and practice of distance education, particularly in the realm of online and virtual learning. His work often focuses on the concept of interaction and the role it plays in effective online education, as well as the development of communities of inquiry in virtual spaces. Randy Garrison, one of the prolific authors in the field is known for his research on online communities of inquiry and the Community of

Inquiry (CoI) framework, which emphasizes the importance of cognitive, social, and teaching presences in online learning environments. His work has helped shape instructional strategies and design principles for virtual learning.

At the same time, Gilly Salmon's work on the five-stage model of online learning has been influential in guiding educators in designing and facilitating effective virtual learning experiences. Her emphasis on structured online activities and fostering online interaction has contributed to the development of engaging virtual learning environments. Another author George Siemens, who is considered to be a prominent figure in the field of educational technology and distance education, known for his work on connectivism, a learning theory that highlights the significance of networked learning in the digital age. His ideas have influenced how educators conceptualize and implement virtual learning environments that leverage the power of networks and social interactions. Clark Quinn's contributions to virtual learning often revolve around the integration of cognitive science principles and instructional design practices in online education. His work emphasizes the importance of designing virtual learning experiences that align with how learners acquire, process, and retain information in digital contexts.

Curtis Bonk is recognized for his research on blended learning and the effective integration of technology in education. His work often explores innovative approaches to virtual learning, such as the use of open educational resources (OER) and massive open online courses (MOOCs), providing valuable insights into the evolving landscape of distance education.

Table 1. Major contributions in the field of virtual reality

SN	Contributor	Contribution
1	Terry Anderson	Known for his work on the Community of Inquiry framework, emphasizing social, cognitive, and teaching presence in online learning.
2	Randy Garrison	Co-creator of the Community of Inquiry framework, focusing on the role of instructor presence and critical thinking skills in virtual classrooms.
3	Tony Bates	His SECTIONS framework evaluates online learning environments, considering factors like technology integration, learner support, and institutional policies.
4	Diana Laurillard	Her Conversational Framework addresses challenges in designing effective learning activities and supporting interactions in virtual environments.
5	Simonson, Smaldino, Albright, and Zvacek	Authors of "Teaching and Learning at a Distance," offering insights on course design, learner support, assessment, and technology integration.

continued on following page

Table 1. Continued

SN	Contributor	Contribution
6	George Siemens	Co-developer of connectivism, exploring learning in the digital age and the role of networks and technology in education.
7	Stephen Downes	Known for his work on open educational resources (OER) and the theory of connectivism, emphasizing distributed learning and networked knowledge.
8	Martin Weller	Author of "The Digital Scholar" and advocate for openness in education, discussing challenges and opportunities in digital scholarship and online learning.
9	Curt Bonk	His work on the TEC-VARIETY framework addresses motivational challenges in online learning, offering practical strategies for engagement and retention.
10	Gilly Salmon	Known for her work on e-tivities and the five-stage model of online learning, emphasizing the importance of structured online activities and peer interaction.
11	Larry R. Squire	His research on the cognitive neuroscience of learning explores the implications of brain science for virtual learning and instructional design.
12	John Seely Brown	Co-author of "The Social Life of Information," discussing the social and cultural dimensions of learning in digital environments.
13	Allison Rossett	Her research on performance support and instructional design addresses challenges in designing effective online learning experiences for workplace training.
14	Clark Quinn	Known for his work on learning technology design, focusing on the alignment of technology with cognitive principles and learning goals.
15	David Wiley	Advocate for open educational resources (OER) and open pedagogy, addressing challenges in access, affordability, and inclusivity in virtual learning environments.
16	Richard E. Mayer	His research on multimedia learning theory explores the design of effective instructional materials for online learning, considering cognitive load and multimedia principles.
17	Nancy White	Known for her work on online facilitation and communities of practice, addressing challenges in fostering collaboration and knowledge sharing in virtual spaces.
18	Bonnie Stewart	Her research on digital identity and networked learning explores the implications of online participation and social media for teaching and learning.
19	Chris Dede	Researcher in educational technology and digital media, addressing challenges in immersive learning environments and virtual worlds.
20	Karen Swan	Her research on online learning communities and student engagement addresses challenges in fostering interaction and collaboration in virtual classrooms.

continued on following page

Table 1. Continued

SN	Contributor	Contribution
21	Alec Couros	Advocate for digital citizenship and networked learning, addressing challenges in online identity, privacy, and safety.
22	Jon Dron	Co-author of "Teaching Crowds," discussing the challenges and affordances of social networking and collective intelligence in online learning.
23	Martin Dougiamas	Creator of Moodle, an open-source learning management system (LMS) addressing challenges in course management and online collaboration.
24	Amy Collier	Her work on digital pedagogy and critical instructional design addresses challenges in equity, inclusion, and social justice in online learning.
25	Jesse Stommel	Advocate for critical digital pedagogy, addressing challenges in power dynamics, agency, and autonomy in online education.
26	Audrey Watters	Critic of ed-tech and advocate for critical perspectives on technology in education, addressing challenges in surveillance, privacy, and data ethics.
27	Maha Bali	Advocate for open education and critical digital pedagogy, addressing challenges in cultural diversity, decolonization, and global collaboration in online learning.
28	Chris Gilliard	Researcher on digital redlining and digital privacy, addressing challenges in equity, surveillance, and algorithmic bias in online education.
29	Henry Jenkins	Scholar of media studies and participatory culture, addressing challenges in digital literacies, remix culture, and participatory learning in virtual spaces.
30	Anya Kamenetz	Author of "DIY U" and advocate for alternative models of education, addressing challenges in affordability, accessibility, and innovation in online learning.
31	Cathy Davidson	Advocate for active learning and the future of higher education, addressing challenges in institutional change, student-centered pedagogy, and digital literacy.
32	Sherry Turkle	Researcher on technology and society, addressing challenges in human connection, empathy, and authenticity in virtual learning environments.
33	Etienne Wenger	Co-author of "Communities of Practice," discussing the challenges and benefits of social learning and knowledge sharing in virtual communities.
34	Paulo Blikstein	Researcher on educational technology and constructionist learning, addressing challenges in project-based learning, maker education, and computational thinking.
35	Howard Rheingold	Author of "Net Smart" and advocate for digital literacies and online community, addressing challenges in attention, critical consumption, and collaboration in digital spaces.

continued on following page

Table 1. Continued

SN	Contributor	Contribution
36	Richard Baraniuk	Founder of Connexions and advocate for open education, addressing challenges in content creation, remix culture, and peer-to-peer learning.
37	Mimi Ito	Researcher on youth culture and digital media, addressing challenges in informal learning, participatory culture, and digital citizenship.
38	Sebastian Thrun	Co-founder of Udacity and advocate for massive open online courses (MOOCs), addressing challenges in scale, access, and credentialing in online education.
39	Kathy Schrock	Advocate for educational technology and digital literacy, addressing challenges in information literacy, media literacy, and digital citizenship.
40	James Paul Gee	Researcher on video games and learning, addressing challenges in game-based learning, situated learning, and identity construction in virtual environments.
41	Sugata Mitra	Known for his "Hole in the Wall" experiments and research on self-directed learning, addressing challenges in learner autonomy and peer collaboration in digital environments.
42	Candace Thille	Researcher on learning analytics and personalized learning, addressing challenges in data-driven decision-making and adaptive learning technologies.
43	Rebecca Eynon	Researcher on digital inequalities and youth digital literacy, addressing challenges in access, participation, and digital skills development in online education.
44	Stephen Heppell	Advocate for innovative learning spaces and technology- enhanced learning, addressing challenges in design thinking, creativity, and collaboration in virtual environments.
45	Jo Boaler	Researcher on mathematics education and online learning, addressing challenges in equitable access, mindset, and instructional design in virtual classrooms.
46	Neil Selwyn	Researcher on digital technology in education, addressing challenges in digital divides, techno-solutionism, and critical perspectives on ed-tech.
47	Cathy N. Davidson	Advocate for active learning and the future of higher education, addressing challenges in institutional change, student-centered pedagogy, and digital literacy.
48	Henry Jenkins	Scholar of media studies and participatory culture, addressing challenges in digital literacies, remix culture, and participatory learning in virtual spaces.
49	Anya Kamenetz	Author of "DIY U" and advocate for alternative models of education, addressing challenges in affordability, accessibility, and innovation in online learning.
50	Michael Grahame Moore	His theory of transactional distance highlights the importance of dialogue, structure, and autonomy in distance education.

3. RESEARCH METHODOLOGY

In order to conduct thorough research and compare the knowledge available regarding the subject at hand, it was necessary to elaborate a set of questions that would motivate the study and resolve its inquiries in the best way possible. Therefore, to optimize the research process, following research questions were proposed:

Table 2. Research questions

SN	Research Question
1	What is the impact regarding the usage of the virtual learning in distance education?
2	What are the applications of the virtual learning in distance education?
3	What are the challenges and advancements presented by the use of the virtual learning in distance education?
4	How does the virtual learning impact the future of distance education?

3.1 Data Collection

For this study, the literature on smart learning in distance education was mapped through Vosviewer software which is a popular tool to analyse and visualize bibliometric data (Naseer et al., 2009; van Eck & Waltman, 2017). Literary work that requires a quantitative study in terms of the bibliometric analysis and bibliometric visualization can be performed using similar kind of softwares as well. Bibliometrics is "the application of mathematical and statistical methods to books and other media of communication" (Kumar & Sharma, 2024; Malighetti et al., 2019; Nandiyanto & Al Husaeni, 2021) to review the chronology of the development of a specific area of literature, through analysing the available scholarly work (Mas-Tur et al., n.d.; Tomyuk et al., 2022; Vermooten et al., 2021; Volkova, 2022). Through bibliometrics, the cited information in terms of publication and frequency can be categorized.

In research, bibliometric visualizing methods are used with the help of Vosviewer to analyze the different outcomes. Co-occurrences of author keywords and bibliographic couplings of the countries, authors, journals, and institutions are depicted via the software. The initial search on Scopus was performed with "Smart Learning or Virtual Learning" and "Distance Education" which fetched 645 documents. Based on the language of the article, the authors found 587 articles which were published in English. The second basis was the source type that included Journal articles, conference proceedings and book chapters and the authors found 472 articles for the study. The remaining articles were either book series, book reviews, book trade journal and were excluded from the study. The search was further refined by excluding articles which were in the press. Hence, the authors found that only 2 articles were in the press, and they were excluded from the data source. The last basis on which the authors selected the database was document type and the authors had only 440 articles (Table 3) remaining that could be included for the analysis.

Table 3. Inclusion and exclusion criteria

Criteria	Criteria description	Status	Remaining Articles
Language	Articles published in English were included	Other language articles excluded	587
Source Type	Journal and conference proceedings were included	Other sources like book series, book, trade journal, book reviews etc were excluded	472
Country	All country included	No exclusion was made based on the country	472
Publication Stage	All articles which were already published, were included	Article in press were excluded	470
Document type	Conference Papers, Articles and book chapters were included	Review, Conference review were excluded	440

Finally, the number of articles remaining for the study was 438 which were inserted to VOSviewer for further analysis.

4. FINDINGS AND INTERPRETATIONS

4.1 Co-Occurrences of Author Keywords

In academic research, author keywords serve as vital descriptors that encapsulate the essence of a study. Analysing the co-occurrence of these keywords provides valuable insights into the thematic connections and trends within the body of literature. Co-occurrence analysis involves identifying patterns of simultaneous occurrence of keywords within scholarly articles. It offers researchers a means to uncover latent relationships and thematic clusters present in literature. By quantifying these relationships, researchers can gain a deeper understanding of the prevailing themes, emerging trends, and interdisciplinary connections within their field.

The dataset used for this analysis consists of 1095 distinct author keywords extracted from a corpus of scholarly articles. To ensure statistical significance, keywords that occur less than 5 times are excluded from the analysis. Subsequently, a threshold is set to identify keywords that co-occur with a frequency above a predefined value, indicating a meaningful association.

Out of the initial pool of 1095 keywords, only 32 keywords meet the threshold criteria, signifying robust co-occurrence patterns within the dataset. These keywords represent focal points around which research themes converge, indicating their prominence within literature. By examining the co-occurrence network, clusters of related keywords emerge, illustrating the interconnectedness of ideas and concepts across different articles.

The identified clusters offer valuable insights into the thematic landscape of the field, highlighting prevalent topics of interest and areas of active research. Researchers can use this information to identify gaps in the literature, explore interdisciplinary connections, and devise future research directions. Moreover, understanding the co-occurrence patterns enables scholars to navigate the vast body of literature more effectively, aiding in literature reviews and knowledge synthesis. Co-occurrence analysis of author keywords offers valuable insights into the thematic connections and trends within the body of literature. By identifying patterns of keyword co-occurrence, researchers can uncover underlying relationships, explore emerging themes, and navigate the scholarly landscape more effectively. Despite its challenges, co- occurrence analysis remains a powerful tool for knowledge discovery and synthesis, with implications spanning academia, information retrieval, and knowledge management. As research methodologies evolve, co-occurrence analysis will continue to facilitate the advancement of knowledge across various domains.

In the current dataset, the keyword co-occurrence analysis has shown a significant pattern. The visualization of the dataset can be seen with figure.

Figure 1. Author keyword co-occurrences

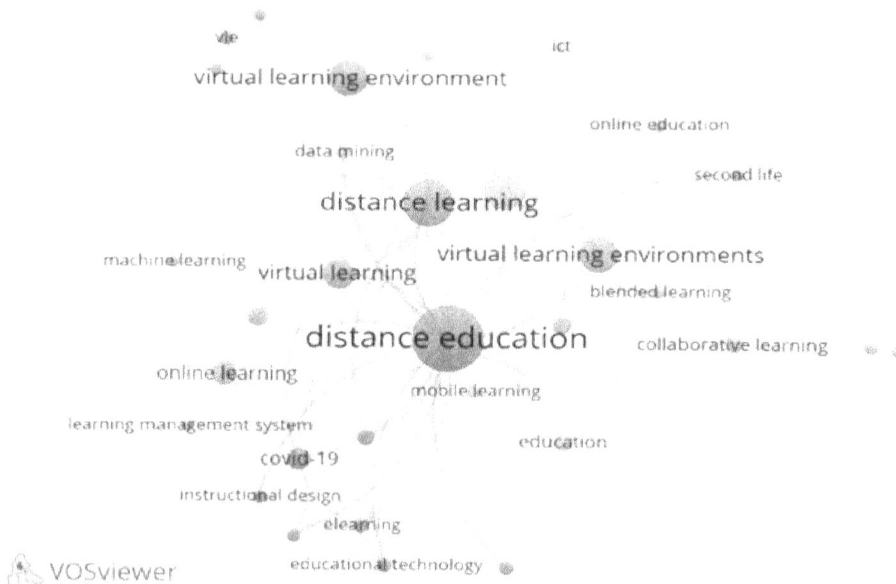

Figure 1 depicts a network visualization of the author keywords' co-occurrences. The keyword occurrence threshold was set at 5. 32 of the 1095 keywords satisfied and met the criteria. The first values in parentheses represent keyword occurrences, while the second represents overall link strength. The most frequently mentioned keywords by the authors are, respectively, distance education (138; 134), distance learning (70; 68), e-learning (45; 57), virtual learning environments (40; 53) and online learning (18;33). These keywords highlight the most often stated concepts in the context of emotional education in literature.

In Figure 1, the different clusters can be seen with different colours. The first cluster shows the concepts that are researched very often with reference to distance education and its impact on various other parameters. Majorly there were 5 clusters found having relationship with other keywords. These cluster are like:

Cluster 1 (8 items)

- Covid-19
- Distance education
- Educational technology
- elearning
- Instructional design
- Medical education

- Nursing
- Virtual reality Cluster 2 (6 items)
- blended learning
- collaborative learning
- computer mediated communication
- distance education and telelearning
- higher education
- virtual learning environment Cluster 3 (6 items)
- Distance learning
- Moodle
- Remote laboratories
- Virtual learning
- Virtual learning environment
- Vle Cluster 4 (4 items)
- Data mining
- eLearning
- ICT
- Internet Cluster 5 (4 items)
- Learning analytics
- Learning management system
- Machine learning
- Online learning

4.2 Bibliographic Coupling of the Countries

Figure 2. Overlay visualization of the bibliographic coupling of the countries

Bibliographic coupling between the countries have been illustrated through the overlay visualization. Minimum 5 published articles and 25 citations were the benchmark created for the study. Only 24 out of 72 countries met the threshold. For all countries, the first numbers show the total publications whereas the second one shows the citation count, and the last one shows the total link strengths.

United States was found to be on top of the list in terms of publications on VR and DL and the total link strength for United States was 506. As far as citations are concerned United States again topped the list with 1712 citations. The top three countries with the highest publications along with United States are the Brazil (89) and United Kingdom (49). United States, United Kingdom, Brazil, Portugal and Spain are the only countries with the highest total link strength in three digits. Figure 2 shows overlay visualization of the bibliographic coupling of the countries, which displays the position of the top countries.

4.3 Bibliographic Coupling of the Authors

Figure 3. Overlay visualization of the bibliographic coupling of the authors

Bibliographic coupling among the researchers can be visualized in Figure 2. Authors with at least 2 documents were taken into consideration. Only 7 out of 436 authors met the threshold. These 7 authors were coupled bibliographically. The link strength was found to be very insignificant as hardly there was a document with any length strength. The highest citations were for Arango F. (20), Meisalo V. (19), Bremgartner V. and Topchyan R. (14) followed by Bobalo Y. (12). Bibliographic coupling of the authors defines that there is a lot of collaborated work required in this field.

4.4 Bibliographic Coupling of the Journals

Figure 4. Network visualization of the bibliographic coupling of the journals

Figure 4 exhibits the bibliographic coupling of the journals with network visualization. Minimum 3 publications and 5 citations (h-index) were set as the basis for this analysis. Of the 325 journals, only 21 could meet the threshold and were coupled bibliographically. Thereafter the top 10 journals were shortlisted and visualized according to their citations and total link strength. The shortlisted journals' citation counts, and the total strength of the bibliographic coupling links were assessed. The most influential journal was found to be *Computers and Education* with 1086 citations and 9 documents followed by education Sciences with 199 citations of 3 documents. *Proceedings - Frontiers in Education Conference, FIE* had 17 documents in its credit. Since the use of virtual learning in distance education is a very new concept, the conference proceedings would have fetched many documents.

5. DISCUSSION

The integration of virtual worlds into distance education has sparked a paradigm shift in how learning is conceptualized and delivered. Smart learning, characterized by the fusion of technology and education, has found a fertile ground in virtual environments. This systematic literature review aims to peep into the myriad applications and implications of virtual learning in distance education, elucidating the opportunities and challenges inherent in this transformative approach. Virtual worlds offer immersive, interactive, and collaborative spaces where learners can engage with content and peers in real-time, transcending the limitations of traditional distance learning. From simulating real-world scenarios for experiential learning to facilitating synchronous interactions through avatars, the possibilities are vast. Educational institutions have leveraged virtual worlds for language learning, Science, Technology, Engineering and Mathematics (STEM) education, professional development, and beyond. These environments provide a dynamic setting where learners can explore, experiment, and construct knowledge collaboratively.

The present study also talks about the growing contribution of virtual platforms in learning atmosphere of the ODL students. One of the primary advantages of virtual worlds in distance education is their ability to enhance learner engagement and immersion. The immersive nature of these environments captivates learners' attention, fostering a sense of presence and agency. By embodying avatars and navigating virtual spaces, learners experience a heightened sense of participation, which is often lacking in traditional online courses. This increased engagement leads to deeper learning experiences and improved knowledge retention. Virtual worlds serve as hubs for collaboration and social learning, transcending geographical barriers. Learners can interact with peers and instructors in real-time, engage in group activities, and co-create content. This collaborative environment mirrors real-world dynamics, fostering teamwork, communication skills, and cultural competence. Additionally, virtual worlds enable educators to facilitate role-playing scenarios, simulations, and problem-based learning activities, enriching the learning experience. The collaborative work displayed here also talks about the growth patterns in virtual learning. However, despite the numerous benefits, the integration of virtual worlds into distance education poses several challenges. Technical barriers, such as hardware and software requirements, accessibility issues, and connectivity constraints, can hinder widespread adoption. Moreover, ensuring the safety and privacy of learners in virtual environments requires robust security measures and vigilant moderation. Additionally, the learning curve associated with navigating virtual worlds may pose challenges for some learners, necessitating adequate training and support.

6. FUTURE DIRECTIONS AND IMPLICATIONS

As virtual worlds continue to evolve, their integration into distance education holds immense potential for innovation and transformation. Future research endeavors should focus on exploring advanced technologies, such as augmented reality and virtual reality, to further enhance the immersive learning experience. Additionally, addressing issues of inclusivity, accessibility, and digital equity will be paramount in ensuring equitable access to virtual learning environments. Moreover, longitudinal studies are needed to assess the long-term efficacy and impact of virtual worlds on learning outcomes and student engagement.

Virtual worlds have already made significant strides in distance education, revolutionizing the way learners interact with content and peers. Looking ahead, several exciting directions emerge for the further integration and enhancement of virtual worlds in distance education. Augmented reality and virtual reality technologies offer unparalleled opportunities for immersive learning experiences. Integrating AR and VR into virtual worlds can elevate the level of immersion and realism, allowing learners to interact with digital content in three-dimensional space. From virtual field trips to complex simulations, AR and VR hold immense potential for enhancing experiential learning in distance education. Leveraging data analytics and artificial intelligence, virtual worlds can be tailored to accommodate individual learning preferences and needs. Personalized avatars, adaptive learning algorithms, and intelligent tutoring systems can dynamically adjust content and pacing to optimize learning outcomes. By catering to learners' unique strengths and challenges, personalized virtual environments can foster deeper engagement and motivation. Ensuring cross-platform accessibility is crucial for broadening the reach of virtual learning environments. Future developments should focus on creating seamless experiences across desktop computers, mobile devices, and emerging technologies. This inclusivity is essential for accommodating diverse learner populations and promoting equitable access to education.

Gamification techniques and interactive narratives can enhance learner engagement and motivation in virtual worlds. By incorporating game elements such as quests, achievements, and leaderboards, educators can transform learning activities into engaging challenges. Interactive narratives, on the other hand, offer immersive storytelling experiences that captivate learners' attention and foster emotional connections with the content. Building upon the collaborative potential of virtual worlds, future developments should focus on creating dynamic learning communities and social spaces. These collaborative environments can facilitate peer-to-peer learning, group projects, and knowledge sharing among learners from diverse backgrounds. By fostering a sense of belonging and community, collaborative learning spaces promote active participation and social interaction. Implementing real-time assessment and feedback mechanisms within virtual worlds can provide valuable insights into learners' progress and comprehension. Interactive quizzes, simulations, and virtual labs enable educators to assess learners' understanding in real-time and provide immediate feedback. This timely feedback loop promotes self-regulated learning and helps learners track their performance effectively. As virtual worlds become increasingly integrated into distance education, it is essential to prioritize ethical considerations and inclusive design practices. This entails ensuring the accessibility of virtual environments for learners with disabilities, fostering diverse representation and cultural sensitivity, and safeguarding learners' privacy and digital rights. By adhering to ethical guidelines and inclusive design principles, virtual learning environments can promote equity, diversity, and inclusivity in education.

7. CONCLUSION

In conclusion, virtual worlds represent a groundbreaking frontier in distance education, offering unprecedented opportunities for immersive, interactive, and collaborative learning experiences. By harnessing the power of technology, educators can transcend the limitations of traditional online learning and cultivate dynamic, engaging environments conducive to knowledge acquisition and skill development. However, addressing technical challenges, ensuring inclusivity, and fostering digital literacy will be essential in realizing the full potential of virtual learning in distance education.

The use of virtual worlds in distance education represents a transformative shift in how learning is conceptualized and delivered. These immersive environments offer a myriad of opportunities for experiential learning, collaboration, and engagement, transcending the limitations of traditional educational approaches. However, realizing the full potential of virtual worlds requires addressing technical challenges, fostering inclusivity and diversity, and embracing emerging technologies and pedagogies. As we navigate the virtual frontier of distance education, let us embark on a journey of innovation and exploration, leveraging the power of virtual worlds to empower learners, inspire creativity, and foster lifelong learning. Together, we can harness the transformative potential of virtual worlds to shape the future of education and build a more inclusive, equitable, and sustainable world for generations to come.

REFERENCES

Arifin, M. H. (2018). The role of student support services in enhancing student persistence in the Open University Context: Lesson from Indonesia Open University. *Turkish Online Journal of Distance Education*, 19(3), 156–168. DOI:10.17718/tojde.445116

Chattopadhyay, S. (2014). Learner Support Services in Open Distance Learning System. *Case Study on IGNOU.*, (June), 1–8.

Hietanen, M., & Svedholm-Häkkinen, A. M. (2023). Transition to Distance Education in 2020 – Challenges among University Faculty in Sweden. *Scandinavian Journal of Educational Research*, 67(3), 433–446. DOI:10.1080/00313831.2021.2021444

Kumar, N., & Sharma, S. (2024). *Demystifying the Technology Adoption by the Asian Cargo Industry*. IGI Global. DOI:10.4018/979-8-3693-1602-3.ch006

Letseka, M. (2016). Open Distance Learning (ODL) through the philosophy of Ubuntu. *Open Distance Learning (ODL) Through the Philosophy of Ubuntu*. Research Gate.

Malighetti, P., Martini, G., Redondi, R., & Scotti, D. (2019). Air transport networks of global integrators in the more liberalized Asian air cargo industry. *Transport Policy*, 80(1), 12–23. DOI:10.1016/j.tranpol.2019.04.021

Martinez-Garcia, A., Horrach-Rosselló, P., & Mulet-Forteza, C. (2023a). Evolution and current state of research into E-learning. *Heliyon*, 9(10), e21016. DOI:10.1016/j.heliyon.2023.e21016 PMID:37867823

Martinez-Garcia, A., Horrach-Rosselló, P., & Mulet-Forteza, C. (2023b). Evolution and current state of research into E-learning. *Heliyon*, 9(10), e21016. DOI:10.1016/j.heliyon.2023.e21016 PMID:37867823

Mas-Tur, A., Modak, N., Merigó, J., & Quantity, N. R.-T.-Q. (2019). *Half a century of Quality & Quantity: a bibliometric review*. Springer. https://link.springer.com/article/10.1007/s11135-018-0799-1

Mir, K. (2016). Design and development of online student support system. *Pak. J. Distance Online Learn*, 3(October), 1–8.

Nandiyanto, A. B. D., & Al Husaeni, D. F. (2021). A bibliometric analysis of materials research in Indonesian journal using VOSviewer. *Journal of Engineering Research (Kuwait)*, 9. DOI:10.36909/jer.ASSEEE.16037

Naseer, M. (2009). Use of bibliometrics in LIS research. *Academia.Edu, 19*(2), 1–12. https://www.academia.edu/download/963587/303n9c3dq8kjbn6.pdf

Pei, L., & Wu, H. (2019). Does online learning work better than offline learning in undergraduate medical education? A systematic review and meta-analysis. *Medical Education Online*, 24(1), 1666538. DOI:10.1080/10872981.2019.1666538 PMID:31526248

Schoech, D., & Helton, D. (2002). Qualitative and Quantitative Analysis of a Course Taught via Classroom and Internet Chatroom. *Qualitative Social Work: Research and Practice*, 1(1), 111–124. DOI:10.1177/1473325002001001748

Seilkhan, A., Abdrassulova, Z., Erkaebaeva, M., Soltan, R., Makhambetov, M., & Ydyrys, A. (2022). Problems of distance education in Kazakhstan during the COVID-19 pandemic. *World Journal on Educational Technology: Current Issues*, 14(2), 380–389. DOI:10.18844/wjet.v14i2.6913

Shtaleva, N. R., Derkho, M. A., Pribytova, O. S., & Shamina, S. V. (2021). Distant learning: Challenges and risks of 2020. *IOP Conference Series. Earth and Environmental Science*, 699(1), 012026. DOI:10.1088/1755-1315/699/1/012026

Singh, V., & Thurman, A. (2019). How Many Ways Can We Define Online Learning? A Systematic Literature Review of Definitions of Online Learning (1988-2018). *American Journal of Distance Education*, 33(4), 289–306. DOI:10.1080/08923647.2019.1663082

Tomyuk, O. N., Diachkova, A. V., Kiseleva, N. A., Kamka, S. V., & Nikolenko, O. I. (2022). Global trends in the education system of high-ranking countries according to PISA-2018. *Perspectives of Science and Education*, 55(1), 10–24. DOI:10.32744/pse.2022.1.1

van Eck, N. J., & Waltman, L. (2017). Citation-based clustering of publications using CitNetExplorer and VOSviewer. *Scientometrics*, 111(2), 1053–1070. DOI:10.1007/s11192-017-2300-7 PMID:28490825

Vermooten, N., & Malan, J. (2021). Relational dynamics amongst personal resources: Consequences for employee engagement. *Sajhrm.Co.Za*, 19(0), 1–12. DOI:10.4102/sajhrm

Volkova, E. N. (2022). Personal characteristics of a 21st-century teacher: An analysis of empirical studies of the problem. *The Education and Science Journal*, 24(3), 126–157. DOI:10.17853/1994-5639-2022-3-126-157

Chapter 12
Virtual Reality (VR)-Based Teaching Strategies for Kindergarten Classes

Maryam Albalushi
Middle East College, Oman

ABSTRACT

This chapter will delve into the world of virtual reality (VR) and its profound impact on kindergarten education. By offering young students immersive experiences that pique their curiosity, encourage exploration, and improve learning outcomes, VR-based teaching strategies present a novel way to engage students. In addition to discussing the many advantages of virtual reality in kindergarten classrooms, this chapter offers educators helpful advice on how to incorporate VR technology into their lesson plans. Furthermore, this chapter contains several sections of VR-based teaching strategies for kindergarten classes.

1. INTRODUCTION

Virtual reality (VR) technology has emerged as both an exciting gaming tool and a technology with a plethora of possible new uses because to the rapid expansion of technological advancements such as high-speed computers, high-resolution graphics, and interface devices (Allcoat & Adrian, 2018). A three-dimensional (3D) computer-generated environment known as virtual reality helps the viewer see the content more realistically. With this technology, the user has a sense of inclusion

DOI: 10.4018/979-8-3693-6407-9.ch012

in the virtual world and gains the ability to perform physical actions and interact with virtual items. (Smith, 2015).

Compared to other forms of media, creating a computer environment that is difficult to tell apart from the actual world enhances the user experience and increases presence and incentive to utilize it (Urech, Krieger, Chesham, Mast, & Berger, 2015).

Virtual reality technology makes it possible to establish an engaging and enjoyable learning environment where students can build their knowledge through active participation, teamwork, and exploration. This increases students' attention and engagement during the learning process (Farahmand, Yadav, & Spafford, 2013).

Research indicates that virtual reality (VR) holds promise as an immersive learning environment and pedagogical tool for students. It offers an authentic context where students can expand their understanding, visualize concepts and situations that cannot be displayed on other media, and gain deeper understanding (Chen, 2016; Huang, Rauch, & Liaw, 2010; Ibáñez et al., 2011).

Moreover, knowledge provided repeatedly and in different ways helps people retain it better, giving educators the chance to cater to each student's "preferred" method of learning (Mayer, 2003). A virtual reality system has the ability to display content repeatedly through many channels or senses and with a variety of delivery methods. In addition to being very visual and aural, it has nonverbal auditory stimuli, which is something that standard teaching approaches lack. This is maybe most significant. Higher levels of cognitive functioning (e.g., interpreting, analyzing, discovering, evaluating, problem-solving, reflective thinking, and memorization) are achieved when learning experiences are more realistic and include auditory cues like the sound of chemical reactions or objects falling to the floor. (Bell and Folger, 1995).

The ability of virtual reality (VR) to present objects that are not typically visible or tangible in the real world is another crucial feature. Examples of such objects include mathematical theories represented on a surface that students can walk on, or students can walk around or inside the nucleus of a cell as it divides or look inside a heart artery in biology class (Persky & McBride, 2009). Students become more engaged with the subject matter and the learning process is enhanced when abstract concepts are represented in a more concrete way. It becomes simpler to interact with and absorb theoretical ideas, which are frequently dry and occasionally challenging to understand.

One important result of this technology is that it fulfills the principles of constructivist learning (Piaget, 1974). Constructivism is a theory that connects learning to the process of making meaning from experience. Its guiding principles include the use of interactive teaching techniques and the development of meaningful learning environments that encourage, inspire, and stimulate students' construction of knowledge (Piaget, 1974). Both immersive and non-immersive virtual reality (VR) can meet these goals by providing students with authentic, contextual, and discovery-based learning activities that foster a diversity of thought patterns and create intrinsic motivation. Students can also take charge of the content, sequencing, and learning strategies to build their own knowledge.

These possibilities are made possible by the computer-generated environment's sensation of presence, which enables more natural interaction between the participant and the VR world and improves learning outcomes (Lee, Wong, & Fung, 2010). By increasing the realism of the stimuli and including the user as an active participant, immersive VR drives users deeper into the simulation as the virtual world feels genuine and all-encompassing (Persky & Eccleston, 2011). According to Sundararajan, Wang, and Bowman (2008), this realism can improve spatial cues and help people create a precise mental map that can be utilized as a memory aid when learning complicated procedures.

Although the majority of the time, this technology has been used with adults, but there are a few pilot projects and ongoing studies that are proving the benefits of using IVR technology with kids in various disciplines. These studies, however, are scarce (Gabyzon, Engel-Yeger, Tresser, & Springer, 2016; Gershon, Zimand, Pickering, Rothbaum, & Hodges, 2004; Passig, Tzuriel, & Eshel-Kedmi, 2016). The makers of VR headsets also include a disclaimer stating that children under the age of 12 or 13 should not use their products; however, they haven't explained why. The available data supports the promise of this technology as a teaching aid, but also casts doubt on how successful it is when used with young learners.

This paper aims to provide an overview of the potential of IVR technology as a teaching tool by describing its uses and potential applications with children in education. Specifically, it will explore the concepts that underlie this potential, as well as the latest research and applications of IVR with children for educational purposes, as well as the constraints and limitations of using IVR in classroom settings.

1.1 Virtual reality: the context

1.1.1. Historical background

The concept of "virtual reality" dates back to 1957, when cinematographer Morton Heiling created the Sensorama Simulator (Heilig, 1961) to pique viewers' senses and deepen their immersion in the story. One of the earliest documented instances of immersive technology is the Sensorama Simulator. According to Srivastava, Chaudhury, and Das (2014), the device could imitate motion with a wide field of vision, stereo noises, fragrances, wind generated by a fan, vibration, and body tilting through the seat.

capable of displaying a large field of vision, stereo audio, scents, wind generated by a fan, and motion simulations such as body tilting and vibration through the seat (Srivastava, Chaudhury, & Das, 2014).

In 1961, Philco Corporation invented the Headsight System, which was the forerunner of today's virtual reality head-mounted display (HMD). The device had a magnetic motion tracking system connected to a closed-circuit camera, as well as a video screen for each of the user's eyes. The technology was designed for the military to replicate hazardous conditions encountered in combat operations and to give helicopter pilots a clean field of vision when flying in the dark (Srivastava et al., 2014). (Mazuryk, Gervautz, & Smith, 2013). The first VR gadget that was made available for purchase and the name "virtual reality" were not developed until the late 1980s (Dixon, 2006).

VR was mostly utilized for medical, aviation simulation, industrial design, and military training between 1970 and 1990. However, by 1994, gaming firms like SEGA and Nintendo had begun to create and market consumer VR games (Mazuryk et al., 2013). Many mainstream IT businesses are now working on VR-related goods. Since 2013, when the business Oculus Rift unveiled a new generation of consumer-priced VR technology, the cost of the technology has significantly decreased (Jensen & Konradsen, 2017). VR technology is increasingly being considered by schools as a teaching tool because it has become more widely available and affordable.

1.1.2. Types of virtual reality systems

To portray the virtual world and enable human interaction, the six different types of VR systems employ various tools and equipment. Even though there is a wide variety of systems available, many of the ones listed in Table 1 cannot be used in educational settings due to either the equipment's costly cost or its unsuitability (i.e., vehicle-base).

Many fields, including education, healthcare, engineering, journalism, and the military, have adopted immersive virtual reality (VR) as a popular tool (Abulrub, Attridge, & Williams, 2011; Allcoat & Adrian, 2018; Bhagat, Liou, & Chang, 2016; Rizzo et al., 2011). Immersion virtual reality (VR) is a perceptually surrounding visual and multisensory computer-simulated environment that gives the user the impression that they are inside or that they may interact with the created world (Blascovich et al., 2002). It is beneficial for a variety of reasons because to its versatility, high degree of realism, and capacity to maintain strict experimental control (Persky & McBride, 2009).

In addition, IVR is always changing, and at this point, the HMD is a necessary part that allows users to see 3D computer-generated visuals within a helmet. The HMD provides a compelling sense of personal, social, and environmental presence and a unique immersion experience by using an inertial and video tracking system to trace the position and orientation of a user's head, hands, or even the entire body by using special gloves, vest, or suit (Blascovich et al., 2002). Additionally, this apparatus has the ability to present and control thermal, haptic, gustatory, auditory, or olfactory stimuli (Persky & McBride, 2009; Smith, 2015).

2. SECTION: UNDERSTANDING THE BENEFITS OF VR FOR KINDERGARTEN EDUCATION

In recent years, there has been an increase in the use of virtual reality (VR) in education. Technological advancements in the twenty-first century and easier access to digital devices like tablets and smartphones have encouraged its acceptance. The question of how widely and profoundly these technologies will be used has replaced the question of when they will be used. As a result, it's critical to consider how new technologies will enhance instruction in early childhood classrooms.

This section will define virtual reality (VR), discuss its advantages, and discuss potential drawbacks for early learning. Principals, educators, legislators, and other stakeholders who are interested in using these digital tools for early education can benefit from our deeper understanding of these tools.

Using head-mounted goggles, headphones, and/or wired clothing, virtual reality (VR) immerses users in a completely made-up environment while simulating certain senses. Through this experience, the user's physical surroundings are obscured, and a digital representation of a separate environment is created. VR uses auditory, visual, and other sensory interactions to give the user the impression of being in a 3D area or another environment. Complete immersion produces the impression of being physically present in a situation that is either artificially created or simulates reality. Users of virtual reality have direct interaction with virtual world things. Wearing a virtual reality headset, kids may investigate an artificial rainforest and uncover insects hidden beneath leaves and pebbles. They can get a taste of life in novel and exotic locations, like residing on an international space station or discovering underwater life.

Virtual reality (VR) has been utilized in a variety of fields, including research, medical, design, the armed forces, athletics, and higher education. Through virtual simulations, VR can help people with physical limitations enhance their fine motor skills and be used during rehabilitation. VR can assist medical practitioners in practicing surgery, learning how to interact with patients, and comprehending medical ideas. Virtual reality (VR) can be used to alleviate anxiety in patients by using exposure therapy and to enhance mental health and well-being by immersing users in mindfulness activities. In educational contexts, virtual reality (VR) offers chances for children to participate in immersive storytelling activities and receive a variety of cultural and historical experiences. It also allows teachers and students to collaborate and work within virtual worlds. (Michelle Margaret Neumann, Meryl Keioskie, David L Neumann and Dale Patterson, 2022)

2.1 Benefits for Early Learning

Virtual reality (VR) offers many prospects for nurturing ingenuity and cooperative education alongside peers. Children can learn to be more involved and self-assured in their ability to complete tasks by using virtual reality.

Early childhood education (ECE) is crucial. Early childhood education is crucial because it lays the groundwork for learning and growth throughout one's life. Early schooling aids in children's development and acquisition of new abilities. Children's early experiences aid in the development of critical skills as per shown in figure 1 below which descript the benefit point of early learning.

Cognitive Growth: Strengthens analytical reasoning, solves problems, and improves academic performance.

Socio-Emotional Development: Promotes positive social interactions and resilience in emotional intelligence.

Physical Development: Through active play, children develop their gross and fine motor skills.

Imagination and creativity: Promotes curiosity, discovery, and original thought.

Formal Schooling Readiness: Provides kids with the knowledge and self-assurance they need to make a smooth transition to elementary school.

Early childhood education program investments build a solid foundation for future success for the child as well as positive ripple effects on families and communities. (WOHM, 2023)

Figure 1. Early childhood education

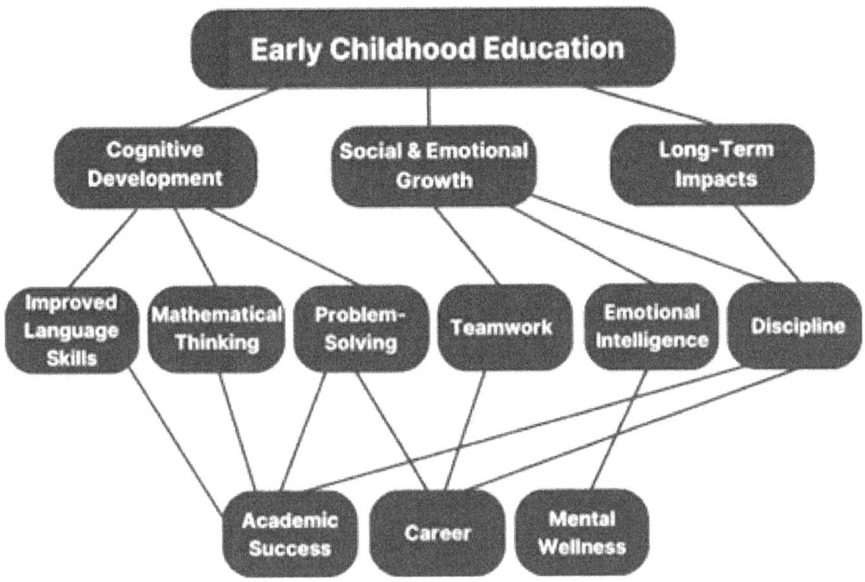

Moreover, there are many factors that influence early childhood education due to the rapid development of technology, so the following points illustrate this:

1. Immersive Technology in Early Elementary: keep the following in mind when considering using immersive technology:
2. Safety: any digital tool used with young children should be designed and tested as safe for their age range.
3. Simplicity: start with tools that are easy to use and explain to young users.
4. Engagement And Interactivity: young students are more likely to stay engaged and benefit if the tool allows for interactivity.
5. Curriculum: content being presented should be connected to the curriculum.

Immersive Learning settings: Describes how virtual reality (VR) submerges kids in virtual worlds to create dynamic and captivating learning settings.

Instances of virtual reality apps that mimic authentic experiences that are pertinent to kindergarten curricula, such discovering the outdoors, historical sites, or creative environments.

Multi-Sensory Stimulation: Multi-sensory virtual reality (VR) activities have the potential to drastically change the way that children are taught since they provide engaging and immersive learning experiences. By combining visual, aural, and tactile stimuli, virtual reality (VR) produces a dynamic and interactive experience that concurrently engages several senses.

Multi-sensory virtual reality exercises provide several advantages for young children, one of which is improved learning retention and engagement. Passive learning is a common teaching strategy used by traditional educators, where students read or listen to lectures before processing the material. On the other hand, youngsters actively participate in the teaching process when they engage in multisensory VR activities. By submerging pupils in virtual environments and presenting knowledge through visual and aural cues, virtual reality (VR) can enhance learning. Combining several sensory inputs results in a multifaceted experience that draws kids in and enhances their memory of the material.

Multi-sensory virtual reality exercises also offer the benefit of experience-based learning opportunities. Through VR simulations, kids can investigate a range of concepts and scenarios in a safe and intact virtual environment. For example, they can visit historical places, delve into the seas, or travel to space. Through these immersive experiences, children may actively participate in the learning process, which fosters a deeper understanding of the material. VR exercises heighten the reality and authenticity of the educational experience by appealing to many senses, creating a sense of presence.

Active learning and problem-solving are further promoted by multimodal VR experiences. Youngsters are encouraged to engage with virtual surroundings and things since it allows them to experiment and modify in ways that aren't feasible in traditional school settings. Children using this hands-on approach to complete virtual jobs and challenges are encouraged to think critically and solve problems. Through the utilization of both cognitive and motor skills, these exercises offer a more comprehensive educational experience.

Diverse learning styles and aptitudes can also be accommodated by multimodal VR exercises. Regarding their learning preferences and strengths, each child is unique. Because virtual reality is multi-sensory, it may be used in many ways to engage learners, including auditory, kinesthetic, and visual learners. Because VR activities offer personalized and flexible learning opportunities, they can also be advantageous for kids with specific needs or learning challenges. By adjusting the content and interaction techniques, virtual reality (VR) can provide a more welcoming and easily accessible learning environment.

Children's imagination and creativity are stimulated by multimodal VR exercises. Users can explore new worlds, interact with objects, and test out ideas because virtual reality is immersive. They are motivated to think creatively since they are free to develop and create. Virtual reality (VR) provides a platform for narrative, artistic production, and imaginative play, which in turn fosters children's creativity and self-expression.

Multisensory virtual reality activities can also facilitate group learning. By connecting numerous VR devices or using shared virtual worlds, children may collaborate and communicate with their peers in real time. They can cooperate on assignments, resolve conflicts as a group, and learn from each other's perspectives. This cooperative component develops communication skills, interpersonal connections, and group dynamics—all essential for their academic and personal growth. Figure 2 illustrates the description of the virtual reality activities.

Figure 2. Virtual reality activities

Although there are many benefits to multimodal VR activities, it's vital to keep in mind that they should be utilized in addition to traditional teaching methods, not in instead of them. They function best when included in a comprehensive curriculum that includes face-to-face communication, hands-on activities, and exposure to the real world. Careful supervision and moderation are also necessary to guarantee that youngsters are using VR for the proper amount of time and with acceptable material. (Group, 2024)

The body and brain arrange internal and exterior stimuli through sensory processing, which enables the body to work efficiently and make sense of the environment. Most people recognize the five main senses. Sight, smell, hearing, touch, and taste are among these senses. I'll briefly review these senses, along with the significance of two less well-known senses for development: vestibular perception and proprioception. The internal sensory and perception systems that comprise nociception (pain) also include proprioception and vestibular perception. Furthermore, there are seven human senses which are vision sense, Hearing sense, smell sense, touch sense, proprioception sense and vestibular sense as per illustration in figure 3.

1. Visual Sense

The process of seeing the world through one's eyes is called sight. It is accomplished by a difficult procedure combining several eye components. Light is perceived by the eye, and it is interpreted as visual representations by the brain.

2. Smell Sense

Information is obtained through smell by stimulating chemical receptors in the upper respiratory tract and nose.

3. Hearing Sense

The brain interprets inner ear vibrations as sound information when we hear.

4. Sense of Taste

The five flavors that are perceived as taste are sweet, salty, sour, bitter, and umami, or savory. The tongue's taste buds are used to detect taste. There is a notion that there are flavor-specific zones on the tongue. All five tastes, however, are detectable on every portion of the tongue, despite the sides of the tongue being more sensitive than the center.

5. Touch Sense

Numerous sensations that are transmitted between skin and brain neurons make up touch. Pressure, discomfort, temperature, and vibration are a few examples of these experiences. It is believed that touch is a sense that is utilized for purposes beyond interacting with the actual environment. It is seen as being crucial to human welfare as well.

6. Proprioception

Proprioception, which encompasses the sense of movement, limb position, and muscular motions, is the awareness of one's presence in space. It enables us to perform tasks like climbing stairs without having to look at them. Individuals with low proprioception could come across as awkward and uncoordinated.

7. Perception of the vestibular system

The sensory system that feeds information about motion, head position, and spatial orientation to our brains is called the vestibular system. (Ross, 2003)

Figure 3. Sensory menu

An investigation of the advantages of multimodal learning for young children's cognitive growth and content engagement.

Personalized and Adaptive Learning: An analysis of the ways in which VR apps can be tailored to kindergarten students' unique learning requirements and preferences.

Instances of VR experiences that are adaptable in that they modify content, tempo, and difficulty levels according to the skills and interests of each child.

3. SECTION: IMPLEMENTING VR-BASED TEACHING STRATEGIES IN KINDERGARTEN CLASSROOMS

Artificial intelligence, computer graphics, sensor technology, and human-computer interface technology have all come together to create the innovative field of virtual reality technology. Utilizing its immersive, interactive, and conceptual qualities, virtual reality technology has been used more and more in the field of education. VR-based learning provides students with a variety of positive emotions, such as relaxation, enjoyment, and interest, in contrast to traditional teaching approaches, which might increase their intrinsic drive to learn. Furthermore, VR technology satisfies the requirements of contextual learning by offering a wide range of perceptual signals and multimodal (such as audio and visual) input, which helps transfer knowledge from virtual scenarios to real-life contexts. For instance, suggested that virtual reality technology is a key tool supporting the revolution of education.

Choosing Relevant VR Content: Instructions for teachers on how to match curriculum-aligned and age-appropriate VR experiences for kindergarten children.

- Factors to consider while evaluating the safety, interaction, and educational value of VR content.

When selecting VR content for kindergarten classes, it's essential to choose experiences that are age-appropriate, engaging, and educational. Here's a detailed guide on how to choose relevant VR content for young children, along with illustrative examples:

Key Considerations for Choosing VR Content for Kindergarten

1. Age Appropriateness
    - **Simplicity**: Ensure the content is simple and intuitive. Young children benefit from straightforward navigation and minimal complexity.
    - **Duration**: VR experiences should be short to match the limited attention span of kindergarteners. Aim for content that lasts between 5 to 15 minutes.
2. Educational Value

- **Learning Goals**: Choose content that aligns with early childhood education goals, such as basic literacy, numeracy, social skills, or understanding of the natural world.
- **Interactive Elements**: Look for interactive content that encourages exploration and learning through play.

3. Safety and Comfort
   - **Comfort**: Ensure the VR content is designed to be comfortable and safe for young children. Avoid content that might cause motion sickness or discomfort.
   - **Parental/Teacher Supervision**: The content should be designed to be used with supervision, considering the role of teachers or parents in guiding the experience.
4. Engaging and Fun
   - **Visual Appeal**: Bright, colorful, and visually stimulating content tends to be more engaging for young children.
   - **Narration and Guidance**: Look for content with friendly characters or narrators that can guide children through the experience.
5. Platform and Hardware Compatibility
   - **User-Friendly Devices**: Ensure the VR hardware is suitable for young children. Many VR headsets may be too large or heavy for kindergarten-aged kids, so consider lightweight options.
   - **Ease of Use**: The VR content should be easy to start and operate with minimal technical requirements.

There are several examples of relevant VR content for kindergarten as follows:

1. Educational Adventures
   - **Example**: *The Curious VR Adventures* – An interactive VR experience where children explore a magical world filled with educational mini-games and puzzles designed for early learners.
2. Exploring Nature
   - **Example**: *Virtual Zoo* – Allows children to explore a virtual zoo where they can learn about different animals through fun and interactive experiences.
3. Storytelling and Imaginative Play
   - **Example**: *Storytime VR* – Provides immersive storytelling experiences where children can interact with characters and environments in classic children's tales.
4. Basic Skills Development

- **Example**: *ABC VR Adventure* – Helps children learn the alphabet through engaging visual and interactive elements that encourage letter recognition and phonics.

There are some tips for implementing VR in the classroom for kindergarten in the future as mentioned below:

- **Trial Runs**: Test the VR content in a classroom setting before full implementation to ensure it works well and engages the children.
- **Teacher Training**: Educators should be familiar with how to use the VR equipment and content effectively.
- **Feedback**: Gather feedback from both children and teachers to refine and improve the VR experiences.

By selecting VR content that aligns with these guidelines, you can provide kindergarten students with enriching and enjoyable learning experiences that foster curiosity and early development.

Including Virtual Reality in Lesson Plans:

Techniques for incorporating VR activities into lesson plans and curriculum goals that are already in place. Suggestions for creating VR-enhanced learning programs that support interactive inquiry and enhance in-class learning.

Encouraging Cooperative Virtual Reality Experiences:

Investigating cooperative virtual reality platforms and tools that promote cooperation and social interaction among kindergarten pupils. The best ways to support conversations, group projects, and cooperative learning in online settings. Imagine witnessing the remains of an old Roman city come to life or strolling along the edge of an active volcano. It is not always necessary to imagine these days. These kinds of rich experiences can be brought to schools using virtual reality (VR), which can stimulate students' minds. Now that this technology has advanced, it is truly starting to reach its full potential. Furthermore, the effects might be particularly significant in the field of education.

In addition, VR in the classroom can have fascinating benefits for schools, as shown by the following points:

1. Concentrated Immersion via Virtual Learning

Although it is mostly a logistical consideration, this is worth highlighting. Because virtual reality is framed within a headset, learners are less likely to be distracted by outside distractions. The actual immersion of learners in learning is a major contributor to the retention of knowledge.

Although it is mostly a logistical consideration, this is worth highlighting. Because virtual reality is framed within a headset, learners are less likely to be distracted by outside distractions. The actual immersion of learners in learning is a major contributor to the retention of knowledge.

With the use of technology, students can receive individualized instruction that has been connected to both higher academic achievement and deeper brain learning. Students absorb information more fully the more personally invested they are in it. A student's brain genuinely transforms and becomes more receptive once they become inspired by a subject.

2. Multi-Sensory Experiences

Tablets have improved the multimedia experience of digital information by adding touchscreen functionality, but they lack the kinesthetic experience that virtual reality offers. Being there, as opposed to being a passive spectator, is the real VR magic that lets you live a tale. Students' thoughts, feelings, and even behavior may be affected by it.

As a result, instead of just seeing what they would have seen in a picture or graphic, kids may truly feel it and perceive it in three dimensions. This firsthand knowledge expands comprehension beyond what can be found in two-dimensional texts and computer screens.

3. Enhanced Involvement in the Classroom

While the average student can recall 20% of what they see and 30% of what they hear, in traditional classroom settings, pupils frequently have limited comprehension of complicated concepts, theories, and subjects due to the limited amount of information provided by illustrations and explanations.

This is due to the fact that even if they may view the explanation on an image, they still need to mentally picture and form an opinion on it. Instead of learning the subject by listening, reading, or simply seeing a two-dimensional picture, people may effortlessly explore numerous realities and views of what they are learning thanks to VR and AR.

Research indicates that when knowledge is acquired through hands-on activities, pupils retain 90% of the content. This demonstrates even further how VR and AR are enhancing education. Figure 4 illustrates the percentage of educators supporting the use of digital technologies in the classroom.

Figure 4. Digital technology in the classroom

Teachers are fully aware that every student has a unique learning style. Some people are happy to lose themselves in a book's pages. On the other hand, other people require exercise, while still others require interactions akin to those in a game. All of these pupils stand to benefit from the use of virtual and augmented reality. For educators, developing a fruitful relationship with pupils can be quite difficult. This is an easily manageable aspect with virtual reality.

4. Education: Pushing the Boundaries

Providing the opportunity to virtually visit remote or physically inaccessible locations is the most popular usage of virtual reality. By making travel and educational opportunities accessible to people who might not otherwise have them, virtual reality (VR) has the potential to democratize education. Virtual field excursions are essentially free, but going on several field trips over the academic year might get expensive. Similar to this, virtual reality (VR) enables educators and learners to see far more of the world from the comforts of the classroom than they could in the past.

5. VR Is Adaptable

There are countless solutions on the market that can accommodate a wide range of financial needs and educational needs. With a variety of multimedia formats, including VR, 3D, and panoramic movies, educational institutions can customize their own VR learning programs. They can also make changes to the program in the future.

6. Establish Cybersecure Classrooms

The hazards usually connected with internet use are eliminated in the classroom when virtual reality technology is used. Students using VR software can only access content that has been specifically designed for them. They won't run the risk of visiting unsuitable websites or reading content meant for younger audiences.

7. Helping Students with Special Needs

With the use of virtual reality, students with disabilities—whether they be psychological or physical—can thrive. Virtual reality has no physical bounds. Programs can be customized using conventional teaching techniques to help those whose growth was previously sluggish. Undoubtedly, it provides access to certain opportunities that were previously thought to be closed. (Group S. M., 2019)

4. SECTION: OVERCOMING CHALLENGES AND ENSURING ETHICAL USE OF VR IN KINDERGARTEN EDUCATION

VR's significance for kindergarten: virtual reality (VR) can help kindergarten teachers achieve several learning objectives, such as social skills, reading, numeracy, and cognitive development. But it's imperative to deal with the related issues and make sure VR is applied morally and successfully. Several points describe the challenges in implementing VR in kindergarten education in more detail as mentioned below:

- **Technical Challenges**
  - **Hardware and Software Compatibility**: VR systems need to be compatible with both the hardware and software used in the classroom. Ensuring that devices are up-to-date, and function properly is essential for a smooth educational experience.

- **Maintenance and Technical Support**: Regular maintenance and reliable technical support are necessary to prevent and address any issues that may arise with VR equipment.

- **Developmental Appropriateness**
  - **Age-Appropriate Content**: Content should be tailored to the developmental level of kindergarten students, ensuring that it is both understandable and engaging.
  - **Attention Span and Interaction**: VR experiences should be short and interactive to match the attention spans and developmental stages of young children.
- **Health and Safety Concerns**
  - **Physical Safety**: Safe use of VR requires clear guidelines and supervised environments to prevent accidents and ensure that children are using the equipment correctly.
  - **Eye Strain and Motion Sickness**: VR content should be designed to minimize risks of eye strain and motion sickness, with breaks and limitations on usage time.
- **Accessibility Issues**
  - **Equity and Access to Technology**: Addressing disparities in access to VR technology ensures that all students have the opportunity to benefit from these experiences.
  - **Adaptations for Diverse Needs**: VR experiences should be adaptable to accommodate children with different learning needs and disabilities.

Handling Technical Considerations: Typical technical obstacles to VR implementation in kindergarten classes and advice for teachers on how to overcome them. Techniques for guaranteeing that students have access to VR equipment and resolving possible inequalities in student technology access.

Ensuring Ethical and Responsible Use: A discussion of privacy, safety, and digital citizenship as well as other ethical issues surrounding the use of VR technology with young children. Instructional materials for teachers on how to minimize hazards and encourage appropriate and responsible behavior in online settings.

Objective:

1. To engage the children of interactive and visually stimulating environments, capturing their attention and enhancing their engagement with the learning material.
2. An extend to Experiential Learning to experience concepts firsthand

3. To stimulate multiple senses simultaneously, providing a rich and multi-dimensional learning experience which caters to different learning styles and preferences.
4. To create and enhance creativity tailored to individual learning needs which allows kindergarten to progress at their own pace and explore topics according to their interests.

All things considered, VR-based teaching techniques have the power to completely transform kindergarten education by offering creative, captivating, and successful learning opportunities that meet the requirements and interests of young students.

Using virtual reality (VR) in kindergarten classrooms can be a creative method to get students interested in learning and improve their academic experience. Here is a suggestion for VR-based kindergarten teaching methods:

1. Interactive Storytelling

Provide virtual reality storytelling experiences that allow kids to participate in the narrative. They can make decisions that affect the story's course, which helps them hone their critical thinking and judgment abilities.

2. Multisensory Learning

Create virtual reality apps that appeal to the senses of touch, sound, and vision. As an illustration, consider a virtual reality gardening simulation that allows kids to sow seeds, water plants, and observe their growth all while experiencing the tactile feedback of the soil and plants.

3. Virtual Manipulatives

With virtual manipulatives, replicate hands-on learning experiences in virtual reality. Kindergarteners can use virtual blocks, shapes, and puzzles to master fundamental math skills including sorting, counting, and spatial thinking.

4. Language Learning

Construct virtual reality spaces where kids can communicate with multilingual characters. This can encourage early language development by introducing children to simple words and phrases in an entertaining and interesting way.

5. Social Skills Development

Create cooperative virtual reality exercises that promote social interaction and teamwork. Cooperative games, such as those that require kids to solve puzzles or do tasks together, can help them develop their collaboration and communication skills.

6. Virtual Art Studio

Give kids access to a virtual creative studio where they may express their imaginations through 3D painting, sculpture, and drawing. Virtual reality tools can provide countless opportunities for exploration and artistic expression.

7. Emotional Regulation Training

Create virtual reality settings that aid kids in recognizing and controlling their emotions. In a secure and regulated virtual setting, they can practice mindfulness exercises, relaxation methods, and conflict resolution strategies.

8. Customizable Learning Environments

Permit educators to alter virtual reality experiences according to each student's unique learning style and needs. Because of its adaptability, learning paths can be tailored to the individual abilities and interests of every child.

5. CONCLUSION

Virtual Reality (VR)-based teaching approaches have great potential to improve kindergarten education by offering individualized, captivating, and immersive learning experiences. Through an awareness of the advantages of virtual reality technology and the application of best practices in the classroom, educators may make the most of this innovative tool to stimulate young minds, encourage curiosity, and develop a lifetime love of learning. Furthermore, by providing immersive, engaging, and enjoyable learning experiences, multi-sensory virtual reality (VR) activities have the potential to drastically alter the way that kids learn. Virtual reality (VR) enhances learning retention, promotes active learning and problem-solving abilities, adapts to different learning styles, stimulates creativity, and facilitates cooperation by appealing to numerous senses. Moreover, Teachers may create dynamic and immersive learning experiences that encourage children's curiosity, creativity, and cognitive development by incorporating VR into kindergarten classrooms. This virtual reality (VR) based teaching techniques have the power to completely transform early childhood education and equip young students for success in the digital age.

REFERENCES

Abulrub, A.-H. G., Attridge, A. N., & Williams, M. A. (2011). Virtual reality in engineering education: The future of creative learning. *2011 IEEE Global Engineering Education Conference (EDUCON)*, (pp. 751–757). IEEE. DOI:10.1109/EDUCON.2011.5773223

Allcoat, D., & Adrian, M. (2018). Learning in virtual reality: Effects on performance, emotion and engagement. *Research in Learning Technology*, 26(1063519), 1–13. DOI:10.25304/rlt.v26.2140

Bell, J. T., & Fogler, H. S. (1995, June). The investigation and application of virtual reality as an educational tool. In *Proceedings of the American society for engineering education annual conference* (Vol. 2513). Research Gate.

Bhagat, K. K., Liou, W.-K., & Chang, C.-Y. (2016). A cost-effective interactive 3D virtual reality system applied to military live firing training. *Virtual Reality (Waltham Cross)*, 20(2), 127–140. DOI:10.1007/s10055-016-0284-x

Blascovich, J., Loomis, J., Beall, A. C., Swinth, K. R., Hoyt, C. L., & Bailenson, J. N. (2002). Immersive Virtual Environment Technology as a Methodological Tool for Social Psychology. *Psychological Inquiry*, 13(2), 103–124. DOI:10.1207/S15327965PLI1302_01

Chen, Y. L. (2016). The effects of virtual reality learning environment on student cognitive and linguistic development. *The Asia-Pacific Education Researcher*, 25(4), 637–646. DOI:10.1007/s40299-016-0293-2

Dixon, S. (2006). A history of virtual reality in performance. *International Journal of Performance Arts and Digital Media*, 2(1), 23–54. DOI:10.1386/padm.2.1.23/1

Farahmand, F., Yadav, A., & Spafford, E. H. (2013). Risks and uncertainties in virtual worlds: An educators' perspective. *Journal of Computing in Higher Education*, 25(2), 49–67. DOI:10.1007/s12528-013-9067-5

Gabyzon, M. E., Engel-Yeger, B., Tresser, S., & Springer, S. (2016). Using a virtual reality game to assess goal-directed hand movements in children: A pilot feasibility study. *Technology and Health Care*, 24(1), 11–19. DOI:10.3233/THC-151041 PMID:26409528

Gershon, J., Zimand, E., Pickering, M., Rothbaum, B. O., & Hodges, L. (2004). A Pilot and Feasibility Study of Virtual Reality as a Distraction for Children With Cancer. *Journal of the American Academy of Child and Adolescent Psychiatry*, 43(10), 1243–1249. DOI:10.1097/01.chi.0000135621.23145.05 PMID:15381891

Heilig, M. L. (1961). US patent 3050870A. https://patents.google.com/patent/US3050870A/en?oq=3%2C050%2C870

Huang, H. M., Rauch, U., & Liaw, S. S. (2010). Investigating learners' attitudes toward virtual reality learning environments: Based on a constructivist approach. *Computers & Education*, 55(3), 1171–1182. DOI:10.1016/j.compedu.2010.05.014

Ibáñez, M. B., García, J. J., Galán, S., Maroto, D., Morillo, D., & Kloos, C. D. (2011). Design and implementation of a 3D multi-user virtual world for language learning. *Journal of Educational Technology & Society*, 14(4), 2–10.

Jensen, L., & Konradsen, F. (2017). A review of the use of virtual reality head-mounted displays in education and training. *Education and Information Technologies*, 23(4), 1515–1529. DOI:10.1007/s10639-017-9676-0

Lee, E. A. L., Wong, K. W., & Fung, C. C. (2010). How does desktop virtual reality enhance learning outcomes? A structural equation modeling approach. *Computers & Education*, 55(4), 1424–1442. DOI:10.1016/j.compedu.2010.06.006

Mayer, R. E. (2003). The promise of multimedia learning: Using the same instructional design methods across different media. *Learning and Instruction*, 13(2), 125–139. DOI:10.1016/S0959-4752(02)00016-6

Mazuryk, T., Gervautz, M., & Smith, K. (2013). Virtual Reality History, Applications, Technology and Future. *Digital Outcasts, 63*(ISIE), 92–98. doi.org/10.1016/B978-0-12-404705-1.00006-6

Neumann, M. M., Keioskie, M. K., Patterson, D., & Neumann, D. L. (2022). Virtual, augmented, and mixed reality: Benefits and barriers for early childhood education. *Childhood Education*, 98(4), 68–79. DOI:10.1080/00094056.2022.2108298

Passig, D., Tzuriel, D., & Eshel-Kedmi, G. (2016). Improving children's cognitive modifiability by dynamic assessment in 3D Immersive Virtual Reality environments. *Computers & Education*, 95, 296–308. DOI:10.1016/j.compedu.2016.01.009

Persky, S., & Eccleston, C. P. (2011). Medical student bias and care recommendations for an obese versus non-obese virtual patient. *International Journal of Obesity*, 35(5), 728–735. DOI:10.1038/ijo.2010.173 PMID:20820169

Persky, S., & McBride, C. M. (2009). Immersive virtual environment technology: A promising tool for future social and behavioral genomics research and practice. *Health Communication*, 24(8), 677–682. DOI:10.1080/10410230903263982 PMID:20183376

Piaget, J. (1974). *Understanding causality.(Trans. D. & M. Miles)*. WW Norton.

Rizzo, A., Parsons, T. D., Lange, B., Kenny, P., Buckwalter, J. G., Rothbaum, B., Difede, J. A., Frazier, J., Newman, B., Williams, J., & Reger, G. (2011). Virtual Reality Goes to War: A Brief Review of the Future of Military Behavioral Healthcare. *Journal of Clinical Psychology in Medical Settings*, 18(2), 176–187. DOI:10.1007/s10880-011-9247-2 PMID:21553133

Ross, M. D. (2003). The evolution of concepts of vestibular peripheral information processing: Toward the dynamic, adaptive, parallel processing macular model. *Acta Oto-Laryngologica*, 123(7), 784–794. DOI:10.1080/00016480310000719 PMID:14575392

Smith, J. W. (2015). Immersive virtual environment technology to supplement environmental perception, preference and behavior research: A review with applications. *International Journal of Environmental Research and Public Health*, 12(9), 11486–11505. DOI:10.3390/ijerph120911486 PMID:26378565

Srivastava, K., Chaudhury, S., & Das, R. (2014). Virtual reality applications in mental health: Challenges and perspectives. *Industrial Psychiatry Journal*, 23(2), 83. DOI:10.4103/0972-6748.151666 PMID:25788795

Urech, A., Krieger, T., Chesham, A., Mast, F. W., & Berger, T. (2015). Virtual reality-based attention bias modification training for social anxiety: A feasibility and proof of concept study. *Frontiers in Psychiatry*, 6, 154. DOI:10.3389/fpsyt.2015.00154 PMID:26578986

WOHM. (2023). *Benefit of early childhood education.* WOHM. https://wohum.org/the-benefits-of-early-childhood-education-and-its-effect-on-future-success/?gad_source=1&gclid=CjwKCAjwko21BhAPEiwAwfaQCIwWOmK2Kp27qFw7sAAjUItKVsCIS2XwjzgnDQNbtNJ3bLbE1H6MChoC8h4QAvD_BwE

Chapter 13
Virtual Reality in Engineering:
Innovations and Applications

S. Suresh
https://orcid.org/0000-0001-8840-0786
Department of Mechanical Engineering, Erode Sengunthar Engineering College, Erode, India India

ABSTRACT

Virtual reality (VR) has transitioned from a futuristic concept to a practical tool with wide-ranging applications in engineering. By immersing users in interactive digital environments, VR enhances spatial understanding, improves design accuracy, and facilitates comprehensive testing. This chapter explores the transformative potential of VR across various engineering fields, emphasizing its impact on design, simulation, training, and maintenance processes. This chapter covers the integration of VR in mechanical, civil, and biomedical engineering, highlighting its benefits in prototyping, fluid dynamics, architectural visualization, safety training, surgical simulation, and more. The future of VR in engineering looks promising, with advancements in AI and sensor technology poised to further revolutionize the field. Through detailed exploration, this chapter provides insights into the multifaceted applications of VR, showcasing its ability to drive innovation and improve outcomes across the engineering industry.

DOI: 10.4018/979-8-3693-6407-9.ch013

1. INTRODUCTION

Virtual Reality (VR) is a simulated experience that can be similar to or completely different from the real world. It immerses users in computer-generated virtual surroundings, allowing them to interact in a seemingly real or physical way through the use of specialized equipment, such as headsets and motion controllers. VR is used in various fields, including gaming, education, healthcare, engineering, and entertainment, to provide immersive experiences that engage the user's senses and allow for interactive exploration.

The various compounds include VR headsets, Motion Controllers, Tracking Systems, Computing Devices, and Software. The interlinking of VR compounds is represented in Figure 1. The most critical component, the VR headset, is worn over the eyes and provides a stereoscopic display. It often includes sensors for tracking head movements, allowing the virtual surroundings to adjust as the user. These handheld devices enable users to engage with the virtual surroundings (Anthes et al., 2016). They typically include buttons, joysticks, and motion sensors to detect hand and arm movements.

Figure 1. Overview of all components included in a VR system

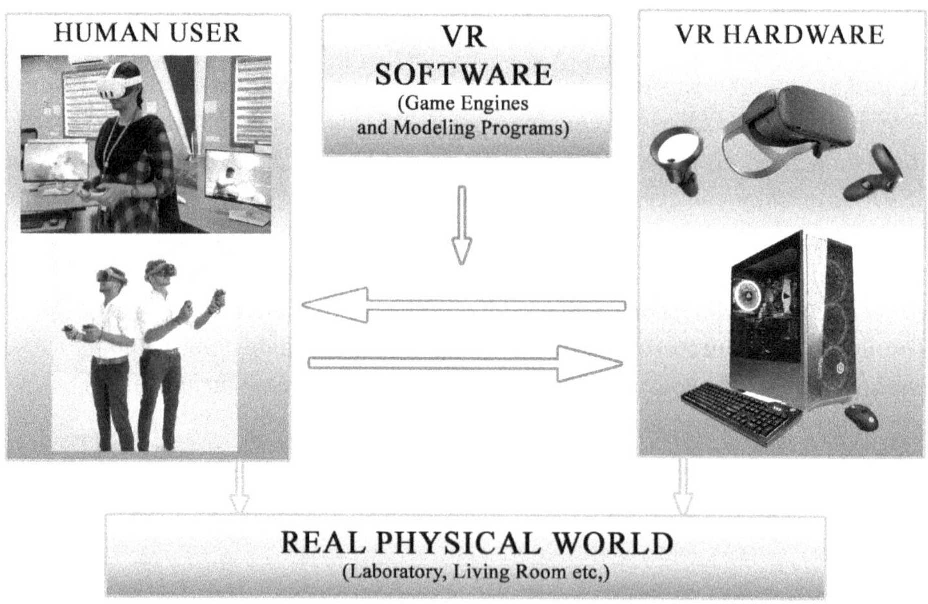

To provide a seamless VR experience, tracking systems use sensors placed around the user or built into the headset to monitor the user's position and actions in real-time. This data is used to regulate the virtual surroundings accordingly. The VR experience is powered by a computer or gaming console that processes the graphics and input data, rendering the virtual environment and ensuring smooth interactions. VR software includes the applications and platforms that create and manage virtual environments. This software is responsible for the graphics, physics, and interactions within the VR space (Kapilan et al., 2021; Singh et al., 2020).

Development in VR systems has gained significant attention in the field of capable Human-Computer Interface (HCI) based research. The main objective of VR systems in HCI is to design a beneficial platform that is feasible and reliable for establishing an effective interaction. Techniques such as hand gesture-based recognition systems and action-based interactive systems play a vital role and are mainly employed in different engineering, empirical, and education-based applications. Figure 2 illustrates different modules involved in the design of an HCI-based VR system. The systems mainly depend on interaction, immersion, and imagination, which complement each other in terms of user attributes, interfacing capabilities, and interaction manners. A closed-loop system that artificially creates communication between the virtual environment and real-time scenarios. A VR system comprises a data acquisition and testing module that takes user instructions as input. Sensors act as an interacting system between the user and the interface. It collects and tracks different interaction modes such as gesture, voice, or touch. The control unit interacts with the virtual environment and provides feedback to users with virtual images being displayed. The user can interrelate with the virtual surroundings usually characterized in the 3D model. The innovation is that each user's interaction with the virtual environment is quantitatively and qualitatively analyzed using the simulation module for simple and complex tasks without the need for intermediate devices.

Figure 2. Human computer interface-based VR system

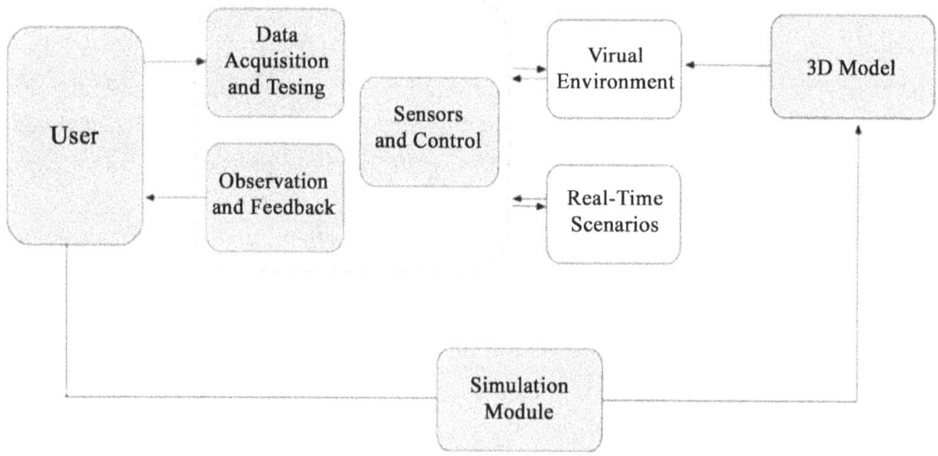

(S.V. et al., 2023)

VR has transitioned from a futuristic concept to a practical tool with wide-ranging applications in various engineering fields. The immersive nature of VR allows engineers to interact with digital environments in ways that were previously unimaginable, leading to significant improvements in design accuracy, training efficacy, and operational efficiency. This chapter will delve into the multifaceted applications of VR in engineering, addressing the mission and concerns associated with its integration (Eswaran & Bahubalendruni, 2022).

The journey of VR technology in engineering began with rudimentary simulations and has evolved into sophisticated, highly immersive environments. Early applications were limited by hardware and software capabilities, but advancements in computational power, graphics rendering, and human-computer interaction have expanded the potential of VR. Today's VR systems are capable of creating realistic, interactive 3D environments that engineers can use for a variety of purposes, from conceptual design to maintenance and repair training (Ardiny & Khanmirza, 2018).

One of the most significant advantages of VR in engineering is the ability to create highly immersive experiences. Unlike traditional computer-aided design (CAD) tools, VR allows engineers to "step inside" their designs. This three-dimensional perspective enables a more intuitive understanding of spatial relationships and potential design issues, which can be difficult to detect on a two-dimensional screen (Leu et al., 2013). Immersion enhances the ability to visualize complex structures and systems, leading to better design decisions and more efficient problem-solving. VR enables engineers to create and manipulate digital prototypes in a virtual environment. This capability is particularly valuable in the early stages of design, where it is essential to identify and resolve potential issues before physical prototypes are built (Murauer, 2018). By using VR, engineers can conduct virtual walkthroughs, assess ergonomic factors, and simulate the assembly process, reducing the need for costly physical prototypes and accelerating the design cycle.

In fields such as aerospace, automotive, and civil engineering, simulation is crucial for testing and validating designs under various conditions. VR provides a platform for conducting virtual simulations that mimic real-world scenarios. Engineers can analyze the behavior of structures under stress, fluid dynamics around a vehicle, or the thermal properties of a building, all within a virtual environment. This approach not only enhances accuracy but also allows for more comprehensive testing than traditional methods. VR is revolutionizing training and education in engineering by providing realistic, hands-on experiences without the associated risks and costs (Kapilan et al., 2021). For example, in mechanical and electrical engineering, VR can simulate equipment and systems, allowing trainees to practice procedures and troubleshoot problems in a safe, controlled environment. This method is particularly effective for complex or hazardous tasks, such as operating heavy machinery or conducting maintenance on live electrical systems. Engineers are using VR to develop interactive maintenance and repair guides that overlay virtual instructions onto real-world equipment. This application, often referred to as augmented reality (AR), helps technicians understand and execute maintenance procedures more accurately and efficiently (Dangelmaier et al., 2005). By visualizing the internal components of a machine and following step-by-step instructions, technicians can reduce errors and improve maintenance outcomes.

Looking ahead, the future of VR in engineering is promising. Advances in Artificial Intelligence (AI), Machine Learning (ML), and sensor technology are expected to further enhance the capabilities of VR systems. For instance, AI-driven simulations could provide even more accurate and dynamic models, while improved haptic feedback systems could offer a more tactile and realistic interaction with virtual objects. As these technologies continue to evolve, VR is poised to become an indispensable tool in the engineering toolkit (L. Kumar et al., 2023)(Rajendra et al., 2022) (Gunasekaran et al., 2024).

VR is transforming engineering practices by offering new ways to visualize, simulate, and interact with designs and systems. Its applications span across design, prototyping, simulation, training, and maintenance, providing important benefits in terms of accuracy, efficiency, and safety. As VR technology continues to advance, its integration into engineering disciplines will undoubtedly deepen, driving innovation and improving outcomes across the industry. This chapter will explore these applications in detail, providing insights into the transformative potential of VR in various engineering fields.

2. APPLICATIONS OF VR IN VARIOUS ENGINEERING FIELDS

2.1 VR in Mechanical Engineering

VR is revolutionizing mechanical engineering by providing immersive and interactive experiences that significantly enhance education, design, simulation, and maintenance processes. This cutting-edge technology bridges the gap between theoretical knowledge and practical application, allowing engineers to visualize and interact with complex systems in ways that were previously unimaginable. The integration of VR in mechanical engineering is not just a technological advancement; it represents a transformative approach to solving engineering challenges, improving efficiency, and fostering innovation in their fields (Impelluso & Metoyer-Guidry, 2001).

Mechanical engineers leverage VR for virtual prototyping, product design, and system simulation. By creating detailed virtual models, engineers can test and refine designs before physical prototypes are made, saving time and resources. VR also enables the simulation of mechanical systems, allowing engineers to analyze performance and identify potential issues. Furthermore, maintenance and repair training using VR provides hands-on experience without the risks associated with real-world scenarios (Kamińska et al., 2017).

Figure 3. JLR is using VR to hold engineering reviews earlier in the vehicle development process

(Https://Virtualspeech.Com/Blog/vr-Applications, n.d.)

Imagine a world where budding engineers can walk through the components of an aircraft engine, understand the dynamics of high-speed machinery, or even participate in a virtual industrial visit to a factory half a world away. This is the potential of VR in mechanical engineering. With a VR headset on, a student is no longer a mere observer. Instead, they become an active participant, zooming into specific components, disassembling them to see their inner workings, and running simulations to witness how changes in one part can affect the whole system. This immersive interaction goes beyond mere observation; it fosters deep understanding and intuition. For example, Figure 3 represents Jaguar Land Rover has been using VR for years to hold design and engineering reviews, prompted by the pandemic to find new alternatives to traditional clay models.

While aircraft engines serve as a vivid example, the scope of VR in mechanical engineering is far more extensive. From understanding the high-speed dynamics of turbomachinery to virtually touring an automotive manufacturing unit, the opportunities are vast and varied. Here are some transformative applications of VR in the mechanical engineering field:

2.1.1. Real-Time Fluid Dynamics

VR allows students to dive into the world of fluid dynamics, watching in real-time how liquids and gases flow and react within systems. This capability provides a tangible understanding of complex concepts like turbulence, laminar flow, and pressure differentials. Students can manipulate variables and instantly see the effects, reinforcing theoretical knowledge with visual and interactive experiences.

2.1.2. Virtual Assembly Lines

Students can walk through virtual factories, understanding automation processes, robotic assemblies, and the ergonomic factors that contribute to efficient production. They can witness the step-by-step construction of products, from raw materials to finished goods, gaining insights into manufacturing processes and workflow optimization without the constraints of physical plant visits. Figure 4 represents a virtual assembly environment.

Figure 4. Virtual representation of assembly environment

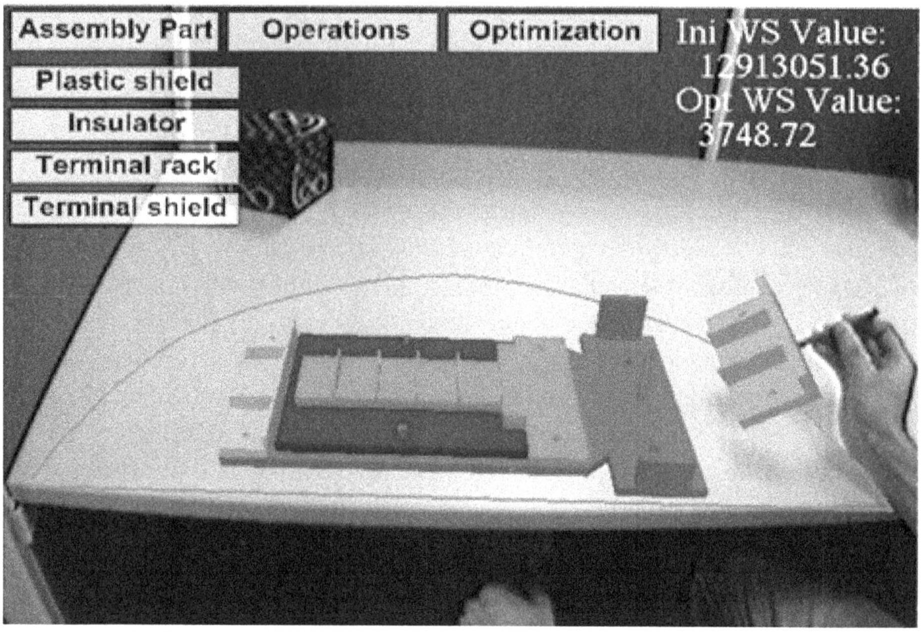

(Ong et al., 2007)

2.1.3. Safety Simulations

Engaging in virtual risk-assessment exercises allows students to experience potential hazards in a controlled environment. They can navigate through scenarios involving machinery malfunctions, chemical spills, or structural failures, learning how to identify risks and implement safety protocols. This hands-on approach to safety training prepares them for real-world challenges, reducing the likelihood of accidents in actual industrial settings.

2.1.4. Global Learning Expeditions

VR enables students to join virtual tours of manufacturing plants in Germany, car assembly lines in Japan, or wind turbine farms in Denmark, all from their classroom or home. These global learning expeditions expose them to different engineering practices, technologies, and cultural approaches, broadening their perspectives and fostering a global mindset. They can interact with experts and peers worldwide, enhancing their learning experience through cross-cultural exchanges (Walsh et al., 2019; Żammit, 2024).

2.1.5. Interactive Component Analysis

VR facilitates detailed analysis of mechanical components, allowing students to disassemble and reassemble parts virtually. They can explore the inner workings of engines, gear systems, and other machinery, understanding the interplay between different elements. This hands-on experience is invaluable for grasping complex mechanical concepts and developing problem-solving skills. Figure 5 illustrates the VR-based Disassemble and Reassemble Mechanical Parts.

Figure 5. VR-based Disassemble and Reassemble Mechanical Parts

(Https://Www.Ixrlabs.Com/Blog/Applications-of-vr-in-Mechanical-Engineering/, n.d.)

2.1.6. Enhanced Design and Prototyping

In the design phase, VR enables engineers to create and test virtual prototypes before committing to physical models. They can visualize designs in 3D, identify potential flaws, and make real-time adjustments. This iterative process speeds up development cycles and reduces costs associated with physical prototyping. Engineers can also simulate the operational performance of their designs, ensuring functionality and reliability before production.

2.1.7. Maintenance and Repair Training

VR provides realistic training environments for maintenance and repair tasks. Technicians can practice procedures on virtual machines, learning to troubleshoot and fix issues without risking damage to actual equipment. This training method enhances their skills and confidence, leading to more efficient and accurate maintenance work in real-world settings.

2.1.8. VR-Based Training in Additive Manufacturing

Additive manufacturing (AM), widely recognized as 3D printing, offers numerous technological advancements and opportunities. However, it also demands specialized knowledge from its practitioners, adopters, and users (Suresh, Kumar, et al., 2024; Suresh, Natarajan, Boopathi, et al., 2024; Suresh, Natarajan, S, et al., 2024). As AM continues to show significant potential and experiences rapid growth across various applications and systems, the need for comprehensive education and training in AM becomes increasingly clear (Huusko et al., 2023).

The concept of incorporating VR into industrial AM training includes microlearning units designed for flexibility and accessibility. Developed as part of an ongoing industrial training project, this approach utilizes VR to provide dynamic and adaptable training experiences. Microlearning and virtual tool-assisted methods represent efficient and responsive strategies for continuous skill development in the industrial sector. By leveraging these tools, companies can customize training programs to meet their specific needs, ensuring that employees stay current with advancing technologies. This customization is essential for effective skill enhancement and knowledge transfer, making the training both relevant and impactful for the evolving industrial landscape (Ostrander et al., 2019).

2.2 VR in Civil Engineering

VR is making significant strides in the field of civil engineering, contributing immersive and interactive skills that enhance design, construction, and training processes. By integrating VR into civil engineering, professionals can visualize projects more effectively, improve collaboration, and reduce errors, ultimately leading to more efficient and innovative outcomes. VR technologies in building business and training have undergone significant evolution over time. Initially, desktop-based VR provided basic virtual experiences (Young et al., 2012). This was followed by the advent of immersive VR, which offered more engaging and realistic simulations. The incorporation of 3D game-based VR further enhanced interactivity and user experience. Nowadays, construction Information model enabled VR represents the cutting edge, allowing for comprehensive project visualization and management (Wang et al., 2018). When applied to the teaching of civil engineering, VR technology has shown encouraging outcomes in recent breakthroughs in the field of education. The current lecture-based classroom format in civil engineering education can only facilitate the flow of information from academic to learner, therefore sustaining a passive learning style (Remolar et al., 2021).

Figure 6. Comparison of a VR lab and a real-world lab (a) VR structures lab; (b) real structures lab; (c) VR heavy structures lab; (d) real heavy structures lab

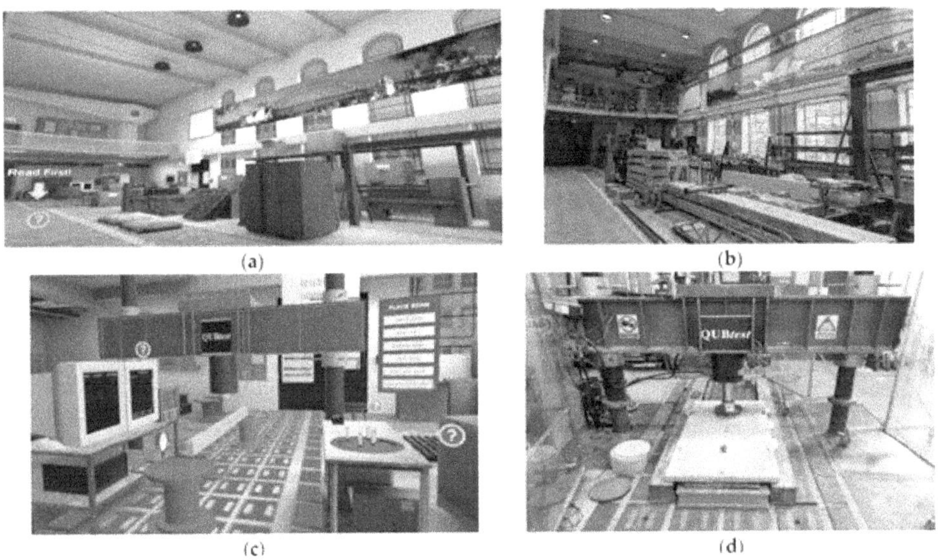

(McCloskey et al., 2024)

Queen's University Belfast (QUB) developed a heavy structures laboratory modeled virtually, allowing students to conduct experiments within a virtual environment (McCloskey et al., 2024). A comparison between the virtually modeled lab and the real-world lab is shown in Figure 6.

In parallel, Augmented Reality (AR) has also gained traction in construction engineering, offering additional layers of information and interactivity by overlaying virtual elements onto the real world. Both VR and AR technologies are being utilized across various aspects of construction engineering, including Architecture Visualization, structural analysis, Health and safety training, and Equipment handling training.

2.2.1 Architecture and Design Visualization

Architectural visualization is one of the main uses of VR in architecture education and design. VR greatly aids students in grasping architectural design principles and allows professors to thoroughly examine students' innovations to uncover hidden errors. VR enables civil engineers to create and explore 3D models of infrastructure projects. By immersing themselves in a virtual environment, engineers can identify design flaws, optimize layouts, and communicate ideas more effectively with stakeholders. This visual and interactive approach helps bridge the gap between conceptual designs and real-world implementation. Figure 7 shows the visual model of the interior view of the lab before construction.

Figure 7. (a, b) Visual and rendered model of the interior view of the lab before construction, and (c) Physical view of the model

Another advantage of VR in Design Visualization is its skill to facilitate simultaneous comparisons of multiple designs. For instance, the 3D interactive virtual surroundings developed by students can navigate and interact with virtual buildings (Kamath et al., 2012). They can also import a CAD model of a building, transform it into a replication, and make modifications as needed. Utilizing virtual environments in architectural learning helps students grasp the core principles of architecture, providing a solid foundation for their future careers. Using VR, engineers can simulate the construction process, identifying potential issues and planning logistics before breaking ground. This allows for better resource management, improved safety measures, and more efficient project timelines. Virtual walkthroughs of construction sites enable teams to foresee challenges and develop solutions proactively.

2.2.2 Construction Safety Training

This is another significant application of VR in civil engineering. The construction industry is inherently high-risk, with a persistently high accident rate. Traditional training methods, such as presentations and videos, often fail to engage trainees effectively and improve their safety performance. To address this, several VR solutions have been developed to enhance safety training practices in construction. For instance, a virtual platform allows university students to right of entry safely in order through smart devices by scanning QR codes (Pedro et al., 2016). Although developing VR apparatus and classifying protection information can be time-consuming, the results have been promising. VR-based training has been shown to increase students' motivation and engagement. To overcome the time constraints, some strategies involve collecting, adapting, and storing objects from previous construction projects in a virtual database. This approach streamlines the creation of VR training materials and ensures a comprehensive and engaging learning experience for trainees (Kuncoro et al., 2023).

In recent years, the mining industry has seen a growing adoption of VR technology. VR visualization offers the ability to thoroughly review past experiences and events, which aids in making more informed decisions. Much of the VR content in this industry involves precise control over equipment operations or responses. VR simulations serve as an outstanding tool for training and education, as well as for simulating abnormal and hazardous conditions in mines and addressing complex issues. Presently, VR is effectively utilized in the mining sector for data visualization, accident reconstruction, simulation applications, risk analysis, hazard awareness, and training (Liao & Lu, 2009).

2.3 VR in Biomedical Engineering (Healthcare)

VR is revolutionizing the healthcare industry by providing innovative solutions for treatment, training, and diagnosis. This technology offers immersive and interactive skills that enhance patient care and medical education (Singh et al., 2020). Here are some of the significant applications of VR in healthcare:

2.3.1 Pain Management and Rehabilitation

VR is making a significant impact on pain management and rehabilitation. VR has gained prominence as an effective and widely adopted method for pain management in patients. In many advanced oncology departments around the world, VR is used to help patients manage discomfort resulting from their condition or medical procedures like biopsies. Studies have indicated that more than half of hospitalized patients experience pain, with approximately one-fifth of them rating their pain as "unbearable" (Sakhri & Boulhart, 2021). Traditionally, pain management has relied heavily on medications such as opioids, which often provide inconsistent and sometimes unsatisfactory results. In contrast, therapeutic VR has emerged as a viable non-drug alternative for treating pain, offering promising results without the drawbacks associated with pharmaceutical approaches. Figure 8 represents the utilization of VR for pain relief in hospitals in Huffpost Canada. VR has also been used as an effective pain relief method for burn injuries, allowing patients to engage in immersive environments that distract them from pain during wound care procedures.

Figure 8. virtual reality for pain relief in hospitals HuffPost Canada 2021

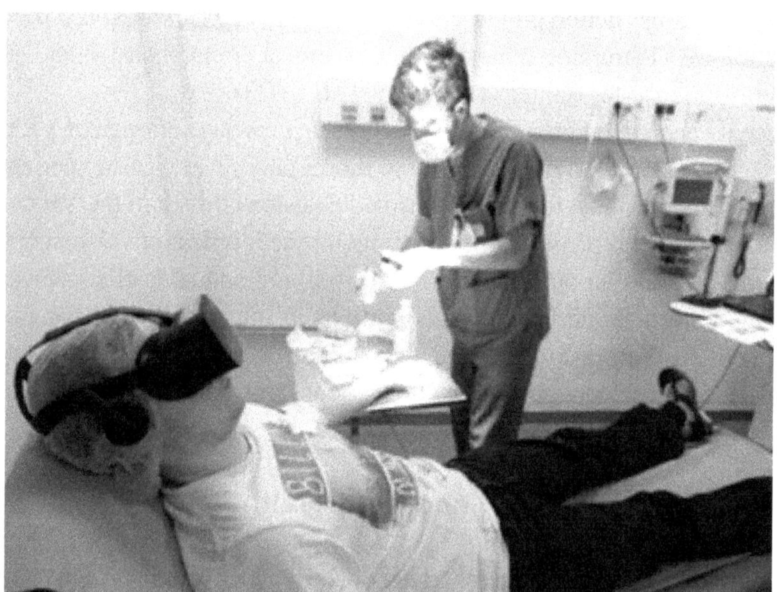

(Sakhri & Boulhart, 2021)

2.3.2 Surgical Training and Simulation

Healthcare professionals can use VR to better prepare for the operating theater. For instance, junior doctors can practice explaining diagnoses and treatment plans, while surgeons can perform virtual surgeries to enhance their skills. Companies like Osso VR enable surgeons to interact with medical devices in VR and practice surgery on virtual bodies, increasing familiarity with new devices and proficiency in implanting them (Cevallos et al., 2022). This hands-on experience is invaluable for improving surgical outcomes and reducing the learning curve for new techniques and technologies (Moro et al., 2017) (Karaliotas, 2011).

2.3.3 Diagnostic Tools and Disease Monitoring

A variety of challenging situations emerge from the diagnosis, treatment, and long-term effects of cancer. Studies have shown that over 10% of cancer patients exhibit clinical symptoms of anxiety disorder, with the prevalence increasing to approximately 17.6% in those who have been living with cancer for more than two years (SAKHRI Selma épse BOULHART, 2022). VR serves not only as a therapeutic tool but also plays a significant role in training and supporting oncology professionals. The integration of VR in medical oncology promises a promising future, enhancing both patient care and professional development.

Figure 9. VR hardware components of the Neurorehabilitation (a complex medical therapy program)

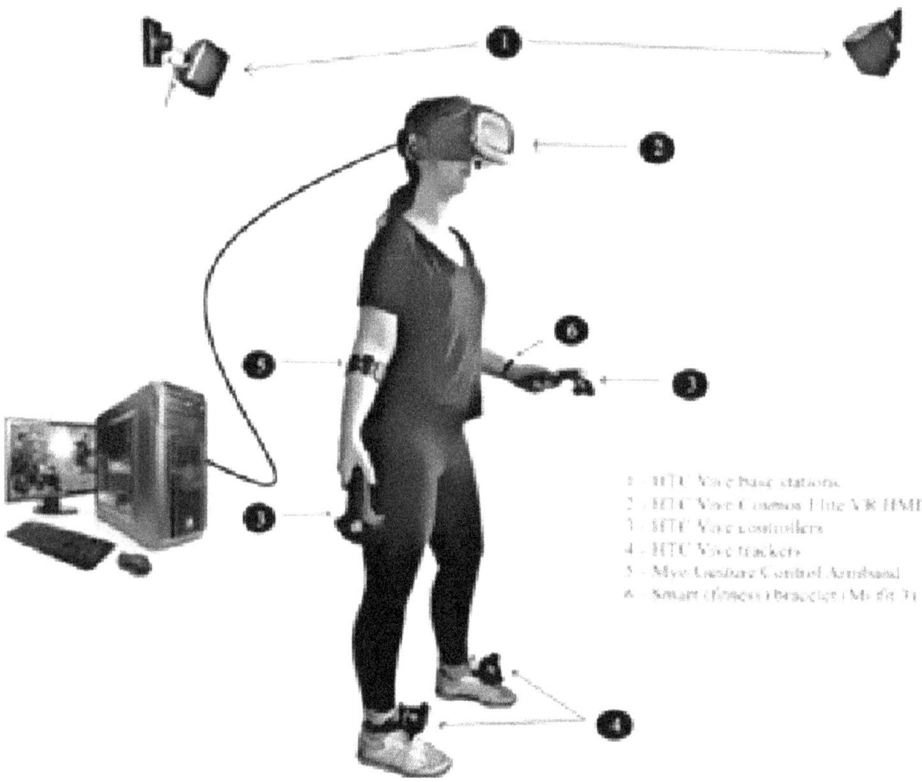

(Stanica et al., 2020)

It introduced Neurorehabilitation exercises using Virtual Reality (INREX-VR), a system for neurorehabilitation that captures real-time user movements, evaluates joint mobility, and records electromyography data (Stanica et al., 2020). It uses a first-person perspective and inverse kinematics for enhanced immersion (Refer to Figure 9). Tutorial exercises are demonstrated by virtual therapists and sessions are configurable via telemedicine. Preliminary tests show promising results and future improvements will focus on accuracy and wireless alternatives using neural networks.

VR, combined with AR and machine learning, is being leveraged to develop advanced diagnostic tools and monitoring systems as illustrated in Figure 10. Companies like Altoida are utilizing XR (extended reality) to create digital biomarkers for neurological diseases such as Alzheimer's (Sahu et al., 2024). This technology platform facilitates earlier diagnosis, participation in clinical trials, and precise monitoring of disease progression and treatment responses. The immersive nature of VR allows for detailed cognitive assessments and more accurate tracking of neurological health.

Figure 10. VR and AR reality-based applications in various fields

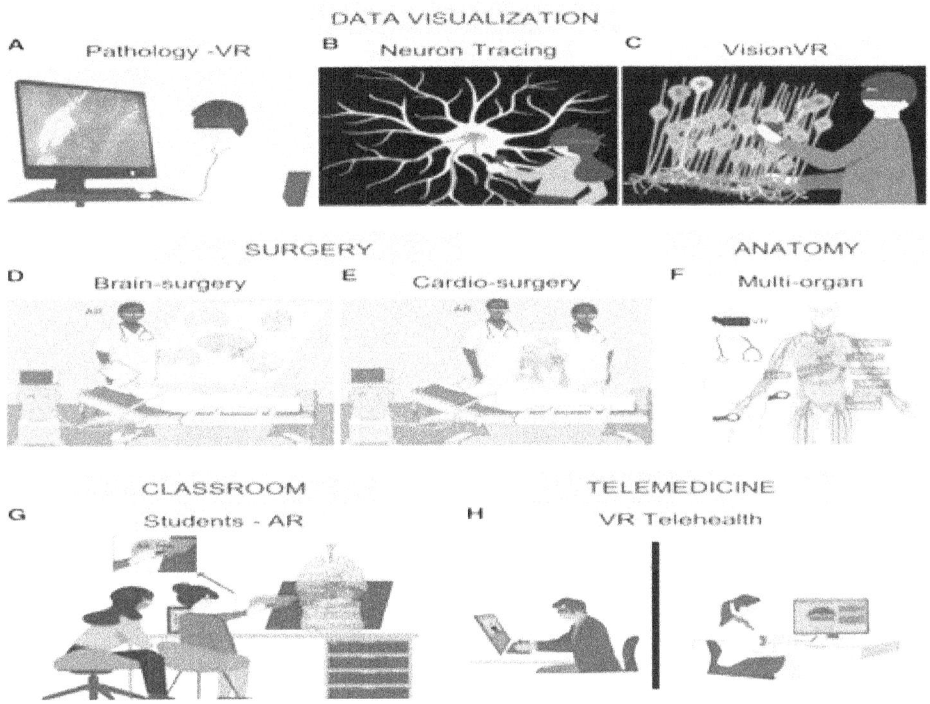

(Venkatesan et al., 2021)

2.3.4 Mental Health Treatment

VR is proving to be a powerful tool in the handling of mental health issues. VR Exposure Therapy is mainly useful in treating post-traumatic stress disorder and anxiety (Powers & Emmelkamp, 2008). Patients are gradually exposed to their fears or traumatic experiences in a restricted virtual environment, helping them to confront and overcome their anxieties. VR environments can also be tailored to simulate various therapeutic settings and provide a protected space for patients to explore and manage their mental health.

Figure 11 shows a typical computer automatic virtual environment (CAVE) system. The CAVE is a multiuser VR system with stereoscopic images projected on the walls of a cubicle. Patients and therapists wear shutter glasses synced with these images and use an electromagnetic tracker for perspective. Movement is natural or aided by a wand. The CAVE system is for individual use, immersing the patient in a virtual environment with screens inside the headset and speakers near the ears. A sensor tracks head movements, adjusting the virtual view accordingly. The therapist monitors and controls the session via a connected computer.

Figure 11. Computer automatic virtual environment

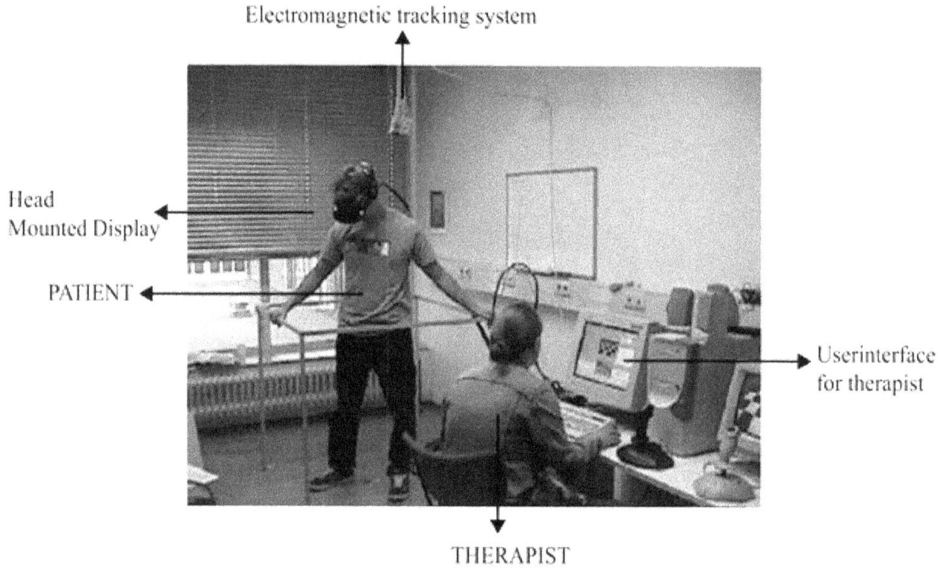

(Krijn et al., 2004)

VR can improve patient education by providing immersive experiences that help patients better comprehend their conditions and treatments. For example, patients can take virtual tours of their anatomy to see how diseases affect their bodies and how treatments will work. This can lead to better-informed patients who are more engaged in their healthcare decisions. VR can also be used to simulate medical procedures, allowing patients to experience them virtually beforehand, which can reduce anxiety and improve compliance with treatment plans.

Biomedical engineering benefits from VR through surgical training, rehabilitation, and medical device design. VR surgical simulators provide realistic practice for surgeons, improving their skills and reducing errors. Rehabilitation programs using VR offer engaging and effective therapies for patients. Additionally, VR aids in the design and testing of medical devices, ensuring functionality and safety before clinical use.

3. CONCLUSION

This chapter summarizes the key points and underscores the transformative potential of VR in various engineering fields. By providing detailed insights and practical examples, it aims to inform and inspire engineers, researchers, and practitioners to embrace VR technology. Its applications span across mechanical, civil, and biomedical engineering, offering significant improvements in design processes, training methodologies, and operational efficiency. VR enables engineers to create immersive, interactive 3D environments that facilitate better decision-making, reduce costs, and enhance safety. The integration of VR in engineering not only bridges the gap between theoretical knowledge and practical application but also fosters a deeper understanding of complex systems. As VR technology continues to advance, its role in engineering will undoubtedly expand, driving further innovation and improving outcomes across various fields.

Despite the numerous benefits, integrating VR into engineering faces technical and ethical challenges. Ensuring the accuracy and reliability of VR simulations, addressing data privacy concerns, and managing the cost of VR implementation are critical issues. The future of VR in engineering lies in its integration with other emerging technologies, such as artificial intelligence (AI) and the Internet of Things (IoT), to create more sophisticated and interconnected systems. Continued research and innovation will drive the evolution of VR applications, opening new horizons for engineering advancements.

4. ACKNOWLEDGMENTS

We would like to acknowledge the financial support received from the Science and Engineering Research Board (SERB) under grant SSY/2023/001464. We gratefully acknowledge the support provided by the ESEC-School of Animation and Gaming, Erode Sengunthar Engineering College, Erode, Tamil Nadu. Their guidance and resources have greatly contributed to the development of this chapter.

REFERENCES

Anthes, C., García-Hernández, R. J., Wiedemann, M., & Kranzlmüller, D. (2016). State of the art of virtual reality technology. *2016 IEEE Aerospace Conference*, (pp. 1–19). IEEE. DOI:10.1109/AERO.2016.7500674

Ardiny, H., & Khanmirza, E. (2018). The Role of AR and VR Technologies in Education Developments: Opportunities and Challenges. *2018 6th RSI International Conference on Robotics and Mechatronics (IcRoM)*, (pp. 482–487). IEEE. DOI:10.1109/ICRoM.2018.8657615

Cevallos, N., Zukotynski, B., Greig, D., Silva, M., & Thompson, R. M. (2022). The Utility of Virtual Reality in Orthopedic Surgical Training. *Journal of Surgical Education*, 79(6), 1516–1525. DOI:10.1016/j.jsurg.2022.06.007 PMID:35821110

Dangelmaier, W., Fischer, M., Gausemeier, J., Grafe, M., Matysczok, C., & Mueck, B. (2005). Virtual and augmented reality support for discrete manufacturing system simulation. *Computers in Industry*, 56(4), 371–383. DOI:10.1016/j.compind.2005.01.007

Eswaran, M., & Bahubalendruni, M. V. A. R. (2022). Challenges and opportunities on AR/VR technologies for manufacturing systems in the context of industry 4.0: A state of the art review. *Journal of Manufacturing Systems*, 65, 260–278. DOI:10.1016/j.jmsy.2022.09.016

Gunasekaran, K., Boopathi, S., Suresh, S., Suresh, P., Vanitha, N. S., & Radhika, K. (2024). Eco-Friendly Smart Agricultural Process Using Artificial Intelligence. In *Reshaping Environmental Science Through Machine Learning and IoT* (pp. 160–175). IGI Global. DOI:10.4018/979-8-3693-2351-9.ch009

Huusko, A., Susi, J., Parchegani, S., Hosseini, H., Tuomisto, A., Helin, A., Piili, H., & Salminen, A. (2023). Virtual Reality-Based Training in Additive Manufacturing: Developing a Service Concept that Adapts to Company-Specific Requirements. *IOP Conference Series. Materials Science and Engineering*, 1296(1), 012004. DOI:10.1088/1757-899X/1296/1/012004

Impelluso, T., & Metoyer-Guidry, T. (2001). Virtual Reality and Learning by Design: Tools for Integrating Mechanical Engineering Concepts. *Journal of Engineering Education*, 90(4), 527–534. DOI:10.1002/j.2168-9830.2001.tb00635.x

Kamath, R. S., Dongale, T. D., & Kamat, R. K. (2012). Development of Virtual Reality Tool for Creative Learning in Architectural Education. *International Journal of Quality Assurance in Engineering and Technology Education*, 2(4), 16–24. DOI:10.4018/ijqaete.2012100102

Kamińska, D., Sapiński, T., Aitken, N., Della Rocca, A., Barańska, M., & Wietsma, R. (2017). Virtual reality as a new trend in mechanical and electrical engineering education. *Open Physics*, 15(1), 936–941. DOI:10.1515/phys-2017-0114

Kapilan, N., Vidhya, P., & Gao, X.-Z. (2021). Virtual Laboratory: A Boon to the Mechanical Engineering Education During Covid-19 Pandemic. *Higher Education for the Future*, 8(1), 31–46. DOI:10.1177/2347631120970757

Karaliotas, C. (2011). When simulation in surgical training meets virtual reality. *Hellenike Cheirourgike. Acta Chirurgica Hellenica*, 83(6), 303–316. DOI:10.1007/s13126-011-0055-9

Krijn, M., Emmelkamp, P. M. G., Olafsson, R. P., & Biemond, R. (2004). Virtual reality exposure therapy of anxiety disorders: A review. *Clinical Psychology Review*, 24(3), 259–281. DOI:10.1016/j.cpr.2004.04.001 PMID:15245832

Kumar, L., Kumar, A., Sharma, R. K., & Kumar, P. (2023). Smart Manufacturing and Industry 4.0. In *Handbook of Smart Manufacturing* (pp. 1–28). CRC Press. DOI:10.1201/9781003333760-1

Kuncoro, T., Ichwanto, M. A., & Muhammad, D. F. (2023). VR-Based Learning Media of Earthquake-Resistant Construction for Civil Engineering Students. *Sustainability (Basel)*, 15(5), 4282. DOI:10.3390/su15054282

Leu, M. C., ElMaraghy, H. A., Nee, A. Y. C., Ong, S. K., Lanzetta, M., Putz, M., Zhu, W., & Bernard, A. (2013). CAD model based virtual assembly simulation, planning and training. *CIRP Annals*, 62(2), 799–822. DOI:10.1016/j.cirp.2013.05.005

Liao, J., & Lu, G. (2009). Research on key techniques of virtual reality applied in mining industry. *Journal of Coal Science and Engineering (China)*, 15(4), 445–448. DOI:10.1007/s12404-009-0420-2

McCloskey, D. W., McAllister, E., Gilbert, R., O'Higgins, C., Lydon, D., Lydon, M., & McPolin, D. (2024). Embedding Civil Engineering Understanding through the Use of Interactive Virtual Reality. *Education Sciences*, 14(1), 6. DOI:10.3390/educsci14010006

Moro, C., Štromberga, Z., Raikos, A., & Stirling, A. (2017). The effectiveness of virtual and augmented reality in health sciences and medical anatomy. *Anatomical Sciences Education*, 10(6), 549–559. https://doi.org/https://doi.org/10.1002/ase.1696. DOI:10.1002/ase.1696 PMID:28419750

Murauer, N. (2018). Design Thinking: Using Photo Prototyping for a user-centered Interface Design for Pick-by-Vision Systems. *Proceedings of the 11th PErvasive Technologies Related to Assistive Environments Conference*, (pp. 126–132). ACM. DOI:10.1145/3197768.3201532

Ong, S. K., Pang, Y., & Nee, A. Y. C. (2007). Augmented Reality Aided Assembly Design and Planning. *CIRP Annals*, 56(1), 49–52. DOI:10.1016/j.cirp.2007.05.014

Ostrander, J. K., Tucker, C. S., Simpson, T. W., & Meisel, N. A. (2019). Evaluating the Use of Virtual Reality to Teach Introductory Concepts of Additive Manufacturing. *Journal of Mechanical Design*, 142(5), 51702. DOI:10.1115/1.4044006

Pedro, A., Le, Q. T., & Park, C. S. (2016). Framework for Integrating Safety into Construction Methods Education through Interactive Virtual Reality. *Journal of Professional Issues in Engineering Education and Practice*, 142(2), 04015011. DOI:10.1061/(ASCE)EI.1943-5541.0000261

Powers, M. B., & Emmelkamp, P. M. G. (2008). Virtual reality exposure therapy for anxiety disorders: A meta-analysis. *Journal of Anxiety Disorders*, 22(3), 561–569. DOI:10.1016/j.janxdis.2007.04.006 PMID:17544252

Rajendra, P., Kumari, M., Rani, S., Dogra, N., Boadh, R., Kumar, A., & Dahiya, M. (2022). Impact of artificial intelligence on civilization: Future perspectives. *Materials Today: Proceedings*, 56, 252–256. DOI:10.1016/j.matpr.2022.01.113

Remolar, I., Rebollo, C., & Fernández-Moyano, J. A. (2021). Learning History Using Virtual and Augmented Reality. *Computers*, 10(11), 146. DOI:10.3390/computers10110146

Sahu, M., Gupta, R., Ambasta, R. K., & Kumar, P. (2024). IoT-driven augmented reality and virtual reality systems in neurological sciences. *Internet of Things : Engineering Cyber Physical Human Systems*, 25, 101098. DOI:10.1016/j.iot.2024.101098

Sakhri, S., & Boulhart, É. (2021). CANCER AND VIRTUAL REALITY VR, THE GREAT CHALLENGE OF THE CENTURY. *Archives of Medical Case Reports and Case Study*, 5(1), 01–07. DOI:10.31579/2692-9392/101

Sakhri, S. (2022). Cancer and Virtual Reality Vr, the Great Challenge of The Century. *Cancer and Virtual Reality Vr, the Great Challenge of The Century*. https://doi.org/DOI:10.31579/2692-9392/0101

Singh, A., Ferry, D., Ramakrishnan, A., & Balasubramanian, S. (2020). Using Virtual Reality in Biomedical Engineering Education. *Journal of Biomechanical Engineering*, 142(11), 111013. DOI:10.1115/1.4048005 PMID:32747925

Stanica, I.-C., Moldoveanu, F., Portelli, G.-P., Dascalu, M.-I., Moldoveanu, A., & Ristea, M. G. (2020). Flexible Virtual Reality System for Neurorehabilitation and Quality of Life Improvement. *Sensors (Basel)*, 20(21), 6045. Advance online publication. DOI:10.3390/s20216045 PMID:33114272

Suresh, S., Kumar, P., Yuvaraj, T., Velmurugan, D., & Natarajan, E. (2024). 4 Adoptability of additive manufacturing process: design perceptive. In A. Kumar, P. Kumar, N. Sharma, & A. K. Srivastava (Eds.), *3D Printing Technologies* (pp. 77–94). De Gruyter. DOI:10.1515/9783111215112-004

Suresh, S., & Natarajan, E. (2024). Additive Manufacturing for a Sustainable Production: Materials, Processes, and Impact. In *Futuristic Technology for Sustainable Manufacturing* (pp. 1–16). IGI Global. DOI:10.4018/979-8-3693-1862-1.ch001

Suresh, S., Natarajan, E., Boopathi, S., & Kumar, P. (2024). 8 Processing of smart materials by additive manufacturing and 4D printing. In A. Kumar, P. Kumar, N. Sharma, & A. K. Srivastava (Eds.), *3D Printing Technologies* (pp. 181–196). De Gruyter. https://doi.org/DOI:10.1515/9783111215112-008k

S.V. S., P., A., & K.R., R. (2023). Practical case studies on human-computer interaction. In S. Bhatia Khan, S. Namasudra, S. Chandna, A. Mashat, & F. Xhafa (Eds.), *Innovations in Artificial Intelligence and Human-Computer Interaction in the Digital Era* (pp. 233–254). Elsevier. DOI:10.1016/B978-0-323-99891-8.00007-3

Venkatesan, M., Mohan, H., Ryan, J. R., Schürch, C. M., Nolan, G. P., Frakes, D. H., & Coskun, A. F. (2021). Virtual and augmented reality for biomedical applications. *Cell Reports Medicine*, 2(7), 100348. DOI:10.1016/j.xcrm.2021.100348 PMID:34337564

Walsh, J., Boyle, F., Moriarty, P., Locke, A., McMahon, D., Katamreddy, S., & Riordan, D. (2019). *The development of VR expeditions for primary school learning*. Edu Learn. DOI:10.21125/edulearn.2019.2118

Wang, P., Wu, P., Wang, J., Chi, H.-L., & Wang, X. (2018). A Critical Review of the Use of Virtual Reality in Construction Engineering Education and Training. *International Journal of Environmental Research and Public Health*, 15(6), 1204. DOI:10.3390/ijerph15061204 PMID:29890627

Young, B., Ellobody, E., & Hu, T. W. C. (2012). 3D Visualization of Structures Using Finite-Element Analysis in Teaching. *Journal of Professional Issues in Engineering Education and Practice*, 138(2), 131–138. DOI:10.1061/(ASCE) EI.1943-5541.0000093

Żammit, J. (2024). Could virtual reality be the next approach for international students learning Maltese? *Educational Technology Research and Development*. DOI:10.1007/s11423-024-10375-9

Chapter 14
Virtual Reality in the Education System

Satyabrata Pandit
Brainware University, India

Saptarshi Kumar Sarkar
Brainware University, India

Sreya Barik
Brainware University, India

Sutapa Shau
Brainware University, India

ABSTRACT

The learning technique that involves the learners in facilitating training in a virtual environment hence extends traditional mode of training that was considered new, is known as virtual reality learning. In this chapter, the author examines experiences of technology use in schools specifically in the classroom and then evaluates implications of the use of virtual reality. This study endeavours to expose the specified literature review approach, the definition and guidelines of the integration of VR in education, a systematic approach and case studies in an endeavour of analysing how this technological innovation could contribute to the students' interest, understanding, and recall of issues, matters, and concepts, regardless of discipline and academic year. Therefore, considering the standpoint of the virtual reality integration as one of the effective learning strategies in education, the issues, including high costs, the technical issue, and the lack of professional development concerning VR for educators, must be addressed for this technology to meet its potential. Besides, the guidelines are given for obtaining the optimal results from VR in context of

DOI: 10.4018/979-8-3693-6407-9.ch014

education and for making sure that the opportunities which are derived out from it are reasonable, reachable, and sustainable in nature, which have also been enclosed in the conclusion part of the chapter.

1. INTRODUCTION

1.1 Background

Traditional techniques of learning, which are based on various cultures and approaches, provided direct teachings, books, and other non-communication devices. These approaches have been used as a model of how learning can be done but in the process may compromise on efficiency. A few shortcomings of effective teaching-learning processes are explained, and one of them is the use of modern technologies like VR. With these technologies in placed, teachers may wish to improve on the efficiency of their teaching strategies (Mantovani, F. (2001), C. (2008) & Johnson,2018).

1.2 Textbooks

Textbooks are considered sources of information since they provide structural knowledge on different topics in school. However, since they are formulaic, unitary, and sequential, they prevent students' interest and may not be suitable for learning styles. This constraint, through written explanation and non-moving graphics, may in fact be inconvenient for students who have dynamic and graphic interactions as their primary priorities, which is what, indeed, these textbooks are majoritarian for (Trowler,2010).

1.3 Lectures

Oral techniques, including teach using a power point display, are approved teaching techniques that entails a teacher presenting content before a class or some learners. These methods provide efficiency when addressing much content within a short period; however, they encourage learning by absorption among students. That leads to a form of learning where the learner is passive and only listens to the teacher without participating. The process above can lead to poor outcome and particularly in the case of a complex piece of knowledge. Therefore, one must ensure the students participate in learning activities as required in the course (Bray, M., Shafique, R., Aljedaani, W.,

Rustam, F., Lee, E., Mehmood, A., & Choi, G. S. (2023), A., & Green, T. D. (2004) et a,2017).

1.4 Static Visual Aids

Little Interactivity Erasers are flash cards, and mirrors, which can be referred to as teaching furniture with resemblance to classroom furniture for holding text and lecturers' backings. These visual tools are inextricably connected with communication, and the reception of entertainment products. As to Sepia, which is rather toned, elegant style, it is appropriate to state that, on the one hand, it may not contribute to the comprehension of subjects by students, on the other hand, it contributes to keeping up the atmosphere of vivacity and sprit. As compared to other elements like over head projectors, LCD projector, live may be interesting to some classes of students with regards to static graphics and multimedia (Song, C., Shin, S. Y., & Shin, K. S. (2023),2019).

1.5 Limitations of Traditional Teaching Methods

The drawbacks of the current models in implementing and managing the learning process again underline the fact that there is potential for a better, more effective way to educate learners, thus creating an improved, interesting learning process(Anderson,2019).

These limitations include:

1.6 Passive Learning

As per the traditional approaches, learners become passive recipients of information and do not get to express the knowledge in a concise, headline manner(Johnson,2020).

1.7 Limited Interactivity

We can notice that having combined the work with textbooks and lectures as the major source of information, the use of the limited number of posters or black/Song, C., Shin, S. Y., & Shin, K. S. (2023) boards as the information board buries students' creativity and weakens their desire to study deeper(Mantovani, F. (2001), C. (2008),2018).

1.8 One-Size-Fits-All Approach

This means that traditional methods of teaching can ignore students' potential tastes and interests in how they are taught with little regard to their learning style preferences(Kaplan-Rakowski, R., Papin, K., & Hartwick, P. M. (2022,2017).

1.9 Abstract Concepts

The aspect of employing traditional instructive tools such as objects, particularly in trying to help the learners grasp some particular matters or ideas can sometimes be proving to be rather difficult for the teachers as it influences the learners' compr ehension and uptake of information(Trowler,2010).

1.10 Inability to Cater to Diverse Learning Styles

Traditional teaching processes can sometimes fail to provide product solutions to the different students' learning commitments because not all students will learn in the same way(Bray, M., Shafique, R., Aljedaani, W., Rustam, F., Lee, E., Mehmood, A., & Choi, G. S. (2023), A., & Green, T. D. (2004) et al,2019).

1.11 The Advent of Virtual Reality (VR)

As for utilizing modern technologies specifically virtual reality technology, it is considered that it can be the effective method to the traditional methods of teaching. Virtual reality locates the learner in a context that provides far greater opportunities for constructive learning andthan can be presented in established approaches to learning and teaching, making it a shift in paradigm. This part deals with the idea of how VR can transform the common forms of learning and how is it effective in comparison with conventional ways of schooling(Song, C., Shin, S. Y., & Shin, K. S. (2023),2021).

1.12 Dynamic and Immersive Learning Environments

A main advantage of VR is the fact that it can offer stunning and realistic learning experiences for them and enable students to learn and manipulate concepts in ways that could not be presented in conventional, rather dull and flat methods. This makes students feel as if they are seated in the classroom because this incubation enhances the sense of presence and participation(Anderson,2020).

1.13 Making Abstract Concepts Tangible and Accessible

To date, there have been theories that tend to have rather abstract concepts and ideas, and VR is a way to make them tangible and easily understandable. It provides the learners with the capacity to understand abstract concepts through models and scenarios that enable the learner to interact with the subject matter. For instance, through the use of VR, the student is able to travel to the galaxies that are so far from him or her Shafique, R., Aljedaani, W., Rustam, F., Lee, E., Mehmood, A., & Choi, G. S. (2023) & Wilson,2019).

1.14 Catering to Diverse Learning Styles

Virtual reality gives the student haptic and customizable learning experience which is in conformity with the students' preferences. It does not require the same approach used in the conventional methods, and it can easily be adapted to the particular needs of the students. While the first type of learners may find it easy to learn from the perspectives given to them through visual modes such as animations and videos, the second type of learner may have better comprehension of similar items and use of object manipulation with the help of VR to perform hands-on research. Applying VR in the classroom can foster student interest, and the integration of Virtual Reality can allow for the creation of the Students for All model(Bray, M., Shafique, R., Aljedaani, W., Rustam, F., Lee, E., Mehmood, A., & Choi, G. S. (2023), A., & Green, T. D. (2004) et al,2021).

1.15 Enhancing Student Engagement and Motivation

It means that by implementing the ideas connected with the usage of virtual reality in learning, students' motivation and their further engagement in the studying process can be boosted. The audience is equally engaged in the content as the method makes people eager to learn new material. This unrestrained and self-generated search for information helps students maintain active participation in learning activities, the studies, and other tasks hence enhancing students' performance and learning(Mantovani, F. (2001), C. (2008),2018).

1.16 Problem Statement

This section discusses the problems associated with traditional classrooms particularly in areas of teaching, how students grasp information given to them, and then how they engage the knowledge to give back the expected result; it then examines Virtual Reality (VR) as a creative solution to these studies in teaching with the aim of embracing learning and work in education(Song, C., Shin, S. Y., & Shin, K. S. (2023),2021) .

1.17 Issues of Engagement in Traditional Classrooms

In a typical classroom setting, the students trouble themselves to stay more engaged and interested in the learning process.

1.18 Several factors contribute to this challenge

1.18.1 Passive Learning

This learning material and resource mostly involve the teacher and the book or stand on the blackboard where the teacher just closes down the interest and energy level in the students by explaining what he or she wants to pass across to them than engaging them in their own learning process(Anderson,2019).

1.18.2 Limited Interactivity

Traditional classes do not expose the students enough to actual participation in class assignments and other group related learning acts due to lack of necessary teaching aids which are not static, no twoway communication channels which are the best in teaching, as most of the teaching aids used are in static form such as blackboards, bulletins, posters etc(Mantovani, F. (2001), C. (2008),2018).

1.18.3 Predictability

Classroom boredom can be worsened by repetitive teaching strategies and course plans, as teachers may lose interest in their subjects if they fail to spark critical thinking and creative expression(Johnson,2020).

1.18.4 Challenges in Knowledge Retention

Shooting the breeze, teachers can aggravate class monotony by using stereotyped teaching approaches and lesson plans, since educators bore in classes fail to engage students' creativity and critical thinking(Bray, M., Shafique, R., Aljedaani, W., Rustam, F., Lee, E., Mehmood, A., & Choi, G. S. (2023), A., & Green, T. D. (2004) et al,2019).

1.18.5 Lack of Contextualization

Shooting the breeze, teachers can aggravate class monotony by using stereotyped teaching approaches and lesson plans, since educators bore in classes fail to engage students' creativity and critical thinking(Song, C., Shin, S. Y., & Shin, K. S. (2023),2021).

1.18.6 Limited Multisensory Engagement

Learners may fail to grasp matters that are taught or explained in a manner that isolates or separates the ideas without presenting real examples that connect such ideas or concepts(Trowler,2010).

1.18.7 Inadequate Feedback Mechanisms

raditional transmission of knowledge still rely on Transmission from the teacher, thus more often using only two modalities of teaching; verbal and visual, while ignoring the other abilities which must exist in a child to decode knowledge as other modalities could be of more help in the storage of knowledge(Kaplan-Rakowski, R., Papin, K., & Hartwick, P. M. (2022,2017).

1.18.8 The Role of VR in Addressing Challenges

Standard types of assessments such as written examinations, quizzes, and reviews can be ineffective in exposing crucial knowledge gaps by showing how much students grasp and apply specific topics once knowledge-check questions are given in a return-minute manner and with useful feedback (Anderson,2019).

1.18.9 Immersive Learning Environments

As a modern technology, virtual reality in education is a revolutionary teaching method that eliminates some of the possibilities of a traditional classroom. It uses technologies and the form of interaction that enables the student to be more interested and focused to lessons. The following is an outline of its strengths that helps VR to avoid or mitigate challenges Shafique, R., Aljedaani, W., Rustam, F., Lee, E., Mehmood, A., & Choi, G. S. (2023) & Wilson,2019).

1.18.10 Active Participation and Exploration

Through virtual reality students can virtually touch information by having the lessons in simulated 3D environments to maximize understanding gained through presence and participation (Bray, M., Shafique, R., Aljedaani, W., Rustam, F., Lee, E., Mehmood, A., & Choi, G. S. (2023), A., & Green, T. D. (2004) et al,2021).

1.18.11 Multisensory Engagement

As a multimodal interaction technology, virtual reality (VR) allows a user to touch or feel objects and perceive what has been developed academically as images of different media with additional senses of touch, sound, and sight simultaneously, at a deeper level than what has been usually achieved in traditional teaching and learning methodologies (Mantovani, F. (2001), C. (2008),2018).

1.18.12 Personalized and Adaptive Learning

Virtual reality (VR) has a dynamic and tailored approach to learning and instructional delivery, where by teachers are able to adapt to the learning capacities of students using virtual interactive and flexible learning modules and setting up simulation (Song, C., Shin, S. Y., & Shin, K. S. (2023),2021).

1.19 Bridging the Gap

Virtual Reality in education has a lot of benefits such as movement and motivation, absorbing knowledge and improve learners' comprehension and recall levels, presentation with multi-learning styles, and practical application. Learnification in VR is very engaging due to the ability of giving students a fully encompassing experience that they will naturally have a desire to learn. It also brings meaningful engagements between students and information as well as enhances application of learnt information in the classroom. Another advantage of VR is that it provides an environment where students learn how to apply the received theoretic data in real-life practice, thus connecting academic and experiential knowledge. Nonetheless, while using VR in teaching, there are some disadvantages and advantages which includes: the problems faced by the teachers in incorporating technology, the learners' interaction and, the comparative advantage of VR in relation to other teaching instruments. Therefore, future studies are required to provide additional insights into the effectiveness of the studied technology concerning the overall learning outcomes and its ability to offer a unprecedented educational model (Anderson,2020; Fleck, S., & Hachet, M. (2016) & Wilson,2019).

1. How does VR impact student engagement and motivation in educational settings?
   Virtual Reality (VR) effectively sharpens students' spatial sensitization, visualization especially in the core courses such as science, engineering and arithmetic. The system offers a range of demonstrations and the real 3D environment where students are enabled to control objects and examine spatial relations. It also assists the learner to develop understanding of the relative positioning of objects as well as relationship between structures and systems hence improving the spatial intelligence. This should convince critics of VR that the experiences offered in the environment improve students' knowledge and analytical skills.
2. What are the cognitive benefits of using VR for learning complex subjects?
   Virtual reality in education sharpens and improves students' three-dimensional perspective and visualization skills when tackling difficult content such as science, engineering, and mathematics. It offers realistic experiences and dynamic context to incorporate physical objects and elements of space and time where students are able to move different objects virtually and comprehend relations between them. This approach in education enables the students to get access to understanding structures and systems, improve on their spatial awareness and skills in critical thinking. A study established that students are more knowledgeable and adept at problem-solving after being subjected to a Virtual Reality lesson.
3. What challenges do educators face when integrating VR into the curriculum?
   The biggest hurdle for the adoption of VR in education is technological as well as structural in essence because of its the nature. These challenges include challenges teachers experience in implementing the VR systems in terms of installation and support, technical problems that may arise, and integration of the systems with current teaching environments. Other challenges are high costs associated with the procurements of VR hardware and software, adequate internet speed and computing

power to support VR; all of these put off the large scale uptake of VR education amongst institutions..

4. How cost-effective is VR implementation in schools compared to traditional educational tools?

   Adopting Virtual Reality in classrooms entail high capital investment costs in acquiring VR equipments, licensing fees, and most importantly in the costs incurred in developing VR contents. Motion controllers, tracking systems, and VR headsets are costly and may take a significant amount of money from schools to purchase; moreover, acquiring these components might be critical for schools to provide teachers with the essentials and educational outcomes they require in terms of professional development and training to help them adapt to new materials.

1.20 Objectives

1.20.1 Examining the Impact and Challenges of VR in Education

R is an innovative technology in learning that exposes learners to realistic worlds in which they can learn. This scholarly research focuses on the impacts of gamification on students' engagement, benefits on cognition and learning, challenges and limitations, as well as cost factors on learning spaces. It entails assessing its cognitive advantages, limitations, and cost.

Finally, the objective aims at evaluating the effectiveness of proposed interventions and methods.

1. **To evaluate how virtual reality affects student motivation and participation.**
   Therefore, the purpose of this research will be to evaluate the efficacy of Virtual Reality (VR) in enhancing student motivation and learning engagement. In promoting the goals of the research, it gathers both the qualitative and quantitative data in order to assess the dynamicity of various student participations in the VR scenarios. Educational VR experiences are explored in terms of the presence and influence on the students' focus, interest, and interactions with educational contents and processes. It aims at finding out those aspects that help in invoking higher level of motivation and active participation in learning trough VR and finding out some of the barriers or conditions that might demotivate learners in VR learning environment (Mantovani, F. (2001), C. (2008) & Joshson,2021).

2. **To evaluate the cognitive benefits of VR-based learning.** The intent of the study is also to assess the extent, reduction of, and/or enhancement of cognitive learning through virtual reality (VR) when learning challenging concepts and sharpening perceived cognitive skills. It will focus on the effects that virtual reality experiences have on such faculties as focusing capacity, memory function, spatial awareness, analytical and logical thinking abilities. As the educational neuroscience and cognitive theories state, the value of learning with the help of virtual reality can be measured and its impact on cognition and learning abilities can be accurately assessed within the frame of intervention conducted through cognitive tests and neuromaging studies (Anderson et al,2019).
3. **To identify the challenges and limitations of VR in education.** The following is the research question: What are the perceptions of teachers in regard to implementation of Virtual Reality (VR) in education? The study will entail surveys, interviews, and focus groups. It aims to examine experiences and obstacles encountered for integrating VR in the learning process – the levels of institutional encouragement, curriculum match, technology complexity, and availability constraints. Specifically, the study aims to establish whether or not these elements affect teachers' attitudes and use of VR technology in the education setting (Kaplan-Rakowski, R., Papin, K., & Hartwick, P. M. (2022 & miller,2020).

1.21 Importance of the Research

This research provides a review on the possible utilization of virtual reality characteristics in the teaching and learning process hence important for educators, policymakers and other stakeholders. The access is an invariant feature, and the advantages and limitations of Virtual Reality implementation are explored and discussed and it underlines potential practical applications in the field with regard to the outcomes of the research Shafique, R., Aljedaani, W., Rustam, F., Lee, E., Mehmood, A., & Choi, G. S. (2023) & Wilson,2019).

1.22 Advancing Educational Technology and Innovation

It is an investigation into VR especially as a teaching aid and as such, looks into the opportunities and risks involved. This stimulates the teachers and organizations to implement the versatile teaching approaches and integrate the new technologies in the educational systems, for example the augmented and virtual reality teaching, which in turn helps to transform the conventional methods of learning and improve the educative experiences (Bray, M., Shafique, R., Aljedaani, W., Rustam, F., Lee, E., Mehmood, A., & Choi, G. S. (2023), A., & Green, T. D. (2004) et al,2021).

1.23 Educating Curriculum Developers and Pedagogical Practices

The opportunity exists to investigate the educational effectiveness of the VR in other aspects of curriculum development and the teaching process in educational organizations. Regarding its cognitive benefits, the paper assesses its effects on motivation and learning outcomes of the students. As to the nature of the findings, the report sheds the light on general provisions on learning design alongside with the effective teaching practices which may assist educators in the process of designing engaging lessons, effective use of the techniques of virtual reality in class, and the creation of the effective approaches to designing the learning activities (Mantovani, F. (2001), C. (2008),2018).

1.24 Enhancing Student Engagement and Learning Outcomes

This paper explores the roles of VR to help improve students' learning motivation and engagement in order to design better learning environment. Its objective is to explain to teachers how the use of VR can enhance teaching and enhance students' achievements, as well as memory consolidation and a clear understanding of complex material. The detailed information about lessons and teachings shows that the students play an important role in their comprehension and effectiveness, and incorporation of VR can foster the students' engagement and interest (Joshson,2020).

1.25 Handling VR Integration's Obstacles and Restrictions

In this study, concerns gathered with regards to implementation issues and barriers of virtual reality (VR) in education are identified and discussed, such as infrastructure requirements, technicality, curriculum integration, and funding considerations. From the paper, it is recommended that strategists of policies and educators should come up with ways on how to eliminate such barriers and enable the utilization of VR technology in learning institutions (Song, C., Shin, S. Y., & Shin, K. S. (2023),2021).

1.26 Directing Allocation of Resources and Policy Decisions

As a result of this study, educational administrators and legislators who make decisions and allocate resources concerning the use of technologies in teaching can be informed by this study. It can inform policy making processes concerning the training opportunities for professional development, technology acquisition, funding sources, and the opportunities and the challenges of using virtual reality as part of education system. The insights can be useful when it comes to making decisions in programs intended for the support of VR technology application and resource management in schools (Anderson,2020).

1.27 Adding to the Body of Information Regarding Educational Technology

It contributes to the more defined understanding of educational technology based on studying prior research and generating empirical data on the application of virtual reality in classes. Altogether, it gives a clear outline on how VR could influence practices of teaching and learning in future, creates a clear road-map for future research and development in this fast growing productive sector and offers a guidance for future studies in educational technology Shafique, R., Aljedaani, W., Rustam, F., Lee, E., Mehmood, A., & Choi, G. S. (2023) & Wilson,2019).

2. LITERATURE REVIEW

2.1 Historical Context of Virtual Reality (VR)

Virtual reality (VR) has been in existence since the mid-twentieth century with such pioneers as motion and sensory systems for prototype video games known as Sensorama and other flight simulators. It became popular in education and other spheres, in the English speaking countries, at the end of the nineties – at the beginning of the two thousand (Christopoulos, A., Mystakidis, S., Pellas, N., & Laakso, M. J. (2021,2018).

2.2 Early VR Origins

2.2.1 Flight Simulators and Sensorama

Morton Heilig's invention of Sensorama in 1957 played an instrumental role in the evolution of the technology; Sensorama was built with the intent to offer viewers the possibility of an immersion in multi sensory-stories, which today constitutes modern VR technology.
During the late 1990s and the early years of the millennia, the growth in computer power, graphic rendering and motion capturing facilitated the creation of complex VR systems, subsequently in different fields.
Flight simulators, at the infancy of VR were at the forefront of VR applications in the sense that they trained pilots in using the aircraft controls and managing the actual situation that might occur in the real world outdoors by simulating the aircraft on VR and thus brought the first VR application in education very closely.
In the late 1990's and the early year 2000, computing capability for graphics, efficient rendering and improved motion capture made for more professional applications of virtual reality in the several fields.
During the late 1990s/early 2000s focused increased computing power, graphics rendering as well as the technological capabilities in motion tracking to produce the complex VR systems that are used in the industries.
Virtual Reality (VR) today is being employed in specific education programmes related to Military operations, Aviation and even in Medical field where real environment requires high risks along with expenses for mock training.
VR flight simulators are a common tool in aviation for pilots and are beneficial for training, starkly representing the craft and flight controls, as well as emergency situations which is valuable to improve pilots as well as familiarize with a broader range of plane models.
well into the late 1990s and the early 2000s, fueled by increased computing capabilities, better graphics and enhanced motion capture and tracking, VR was then tested in serious applications for different industries.
Some of the roles of virtual reality in a program enables the surgical doctors to perform what could be termed as mock surgery in computer generated surgical theaters before conducting real surgeries on patients. Educational patient engagement is another area where VR can be leveraged as with the use of actual virtual environments for displaying and demonstrating the patient medical procedures as well as body structures.

Some of the application of VR training simulations includes identification of operations of equipment during combat, tactical movements, as well as, other combats. These simulations offer realistic setting as needed for different operations that help troops train in actual settings, develop decision-making, coordination and collaboration skill required for military application.
Explaining the history of virtual reality, one has to state that during the late 1990 and the early years of the Gerntury, real-life uses of VR that went beyond just demonstrations of rather contrived prototypes that have been made possible by improvements in the computing power of computers, advances in graphics rendering technology as well as in motion tracking technology that allowed for the creation of advanced virtual reality systems' across the variety of industries.

2.2.2 Showcasing Virtual Reality's Educational Potential

the use of Virtual reality (VR) also presents some promise across different levels of education such as the K-12 education, colleges, and in vocational training. Its blended nature engages learners making your learning environment practical and rich. Due to the increasing popularity of the newest technologies, teachers have recently started investigating the possibility of using VR technology in such environments.
The two latter decades of the 20 th century presented real world use which took tangible shape for the use of VR over and above experimental modelling due to superior computing capacities, graphics and, motion tracking technologies which enabled robust VR systems in several domains.
A study on the awareness of virtual reality (VR) in the education arena reveals that VR has gained acceptance by educators and learners in the teaching learning environment in view of the enhanced and developing technologies. It has impacted fields such as physics engineering and history among other fields and has been boosted by remote and hybrid learning. In the case of virtual reality the benefits include; Its ability to offer real immersion virtual reality can be termed to have had a revolutionary impact on education due to its ability to transcend the differences between online learning and traditional classroom teaching and learning.

2.2.3 Developments in Virtual Reality Technology

As for the forming virtual reality technology, the progression has been gradual since the emergence of head mounted display if it is observed in the context of the spec, software, and graphics rendering. In terms of tracking, observers have been subjects to the powerful GPUs, enhanced tracking systems, and clearer screens which enhanced virtual reality. Lastly, the present day independence of almost all next-generation VR headsets such as HTC Vive Focus or Oculus Quest to the wired PC interface has reduced the question of connection and enhanced the actuality of VR execution (Doran, A, Mihalidis, P & Schaeche, A.2020).

2.2.4 Accessibility and Affordability

Wearable VR peripherals are also now becoming cheaper and more obtainable making virtual learning mechanisms possible within colleges and universities. There have been offers such as student discounts and scholarships and such funding systems have also made the implementation of VR technology easier because it has treated ''all'' students to be weavers of their own learning tools and a majority of them would not be in a position to finance it (Doran, Mihailidis, & Schaeche, 2020).

2.2.5 Integration Into Curricula

The prospect of applying VR in different learning domains has been identified by teachers to a significant extent. Universities and other establishments are adopting use of VR to supplement or broaden conventional learning models and offer richer experiences for learners. The areas in science learning where VR is practical include learning facts and concepts about the molecular biology and astronomy, performance of experiments in virtual environment, and emulation of the events in sciences. Depending on its design it can also guide students to historical sites and events allowing them to be historically alive (Doran, Mihailidis, & Schaeche, 2020).

2.2.6 Immersive Learning Experiences

Virtual learning is a great innovation which focuses on the use of simulation techniques which cover students in the process. VR allows for learning that is more engaging and one that the veteran cannot achieve when reading through material. Students can search for information and reorganize it in order to interpret it and consolidate it in their knowledge. VR can mimic field trips to areas that are otherwise unreachable due to distance and time constraints; Students can visit virtual museums, historical sites and even cultural events. It also provides an intriguing portrayal of past events and their details (Merchant Group, 2019).

2.2.7 Bridging the Gap in Remote and Hybrid Learning

Doran, Mihailidis, & Schaeche, 2020 acknowledged the use of virtual learning in response to the COVID-19 pandemic and identified VR as the integration of classroom and online learning. This makes it fulfill the student's social needs beyond the degree of asynchronous platform or even video conferencing where such requirements are limited to only one or two aspects of the learning, making VR to include virtual classroom, simulation, and virtual environments to bring presence and or community into the distant learning .

2.2.8 Theoretical Framework for Virtual Reality (VR) in Education

This section also composes theoretical supports that one need to realise and implement VR-based educational interventions, particularly such principals based on constructivism by Jean Piaget and more on Lev Vygotsky and David Kolb's experiential learning theory. It is through these theories that one can appreciate how VR improves opportunities for practical learning and also minimizes the complexity involved in knowledge acquisition through practical learning and engagement, explaining why VR is widely used in learning (Merchant Group, 2019).

2.2.9 Experiential Learning Theory

David Kolb's experiential learning theory, developed in the 1980s, posits that learning is a lifelong process involving four stages: observing-reflecting-thinking, hypothesizing-testing-verifying, experimenting-conferring-acting; active participation, thinking through and acting out, emergency education plan used by the students; theoretical and practical experience (Merchant Group, 2019).

2.2.10 Application to VR in Education

Another (Teaching Method) that correlates well with experiential learning is the Virtual Reality (VR) because it integrates students into simulated environments where they can engage in real life experiences. This strategy improves learning hence helping student to achieve objectives set as well as offers practical distinction and experience in performing real-life exercises. Furthermore, the skills and achievements captured in the real environment are augmented with reflective observation that inspires students to assess outcomes and look for improvements. Being an effective and enjoyable teaching and learning tool, its interactive learning format enables students engage them in a process where knowing is done actively; a process where students are able to not only try out concepts and ideas, work out problems as well as think through challenges and apply knowledge in concrete situations, all of which enhances the learning process (Merchant Group, 2019).

2.2.11 Constructivist Theories

Some constructivist theories; the cognitive development theory by Jean Piaget, the socio-cultural theory by Lev Vygotsky also support the notion that learners actively build their conceptual systems in relation to the surroundings. In structural development, Piaget named four types of stages of cognitive development, while in sociocultural development, Vygotsky emphasized that cognitive social intercourse and cultural history play a vital role in the process of cognitive development. Achievement for Vygotsky required teaching and interaction; he postulated that learning is a social affair occurring through cooperation, construction, and apprenticeship (Doran, Mihailidis, & Schaeche, 2020).

2.2.12 Application to VR in Education

Virtual reality (VR) is another tool fully embedded in interactive educational environment which allows students to navigate through the virtual world, enhancing the substantial and, therefore, information comprehension. Instead of passive reception of information, it enables creating students' perception based on their problem solving and team work. It also provides support, criticisms, encouragements making it possible for the students and teachers to participate in a socializes and cooperate (Merchant Group, 2019).

2.3 Previous Studies on the Impact of Virtual Reality (VR) in Education

his section discusses the growing body of studies on the training of VR on education: the findings and strategies within these papers, and consequently the potential of VR for educational practice (Doran, Mihailidis, & Schaeche, 2020).

2.3.1 Systems Reviews and Meta-Analyses

In an independent study involving the Merchant Group, meta-analysis research was done regarding the impact of virtual reality (VR) on teaching; results showed boosted results with emphasis on science and engineering most significantly. Describing the difference from conventional teaching methods, the participants observed that the physical presence, interaction, and recall of the concept through the VR environments boosted motivation. At the same time, it pointed to issues that critics have long railed against, such as high costs and technology problems (Merchant Group, 2019).

2.4 Research on Experiments and Semi-Experiments

2.4.1 Wu and associates (2013)

USing an experimental research design, Wu et al sought to determine the effects of learning through the use of Virtual Reality in geometry lessons on the understanding of the topic by students. According to the outcomes of the study, students who learned geometry using a virtual reality environment comprehended and retained geometry concepts better than other students who learned the concepts in a traditional classroom setting. Hence, the students were active in the seemingly impractical geometric ideas because of the whole and encompassing features of VR simulations.

2.4.2 Ke and Im (2014)

The effects of problem solving in physics among leveled students through the implementation of VR-based learning were studied by Ke & Im. It sought to establish differences between the group of students who were subjected to VR simulations and the students who were subjected to traditional teaching approaches. This work revealed that by getting the Perkins' model implemented within the VR based learning environment students are able to practice more and carry out better experiments, change the variables, and observe the outcomes in real time (ke & Im,2014).

2.5 Observational Studies and Case Studies

2.5.1 The Erickson group (2017)

Erickson et al. explored the applicability of using VR technology to teach High school Biology in a case study research. They established that introduction of VR provides enhanced student interaction and a better understanding of biodiverse subjects. However, some of the issues also emerged which included; for instance, inadequate access to the different types of VR gear and fewer professionals qualified to help with the usage of the gear (Erickson,2017).

2.5.2 Yang and Lai (2020)

Lai and Yang distributed an observational study on technology acceptance of college engineering courses through embodied actuality of VR simulations. Studying case, the authors elaborated that such use of VR simulations enhance student collaboration, problem solving and engagement. Students were able to obviously conceptually concisely, play around design methodologies and get the response immediately. Nonetheless, the use of the technologies was hindered by the technical flu that it had such barriers of motion sickness and equipment failure (Yang & Lai,2020).

2.6 Research on Virtual Reality (VR) in Education Is Still Lacking

Allowing for the fact that the investigation of the use of virtual reality (VR) in education has progressed relatively recently, there are questions that remain open, and further research directions. Future studies should incorporate these considerations in a great detail, mentioning key issues with the present state of research Shafique, R., Aljedaani, W., Rustam, F., Lee, E., Mehmood, A., & Choi, G. S. (2023) & Mantovani, F. (2001), C. (2008), 2021).

2.7 Insufficient Longitudinal Research

While VR is being adopted in education, assessments of the effects of virtual learning have been largely cross-sectional and few studies examined lasting changes in student achievement. For now, the published studies address only the Short-term effects and Instant 'learning' effects while the longevity, the permanency and the long-term dynamics of the VR-models remain underexplored. Longitudinal designs are particularly informative for understanding the effectiveness of applied techniques of learning through VR Shafique, R., Aljedaani, W., Rustam, F., Lee, E., Mehmood, A., & Choi, G. S. (2023) & Mantovani, F. (2001), C. (2008), 2021).

2.8 Insufficient Study on Scalability and Cost-Effectiveness

The first research gap revolves around the strained literature on education, in that there is no extensive substantive research in relation to the sustainability and cost-effectiveness of Virtual Reality (VR). Although VR may improve learning, issues related to the application of VR and concerns with its affordances need further considerations. More experimental studies are required to investigate the applicability of VR across and within the context of K-12 schooling, higher education, and vocational training programmes (Bray, M., Shafique, R., Aljedaani, W., Rustam, F., Lee, E., Mehmood, A., & Choi, G. S. (2023), A., & Green, T. D. (2004) & Johnson, 2020).

2.9 Lack of Research on Educator Support Needs and Challenges

As with the interest in the use of VR technology increases, there is scant literature exploring the problems that teachers face in incorporating VR into lessons. Barriers are characterized by lack of knowledge in technology, fewer promotional chances within their working stations as well as restricted access to resources. Knowledge of these issues is instrumental in devising proper measures and actions to manage VR applied to educational endeavours, like endowing teachers with VR tools for professional development activities, designing training programs, and creating VR instructions (Lopez & Carter, 2019).

2.10 Insufficient Examination of Issues Related to Equity and Inclusion

The current literature review points to an area of the research that has yet addressed on the impact of VR in education and specifically on inclusion and equity. Issues like access and participation rates will compel many students of color and first-generation college students into questioning. They were asked about challenges that need to be solved to make sure all students receive benefits from VR technologies if the later is implemented into education environment: In this aspect, Underrepresentation of these communities, digital literacy, relevance of VR material to cultural context, and, at last, accessibility of VR equipment and software, including its cost, need solutions (Peters & Thomas, 2022).

2.11 Insufficient Attention to Ethical and Social Consequences

The adoption of VR in the education sector come in several challenges regarding privacy, security, and citizenship, moreover; how students relationships and overall wellbeing might be affected. CT researchers and educators should address such concerns as the legal protection for data privacy, participants' consent, appropriate use of VR material, and other principles of responsible virtual citizenship focusing on the ways VR therapies would uphold moral standards of virtual practices for the sake of both participants' well-being and the general population (Omasta, M., & Snyder-Young, D. (2022) & Martin, 2020).

2.12 Approach

The research method chapter of a research proposal outlines the approaches to the research, the methods and tools employed in the collection of data and the techniques used in quantifying the effects of VR on learning performance and learners' engagement in learning using population data through a mixed method research design (Omasta, M., & Snyder-Young, D. (2022) & Martin, 2020).

2.13 Mixed-Methods Research Design Approach

The study by this writer implements an experimental research methodology that uses both quantitative and qualitative methods in analyzing the usage of virtual reality technology, teaching approaches, and learning achievement. The approach accrues various information from surveys, experiment, focus group, and interviews, which helps in getting views of various angles of the study issue (Omasta, M., & Snyder-Young, D. (2022) & Martin, 2020).

2.14 The Quantitative Aspect

It tests hypothesis about the effects of VR on learning achievement and learners' interaction employing survey-based research and experimental research study. Surveys collect information from different people, while experimental research measures the changes in dependent variables brought on by changing independent variables; causes and effects are assessed (Omasta, M., & Snyder-Young, D. (2022) & Martin, 2020).

2.15 The Qualitative Aspect

The study is of qualitative nature and the primary data is therefore collected by way of focus groups and interviews where educators and students express their opinions on virtual reality at schools. Such an approach helps to avoid the identification of straightforward pros and cons of using VR in education and enables the participants to share their ideas of how VR usage in this context can be further developed and improved .

2.16 Data Gathering Techniques

Surveys will be employed as for data collection in relation to students' engagement, perceptions and achievements in environments that incorporate Virtual Reality in learning, and these include Demographic Questions, Likert Scale and closed Questions. Data will be varnish and studied by means of descriptive, comparative and concluding methods (Omasta, M., & Snyder-Young, D. (2022) & Martin, 2020).

2.17 Pilot Research

The effects of VR interventions as a teaching method will also be examined on students' academic performance through comparing between the group that received VR intervention and the group that used traditional method of learning. Assessments will be in form of pre-test and post-test to determine the retention level, and new information gained along the course of the training. The research hypothesis for the study is as follows: H1: VR therapies are effective in treating AD The following inferential statistical tests will be used in the study: t-tests and ANOVA tests (Omasta, M., & Snyder-Young, D. (2022) & Martin, 2020).

2.18 Conversations

Teachers will sit for semi-structured interviews whereby they will be asked about their outstanding experience and difficulties they have encountered in implementing virtual reality in lessons. Some of the areas that fall under it include curriculum integration, students' engagement, technological assistance, and business instructional processes. In this study, the process of categorization will be used and through thematic analysis, the common themes will be determined (Omasta, M., & Snyder-Young, D. (2022) & Martin, 2020).

2.19 Focus Groups

Students will attend focus group involving discussion on specified concept of virtual reality in learning environment, more specifically focusing on usability, immersion, relevance and subsequent result. The type of analysis that will be used is thematic analysis with the objectives of identifying the themes of the lesson, the opposing views, and potential changes (Omasta, M., & Snyder-Young, D. (2022) & Martin, 2020).

2.20 Methods of Data Analysis

Descriptive, correlational and inferential statistical tools would be applied on quantitative data collected from survey, and experiments research regarding demographic characteristics, students' participation and relevance, and effects of VR treatments on learning outcome (Omasta, M., & Snyder-Young, D. (2022) & Martin, 2020).

2.21 Analysis of Qualitative Data

Since focus group data and interviews collected will be in form of interviews, thematic content analysis technique will be adopted so as to discover themes that are of core essence in the research study. Interrogative, most: Open coding of participants' individual experience with and perception of VW in education will be performed line by line with, in addition, member check and data triangulation to ensure the study's reliability (Omasta, M., & Snyder-Young, D. (2022) & Martin, 2020).

2.22 The Sample and Population

The demographic and sample part of a study under the area of interest in this regard is vital for analyzing the impact of Virtual Reality as a significant aspect of learning; it also entails determining the sample size as well as the sampling method and population target.

2.23 The Aim Audience

The research will focus on both current K-12 and higher education teachers and students, who actively implement virtual reality in their classes, with the view of acknowledging a variety of perspectives on VR use in education.

2.24 Quantity of Sample

To capture different perceptions of VR use in FAWE, the study targets fifty teachers -and 300 students. Please note that the sample size is moderate and equal for learners and instructors in order to capture both their attitudes and outcomes.

2.25 Techniques for Gathering Data

These approaches involve focus group, questionnaires, interviews and experimental research to establish the impacts of virtual reality in education where data is collected quantitatively and qualitatively in terms of learning, instructors' perception and learners' engagement.

2.26 Questionnaires

This research incorporates surveying as a methodology for assessing quantitative data of students' VR-based learning experience concerning the perceived outcomes, motivation, satisfaction and engagement. Some survey questions also concern the teaching practices, including instructional practices, technologies, and professional learning needs.

2.27 Benefits of Surveys

Efficiency: Researchers are able, quickly and at a short notice, to obtain information from a large pool of people through surveys.
Standardization: The use of questionnaires makes it easy to have consistent data across groups as well as across participants and also makes the identification of participants in similar groups easier.
Quantitative Analysis: Survey replies can be analyzed quantitatively so that the researchers can have an understanding of the pattern, trend, and relations in the obtained results.

2.28 Conversations

This research employs face-to-face, semi-structured interviews as a data collection tool to obtain teachers' qualitative views regarding the implementation of virtual reality in learning environments, including the pedagogical potential benefits of using VR, the technological challenges they face when incorporating technologies such as VR in their class, strategies they employ to facilitate effective use of virtual reality in class, and recommendations they have for improvement of the use of such technologies as VR.

2.29 Benefits of Interviewing

Depth: The participants expressing their thoughts, experiences and opinions in their own words during interviews yield the respondents' elaborate data.
Flexibility: Though a semi-structured interview retains some structure to guide the discussion, it allows the researcher to cover new issues that arise in the exploration.
Participant Perspective: Qualitative interviews may help researchers gain a substantially richer insight into participants' perceptions as the interviews give a voice to the participants.

2.30 Discussion Groups

Focus groups are another form of data collection tools that are used to analyze the personal viewpoints and encounters of students concerning VR-based learning, A simplistic moderator focuses on usability, immersion, engagement and perceived advantages and difficulties of a certain product then people from the group express their ideas and opinions.
The benefits of focus groups:The technique permits discussion and communication and increases the probability of studying diverse experiences and opinions due to the members in focus groups.
Peer Influence: Other effects like the reciprocal encouragement of the members of the group and the resultant fulfillment and stimulation may also come out from the identification of group dynamics.
Rich Data: Responding to how the study collected detailed, qualitative data that portray the comprehensive picture on experiences and perceptions of participants, the author notes that focus group discussions mirror the complexities of focus group discussions.

2.31 Research via Experiments

Finally, the experimental research are quantitative research type that help understand causal relationships between factors. In performing research studies, the efficacy of the VR treatments is assessed in relation to learning outcomes tied to VR students while ascertaining whether or not the VR students outperform traditional classroom methods by conducting controlled experiments.

2.32 Benefits of Research using Experiments

Causality: To untangle confounding factors, experimental research designs help distinguish the effects of relations between independent and dependent variables.
Control: Because the experimenters have control over the environment, they can study any variables they wish and ensure that the amounts can be precisely controlled.
Generalizability: High internal designs enhance the validity of the results as it reduces mere probability of getting similar results upon testing the same hypothesis on a different population by the researchers.

2.33 Process

The operational part of a research process describes the ways and means of acquiring data, procedures of acting on subjects, as well as assessing the intervention effects, for example, Virtual Reality on learning (Mantovani, F. (2001), C. (2008) & Jackson, 2021).

2.34 Distribution of Surveys

Surveys are delivered electronically either by email list or online platforms and have a potential coverage, ease of dicharging and efficiency added by features such as reminders for participation (Check, J., & Schutt, R. K. (2011) & Song, C., Shin, S. Y., & Shin, K. S. (2023), 2019).

2.35 Holding Focus Groups and Interviews

Sharing online observation of focus groups and interviews is carried out using online video conferencing platforms such as Zoom, Microsoft Teams, and Google Meet whereby the researcher communicates with participants through video conferencing in a predetermined order and following their consent (Omasta, M., & Snyder-Young, D. (2022) & Martin, 2020).

2.36 Partially Organized Format

Focus groups that are semi-structured and interviews give the researcher the chance to have different questions while at the same time remaining consistent with responses that are gained; the facilitators of such tours invited participants to express their opinions regarding virtual reality in education (Omasta, M., & Snyder-Young, D. (2022) & Martin, 2020).

2.37 Configuration for the Experiment

Collectively, experimental investigations involve a split-up of the participants into the control group and the experimental group, whereby the participants are always grouped by a random process to help in the elimination of such biases. The strategies used here involve implementing VR interventions to the experimental group while the control group is taught in conventional methods (Mantovani, F. (2001), C. (2008) & Jackson, 2021).

2.38 VR Educational Resources

Those modules that use Virtual Reality as a learning tool are incorporated in experimental groups to build, support, develop interest and provide knowledge through application of learning via different interfaces and using apps and simulation (Mantovani, F. (2001), C. (2008) & Jackson, 2021).

2.39 Gathering and Examining Data

Tools of descriptive and inferential statistics are used to compare the data gathered via experiments and surveys and to assess the correlation between the groups being compared (Check, J., & Schutt, R. K. (2011) & Song, C., Shin, S. Y., & Shin, K. S. (2023), 2019).

2.40 Qualitative Information

Thematic analysis applied to analyze the qualitative data collected from the focus group and interview and usually involves coding the data, looking for the data relating to theme and making overall patterns on the identified themes while making the participants'quote to keep the discussion open (Omasta, M., & Snyder-Young, D. (2022) & Martin, 2020).

2.41 Examining Data

Data analysis involves the use of various techniques to make data intelligible after going through the process of data collection and compilation. Qualitative research was employed in this study to assess the impact of the adoption of VR on the learning sector (Omasta, M., & Snyder-Young, D. (2022) & Martin, 2020).

2.42 Analysis of Quantitative Data

Descriptive and inferential statistics are applied in this study to analyze actual survey question responses and objective participant data with perspectives of trends, relationships and regularity (Check, J., & Schutt, R. K. (2011) & Song, C., Shin, S. Y., & Shin, K. S. (2023), 2019).

2.43 Typical Statistics

Descriptive statistics offers full picture of the characteristics of the sample being investigated, as well as variability and distribution of variables which helps in comprehending the variability, core pattern and distributional features of surveys and experiments data (Check, J., & Schutt, R. K. (2011) & Song, C., Shin, S. Y., & Shin, K. S. (2023), 2019).

2.44 Inferential Statistics

This research uses post hoc and comparisons tests such as regression analysis, correlation analysis, ANOVA, and t-tests to analyze the differences between the groups, relationships between variables, and overall significance of findings (Check, J., & Schutt, R. K. (2011) & Song, C., Shin, S. Y., & Shin, K. S. (2023), 2019).

2.45 Analysis of Qualitative Data

TIn this research, the approach used for analyzing the data set is qualitative analysis as it is aimed at developing themes, patterns, and meanings in the focus group transcripts and instructor and student interviews (Omasta, M., & Snyder-Young, D. (2022) & Martin, 2020).

2.46 Analysis by Theme

Thematic analysis is an iterative procedure used for identifying and categorizing the pattern in the data collected, which can help researchers understand the participant experience, perception, and vision of incorporating VR technology in learning institution (Omasta, M., & Snyder-Young, D. (2022) & Martin, 2020).

2.47 Coding Methods

Coding techniques are used in analysis of qualitative data with a view of categorizing the data into useful units by means of which the researcher is in a position to find out what is being repeated; to realize something new; and to get a total understanding of the data (Omasta, M., & Snyder-Young, D. (2022) & Martin, 2020).

2.48 Moral Points to Remember

CONCLUSION Ethical procedures and principles are vital in carrying out research involving human subjects, particularly in the case of educational use of virtual reality (Peters & Thomas, 2022).

2.49 Knowledgeable Assent

An example of an ethical principle is informed consent whereby participants must be aware of the kind of project that the researcher will conduct, its purposes, the risks involved, and possible benefits. Far-reaching information on processes, risk and/or outcome, confidentiality and the rights to resignation without prejudice are featured in this study (Peters & Thomas, 2022).

2.50 Confidentiality and Anonymity

To safeguard identifiable information of participants in the study, this study will assign each participant a code and will keep information that will identify him/her separately from the study data. Records of data collected are ordinarily kept in locked cabinets or computers or other storage sections requiring passwords to gain entry in the hands of qualified researchers (Peters & Thomas, 2022).

Steps to Guarantee Confidentiality and Anonymity:

The use of participant IDs or codes where the actual identity of the participant is not used but rather generated codes.

differentiation of the contents of the science section from individual information that a user might not wish to share.

limited access to data for only official workers and those participants who are included in the research.

Secure or enclosed or encrypted forms of digital or electronic systems cavinents.

2.51 Approval by Ethics

Where the research involves human participants, the researcher must have permission from the Institutional Review Board (IRB) or ethical clearance from an ethics committee. The IRB has oversight of the specifics of study matters of the kind such as; design of the study, clearance of informed consent, data collection plans among others with the aim of conforming to established ethical standards (Christopoulos, A., Mystakidis, S., Pellas, N., & Laakso, M. J. (2021 & Harris, 2018).

2.52 Procedure for Getting Ethical Approval

The study protocol was submitted to the institutional review board of the experiment.

Reviewing, specifically, the protocols, the informed consent forms and the overall construction of the research.

Assessment of risk that can be faced to participants and measures to avoid them.

Provision with the research's IRB or an ethics committee (Mantovani, F. (2001), C. (2008), 2021).

2.53 Findings

The section called outcomes typically includes the results of the study which is referred to goals and questions of the research. It entails computed answers to administered questionnaires, research experiments, and comprehensive qualitative data and in its presentation it incorporates figures such as tables, graphs and charts Shafique, R., Aljedaani, W., Rustam, F., Lee, E., Mehmood, A., & Choi, G. S. (2023) & Miller, 2020).

2.54 Data Presentation

The results of the study can be highlighted as coherent by using clear tables, graphs, charts, inferential statistics, and descriptive statistics, which enhance understanding for readers (Bray, M., Shafique, R., Aljedaani, W., Rustam, F., Lee, E., Mehmood, A., & Choi, G. S. (2023), A., & Green, T. D. (2004) & Roberts, 2019).

2.55 Tables;

Tables are a structured way of displaying quantitative information, which is generally used to present a précised summary of experiments, questionnaires, and manners of summarizing data (Song, C., Shin, S. Y., & Shin, K. S. (2023) & Black, 2019).

2.56 Graphs

This work relies on graphical presentment to make representations of data and their developments, relations and associations on scatter diameters, line chart and bar chart. Line graphs are used to demonstrate trends as those in Figure 2, whereas bar graphs compare the mean scores as in Figure 4 and scatter plots illustrate data relationships as in Figure (Johnson & Clark, 2020).

2.57 Diagrams

Pie charts and radar charts and other related charts are best used for revealing relationships and various data based on category and response hence, offering different angles in presenting the findings Shafique, R., Aljedaani, W., Rustam, F., Lee, E., Mehmood, A., & Choi, G. S. (2023), 2018).

2.58 Important Results

The area of the research paper focuses on the results of the conducted research on the consequences of using virtual reality in the learning process, the impact on the learners and instructors, the level of learners' engagement, and cost-efficiency (Lopez & Carter, 2019).

2.59 Participation of Students

Some of the specific observations gathered from them include ; ¬According to the survey, students who have applied the VR technology in education express great motivation as compared to the conventional methods. The engagement and interactivity resulting from the comparatively 'virtual' nature of VR environments work to engage students more effectively, thereby providing a more stimulating learning process (Mantovani, F. (2001), C. (2008) & Johnson, 2020).

2.60 Analysis

The use of virtual reality in education to enhance information delivery and achieve effective utilization of the systems tools can as well act as a catalyst for active participation of students in class by offering them virtual relativity. One can develop virtual scenarios which supplements the content to be taught to the learners in the classrooms, to support deeper learning experiences (Christopoulos, A., Mystakidis, S., Pellas, N., & Laakso, M. J. (2021 & Harris, 2018).

2.61 Learning Results

In a study highlighted in this literature, students who are taught using the VR technology proved to have better understanding, skills in visualization, knowledge retention, test performance, and practical application correlated with VR usage (Song, C., Shin, S. Y., & Shin, K. S. (2023) & Black, 2019).

2.62 Analysis

These include learning from the study that the integration of virtual reality (VR) technology in teaching and learning process improves the students scores and cognitive skills due to the interactive and immersive nature of the course (Johnson & Clark, 2020).

2.63 Teacher Difficulties

Survey questions asked during the interviews shown below expose various problems arising from the application of VR technology in teaching approaches: Technical difficulties, lack of support, inadequate or unavailable training, and expensive costs (Mantovani, F. (2001), C. (2008), 2021).

2.64 Analysis

The practice challenges educators to transcend the technology, training, and resource hurdles with regard to the successful adoption of VR technology in education, while institutions offering financing and technical support and professional development for instructors (Lopez & Carter, 2019).

2.65 Comprehensive Evaluation

I had written the section of analysis after the research study and here, I have analyzed the effect of Virtual Reality (VR) on the students' engagement and the future perception of education Shafique, R., Aljedaani, W., Rustam, F., Lee, E., Mehmood, A., & Choi, G. S. (2023) & Mantovani, F. (2001), C. (2008), 2021).

2.66 Involvement of Students

STUDY RESULT: From the innovation of utilizing virtual reality in teaching students, it is very evident that motivation to learn and learning interest is greatly enhanced as opposed to normal teaching methods. In their current state, availability of VR experiences is paramount for keeping users engaged due to the depth of the platforms. Issues related to educational practice are discerned from the findings of this study (Christopoulos, A., Mystakidis, S., Pellas, N., & Laakso, M. J. (2021 & Harris, 2018).

2.67 A Higher Level of Student Engagement Can Be Attained via Immersion and Interactivity

VR setting makes my teaching interesting and dynamic whereby the students are provoked to learn by creating a setting that captures their virtual world of interest. The goal of using Virtual Reality Application based on concepts and phenomena is that VR is three-dimensional, multisensorial space that makes learning concepts and phenomena more effective and interesting for pupils (Mantovani, F. (2001), C. (2008) & Johnson, 2020).

2.68 Possibilities for Active Learning

Some of the benefits of virtual reality (VR) for students include creating opportunities for students to solve problems, handling virtual objects and changing the data. This makes students' engagement to be determined by their desire as most of the VRs are experiential hence students would feel like they are in control .

2.69 Personalized Learning Environments

Virtual Reality could be chosen according to the needs and inclinations of a learner or determined individually, which will allow learners to work with the content at their pace and with emphasis on the approaches that they find most comfortable.

2.70 Real-World Relevance

virtual reality simulations and experience create enhanced and more related feeling with actuality where learning takes place therefore makes the learning sessions more meaningful and impactful for the pupils. Virtual learning (VL) solves the problem of a conceptual understanding and disconnection with practical implementation by transferring theories and concepts into the virtual reality environment (Song, C., Shin, S. Y., & Shin, K. S. (2023) & Black, 2019).

2.71 Intrinsic Motivation

A self-interest or motivation comes from students engaging the content by the mere excitement of using VR in learning contexts. 'By their nature, students become intrigued by various phenomena, and investigations initiated with VR gear are fun, interesting and require no extra encouragement since students are eager to discover things on their own (Bray, M., Shafique, R., Aljedaani, W., Rustam, F., Lee, E., Mehmood, A., & Choi, G. S. (2023), A., & Green, T. D. (2004) & Roberts, 2019).

2.72 VR Technology Integration's Implications for Educational Practice

Proficient use of virtual reality in classes may assist teachers to create better opportunities of motivated teaching so as to enhance the learners' motivation (Lopez & Carter, 2019).

2.73 Multimodal Learning Approaches

Virtual reality (VR) is an effective and enhanced means of learning, and if provided along with the traditional practices of learning, will prove helpful in a range of learning styles. To integrate VR, educators could enhance learning by integrating VR as additional rather than a replacement for traditional pass readiness techniques, texts, blackboards, and implements (Johnson & Clark, 2020).

2.74 Professional Development and Training

When preparing to integrate the use of Virtual Reality technology into their teaching, other professionals in the field assert that teachers require enough practice and resources. Professional development programs for, say, VR-enhanced teaching have to provide teachers with the information, skills, and resources with which they can successfully design and implement the teaching of VR-enhanced classes Shafique, R., Aljedaani, W., Rustam, F., Lee, E., Mehmood, A., & Choi, G. S. (2023) & Mantovani, F. (2001), C. (2008), 2021).

2.75 Assessment and Evaluation

Due to shifts in educational practice, incorporating VR technology into teaching and learning spaces, there is a need to establish adequate and reliable assessments together with evaluation criteria to determine the impact of VR on learning and student learning. To address this line, the following evaluations can be proposed to give educators a more comprehensive picture of the learning experience, since it is within the context of virtual reality where learning is immersive and interactive (Bray, M., Shafique, R., Aljedaani, W., Rustam, F., Lee, E., Mehmood, A., & Choi, G. S. (2023), A., & Green, T. D. (2004) & Roberts, 2019).

3. FUTURE RESEARCH DIRECTIONS

3.1 Long-Term Effects

Further research is needed to better understand with VR helps students remain motivated and productive, and what impact this has on students' achievement in the longer term. Extensive three, four or five-year longitudinal studies may reveal how the technology influences learning outcomes for the learners in the long run, besides how effective it is when used in education .

3.2 Effectiveness Across Disciplines

Future research has to explore how responsive is VR technology in other professions and branches. In turn, the scholars can investigate the various impacts of VR in different learning contexts to identify the optimal methodologies and strategies to integrate VR across a diverse set of courses.

3.3 Accessibility and Equity

Equality and additional access options must be considered when using VR technology especially when applying it in teaching and learning contexts. Subsequent research must address issues of access, such as cost and technical factors and digital literacy, so that the potential benefit on learning outcomes of virtual reality-based learning is available to all learners.

3.4 Pedagogical Strategies

To get maximum of the educational benefits from the application of virtual reality technologies, the research should focus on such topics as identification of the effective approaches to instructions. It may thus be important for teachers to learn how to implement and facilitate VR-enhanced lectures that will ensure students remain engaged and achieve the best results possible.

3.5 Learning Outcomes

A study paper learning outcomes section in a study paper virtually provides a detailed analysis of how with reference to tests and evaluations, Virtual Reality (VR) impacts students' performance. This section analyses the findings from the experimental studies that compared the student outcomes when using virtual reality to other conventional teaching and learning methods. The appropriation of the application is explored in aspects related to en hancement of learning results in areas where visualization of complicated concepts is important, for instance, in science and engineering disciplines. It also examines the way the use of VR technology enhances student engagement in relation to the material, thus making learning smoother, easier, and more effective in terms of understanding and recall.

3.6 Experimental Studies and Assessment Results

Results of the experimental investigations, which were conducted in the framework of the research, indicated that in the case of using the VR technology instead of more traditional methods, students cleared the evaluations significantly better. The findings pointed to the reality that virtual reality together with learner centered approaches enhanced the scores since those learners who participated in the learning activities achieved better performance on tests in various content areas but science and engineering particularly.

3.7 Quantitative Analysis of Assessment Scores

When comparing the results of the questionnaire with the performance of other pupils and distinguishing the effect of using virtual reality, the following conclusions were made: Quantity analysis provided a statistically significant proof of the positive impact of virtual reality on the performance of pupils comparing to traditional learning approaches. This study also proves the importance of using the VR technology in learning by comparing the mean score of students in the VR group and the control group whereby the former record a higher mean students throughout.

3.8 Subject-Specific Improvements

Particularly, the experimental group revealed a statistically significant improvement in overall achievements such as physics and engineering that heavily relies on the use of virtual environment. According to assessment tests, pupils with virtual reality have better understanding of abstract notions and propositions as compare to traditional knowledge assessment.

3.9 Enhancing Understanding and Retention

Through use of virtual reality technology the users were able to interact with content in ways which enhanced knowledge retention among pupils for the topic being taught. Due to VR, students also could do experiments, solve the tasks in three dimensions, explore, and control virtual objects during the learning process while maintaining the interest to the subject.

3.10 Spatial Understanding and Visualization

The capability of VR technology in enhancing certain cognitive skills that are important in scientific and engineering disciplines including space creation and navigation is one of the noteworthy benefits. Considering the use of VR, students could perceive concepts and the phenomena of a particular area as natural as interesting; this would assist them in comprehending the material and memorizing it.

3.11 Experiential Learning Opportunities

Settings of virtual reality give pupils opportunities for learning experiences that cannot be posed in regular class teaching and learning practices. One major advantage of student engagement that was identified was the ability to apply theoretical knowledge within real-life scenarios owing to the use of virtual reality where actual event and surrounding were mimicked Students thus, attained a better understanding of the information that was being passed on to them.

3.12 Engagement and Motivation

Some of the benefits that have impelled motivation and engaged; student I include: A key feature that has been attributed to attainment of these results include; Investigation on the effects of VR-enhanced classes revealed that the propensity and participation level of students in a class was enhanced due to the VR and hence their involvement, attention and interest in the content was equally increased.

3.13 Implications for Educational Practice

The consequences involved with the findings with regard to learning outcomes impact on practice of education specifically in the realms of science and engineering. Educational administrators may enhance deliver – y strategies to make course content richer for student flow as well as comprehension, recall, and academic performance by having instructing staff integrate VR into class lessons.

3.14 Curriculum Design and Instructional Strategies

From the angle of Virtual Reality technologies, the educators might possibly design curricula and instructional procedures that enhance the concept of learning through experience, spatial learning, and imaging. Teachers can engage students and facilitate meaningful lessons by incorporating virtual environments, equipment, and various learning exercices into class.

3.15 Professional Development and Training

In employing virtual reality technology for the enhancement of teaching methods, the educators require adequate training and assistance since they initially come across the technologies as learners. For a professional development program to be effective, it has to provide teachers with the knowledge and skills essential for delivering VR-enabled lessons successfully.

3.16 Assessment and Evaluation

The enhancement of practices in education through the integration of virtual reality (VR) technology as a teaching aid requires the presence of effective assessment tools and evaluation criteria in order to measure impact of the VR implementation on learning. To embrace the overarchingly transformative conditions of learning, the educators should offer proper assessments in tune with the explorative and engaging processes inherent in the virtual reality environment.

3.17 Educator Challenges

The consideration of challenges affecting educators is a section that discusses the results from the interviews conducted with the teachers where it seeks to explain those challenges that teachers encounter when incorporating Virtual Reality (VR) into teaching and learning process. The study looks at what happens subsequent to these common issues, particularly with regards to how they affect educational practice and policy, and further contains an identification of issues which include: Technology constraints, lack of knowledge, and resource constraints. It is in this section that the writer seeks to offer educators a comprehensive preview of the challenges they are likely to face with the use of VR technology and gives possible recommendations on such issues.

3.18 Common Challenges Faced by Educators

3.18.1 Technical Difficulties

Among all the concerns which were identified, one of the most crucial is the problem of technicalities that concern virtual reality technology. Tenders with network connections, software compatibility issues and failure of devices often limit the effective utilization of VR in educational processes. But teachers are rather annoyed by these technological barriers while they cannot use VR tools and applications to provide unique and effective learning courses.

3.18.2 Lack of Training and Support

A portion of teachers has reported the lack of support and training with VR technology making them uncomfortable in the integration of the technology in their classes. They suggest a requirement for opportunities of professional training which will provide general guidelines on application of vr technologies and applications into learning contexts. To incorporate VR technology into the course, teachers may experience difficulty distinguishing the nature of VR as a medium on their own, and may be hesitant to integrate this into their teaching should they lack proper training on the matter.

3.18.3 High Costs and Limited Resources

They also noted on their research that for many schools, the cost of implementing VR technology is extremely high hence a major hurdle. VR hardware, software, and other accessories that include related equipment often require more money to purchase, which is often beyond the available financial resources of many schools, colleges, and universities with limited funding. In addition, the cost of maintaining and supporting the technology creates more pressure on the always-squeezed budgets of schools which can no longer afford to finance the costs of using VR beyond a certain point.

3.18.4 Implications for Educational Practice

It is essential to fund professional development initiatives that provide instructors the guidance and assistance they need to successfully incorporate virtual reality technology into their lesson plans. Educational institutions may enable teachers to employ VR technologies and applications to improve student learning outcomes by providing workshops, seminars, and online courses on VR pedagogy and instructional design.

3.18.5 Professional Development and Training

Infrastructure and technological assistance should be given top priority by educational institutions in order to handle the technical challenges posed by VR technology. The establishment of specialized IT support teams and helpdesk services may offer educators prompt support in resolving hardware and software problems, guaranteeing the seamless integration and functioning of virtual reality technology in educational environments.

3.18.6 Technical Support and Infrastructure

In order to facilitate the adoption and integration of virtual reality technology in educational institutions, policy makers and leaders in the field of education must allot enough funds and resources. Policymakers may help lower costs and promote a wider uptake of VR-enhanced learning experiences by setting aside money for the acquisition of VR gear, software licenses, and related equipment, as well as for continuing maintenance and support.

3.18.7 Funding and Resource Allocation

The financial aspects of integrating Virtual Reality (VR) technology in educational contexts are examined in the section on cost-effectiveness. Although VR technology, software, and infrastructure need an initial investment, the research indicates that VR has the potential to yield long-term advantages that outweigh the expenditures. This section examines the elements that make virtual reality (VR) in education cost-effective, such as enhanced learning outcomes and possible declines in dropout rates. It also showcases the experiences of educational institutions that have effectively used virtual reality, demonstrating how the advantages have outweighed the drawbacks.

3.18.8 Cost-Effectiveness

In the cost analysis, the feasibility of incorporating Virtual Reality (VR) into learning environments is discussed based on the financial repercussions that are incurred. The studies show that VR technology and software as well as VR infrastructure require an initial investment, yet the research illustrates that VR might bring more long-term benefits to an investment than the costs. The following sub-section looks at factors within VR in education that have a cost-savings potential including but not limited to; improved learning achievements and potential reduced drop-out rates. Virtual reality implementation in education Some LEA experiences have been presented also, explaining how the promised advantages have overcome such shortcomings.

3.19 Factors Contributing to Cost-Effectiveness

3.19.1 Improved Learning Outcomes

A fundamental factor contributing to the improvement of economic efficiency of VR is the effectiveness of using the technology in improving learning outcomes. The findings presented prove that there are apparent benefits of applying virtual reality in teaching and learning processes, making those students who participate in the VR courses to be more engaged, understand the content better, and retain it in contrast to their non VR-course counterparts. It has therefore contributes to the provision of more interesting and appealing learning facilities using virtual reality (VR) technology, which in one way boosts student understanding and mastery of the learning content and thereby improves pass rates as well as performance in examinations.

3.19.2 Potential Reductions in Dropout Rates

Failure rate reduction, leading to high enrollment retention, is also a feature of virtual reality, which makes the idea economically beneficial to apply for education. Increased levels of learning attainment and persistence are possible outcomes derived from the elements of student interest incorporated in studies using virtual reality systems. These can just as well raise motivation, curiosity, and joy related to the learning process in students. The benefit of VR technology is that it helps lowering down the ratio of students who decided to drop out schools or universities, making learning process more pleasant, which, in long perspective, will minimize expenses of educational institutes.

3.19.3 Cost-Benefit Analysis

Despite the fact that investment for adopting VR scenario may involve a one-time high cost, which have been estimated in the analysis section; cost-benefit analysis show that the benefits outweigh the costs and hysterics in the long run. The integration of VR technology is considered because of financial capacity to focus on prospective aspects of introducing the technology, such as lower dropout rates, higher learning outcomes, and the like. The improvements rising from integration of the virtual reality technology have generated outstanding returns on investment in terms of enhancing the performance, satisfaction and retention rates among the students of the educational facilities.

3.19.4 Experiences of Schools with VR Integration

Insights from research that have focused on the schools that have benefited from the application of virtual reality technology provide understandings on the economical applicability of VR in tackling challenges in education. There are three benefits that these educational institutions have experienced as a result of incorporating virtual reality in their teachings: improved student attendance, performance, and shedding off unsatisfactory rates. While having to consider the long term effects that the VR technology would have on their budget and financial plan of the organizations involved, most of them have had to spend significantly but gain even bigger advantages in the long run. To be effective and for VR integration programs to have the potential of standing the test of time and garner positive results, scholars emphasize that cognizant planning, the engagement of relevant parties in the acceptance and endorsement of the change, and ongoing and consistent support and follow-through.

3.19.5 Implications for Educational Practice

Virtual reality's economic groundedness for education has a large influence on educational policy and practice. Organizations especially the educational institutions may choose to invest optimally in VR integration projects through a realization of the long-term gains and functions that can embrace cost minimization revolving around the VR technology.

3.20 Key Considerations Include

3.21 Strategic Planning and Budgeting

Another factor that has to be utilized by educational institutions is the strategic planning and budgeting guidelines that would help to assess the feasibility and cost-effectiveness of the VR integration initiatives. Overall need assessments, cost-effective analyses, and stakeholder listening, educational institutions can establish realistic and guiding implementation plans and a believable budget that harmonises the institution's objectives and requirements.

3.22 Stakeholder Buy-In and Support

Although many educators and administrators may be aware of the usefulness of VR technology, students, parents, and other members of the community may know little about it so funding is required for the employment of this technology in learning institutions. Thus, educational leaders should engage stakeholders in decision-making and with permission of their involvement, ensure they are informed about the potential benefits of VR integration.

3.23 Ongoing Evaluation and Improvement

This indicates that efforts toward the incorporation of VR require evaluation and occasional readjustment to ensure their sustainability and usefulness. In order to fairly assess the impact of VR technology for teaching and learning related applications, schools should collect data for student performance, satisfaction and interaction rate. Through the evaluation, institutions are in a position to identify the areas that require improvement or need to be adjusted further in implementing VR integration plan.

4. DISCUSSION

Importance of VR is evident in that it can enhance education particularly the discussion part that presents an explanation of the research information. In this section, the author enlists the major strengths and weaknesses of the utilization of VR technology, links the outcomes to the educational practice and possibly policies. It also includes recommendation of areas of study or application of the context.

4.1 Interpretation of Findings

Conclusion derived from this study suggests that the technology of VR has the possibilities of enhancing students' learning gains and engagement in learning process in classroom setting. To the characteristics of VR, students will achieve a more positive and effective learning result since VR learning uniquely addresses people's learning needs and conforms successfully to the theoretical beliefs of experiential and constructivism learning theories. Through the use of the virtual reality (VR), education transforms into another level of experience where students are allowed to engage with information in three-dimensional environment, thus facilitating the understanding, memorizing and learning process and skill acquisition in multiple disciplines of study.

4.2 Alignment With Learning Theories

Possibilities for implementing VR technology is discussed focusing on practices of utilizing technology in the frameworks of the experiential method or constructivism. David Kolb has focused on the issue of experiential learning while emphasizing the role of experience, reflection as well as construction. Virtual reality learning environments are contextualized settings with student activities that involve engagement as a key process aspect, alongside building knowledge. For Erkenntnistheorien such as Konstruktionismus auch wie die Lev Vygotsky and Jean Piaget give significance to societal engagement and environmental investigation in the action of getting wisdom. Virtual reality technology is a unique way of providing students with the methodologies of learning that involve exploration, problem solving and critical thinking as well as develop teamwork skills.

4.3 Addressing Challenges

Concisely, as observed in the study and application of virtual reality technology as a useful tool in education, there are effects which denote certain challenges that still need to be further tackled in order to achieve the full potential of this technology in this aspect. It has been most affected by the high cost of having the VR gears, apps, software and infrastructures, technical issues such as the compatibility of some software, and technical hitches in the devices used for VR. Three concerns were raised regarding support and preparation for the use of VR in class: teachers' lack of help and preparation for an adequate use of VR in teaching. To address these issues and strip off barriers to VR acceptance and to enhance its impacts on teaching and learning, these questions must be solved.

4.4 Implications for Educational Practice and Policy

In the conversation the need to incorporate virtual reality technology as part of learning curriculum cannot be overemphasized to facilitate positive results on the results of the students. As for activity, teachers can apply VR in teaching as it creates rich learning contexts that would meet preferences and needs of students and their learning styles. The use of virtual reality models, virtual experiments, and interactive modes in teaching enable instructors to offer stimulating contexts that focus on appeal to curiosity, exploration, and learning among learners.

4.5 Professional Development and Support

A lot of attention should be devoted to providing the necessary support to the teachers, which will help them implement VR technology into the curricula effectively. Thus, professional development in the context of VR tools and applications should contain information regarding the best practices to implement VR tools and apps into to education, the best approaches and techniques to use VR tools and apps in the teaching-learning process, as well as instructions for properly managing VR tools and applications. The use of mentors in providing day-to-day support may enable teachers to address the challenges that hinder the implementation of virtual reality technology, and enhance the instructional benefits of the application in the classroom.

4.6 Addressing Equity and Access

To ensure that all students are equally afforded an opportunity to access VR technologies in their learning, it is important that the following principles of educational equity and inclusion are upheld. To remove those barriers which are in the way of access to virtual reality by students and schools, policy makers and the leaders of education must provide adequate and necessary infrastructure, resources and support services with special focus on the maximum utilization of such technologies. Different forms of underprivileged groups and altogether disadvantaged populations need to be prioritized in order to help every student make full use of the things that VR technology can offer to the table when it comes to learning.

4.7 Strengths and Limitations

Several benefits for using VR technology in talk include the ability to deliver novel and exciting learning solutions, promote engagement and enquiry and help to understand and recall content. An umbrella for a set of techniques that give students the power to probe deeper into challenging concepts and explore virtual experiments besides using simulations that cannot be done through traditional educational models is known as Virtual Reality (VR).

4.8 Limitations and Challenges

VR, in this point enable technological advantages and facilitations However, each technological system and creation has its difficulties and drawbacks that must be considered. The problem with adopting VR is that the costs of infrastructure and software as well as hardware are high which makes it difficult for many education institutions to incorporate into their learning system. It is possible to encounter certain technical difficulties when it comes to integrate VR into learning and teaching process. These are issues such as hardware failure or malfunction, compatibility issues that characterize some of the software, and issues in connectivity that characterizes the network. Another weakness is the lack of support, specifically help and guidance for teachers to implement VR in their curriculum without challenges.

4.9 Recommendations for Future Research

Special emphasis should be made on longitudinal studies to evaluate the effectiveness of the VR technology for students, achievement in academic results, rate of learning accomplishment, and general student interest in the progress of undertaking the educational programs. Research employing a longitudinal design can make a contribution to understanding the subject's lasting outcomes on students' learning development, which has implications on educational practice and policy.

4.10 Cost-Effectiveness Analysis

Hence, if scholars focus on the expenditures and revenue associated with virtual reality technology, they may present unique insights into how to make VR practical within a given school or school system's budget and how to maximize the benefits while remaining financially reasonable.

4.11 Equity and Inclusion

Other considerations which should also be studied by research include Equity and inclusion in the adoption of VR. Concerning the method, as scholars compare the levels of student and school access to the VR kits, they might identify factors preventing equal access and develop.

4.12 Implications for Educators

rows of teachers have consequences in the use of virtual reality (VR) in the classroom. Among the benefits: students' interest to courses and learning Performance while among the challenges are concerns to technical proficiency and in resource management. To understand the implications of VR adoption for educators that are necessary to leverage the benefits of the immersive technology in teaching and learning processes this section presents the potential effects of VR implementation for educators and the need for their training, support, and professional development.

4.13 Leveraging VR for Active Learning

Virtual Reality (VR) may also be used by teachers to give outlooks that make the learners engage in the class more than they would otherwise. In this way, teachers may cultivate curiosity, inquiry, and discovery by allowing students an opportunity to intersect with electronic simulations and participation in virtual experiments or in other ethereal contexts. Hence, teachers can establish the students' points of view and utilize virtual reality to use active-teaching methods and engage the students in the types of learning activities that may capture their attention and adhere to voguish approaches to learning typology.

4.14 Personalizing Learning Experiences

Teaching learning using virtual reality might get to a point where the tutors will teach according to the requirement, as well as the choice, and the capability of the learners. Teachers and facilitators can further open environments for continuing learning in which the learners can make choices themselves by identifying the area of learning interests and choices that can be enabled by self-directed learning through virtual simulations that is in alignment with the learning outcomes. During the regular classes the teacher is able to come up with VR simulation or situations related to some of the learning objectives for differentiation of instructions in order to accommodate the learning disabled students based on achievement level.

4.15 Addressing Technical Proficiency

The lack of technical competence in using VR tools and apps is one of the main challenges that lectures face when the adoption of VR in their learning-teaching process. This might cause apprehension and doubt over the application of VR technology because most instructors in this study are likely to be unfamiliar with it. It makes sense to mention that to avoid these issues teachers require special training and professional development encompassing detailed familiarisation with VR technology, software, and content creation instruments inasmuch as practicing with the above-discussed tools. This may best be done by teachers exercising caution in the use of VR technology in the classroom, after which they seek the help that is usually availed by technical support and troubleshooting services.

4.16 Ensuring Access and Equity

Similarly, another concern when it comes to inclusion of VR comes in when trying to establish that student and or schools get fair access to technology. Ideally, if people have different access to VR technology, software, as well as the structure of the whole environment, inequality in educational opportunities or results may rise. As with many contexts, particular care should be taken when implementing VR ideas in practice that equity considerations are not forgotten about. To this end they should also advocate for resources and policies that would guarantee equal opportunities in engagement in and access to en Abbas forces learning environment for ALL students. Incorporating the stake along with the help of administrators, legislatures, and other partners may also ensure that VR technology is availed as much as possible to students of different settings and backgrounds through removing systematic barriers to access.

4.17 Investing in Professional Development

Apart from this, if the intention is to support the teachers in incorporating VR technology into their teaching practices, then the money has to be invested in professional development courses. Professional development must focus on VR as an education delivery method, effective instructional design, technology savvy, norming all teachers about how to apply and leverage VR technologies and apps in classroom instruction for the enhancement of learning outcomes among students. Many practices involving workshops, virtual or face-to-face classes, and cooperative learning may also denote the ability of the instructors themselves to share the information they have as well as learn from each other to enhance a culture of creativity and innovation.

4.18 Providing Technical Support

In order to scale VR-related barriers and problems that impede its use, educators require not only technical support, but also professional development. In order to cater for the immediate support and direction of these instructors, the educational institutions should establish special pass throughs such as help-desk services and forums. Technical support people can explain settings for wearing VR gear and software, general issues that are encountered and ways to improve the use of VR in education endeavors. A focus on the technical aspect suggests that such needs matter to help educational institutions optimise the use of virtual reality in the classroom, helping teachers overcome the challenges that hinder the use of the innovation.

4.19 Collaborating With Peers

Facilitating the use of VR, educators should work on redesigning lessons with colleagues, experiment with different ways, and share knowledge, ideas, and strategies of integrating the technology while participating in interdisciplinary teaching groups and professional learning communities.

4.20 Encouraging Experimentation and Exploration

Based on the above analysis, assistance offered to the educators in exploring virtual reality technology used in the class is the key to unfolding creativity and innovation. Schools should promote innovation and allow the educational process to be more open to experimentation, deviating from the traditional practices and adopting new tools that can be offered by immersive technologies.

4.21 Policy Recommendations

Education stakeholders must ensure the formulation of effective policies that put emphasis on VR technology; the establishment of proper rules and regulations that would foster cooperation between the Ministry of Education and other offices, schools, colleges and universities, businesses among others to transform the teaching and learning fraternity by availing and implementing effective technology such as VR especially in the poor and rural regions.

4.22 Investing in VR Technology

4.22.1 Equitable Funding Allocation

Public policy makers should therefore ensure that funding for VR technology infrastructure in school is targeted at schools in the deprived and rural areas. Targeted grants and subsidies can level the playing field by providing the finest teaching aids to schools and subsequently negate inherent limitations in VR technology accessibility.

4.22.2 Establishing Technology Grants

Governments and charitable institutions should provide technology subsidies that apply to the incorporation of virtual reality into all educational levels to provide schools with the necessary funding to purchase equipment, develop content, and staff experienced educators.

4.23 Supporting Educator Training and Development

4.23.1 Professional Development Programs

Pausing for a moment, focusing on teachers' professional development programs, and allocating more resources to them can help teachers, who are in charge of preparing lessons with virtual reality technology, attend seminars, obtain certifications, undergo practical training, join peer groups, and gain access to the various learning communities.

4.23.2 Technical Assistance and Support

Furthermore, the financing to cover the technical support regards teachers can improve and guidance for the teachers that use VR technology in the classrooms along with the professional development that will help the teachers tackling with technological issues and giving out a way to minimize VR adoption barriers.

4.24 Developing Standardized VR Content

4.24.1 Curriculum Integration

In light of this, the authorities need to focus on the development of the homogenized virtual reality material that could effectively fit the curriculum and educational requirements. Working with selected content makers, industries and specialists of education can help in developing learning objectives, incorporating the use of VR systems that makes a virtue beneficial to students.

4.24.2 Open Educational Resources

Governmental and institutional leaders should encourage the production of OER for use in creating and using VR material for ease of access and affordable solutions as well as foster an open classroom environment and for teachers to address students' learning requirements.

4.25 Promoting Research and Evaluation

4.25.1 Research Grants

Goal Based Funding Recommendations: Policies should dedicate money for research on the effectiveness of VR technology in education environment and comparisons, cross-sectional, randomized control trails, and longitudinal studies in order to equip policymaker with more empirical information for policy decisions in the future.

4.25.2 Program Evaluation

Through funding, policymakers allocate more resources for assessment and research of programs relating to virtual reality in learning environments. It is useful to find out such strengths, weaknesses, opportunities and threats that are involved in certain activities. There is also a need to consult with other academic institutions, researches and evaluators.

4.25.3 Future Research Dirctions

A more pointed focus is needed on the exhaustive investigation of an efficacy, cost efficiency, and prospects of the super-large-scale utilization and combination of the VR equipment in the sphere of education in order to improve the existing knowledge and optimize the perspectives of utilizing VR equipment in education.

4.26 Longitudinal Studies

4.26.1 Understanding Long-Term Effects

Subsequent research should involve time series analysis of the effects of VR technology on learning achievements, teaching effectiveness, and wellbeing on emergent learning paradigms with regard to trends, patterns, and control variables affecting VR effectiveness for learning.

4.26.2 Examining Transferability of Skills

Presently, researchers are exploring how VR-based learning environment could be applied in real life contexts and in pursuing advanced education. They intend to foster an appreciation of the effectiveness of VR in complementing conventional education and transferring value education skills such as critical and creative thinking into practical real life situations such as problem-solving.

4.27 Cost-Effectiveness and Scalability

4.27.1 Evaluating Cost-Effectiveness

Subsequent studies should employ cost-utility comparisons to illustrate the financial costs and returns on investments in VR as an assessment tool in learning. This will encompass trainers, professional development, learning achievement, and performance of students to offer a research-driven rationale to politicians, chief administrators, funders, and other stakeholders in charge of resource and financial allocations.

4.27.2 Investigating Scalability

Scaleability research of VR technology is important to this model's applicability to a broad range of educational settings. In this paper, the possibility of utilizing VR solutions in different institutions is reviewed and the issues that arise when using VR systems include limited infrastructure and technological issues.

4.28 Adaptive VR Systems

4.28.1 Developing Personalized Learning Experiences

Finally, future research should actively explore more flexible configurations of Distance education class, since different forms of virtual environment appeal to different students. These systems employ ART and ML to adapt materials, scholarly difficulties and learning strategies based on students' performance.

4.28.2 Investigating Effectiveness

An investigation on the efficiency within Adaptive VR treatment ought to look at the efficiency on learning outcomes, on cognitive advancement, and affective interest with students under adaptive VR treatment, the non-adaptive VR treatment, and traditional methods.

4.29 Integration with Emerging Technologies

4.29.1 Exploring Synergies with AR and AI

Subsequent research should consider merging VR technology with AI topographical inventions and augmentation reality breakthroughs to achieve an ordinary level of learning environment. 'Finally, integration of artificial intelligence in VR applications can provide flexible suggestions, progressive feedback, and resourceful training, hence improving the effectiveness of education.

4.29.2 Investigating Multimodal Learning Environments

Exploratory studies related to the combination of VR, AR, and AI have to concentrate on developing human–computer interfaces that would engage all four types of learning modalities – visuals, audições, touch, and space. This can help activate all the abilities of the human brain, make them work on different senses and develop more profound comprehension of the concepts.

5. CONCLUSION

The use of VR in learning therefore brings a significant positive change through enhancement of learners' learning experiences through immersion. This area focuses on several weaknesses which are still worthy to be further investigated as the advantages of adopting VR in education are overwhelming. "

REFERENCES

Al-Ansi, A. M., Jaboob, M., Garad, A., & Al-Ansi, A. (2023). Analyzing augmented reality (AR) and virtual reality (VR) recent development in education. *Social Sciences & Humanities Open*, 8(1), 100532. DOI:10.1016/j.ssaho.2023.100532

AlGerafi, M. A., Zhou, Y., Oubibi, M., & Wijaya, T. T. (2023). Unlocking the potential: A comprehensive evaluation of augmented reality and virtual reality in education. *Electronics (Basel)*, 12(18), 3953. DOI:10.3390/electronics12183953

Arriagada, C. (2024). *Early Childhood Educators' Perceptions, Attitudes, And Beliefs On Use Of The Modern Classrooms Project: A Case Study.*

Bowen, M. M. (2018). *Effect of virtual reality on motivation and achievement of middle-school students.* The University of Memphis.

Bray, M., Shafique, R., Aljedaani, W., Rustam, F., Lee, E., Mehmood, A., & Choi, G. S. (2023). *Technology and the diverse learner: A guide to classroom practice.* Corwin Press.

Check, J., & Schutt, R. K. (2011). *Research methods in education.* Sage publications.

Christopoulos, A., Mystakidis, S., Pellas, N., & Laakso, M. J. (2021). ARLEAN: An Augmented Reality Learning Analytics Ethical Framework. *Computers*, 2021(10), 92. DOI:10.3390/computers10080092

Daim, T. U., Blanton, S., Basoglu, A. N., & Ding, A. (2011). Exploring information technology adoption in the classroom: Case of online learning technology. *International Journal of Business Information Systems*, 7(3), 327–340. DOI:10.1504/IJBIS.2011.039334

Dhawan, S. (2020). Online learning: A panacea in the time of COVID-19 crisis. *Journal of Educational Technology Systems*, 49(1), 5–22. DOI:10.1177/0047239520934018

Di, X., & Zheng, X. (2022). A meta-analysis of the impact of virtual technologies on students' spatial ability. *Educational Technology Research and Development*, 70(1), 73–98. DOI:10.1007/s11423-022-10082-3

Fleck, S., & Hachet, M. (2016). Making tangible the intangible: Hybridization of the real and the virtual to enhance learning of abstract phenomena. *Frontiers in ICT (Lausanne, Switzerland)*, 3, 30. DOI:10.3389/fict.2016.00030

Florea, A., & Gellert, A. (2014). Different Approaches For Solving Optimization Problems Using Interactive E-Learning Tools. *eLearning & Software for Education*, (2).

Höffler, T., Schmeck, A., Höffler, A. O. T. N., Schmeck, A., & Opfermann, M. (2013). Static and dynamic visual representations. *Learning through visual displays: Current perspectives on cognition, learning, and instruction*, 133-163.

Houston, D. L. (2018). *At-risk middle school boys' engagement in the iEngage model* [Doctoral dissertation, Walden University].

Ismail, H., Hussein, N., Harous, S., & Khalil, A. (2023). Survey of personalized learning software systems: A taxonomy of environments, learning content, and user models. *Education Sciences*, 13(7), 741. DOI:10.3390/educsci13070741

Jewitt, C. (2008). *The visual in learning and creativity: A review of the literature.* Arts Council.

Jiang, H., Vimalesvaran, S., Wang, J. K., Lim, K. B., Mogali, S. R., & Car, L. T. (2022). Virtual reality in medical students' education: Scoping review. *JMIR Medical Education*, 8(1), e34860. DOI:10.2196/34860 PMID:35107421

Kaplan-Rakowski, R., Papin, K., & Hartwick, P. M. (2022). Language teachers' perceptions and use of extended reality. *Available atSSRN* 4096263. DOI:10.2139/ssrn.4096263

Klingenberg, S., Jørgensen, M. L., Dandanell, G., Skriver, K., Mottelson, A., & Makransky, G. (2020). Investigating the effect of teaching as a generative learning strategy when learning through desktop and immersive VR: A media and methods experiment. *British Journal of Educational Technology*, 51(6), 2115–2138. DOI:10.1111/bjet.13029

Kümmel, E., Moskaliuk, J., Cress, U., & Kimmerle, J. (2020). Digital learning environments in higher education: A literature review of the role of individual vs. social settings for measuring learning outcomes. *Education Sciences*, 10(3), 78. DOI:10.3390/educsci10030078

Lai, J. W., & Cheong, K. H. (2022). Educational opportunities and challenges in augmented reality: Featuring implementations in physics education. *IEEE Access : Practical Innovations, Open Solutions*, 10, 43143–43158. DOI:10.1109/ACCESS.2022.3166478

Lewis, L. H., & Williams, C. J. (1994). Experiential learning: Past and present. *New Directions for Adult and Continuing Education*, 1994(62), 5–16. DOI:10.1002/ace.36719946203

Lewis, L. S. (2023). *Literacy-based Instruction in Low-SES Schools During COVID-19 Distance Learning* [Doctoral dissertation, Azusa Pacific University].

Makransky, G., Andreasen, N. K., Baceviciute, S., & Mayer, R. E. (2021). Immersive virtual reality increases liking but not learning with a science simulation and generative learning strategies promote learning in immersive virtual reality. *Journal of Educational Psychology*, 113(4), 719–735. DOI:10.1037/edu0000473

. Mantovani, F. (2001). 12 VR learning: Potential and challenges for the use of 3d environments in education and training. *Towards cyberpsychology: mind, cognition, and society in the Internet age, 2*(207).

. Mantovani, F. (2001). 12 VR learning: Potential and challenges for the use of 3d environments in education and training. *Towards cyberpsychology: mind, cognition, and society in the Internet age, 2*(207).

McKleroy, V. S., Galbraith, J. S., Cummings, B., Jones, P., Harshbarger, C., Collins, C., Gelaude, D., & Carey, J. W.ADAPT Team. (2006). Adapting evidence–based behavioral interventions for new settings and target populations. *AIDS Education and Prevention*, 18(supp), 59–73. DOI:10.1521/aeap.2006.18.supp.59 PMID:16987089

Merchant, Z., Goetz, E. T., Cifuentes, L., Keeney-Kennicutt, W., & Davis, T. J. (2014). Effectiveness of virtual reality-based instruction on students' learning outcomes in K-12 and higher education: A meta-analysis. *Computers & Education*, 70, 29–40. DOI:10.1016/j.compedu.2013.07.033

Merchant, Z., Goetz, E. T., Cifuentes, L., Keeney-Kennicutt, W., & Davis, T. J. (2014). Effectiveness of virtual reality-based instruction on students' learning outcomes in K-12 and higher education: A meta-analysis. *Computers & Education*, 70, 29–40. DOI:10.1016/j.compedu.2013.07.033

Neamtu, C., Comes, R., Matescu, R., Ghinea, R., & Daniel, F. (2012, November). Using virtual reality to teach history. In *Proceedings of the 7th International Con ference on Virtual Learning (Bucure ti: Editura Universitatii din Bucuresti)* (pp. 303-310). Research Gate.

Negahban, A. (2024). Simulation in engineering education: The transition from physical experimentation to digital immersive simulated environments. *Simulation*, 100(7), 00375497241229757. DOI:10.1177/00375497241229757

Ntaba, A., & Jantjies, M. (2021). Open distance learning and immersive technologies: a literature analysis. *Balancing the Tension between Digital Technologies and Learning Sciences*, (pp. 183-198). IEEE.

Omasta, M., & Snyder-Young, D. (2022). Methodologies and methods. *Impacting Theatre Audiences: Methods for Studying Change.*

Ouariach, S., Khaldi, M., Mohamed, E., & Khaldi, M. (2023). The Flipped Classroom: From Passive Information Absorption to Active Learning. In *Handbook of Research on Language Teacher Identity* (pp. 269-293). IGI Global.

Pallavicini, F., Pepe, A., Clerici, M., & Mantovani, F. (2022). Virtual reality applications in medicine during the COVID-19 pandemic: Systematic review. *JMIR Serious Games*, 10(4), e35000. DOI:10.2196/35000 PMID:36282554

Piaget, J. (1970). *Piaget's theory* (Vol. 1). Wiley.

Qu, Z., Lau, C. W., Simoff, S. J., Kennedy, P. J., Nguyen, Q. V., & Catchpoole, D. R. (2022). Review of innovative immersive technologies for healthcare applications. *Innovations in Digital Health, Diagnostics, and Biomarkers*, 2(2022), 27–39. DOI:10.36401/IDDB-21-04

Roberts, L. D., & Allen, P. J. (2015). Exploring ethical issues associated with using online surveys in educational research. *Educational Research and Evaluation*, 21(2), 95–108. DOI:10.1080/13803611.2015.1024421

Routh, D. K. (1994). *Clinical psychology since 1917: Science, practice and organization*. Springer Science & Business Media. DOI:10.1007/978-1-4757-9712-1

Russell, M. (2022). *Statistics in Natural Resources: Applications with R*. Chapman and Hall/CRC. DOI:10.1201/9781003285809

Shafique, R., Aljedaani, W., Rustam, F., Lee, E., Mehmood, A., & Choi, G. S. (2023). Role of Artificial Intelligence in Online Education: A Systematic Mapping Study. *IEEE Access : Practical Innovations, Open Solutions*, 11, 52570–52584. DOI:10.1109/ACCESS.2023.3278590

Slade, S., & Prinsloo, P. (2013). Learning analytics: Ethical issues and dilemmas. *The American Behavioral Scientist*, 57(10), 1510–1529. DOI:10.1177/0002764213479366

Song, C., Shin, S. Y., & Shin, K. S. (2023). Optimizing foreign language learning in virtual reality: A comprehensive theoretical framework based on constructivism and cognitive load theory (VR-CCL). *Applied Sciences (Basel, Switzerland)*, 13(23), 12557. DOI:10.3390/app132312557

Strati, A. D., Schmidt, J. A., & Maier, K. S. (2017). Perceived challenge, teacher support, and teacher obstruction as predictors of student engagement. *Journal of Educational Psychology*, 109(1), 131–147. DOI:10.1037/edu0000108

Termos, M. H. (2013). The Effects of the Classroom Performance System on Student Participation, Attendance, and Achievement. *International Journal on Teaching and Learning in Higher Education*, 25(1), 66–78.

. Trowler, V. (2010). Student engagement literature review. *The higher education academy, 11*(1), 1-15.

Vygotsky, L. S., & Cole, M. (1978). *Mind in society: Development of higher psychological processes*. Harvard university press.

Wu, H. K., Lee, S. W. Y., Chang, H. Y., & Liang, J. C. (2013). Current status, opportunities and challenges of augmented reality in education. *Computers & Education*, 62, 41–49. DOI:10.1016/j.compedu.2012.10.024

Chapter 15
VR Headset Selection via CODAS Based on Pythagorean Fuzzy Set

Elif Çaloğlu Büyükselçuk
https://orcid.org/0000-0002-5976-6727
Fenerbahçe University, Turkey

ABSTRACT

Thanks to the developing technology, innovative activities emerge in the education sector, as in every sector. Contrary to traditional teaching and learning methods, novel models have started to be used in the education sector with the opportunities offered by virtual reality (VR), augmented reality (AR) or mixed reality (MR) technologies used in many different sectors. In this study, a model developed for use in the education sector in Turkey, which is named MEB-VR, has been introduced and the solution of a problem encountered in this model has been discussed. MEB-VR has been developed especially for applied and laboratory courses. The problem of determining the best headsets to be used in the model, in which the VR-based education approach is adopted, has been tried to be solved in this study. For this purpose, the most suitable VR headset was determined using the combinative distance based assessment (CODAS) method based on circular pythagorean fuzzy sets (C-PFS).

1. INTRODUCTION

Education is an important issue that shapes the lives of people and societies in a positive way and directs their futures. Though the pace of the technological development in education is slow, different innovative technologies are applied to this sector (Allcoat et al., 2021). For this reason, all necessary investments should be

DOI: 10.4018/979-8-3693-6407-9.ch015

made in the field of education, and it should be ensured that all individuals receive equal and quality education. To achieve this quality and equality, it has become inevitable to take advantage of the opportunities offered by technology (Thangeda et al., 2016; OECD, 2012). All necessary technological developments should be used to amplify the teaching process in education. Mostly, traditional teaching methods such as auditory or visual, are widely used. Multisensory teaching methods can be used for more permanent and effective learning. The use of Virtual Reality technology in education is a tool that supports multisensory teaching methods (Horváth, 2021; Chen et al., 2014).

Virtual Reality (VR) is an advanced technology that excites individuals, supports, and encourages their learning processes. Thanks to this technology, the user feels as a part of the environment s/he is in, that is, s/he learns by living in that environment (Pantelidis, 2021). VR has been used in many different fields such as education, healthcare, manufacturing, entertainment, design, construction, and military fields (Albahbah et al., 2021). Lege and Bonner stated that VR experience is actively used and experienced especially in the entertainment industry. Although students have had this experience, it is still an effective and attractive learning tool for the education sector (Lege & Bonner, 2021). There have been discussions about the necessity of VR technology in the education sector for years. In the beginning, it was clear that institutions would not be able to afford such a large investment. However, with the advancements in VR technology over time, the costs have also decreased (Hussein & Nätterdal, 2015).

Different studies were found when it has been researched on the concepts of education and VR in the literature. VR is applied in different education fields such as science, engineering and even language learning (Frazier et al., 2021). Tang emphasized the importance of VR technology, which is a new teaching media, college physical education. In the study, it was investigated how VR technology is beneficial in increasing the quality of physical education. At the end of the research, it was concluded that this technology contributed a lot in increasing the quality of physical education (Tang, 2021). Ling and Rui applied VR glasses and Leap Motion to situational and practical courses and made some suggestions. They suggested that with this innovative educational environment in the History lesson, the students can feel themselves in that period, in the costumes and events of that period. With this feeling, a more permanent and effective learning environment can be provided for the students. Likewise, with an application made in the chemistry laboratory, a more effective learning environment can be provided by reducing the dangers and risks of the experiments, as well as the costs. It can be used in many different areas and for many different purposes, and the miracle results are provided (Ling & Rui, 2016).

A study was conducted to investigate the efficiency of using mixed reality and augmented reality technologies together with VR in education. The result of the research is interesting that when these innovative technologies are compared with traditional education models, similar performances have been achieved in the learning processes of students. However, it was concluded that students were more excited and interested in this innovative learning model (Allcoat et al., 2021).

A project has been developed at Victoria University of Wellington on the use of VR technology in the teaching library design, especially for users with physical impairments. As a result of the interviews and surveys made with the users, it was concluded that the use of this innovation is very exciting, impressive, and enjoyable. According to the results of the research, with the cheaper and more widespread use of VR head mounted displays, VR libraries will also be used more widely (Calvert, 2019). Checa and Bustillo worked especially with undergraduate students on cultural heritage to explore the limitations and possibilities of virtual reality environments. It has been observed that high efficiency is achieved in the virtual reality environment in spatial positioning. With the intense interest in VR technology, positive developments have also been achieved in the learning processes of students. Depending on the locomotion procedure in the virtual reality environment, differences in the behaviours of the users have been detected (Checa & Bustillo, 2020). Kim et al. developed a learning management system for VR education in a chemistry experiment. The supervisor monitored the learning performances and interaction behaviours of the students. The developed system has two sub-units. One of them is the student unit. With the HMD-based VR learning method, students can access the content and communicate with their teacher, when necessary, in the student unit. The other unit is the supervisor or server unit. In the server unit, student learning performance is reported by monitoring students' relationships and interactions between them. This unit is the learning management system (Kim et al., 2019).

In a study, the VR education model have been compared to the traditional education model in architectural history courses. Experiments were conducted to test students' learning abilities and interesting results were obtained. As a result of the study, it was determined that VR education has been more effective than the traditional one and students got higher scores. In the VR environment, their analytical and critical thinking skills have improved especially in male students. Female students complained of the weight of tools and equipment and nausea (Ibrahim et al., 2021).

Instead of classical real estate education, VR based educational model is applied in Hong Kong. This model was developed for different purposes. It was aimed to increase students' curiosity with built environment digitally; to improve their insights with sustainable built environment; to combine real-life applications with classroom learning experiences; and to provide them with the opportunity to be intertwined with technology in real estate applications. At the end of the study, students reported that they were very satisfied with this innovative education model. VR tool cannot only be a tool in the classroom education, it also improves students' innovative and creative thinking. In addition to these, it enables students to make connections between real estate course curriculum and real-life applications (Hou & Wu, 2020).

Because of the widespread use and advantages of VR technology in education, a VR-based education model has also been developed for Turkey. An education model called MEB-VR has been proposed and developed in distance or face to face learning to conduct the courses, especially the laboratory and applied courses in schools affiliated to the Ministry of National Education. Its scope is very broad, and it aims to offer equal opportunities to students in education. MEB-VR provides support for students to learn the course subjects permanently. In the model, the student follows the lectures using VR technology, and the student's performance is measured by applying an exam at the end of the course. Those who fail the course are asked to repeat the course. The system automatically sends the reports of students by e-mail to the institution and student. With this developed education model, it provides students with a more effective and efficient education opportunity, especially in schools that do not have adequate laboratory facilities. In this study, one of the problems encountered in this developed model will be discussed and examined. The first question that came up in the implementation of this model was about which headsets to choose. In fact, this problem is the same as a selection problem made by considering certain criteria and performance indicators. For this purpose, the research was conducted on determining the best VR headset. This problem is a multi-criteria decision-making (MCDM) problem, and this study has been aimed to determine which criteria should be considered in the selection of headsets used for MEB-VR and to choose the best among the headsets available in the market. COPRAS method based on circular Pythagorean fuzzy set was used to determine the best one.

2. MATERIALS AND METHODS

2.1. Virtual Reality

Virtual reality is the combination of reality and imagination with fictions created using technology. Virtual learning environments are platforms designed to enrich students' learning experiences with the inclusion of developing technology in educational environments (Lee & Hwang, 2022; Joyce et al., 2021). In recent years, VR technology has found a more common usage area because it can be obtained more affordable than past (Frazier et al., 2021). The use of VR technology in the education sector offers students experiences they have never experienced before.

It gives them the opportunity to repeat this experience, experiments, or situations over and over. VR technology, which prevents the use of real resources and allows learning to take place in a safe environment, can also be easily adapted to many different educational areas (Paszkiewicz et al., 2021). It is possible to say that there are disadvantages as well as advantages. Education with VR incurs both hardware and software costs. In addition, more effort and time is needed for the preparation of content and virtual environments compared to the classical education model. In addition, from the perspective of the user, it causes them to be dependent on the virtual environment, limited interpersonal communication and some health problems (Paszkiewicz et al., 2021).

At its most basic level, a VR headset is a device used in the delivery of VR technology. The VR headsets are worn tightly around the eyes to provide a realistic and immersive experience (Wang et al., 2020). Today, there are a wide variety of headsets with different features and types available for sale on the market. Headsets, whether used in VR, Augmented Reality (AR) or Mixed Reality (MR) can be grouped under three groups.

2.1.1. Mobile Headsets

Smartphones are used in mobile headsets. Perception of the screen by the eyes takes place with the help of two different lenses. Here, smartphones work like a VR device. Since the system runs on the smartphone, there is no need for any cable connection. They are troublesome as there is no accurate location tracking feature. They use three degrees of freedom motion tracking, which means they can accurately track the direction you are looking at, but not which direction you are moving (Noble, 2019). Mobile headsets, which require less investment than other headsets, are devices that require easy installation and are user-friendly. Such headsets are limited in terms of the content they support. That's why smartphone headsets are the least powerful type of VR headset (Smith, 2021). They cannot handle most VR games or complex content.

2.1.2. Standalone (Untethered) Headsets

Standalone (untethered) headsets do not require any equipment. They contain screens and Android-based smart phones in their body. In the case of using these headsets, no cables are required for the VR experience (Smith, 2021). Due to their wireless feature, these devices provide extra freedom and range of motion. Although they provide total freedom of movement, they can cause higher costs in the process of buying. In some cases, it may be impossible for them to compete with other tethered headsets depending on the VR content. These devices require a Wi-Fi connection to receive and transmit VR content. Although not as powerful as tethered headsets, they are devices that have the potential to offer an impressive and immersive VR experience (Smith, 2021).

2.1.3. Tethered Headsets

Tethered headsets are used by connecting to devices such as a PC or a video game console. The connection cable allows the PC or console to transmit VR signals to the headset, which are then passed on to the user for them to experience. They can be thought that tethered headsets as the most powerful type of VR headsets (Smith, 2021). They offer more options as they connect to another device and could offer more experience as they can draw more power. It also offers more movement opportunities as it provides 6 degrees of freedom motion tracking (Angelov et al., 2020). More power will provide a more effective and immersive VR experience in every sense. It will enable the rendering of more graphics-intensive applications, and this means more content. Although to this power, they are headsets that limit the user's mobility due to the wired connection. The cable can become entangled in people's legs, causing discomfort and sometimes even injury to them (Smith, 2021).

2.2. Multi Criteria Decision Making (MCDM) Based on Pythagorean Fuzzy Sets

As a result of a search with the keyword "Pythagorean fuzzy" and "MCDM" on Web of Science Core Collection on July 12, 2023, 216 publications were found. The distribution of these publications by years is given in Figure 1. 206 of these publications are articles, 10 of them are early access, and 13 of them are proceeding paper. Table 1 summarizes the studies on the subject.

Figure 1. Number of publications due to years

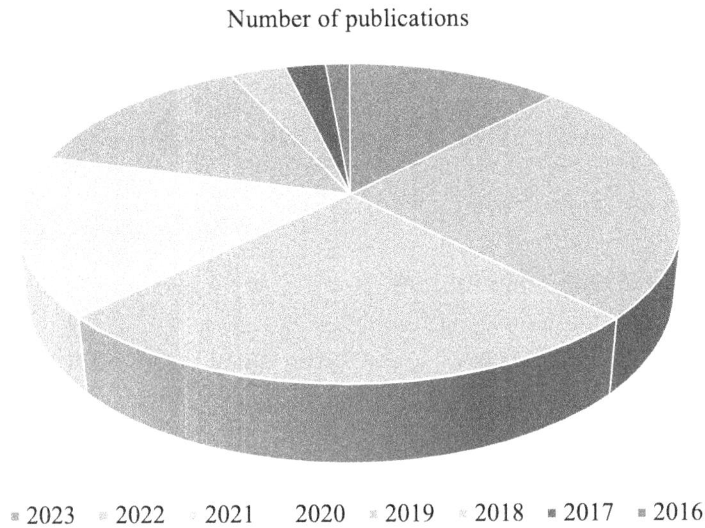

Table 1. Summary of Pythagorean fuzzy sets

Author(s)	Aim
Rani et al., 2023	Determining criteria weight by using standard deviation based on Pythagorean fuzzy set and MAIRCA methods for MCDM problem solution
Ejegwa, 2021	Generalizing the correlation coefficient for PFSs to give better results in solving multi-criteria decision-making problems
Rani et al., 2019	Determining renewable energy technologies by using VIKOR based on entropy and divergence measures of Pythagorean fuzzy sets
Rani et al., 2020	Selecting sustainable recycling partner by using TOPSIS based on Pythagorean fuzzy sets
Mishra et al., 2022	Evaluating waste-to-energy technology selection by using COPRAS based on Pythagorean fuzzy set
Liu et al., 2022	Determining sustainable circular supplier selection in the manufacturing industry via EDAS based on Pythagorean fuzzy sets
Sarkar & Biswas, 2022	Evaluating strategy prioritization of a tiles manufacturing company by using MULTIMOORA based on Pythagorean fuzzy sets
Peng & Ma, 2020	Constructing a new algorithm for MCDM problem solution based on CODAS and Pythagorean fuzzy sets
Mohd et al., 2020	Evaluating green supplier development program via MCDM based on Pythagorean fuzzy sets
Molla et al., 2021	Solving medical diagnosis problems by PROMETHEE method with Pythagorean fuzzy sets

2.2.1. Some Preliminaries

Intuitive fuzzy sets, in which the membership function and the non-membership function are evaluated together, were first introduced to the literature by Atanassov (Atanassov, 1999).

Definition 1. An intuitionistic fuzzy set (IFS) F in the universal set (U) is defined by

$$F = \{\langle u, \mathfrak{M}_F(u), \mathfrak{N}_F(u)\rangle : u \in U\} \tag{1}$$

where $\mathfrak{M}_F$ (membership function) and $\mathfrak{N}_F$ (non-membership function): $U \to [0,1]$ are functions with the condition $\mathfrak{M}_F + \mathfrak{N}_F \leq 1$.

Definition 2. The concept of Pythagorean fuzzy set (PFS) was developed by Yager (Yager, 2013a; Yager, 2013b) and it is a general form of IFS. A PFS P in U is defined by

$$P = \{\langle u, \mathfrak{M}_P(u), \mathfrak{N}_P(u)\rangle : u \in U\} \tag{2}$$

where $\mathfrak{M}_P$ (membership function) and $\mathfrak{N}_P$ (non-membership function): $U \to [0,1]$ are functions with the condition $\mathfrak{M}_P^2(u) + \mathfrak{N}_P^2(u) \leq 1$.

Then the pair $\mathfrak{a} = \langle \mathfrak{M}_\mathfrak{a}, \mathfrak{N}_\mathfrak{a}\rangle$ is called Pythagorean fuzzy value (PFV).

Definition 3. Let $\mathfrak{r} \in [0,1]$. A circular PFS $P_\mathfrak{r}$ in U is defined by

$$P_\mathfrak{r} = \{\langle u, \mathfrak{M}_P(u), \mathfrak{N}_P(u); \mathfrak{r}\rangle : u \in U\} \tag{3}$$

where $\mathfrak{r}$ is the radius of $(\mathfrak{M}_P(u), \mathfrak{N}_P(u))$ on the plane. The radius shows the membership and non-membership degree of $u \in U$.

Definition 4. Let $\mathfrak{M}_\mathfrak{a}, \mathfrak{N}_\mathfrak{a}, \mathfrak{r}_\mathfrak{a} \in [0,1]$ and $\mathfrak{M}_\mathfrak{a}^2 + \mathfrak{N}_\mathfrak{a}^2 \leq 1$. Then this is called a circular PFV (C-PFV) $(\mathfrak{a} = \langle \mathfrak{M}_\mathfrak{a}, \mathfrak{N}_\mathfrak{a}; \mathfrak{r}_\mathfrak{a}\rangle)$.

2.2.2. Circular Pythagorean CODAS Method

Different methods have been developed and used in the solution of multi-criteria decision- making problems. In this section, CODAS method based on circular Pythagorean fuzzy set will be explained. In this method, the Euclidean and Hamming distance measures are used. The steps of the method are as follows (Khan et al., 2023):

Step 1. Let $A = \{A_1, A_2, \ldots, A_m\}$ be the set of m alternatives and $C = \{C_1, C_2, \ldots, C_n\}$ the set of n criteria. Let $DM = \{DM_1, DM_2, \ldots, DM_l\}, l = 1,2,\ldots,k$ defines the set of decision makers. All alternatives are evaluated due to each criterion by every decision maker. With these evaluations, the mxn decision matrix is obtained and as shown below.

$$M^k = (\mathfrak{a}_{ij})^k = \begin{matrix} \\ A_1 \\ A_2 \\ \vdots \\ A_m \end{matrix} \begin{pmatrix} C_1 & C_2 & \cdots & C_n \\ (\mathfrak{M}^k_{11}, \mathfrak{N}^k_{11}, \mathfrak{h}^k_{11}) & (\mathfrak{M}^k_{12}, \mathfrak{N}^k_{12}, \mathfrak{h}^k_{12}) & \cdots & (\mathfrak{M}^k_{1n}, \mathfrak{N}^k_{1n}, \mathfrak{h}^k_{1n}) \\ (\mathfrak{M}^k_{21}, \mathfrak{N}^k_{21}, \mathfrak{h}^k_{21}) & (\mathfrak{M}^k_{22}, \mathfrak{N}^k_{22}, \mathfrak{h}^k_{22}) & \cdots & (\mathfrak{M}^k_{2n}, \mathfrak{N}^k_{2n}, \mathfrak{h}^k_{2n}) \\ \vdots & \vdots & \ddots & \vdots \\ (\mathfrak{M}^k_{m1}, \mathfrak{N}^k_{m1}, \mathfrak{h}^k_{m1}) & (\mathfrak{M}^k_{m2}, \mathfrak{N}^k_{m2}, \mathfrak{h}^k_{m2}) & \cdots & (\mathfrak{M}^k_{mn}, \mathfrak{N}^k_{mn}, \mathfrak{h}^k_{mn}) \end{pmatrix} \quad (4)$$

where $\mathfrak{h}$ is the hesitancy degree and calculated as follows:

$$\mathfrak{h} = \sqrt{1 - \left(\mathfrak{M}^2_P(u) - \mathfrak{N}^2_P(u)\right)} \quad (5)$$

Step 2. The following equation is used to aggregate decision matrices obtained as a result of the evaluation of alternatives according to the criteria by each decision maker in a single matrix. The weights of decision makers are not same and decision makers' weight vector is constructed as $\mathfrak{w} = [\mathfrak{w}_1, \mathfrak{w}_2, \ldots, \mathfrak{w}_k]$.

$$\left\{\langle \mathfrak{M}^1_{ij}, \mathfrak{N}^1_{ij}\rangle, \langle \mathfrak{M}^2_{ij}, \mathfrak{N}^2_{ij}\rangle, \ldots, \langle \mathfrak{M}^l_{ij}, \mathfrak{N}^l_{ij}\rangle\right\}, l = 1,2,\ldots,k$$

$$\langle m_{ij}, n_{ij}\rangle = \left\langle \sqrt{\frac{\sum_{l=1}^{k} \mathfrak{w}_l \left(\mathfrak{M}^l_{ij}\right)^2}{k}}, \sqrt{\frac{\sum_{l=1}^{k} \mathfrak{w}_l \left(\mathfrak{N}^l_{ij}\right)^2}{k}} \right\rangle \quad (6)$$

Step 3. The radius of all PFVs is calculated as follows:

$$r_{ij} = min\left\{ \max_{1 \le l \le k} \sqrt{\left(m_{ij} - \mathfrak{M}^l_{ij}\right)^2 + \left(n_{ij} - \mathfrak{N}^l_{ij}\right)^2}, 1 \right\} \quad (7)$$

Step 4. The criteria weights are not same in real life MCDM problems. The criteria weights are calculated by using the chi-square distance-based divergence measure (Çaloğlu Büyükselçuk & Sarı, 2023).

Let $P_1 = \left\{ \left(u_i, \mathfrak{M}_{P_1}(u_i), \mathfrak{N}_{P_1}(u_i); \mathfrak{r}_{P_1}(u_i)\right) \middle| \text{ i} = 1,2,\ldots,\text{n} \right\}$ and $P_2 = \left\{ \left(u_i, \mathfrak{M}_{P_2}(u_i),\right.\right.$ $\left.\left.\mathfrak{N}_{P_2}(u_i); \mathfrak{r}_{P_2}(u_i)\right) \middle| \text{ i} = 1,2,\right.$

$\left.\ldots,\text{n}\right\}$

$\overline{D}(P_1, P_2)$

$$= \frac{1}{n}\sum_{i=1}^{n}\left[\frac{\left(\mathfrak{M}_{P_1}(u_i) - \mathfrak{M}_{P_2}(u_i)\right)^2}{1 + \mathfrak{M}_{P_1}(u_i) + \mathfrak{M}_{P_2}(u_i)} + \frac{\left(\mathfrak{N}_{P_1}(u_i) - \mathfrak{N}_{P_2}(u_i)\right)^2}{1 + \mathfrak{N}_{P_1}(u_i) + \mathfrak{N}_{P_2}(u_i)} + \frac{\left(\mathfrak{r}_{P_1}(u_i) - \mathfrak{r}_{P_2}(u_i)\right)^2}{1 + \mathfrak{r}_{P_1}(u_i) + \mathfrak{r}_{P_2}(u_i)}\right] \tag{8}$$

$$w_j = \frac{\frac{1}{k}\sum_{i=1}^{k}\left[\frac{\left(\mathfrak{M}_{P_1}(u_i) - \mathfrak{M}_{P_2}(u_i)\right)^2}{1 + \mathfrak{M}_{P_1}(u_i) + \mathfrak{M}_{P_2}(u_i)} + \frac{\left(\mathfrak{N}_{P_1}(u_i) - \mathfrak{N}_{P_2}(u_i)\right)^2}{1 + \mathfrak{N}_{P_1}(u_i) + \mathfrak{N}_{P_2}(u_i)} + \frac{\left(\mathfrak{r}_{P_1}(u_i) - \mathfrak{r}_{P_2}(u_i)\right)^2}{1 + \mathfrak{r}_{P_1}(u_i) + \mathfrak{r}_{P_2}(u_i)}\right]}{\sum_{j=1}^{n}\frac{1}{n}\sum_{i=1}^{n}\left[\frac{\left(\mathfrak{M}_{P_1}(u_i) - \mathfrak{M}_{P_2}(u_i)\right)^2}{1 + \mathfrak{M}_{P_1}(u_i) + \mathfrak{M}_{P_2}(u_i)} + \frac{\left(\mathfrak{N}_{P_1}(u_i) - \mathfrak{N}_{P_2}(u_i)\right)^2}{1 + \mathfrak{N}_{P_1}(u_i) + \mathfrak{N}_{P_2}(u_i)} + \frac{\left(\mathfrak{r}_{P_1}(u_i) - \mathfrak{r}_{P_2}(u_i)\right)^2}{1 + \mathfrak{r}_{P_1}(u_i) + \mathfrak{r}_{P_2}(u_i)}\right]} \quad j = 1,2,\ldots,n \tag{9}$$

Step 5. The decision matrix is normalized according to whether the criteria are benefit or cost oriented.

$$\mathfrak{a}'_{ij} = \left\langle m'_{ij}, n'_{ij}; r'_{ij}\right\rangle = \left\{\begin{matrix} m_{ij}, n_{ij}; r_{ij}\ for\ benefit\ criteria \\ n_{ij}, m_{ij}; r_{ij}\ for\ cost\ criteria \end{matrix}\right\} \tag{10}$$

Step 6. In this step, the normalized vector is weighted as follows:

$$w_j.\mathfrak{a}'_{ij} = \left(\mu_{ij}, \varphi_{ij}; \delta_{ij}\right) = \left(\sqrt{1 - \left(1 - m_{ij}^2\right)^{w_j}}, n_{ij}^{w_j}; r_{ij}\right) \tag{11}$$

Step 7. For each criterion, calculate the negative ideal (NI) C-PFVs as follows:

$$NI = \left\{\left(\overline{\mu}_j, \overline{\varphi}_j; \overline{\delta}_j\right) \middle| j = 1,2,\ldots,n\right\}$$

$$NI = \left\{\left(\min_{i=1,\ldots,m}(\mu_{ij}), \max_{i=1,\ldots,m}(\varphi_{ij}); \min_{i=1,\ldots,m}(\delta_{ij})\right) \middle| j = 1,2,\ldots,n\right\} \tag{12}$$

Step 8. Calculate the Hamming and Euclidean distances of each alternative from NI.

$$\overline{E}_i = \frac{1}{2}\left(\frac{1}{n}\sum_{j=1}^{n}\frac{\left|\delta_{ij} - \overline{\delta}_j\right|}{\sqrt{2}} + \sqrt{\frac{1}{2n}\sum_{j=1}^{n}\left[\left(\mu_{ij}^2 - \overline{\mu}_j^2\right)^2 + \left(\varphi_{ij}^2 - \overline{\varphi}_j^2\right)^2\right]}\right) \tag{13}$$

$$\overline{H}_i = \frac{1}{2n}\sum_{j=1}^{n}\left(\frac{\left|\delta_{ij} - \overline{\delta}_j\right|}{\sqrt{2}} + \frac{1}{2}\left(\left|\mu_{ij}^2 - \overline{\mu}_j^2\right| + \left|\varphi_{ij}^2 - \overline{\varphi}_j^2\right|\right)\right) \tag{14}$$

Step 9. Construct the relative assessment matrix due to the Euclidean and Hamming distances that calculated in the previous step.

$$Ram = \left[R_{ik}\right]_{mxm} \tag{15}$$

$$R_{ik} = (\bar{E}_i - \bar{E}_k) + [\lambda_{ik}(\bar{E}_i - \bar{E}_k)x(\bar{H}_i - \bar{H}_k)] \tag{16}$$

where λ_{ik} means the threshold function. It can be used to identify whether two alternatives' Euclidean distances are same.

$$\lambda_{ik} = \begin{Bmatrix} 1 \; if |\bar{E}_i - \bar{E}_k| \leq \tau \\ 0 \; if |\bar{E}_i - \bar{E}_k| > \tau \end{Bmatrix} \tag{17}$$

where τ is the threshold criterion and is between 0.01 and 0.05.

Step 10. Each alternatives' evaluation score is calculated by using Ram, shown as below:

$$R_i = \sum_{k=1}^{n} R_{ik} \tag{18}$$

Step 11. Alternatives are ranked due to decreasing evaluation score values.

3. DETERMINATION OF THE BEST VR HEADSET

In this study, a model has been developed on the selection of the most suitable VR headsets with different features sold in the market to be used in the MEB-VR education model, which was developed to provide equal opportunity in education. This problem can be solved as a multi-criteria decision-making problem. The first question is which selection criteria should be considered and what should be their importance. The second question is which headset should be preferred under these criteria and importance levels. The flow chart of this study is as given in Figure 2.

Figure 2. Flow chart of the problem

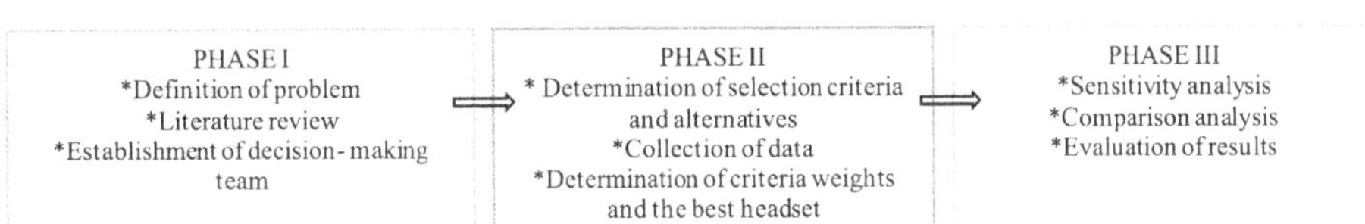

Phase I. At the first step, the problem to be dealt with is correctly and clearly defined. After a detailed literature review on the subject, a decision-making team is formed to guide the study. This decision-making team consists of 6 people. This team is made up of individuals with different education and experience. This team consists of MEB-VR Project coordinator, MEB-VR information technology consultants, and academicians.

Phase II. The problem here is how to determine the headsets required for virtual reality technology to be used especially in applied and laboratory courses during the distance or face-to-face education in MEB-VR model. This problem is one of the most frequently encountered multi-criteria decision-making problems in the literature. To solve this problem, the criteria which evaluate the alternatives should be determined. At this stage of the study, it is decided to create selection criteria based on only the technical features of the headsets. The criteria determined to evaluate the alternatives are defined in Table 2. At this stage, among the criteria to be considered in the selection of the most suitable headsets, the criteria that the users can experience with their usage are not included. Among the different types of headsets, especially standalone types were preferred. Decision makers have decided to use standalone headsets in this education model because they are portable, do not require connection and provide free movement to the user. Two of the standalone headphones (A_1 and A_2) available on the market are products of different brands made in China. One (A_3) is manufactured in Taiwan. The remaining two (A_4 and A_5) are two different models produced in the USA and belonging to the same brand. Alternatives are evaluated according to the criteria and an initial decision matrix is created. The technical specifications of each alternative have been obtained from the official websites of them and websites that make some comparisons on the subject. The best VR headset is selected by applying the steps of the CODAS method based on the circular Pythagorean fuzzy values.

Table 2. Evaluation criteria for virtual reality headsets

Criteria	Code	Definition
Display screen resolution (Zhan et al., 2020)	C_1	When using the headsets, it is important that the screen resolution is as high as possible to have a clear view.
Field of view (FOV) (Arthur, 2000)	C_2	It is the angle of view. If it is too narrow, unnatural head turns may occur.
Refresh rate (Hz) (Intel, 2022)	C_3	It refers to how many times per second the screen can draw a new image. This is measured in Hertz (Hz). For example, if the screen has a refresh rate of 144 Hz, this means that it refreshes the image 144 times per second.
Weight (Mehrfard et al., 2019)	C_4	It is the weight of headset. The weight of the device should be as low as possible in order not to disturb the individual.
Battery (Al Janabi et al., 2020)	C_5	It is the power source, and it is an important criterion that affects the duration of use.
Degrees of freedom (DoF) (Veit et al., 2009)	C_6	It is the number of directions an object can move or turn.

continued on following page

Table 2. Continued

Criteria	Code	Definition
Random access memory (RAM) (GB) (Britannica, 2023a)	C_7	Random access memory is a type of data store used in microprocessor systems that can be read and changed in any order, often used to store operating data and machine code.
Central processing unit (CPU) (GHz) (Britannica, 2023b)	C_8	It is the part of digital computers that processes data and performs software commands.
Graphics processing unit (GPU) (MHz) (Britannica, 2023c)	C_9	It is the device used for graphic creation in personal computers, workstations, or game consoles.
Price (USD)	C_{10}	It is the selling price of the product.

Phase III. At this stage, sensitivity analysis is performed to determine how the outcome of the problem will be affected under different conditions. In addition, the same problem is solved with different MCDM methods, and the comparison is made. Obtained results are discussed in detail.

To determine the best headset, the CODAS method based on Pythagorean fuzzy set, which was given in the previous step, will be applied. First, the evaluation of the alternatives according to the criteria was made using linguistic values via Table 3 (Thakur et al., 2022) by each decision maker and the results are given in Table 4.

Table 3. Linguistic values to evaluate alternatives

Linguistic Terms	Score	Pythagorean Fuzzy Numbers	
		$\mathfrak{M}$	$\mathfrak{N}$
Excellent good	7	0.95	0.27
Very good	6	0.85	0.44
Good	5	0.76	0.63
Medium good	4	0.65	0.73
Fair	3	0.57	0.79
Medium bad	2	0.49	0.87
Bad	1	0.41	0.93

Table 4. Evaluation results for alternatives by each decision maker

DM_s	Alternatives	Criteria									
		C_1	C_2	C_3	C_4	C_5	C_6	C_7	C_8	C_9	C_{10}
DM_1	A_1	4	4	5	7	7	3	3	5	5	3
	A_2	4	6	5	3	1	5	6	7	6	4
	A_3	7	6	6	2	2	5	5	7	6	5
	A_4	5	3	3	6	2	3	4	3	3	7
	A_5	6	5	4	5	1	6	6	7	6	4
DM_2	A_1	3	4	6	6	7	4	3	6	5	3
	A_2	3	5	4	4	2	5	5	6	7	5
	A_3	6	5	6	2	1	4	4	6	6	4
	A_4	4	2	3	7	3	3	4	2	2	6
	A_5	7	6	5	4	2	6	7	7	5	5
DM_3	A_1	2	3	4	6	7	3	4	5	6	4
	A_2	5	5	6	2	2	4	5	6	7	2
	A_3	7	6	5	3	2	4	4	6	7	6
	A_4	4	5	3	5	3	3	4	2	3	6
	A_5	6	6	4	5	2	7	7	7	6	5
DM_4	A_1	3	4	6	7	6	4	3	6	5	3
	A_2	5	6	5	4	2	6	7	6	6	3
	A_3	6	6	5	3	4	4	5	6	7	6
	A_4	6	4	4	5	4	4	3	2	4	5
	A_5	5	5	6	4	2	7	6	7	7	5
DM_5	A_1	4	5	4	6	6	4	5	6	6	3
	A_2	5	5	6	4	2	5	7	7	6	3
	A_3	6	7	7	3	4	4	5	7	5	6
	A_4	5	4	5	6	4	4	5	3	3	6
	A_5	7	6	5	5	1	6	5	7	6	5
DM_6	A_1	5	4	6	6	7	4	3	4	4	3
	A_2	4	5	6	4	1	5	5	7	6	2
	A_3	7	7	6	3	2	4	5	7	5	4
	A_4	4	4	3	5	3	4	5	4	2	4
	A_5	5	4	6	7	1	6	7	6	5	3

An example of the decision matrix obtained as a result of the evaluations made by DM_3 is represented below. For the readers to understand calculations more easily, some calculation examples will be given after each step. Values whose calculations are given in italics in the tables. Calculations on how the numbers written in italics in the tables are obtained will be given in detail at each step.

$$M^3 = (\mathfrak{a}_{ij})^3 = \begin{matrix} \\ A_1 \\ A_2 \\ \vdots \\ A_5 \end{matrix} \begin{pmatrix} C_1 & C_2 & \cdots & C_{10} \\ (0.49,0.87,1.232) & (0.57,0.79,1.14) & \cdots & (0.57,0.79,1.14) \\ (0.76,0.63,0.906) & (0.76,0.63,0.906) & \cdots & (0.49,0.87,1.232) \\ \vdots & \vdots & \ddots & \vdots \\ (0.85,0.44,0.687) & (0.85,0.44,0.687) & \cdots & (0.76,0.63,0.906) \end{pmatrix}$$

By using Equation 5, the hesitancy degree is calculated as follows:

$$\mathfrak{h}^3_{11} = \sqrt{1 - (0.49^2 - 0.87^2)} = 1.232$$

The decision matrices obtained as a result of the evaluations made by each decision maker are reduced to a single aggregate matrix using Equation 6 (Table 5). Since the experiences of the decision makers were considered equal, the weights of the decision makers were not taken into account.

Table 5. Aggregate decision matrix

m_{ij}, n_{ij}	C_1	C_2	...	C_9	C_{10}
A1	(0.621,0.760)	(0.657,0.725)	...	(0.775,0.593)	(0.584,0.780)
A2	(0.696,0.693)	(0.791,0.573)	...	(0.885,0.392)	(0.596,0.784)
A3	(0.901,0.365)	(0.871,0.433)	...	(0.857,0.470)	(0.774,0.584)
A4	(0.724,0.657)	(0.634,0.750)	...	(0.559,0.808)	(0.824,0.514)
A5	(0.857,0.470)	(0.790,0.564)	...	(0.839,0.491)	(0.714,0.676)

$$\langle m_{11}, n_{11} \rangle = \Bigg\langle \sqrt{\frac{0.65^2 + 0.57^2 + 0.49^2 + 0.57^2 + 0.65^2 + 0.76^2}{6}},$$

$$\sqrt{\frac{0.73^2 + 0.79^2 + 0.87^2 + 0.79^2 + 0.73^2 + 0.63^2}{6}} \Bigg\rangle = \langle (0.621,0.760) \rangle$$

Radius of Pythagorean fuzzy values are calculated by using Equation 7 and are shown in the Table 6.

Table 6. Radius of PFVs

r_{ij}	C_1	C_2	...	C_9	C_{10}
A1	0.191	0.140	...	0.185	0.083
A2	0.159	0.146	...	0.138	0.225
A3	0.107	0.226	...	0.221	0.192
A4	0.251	0.187	...	0.120	0.277
A5	0.221	0.217	...	0.247	0.183

$$r_{11} = \min\left(\left\{\max\begin{pmatrix}\sqrt{(0.62-0.65)^2+(0.76-0.73)^2}, \sqrt{(0.62-0.57)^2+(0.76-0.79)^2}, \\ \sqrt{(0.62-0.49)^2+(0.76-0.87)^2}, \sqrt{(0.62-0.57)^2+(0.76-0.79)^2}, \\ \sqrt{(0.62-0.65)^2+(0.76-0.73)^2}, \sqrt{(0.62-0.76)^2+(0.76-0.63)^2}\end{pmatrix}\right\}, 1\right) = 0.191$$

The criteria that are the subject of the problem were evaluated using Table 7 [49] and the evaluations made by each decision maker are given in Table 8.

Table 7. Linguistic values to evaluate criteria

Linguistic Terms	Score	Pythagorean Fuzzy Numbers	
		$\mathfrak{M}$	$\mathfrak{N}$
Much more important	5	0.96	0.27
More important	4	0.83	0.46
Important	3	0.65	0.54
Low important	2	0.46	0.73
Very low important	1	0.38	0.84

Table 8. Criteria evaluations by decision makers

Criteria	Decision makers					
	DM_1	DM_2	DM_3	DM_4	DM_5	DM_6
C_1	4	5	5	4	4	5
C_2	2	1	2	2	4	3
C_3	3	5	5	5	3	5
C_4	4	4	4	3	5	4
C_5	1	1	1	3	3	2
C_6	1	3	2	1	1	1
C_7	5	2	4	5	5	4
C_8	5	3	3	4	2	2

Criteria	Decision makers					
	DM_1	DM_2	DM_3	DM_4	DM_5	DM_6
C_9	3	4	3	1	2	3
C_{10}	2	2	1	2	1	1

Aggregated criteria weight matrix is represented in Table 9. By using Equations 8 and 9, the weights of the criteria were determined and given in Figure 3.

Table 9. Aggregated criteria matrix

Criteria	m	n	r
C_1	0.897	0.377	0.124
C_2	0.561	0.684	0.350
C_3	0.869	0.382	0.270
C_4	0.827	0.449	0.223
C_5	0.498	0.734	0.246
C_6	0.449	0.780	0.313
C_7	0.852	0.442	0.486
C_8	0.693	0.568	0.400
C_9	0.621	0.622	0.325
C_{10}	0.422	0.787	0.068

Figure 3. Criteria weights

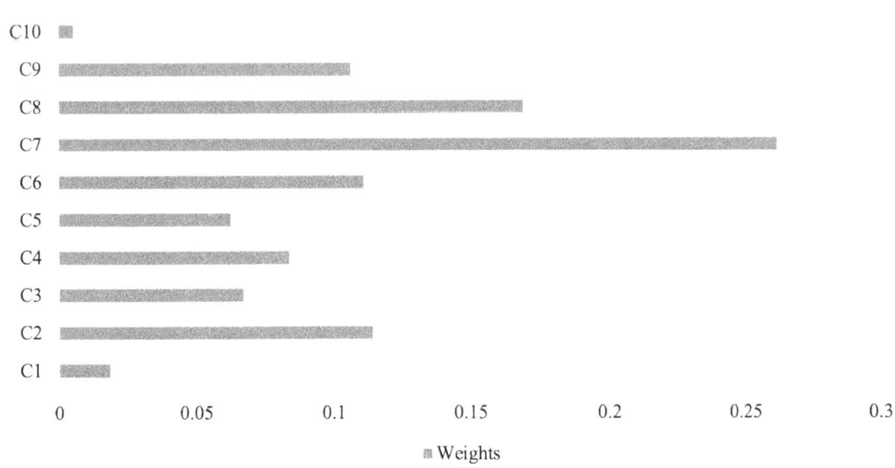

It has been determined that the most important criteria for standalone headsets are RAM (weight: 0.262), CPU and FOV criteria are in the second and third places. It is the price criterion that has the least weight. The order of the criteria according to the weights is $C_7 > C_8 > C_2 > C_6 > C_9 > C_4 > C_3 > C_5 > C_1 > C_{10}$. Since it is intended for use in the education sector, the price criterion has been determined as the least important criterion by the decision makers.

The initial decision matrix is normalized using Equation 10. The 4th and 10th criteria are cost-oriented, while the remaining criteria are benefit-oriented. The normalized decision matrix is as shown in the Table 10.

Table 10. Normalized decision matrix

$m_{ij}, n_{ij}; r_{ij}$	C_1	...	C_4	...	C_9	C_{10}
A_1	(0.621,0.760;0.191)	...	(0.392,0.885;0.138)	...	(0.775,0.593;0.185)	(0.780,0.584;0.083)
A_2	(0.696,0.693;0.159	...	(0.765,0.613;0.162)	...	(0.885,0.392;0.138)	(0.784,0.596;0.225)
A_3	(0.901,0.365;0.107)	...	(0.818,0.545;0.076)	...	(0.857,0.470;0.221)	(0.584,0.774;0.192)
A_4	(0.724,0.657;0.250)	...	(0.525,0.825;0.284)	...	(0.559,0.808;0.120)	(0.514,0.824;0.277)
A_5	(0.857,0.470;0.221)	...	(0.623,0.762;0.400)	...	(0.839,0.491;0.247)	(0.676,0.714;0.183)

The normalized matrix is multiplied by the criterion weights (Equation 11) to obtain the weighted normalized matrix (Table 11).

Table 11. Weighted normalized decision matrix

$(\mu_{ij}, \varphi_{ij}; \delta_{ij})$	C_1	C_2	...	C_{10}
A_1	*(0.0950,0.9949;0.1906)*	(0.2502,0.9639;0.1398)	...	(0.0716,0.9971;0.0829)
A_2	(0.1107,0.9932;0.1587)	(0.3259,0.9385;0.1461)	...	(0.0722,0.9972;0.2254)
A_3	(0.1753,0.9814;0.1067)	(0.3870,0.9088;0.2263)	...	(0.0477,0.9986;0.1916)
A_4	(0.1173,0.9922;0.2505)	(0.2387,0.9677;0.1872)	...	(0.0409,0.9989;0.2773)
A_5	(0.1563,0.9860;0.2209)	(0.3252,0.9366;0.2173)	...	(0.0578,0.9982;0.1834)

$$(\mu_{11}, \varphi_{11}; \delta_{11}) = \left(\sqrt{1-(1-0.6208^2)^{0.0187}}, 0.7602^{0.0187}; 0.1906\right) = (0.0950, 0.9949; 0.1906)$$

For each criterion, the negative ideal C-PFVs are calculated using Equation 12 and represented in Table 12.

Table 12. NI C-PFVs for each criterion

Criteria	C_1	C_2	...	C_{10}
NI	*(0.0951,0.9949;0.1067)*	(0.2387,0.9677;0.1398)	...	(0.0409,0.9989;0.0829)

$$NI = \left\{ \begin{array}{c} min(0.0951,0.1107,0.1753,0.1173,0.1563), max(0.9949,0.9932,0.9814,0.9922,0.9860)\ ; \\ min(0.1906,0.1587,0.1067,0.2505,0.2209) \end{array} \right\}$$

$$= (0.0951,0.9949;0.1067)$$

The Euclidean and Hamming distances of each alternative from NI are calculated using Equations 13 and 14 (Table 13).

Table 13. Euclidean and Hamming distances

Alternatives	$\overline{E}_i$	$\overline{H}_i$
A_1	*0.0433*	*0.0332*
A_2	0.0717	0.0576
A_3	0.0623	0.0507
A_4	0.0316	0.0291
A_5	0.0964	0.0773

$$\overline{E}_i = \frac{1}{2}\left(\frac{1}{10}\left(\frac{|0.1906 - 0.1067|}{\sqrt{2}} + \frac{|0.1398 - 0.1398|}{\sqrt{2}} + \frac{|0.1916 - 0.1888|}{\sqrt{2}} + \ldots + \frac{|0.0829 - 0.0829|}{\sqrt{2}}\right)\right.$$

$$\left. + \sqrt{\frac{1}{2*10}([(0.095^2 - 0.095^2)^2 + (0.9949^2 - 0.9949^2)^2] + \ldots + [(0.1176^2 - 0.1176^2)^2 + (0.9898^2 - 0.9898^2)^2])}\right) = 0.0433$$

$$\overline{H}_i = \frac{1}{2*10}\left[\left(\frac{|0.1906 - 0.1067|}{\sqrt{2}} + \frac{1}{2}((0.095^2 - 0.095^2) + (0.9949^2 - 0.9949^2))\right)\right.$$

$$\left. + \left(\frac{|0.1398 - 0.1398|}{\sqrt{2}} + \frac{1}{2}((0.2502^2 - 0.2387^2) + (0.9639^2 - 0.9677^2))\right) + \ldots\right] = 0.0332$$

Using equation 16, the relative assessment matrix is obtained as follows. The Threshold criterion was set at 0.04.

$$RAM = \begin{pmatrix} 0.0000 & 0.0290 & 0.0193 & -0.0117 & 0.0530 \\ -0.0277 & 0.0000 & -0.0093 & -0.0390 & 0.0252 \\ -0.0187 & 0.0094 & 0.0000 & -0.0301 & 0.0350 \\ 0.0118 & 0.0401 & 0.0314 & 0.0000 & 0.0648 \\ -0.0507 & -0.0242 & -0.0331 & -0.0617 & 0.0000 \end{pmatrix}$$

$$R_{12} = (0.0433 - 0.0717) + (1*(0.0433 - 0.0717)*(0.0332 - 0.0576)) = -0.0277$$

Evaluation score of each alternative is equal to the sum of Rams. The alternative with the highest score will be the best option. The final results are as shown in the Figure 4.

Figure 4. Evaluation scores of each alternatives

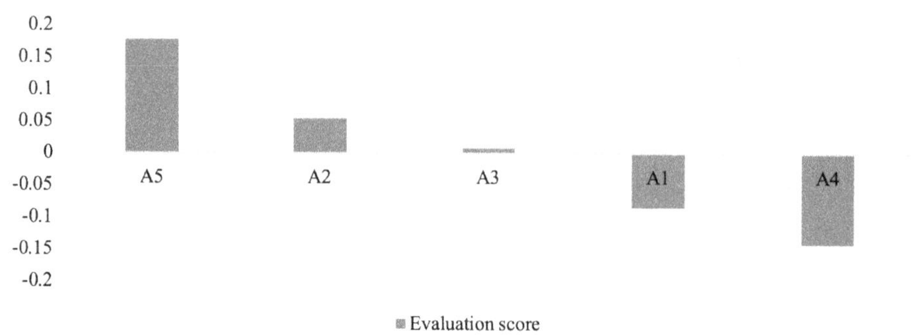

When all the results are evaluated, the three most important criteria for choosing a standalone VR headset in the education sector are RAM, CPU and FOV. In the light of the determined criteria, it has been determined that the best headset is one of the models produced in America (A5).

4. RESULTS AND DISCUSSION

In this section, the sensitivity analysis of the problem and the comparison of the obtained results when the problem is solved with other methods will be made.

4.1. Sensitivity Analysis

In this section, an analysis of how the problem subject to the study will react under different conditions will be given. First of all, if the threshold criterion value used to determine the scores of the alternatives changes between 0.01 and 0.05, how the alternative rankings will change was analysed and the results are given in Figure 5.

Figure 5. Ranking of alternatives due to different Threshold criterion value

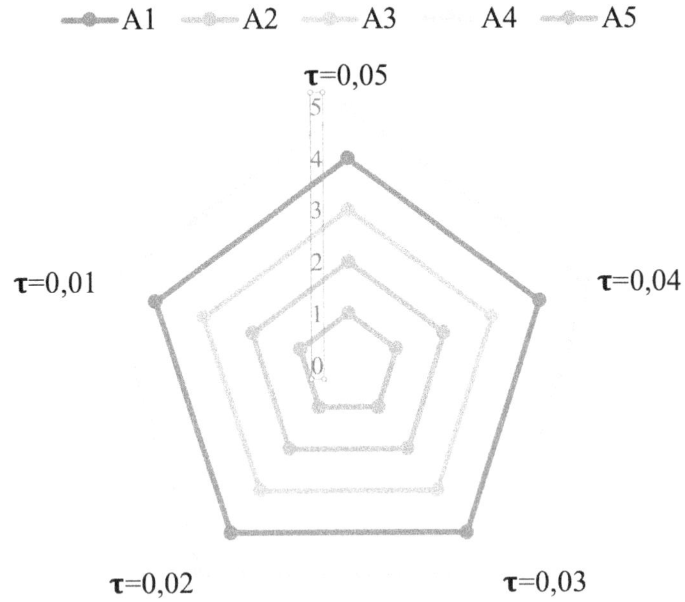

As can be seen from the graph, it has been observed that there is no change in the ranking of the alternatives for different threshold criterion values. According to 10 different criteria of alternatives, 7 different evaluation scales and 70 different scenarios were developed, and the rankings of the alternatives were evaluated. It was concluded that there was no change in the rankings for each different scenario ($A_5>A_2>A_3>A_1>A_4$).

4.2. Comparison Analysis

In the study, CODAS method based on circular Pythagorean fuzzy numbers was used to solve the problem. In this section, it will be discussed how the obtained result changes when the problem is solved with other multi-criteria decision-making methods. For this purpose, ARAS, MOORA, EDAS, COPRAS and CODAS methods based on triangular fuzzy numbers (TFNs) were used to solve the problem and the results are given in Table 14.

Table 14. Comparison of alternatives' ranking according to different MCDM methods

MCDM methods	Ranking
CODAS based on C-PFN	$A_5>A_2>A_3>A_1>A_4$
CODAS based on TFN	$A_5>A_2>A_3>A_1>A_4$
COPRAS based on TFN	$A_3>A_2>A_5>A_1>A_4$
EDAS based on TFN	$A_5>A_2>A_1>A_3>A_4$
ARAS based on TFN	$A_5>A_3>A_2>A_1>A_4$
MOORAS based on TFN	$A_5>A_2>A_1>A_3>A_4$

When the Table 14 is examined, the best alternative was obtained as A_5 according to the results found in the MCDM methods applied other than the COPRAS based on TFN method. However, there were some minor changes because of closeness coefficients in the ranking of the other alternatives. When Spearman's rank correlation coefficient was calculated, it was found as 0.900 between all fuzzy MCDM methods except COPRAS method (0.6000). It has been easily observed that there is a strong and positive relationship between the proposed method and other methods.

5. CONCLUSION

The developments in technology and informatics have made positive contributions in the education sector as well as in all sectors. virtual reality, augmented reality or mixed reality technology is widely used in education, both in face-to-face and distance education. The use of this technology, especially in practice and laboratory courses, positively affects the learning efficiency of students. In this study, it is aimed to determine the virtual reality headsets to be used in the MEB-VR model developed for this purpose. First, it has been preferred to use standalone headsets among headsets in different categories. Thanks to this type of headsets, they will be more flexible in student movements and can be more expensive in terms of cost. However, these devices are not very suitable from an ergonomic point of view, they may be heavier than other types.

Determining the best headset is a typical multi-criteria decision-making problem. Although there are many techniques used to solve these problems, in this study CODAS based on circular Pythagorean fuzzy set was applied to determine the best standalone headset. In order to overcome the uncertainty and ambiguity that arise in many practical situations, it is preferred to use circular Pythagorean fuzzy sets. When the problem is handled and solved by considering the determined criteria, A_5 emerges as the best standalone VR headset. This study will contribute to school administrators, purchasing and IT department employees, students, and their parents to make more effective and correct decisions, especially in the choice of standalone virtual reality headsets to be used in the education sector.

Some limitations were encountered in the study. The biggest problem faced here is that the most appropriate headsets were chosen based on the experiences of the decision maker team consisting of only six people. A limitation is that not all headsets available in the market can be tested on students. Such a study is planned to be carried out in the future. If sufficient budget can be provided, different course contents and different headsets will be tested on students of different age groups. Here, not only the technical features of the device will be tested, but also the physical, social, and psychological dimensions of the experience of the students will be discussed, and broader selection criteria and accordingly alternatives will be evaluated. All these results will be analysed, and studies and investments will be made for the design of the most suitable VR headset that can be used in the MEB-VR education model. It is planned to produce headsets that will be used especially in the education model and designed by considering the wishes of the students, school administrators and teachers in every aspect.

5.1 Data Availability

The data used to support the findings of this study are included within the article.

5.2 Conflicts of Interest

The author declares that there is no conflict of interest regarding the publication of this paper.

5.3 Funding Statement

This research received no external funding.

REFERENCES

Al Janabi, H. F., Aydin, A., Palaneer, S., Macchione, N., Al-Jabir, A., Khan, M. S., & Ahmed, K. (2020). Effectiveness of the HoloLens mixed-reality headset in minimally invasive surgery: A simulation-based feasibility study. *Surgical Endoscopy*, 34(3), 1143–1149. DOI:10.1007/s00464-019-06862-3 PMID:31214807

Albahbah, M., Kıvrak, S., & Arslan, G. (2021). Application areas of augmented reality and virtual reality in construction project management: A scoping review. *Journal of Construction Engineering and Management & Innovation*, 4(3), 151–172. DOI:10.31462/jcemi.2021.03151172

Allcoat, D., Hatchard, T., Azmat, F., Stansfield, K., Watson, D., & von Mühlenen, A. (2021). Education in the digital age: Learning experience in virtual and mixed realities. *Journal of Educational Computing Research*, 59(5), 795–816. DOI:10.1177/0735633120985120

Angelov, V., Petkov, E., Shipkovenski, G., & Kalushkov, T. (2020, June) Modern virtual reality headsets. In *2020 International congress on human-computer interaction, optimization and robotic applications (HORA)* (pp. 1-5). IEEE.

Arthur, K. W. (2000). *Effects of field of view on performance with head-mounted displays*. The University of North Carolina at Chapel Hill.

Atanassov, K. T. (1999). *Intuitionistic fuzzy sets. In intuitionistic fuzzy steps*. Physica. DOI:10.1007/978-3-7908-1870-3

Çaloğlu Büyükselçuk, E., & Sarı, Y. C. (2023). The best whey protein powder selection via VIKOR based on circular intuitionistic fuzzy sets. *Symmetry*, 15(7), 1313. DOI:10.3390/sym15071313

Calvert, P. (2019). Virtual reality as a tool for teaching library design. *Education for Information*, 35(4), 439–450. DOI:10.3233/EFI-170150

Checa, D., & Bustillo, A. (2020). Advantages and limits of virtual reality in learning processes: Briviesca in the fifteenth century. *Virtual Reality (Waltham Cross)*, 24(1), 151–161. DOI:10.1007/s10055-019-00389-7

Chen, C. J., Toh, S. C., & Ismail, W. M. F. W. (2014). Are learning styles relevant to virtual reality? *Journal of Research on Technology in Education*, 38(2), 123–141. DOI:10.1080/15391523.2005.10782453

Ejegwa, P. A. (2021). Generalized triparametric correlation coefficient for Pythagorean fuzzy sets with application to MCDM problems. *Granular Computing*, 6(3), 557–566. DOI:10.1007/s41066-020-00215-5

Frazier, E., Lege, R., & Bonner, E. (2021). Making virtual reality accessible for language learning: Applying VR application analysis framework. *The Journal of Teaching English with Technology*, 21(1), 128–140.

Horváth, I. (2021). An analysis of personalized learning opportunities in 3D VR. *Frontiers of Computer Science*, 3(673826).

Hou, H., & Wu, H. (2020). Technology for real estate education and practice: A VR technology perspective. *Property Management*, 38(2), 311–324. DOI:10.1108/PM-08-2019-0046

Hussein, M., & Nätterdal, C. (2015). *The benefits of using virtual reality in education. A comparison study*. [Dissertation, University of Gothenburg & Chalmers University of Technology, Göteborg, Sweden].

Ibrahim, A., Al-Rababah, A. I., & Baker, Q. B. (2021). Integrating virtual reality technology into architecture education: The case of architectural history courses. *Open House International*, 46(4), 498–509. DOI:10.1108/OHI-12-2020-0190

Intel (2023, February 20) What is refresh rate and why is it important? https://www.intel.com/content/www/us/en/gaming/resources/highest-refresh-rate-gaming.html

Joyce, T. S. L., & Enoch, E. N. (2021). The use of virtual reality in pharmacy education in Hong Kong: Lessons learnt. *Frontiers in Education*, 6, 639126. DOI:10.3389/feduc.2021.639126

Khan, M. J., Alcantud, J. C. R., Kumam, W., Kumam, P., & Alreshidi, N. A. (2023). Expanding Pythagorean fuzzy sets with distinctive radii: Disc Pythagorean fuzzy sets. *Complex & Intelligent Systems*, 9(6), 1–18. DOI:10.1007/s40747-023-01062-y

Kim, H., Nah, S., Oh, J., & Ryu, H. (2019, March). VR-MOOCs: A learning management system for VR education. In *2019 IEEE Conference on Virtual Reality and 3D User Interfaces (VR)* (pp. 1325-1326). IEEE. DOI:10.1109/VR.2019.8798106

Lee, H. J., & Hwang, Y. (2022). Technology-enhanced education through VR-making and metaverse-linking to foster teacher readiness and sustainable learning. *Sustainability (Basel)*, 14(8), 4786. DOI:10.3390/su14084786

Lege, R., & Bonner, E. (2020). Virtual reality in education: The promise, progress, and challenge. *The JALT CALL Journal*, 16(3), 167–180. DOI:10.29140/jaltcall.v16n3.388

Ling, H., & Rui, L. (2016). *VR glasses and leap motion trends in education*. The 11th International Conference on Computer Science & Education, Nagoya University, Japan.

Liu, C., Rani, P., & Pachori, K. (2022). Sustainable circular supplier selection and evaluation in the manufacturing sector using Pythagorean fuzzy EDAS approach. *Journal of Enterprise Information Management*, 35(4/5), 1040–1066. DOI:10.1108/JEIM-04-2021-0187

Mehrfard, A., Fotouhi, J., Taylor, G., Forster, T., Navab, N., & Fuerst, B. (2019). A comparative analysis of virtual reality head-mounted display systems. arXiv preprint arXiv:1912.02913.

Mishra, A. R., Pamučar, D., Hezam, I. M., Chakrabortty, R. K., Rani, P., Božanić, D., & Ćirović, G. (2022). Interval-valued pythagorean fuzzy similarity measure-based complex proportional assessment method for waste-to-energy technology selection. *Processes (Basel, Switzerland)*, 10(5), 1015. DOI:10.3390/pr10051015

Mohd, W. W., Abdullah, L., Yusoff, B., Taib, C. M. I. C., & Merigo, J. M. (2019). An integrated MCDM model based on Pythagorean fuzzy sets for green supplier development program. *Malaysian Journal of Mathematical Science*, 13, 23–37.

Molla, M. U., Giri, B. C., & Biswas, P. (2021). Extended PROMETHEE method with Pythagorean fuzzy sets for medical diagnosis problems. *Soft Computing*, 25(6), 4503–4512. DOI:10.1007/s00500-020-05458-7

Noble, S. (2023, January 3) *The ultimate VR, AR, MR guide*. ANIWAA. https://www.aniwaa.com/guide/vr-ar/ultimate-vr-ar-mr-guide/

OECD. (2012). *Equity and quality in education: Supporting disadvantaged students and schools*. OECD Publishing. DOI:10.1787/9789264130852-

Pantelidis, V. S. (2021). Reasons to use virtual reality in education and training courses and a model to determine when to use virtual reality. *Themes in Science and Technology Education*, 2, 59–70.

Paszkiewicz, A., Salach, M., Dymora, P., Bolanowski, M., Budzik, G., & Kubiak, P. (2021). Methodology of implementing virtual reality in education for industry 4.0. *Sustainability (Basel)*, 13(9), 5049. DOI:10.3390/su13095049

Peng, X., & Ma, X. (2020). Pythagorean fuzzy multi-criteria decision making method based on CODAS with new score function. *Journal of Intelligent & Fuzzy Systems*, 38(3), 3307–3318. DOI:10.3233/JIFS-190043

Rani, P., Chen, S. M., & Mishra, A. R. (2023). Multiple attribute decision making based on MAIRCA, standard deviation-based method, and Pythagorean fuzzy sets. *Information Sciences*, 644, 119274. DOI:10.1016/j.ins.2023.119274

Rani, P., Mishra, A. R., Pardasani, K. R., Mardani, A., Liao, H., & Streimikiene, D. (2019). A novel VIKOR approach based on entropy and divergence measures of Pythagorean fuzzy sets to evaluate renewable energy technologies in India. *Journal of Cleaner Production*, 238, 117936. DOI:10.1016/j.jclepro.2019.117936

Rani, P., Mishra, A. R., Rezaei, G., Liao, H., & Mardani, A. (2020). Extended Pythagorean fuzzy TOPSIS method based on similarity measure for sustainable recycling partner selection. *International Journal of Fuzzy Systems*, 22(2), 735–747. DOI:10.1007/s40815-019-00689-9

Sarkar, B., & Biswas, A. (2022). A multi-criteria decision making approach for strategy formulation using Pythagorean fuzzy logic. *Expert Systems: International Journal of Knowledge Engineering and Neural Networks*, 39(1), e12802. DOI:10.1111/exsy.12802

Smith, M. B. (2021, January 3). *Virtual reality headsets: A buying guide*. BH Photo Video. https://www.bhphotovideo.com/explora/computers/buying-guide/virtual-reality-headset-a-buying-guide

Tang, H. (2021). Applied research of VR technology in physical education. *The International Journal of Electronic Engineering Education*. .DOI:10.1177/00207209211007774

Thakur, P., Kizielewicz, B., Gandotra, N., Shekhovtsov, A., Saini, N., & Sałabun, W. (2022). The group decision-making using Pythagorean fuzzy entropy and the complex proportional assessment. *Sensors (Basel)*, 22(13), 4879. DOI:10.3390/s22134879 PMID:35808377

Thangeda, A., Baratiseng, B., & Mompati, T. (2016). Education for sustainability: Quality education Is a necessity in modern day. How far do the educational institutions facilitate quality education? *Journal of Education and Practice*, 7(2), 9–17.

Veit, M., Capobianco, A., & Bechmann, D. (2009, November). Influence of degrees of freedom's manipulation on performances during orientation tasks in virtual reality environments. In *Proceedings of the 16th ACM Symposium on Virtual Reality Software and Technology* (pp. 51-58). ACM. DOI:10.1145/1643928.1643942

Wang, Z., He, R., & Chen, K. (2020). Thermal comfort and virtual reality headsets. *Applied Ergonomics*, 85, 103066. DOI:10.1016/j.apergo.2020.103066 PMID:32174354

Yager, R. R. (2013a). Pythagorean membership grades in multicriteria decision making. *IEEE Transactions on Fuzzy Systems*, 22(4), 958–965. DOI:10.1109/TFUZZ.2013.2278989

Yager, R. R. (2013b, June) Pythagorean fuzzy subsets. In *2013 joint IFSA world congress and NAFIPS annual meeting (IFSA/NAFIPS)* (pp. 57-61). IEEE. DOI:10.1109/IFSA-NAFIPS.2013.6608375

Zhan, T., Yin, K., Xiong, J., He, Z., & Wu, S. T. (2020). Augmented reality and virtual reality displays: Perspectives and challenges. *iScience*, 23(8), 101397. DOI:10.1016/j.isci.2020.101397 PMID:32759057

Chapter 16
Improving Academic Specialization Choice in Higher Education in Oman Using Virtual Reality (VR) Experiential Learning

Shaik Asif Hussain
https://orcid.org/0000-0001-5312-4320
Middle East College, Oman

ABSTRACT

For any student, picking an area of academic specialization is a pivotal moment that impacts their future career progression and personal fulfillment. Traditional methods like career counseling and information sessions often fail to give learners the necessary experiences to help them make informed choices. This realization necessitates a comprehension of pupils' transitions between academic disciplines. For this reason, this chapter has been rolled out to investigate the potential use of immersive virtual reality (VR) as a novel tool to enhance experiential learning and aid students in their academic specialization selection process. The work helps to assist students better if they understand the elements that contribute to happiness or discontent while choosing a study major. Teachers, career counsellors, students, and employers making decisions about their educational route may all benefit from insight into the variables influencing the choice of study and the link between decision-making processes and the degree of satisfaction after using the virtual reality platform.

DOI: 10.4018/979-8-3693-6407-9.ch016

1. INTRODUCTION

The traditional methods of exploring academic selections come with several limitations. First, the method is attributed to a lack of immersive experiences as the methods fail to offer students the hands-on and interactive experiences required to get a proper understanding of diverse fields (Hawes & Arya. 2023). The students make misinformed choices due to the reliance on static information and limited engagement. The method also comes with inaccurate representations as they only give an idealized picture of academic specializations, thereby neglecting the challenges and realities of this field. This disconnect mostly leads to disappointments once the students begin their academic journeys. The traditional methods also come with the disadvantage of limiting information to students regarding various academic specializations especially those that are offered in other institutions and niche fields. This results in students being restricted in their exploration journey, limiting their potential choices. The other disadvantage is that traditional methods offer limited opportunities for students to assess their interests, skills, and motivations in specific academic fields. This can make it challenging for them to identify the specialization that aligns best with their aspirations. The other challenge is seen in that the traditional methods also come with a lack of support for the students to enable them to make decisions during the academic specialization selection process (Hawes & Arya, 2023). This usually leads to confusion anxiety, and eventually suboptimal choices. Furthermore, existing research, as exemplified by Silver's study, has predominantly focused on quantitative analysis of significant changes, overlooking the qualitative aspects and the transitional experience of students between specializations. He found that around 38 students, influenced by external factors such as parental desires, find themselves on unsuitable academic paths, leading to a lack of enthusiasm for their chosen field (Silver, 2023).

Therefore, many ways contribute to solving this problem, such as using virtual reality with artificial intelligence techniques. Virtual Reality is a simulated experience that employs pose tracking and 3D near-eye displays to give the user an immersive feel of a virtual world. This is what is essential that the student feels the virtual environment is reality (Soliman et al., 2021). Previous studies have developed Virtual Reality (VR) in different domains like Education, Engineering Experiments, Healthcare Training, Treatments, and Consultations. For example, the existing research done by (Barkokebas et al., 2019), this work proposes an approach to assess the training for assembly/disassembly and maintenance of machines developed for the construction manufacturing industry by using immersive virtual reality. In addition, another research paper was done by Christie Hurrell and Jeremiah Baker in 2021. This paper describes the configuration, access policies, and outreach activities around the library's VR services and spaces and discusses in more detail how VR has been used VR in undergraduate classes, including kinesiology, dance, literature, and art history. However, there are no effective methods yet other than descriptive methods or field visits, which do not significantly contribute to understanding the disciplines (Hurrell & Baker, 2021).

For any student, selecting a suitable area of academic specialization is a pivotal moment in their life that impacts their future career progression and personal fulfillment. This information relies on information available to a learner concerning the various academic fields. Currently, traditional methods like career counseling and information sessions often fail to give learners the necessary experiences to help them make informed choices (Beck et al., 2023). For this reason, this research has been rolled out to investigate the potential of immersive virtual reality (VR) as a novel tool to enhance experiential learning and aid students in their academic specialization selection process.

1.1 Problem Statement

One of the most important decisions a student makes in college is choosing a major. Despite the common perception that choosing a major is a distinct decision made at one specific moment, many students change their majors at least once during their higher education journey. Primary selection is frequently considered a distinct decision that students make at a certain period despite its importance. However, studies reveal that a third of undergraduate students alter their major at least once. This realization necessitates a more profound comprehension of pupils' transitions between academic disciplines. The process of switching majors is examined in this work as a crucial educational transition. By compiling firsthand stories of transition, one may get insight into students' views, interpretations, and meaning-making around these periods of change in higher education. It finds that the most common reasons include academic difficulty, lack of interest, and career uncertainty. There are three phases to the realization of the research aim. Two surveys will be conducted as primary sources utilizing an internet questionnaire to collect the data for the first stage. The experimentation step involves working with focus groups on the VR platform. In-depth insights into students' experiences are gathered through interviews (focus groups) with those active in the VR platform, and user interactions are monitored by analytics inside the VR platform. After implementing the system, it is expected that the research will study the major issue behind making the students change their majors during the study and observe the extent of the implemented VR platform's influence on decision-making. Furthermore, the study will pinpoint several elements that might aid students in making an informed choice before beginning their studies. From the solutions obtained the Educators and counselors may be able to assist students better if they understand the elements that contribute to happiness or discontent while choosing a study major. Teachers, career counselors, students, and employers making decisions about their educational route may all benefit from insight into the variables influencing the choice of area of study and the link between decision-making processes and the degree of satisfaction after using the proposed VR platform. By embracing VR technology, we can transform the way students approach academic specialization selection, paving the way for a more informed, engaged, and fulfilling learning experience in higher education.

2. RESEARCH METHODOLOGY

Table 1. Research Methodology

Methodology in a research proposal	
Research type	**The study will employ a mixed-methods approach, combining quantitative surveys to measure changes in understanding and confidence levels, qualitative interviews to gather in-depth insights into students' experiences, and analytics within the VR to track user interactions. A pre-and-post intervention design will be utilized to assess changes in participants' knowledge and perceptions. The experimental group will engage with the VR, while the control group will follow traditional vocational guidance methods.** **Research method Primary /secondary Qualitative/ Quantitative** **Survey Primary Quantitative** **Interview/focus group Primary Qualitative** **Experiment- focus group Primary Quantitative**
Population and sample	The study will focus on students in college or university with different specializations in Oman. The table will highlight the population and different sample sizes in each research method. pre-and-post-intervention design Research method Population Sample size Pre-intervention design Survey 1 Around 150 students at a private college in Oman It needs to be checked (50 for each specialization) to classify the most specializations that make students change their field during their study. Check most academic specializations that students change their majors after finishing the survey1. With or in - intervention design Experiment- focus group 10 for the most academic specializations students change their majors from and to. Post-intervention design Interview/focus group Ten focus students for each academic specialization that students change their majors (from and to), after applying the Experiment by using VR method When: Two years are required to finish the different research methods.
Research methods	To gather in-depth insights into students' experiences and analytics within the VR platform to track user interactions.

continued on following page

Table 1. Continued

Methodology in a research proposal	
Research type	**The study will employ a mixed-methods approach, combining quantitative surveys to measure changes in understanding and confidence levels, qualitative interviews to gather in-depth insights into students' experiences, and analytics within the VR to track user interactions. A pre-and-post intervention design will be utilized to assess changes in participants' knowledge and perceptions. The experimental group will engage with the VR, while the control group will follow traditional vocational guidance methods. Research method Primary /secondary Qualitative/ Quantitative Survey Primary Quantitative Interview/focus group Primary Qualitative Experiment- focus group Primary Quantitative**
Practicalities	10-23 months, depending on research method types and complexity of analysis. Physical access refers to the ability to get in direct face-to-face.

2.1 Hypothesis

Experiential learning stresses hands-on experience in obtaining knowledge and skills (Stavroulia et al., 2019). This approach helps learners directly participate in the subject matter, thereby realizing a more profound understanding, critical thinking, and problem-solving abilities. In the academic setup, experiential learning helps students gain good insights into different fields' changing aspects, enabling them to assess their fit and interests. However, the traditional methods of exploring academic specializations come with huge shortcomings and, therefore, fail to make this experience possible. The Career counseling sessions rely heavily on verbal descriptions and limited resources, whereas information sessions mostly fail to capture the genuine quintessence of the everyday work and the challenges involved. This lack of harmonious engagement often leads to students making uninformed choices due to inaccurate and incomplete information.

2.2 Anticipated Analysis

Career guidance services provide different activities and programs that should be implemented in schools and academic institutions. Services assist and help students to make their academic decisions as per their choices and provide insight into job opportunities, including visits, field surveys, trips, work sites, organization visits, and various training and development programs that enhance the experience level and professionalism among students while studying. This increases the credibility, knowledge, and awareness of their personal and professional growth. Research outcomes reflect that most of the students cannot choose their field according to their desires; instead, they choose a field according to their families' desires. This resulted in a lack of interest, concentration, and happiness in their studies. Moreover, decision plays an essential role in every student's life; selecting specialization as per one's own desire and wish can develop more interest, happiness, and awareness among students (Jóźwiak et al., 2023). Research outcomes done by (Silver, 2023) reflected around 38 students changed their fields and found six themes emerged about three phases of transition: endings, neutral zones, and new beginnings. He suggested that future research could extend the work by exploring factors influencing students' experiences in their destination major and the experiences of students who change majors multiple times. (Abdelkarim, Ra'ed Mohammad, 2020; Neupane et al., 2023) conducted the studies on students' learning styles and multiple intelligences (MI), they found that around 34.51% preferred Kinesthetic learning styles, followed by, 32.01% preferred Auditory learning styles and 33.48% respondents preferred Visual learning styles to understand the contents. Also, the study finds that the students from the specializations: Computer, Mathematics, Languages, Social Sciences, Accounting and Finance, Management Information Systems, and Law made a good decision about selecting their college programs. On the other hand, the study reports that the students from Architecture do not match the intelligence profiles required, which means the learning style of teaching needs improvement- respectively. Additionally, (Soliman et al., 2021) used the VR method to improve the student's understanding of the subjects, performance, and education experience and observed that integrating the constructivist and variation learning theory/approach by the VR application will enhance the learning of education and will yield pedagogical benefits to the students in education. To apply a model or platform using the VR method, which is stated in the (Soliman et al., 2021) paper, to serve the problem mentioned and test it on a percentage of students. Then, the results will be analyzed after implementation.

2.3 Objectives

1. **To develop a** Virtual Reality (VR) platform that provides an in-depth understanding of different specializations during the university admission stage.
2. **To evaluate** the impact of VR on students' decision-making confidence and satisfaction with their chosen specialization.
3. **To compare** the effectiveness of VR-based experiential learning with traditional methods for academic specialization selection in terms of knowledge retention, engagement, and long-term career satisfaction.
4. **Identify specific VR scenarios and activities** most effective for different specialization choices and learning styles.

2.4 Relevance to Augmented Reality

The idea of the work is to develop the concept with VR completely virtual and thereafter use the real-world setting to sync with Augmented reality to enhance both the virtual and real world. It was great challenge to change from on-site (face to face) to VR classroom. Because VR learning environment requires special attention to your students to build relationships with each other and also design the course activities in such a way to achieve the goals of the module. It is proud to say that from the first day of online learning Middle East College (MEC) has provided online learning platform with IT support team to facilitate the delivery of online teaching smoothly through Microsoft teams and big blue Button. At this point I found VR for any Multimedia communications and IoT module keeps you engaging and interactive experience with available technology tools. To happen learning and deep thinking for my module the following were kept ready one week ahead to make my students active learners. The scheduled topics for the online class were provided with voice over in small chunks so that students can accustomed to my tone, voice and personality. Similarly, the numerical of the topic were already solved with posted comments to convey the right meaning and understanding. Actual intention of providing all this material of voice over power points, numerical solved, video links and formative assessments through Moodle and streaming server is to bring online classroom alive with links, digital tools and media. Sometimes I felt it's critical to build each week topics as a mindful address to interact with my students. However, it is very important that how you reach out to your students will draw the connection on their own. Although the online class taught was also recorded and shared among the peers to keep a record of each week activity and help out the class missed students. Apart from above activities during the online class few things were also addressed simultaneously

- Interacting and talking with the students using the VR in online class
- Discussing the forth coming announcements of the module
- Giving short breaks to refresh them from continuous online topic delivery.
- Respond to their questions through the immersive learning.
- Posting a quick video covering animated view to clarify any misconceptions on the topics covered.

3. CONCLUSION AND RECOMMENDATIONS

One of the significant effects is better learning could happen with the state of academic standards for accountability measures and evaluation of curriculum in specific areas of technology. It includes the common goals of Learn and build my knowledge through shared learning from peers. VR involvement, to stand out from my colleagues and create an inspiration to follow the success path. The use of VR directly affects the professional growth, quality and decision making to embrace my knowledge and build better skilled society in future.

There are few health risks when subjected to a stipulated duration. Furthermore, the security and privacy risk is greater when used in real-world settings and interactions with the physical world. However, when adapting the technology, the risks are very common, and later, they are used when technology immerses the needs and supports the requirements.

Cost and accessibility: VR technology can be expensive, and ensuring equitable access to VR experiences for all students remains challenging.

Technical limitations: Current VR technology may not be able to replicate all aspects of real-world experiences perfectly.

Pedagogical design: Integrating VR into the curriculum requires careful planning and development of engaging VR learning experiences.

Despite these challenges, the potential of VR for enhancing academic specialization selection is undeniable. As VR technology evolves and becomes more accessible, we can expect its transformative impact on higher education, empowering students to make informed and confident choices about their academic and professional futures.

Time limit (Not able to finish the VR design on time as it requires deep analysis from the students (feedback survey, intervention, focus group (Test)).

REFERENCES

Barkokebas, R., Ritter, C., Sirbu, V., Li, X., & Al-Hussein, M. (2019). Application of virtual reality in task training in the construction manufacturing industry. In *Isarc. proceedings of the international symposium on automation and robotics in construction* (Vol. 36, pp. 796–803). IAARC Publications. DOI:10.22260/ISARC2019/0107

Beck, D., Morgado, L., & O'Shea, P. (2023). Educational practices and strategies with immersive learning environments: Mapping of reviews for using the metaverse. *IEEE Transactions on Learning Technologies*.

Hawes, D., & Arya, A. (2023). Technology solutions to reduce anxiety and increase cognitive availability in students. *IEEE Transactions on Learning Technologies*, 16(2), 1. DOI:10.1109/TLT.2023.3239985

Hurrell, C., & Baker, J. (2021). Immersive learning: Applications of virtual reality for undergraduate education. *College & Undergraduate Libraries*, 27(2-4), 197–209. DOI:10.1080/10691316.2020.1796879

Jóźwiak, M., Kolemba, A., Waligórska, H., Waligórska, H., Jóźwiak, M., & Kolemba, A. (2023). *Career Interest Preferences, Randomness of Study Program Choice, and Competencies vs. Academic Major Reselection.* Silesian University of Technology Publishing House. .DOI:10.29119/1641-3466.2023.179.34

Neupane, D., Pant, S., & Bhattarai, P. (2023). Preferred Learning Techniques among Bachelor's Level Students. *Nepal Journal of Multidisciplinary Research*, 6(2), 145–154. DOI:10.3126/njmr.v6i2.57660

Silver, B. R. (2023). Major transitions: How college students interpret the process of changing fields of study. *Higher Education*. DOI:10.1007/s10734-023-01050-8 PMID:37362756

Soliman, M., Pesyridis, A., Dalaymani-Zad, D., Gronfula, M., & Kourmpetis, M. (2021). The application of virtual reality in engineering education. *Applied Sciences (Basel, Switzerland)*, 11(6), 2879. Advance online publication. DOI:10.3390/app11062879

Stavroulia K. E. Christofi M. Baka E. Michael-Grigoriou D. Magnenat-Thalmann N. & Lanitis A. (2019). Assessing the emotional impact of virtual reality-based teacher training. *The International Journal of Information and Learning Technology*, 192–217.

Compilation of References

. Mantovani, F. (2001). 12 VR learning: Potential and challenges for the use of 3d environments in education and training. *Towards cyberpsychology: mind, cognition, and society in the Internet age, 2*(207).

. Trowler, V. (2010). Student engagement literature review. *The higher education academy, 11*(1), 1-15.

Abulrub, A.-H. G., Attridge, A. N., & Williams, M. A. (2011). Virtual reality in engineering education: The future of creative learning. *2011 IEEE Global Engineering Education Conference (EDUCON)*, (pp. 751–757). IEEE. DOI:10.1109/EDUCON.2011.5773223

Acharya, M., & Mohbey, K. K. (2024). *Virtual Environment Role in Higher Education Students Learning Enhancement with Intellectual Disabilities Applied Assistive Technologies and Informatics for Students with Disabilities*. Springer.

Adams, D., Bah, A., Barwulor, C., Musaby, N., Pitkin, K., & Redmiles, E. M. (2018). Ethics emerging: The story of privacy and security perceptions in virtual reality. *Fourteenth Symposium on Usable Privacy and Security (SOUPS 2018)*, (pp. 427–442). USENIX. https://www.usenix.org/conference/soups2018/presentation/adams

Adetayo, A. J., Aborisade, M. O., & Sanni, B. A. (2024). Microsoft Copilot and Anthropic Claude AI in education and library service. *Library Hi Tech News*. Advance online publication. DOI:10.1108/LHTN-01-2024-0002

Aithal, P., & Aithal, S. (2024). Future of Higher Education through Technology Prediction and Forecasting. *Poornaprajna International Journal of Management* [PIJMESS]. *Education & Social Science*, 1(1), 1–50.

Akdere, M., Jiang, Y., & Acheson, K. (2023). To simulate or not to simulate? Comparing the effectiveness of video-based training versus virtual reality-based simulations on interpersonal skills development. *Human Resource Development Quarterly*, 34(4), 437–462. DOI:10.1002/hrdq.21470

Akhtar, M. H., Anderson, M., & Cochrane, T. (2024). Implementing Augmented Reality and Virtual Reality for authentic healthcare education. *Pacific Journal of Technology Enhanced Learning*, 6(1), 2–3. DOI:10.24135/pjtel.v6i1.177

Al Janabi, H. F., Aydin, A., Palaneer, S., Macchione, N., Al-Jabir, A., Khan, M. S., & Ahmed, K. (2020). Effectiveness of the HoloLens mixed-reality headset in minimally invasive surgery: A simulation-based feasibility study. *Surgical Endoscopy*, 34(3), 1143–1149. DOI:10.1007/s00464-019-06862-3 PMID:31214807

Alahi, M. E. E., Sukkuea, A., Tina, F. W., Nag, A., Kurdthongmee, W., Suwannarat, K., & Mukhopadhyay, S. C. (2023). Integration of IoT-enabled technologies and artificial intelligence (AI) for smart city scenario: Recent advancements and future trends. *Sensors (Basel)*, 23(11), 5206. DOI:10.3390/s23115206 PMID:37299934

Alalwan, N., Cheng, L., Al-Samarraie, H., Yousef, R., Alzahrani, A. M., & Sarsam, S. M. (2020). Challenges and prospects of virtual reality and augmented reality utilization among primary school teachers: A developing country perspective. *Studies in Educational Evaluation*, 66, 66. DOI:10.1016/j.stueduc.2020.100876

Al-Ansi, A. M., Jaboob, M., Garad, A., & Al-Ansi, A. (2023). Analyzing augmented reality (AR) and virtual reality (VR) recent development in education. *Social Sciences & Humanities Open*, 8(1), 100532. DOI:10.1016/j.ssaho.2023.100532

Albahbah, M., Kıvrak, S., & Arslan, G. (2021). Application areas of augmented reality and virtual reality in construction project management: A scoping review. *Journal of Construction Engineering and Management & Innovation*, 4(3), 151–172. DOI:10.31462/jcemi.2021.03151172

AlGerafi, M. A., Zhou, Y., Oubibi, M., & Wijaya, T. T. (2023). Unlocking the potential: A comprehensive evaluation of augmented reality and virtual reality in education. *Electronics (Basel)*, 12(18), 3953. DOI:10.3390/electronics12183953

Alghamdi, F. (2020). Trends in Educational Technology. In *JAAR* (*Vol. 8*, Issue 3). https://www.american-journals.com

Alim, E., Coşkun, Ö., & Peker, T. V. (2022). *Comparison and Evaluation of the Effectiveness of Traditional Neuroanatomy Teaching in Medical Education with Virtual-Reality Application Based on 3D Virtual Neuroanatomical Models, Which Is an Innovative Approach*. Research Square. DOI:10.21203/rs.3.rs-2351422/v1

Allcoat, D., Hatchard, T., Azmat, F., Stansfield, K., Watson, D., & von Mühlenen, A. (2021). Education in the digital age: Learning experience in virtual and mixed realities. *Journal of Educational Computing Research*, 59(5), 795–816. DOI:10.1177/0735633120985120

Allcoat, D., & von Mühlenen, A. (2018). Learning in virtual reality: Effects on performance, emotion and engagement. *Research in Learning Technology*, 26(0). https://journal.alt.ac.uk/index.php/rlt/article/view/2140. DOI:10.25304/rlt.v26.2140

Al-Mughairi, H., & Bhaskar, P. (2024). Exploring the factors affecting the adoption AI techniques in higher education: insights from teachers' perspectives on ChatGPT. *Journal of Research in Innovative Teaching & Learning*. DOI:10.1108/JRIT-09-2023-0129

Alnagrat, A. J. A., Alkhallas, M. I., Mohamed, A. S. I., Ismail, R. C., Idrus, S. Z. S., & Saed, H. S. (2023). Virtual Reality Semiconductor Laboratory: Usability Testing to Improve User Experience (UX) in Virtual Environments. *2023 IEEE 3rd International Maghreb Meeting of the Conference on Sciences and Techniques of Automatic Control and Computer Engineering (MI-STA)*, (pp. 469–473). IEEE. https://ieeexplore.ieee.org/abstract/document/10169788/

Alnagrat, A., Ismail, R. C., & Idrus, S. Z. S. (2022). The opportunities and challenges in virtual reality for virtual laboratories. *Innovative Teaching and Learning Journal*, 6(2), 73–89. DOI:10.11113/itlj.v6.91

Alshammari, S. H. (2019). The role of virtual reality in enhancing students' learning. *International Journal of Educational Technology and Learning*, 7(1), 1–6. DOI:10.20448/2003.71.1.6

Altarteer, S., & Charissis, V. (2019). Technology acceptance model for 3D virtual reality system in luxury brands online stores. *IEEE Access : Practical Innovations, Open Solutions*, 7, 64053–64062. DOI:10.1109/ACCESS.2019.2916353

Alvarez, A. V. (2020). The phenomenon of learning at a distance through emergency remote teaching amidst the pandemic crisis. *Asian Journal of Distance Education*, 15(1). https://files.eric.ed.gov/fulltext/EJ1289949.pdf

Angelova, N. V. (2021). Technology and psychology: The application of vr technology. *Psychological Thought*, 14(2), 269–281. DOI:10.37708/psyct.v14i2.656

Angelov, V., Petkov, E., Shipkovenski, G., & Kalushkov, T. (2020, June) Modern virtual reality headsets. In *2020 International congress on human-computer interaction, optimization and robotic applications (HORA)* (pp. 1-5). IEEE.

Anthes, C., García-Hernández, R. J., Wiedemann, M., & Kranzlmüller, D. (2016). State of the art of virtual reality technology. *2016 IEEE Aerospace Conference*, (pp. 1–19). IEEE. DOI:10.1109/AERO.2016.7500674

Ardiny, H., & Khanmirza, E. (2018). The Role of AR and VR Technologies in Education Developments: Opportunities and Challenges. *2018 6th RSI International Conference on Robotics and Mechatronics (IcRoM)*, (pp. 482–487). IEEE. DOI:10.1109/ICRoM.2018.8657615

Arif, Y. M., Ayunda, N., Diah, N. M., & Garcia, M. B. (2024). A Systematic Review of Serious Games for Health Education: Technology, Challenges, and Future Directions. *Transformative Approaches to Patient Literacy and Healthcare Innovation*, 20-45.

Arifin, M. H. (2018). The role of student support services in enhancing student persistence in the Open University Context: Lesson from Indonesia Open University. *Turkish Online Journal of Distance Education*, 19(3), 156–168. DOI:10.17718/tojde.445116

Aroesty, S. V. (2021). *Development of a Conceptual Framework for Peer Surgical Coaching Programs*. McGill University.

Arora, C. S., & Kaistha, S. (2022). Virtual meet-ups: A purported mechanism for the 21st century work culture. *JIMS 8M, 27*(1), 56–64. DOI:10.5958/0973-9343.2022.00007.2

Arriagada, C. (2024). *Early Childhood Educators' Perceptions, Attitudes, And Beliefs On Use Of The Modern Classrooms Project: A Case Study*.

Arthur, K. W. (2000). *Effects of field of view on performance with head-mounted displays*. The University of North Carolina at Chapel Hill.

Artisantg. (2024). *TDS220 Tektronix Two Channel Digital Real-Time Oscilloscope*. Artisantg. https://www.artisantg.com/TestMeasurement/67520-1/Tektronix-TDS220-Two-Channel-Digital-Real-Time-Oscilloscope

Asad, M. M., Naz, A., Churi, P., & Tahanzadeh, M. M. (2021). Virtual reality as pedagogical tool to enhance experiential learning: A systematic literature review. *Education Research International*, 2021, 1–17. DOI:10.1155/2021/7061623

Atanassov, K. T. (1999). *Intuitionistic fuzzy sets. In intuitionistic fuzzy steps*. Physica. DOI:10.1007/978-3-7908-1870-3

Baby, B., Singh, R., Suri, A., Dhanakshirur, R. R., Chakraborty, A., Kumar, S., Kalra, P. K., & Banerjee, S. (2020). A review of virtual reality simulators for neuroendoscopy. *Neurosurgical Review*, 43(5), 1255–1272. DOI:10.1007/s10143-019-01164-7 PMID:31444716

Bacus, J. (2020, February 16). Information modeling in SketchUp. *SketchUp Blog*. https://blog.sketchup.com/article/information-modeling-sketchup

Bae, J., Lee, J., Jang, Y., & Lee, Y. (2019). Development of simulation education debriefing protocol with faculty guide for enhancement clinical reasoning. *BMC Medical Education*, 19(1), 1–7. DOI:10.1186/s12909-019-1633-8 PMID:31185972

Bailenson, J. (2018). *Experience on demand: What virtual reality is, how it works, and what it can do*. Norton & Company.

Baniasadi, T., Ayyoubzadeh, S. M., & Mohammadzadeh, N. (2020). Challenges and practical considerations in applying virtual reality in medical education and treatment. *Oman Medical Journal*, 35(3), 1–10. DOI:10.5001/omj.2020.43 PMID:32489677

Barger, S. (2018). *Vicarious learning and perceived self-efficacy among pre-licensure nursing students during pediatric end-of-life situations*. The University of Alabama.

Barkokebas, R., Ritter, C., Sirbu, V., Li, X., & Al-Hussein, M. (2019). Application of virtual reality in task training in the construction manufacturing industry. In *Isarc. proceedings of the international symposium on automation and robotics in construction* (Vol. 36, pp. 796–803). IAARC Publications. DOI:10.22260/ISARC2019/0107

Barrow, J. (2022). *The Future with Extended Reality, Three-Dimensional, and Advanced Imaging for Molecules, Microscopy, and Anatomy Technologies in Biomedical and Life Sciences Education: Approaches and Evidence of Efficacy for Learning*. Springer.

Barteit, S., Lanfermann, L., Bärnighausen, T., Neuhann, F., & Beiersmann, C. (2021). Augmented, mixed, and virtual reality-based head-mounted devices for medical education: Systematic review. *JMIR Serious Games*, 9(3), e29080. DOI:10.2196/29080 PMID:34255668

Bassano, C., Chessa, M., Fengone, L., Isgrò, L., Solari, F., Spallarossa, G., Tozzi, D., & Zini, A. (2020). Virtual reality system for ship handling simulations: A case study on nautical personnel performance, observed behaviour, sense of presence and sickness. In *Communications in Computer and Information Science* (pp. 101–127). Springer International Publishing.

Baxter, G., & Hainey, T. (2023). Using immersive technologies to enhance the student learning experience. *Interactive Technology and Smart Education*.

Bazin, S. J. (2019). *The Relationship between Reading, Math, Science, and English/Language Usage and National Council Licensure Exam Success for Nursing Students*. Northcentral University.

Beck, D., Morgado, L., & O'Shea, P. (2023). Educational practices and strategies with immersive learning environments: Mapping of reviews for using the metaverse. *IEEE Transactions on Learning Technologies*.

Belani, M., Singh, H. V., Parnami, A., & Singh, P. (2023). Investigating spatial representation of learning content in virtual reality learning environments. *2023 IEEE Conference Virtual Reality and 3D User Interfaces (VR)*, (pp. 33–43). IEEE. https://ieeexplore.ieee.org/abstract/document/10108413/

Bell, J. T., & Fogler, H. S. (1995, June). The investigation and application of virtual reality as an educational tool. In *Proceedings of the American society for engineering education annual conference* (Vol. 2513). Research Gate.

Bell, I. H., Nicholas, J., Alvarez-Jimenez, M., Thompson, A., & Valmaggia, L. (2020). Virtual reality as a clinical tool in mental health research and practice. *Dialogues in Clinical Neuroscience*, 22(2), 169–177. DOI:10.31887/DCNS.2020.22.2/lvalmaggia PMID:32699517

Belliger, A., & Krieger, D. J. (2024). *From Systems to Actor-Networks: A Paradigm Shift in the Social Sciences*. Ethics International Press Limited.

Bhagat, K. K., Liou, W.-K., & Chang, C.-Y. (2016). A cost-effective interactive 3D virtual reality system applied to military live firing training. *Virtual Reality (Waltham Cross)*, 20(2), 127–140. DOI:10.1007/s10055-016-0284-x

Bhardwaj, H., Noumani, A., Himanshu, J. K., Chakravorty, S., & Solanki, P. R. (2024). Recent advancement in the detection of potential cancer biomarkers using the nanomaterial integrated electrochemical sensing technique: A detailed review. *Materials Advances*, 5(2), 475–503. DOI:10.1039/D3MA00621B

Bhatia, A., & Buvanendran, A. (2019). Anesthesia and postoperative pain control—Multimodal anesthesia protocol. *Journal of Spine Surgery*, 5(S2, Suppl 2), S160–S165. DOI:10.21037/jss.2019.09.33 PMID:31656870

Bibbò, L., & Morabito, F. C. (2022). Neural network design using a virtual reality platform. *Global Journal of Computer Science and Technology*, 22(D1), 45–61. DOI:10.34257/GJCSTDVOL22IS1PG45

Birkheim, S. L., Calogiuri, G., & Martinsen, R. (2023). Advancing immersive virtual reality-based simulation practices: Developing an evidence-based and theory-driven pedagogical framework for VR-based simulations of non-technical skills among healthcare professionals. *Interactive Learning Environments*, 1–13. DOI:10.1080/10494820.2023.2186896

Blankenship, D. M. (2023). *Simulation as Orientation to Perinatal Clinical Experiences: Effects on Anxiety and Confidence in Prelicensure Nursing Students*. Wilmington University.

Blascovich, J., Loomis, J., Beall, A. C., Swinth, K. R., Hoyt, C. L., & Bailenson, J. N. (2002). Immersive Virtual Environment Technology as a Methodological Tool for Social Psychology. *Psychological Inquiry*, 13(2), 103–124. DOI:10.1207/S15327965PLI1302_01

Boschee, P. (2023). Comments: AI language tools hit the books . . . And technical content? *Journal of Petroleum Technology*, 75(04), 8–9. DOI:10.2118/0423-0008-JPT

Botha, A., Smuts, H., & De Villiers, C. (2018). *Emerging technologies for education*. Springer Nature.

Bowen, M. M. (2018). *Effect of virtual reality on motivation and achievement of middle-school students*. The University of Memphis.

Bowman, D. A., & McMahan, R. P. (2007). Virtual reality: How much immersion is enough? *Computer*, 40(7), 36–43. DOI:10.1109/MC.2007.257

Bray, M., Shafique, R., Aljedaani, W., Rustam, F., Lee, E., Mehmood, A., & Choi, G. S. (2023). *Technology and the diverse learner: A guide to classroom practice*. Corwin Press.

Brook, K. (2020). *Oculus Quest 2 Hands On – The Best VR Headset For Fitness*. VR Fitness Insider. https://www.vrfitnessinsider.com/oculus-quest-2-hands-on-the-best-vr-headset-for-fitness/

Brunzini, A., Grandi, F., Peruzzini, M., & Pellicciari, M. (2023). An integrated methodology for the assessment of stress and mental workload applied on virtual training. *International Journal of Computer Integrated Manufacturing*, 1–19. DOI:10.1080/0951192X.2023.2189311

Bryson, S. (2013). *Virtual Reality: A Definition History - A Personal Essay* (arXiv:1312.4322). arXiv. http://arxiv.org/abs/1312.4322

Burbules, N. C., Fan, G., & Repp, P. (2020). Five trends of education and technology in a sustainable future. *Geography and Sustainability*, 1(2), 93–97. DOI:10.1016/j.geosus.2020.05.001

Burdea, G., & Coiffet, P. (2017). *Virtual reality technology*. Wiley.

Caldas, O. I., Sanchez, N., Mauledoux, M., Avilés, O. F., & Rodriguez-Guerrero, C. (2022). Leading presence-based strategies to manipulate user experience in virtual reality environments. *Virtual Reality (Waltham Cross)*, 26(4), 1507–1518. DOI:10.1007/s10055-022-00645-3

Çaloğlu Büyükselçuk, E., & Sarı, Y. C. (2023). The best whey protein powder selection via VIKOR based on circular intuitionistic fuzzy sets. *Symmetry*, 15(7), 1313. DOI:10.3390/sym15071313

Calvert, P. (2019). Virtual reality as a tool for teaching library design. *Education for Information*, 35(4), 439–450. DOI:10.3233/EFI-170150

Cant, R., Cooper, S., & Ryan, C. (2022). Using virtual simulation to teach evidence-based practice in nursing curricula: A rapid review. *Worldviews on Evidence-Based Nursing*, 19(5), 415–422. DOI:10.1111/wvn.12572 PMID:35261156

Cao, K. (2024). Predicting the behavior intention of intelligent office software. *SHS Web of Conferences, 181*, 01009. SHS. DOI:10.1051/shsconf/202418101009

Capasa, L., Zulauf, K., & Wagner, R. (2022). Virtual reality experience of mega sports events: A technology acceptance study. *Journal of Theoretical and Applied Electronic Commerce Research*, 17(2), 686–703. DOI:10.3390/jtaer17020036

Carpenter, R. E., McWhorter, R., & Stone, K. (2023). *Adopting Virtual Reality for Education: Exploring Teachers' Perspectives on Readiness, Opportunities, and Challenges*. Scholar Works. https://scholarworks.uttyler.edu/hrd_fac/43/

Carreon, A., Criss, C., & Mosher, M. (2023). Classroom virtual reality for students with disabilities: A PRELIMINARY GUIDE TO AVAILABLE virtual content. *Journal of Special Education Technology*, 39(1), 143–150. DOI:10.1177/01626434231170593

Carr, K., & England, R. (2023). *Simulated and virtual realities: Elements of perception*. CRC Press.

Cevallos, N., Zukotynski, B., Greig, D., Silva, M., & Thompson, R. M. (2022). The Utility of Virtual Reality in Orthopedic Surgical Training. *Journal of Surgical Education*, 79(6), 1516–1525. DOI:10.1016/j.jsurg.2022.06.007 PMID:35821110

Chaijaroen, N., Jackpeng, S., & Chaijaroen, S. (2020). The Development of Constructivist Web-Based Learning Environments to Enhance Learner's Information Processing and Reduce Cognitive Load. In Huang, T.-C., Wu, T.-T., Barroso, J., Sandnes, F. E., Martins, P., & Huang, Y.-M. (Eds.), *Innovative Technologies and Learning* (Vol. 12555, pp. 475–482). Springer International Publishing. DOI:10.1007/978-3-030-63885-6_52

Chattopadhyay, S. (2014). Learner Support Services in Open Distance Learning System. *Case Study on IGNOU.*, (June), 1–8.

Checa, D., & Bustillo, A. (2020). Advantages and limits of virtual reality in learning processes: Briviesca in the fifteenth century. *Virtual Reality (Waltham Cross)*, 24(1), 151–161. DOI:10.1007/s10055-019-00389-7

Check, J., & Schutt, R. K. (2011). *Research methods in education*. Sage publications.

Chen, B., Wang, Y., & Wang, L. (2022). The effects of virtual reality-assisted language learning: A meta-analysis. *Sustainability (Basel)*, 14(6), 3147. DOI:10.3390/su14063147

Chen, C. J. (2006). The design, development and evaluation of a virtual reality based learning environment. *Australasian Journal of Educational Technology*, 22(1). https://ajet.org.au/index.php/ajet/article/view/1306. DOI:10.14742/ajet.1306

Chen, C. J., Toh, S. C., & Ismail, W. M. F. W. (2005). Are Learning Styles Relevant To Virtual Reality? *Journal of Research on Technology in Education*, 38(2), 123–141. DOI:10.1080/15391523.2005.10782453

Chen, C.-H., Huang, C.-Y., & Chou, Y.-Y. (2019). Effects of augmented reality-based multidimensional concept maps on students' learning achievement, motivation and acceptance. *Universal Access in the Information Society*, 18(4), 257–268. DOI:10.1007/s10209-017-0595-z

Chen, S.-C., Liu, M.-L., & Lin, C.-P. (2013). Integrating technology readiness into the expectation–confirmation model: An empirical study of mobile services. *Cyberpsychology, Behavior, and Social Networking*, 16(8), 604–612. DOI:10.1089/cyber.2012.0606 PMID:23790359

Chen, Y. L. (2016). The effects of virtual reality learning environment on student cognitive and linguistic development. *The Asia-Pacific Education Researcher*, 25(4), 637–646. DOI:10.1007/s40299-016-0293-2

Chi, P.G., ZaffwanIdris, M.Z. & Nugrahan, R. (2021). Virtual Reality (VR) in 21st: century education: the opportunities and challenges of digital learning in classroom. *Asian Pendidikan*, 1(2), 105–110.

Choi, J., Thompson, C. E., Choi, J., Waddill, C. B., & Choi, S. (2022). Effectiveness of immersive virtual reality in nursing education: Systematic review. *Nurse Educator*, 47(3), E57–E61. DOI:10.1097/NNE.0000000000001117 PMID:34657101

Christopoulos, A., Mystakidis, S., Pellas, N., & Laakso, M. J. (2021). ARLEAN: An Augmented Reality Learning Analytics Ethical Framework. *Computers*, 2021(10), 92. DOI:10.3390/computers10080092

Clarke, E. (2021). Virtual reality simulation—The future of orthopaedic training? A systematic review and narrative analysis. *Advances in Simulation (London, England)*, 6(1), 1–11. DOI:10.1186/s41077-020-00153-x PMID:33441190

Coldham, G., & Cook, D. M. (2017). VR usability from elderly cohorts: Preparatory challenges in overcoming technology rejection. *2017 National Information Technology Conference (NITC)*. IEEE. DOI:10.1109/NITC.2017.8285645

Conte, G., Arrigoni, C., Magon, A., Stievano, A., & Caruso, R. (2023). Embracing Digital and Technological Solutions in Nursing: A scoping review and conceptual framework. *International Journal of Medical Informatics*, 177, 105148. DOI:10.1016/j.ijmedinf.2023.105148 PMID:37453178

Courtwright, S. E., Turi, E., Barr, E. A., Burns, J. C., Gigli, K. H., Bennett, C. R., Sonney, J., Francis, L., & Poghosyan, L. (2024). Facilitators and Barriers to Pediatric Nurse Practitioner Practice in the United States: A Systematic Review. *Journal of Pediatric Health Care*, 38(4), 520–543. DOI:10.1016/j.pedhc.2023.12.003 PMID:38284964

Creed, C., Al-Kalbani, M., Theil, A., Sarcar, S., & Williams, I. (2024). Inclusive AR/VR: Accessibility barriers for immersive technologies. *Universal Access in the Information Society*, 23(1), 59–73. DOI:10.1007/s10209-023-00969-0

Cumming, T. M., & Rose, M. C. (2022). Exploring universal design for learning as an accessibility tool in higher education: A review of the current literature. *Australian Educational Researcher*, 49(5), 1025–1043. DOI:10.1007/s13384-021-00471-7

Daim, T. U., Blanton, S., Basoglu, A. N., & Ding, A. (2011). Exploring information technology adoption in the classroom: Case of online learning technology. *International Journal of Business Information Systems*, 7(3), 327–340. DOI:10.1504/IJBIS.2011.039334

Daley, D., & Dale, A. M. (2024). *Promoting Occupational Health and Productivity: Adults Interprofessional Perspectives for Community Practice*. Routledge. DOI:10.4324/9781003524649-15

Dalgarno, B., & Lee, M. J. (2010). What are the learning affordances of 3-D virtual environments? *British Journal of Educational Technology*, 41(1), 10–32. DOI:10.1111/j.1467-8535.2009.01038.x

Damanpour, F., & Schneider, M. (2006). Phases of the adoption of innovation in organizations: Effects of environment, organization and top managers. *British Journal of Management*, 17(3), 215–236. DOI:10.1111/j.1467-8551.2006.00498.x

Damaševicius, R., & Sidekerskiene, T. (2024). Virtual worlds for learning in metaverse: A narrative review. *Sustainability*, 16(5), 1–41. DOI:10.3390/su16052032 PMID:38510213

Damerji, H., & Salimi, A. (2021). Mediating effect of use perceptions on technology readiness and adoption of artificial intelligence in accounting. *Accounting Education*, 30(2), 107–130. DOI:10.1080/09639284.2021.1872035

Dangelmaier, W., Fischer, M., Gausemeier, J., Grafe, M., Matysczok, C., & Mueck, B. (2005). Virtual and augmented reality support for discrete manufacturing system simulation. *Computers in Industry*, 56(4), 371–383. DOI:10.1016/j.compind.2005.01.007

Darcy-Mahoney, A., Carter, B., Green, K., Mullan, F., & Beard, K. V. (2020). Looking backwards to move forward: Using a social mission lens in nursing education. *Journal of Professional Nursing*, 36(5), 412–416. DOI:10.1016/j.profnurs.2020.03.005 PMID:33039077

Davila Delgado, J. M., Oyedele, L., Beach, T., & Demian, P. (2020). Augmented and Virtual Reality in Construction: Drivers and Limitations for Industry Adoption. *Journal of Construction Engineering and Management*, 146(7), 04020079. DOI:10.1061/(ASCE)CO.1943-7862.0001844

Davis, (2020). The challenges of data privacy and security in education technology. *Journal of Information Technology Education*, 19, 1–14.

De Troyer, O., Kleinermann, F., & Ewais, A. (2010). Enhancing Virtual Reality Learning Environments with Adaptivity: Lessons Learned. In Leitner, G., Hitz, M., & Holzinger, A. (Eds.), *HCI in Work and Learning, Life and Leisure* (Vol. 6389, pp. 244–265). Springer Berlin Heidelberg., DOI:10.1007/978-3-642-16607-5_16

Dede, , C. (2009). Immersive interfaces for engagement and learning. *Science*, 323(5910), 66–69. DOI:10.1126/science.1167311 PMID:19119219

Dede, C. (2018). *Immersive interfaces for learning: The future of learning in a digital world*. MIT Press.

Dede, C., Jacobson, J., & Richards, J. (2017). *Virtual, augmented, and mixed realities in education*. Springer.

Dehghani, M., Acikgoz, F., Mashatan, A., & Lee, S. H. (2022). A holistic analysis towards understanding consumer perceptions of virtual reality devices in the post-adoption phase. *Behaviour & Information Technology*, 41(7), 1453–1471. DOI:10.1080/0144929X.2021.1876767

Dhawan, S. (2020). Online learning: A panacea in the time of COVID-19 crisis. *Journal of Educational Technology Systems*, 49(1), 5–22. DOI:10.1177/0047239520934018

Díaz, M. J., Mantell, C., Caro, I., de Ory, I., Sánchez, J., & Portela, J. R. (2022). Creation of immersive resources based on virtual reality for dissemination and teaching in chemical engineering. *Education Sciences*, 12(8), 572. DOI:10.3390/educsci12080572

Ding, X., & Li, Z. (2022). A review of the application of virtual reality technology in higher education based on Web of Science literature data as an example. Paper presented at the *Frontiers in Education*. IEEE. DOI:10.3389/feduc.2022.1048816

Di, X., & Zheng, X. (2022). A meta-analysis of the impact of virtual technologies on students' spatial ability. *Educational Technology Research and Development*, 70(1), 73–98. DOI:10.1007/s11423-022-10082-3

Dixon, S. (2006). A history of virtual reality in performance. *International Journal of Performance Arts and Digital Media*, 2(1), 23–54. DOI:10.1386/padm.2.1.23/1

Domingueti, D., Barbosa Feres Carvalho, D., Colombo Dias, D. R., & Oliveira, V. C. (2022). Software-Based Simulation on a 3D Environment for Vaccination Teaching and Learning: Design Science Research. *JMIR Medical Education*, 8(4), e35712. DOI:10.2196/35712 PMID:36459390

Dubovi, I. (2023). Facial expressions capturing emotional engagement while learning with desktop VR: The impact of emotional regulation and personality traits. *Interactive Learning Environments*, 1–17. DOI:10.1080/10494820.2023.2208173

Duffy, J. R. (2022). *Quality caring in nursing and health systems: Implications for clinicians, educators, and leaders*. Springer Publishing Company. DOI:10.1891/9780826136961

Dwivedi, Y. K., Hughes, L., Baabdullah, A. M., Ribeiro-Navarrete, S., Giannakis, M., Al-Debei, M. M., Dennehy, D., Metri, B., Buhalis, D., Cheung, C. M. K., Conboy, K., Doyle, R., Dubey, R., Dutot, V., Felix, R., Goyal, D. P., Gustafsson, A., Hinsch, C., Jebabli, I., & Wamba, S. F. (2022). Metaverse beyond the hype: Multidisciplinary perspectives on emerging challenges, opportunities, and agenda for research, practice and policy. *International Journal of Information Management*, 66(102542), 102542. DOI:10.1016/j.ijinfomgt.2022.102542

Dyke, C., Franklin, B. R., Sweeney, W. B., & Ritter, E. M. (2021). Early implementation of Fundamentals of Endoscopic Surgery training using a simulation-based mastery learning curriculum. *Surgery*, 169(5), 1228–1233. DOI:10.1016/j.surg.2020.12.005 PMID:33583604

Ejegwa, P. A. (2021). Generalized triparametric correlation coefficient for Pythagorean fuzzy sets with application to MCDM problems. *Granular Computing*, 6(3), 557–566. DOI:10.1007/s41066-020-00215-5

Elendu, C., Amaechi, D. C., Okatta, A. U., Amaechi, E. C., Elendu, T. C., Ezeh, C. P., & Elendu, I. D. (2024). The impact of simulation-based training in medical education. *Revista de Medicina (São Paulo)*, 103(27), e38813. PMID:38968472

Enders, L. R., Smith, R. J., Gordon, S. M., Ries, A. J., & Touryan, J. (2021). Gaze behavior during navigation and visual search of an open-world virtual environment. *Frontiers in Psychology*, 12, 681042. DOI:10.3389/fpsyg.2021.681042 PMID:34434140

Endomicroscopy, P.-B. C. L., Diana, M., Dallemagne, B., Chung, H., Nagao, Y., Halvax, P., & Demartines, N. (2014). 2014 Scientific Session of the Society of American Gastrointestinal and Endoscopic Surgeons (SAGES), Salt Lake City, Utah, USA, 2–5 April 2014. *Surgical Endoscopy*, 28(S1), S311–S445. DOI:10.1007/s00464-014-3476-z

Englar, R. E. (2017). A novel approach to simulation-based education for veterinary medical communication training over eight consecutive pre-clinical quarters. *Journal of Veterinary Medical Education*, 44(3), 502–522. DOI:10.3138/jvme.0716-118R1 PMID:28876987

Erdoğmuş, N., & Esen, M. (2011). An investigation of the effects of technology readiness on technology acceptance in e-HRM. *Procedia: Social and Behavioral Sciences*, 24, 487–495. DOI:10.1016/j.sbspro.2011.09.131

ESTAARMAX. (n.d.). *Best 3D Max Course in Chennai*. ESTAARMAX. https://www.estaarmax.in/3ds-max-design/

Eswaran, M., & Bahubalendruni, M. V. A. R. (2022). Challenges and opportunities on AR/VR technologies for manufacturing systems in the context of industry 4.0: A state of the art review. *Journal of Manufacturing Systems*, 65, 260–278. DOI:10.1016/j.jmsy.2022.09.016

Etambakonga, C. L. (2021). The rise of virtual reality in online courses: Ethical issues and policy recommendations. *Factoring Ethics in Technology, Policy Making, Regulation and AI*. https://books.google.com/books?hl=en&lr=&id=9a5aEAAAQBAJ&oi=fnd&pg=PA131&dq=ethical+considerations+of+virtual+reality,+such+as+data+privacy,+content+appropriateness,+and+digital+equity,+raise+important+questions+about+the+responsible+and+ethical+use+of+VR+technology+in+educational+settings+&ots=gX989_AQmX&sig=GeYFOHMZpKzkTp1PQ4OMCcmJmXk

eZainab, H., Bawany, N. Z., Rehman, W., & Imran, J. (2024). Design and development of virtual reality exposure therapy systems: Requirements, challenges and solutions. *Multimedia Tools and Applications*, 83(2), 6137–6160. DOI:10.1007/s11042-023-15756-5

Fakahani, L., Aljehani, S., Baghdadi, R., & El-Shorbagy, A.-M. (2022). The use and challenges of virtual reality in architecture. *Civil Engineering and Architecture*, 10(6), 2754–2763. DOI:10.13189/cea.2022.100638

Familoni, B. T., & Onyebuchi, N. C. (2024). Augmented and virtual reality in us education: a review: analyzing the impact, effectiveness, and future prospects of ar/vr tools in enhancing learning experiences. *International Journal of Applied Research in Social Sciences*, 6(4), 642–663. DOI:10.51594/ijarss.v6i4.1043

Fang, S., & Yatani, K. (2023). Towards Understanding Sense of Inclusion in Social VR Onboarding. *Extended Abstracts of the 2023 CHI Conference on Human Factors in Computing Systems*, (pp. 1–8). ACM. DOI:10.1145/3544549.3585751

Farahmand, F., Yadav, A., & Spafford, E. H. (2013). Risks and uncertainties in virtual worlds: An educators' perspective. *Journal of Computing in Higher Education*, 25(2), 49–67. DOI:10.1007/s12528-013-9067-5

Farsi, G. A., Yusof, A. B. M., Fauzi, W. J. B., Rusli, M. E. B., Malik, S. I., Tawafak, R. M., Mathew, R., & Jabbar, J. (2021). The practicality of virtual reality applications in education: Limitations and recommendations. *Hunan Daxue Xuebao. Shehui Kexue Ban*, 48(7), 142–155.

Fasihuddin, H. (2023). Virtual Reality Technology in Teaching Computer Hardware: A Prototype and Assessment from User Perspectives. *TEM Journal*, 12(2), 899–907. DOI:10.18421/TEM122-36

Fei, T., Mao, Q., Wu, F., & Yu, P. (2023). The Future Prospects of Importance of VR's Impact on Education. *Highlights in Science. Engineering and Technology*, 39, 111–120.

Feng, M., & Xia, X. (2023). Discussing the Effect of Computer-Based Instruction on College Students' Learning Outcomes in Statistics. *2023 IEEE 12th International Conference on Educational and Information Technology, ICEIT 2023*, (pp. 59–62). IEEE. DOI:10.1109/ICEIT57125.2023.10107772

Fiani, B., De Stefano, F., Kondilis, A., Covarrubias, C., Reier, L., & Sarhadi, K. (2020). Virtual reality in neurosurgery:"can you see it?"–a review of the current applications and future potential. *World Neurosurgery*, 141, 291–298. DOI:10.1016/j.wneu.2020.06.066 PMID:32561486

Fleck, S., & Hachet, M. (2016). Making tangible the intangible: Hybridization of the real and the virtual to enhance learning of abstract phenomena. *Frontiers in ICT (Lausanne, Switzerland)*, 3, 30. DOI:10.3389/fict.2016.00030

Florea, A., & Gellert, A. (2014). Different Approaches For Solving Optimization Problems Using Interactive E-Learning Tools. *eLearning & Software for Education*, (2).

Fluke Corporation. (2023). *What is an Oscilloscope?* Fluke Corporation. https://www.fluke.com/en-us/learn/blog/electrical/what-is-an-oscilloscope

Fontenot, J., & McMurray, P. (2020). Decolonizing entry to practice: Reconceptualizing methods to facilitate diversity in nursing programs. *Teaching and Learning in Nursing*, 15(4), 272–279. DOI:10.1016/j.teln.2020.07.002

Foronda, C. L., Gonzalez, L., Meese, M. M., Slamon, N., Baluyot, M., Lee, J., & Aebersold, M. (2024). A comparison of virtual reality to traditional simulation in health professions education: A systematic review. *Simulation in Healthcare*, 10, 1097. PMID:37651101

Fortune Business Insights. (2019). Virtual reality market size, share & industry analysis. *Fortune Business Insights.* https://www.fortunebusinessinsights.com/industry-reports/virtual-reality-market-101378

Foster, T. C., Moroney, W. F., Phillips, H. L., & Lilienthal, M. G. (2024). Human Factors in Simulation and Training: An Overview. *Human Factors in Simulation and Training*, (pp. 1-64). Research Gate.

Foster, T. C., Moroney, W. F., Phillips, H. L., & Lilienthal, M. G. (2024). Human Factors in Simulation and Training: An Overview. *Human Factors in Simulation and Training*, 1-64.

Fowler, C. (2015). *Virtual reality and augmented reality in education: A new frontier for learning*. Routledge.

Fransson, G., Holmberg, J., & Westelius, C. (2020). The challenges of using head mounted virtual reality in K-12 schools from a teacher perspective. *Education and Information Technologies*, 25(4), 3383–3404. DOI:10.1007/s10639-020-10119-1

Frazier, E., Lege, R., & Bonner, E. (2021). Making virtual reality accessible for language learning: Applying VR application analysis framework. *The Journal of Teaching English with Technology*, 21(1), 128–140.

Frehlich, C. (2020). *Immersive learning: A practical guide to virtual reality's superpowers in education*. Rowman & Littlefield.

Freina, L., & Ott, M. (2015, April). A literature review on immersive virtual reality in education: state of the art and perspectives. In *The international scientific conference elearning and software for education* (*Vol. 1*, No. 133, pp. 10-1007). Research Gate. DOI:10.12753/2066-026X-15-020

Freina, L., & Ott, M. (2015). *A literature review on immersive virtual reality in education: The State of the art*. Springer.

Fried, M. P., Satava, R., Weghorst, S., Gallagher, A., Sasaki, C., Ross, D., & Zeltsan, M. (2005). The use of surgical simulators to reduce errors. *Advances in patient safety: from research to implementation, 4*, 165-177.

Fromm, J., Radianti, J., Wehking, C., Stieglitz, S., Majchrzak, T. A., & vom Brocke, J. (2021). More than experience?-On the unique opportunities of virtual reality to afford a holistic experiential learning cycle. *The Internet and Higher Education*, 50, 100804. DOI:10.1016/j.iheduc.2021.100804

Fussell, S. G., & Truong, D. (2023). Accepting virtual reality for dynamic learning: An extension of the technology acceptance model. *Interactive Learning Environments*, 31(9), 5442–5459. DOI:10.1080/10494820.2021.2009880

Gabyzon, M. E., Engel-Yeger, B., Tresser, S., & Springer, S. (2016). Using a virtual reality game to assess goal-directed hand movements in children: A pilot feasibility study. *Technology and Health Care*, 24(1), 11–19. DOI:10.3233/THC-151041 PMID:26409528

Galleguillos, M. R., Eloiriachi, A., Serdar, B., & Coşkun, A. (2022). Design Strategies to Promote Intercultural Meaningful Social Interactions. *Proceedings of the Design Society*, 2, 2203–2212. DOI:10.1017/pds.2022.223

Gandolfi, E., Kosko, K. W., & Ferdig, R. E. (2021). Situating presence within extended reality for teacher training: Validation of the extended Reality Presence Scale (XRPS) in preservice teacher use of immersive 360 video. *British Journal of Educational Technology*, 52(2), 824–841. DOI:10.1111/bjet.13058

Garber, K., Chike-Harris, K., Vetter, M. J., Kobeissi, M., Heidesch, T., Arends, R., Teall, A. M., & Rutledge, C. (2023). Telehealth policy and the advanced practice nurse. *The Journal for Nurse Practitioners*, 19(7), 104655. DOI:10.1016/j.nurpra.2023.104655 PMID:37235075

García-Avilés, J. A. (2020). *The international encyclopedia of media psychology*. Wiley.

Gerolamo, A. M., Delaney, K. R., Phoenix, B., Black, P., Rushton, A., & Stallings, J. (2024). Psychiatric nursing workforce survey: Results and implications. *Journal of the American Psychiatric Nurses Association*, 30(3), 690–696. DOI:10.1177/10783903221146190 PMID:36582042

Gershon, J., Zimand, E., Pickering, M., Rothbaum, B. O., & Hodges, L. (2004). A Pilot and Feasibility Study of Virtual Reality as a Distraction for Children With Cancer. *Journal of the American Academy of Child and Adolescent Psychiatry*, 43(10), 1243–1249. DOI:10.1097/01.chi.0000135621.23145.05 PMID:15381891

Glancova, A., Do, Q. T., Sanghavi, D. K., Franco, P. M., Gopal, N., Lehman, L. M., Dong, Y., Pickering, B. W., & Herasevich, V. (2021). Are we ready for video recognition and computer vision in the intensive care unit? A survey. *Applied Clinical Informatics*, 12(01), 120–132. DOI:10.1055/s-0040-1722614 PMID:33626583

Godoe, P., & Johansen, T. S. (2012). Understanding adoption of new technologies: Technology readiness and technology acceptance as an integrated concept. *Journal of European Psychology Students*, 3, 38. DOI:10.5334/jeps.aq

Gomes, N., Lou, Y., Patwardhan, V., Moyer, T., Vavala, V., & Barros, C. (2020). The Effects of Virtual Reality Learning Environments on Improving the Retention, Comprehension, and Motivation of Medical School Students. In Ahram, T., Taiar, R., Colson, S., & Choplin, A. (Eds.), *Human Interaction and Emerging Technologies* (Vol. 1018, pp. 289–296). Springer International Publishing. DOI:10.1007/978-3-030-25629-6_45

Guazzaroni, G., & Pillai, A. S. (2020). *Virtual and augmented reality in education, art, and museums*. Springer. DOI:10.4018/978-1-7998-1796-3

Gunasckaran, K., Boopathi, S., Suresh, S., Suresh, P., Vanitha, N. S., & Radhika, K. (2024). Eco-Friendly Smart Agricultural Process Using Artificial Intelligence. In *Reshaping Environmental Science Through Machine Learning and IoT* (pp. 160–175). IGI Global. DOI:10.4018/979-8-3693-2351-9.ch009

Guo, Q., Zhu, D., Li, F., Wang, X., & Shu, Y. (2024). Tourists' adoption of extended reality technologies: A MetaAnalytical structural equation modeling. *Journal of Hospitality & Tourism Research (Washington, D.C.)*, 48(3), 450–463. DOI:10.1177/10963480221108906

Gustad, L. T., Bangstad, I.-L., Torsvik, M., & Rise, M. B. (2024). Nurses' and Physicians' Experiences After Implementation of a Quality Improvement Project to Improve Sepsis Awareness in Hospitals. *Journal of Multidisciplinary Healthcare*, 17, 29–41. DOI:10.2147/JMDH.S439017 PMID:38192738

Gyll, S. P., Shader, K. K., Zikas, P., & Papagiannakis, G. (2023). Design, Technology, and Measurement Considerations in Virtual-Reality Assessment. *Designing Context-Rich Learning by Extending Reality*, 132–160.

Haker, L. J. (2024). *A Constructivist Grounded Theory on CPS Social Worker's Conceptualization of the Access Screening Tool in Relation With Their Experiences, Training, and Values*. Saybrook University.

Hamilton, D., McKechnie, J., Edgerton, E., & Wilson, C. (2021). Immersive virtual reality as a pedagogical tool in education: A systematic literature review of quantitative learning outcomes and experimental design. *Journal of Computers in Education*, 8(1), 1–32. DOI:10.1007/s40692-020-00169-2

Haney, B. (2023). 35th Annual APRN legislative update: Updates to APRN practice authority in the United States. *The Nurse Practitioner*, 48(1), 20–47. DOI:10.1097/01.NPR.0000903012.03553.a4 PMID:36573856

Hassmiller, S. B., & Wakefield, M. K. (2022). The future of nursing 2020–2030: Charting a path to achieve health equity. *Nursing Outlook*, 70(6), S1–S9. DOI:10.1016/j.outlook.2022.05.013 PMID:36446536

Hauze, S. W., Hoyt, H. H., Frazee, J. P., Greiner, P. A., & Marshall, J. M. (2019). Enhancing nursing education through affordable and realistic holographic mixed reality: The virtual standardized patient for clinical simulation. *Advances in Experimental Medicine and Biology*, 1, 1–13. DOI:10.1007/978-3-030-06070-1_1 PMID:30919290

Hawes, D., & Arya, A. (2023). Technology solutions to reduce anxiety and increase cognitive availability in students. *IEEE Transactions on Learning Technologies*, 16(2), 1. DOI:10.1109/TLT.2023.3239985

Hazarika, A., & Rahmati, M. (2023). Towards an evolved immersive experience: Exploring 5G-and beyond-enabled ultra-low-latency communications for augmented and virtual reality. *Sensors (Basel)*, 23(7), 3682. DOI:10.3390/s23073682 PMID:37050742

Heever, H., & Oosthuizen, R. (2024). Application of cognitive work analysis in support of systems engineering of a socio-technical system. *International Journal of Industrial and Systems Engineering*, 46(1), 90–106. DOI:10.1504/IJISE.2024.135830

Heilig, M. L. (1961). US patent 3050870A. https://patents.google.com/patent/US3050870A/en?oq=3%2C050%2C870

Heinz, M. S. (2018). *Exploring predictors of technology adoption among older adults*. Iowa State University.

Heitzman, N., Seidel, T., Opitz, A., Hetmanek, A., Wecker, C., Fischer, M., & Siebeck, M. (2019). Facilitating diagnostic competences in simulations: A conceptual framework and a research agenda for medical and teacher education. *Frontline Learning Research*, 7(4), 1–24. DOI:10.14786/flr.v7i4.384

Herath, H., & Mittal, M. (2022). Adoption of artificial intelligence in smart cities: A comprehensive review. *International Journal of Information Management Data Insights*, 2(1), 100076. DOI:10.1016/j.jjimei.2022.100076

Hietanen, M., & Svedholm-Häkkinen, A. M. (2023). Transition to Distance Education in 2020 – Challenges among University Faculty in Sweden. *Scandinavian Journal of Educational Research*, 67(3), 433–446. DOI:10.1080/00313831.2021.2021444

Hiran, K. K., Doshi, R., & Patel, M. (2024b). Modern Technology in Healthcare and Medical Education: Blockchain, IoT, AR, and VR: Blockchain, IoT, AR, and VR: IGI Global.

Hiran, K. K., Doshi, R., & Patel, M. (2024a). *Applications of Virtual and Augmented Reality for Health and Wellbeing*. IGI Global. DOI:10.4018/979-8-3693-1123-3

Höffler, T., Schmeck, A., Höffler, A. O. T. N., Schmeck, A., & Opfermann, M. (2013). Static and dynamic visual representations. *Learning through visual displays: Current perspectives on cognition, learning, and instruction*, 133-163.

Horváth, I. (2021). An analysis of personalized learning opportunities in 3D VR. *Frontiers of Computer Science*, 3(673826).

Hou, H., & Wu, H. (2020). Technology for real estate education and practice: A VR technology perspective. *Property Management*, 38(2), 311–324. DOI:10.1108/PM-08-2019-0046

Houston, D. L. (2018). *At-risk middle school boys' engagement in the iEngage model* [Doctoral dissertation, Walden University].

Hsieh, M.-C., & Lee, J.-J. (2018). Preliminary study of VR and AR applications in medical and healthcare education. *J Nurs Health Stud*, 3(1), 1. DOI:10.21767/2574-2825.100030

Huang, J., Lucash, M. S., Simpson, M. B., Helgeson, C., & Klippel, A. (2019). Visualizing natural environments from data in virtual reality: Combining realism and uncertainty. *2019 IEEE Conference on Virtual Reality and 3D User Interfaces (VR)*, (pp. 1485–1488). IEEE. https://ieeexplore.ieee.org/abstract/document/8797996/

Huang, T, (2019). Toward a scale for measuring the cognitive learning performance of virtual reality education. *Computers & Education*, 137, 51-64.

Huang, T.-C., Limniou, M., & Wu, W.-C. V. (2023). Virtual learning environments in educational institutions. In *Frontiers in Virtual Reality* (*Vol. 4,* p. 1138660). Frontiers Media SA. https://www.frontiersin.org/articles/10.3389/frvir.2023.1138660/full

Huang, , Rauch, U., & Liaw, S.-S. (2010). H. M ET AL., 2010., Rauch, U., & Liaw, S. S. (2010). Investigating learners' attitudes toward virtual reality learning environments: Based on a constructivist approach. *Computers & Education*, 55(3), 1171–1182. DOI:10.1016/j.compedu.2010.05.014

Huang, T. C., & Liaw, S. S. (2021). *Virtual reality in education: A new paradigm for learning and teaching*. Springer.

Huang, X., Huss, J., North, L., Williams, K., & Boyd-Devine, A. (2023). Cognitive and motivational benefits of a theory-based immersive virtual reality design in science learning. *Computers and Education Open*, 4, 100124. DOI:10.1016/j.caeo.2023.100124

Hu-Au, E., & Lee, J. J. (2018). Virtual reality in education: A tool for learning in the experience age. *International Journal of Innovation in Education*, 4(4), 215–226. DOI:10.1504/IJIIE.2017.091481

Hung, S.-W., & Cheng, M.-J. (2013). Are you ready for knowledge sharing? An empirical study of virtual communities. *Computers & Education*, 62, 8–17. DOI:10.1016/j.compedu.2012.09.017

Hurrell, C., & Baker, J. (2021). Immersive learning: Applications of virtual reality for undergraduate education. *College & Undergraduate Libraries*, 27(2-4), 197–209. DOI:10.1080/10691316.2020.1796879

Hussain, S., Ameri Sianaki, O., & Ababneh, N. (2019). A Survey on Conversational Agents/Chatbots Classification and Design Techniques. In *Advances in Intelligent Systems and Computing* (pp. 946–956). Springer International Publishing.

Hussain, S., Mubeen, I., Ullah, N., Shah, S. S. U. D., Khan, B. A., Zahoor, M., Ullah, R., Khan, F. A., & Sultan, M. A. (2022). Modern diagnostic imaging technique applications and risk factors in the medical field: A review. *BioMed Research International*, 2022(1), 5164970. DOI:10.1155/2022/5164970 PMID:35707373

Hussein, M., & Nätterdal, C. (2015). *The benefits of using virtual reality in education. A comparison study*. [Dissertation, University of Gothenburg & Chalmers University of Technology, Göteborg, Sweden].

Huusko, A., Susi, J., Parchegani, S., Hosseini, H., Tuomisto, A., Helin, A., Piili, H., & Salminen, A. (2023). Virtual Reality-Based Training in Additive Manufacturing: Developing a Service Concept that Adapts to Company-Specific Requirements. *IOP Conference Series. Materials Science and Engineering*, 1296(1), 012004. DOI:10.1088/1757-899X/1296/1/012004

I3-Technologies. (2023). *VR in the classroom: benefits and drawbacks.* I3 Technologies. https://www.i3-technologies.com/en/blog/stories/education/vr-in-the-classroom-benefits-and-drawbacks/#:~:text=Some%20benefits%20of%20using%20VR,retention%20and%20comprehension%20of%20concepts

Ibáñez, M. B., García, J. J., Galán, S., Maroto, D., Morillo, D., & Kloos, C. D. (2011). Design and implementation of a 3D multi-user virtual world for language learning. *Journal of Educational Technology & Society*, 14(4), 2–10.

Ibrahim, A., Al-Rababah, A. I., & Baker, Q. B. (2021). Integrating virtual reality technology into architecture education: The case of architectural history courses. *Open House International*, 46(4), 498–509. DOI:10.1108/OHI-12-2020-0190

Impelluso, T., & Metoyer-Guidry, T. (2001). Virtual Reality and Learning by Design: Tools for Integrating Mechanical Engineering Concepts. *Journal of Engineering Education*, 90(4), 527–534. DOI:10.1002/j.2168-9830.2001.tb00635.x

Intel (2023, February 20) What is refresh rate and why is it important? https://www.intel.com/content/www/us/en/gaming/resources/highest-refresh-rate-gaming.html

Ismail, H., Hussein, N., Harous, S., & Khalil, A. (2023). Survey of personalized learning software systems: A taxonomy of environments, learning content, and user models. *Education Sciences*, 13(7), 741. DOI:10.3390/educsci13070741

Iwamoto, S. (2023). *Developing a Theory of Community Caring for Public Health Nursing*. Paper presented at the Healthcare. DOI:10.3390/healthcare11030349

Jadhav, P. P., Samnani, A., Alachiya, A., Shah, V., & Selvam, A. (2022). Intelligent chatbot. *International Journal of Advanced Research in Science. Tongxin Jishu*, 679–683, 679–683. Advance online publication. DOI:10.48175/IJARSCT-3996

Jagatheesaperumal, S. K., Ahmad, K., Al-Fuqaha, A., & Qadir, J. (2024). Advancing education through extended reality and internet of everything enabled metaverses: Applications, challenges, and open issues. *IEEE Transactions on Learning Technologies*, 17, 1120–1139. DOI:10.1109/TLT.2024.3358859

Jeffries, P. (2022). *Clinical simulations in nursing education: Advanced concepts, trends, and opportunities*. Lippincott Williams & Wilkins.

Jensen, L., & Konradsen, F. (2017). A review of the use of virtual reality head-mounted displays in education and training. *Education and Information Technologies*, 23(4), 1515–1529. DOI:10.1007/s10639-017-9676-0

Jewitt, C. (2008). *The visual in learning and creativity: A review of the literature.* Arts Council.

Jiang, H., Vimalesvaran, S., Wang, J. K., Lim, K. B., Mogali, S. R., & Car, L. T. (2022). Virtual reality in medical students' education: Scoping review. *JMIR Medical Education*, 8(1), e34860. DOI:10.2196/34860 PMID:35107421

Jibril, A. U., Abdullahi, N. M., Ali, A. S., Abdulkadir, H., Matthew, U. O., & Haruna, K. (2022). Motivational aspects of digital games in learning process. *Science in Information Technology Letters*, 3(1), 1–9. DOI:10.31763/sitech.v3i1.885

Johnson, A. M., Jacovina, M. E., Russell, D. G., & Soto, C. M. (2023). *Challenges and solutions when using technologies in the classroom.* Taylor & Francis. https://www.taylorfrancis.com/chapters/edit/10.4324/9781315647500-2/challenges-solutions-using-technologies-classroom-amy-johnson-matthew-jacovina-devin-russell-christian-soto

Jollibekova, M. (2024). THE USE OF INFORMATION AND COMMUNICATION TECHNOLOGIES IN LEARNING ENGLISH LANGUAGE. *Евразийский Журнал Академических Исследований*, 4(3), 76–80.

Joseph, S., S, B. P., R, P., M, S. K., S, S., V, J., & R, S. P. (2023). IoT Empowered AI: Transforming Object Recognition and NLP Summarization with Generative AI. *2023 IEEE International Conference on Computer Vision and Machine Intelligence (CVMI)*. IEEE. DOI:10.1109/CVMI59935.2023.10465077

Joyce, T. S. L., & Enoch, E. N. (2021). The use of virtual reality in pharmacy education in Hong Kong: Lessons learnt. *Frontiers in Education*, 6, 639126. DOI:10.3389/feduc.2021.639126

Jóźwiak, M., Kolemba, A., Waligórska, H., Waligórska, H., Jóźwiak, M., & Kolemba, A. (2023). *Career Interest Preferences, Randomness of Study Program Choice, and Competencies vs. Academic Major Reselection.* Silesian University of Technology Publishing House. .DOI:10.29119/1641-3466.2023.179.34

Jumani, A. K., Siddique, W. A., Laghari, A. A., Abro, A., & Khan, A. A. (2022). *Virtual reality and augmented reality for education Multimedia computing systems and virtual reality.* CRC Press.

Jungherr, A. (2023). Using ChatGPT and other large language model (LLM) applications for academic paper assignments. In *SocArXiv*. DOI:10.31235/osf.io/d84q6

Junsawang, S., Chaveesuk, S., & Chaiyasoonthorn, W. (2022). Testing and measurement on willingness to use augmented reality, virtual reality, and AI-enabled checkouts. *2022 5th International Conference on Artificial Intelligence and Big Data (ICAIBD).*

Kamath, R. S., Dongale, T. D., & Kamat, R. K. (2012). Development of Virtual Reality Tool for Creative Learning in Architectural Education. *International Journal of Quality Assurance in Engineering and Technology Education*, 2(4), 16–24. DOI:10.4018/ijqaete.2012100102

Kamińska, D., Sapiński, T., Aitken, N., Della Rocca, A., Barańska, M., & Wietsma, R. (2017). Virtual reality as a new trend in mechanical and electrical engineering education. *Open Physics*, 15(1), 936–941. DOI:10.1515/phys-2017-0114

Kamińska, D., Sapiński, T., Wiak, S., Tikk, T., Haamer, R. E., Avots, E., Helmi, A., Ozcinar, C., & Anbarjafari, G. (2019). Virtual reality and its applications in education: Survey. *Information (Basel)*, 10(10), 318. DOI:10.3390/info10100318

Kapilan, N., Vidhya, P., & Gao, X.-Z. (2021). Virtual Laboratory: A Boon to the Mechanical Engineering Education During Covid-19 Pandemic. *Higher Education for the Future*, 8(1), 31–46. DOI:10.1177/2347631120970757

Kaplan, A. D., Cruit, J., Endsley, M., Beers, S. M., Sawyer, B. D., & Hancock, P. A. (2021). The effects of virtual reality, augmented reality, and mixed reality as training enhancement methods: A meta-analysis. *Human Factors*, 63(4), 706–726. DOI:10.1177/0018720820904229 PMID:32091937

Kaplan-Rakowski, R., Papin, K., & Hartwick, P. M. (2022). Language teachers' perceptions and use of extended reality. *Available atSSRN* 4096263. DOI:10.2139/ssrn.4096263

Karaliotas, C. (2011). When simulation in surgical training meets virtual reality. *Hellenike Cheirourgike. Acta Chirurgica Hellenica*, 83(6), 303–316. DOI:10.1007/s13126-011-0055-9

Karwasz, G. P., & Wyborska, K. (2023). How constructivist environment changes perception of learning: Physics is fun. *Education Sciences*, 13(2), 195. DOI:10.3390/educsci13020195

Katelin Hoskins, M. (2018). Ethics education in nursing: Instruction for future generations of nurses. *Online Journal of Issues in Nursing*, 23(1), 1–11.

Kay, T., Raswan, M., Camarillo-Abad, H. M., Qi, T. D., & Cibrian, F. L. (2023). Using Virtual Reality to Foster Creativity for Co-design a New Self-Expression and Relaxation Virtual Environment for Students. *Creativity and Cognition*, 365–367, 365–367. DOI:10.1145/3591196.3596611

Keenan-Lindsay, L., & Leifer, G. (2023). *Leifer's Introduction to Maternity & Pediatric Nursing in Canada-E-Book: Leifer's Introduction to Maternity & Pediatric Nursing in Canada-E-Book*. Elsevier Health Sciences.

Kelly, M. A., Berragan, E., Husebø, S. E., & Orr, F. (2016). Simulation in nursing education—International perspectives and contemporary scope of practice. *Journal of Nursing Scholarship*, 48(3), 312–321. DOI:10.1111/jnu.12208 PMID:27061858

Khan, M. J., Alcantud, J. C. R., Kumam, W., Kumam, P., & Alreshidi, N. A. (2023). Expanding Pythagorean fuzzy sets with distinctive radii: Disc Pythagorean fuzzy sets. *Complex & Intelligent Systems*, 9(6), 1–18. DOI:10.1007/s40747-023-01062-y

Kihlström, K., & Vahlgren, A. (2022). *Innovation implementation as a dynamic process with multiple outcomes: A single case study at Saab. MSc Business Administration*. Linköping University.

Kim, H., Nah, S., Oh, J., & Ryu, H. (2019, March). VR-MOOCs: A learning management system for VR education. In *2019 IEEE Conference on Virtual Reality and 3D User Interfaces (VR)* (pp. 1325-1326). IEEE. DOI:10.1109/VR.2019.8798106

Kirk, D. (2016). *The immersive learning revolution: how virtual reality is transforming education*. Routledge.

Klingenberg, S., Jørgensen, M. L., Dandanell, G., Skriver, K., Mottelson, A., & Makransky, G. (2020). Investigating the effect of teaching as a generative learning strategy when learning through desktop and immersive VR: A media and methods experiment. *British Journal of Educational Technology*, 51(6), 2115–2138. DOI:10.1111/bjet.13029

Klunder-Rosser, J. (2020). Should the development of orthopaedic trauma nursing be a priority in low to middle income countries? A scoping review. *International Journal of Orthopaedic and Trauma Nursing*, 37, 100749. DOI:10.1016/j.ijotn.2019.100749 PMID:32001191

Kolsi, T. (2023). *Accelerating the innovation adoption rate of laggards in B2B context*. Master's Programme in International Marketing Management. Lahti University of Technology

Kooijman, L., Asadi, H., Mohamed, S., & Nahavandi, S. (2023). A virtual reality study investigating the train illusion. *Royal Society Open Science*, 10(4), 221622. DOI:10.1098/rsos.221622 PMID:37063997

Kouijzer, M. M. T. E., Kip, H., Bouman, Y. H. A., & Kelders, S. M. (2023). Implementation of virtual reality in healthcare: A scoping review on the implementation process of virtual reality in various healthcare settings. *Implementation Science Communications*, 4(1), 67. DOI:10.1186/s43058-023-00442-2 PMID:37328858

Kouijzer, M., Kip, H., Kelders, S. M., & Bouman, Y. (2024). The introduction of virtual reality in forensic mental healthcare–an interview study on the first impressions of patients and healthcare providers regarding VR in treatment. *Frontiers in Psychology*, 15, 1284983. DOI:10.3389/fpsyg.2024.1284983 PMID:38746916

Kress, B. C. (2019). *Digital optical elements and technologies (EDO19): applications to AR/VR/MR.* Paper presented at the Digital Optical Technologies 2019.

Krijn, M., Emmelkamp, P. M. G., Olafsson, R. P., & Biemond, R. (2004). Virtual reality exposure therapy of anxiety disorders: A review. *Clinical Psychology Review*, 24(3), 259–281. DOI:10.1016/j.cpr.2004.04.001 PMID:15245832

Kumar, L., Kumar, A., Sharma, R. K., & Kumar, P. (2023). Smart Manufacturing and Industry 4.0. In *Handbook of Smart Manufacturing* (pp. 1–28). CRC Press. DOI:10.1201/9781003333760-1

Kumar, N., & Sharma, S. (2024). *Demystifying the Technology Adoption by the Asian Cargo Industry*. IGI Global. DOI:10.4018/979-8-3693-1602-3.ch006

Kumar, V. V., Carberry, D., Beenfeldt, C., Andersson, M. P., Mansouri, S. S., & Gallucci, F. (2021). Virtual reality in chemical and biochemical engineering education and training. *Education for Chemical Engineers*, 36, 143–153. DOI:10.1016/j.ece.2021.05.002

Kümmel, E., Moskaliuk, J., Cress, U., & Kimmerle, J. (2020). Digital learning environments in higher education: A literature review of the role of individual vs. social settings for measuring learning outcomes. *Education Sciences*, 10(3), 78. DOI:10.3390/educsci10030078

Kuna, P., Hašková, A., & Borza, L. (2023). Creation of virtual reality for education purposes. *Sustainability (Basel)*, 15(9), 7153. DOI:10.3390/su15097153

Kun, B., Yan, W., & Han, D. (2023). Exploring Interactive Design Strategies of Online Learning Platform Based on Cognitive Load Theory. *Human Factors and Systems Interaction*, 84(84). Advance online publication. DOI:10.54941/ahfe1003585

Kuncoro, T., Ichwanto, M. A., & Muhammad, D. F. (2023). VR-Based Learning Media of Earthquake-Resistant Construction for Civil Engineering Students. *Sustainability (Basel)*, 15(5), 4282. DOI:10.3390/su15054282

Kunnumpurath, B., Menon, V. A., & Paul, A. (2024b). ChatGPT and virtual experience. In *Advances in computational intelligence and robotics book series* (pp. 32–50). IGI Global. DOI:10.4018/979-8-3693-4268-8.ch003

Kutzin, J., Kipper, K., & Dahl, W. (2021). Emergency Nursing Continuing Professional Development Using Simulation. *Comprehensive Healthcare Simulation: Emergency Medicine*, 181-188.

Kyaw, B. M., Saxena, N., Posadzki, P., Vseteckova, J., Nikolaou, C. K., George, P. P., & Zary, N. (2019). Virtual reality for health professions education: Systematic review and meta-analysis by the digital health education collaboration. *Journal of Medical Internet Research*, 21(1), e12959. DOI:10.2196/12959 PMID:30668519

L'her, E., Geeraerts, T., Desclefs, J.-P., Benhamou, D., Blanié, A., Cerf, C., & Ouanes, I. (2020). Simulation-based teaching in critical care, anaesthesia and emergency medicine. *Anaesthesia Critical Care & Pain Medicine*, 39(2), 311–326. DOI:10.1016/j.accpm.2020.03.010 PMID:32223994

Lai, J. W., & Cheong, K. H. (2022). Educational opportunities and challenges in augmented reality: Featuring implementations in physics education. *IEEE Access : Practical Innovations, Open Solutions*, 10, 43143–43158. DOI:10.1109/ACCESS.2022.3166478

LaMorte, W. W. (2022). *Diffusion of innovation theory*. Boston University School of Public Health.

Lampropoulos, G., & Kinshuk, N. (2024). Virtual reality and gamification in education: A systematic review. *Educational Technology Research and Development*, 72(3), 1691–1785. DOI:10.1007/s11423-024-10351-3

Lämsä, J., Mannonen, J., Tuhkala, A., Heilala, V., Helovuo, A., Tynkkynen, I., Lampi, E., Sipiläinen, K., Kärkkäinen, T., & Hämäläinen, R. (2023). Capturing cognitive load management during authentic virtual reality flight training with behavioural and physiological indicators. *Journal of Computer Assisted Learning*, 39(5), 1553–1563. DOI:10.1111/jcal.12817

Lauring, J., Jonasson, C., & Jackowska, M. (2023). Virtuality and inclusiveness in organizations. In *Handbook of Virtual Work* (pp. 384–402). Edward Elgar Publishing. https://www.elgaronline.com/edcollchap/book/9781802200508/book-part-9781802200508-31.xmlDOI:10.4337/9781802200508.00031

LaVille, S. M. (2023). *Virtual Reality*. Cambridge University Press. DOI:10.1017/9781108182874

Le Traon, Y., & Xie, T. (2023). Model-based testing, test case prioritization and testing of virtual reality applications. *Software Testing, Verification & Reliability*, 33(8), e1868. DOI:10.1002/stvr.1868

Lee, E. A. L., Wong, K. W., & Fung, C. C. (2010). How does desktop virtual reality enhance learning outcomes? A structural equation modeling approach. *Computers & Education*, 55(4), 1424–1442. DOI:10.1016/j.compedu.2010.06.006

Lee, H. J., & Hwang, Y. (2022). Technology-enhanced education through VR-making and metaverse-linking to foster teacher readiness and sustainable learning. *Sustainability (Basel)*, 14(8), 4786. DOI:10.3390/su14084786

Lee, H., Xu, Y., & Porterfield, A. (2019). *Consumers' adoption of virtual fitting rooms: Antecedents and moderating factors*. Iowa State University. *The Library*.

Lee, J., Kim, J., & Choi, J. Y. (2019). The adoption of virtual reality devices: The technology acceptance model integrating enjoyment, social interaction, and strength of the social ties. *Telematics and Informatics*, 39, 37–48. DOI:10.1016/j.tele.2018.12.006

Lee, M. J. W., Dalgarno, B., & Chan, C. (2019). How immersive are three-dimensional virtual learning environments? An exploration of their cognitive and affective affordances. *British Journal of Educational Technology*, 40(3), 457–479.

Lege, R., & Bonner, E. (2020). Virtual reality in education: The promise, progress, and challenge. *The JALT CALL Journal*, 16(3), 167–180. DOI:10.29140/jaltcall.v16n3.388

Leigh, L. Y., Vannelli, P., Crow, H. C., Desai, S., Lepore, M., Anolik, R., & Glick, M. (2021). Diseases of the respiratory tract. *Burket's Oral Medicine*, 469-504.

Letseka, M. (2016). Open Distance Learning (ODL) through the philosophy of Ubuntu. *Open Distance Learning (ODL) Through the Philosophy of Ubuntu*. Research Gate.

Leu, M. C., ElMaraghy, H. A., Nee, A. Y. C., Ong, S. K., Lanzetta, M., Putz, M., Zhu, W., & Bernard, A. (2013). CAD model based virtual assembly simulation, planning and training. *CIRP Annals*, 62(2), 799–822. DOI:10.1016/j.cirp.2013.05.005

Levy, J., & Liu, D. (2022). Extended Reality (XR) environments for flood risk management with 3D GIS and open source 3D graphics cross-platform game engines: advances in immersive sea level rise planning technologies for student learning and community engagement. *Paper presented at the International Conference on Intelligent Technologies*. Research Gate.

Lewis, L. S. (2023). *Literacy-based Instruction in Low-SES Schools During COVID-19 Distance Learning* [Doctoral dissertation, Azusa Pacific University].

Lewis, L. H., & Williams, C. J. (1994). Experiential learning: Past and present. *New Directions for Adult and Continuing Education*, 1994(62), 5–16. DOI:10.1002/ace.36719946203

Liao, J., & Lu, G. (2009). Research on key techniques of virtual reality applied in mining industry. *Journal of Coal Science and Engineering (China)*, 15(4), 445–448. DOI:10.1007/s12404-009-0420-2

Liao, R. (2024). *Virtual reality technology in art education system*. China Academic of Art. DOI:10.3233/FAIA231425

Li, C.-H. (2023). Instructional Design, Learning Satisfaction, and Learning Outcome in a Virtual Reality Learning Environment Aimed at Improving the Cognition of Computer Hardware Components. *International Journal of Engineering & Technology Innovation*, 13(2). https://search.ebscohost.com/login.aspx?direct=true&profile=ehost&scope=site&authtype=crawler&jrnl=22235329&AN=162741872&h=DhnNrK88ug4kEmy1matB9PKSQezB1M%2BdbZqYkg0phZsyFgVSAEvB3hgay4GDRf3n1C5M4M%2BDjRhzjtztpSiEnw%3D%3D&crl=c

Liesa-Orús, M., Latorre-Cosculluela, C., Vázquez-Toledo, S., & Sierra-Sánchez, V.LiesaOrús. (2020). The technological challenge facing higher education professors: Perceptions of ICT tools for developing 21st Century skills. *Sustainability (Basel)*, 12(13), 5339. DOI:10.3390/su12135339

Li, J., Zhang, H., & Jiang, X. (2017). The effect of virtual reality training on medical students' learning outcomes. *Journal of Medical Education*, 45(4), 299–305.

Lin, C.-H., Shih, H.-Y., & Sher, P. J. (2007). Integrating technology readiness into technology acceptance: The TRAM model. *Psychology and Marketing*, 24(7), 641–657. DOI:10.1002/mar.20177

Ling, H., & Rui, L. (2016). *VR glasses and leap motion trends in education*. The 11th International Conference on Computer Science & Education, Nagoya University, Japan.

Lin, Y., & Yu, Z. (2023). A meta-analysis of the effects of augmented reality technologies in interactive learning environments (2012–2022). *Computer Applications in Engineering Education*, 31(4), 1111–1131. DOI:10.1002/cae.22628

Liu, D., Bhagat, K. K., Gao, Y., Chang, T.-W., & Huang, R. (2017). The potentials and trends of virtual reality in education: A bibliometric analysis on top research studies in the last two decades. *Virtual, augmented, and mixed realities in education*, 105-130.

Liu, Q., Geertshuis, S., & Grainger, R. (2020). Understanding academics' adoption of learning technologies: A systematic review. *Science Direct, 151*. https://www.sciencedirect.com/science/article/abs/pii/S0360131520300579

Liu, C.-H., & Huang, Y.-M. (2015). An empirical investigation of computer simulation technology acceptance to explore the factors that affect user intention. *Universal Access in the Information Society*, 14(3), 449–457. DOI:10.1007/s10209-015-0402-7

Liu, C., Rani, P., & Pachori, K. (2022). Sustainable circular supplier selection and evaluation in the manufacturing sector using Pythagorean fuzzy EDAS approach. *Journal of Enterprise Information Management*, 35(4/5), 1040–1066. DOI:10.1108/JEIM-04-2021-0187

Liu, J. Y. W., Yin, Y.-H., Kor, P. P. K., Cheung, D. S. K., Zhao, I. Y., Wang, S., Su, J. J., Christensen, M., Tyrovolas, S., & Leung, A. Y. (2023). The effects of immersive virtual reality applications on enhancing the learning outcomes of undergraduate health care students: Systematic review with meta-synthesis. *Journal of Medical Internet Research*, 25, e39989. DOI:10.2196/39989 PMID:36877550

Li, W., Liu, X., Zhang, Q., Zhou, B., & Wang, B. (2023). VR-Enhanced Cognitive Learning: Method, Framework, and Application. *Applied Sciences (Basel, Switzerland)*, 13(8), 4756. DOI:10.3390/app13084756

Li, Y., Ch'ng, E., & Cobb, S. (2023). Factors Influencing Engagement in Hybrid Virtual and Augmented Reality. *ACM Transactions on Computer-Human Interaction*, 30(4), 1–27. DOI:10.1145/3589952

Lopez, M., Arriaga, J. G., Nigenda Álvarez, J. P., González, R. T., Elizondo-Leal, J. A., Valdez-García, J. E., & Carrión, B. (2021). Virtual reality vs traditional education: Is there any advantage in human neuroanatomy teaching? *Computers &amp. Computers & Electrical Engineering*, 93, 107282. DOI:10.1016/j.compeleceng.2021.107282

Lougiakis, C., González, J. J., Ganias, G., Katifori, A., & Roussou, M. (2024). Comparing Physics-based Hand Interaction in Virtual Reality: Custom Soft Body Simulation vs. Off-the-Shelf Integrated Solution.*Paper presented at the 2024 IEEE Conference Virtual Reality and 3D User Interfaces (VR).* IEEE. DOI:10.1109/VR58804.2024.00094

Lowman, G. H., & Harms, P. D. (2022). Addressing the nurse workforce crisis: A call for greater integration of the organizational behavior, human resource management and nursing literatures. *Journal of Managerial Psychology*, 37(3), 294–303. DOI:10.1108/JMP-04-2022-713

Lowy, R., Gao, L., Hall, K., & Kim, J. G. (2023). Toward Inclusive Mindsets: Design Opportunities to Represent Neurodivergent Work Experiences to Neurotypical Co-Workers in Virtual Reality. *Proceedings of the 2023 CHI Conference on Human Factors in Computing Systems*, (pp. 1–17). ACM. DOI:10.1145/3544548.3581399

Lui, L. F., Radhakrishnan, U., Chinello, F., & Koumaditis, K. (2023). Adaptive Immersive VR Training Based on Performance and Self-Efficacy. *2023 IEEE Conference on Virtual Reality and 3D User Interfaces Abstracts and Workshops (VRW)*, (pp. 25–29). IEEE. https://ieeexplore.ieee.org/abstract/document/10108645/

Lv, Z. (2020). Virtual reality in the context of Internet of Things. *Neural Computing & Applications*, 32(13), 9593–9602. DOI:10.1007/s00521-019-04472-7

MacQuarrie, A., & Steed, A. (2017). Cinematic virtual reality: Evaluating the effect of display type on the viewing experience for panoramic video. *2017 IEEE Virtual Reality (VR)*, (pp. 45–54). IEEE. https://ieeexplore.ieee.org/abstract/document/7892230/

Magnenat-Thalmann, N., Stephanidis, C., Wu, E., Thalmann, D., Sheng, B., Kim, J., Papagiannakis, G., & Gavrilova, M. (Eds.). (2020). *Advances in computer graphics: 37Th computer graphics international conference, CGI 2020, Geneva, Switzerland, October 20-23, 2020, proceedings*. Springer International Publishing.

Maher, S. (2020). Chatbots & Its Techniques using AI: A Review. *International Journal for Research in Applied Science and Engineering Technology*, 8(12), 503–508. DOI:10.22214/ijraset.2020.32537

Mahmoud, K. F., Finnell, D. S., Sereika, S. M., Lindsay, D., & Mitchell, A. M. (2024). Comparing Medical-Surgical, Psychiatric–Mental Health, and Addiction Specialty Nurses' Personal Attitudes, Professional Attitudes, and Motivation Toward Working With Individuals With Alcohol and Opioid Use Problems: Implications for the Nursing Workforce Using a Nationwide Sample. *Journal of Nursing Regulation*, 15(2), 17–27. DOI:10.1016/S2155-8256(24)00052-8

Mäkinen, H., Haavisto, E., Havola, S., & Koivisto, J.-M. (2022). User experiences of virtual reality technologies for healthcare in learning: An integrative review. *Behaviour & Information Technology*, 41(1), 1–17. DOI:10.1080/0144929X.2020.1788162

Makransky, G., Andreasen, N. K., Baceviciute, S., & Mayer, R. E. (2021). Immersive virtual reality increases liking but not learning with a science simulation and generative learning strategies promote learning in immersive virtual reality. *Journal of Educational Psychology*, 113(4), 719–735. DOI:10.1037/edu0000473

Makransky, G., & Lilleholt, L. (2018). A structural equation modeling investigation of the emotional value of immersive virtual reality in education. *Educational Technology Research and Development*, 66(5), 1141–1164. DOI:10.1007/s11423-018-9581-2

Makransky, G., Lilleholt, L., & Aaby, A. (2019). Development and validation of the Multimodal Presence Scale for virtual reality environments: A confirmatory factor analysis and item response theory approach. *Computers & Education*, 141, 103607.

Makransky, G., & Mayer, R. E. (2020). Benefits of immersive virtual reality in education. *Journal of Educational Psychology*, 112(4), 794–806.

Makransky, G., Terkildsen, T. S., & Mayer, R. E. (2019). Adding immersive virtual reality to a science lab simulation causes more presence but less learning. *Learning and Instruction*, 60, 225–236. DOI:10.1016/j.learninstruc.2017.12.007

Malekzadeh, S. (2017). *Simulation in Otolaryngology, An Issue of Otolaryngologic Clinics of North: Simulation in Otolaryngology, An Issue of Otolaryngologic Clinics of North* (Vol. 50). Elsevier Health Sciences.

Malighetti, P., Martini, G., Redondi, R., & Scotti, D. (2019). Air transport networks of global integrators in the more liberalized Asian air cargo industry. *Transport Policy*, 80(1), 12–23. DOI:10.1016/j.tranpol.2019.04.021

Markwell, L. T., Velten, J. R., Partridge, J. A., & Porter, J. M. (2023). Virtual motivation: The psychological and transfer of learning effects of immersive virtual reality practice. *Journal of Motor Learning and Development, 1*(aop), (pp. 1–15). Research Gate.

Marougkas, A., Troussas, C., Krouska, A., & Sgouropoulou, C. (2023). Virtual Reality in education: A review of learning theories, approaches and methodologies for the last decade. *Electronics (Basel)*, 12(13), 2832. DOI:10.3390/electronics12132832

Marougkas, A., Troussas, C., Krouska, A., & Sgouropoulou, C. (2024). How personalized and effective is immersive virtual reality in education? A systematic literature review for the last decade. *Multimedia Tools and Applications*, 83(6), 18185–18233. DOI:10.1007/s11042-023-15986-7

Martarelli, C., Dubach, J., Schelleis, N., Cacchione, T., & Tempelmann, S. (2023). *Virtual reality in primary science education: Improving knowledge of the water cycle*. https://osf.io/preprints/psyarxiv/qj2a5/DOI:10.31234/osf.io/qj2a5

Martinez-Garcia, A., Horrach-Rosselló, P., & Mulet-Forteza, C. (2023a). Evolution and current state of research into E-learning. *Heliyon*, 9(10), e21016. DOI:10.1016/j.heliyon.2023.e21016 PMID:37867823

Martinez-Ulloa, L., Flores, A., Maldonado-Aguayo, Y., Fuentealba-Urra, S., Rubio, A., Guerreo, J., & Ravazzano, C. (2024). Incorporation of a digital health literacy model into the curricula of medical and rehabilitation science courses in higher education. *Salud, Ciencia y Tecnología*, 4, 909–909. DOI:10.56294/saludcyt2024909

Martín-Gutiérrez, J., Mora, C. E., Añorbe-Díaz, B., & González-Marrero, A. (2017). Virtual technologies trends in education. *Eurasia Journal of Mathematics, Science and Technology Education*, 13(2), 469–486.

Mas-Tur, A., Modak, N., Merigó, J., & Quantity, N. R.-T.-Q. (2019). *Half a century of Quality & Quantity: a bibliometric review*. Springer. https://link.springer.com/article/10.1007/s11135-018-0799-1

Mathew, P. S., & Pillai, A. S. (2020). Role of immersive (XR) technologies in improving healthcare competencies: a review. *Virtual and Augmented Reality in Education, Art, and Museums*, 23-46.

Matthew, U. O., Kazaure, J. S., Kazaure, A. S., Onyedibe, O. N., & Okafor, A. N. (2022). The twenty first century E-learning education management & implication for media technology adoption in the period of pandemic. *EAI Endorsed Transactions on e-Learning, 8*(1).

Matthew, U. O. (2019). Information System Management & Multimedia Applications in an E-Learning Environment. [IJICTHD]. *International Journal of Information Communication Technologies and Human Development*, 11(3), 21–41. DOI:10.4018/IJICTHD.2019070102

Matthew, U. O., Kazaure, A. S., Kazaure, J. S., Hassan, I. M., Nwanakwaugwu, A. C., & Okafor, N. U. (2022). Educational Technology Adaptation & Implication for Media Technology Adoption in the Period of COVID-19. *Journal of Trends in Computer Science and Smart Technology*, 4(4), 226–245. DOI:10.36548/jtcsst.2022.4.002

Matthew, U. O., & Kazaure, J. S. (2020). Multimedia e-learning education in nigeria and developing countries of Africa for achieving SDG4. [IJICTHD]. *International Journal of Information Communication Technologies and Human Development*, 12(1), 40–62. DOI:10.4018/IJICTHD.2020010103

Matthew, U. O., Kazaure, J. S., Amaonwu, O., Adamu, U. A., Hassan, I. M., Kazaure, A. A., & Ubochi, C. N. (2021). *Role of internet of health things (IoHTs) and innovative internet of 5G medical robotic things (IIo-5GMRTs) in COVID-19 global health risk management and logistics planning Intelligent Data Analysis for COVID-19 Pandemic*. Springer.

Matthew, U. O., Kazaure, J. S., & Haruna, K. (2020). Multimedia Information System (MIS) for Knowledge Generation and ICT Policy Framework in Education: Innovative Sustainable Educational Investment. [IJICTHD]. *International Journal of Information Communication Technologies and Human Development*, 12(3), 28–58. DOI:10.4018/IJICTHD.2020070102

Matthew, U. O., Kazaure, J. S., Kazaure, A. S., Nwamouh, U. C., & Chinonso, A. (2022). ICT Policy Implementation as Correlate for Achieving Educational Sustainability: Approaching Development in Multi ICT Dimensions. *Journal of Information Technology*, 4(4), 250–269.

Matthew, U. O., Kazaure, J. S., Ndukwu, C. C., Ebong, G. N., Nwanakwaugwu, A. C., & Nwamouh, U. C. (2024). *Artificial Intelligence Educational Pedagogy Development: ICT Pedagogy Development for Education 5.0 Educational Perspectives on Digital Technologies in Modeling and Management*. IGI Global. DOI:10.4018/979-8-3693-2314-4.ch003

Matthew, U. O., Kazaure, J. S., & Okafor, N. U. (2021). Contemporary development in E-Learning education, cloud computing technology & internet of things. *EAI Endorsed Transactions on Cloud Systems*, 7(20), e3–e3.

Matthew, U. O., Kazaure, J. S., & Okochi, P. I. (2022). 5G Mid-Range Electromagnetic Spectrum Implementation for Critical Infrastructure Development: Electromagnetic Spectrum Sustainability. [IJITN]. *International Journal of Interdisciplinary Telecommunications and Networking*, 14(1), 1–26. DOI:10.4018/IJITN.307103

Matthew, U. O., Onumaku, V. C., Fatai, L. O., Adekunle, T. S., Waliu, A. O., Ndukwu, C. C., & Ebong, G. N. (2024). *E-Healthcare Data Warehouse Design and Data Mining Using ML Approach Reshaping Healthcare with Cutting-Edge Biomedical Advancements*. IGI Global.

Mayer, R. E. (2003). The promise of multimedia learning: Using the same instructional design methods across different media. *Learning and Instruction*, 13(2), 125–139. DOI:10.1016/S0959-4752(02)00016-6

Mazuryk, T., Gervautz, M., & Smith, K. (2013). Virtual Reality History, Applications, Technology and Future. *Digital Outcasts, 63*(ISIE), 92–98. doi.org/10.1016/B978-0-12-404705-1.00006-6

McBride, A. B., Campbell, J., Barr, T., Duffy, J., Haozous, E., Mallow, J., Narsavage, G., Ridenour, N., & Theeke, L. (2017). The impact of the nurse faculty scholars program on schools of nursing. *Nursing Outlook*, 65(3), 327–335. DOI:10.1016/j.outlook.2017.01.013 PMID:28416201

McCloskey, D. W., McAllister, E., Gilbert, R., O'Higgins, C., Lydon, D., Lydon, M., & McPolin, D. (2024). Embedding Civil Engineering Understanding through the Use of Interactive Virtual Reality. *Education Sciences*, 14(1), 6. DOI:10.3390/educsci14010006

McGarr, O., & Gallchóir, C. Ó. (2020). Exploring the digital divide in post-primary schools. *British Journal of Educational Technology*, 51(6), 2116–2130.

McGonigle, D., & Mastrian, K. (2024). *Nursing informatics and the foundation of knowledge*. Jones & Bartlett Learning.

McKinnon, L. D., & North, M. M. (2004). A comparative study of presence in virtual reality vs. presence in the real world. *Proceedings of the 42nd Annual Southeast Regional Conference*. ACM. DOI:10.1145/986537.986597

McKleroy, V. S., Galbraith, J. S., Cummings, B., Jones, P., Harshbarger, C., Collins, C., Gelaude, D., & Carey, J. W.ADAPT Team. (2006). Adapting evidence–based behavioral interventions for new settings and target populations. *AIDS Education and Prevention*, 18(supp), 59–73. DOI:10.1521/aeap.2006.18.supp.59 PMID:16987089

Mehrfard, A., Fotouhi, J., Taylor, G., Forster, T., Navab, N., & Fuerst, B. (2019). A comparative analysis of virtual reality head-mounted display systems. arXiv preprint arXiv:1912.02913.

Merchant, Z., Goetz, E. T., Cifuentes, L., Keeney-Kennicutt, W., & Davis, T. J. (2014). Effectiveness of virtual reality-based instruction on students' learning outcomes in K-12 and higher education: A meta-analysis. *Computers & Education*, 70, 29–40. DOI:10.1016/j.compedu.2013.07.033

Mhatre, N., Motani, K., Shah, M., & Mali, S. (2016). Donna Interactive Chat-bot acting as a Personal Assistant. *International Journal of Computer Applications*, 140(10), 6–11. DOI:10.5120/ijca2016909460

Mikropoulos, T. A., & Natsis, A. (2016). *Educational virtual reality: A new era for learning*. Springer.

Miller, D. (2022). *Ethics of virtual reality: A philosophical perspective*. Routledge.

Miranda, M.Q., Miranda, J.S., Schwartz, C.A. & Almeida, J.P.L. (2016). Technology adoption in diffusion of innovations perspective: introduction of an ERP system in a non-profit organization. *Scientific Information System*, 103-124.

Mir, K. (2016). Design and development of online student support system. *Pak. J. Distance Online Learn*, 3(October), 1–8.

Mishra, A. R., Pamučar, D., Hezam, I. M., Chakrabortty, R. K., Rani, P., Božanić, D., & Ćirović, G. (2022). Interval-valued pythagorean fuzzy similarity measure-based complex proportional assessment method for waste-to-energy technology selection. *Processes (Basel, Switzerland)*, 10(5), 1015. DOI:10.3390/pr10051015

Mishra, S. P., Kulshreshtha, D., Srivastava, A. K., Gandhi, A. K., & Rastogi, M. (2019). *Gamification to promote the engagement in healtcare and wellness of patients under therapeutic care: gamification and healthcare Application of Gaming in New Media Marketing*. IGI Global. DOI:10.4018/978-1-5225-6064-7.ch015

Mizota, T., Anton, N. E., Huffman, E. M., Guzman, M. J., Lane, F., Choi, J. N., & Stefanidis, D. (2020). Development of a fundamentals of endoscopic surgery proficiency-based skills curriculum for general surgery residents. *Surgical Endoscopy*, 34(2), 771–778. DOI:10.1007/s00464-019-06827-6 PMID:31102077

Mohd, W. W., Abdullah, L., Yusoff, B., Taib, C. M. I. C., & Merigo, J. M. (2019). An integrated MCDM model based on Pythagorean fuzzy sets for green supplier development program. *Malaysian Journal of Mathematical Science*, 13, 23–37.

Molla, M. U., Giri, B. C., & Biswas, P. (2021). Extended PROMETHEE method with Pythagorean fuzzy sets for medical diagnosis problems. *Soft Computing*, 25(6), 4503–4512. DOI:10.1007/s00500-020-05458-7

Mordor Intelligence. (2024). Virtual Reality (VR) Market Size. https://www.mordorintelligence.com/industry-reports/virtual-reality-market/market-size

Moro, C., Štromberga, Z., Raikos, A., & Stirling, A. (2017). The effectiveness of virtual and augmented reality in health sciences and medical anatomy. *Anatomical Sciences Education*, 10(6), 549–559. https://doi.org/https://doi.org/10.1002/ase.1696. DOI:10.1002/ase.1696 PMID:28419750

Morsiani, G., Bagnasco, A., & Sasso, L. (2017). How staff nurses perceive the impact of nurse managers' leadership style in terms of job satisfaction: A mixed method study. *Journal of Nursing Management*, 25(2), 119–128. DOI:10.1111/jonm.12448 PMID:27917561

Mozumder, I., Athar, A., & Sheeraz, M. (2022). *Technological Roadmap of the Future Trend of Metaverse based on IoT, Blockchain, and AI Techniques in Metaverse Education*. IEEE. https://ieeexplore.ieee.org/document/9728808

Mukkawar, V. V., Netak, L. D., & Nikam, V. B. (2021). Architectural view of non-face-to-face experiential learning through the immersive technologies. *Paper presented at the International Conference on Intelligent Human Computer Interaction*. Research Gate.

Mulders, M., Buchner, J., & Kerres, M. (2020). A framework for the use of immersive virtual reality in learning environments. [iJET]. *International Journal of Emerging Technologies in Learning*, 15(24), 208–224. DOI:10.3991/ijet.v15i24.16615

Münster, S., Maiwald, F., Bruschke, J., Kröber, C., Sun, Y., Dworak, D., Komorowicz, D., Munir, I., Beck, C., & Münster, D. L. (2024). A digital 4D information system on the world scale: Research challenges, approaches, and preliminary results. *Applied Sciences (Basel, Switzerland)*, 14(5), 1992. DOI:10.3390/app14051992

Murauer, N. (2018). Design Thinking: Using Photo Prototyping for a user-centered Interface Design for Pick-by-Vision Systems. *Proceedings of the 11th PErvasive Technologies Related to Assistive Environments Conference*, (pp. 126–132). ACM. DOI:10.1145/3197768.3201532

Mystakidis, S., & Lympouridis, V. (2023). Immersive learning. *Encyclopedia*, 3(2), 396–405. DOI:10.3390/encyclopedia3020026

Nacke, L. E., Mirza-Babaei, P., & Drachen, A. (2023). User Experience Design and Research in Games. *Extended Abstracts of the 2023 CHI Conference on Human Factors in Computing Systems*, (pp. 1–3). ACM. DOI:10.1145/3544549.3574181

Naef, M., Staadt, O., & Gross, M. (2002). Spatialized audio rendering for immersive virtual environments. *Proceedings of the ACM Symposium on Virtual Reality Software and Technology*, (pp. 65–72). ACM. DOI:10.1145/585740.585752

Nandiyanto, A. B. D., & Al Husaeni, D. F. (2021). A bibliometric analysis of materials research in Indonesian journal using VOSviewer. *Journal of Engineering Research (Kuwait)*, 9. DOI:10.36909/jer.ASSEEE.16037

Naseer, M. (2009). Use of bibliometrics in LIS research. *Academia.Edu, 19*(2), 1–12. https://www.academia.edu/download/963587/303n9c3dq8kjbn6.pdf

Nasrabadi, A. T., Mahzari, A., Beshay, J. D., & Prakash, R. (2017). Adaptive 360-degree video streaming using Scalable Video coding. *Proceedings of the 25th ACM International Conference on Multimedia*. DOI:10.1145/3123266.3123414

Navab, E., Hoseini Azizi, T., & Darvish, A. (2024). Comparative study of master's degree curricula in nursing informatics at Tehran University of Medical Sciences and the University of Maryland. *Journal of Medical Education Development*, 17(53), 91–100.

Neamtu, C., Comes, R., Matescu, R., Ghinea, R., & Daniel, F. (2012, November). Using virtual reality to teach history. In *Proceedings of the 7th International Conference on Virtual Learning (Bucure ti: Editura Universitatii din Bucuresti)* (pp. 303-310). Research Gate.

Negahban, A. (2024). Simulation in engineering education: The transition from physical experimentation to digital immersive simulated environments. *Simulation*, 100(7), 00375497241229757. DOI:10.1177/00375497241229757

Neumann, M. M., Keioskie, M. K., Patterson, D., & Neumann, D. L. (2022). Virtual, augmented, and mixed reality: Benefits and barriers for early childhood education. *Childhood Education*, 98(4), 68–79. DOI:10.1080/00094056.2022.2108298

Neupane, D., Pant, S., & Bhattarai, P. (2023). Preferred Learning Techniques among Bachelor's Level Students. *Nepal Journal of Multidisciplinary Research*, 6(2), 145–154. DOI:10.3126/njmr.v6i2.57660

Newman, M., Gatersleben, B., Wyles, K. J., & Ratcliffe, E. (2022). The use of virtual reality in environment experiences and the importance of realism. *Journal of Environmental Psychology*, 79, 101733. DOI:10.1016/j.jenvp.2021.101733

Newton, M. H., & Annetta, L. A. (2024). The Influence of Extended Reality on Climate Change Education. *Science & Education*, 1–21. DOI:10.1007/s11191-024-00518-y

Nganji, J. T., & Brayshaw, M. (2017). Disability-aware adaptive and personalised learning for students with multiple disabilities. *The International Journal of Information and Learning Technology*, 34(4), 307–321. DOI:10.1108/IJILT-08-2016-0027

Nikolić, D., & Whyte, J. (2021). Visualizing a new sustainable world: Toward the next generation of virtual reality in the built environment. *Buildings*, 11(11), 546. DOI:10.3390/buildings11110546

Noble, S. (2023, January 3) *The ultimate VR, AR, MR guide*. ANIWAA. https://www.aniwaa.com/guide/vr-ar/ultimate-vr-ar-mr-guide/

Nordin, S., Sturge, J., Ayoub, M., Jones, A., McKee, K., Dahlberg, L., Meijering, L., & Elf, M. (2021). The role of information and communication technology (ICT) for older adults' decision-making related to health, and health and social care services in daily life—A scoping review. *International Journal of Environmental Research and Public Health*, 19(1), 151. DOI:10.3390/ijerph19010151 PMID:35010408

Ntaba, A., & Jantjies, M. (2021). Open distance learning and immersive technologies: a literature analysis. *Balancing the Tension between Digital Technologies and Learning Sciences*, (pp. 183-198). IEEE.

Nuguri, S. S., Calyam, P., Oruche, R., Gulhane, A., Valluripally, S., Stichter, J., & He, Z. (2021). vSocial: A cloud-based system for social virtual reality learning environment applications in special education. *Multimedia Tools and Applications*, 80(11), 16827–16856. DOI:10.1007/s11042-020-09051-w

Oculus. (2023). *OCULUS LOGO*. https://1000logos.net/oculus-logo/

OECD. (2012). *Equity and quality in education: Supporting disadvantaged students and schools*. OECD Publishing. DOI:10.1787/9789264130852-

Oh, K., & Nussli, N. (2014). Teacher training in the use of a three-dimensional immersive virtual world: Building understanding through first-hand experiences. *Journal of Teaching and Learning with Technology*, 33–58.

Oh, H., & Son, W. (2022). Cybersickness and its severity arising from virtual reality content: A comprehensive study. *Sensors (Basel)*, 22(4), 1314. DOI:10.3390/s22041314 PMID:35214216

Okwudili, U. M., & Kazaure, J. S. (2020). Digital activism and digital revolution in objective journalism. [IJICST]. *International Journal of Interactive Communication Systems and Technologies*, 10(2), 39–56. DOI:10.4018/IJICST.2020070104

Olechowski, A., Eppinger, S. D., & Joglekar, N. (2015). Technology readiness levels at 40: A study of state-of-the-art use, challenges, and opportunities. *2015 Portland International Conference on Management of Engineering and Technology (PICMET)*. IEEE. DOI:10.1109/PICMET.2015.7273196

Omasta, M., & Snyder-Young, D. (2022). Methodologies and methods. *Impacting Theatre Audiences: Methods for Studying Change*.

Ong, S. K., Pang, Y., & Nee, A. Y. C. (2007). Augmented Reality Aided Assembly Design and Planning. *CIRP Annals*, 56(1), 49–52. DOI:10.1016/j.cirp.2007.05.014

Onyesolu, M. O., & Eze, F. U. (2011). Understanding virtual reality technology: Advances and applications. *Advances in Computational Science and Engineering*, 1, 53–70.

Onyesolu, M. O., Nwasor, V. C., Ositanwosu, O. E., & Iwegbuna, O. N. (2013). Pedagogy: Instructivism to socio-constructivism through virtual reality. *International Journal of Advanced Computer Science and Applications*, 4(9).

Ostrander, J. K., Tucker, C. S., Simpson, T. W., & Meisel, N. A. (2019). Evaluating the Use of Virtual Reality to Teach Introductory Concepts of Additive Manufacturing. *Journal of Mechanical Design*, 142(5), 51702. DOI:10.1115/1.4044006

Ouariach, S., Khaldi, M., Mohamed, E., & Khaldi, M. (2023). The Flipped Classroom: From Passive Information Absorption to Active Learning. In *Handbook of Research on Language Teacher Identity* (pp. 269-293). IGI Global.

Oyekunle, D., Ugochukwu, O. M., Rosa, R. L., Rodriguez, D. Z., & Fatai, L. O. (2024). Novel Approaches in Clinical Simulation: Immersive Educational Technology to Enhance Nursing Education. *INFOCOMP Journal of Computer Science, 23*(1).

Oyewole, A. T., Adeoye, O. B., Addy, W. A., Okoye, C. C., Ofodile, O. C., & Ugochukwu, C. E. (2024). Augmented and virtual reality in financial services: A Review of Emerging Applications. *World Journal of Advanced Research and Reviews*, 21(3), 551–567. DOI:10.30574/wjarr.2024.21.3.0623

Özekici, Y. K., & Küçükergin, K. G. (2023). The role of COVID-19 anxiety and social contact within technology readiness and acceptance model for virtual reality. *Journal of Vacation Marketing*, 29(4), 498–521. DOI:10.1177/13567667221109268

Paiva, H. W. A., Golçalves, J. G., Rodrígues, D. Z., & Rosa, R. L. (2024). A Comprehensive Analysis of Virtual Reality Applications in Healthcare. *INFOCOMP Journal of Computer Science, 23*(1).

Pallavicini, F., Pepe, A., Clerici, M., & Mantovani, F. (2022). Virtual reality applications in medicine during the COVID-19 pandemic: Systematic review. *JMIR Serious Games*, 10(4), e35000. DOI:10.2196/35000 PMID:36282554

Pantelidis, V. S. (2021). Reasons to use virtual reality in education and training courses and a model to determine when to use virtual reality. *Themes in Science and Technology Education*, 2, 59–70.

Paolanti, M., Puggioni, M., Frontoni, E., Giannandrea, L., & Pierdicca, R. (2023). Evaluating Learning Outcomes of Virtual Reality Applications in Education: A Proposal for Digital Cultural Heritage. *Journal on Computing and Cultural Heritage*, 16(2), 1–25. DOI:10.1145/3593432

Papanastasiou, G., Drigas, A., Skianis, C., & Lytras, M. D. (2018). Virtual and augmented reality effects on K-12, higher and tertiary education students' twenty-first century skills. *Virtual Reality (Waltham Cross)*, 22(4), 573–589.

Parasuraman, A. (2000). Technology readiness index (Tri): A multiple-item scale to measure readiness to embrace new technologies. *Journal of Service Research*, 2(4), 307–320. DOI:10.1177/109467050024001

Pasklinsky, N., & Latimer, B. (2024). Simulation Modalities for Undergraduate Nursing Education *Comprehensive Healthcare SimulationNursing*, 27–33.

Passig, D., Tzuriel, D., & Eshel-Kedmi, G. (2016). Improving children's cognitive modifiability by dynamic assessment in 3D Immersive Virtual Reality environments. *Computers & Education*, 95, 296–308. DOI:10.1016/j.compedu.2016.01.009

Paszkiewicz, A., Salach, M., Dymora, P., Bolanowski, M., Budzik, G., & Kubiak, P. (2021). Methodology of implementing virtual reality in education for industry 4.0. *Sustainability (Basel)*, 13(9), 5049. DOI:10.3390/su13095049

Patel, N. S., Puah, S., & Kok, X.-F. K. (2024). Shaping future-ready graduates with mindset shifts: studying the impact of integrating critical and design thinking in design innovation education. *Paper presented at the Frontiers in Education*. IEEE. DOI:10.3389/feduc.2024.1358431

Pearson, I. (2006). A trip into the future [virtual reality and artificial intelligence]. *IET 2nd International Technology and Innovation Conference*. Research Gate.

Pedro, A., Le, Q. T., & Park, C. S. (2016). Framework for Integrating Safety into Construction Methods Education through Interactive Virtual Reality. *Journal of Professional Issues in Engineering Education and Practice*, 142(2), 04015011. DOI:10.1061/(ASCE)EI.1943-5541.0000261

Pei, L., & Wu, H. (2019). Does online learning work better than offline learning in undergraduate medical education? A systematic review and meta-analysis. *Medical Education Online*, 24(1), 1666538. DOI:10.1080/10872981.2019.1666538 PMID:31526248

Pellas, N., Mystakidis, S., & Kazanidis, I. (2021). Immersive Virtual Reality in K-12 and Higher Education: A systematic review of the last decade scientific literature. *Virtual Reality (Waltham Cross)*, 25(3), 835–861. DOI:10.1007/s10055-020-00489-9

Peng, X., & Ma, X. (2020). Pythagorean fuzzy multi-criteria decision making method based on CODAS with new score function. *Journal of Intelligent & Fuzzy Systems*, 38(3), 3307–3318. DOI:10.3233/JIFS-190043

PenjIšević, A., Sančanin, B., & Bogdanova, M. (2023). AN ETHICS CRISIS IN VIRTUAL MEDIA SPACE. *Social Informatics Journal*, 2(1), 7–13. DOI:10.58898/sij.v2i1.07-13

Persky, S., & Eccleston, C. P. (2011). Medical student bias and care recommendations for an obese versus non-obese virtual patient. *International Journal of Obesity*, 35(5), 728–735. DOI:10.1038/ijo.2010.173 PMID:20820169

Persky, S., & McBride, C. M. (2009). Immersive virtual environment technology: A promising tool for future social and behavioral genomics research and practice. *Health Communication*, 24(8), 677–682. DOI:10.1080/10410230903263982 PMID:20183376

Peterson, A., Charles, V., Yeung, D., & Coyle, K. (2021). The health equity framework: A science-and justice-based model for public health researchers and practitioners. *Health Promotion Practice*, 22(6), 741–746. DOI:10.1177/1524839920950730 PMID:32814445

Piaget, J. (1970). *Piaget's theory* (Vol. 1). Wiley.

Piaget, J. (1974). *Understanding causality.(Trans. D. & M. Miles)*. WW Norton.

Pickering, B., Bartholomew, R., Nouri Janian, M., López Moreno, B., & Surridge, M. (2020). Ask me no questions: Increasing empirical evidence for a qualitative approach to technology acceptance. In *Human-Computer Interaction. Design and User Experience* (pp. 125–136). Springer International Publishing.

Pillai, J. S., Schmidt, C., & Richir, S. (2013). Achieving presence through evoked reality. *Frontiers in Psychology*, 4, 86. DOI:10.3389/fpsyg.2013.00086 PMID:23550234

Piovesan, S. D., Passerino, L. M., & Pereira, A. S. (2012). Virtual Reality as a Tool in the Education. *International Association for Development of the Information Society*. https://eric.ed.gov/?id=ED542830

Piragauta, J. A. R., & De Oliveira, J. M. (2023). Do Ethics and Values Play a Role in Virtual Education? A Study on the Perception of Students and Teachers. *Journal of Academic Ethics*, 21(2), 343–356. DOI:10.1007/s10805-022-09459-z PMID:36247220

Plotzky, C., Lindwedel, U., Bejan, A., König, P., & Kunze, C. (2021). Virtual Reality in healthcare skills training: The effects of presence on acceptance and increase of knowledge. *I-Com*, 20(1), 73–83. DOI:10.1515/icom-2021-0008

Pollard, K. A., Oiknine, A. H., Files, B. T., Sinatra, A. M., Patton, D., Ericson, M., Thomas, J., & Khooshabeh, P. (2020). Level of immersion affects spatial learning in virtual environments: Results of a three-condition within-subjects study with long intersession intervals. *Virtual Reality (Waltham Cross)*, 24(2), 783–796. DOI:10.1007/s10055-019-00411-y

Poutiainen, A., & Krzywacki, H. (2023). Virtual reality in pre-service teacher education: Challenges of realization in music education. *International Conference on Education and New Developments END2023*, (pp. 330–334). Research Portal. https://researchportal.helsinki.fi/files/275544512/Poutiainen_Krzywacki_VR_in_pre_service_teacher_education_2023_END.pdf

Powers, M. B., & Emmelkamp, P. M. G. (2008). Virtual reality exposure therapy for anxiety disorders: A meta-analysis. *Journal of Anxiety Disorders*, 22(3), 561–569. DOI:10.1016/j.janxdis.2007.04.006 PMID:17544252

Predescu, S.-L., Caramihai, S. I., & Moisescu, M.-A. (2023). Impact of VR application in an academic context. *Applied Sciences (Basel, Switzerland)*, 13(8), 4748. DOI:10.3390/app13084748

Priatna, T., Maylawati, D., Sugilar, H., & Ramdhani, M. (2020). The key success factors for implementing e-learning in higher education. *International Journal of Emerging Learning Technologies*, 15(17), 101–114. DOI:10.3991/ijet.v15i17.14293

Program-ace. (2022). *Metaverse in Unity vs. Unreal: Clash of Engines*. Program-ace. https://program-ace.com/blog/metaverse-unity-vs-unreal/

Pyae, A., Ravyse, W., Luimula, M., Pizarro-Lucas, E., Sanchez, P. L., Dorado-Diaz, I. P., & Thaw, A. K. (2023). Exploring user experience and usability in a metaverse learning environment for students: A Usability Study of the Artificial Intelligence, Innovation, and Society (AIIS). *Electronics (Basel)*, 12(20), 4283. DOI:10.3390/electronics12204283

Qayyum, A., Butt, M. A., Ali, H., Usman, M., Halabi, O., Al-Fuqaha, A., Abbasi, Q. H., Imran, M. A., & Qadir, J. (2024). Secure and trustworthy artificial intelligence-extended reality (AI-XR) for metaverses. *ACM Computing Surveys*, 56(7), 1–38. DOI:10.1145/3614426

Qorbani, H. S., Abdinejad, M., Arya, A., & Joslin, C. (2022). Improving accessibility of elevation control in an immersive virtual environment. *2022 IEEE International Conference on Artificial Intelligence and Virtual Reality (AIVR)*, (pp. 26–35). IEEE. https://ieeexplore.ieee.org/abstract/document/10024457/

Quail, M., Brundage, S. B., Spitalnick, J., Allen, P. J., & Beilby, J. (2016). Student self-reported communication skills, knowledge and confidence across standardised patient, virtual and traditional clinical learning environments. *BMC Medical Education*, 16(1), 1–12. DOI:10.1186/s12909-016-0577-5 PMID:26919838

Qu, Z., Lau, C. W., Simoff, S. J., Kennedy, P. J., Nguyen, Q. V., & Catchpoole, D. R. (2022). Review of innovative immersive technologies for healthcare applications. *Innovations in Digital Health, Diagnostics, and Biomarkers*, 2(2022), 27–39. DOI:10.36401/IDDB-21-04

Rahayu, A., Sulastri, S., Wibowo, L. A., & Gaffar, V. (2022). Effect of technology readiness towards acceptance technology in using information system. *Proceedings of the 6th Global Conference on Business, Management, and Entrepreneurship (GCBME 2021)*. IEEE. DOI:10.2991/aebmr.k.220701.101

Rajendra, P., Kumari, M., Rani, S., Dogra, N., Boadh, R., Kumar, A., & Dahiya, M. (2022). Impact of artificial intelligence on civilization: Future perspectives. *Materials Today: Proceedings*, 56, 252–256. DOI:10.1016/j.matpr.2022.01.113

Ramos, M. (2024). Emerging Technologies in Radiotherapy: Advances in Health Literacy and Healthcare Practice. *Transformative Approaches to Patient Literacy and Healthcare Innovation*, (pp. 89-110). Research Gate.

Rani, P., Chen, S. M., & Mishra, A. R. (2023). Multiple attribute decision making based on MAIRCA, standard deviation-based method, and Pythagorean fuzzy sets. *Information Sciences*, 644, 119274. DOI:10.1016/j.ins.2023.119274

Rani, P., Mishra, A. R., Pardasani, K. R., Mardani, A., Liao, H., & Streimikiene, D. (2019). A novel VIKOR approach based on entropy and divergence measures of Pythagorean fuzzy sets to evaluate renewable energy technologies in India. *Journal of Cleaner Production*, 238, 117936. DOI:10.1016/j.jclepro.2019.117936

Rani, P., Mishra, A. R., Rezaei, G., Liao, H., & Mardani, A. (2020). Extended Pythagorean fuzzy TOPSIS method based on similarity measure for sustainable recycling partner selection. *International Journal of Fuzzy Systems*, 22(2), 735–747. DOI:10.1007/s40815-019-00689-9

Ratnam, T. (2023). Exploring the notion of inclusivity as facilitating students' ontological engagement for personally relevant learning. *European Journal of Education*, 58(2), 277–288. DOI:10.1111/ejed.12552

Rauschnabel, P. A., Felix, R., Hinsch, C., Shahab, H., & Alt, F. (2022). What is XR? Towards a framework for augmented and virtual reality. *Computers in Human Behavior*, 133, 107289. DOI:10.1016/j.chb.2022.107289

Ravichandran, R., & Mahapatra, J. (2023). Virtual Reality in vocational education and training: Challenges and possibilities. *Journal of Digital Learning and Education*, 3(1), 25–31. DOI:10.52562/jdle.v3i1.602

Remolar, I., Rebollo, C., & Fernández-Moyano, J. A. (2021). Learning History Using Virtual and Augmented Reality. *Computers*, 10(11), 146. DOI:10.3390/computers10110146

Richardson, H., Goldsamt, L. A., Simmons, J., Gilmartin, M., & Jeffries, P. R. (2014). Increasing faculty capacity: Findings from an evaluation of simulation clinical teaching. *Nursing Education Perspectives*, 35(5), 308–314. DOI:10.5480/14-1384 PMID:25291926

Riesen, M., Hoekman, J., & Björkelund, K. (2023). *Global Development of Nurse Anesthesia Education from Mid-Nineteenth Century into Today's Advanced Nursing Practice Nurse Practitioners and Nurse Anesthetists: The Evolution of the Global Roles*. Springer.

Rishard, M. A. M., Jayasekara, S. L., Ekanayake, E., Wickramathilake, K., Reyal, S., Manathunga, K., & Wickramarathne, J. (2022). Adaptivo: A Personalized Adaptive E-Learning System based on Learning Styles and Prior Knowledge. *2022 Seventh International Conference on Informatics and Computing (ICIC)*, (pp. 1–9). IEEE. https://ieeexplore.ieee.org/abstract/document/10007006/

Rizzo, A., Parsons, T. D., Lange, B., Kenny, P., Buckwalter, J. G., Rothbaum, B., Difede, J. A., Frazier, J., Newman, B., Williams, J., & Reger, G. (2011). Virtual Reality Goes to War: A Brief Review of the Future of Military Behavioral Healthcare. *Journal of Clinical Psychology in Medical Settings*, 18(2), 176–187. DOI:10.1007/s10880-011-9247-2 PMID:21553133

Roberts, L. D., & Allen, P. J. (2015). Exploring ethical issues associated with using online surveys in educational research. *Educational Research and Evaluation*, 21(2), 95–108. DOI:10.1080/13803611.2015.1024421

Roberts, T., & Hernandez, K. (2019). Digital Access is not Binary: The 5'A's of Technology Access in the Philippines. *The Electronic Journal on Information Systems in Developing Countries*, 85(4), e12084. Advance online publication. DOI:10.1002/isd2.12084

Rodríguez, J. H., de Cortez, M. H., Gómez, J. L., Pérez, J. L., & Huuskonen, A. (2024). *3.4 Professional Growth in Nursing Education*. SmartNurse.

Rogers, E. M. (1962). *Diffusion of innovations*. Free Press.

Romero-Sanchez, D., & Barrios, D. (2022). Technological acceptance of virtual platforms in university students: An analysis in times of pandemic. *IEEE Revista Iberoamericana de Technologias del Aprendizaje*, 17(1), 17–20. DOI:10.1109/RITA.2022.3149782

Rong, Q., Lian, Q., & Tang, T. (2022). Research on the Influence of AI and VR Technology for Students' Concentration and Creativity. *Frontiers in Psychology*, 13, 767689. Advance online publication. DOI:10.3389/fpsyg.2022.767689 PMID:35401322

Roser, D., Nagl, S., & Ebigbo, A. (2024). Navigating the Learning Landscape: Comprehensive Training in Third Space Endoscopy Training, Techniques, and Practical Recommendations. *Best Practice & Research. Clinical Gastroenterology*, 71, 101918. DOI:10.1016/j.bpg.2024.101918 PMID:39209422

Ross, M. D. (2003). The evolution of concepts of vestibular peripheral information processing: Toward the dynamic, adaptive, parallel processing macular model. *Acta Oto-Laryngologica*, 123(7), 784–794. DOI:10.1080/00016480310000719 PMID:14575392

Rossoni, M., Spadoni, E., Carulli, M., Barone, C., Colombo, G., & Bordegoni, M. (2024). Virtual Reality in Education to Enable Active Learning and Hands-on Experience. *Computer-Aided Design and Applications*, 21(2), 258–269.

Rouleau, G., Gagnon, M.-P., Côté, J., Payne-Gagnon, J., Hudson, E., & Dubois, C.-A. (2017). Impact of information and communication technologies on nursing care: Results of an overview of systematic reviews. *Journal of Medical Internet Research*, 19(4), e122. DOI:10.2196/jmir.6686 PMID:28442454

Roussou, M. (2004). Learning by doing and learning through play: An exploration of interactivity in virtual environments for children. *Computers in Entertainment*, 2(1), 10–10. DOI:10.1145/973801.973818

Roussou, M., Oliver, M., & Slater, M. (2006). The virtual playground: An educational virtual reality environment for evaluating interactivity and conceptual learning. *Virtual Reality (Waltham Cross)*, 10(3–4), 227–240. DOI:10.1007/s10055-006-0035-5

Routh, D. K. (1994). *Clinical psychology since 1917: Science, practice and organization*. Springer Science & Business Media. DOI:10.1007/978-1-4757-9712-1

Russell, M. (2022). *Statistics in Natural Resources: Applications with R*. Chapman and Hall/CRC. DOI:10.1201/9781003285809

Rutkowski, S., Kiper, P., Cacciante, L., Cieslik, B., Mazurek, J., Turolla, A., & Szczepanska-Gieracha, J. (2020). Use of virtual reality-based training in different fields of rehabilitation: A systematic review and meta-analysis. *Journal of Rehabilitation Medicine*, 52(11), 1–16. DOI:10.2340/16501977-2755 PMID:33073855

Ryan, E., & Poole, C. (2019). Impact of virtual learning environment on students' satisfaction, engagement, recall, and retention. *Journal of Medical Imaging and Radiation Sciences*, 50(3), 408–415. DOI:10.1016/j.jmir.2019.04.005 PMID:31229502

Ryan, G. V., Callaghan, S., Rafferty, A., Higgins, M. F., Mangina, E., & McAuliffe, F. (2022). Learning outcomes of immersive technologies in health care student education: Systematic review of the literature. *Journal of Medical Internet Research*, 24(2), e30082. DOI:10.2196/30082 PMID:35103607

Ryan, M.-L. (1999). Immersion vs. interactivity: Virtual reality and literary theory. *SubStance*, 28(2), 110–137. DOI:10.1353/sub.1999.0015

Ryder, M., Browne, F., Curtin, M., Furlong, E., Connolly, M., Larkin, J., & Zampiero, N. (2024). *A Report of the Review of Undergraduate Nursing and Midwifery Curriculum leading to Registration in Ireland*. Research Gate.

S.V. S., P., A., & K.R., R. (2023). Practical case studies on human-computer interaction. In S. Bhatia Khan, S. Namasudra, S. Chandna, A. Mashat, & F. Xhafa (Eds.), *Innovations in Artificial Intelligence and Human-Computer Interaction in the Digital Era* (pp. 233–254). Elsevier. DOI:10.1016/B978-0-323-99891-8.00007-3

Sadowski, W., & Stanney, K. (2002). Presence in virtual environments. In *Handbook of virtual environments* (pp. 831–846). CRC Press. https://www.taylorfrancis.com/chapters/edit/10.1201/9780585399102-51/presence-virtual-environments-wallace-sadowski-kay-stanney

Sagnier, C., Loup-Escande, E., Lourdeaux, D., Thouvenin, I., & Valléry, G. (2020). User acceptance of virtual reality: An extended technology acceptance model. *International Journal of Human-Computer Interaction*, 36(11), 993–1007. DOI:10.1080/10447318.2019.1708612

Sahin, I. (2006). Detailed review of Rogers' diffusion of innovations theory and educational technology-related studies based on Rogers' theory. *The Turkish Online Journal of Educational Technology*, 5(2), 1–10.

Sahu, M., Gupta, R., Ambasta, R. K., & Kumar, P. (2024). IoT-driven augmented reality and virtual reality systems in neurological sciences. *Internet of Things : Engineering Cyber Physical Human Systems*, 25, 101098. DOI:10.1016/j.iot.2024.101098

Saini, S. S., Malhi, S. S., Saro, B. K., Khan, M. S., & Kaur, A. (2022). Virtual reality: A survey of enabling technologies and its applications in IoT. *2022 International Conference on Electronics and Renewable Systems (ICEARS)*. IEEE. DOI:10.1109/ICEARS53579.2022.9752424

Sakai, D., Joyce, K., Sugimoto, M., Horikita, N., Hiyama, A., Sato, M., Devitt, A., & Watanabe, M. (2020). Augmented, virtual and mixed reality in spinal surgery: A real-world experience. *Journal of Orthopaedic Surgery (Hong Kong)*, 28(3), 2309499020952698. DOI:10.1177/2309499020952698 PMID:32909902

Sakhri, S. (2022). Cancer and Virtual Reality Vr, the Great Challenge of The Century. *Cancer and Virtual Reality Vr, the Great Challenge of The Century*. https://doi.org/DOI:10.31579/2692-9392/0101

Sakhri, S., & Boulhart, É. (2021). CANCER AND VIRTUAL REALITY VR, THE GREAT CHALLENGE OF THE CENTURY. *Archives of Medical Case Reports and Case Study*, 5(1), 01–07. DOI:10.31579/2692-9392/101

Saric, J., Aerts, A., Anne, M., Barboza, J., Boch, J., Dashdorj, N., & Rollemberg, S. M. S. (2024). Assessing the contributions of an urban population health initiative to shift political priority towards cardiovascular health: Three case studies from Brazil, Mongolia and Senegal. *BMC Health Services Research*, 24(1), 16. DOI:10.1186/s12913-023-10432-8 PMID:38178108

Sarkar, B., & Biswas, A. (2022). A multi-criteria decision making approach for strategy formulation using Pythagorean fuzzy logic. *Expert Systems: International Journal of Knowledge Engineering and Neural Networks*, 39(1), e12802. DOI:10.1111/exsy.12802

Satell, G. (2017). *Mapping innovation: a playbook for navigating a disruptive age*. McGraw-Hill.

Scavarelli, A., Arya, A., & Teather, R. J. (2020). Virtual reality and augmented reality in social learning spaces: A literature review. *Virtual Reality (Waltham Cross)*, 25(1), 257–277. DOI:10.1007/s10055-020-00444-8

Schoech, D., & Helton, D. (2002). Qualitative and Quantitative Analysis of a Course Taught via Classroom and Internet Chatroom. *Qualitative Social Work: Research and Practice*, 1(1), 111–124. DOI:10.1177/1473325002001001748

Schröder-Dering, C., Zachmann, G., & Weller, R. (2022). Dynparity: Dynamic disparity adjustment to avoid stereo window violations on stationary stereoscopic displays. *Computer Animation and Virtual Worlds*, 33(6), e2099. DOI:10.1002/cav.2099

Schwingrouber, J., Bryant-Lukosius, D., Kilpatrick, K., Mayen, S., & Colson, S. (2024). Evaluation of the implementation of advanced practice nursing roles in France: A multiple case study. *Journal of Advanced Nursing*, 80(3), 977–992. DOI:10.1111/jan.15840 PMID:37658619

Seetohul, J., Shafiee, M., & Sirlantzis, K. (2023). Augmented reality (AR) For surgical robotic and autonomous systems: State of the art, challenges, and solutions. *Sensors (Basel)*, 23(13), 6202. DOI:10.3390/s23136202 PMID:37448050

Seilkhan, A., Abdrassulova, Z., Erkaebaeva, M., Soltan, R., Makhambetov, M., & Ydyrys, A. (2022). Problems of distance education in Kazakhstan during the COVID-19 pandemic. *World Journal on Educational Technology: Current Issues*, 14(2), 380–389. DOI:10.18844/wjet.v14i2.6913

Serin, H. (2020). Virtual reality in education from the perspective of teachers. *Amazonia Investiga*, 9(26), 291–303. DOI:10.34069/AI/2020.26.02.33

Shafique, R., Aljedaani, W., Rustam, F., Lee, E., Mehmood, A., & Choi, G. S. (2023). Role of Artificial Intelligence in Online Education: A Systematic Mapping Study. *IEEE Access : Practical Innovations, Open Solutions*, 11, 52570–52584. DOI:10.1109/ACCESS.2023.3278590

Shahzad, R., & Gorur, R. (2024). Actor-Network Theory: A material-semiotic approach to policy analysis. *AnalysingEducational Policy*, 157–170. Routledge.

Shankar, A. U., Tewari, V., Rahman, M., Mishra, A., & Bajaj, K. K. (2023). Impact of virtual reality (Vr) and augmented reality (Ar) in education. *Tuijin Jishu/Journal of Propulsion Technology, 44*(4), 1310–1318.

Sharma, D. K., Khera, A., & Singh, D. (2020). Using Artificial Intelligence to Bring Accurate Real-Time Simulation to Virtual Reality. *Advanced Computational Intelligence Techniques for Virtual Reality in Healthcare*, (pp. 141-163). Research Gate.

Shaukat, S. M. (2023). Exploring the Potential of Augmented Reality (AR) and Virtual Reality (VR) in Education. *International Journal of Advanced Research in Science. Tongxin Jishu.*

Shin, D. (2018). Empathy and embodied experience in virtual environment: To what extent can virtual reality stimulate empathy and embodied experience? *Computers in Human Behavior*, 78, 64–73. DOI:10.1016/j.chb.2017.09.012

Sholihin, M., Sari, R. C., Yuniarti, N., & Ilyana, S. (2020). A new way of teaching business ethics: The evaluation of virtual reality-based learning media. *International Journal of Management Education*, 18(3), 1–13. DOI:10.1016/j.ijme.2020.100428

Shorey, S., & Ng, E. D. (2021). The use of virtual reality simulation among nursing students and registered nurses: A systematic review. *Nurse Education Today*, 98, 98. DOI:10.1016/j.nedt.2020.104662 PMID:33203545

Shtaleva, N. R., Derkho, M. A., Pribytova, O. S., & Shamina, S. V. (2021). Distant learning: Challenges and risks of 2020. *IOP Conference Series. Earth and Environmental Science*, 699(1), 012026. DOI:10.1088/1755-1315/699/1/012026

Silver, B. R. (2023). Major transitions: How college students interpret the process of changing fields of study. *Higher Education*. DOI:10.1007/s10734-023-01050-8 PMID:37362756

Simon-Liedtke, J. T., & Baraas, R. C. (2022). The need for universal design of eXtended Reality (XR) technology in primary and secondary education: identifying opportunities, challenges, and knowledge gaps from the literature.*Paper presented at the International Conference on Human-Computer Interaction*. Springer. DOI:10.1007/978-3-031-06015-1_9

Singh, H., Praveena, K. V. S., Raja, M., Kumar, T., & Tongkachok, K. (2022). Adaptive 3D and VFX Films Virtual Learning Environments. *2022 5th International Conference on Contemporary Computing and Informatics (IC3I)*, (pp. 1129–1134). IEEE. https://ieeexplore.ieee.org/abstract/document/10073177/

Singh, A., Ferry, D., Ramakrishnan, A., & Balasubramanian, S. (2020). Using Virtual Reality in Biomedical Engineering Education. *Journal of Biomechanical Engineering*, 142(11), 111013. DOI:10.1115/1.4048005 PMID:32747925

Singh, V., & Thurman, A. (2019). How Many Ways Can We Define Online Learning? A Systematic Literature Review of Definitions of Online Learning (1988-2018). *American Journal of Distance Education*, 33(4), 289–306. DOI:10.1080/08923647.2019.1663082

Sipilä, J. (2020). *Benefits and challenges of adopting virtual reality in primary education*. [Bachelor's Thesis in Information Processing Science, University of Oulu].

Skulmowski, A. (2023). Ethical issues of educational virtual reality. *Computers & Education: X Reality, 2*, 100023.

Skulmowski, A. (2023). Ethical issues of educational virtual reality. *Computers & Education: X Reality, 2*, 100023. DOI:10.1016/j.cexr.2023.100023

Slade, S., & Prinsloo, P. (2013). Learning analytics: Ethical issues and dilemmas. *The American Behavioral Scientist*, 57(10), 1510–1529. DOI:10.1177/0002764213479366

Slater, M., Khanna, P., Mortensen, J., & Yu, I. (2009). Visual realism enhances realistic response in an immersive virtual environment. *IEEE Computer Graphics and Applications*, 29(3), 76–84. DOI:10.1109/MCG.2009.55 PMID:19642617

Slater, M., & Sanchez-Vives, M. V. (2016). Enhancing our lives with immersive virtual reality. *Frontiers in Robotics and AI*, 3, 74. DOI:10.3389/frobt.2016.00074

Slater, M., & Wilbur, S. (2019). *A framework for immersive virtual environments (five): Speculations on the future of virtual reality*. Springer.

Smith, M. B. (2021, January 3). *Virtual reality headsets: A buying guide*. BH Photo Video. https://www.bhphotovideo.com/explora/computers/buying-guide/virtual-reality-headset-a-buying-guide

Smith, A. (2020). Virtual reality in education: The promises and challenges of a novel technology. *Computers & Education*, 144, 103688.

Smith, J. W. (2015). Immersive virtual environment technology to supplement environmental perception, preference and behavior research: A review with applications. *International Journal of Environmental Research and Public Health*, 12(9), 11486–11505. DOI:10.3390/ijerph120911486 PMID:26378565

Soliman, M., Pesyridis, A., Dalaymani-Zad, D., Gronfula, M., & Kourmpetis, M. (2021). The application of virtual reality in engineering education. *Applied Sciences (Basel, Switzerland)*, 11(6), 2879. Advance online publication. DOI:10.3390/app11062879

Song, C., Shin, S. Y., & Shin, K. S. (2023). Optimizing foreign language learning in virtual reality: A comprehensive theoretical framework based on constructivism and cognitive load theory (VR-CCL). *Applied Sciences (Basel, Switzerland)*, 13(23), 12557. DOI:10.3390/app132312557

Son, M., & Han, K. (2011). Beyond the technology adoption: Technology readiness effects on post-adoption behavior. *Journal of Business Research*, 64(11), 1178–1182. DOI:10.1016/j.jbusres.2011.06.019

Southgate, E., Smith, S. P., Cividino, C., Saxby, S., Kilham, J., Eather, G., Scevak, J., Summerville, D., Buchanan, R., & Bergin, C. (2019). Embedding immersive virtual reality in classrooms: Ethical, organisational and educational lessons in bridging research and practice. *International Journal of Child-Computer Interaction*, 19, 19–29. DOI:10.1016/j.ijcci.2018.10.002

Souza, A. M. C., Manzolli, J., Campos, C. D. S., & Rennó-Costa, C. (2022). Playing the Hypercube–Using Augmented Reality to Enhance a Multimodal Musical Performance. Paper presented at *the Proceedings of the 24th Symposium on Virtual and Augmented Reality*. ACM. DOI:10.1145/3604479.3604530

Sox, H. C., Higgins, M. C., Owens, D. K., & Schmidler, G. S. (2024). *Medical decision making*. John Wiley & Sons. DOI:10.1002/9781119627876

Spike, J., Xie, Y., Spike, J., & Xie, Y. (2025). *Using VR for Collaborative Learning: A Theoretical and Practical Lens.* IGI Global. Https://Services.Igi-Global.Com/Resolvedoi/Resolve.Aspx?Doi=10.4018/978-1-6684-7366-5.Ch040

Srivastava, K., Chaudhury, S., & Das, R. (2014). Virtual reality applications in mental health: Challenges and perspectives. *Industrial Psychiatry Journal*, 23(2), 83. DOI:10.4103/0972-6748.151666 PMID:25788795

Stachoň, Z., Kubíček, P., Málek, F., Krejčí, M., & Herman, L. (2018). The role of Hue and realism in virtual reality. *7th International Conference on Cartography and GIS.(Jun. 2018)*, 932–941. https://iccgis2018.cartography-gis.com/7ICCGIS_Proceedings/7_ICCGIS_2018%20(104).pdf

Stanica, I.-C., Moldoveanu, F., Portelli, G.-P., Dascalu, M.-I., Moldoveanu, A., & Ristea, M. G. (2020). Flexible Virtual Reality System for Neurorehabilitation and Quality of Life Improvement. *Sensors (Basel)*, 20(21), 6045. Advance online publication. DOI:10.3390/s20216045 PMID:33114272

Starks, A. C., & Reich, S. M. (2023). *"What about special ed?":* Barriers and enablers for teaching with technology in special education. *Computers and Education, 193.* DOI:10.1016/j.compedu.2022.104665

Stavroulia K. E. Christofi M. Baka E. Michael-Grigoriou D. Magnenat-Thalmann N. & Lanitis A. (2019). Assessing the emotional impact of virtual reality-based teacher training. *The International Journal of Information and Learning Technology*, 192–217.

Steindorff, J.-V., Redlich, L.-M., Paulicke, D., & Jahn, P. (2024). Use and Design of Virtual Reality–Supported Learning Scenarios in the Vocational Qualification of Nursing Professionals: Scoping Review. *JMIR Serious Games*, 12, e53356. DOI:10.2196/53356 PMID:38976873

Stenseth, H. V., Steindal, S. A., Solberg, M. T., Ølnes, M. A., Mohallem, A., Sørensen, A. L., & Riegel, F. (2022). Simulation-based learning supported by technology to enhance critical thinking in nursing students: Protocol for a scoping review. *JMIR Research Protocols*, 11(4), e36725. DOI:10.2196/36725 PMID:35373777

Stoll, K. H., Downe, S., Edmonds, J., Gross, M. M., Malott, A., McAra-Couper, J., & Team, I. S. (2020). A survey of university students' preferences for midwifery care and community birth options in 8 high-income countries. *Journal of Midwifery & Women's Health*, 65(1), 131–141. DOI:10.1111/jmwh.13069 PMID:31957228

Stonum, R. (1998). *A survey of immersive technology for maintenance evaluations*. Defense Technical Information Center. DOI:10.21236/ADA349708

Stoumpos, A. I., Kitsios, F., & Talias, M. A. (2023). Digital transformation in healthcare: Technology acceptance and its applications. *International Journal of Environmental Research and Public Health*, 20(4), 3407. DOI:10.3390/ijerph20043407 PMID:36834105

Strati, A. D., Schmidt, J. A., & Maier, K. S. (2017). Perceived challenge, teacher support, and teacher obstruction as predictors of student engagement. *Journal of Educational Psychology*, 109(1), 131–147. DOI:10.1037/edu0000108

Sudharson, D., Malik, R., Sathya, R. R., Vaishali, V., Balavedhaa, S., & Gautham, S. (2024). A Novel Adaptive Framework for Immersive Learning Using VR in Education. *Transforming Education with Virtual Reality*, 1-26.

Sumardani, D., & Lin, C.-H. (2023). *Investigating the Factor that Influences the Implementation of Virtual Reality for Science Learning*. Research Square. https://www.researchsquare.com/article/rs-2737402/latest

Sun, Y., Pandita, S., Madden, J., Kim, B., Holmes, N. G., & Won, A. S. (2023). Exploring Interaction, Movement and Video Game Experience in an Educational VR Experience. *Extended Abstracts of the 2023 CHI Conference on Human Factors in Computing Systems*, (pp. 1–6). ACM. DOI:10.1145/3544549.3585882

Sundar, S. S., Oeldorf-Hirsch, A., & Garga, A. (2008). A cognitive-heuristics approach to understanding presence in virtual environments. *PRESENCE 2008: Proceedings of the 11th Annual International Workshop on Presence*, (pp. 219–228). Research Gate.

Sun, S., Lee, P. C., Law, R., & Hyun, S. S. (2020). An investigation of the moderating effects of current job position level and hotel work experience between technology readiness and technology acceptance. *International Journal of Hospitality Management*, 90(102633), 102633. DOI:10.1016/j.ijhm.2020.102633

Sun, Y., & Li, J. (2023). User Interface Design and Interactive Experience Based on Virtual Reality. *Computer-Aided Design and Applications*, 184–195. DOI:10.14733/cadaps.2023.S13.184-195

Suresh, S., & Natarajan, E. (2024). Additive Manufacturing for a Sustainable Production: Materials, Processes, and Impact. In *Futuristic Technology for Sustainable Manufacturing* (pp. 1–16). IGI Global. DOI:10.4018/979-8-3693-1862-1.ch001

Suresh, S., Kumar, P., Yuvaraj, T., Velmurugan, D., & Natarajan, E. (2024). 4 Adoptability of additive manufacturing process: design perceptive. In A. Kumar, P. Kumar, N. Sharma, & A. K. Srivastava (Eds.), *3D Printing Technologies* (pp. 77–94). De Gruyter. DOI:10.1515/9783111215112-004

Suresh, S., Natarajan, E., Boopathi, S., & Kumar, P. (2024). 8 Processing of smart materials by additive manufacturing and 4D printing. In A. Kumar, P. Kumar, N. Sharma, & A. K. Srivastava (Eds.), *3D Printing Technologies* (pp. 181–196). De Gruyter. https://doi.org/DOI:10.1515/9783111215112-008k

Syamlan, A., Fathurachman, , Denis, K., Vander Poorten, E., Pramujati, B., & Tjahjowidodo, T. (2022). Haptic/virtual reality orthopedic surgical simulators: A literature review. *Virtual Reality (Waltham Cross)*, 26(4), 1795–1825. DOI:10.1007/s10055-022-00666-y

Sykownik, P., Karaosmanoglu, S., Emmerich, K., Steinicke, F., & Masuch, M. (2023). VR Almost There: Simulating Co-located Multiplayer Experiences in Social Virtual Reality. *Proceedings of the 2023 CHI Conference on Human Factors in Computing Systems*, (pp. 1–19). ACM. DOI:10.1145/3544548.3581230

Tahsin, F., Armas, A., Kirakalaprathapan, A., Kadu, M., Sritharan, J., & Steele Gray, C. (2023). Information and communications technologies enabling integrated primary care for patients with complex care needs: Scoping review. *Journal of Medical Internet Research*, 25, e44035. DOI:10.2196/44035 PMID:37074779

Takian, A., Raoofi, A., & Haghighi, H. (2022). *COVID 19 pandemic: The fears and hopes for SDG 3, with focus on prevention and control of noncommunicable diseases (SDG 3.4) and universal health coverage (SDG 3.8) COVID-19 and the Sustainable Development Goals*. Elsevier.

Tang, H. (2021). Applied research of VR technology in physical education. *The International Journal of Electronic Engineering Education*. .DOI:10.1177/00207209211007774

Tarasova, L., Pozdeeva, T., & Baranova, A. (2022). Study of the readiness of students to use VR technologies during a course in engineering geometry and computer graphics. *2022 VI International Conference on Information Technologies in Engineering Education (Inforino)*. IEEE. DOI:10.1109/Inforino53888.2022.9782995

Termos, M. H. (2013). The Effects of the Classroom Performance System on Student Participation, Attendance, and Achievement. *International Journal on Teaching and Learning in Higher Education*, 25(1), 66–78.

Thakur, P., Kizielewicz, B., Gandotra, N., Shekhovtsov, A., Saini, N., & Sałabun, W. (2022). The group decision-making using Pythagorean fuzzy entropy and the complex proportional assessment. *Sensors (Basel)*, 22(13), 4879. DOI:10.3390/s22134879 PMID:35808377

Thangeda, A., Baratiseng, B., & Mompati, T. (2016). Education for sustainability: Quality education Is a necessity in modern day. How far do the educational institutions facilitate quality education? *Journal of Education and Practice*, 7(2), 9–17.

Theobald, K. A., Tutticci, N., Ramsbotham, J., & Johnston, S. (2021). Effectiveness of using simulation in the development of clinical reasoning in undergraduate nursing students: A systematic review. *Nurse Education in Practice*, 57, 103220. DOI:10.1016/j.nepr.2021.103220 PMID:34781195

Thirunavukarasu, A. J., Hu, M. L., Foster, W. P., Xue, K., Cehajic-Kapetanovic, J., & MacLaren, R. E. (2024). Robot-Assisted Eye Surgery: A Systematic Review of Effectiveness, Safety, and Practicality in Clinical Settings. *Translational Vision Science & Technology*, 13(6), 20–20. DOI:10.1167/tvst.13.6.20 PMID:38916880

Timotheou, S., Miliou, O., Dimitriadis, Y., Sobrino, S. V., Giannoutsou, N., Cachia, R., Monés, A. M., & Ioannou, A. (2023). Impacts of digital technologies on education and factors influencing schools' digital capacity and transformation: A literature review. *Education and Information Technologies*, 28(6), 6695–6726. DOI:10.1007/s10639-022-11431-8 PMID:36465416

Tiwari, R. G., Agarwal, A. K., & Husain, M. (2023). 13 Integration of virtual reality in the e-learning environment. *Augmented and Virtual Reality in Industry, 5*(2), 253.

Tlili, A., Huang, R., Shehata, B., Liu, D., Zhao, J., Metwally, A. H. S., Wang, H., Denden, M., Bozkurt, A., Lee, L. H., Beyoglu, D., Altinay, F., Sharma, R. C., Altinay, Z., Li, Z., Liu, J., Ahmad, F., Hu, Y., Salha, S., . . . Burgos, D. (2022). Is Metaverse in education a blessing or a curse: a combined content and bibliometric analysis. In *Smart Learning Environments* (*Vol. 9*, Issue 1). Springer. DOI:10.1186/s40561-022-00205-x

Tomyuk, O. N., Diachkova, A. V., Kiseleva, N. A., Kamka, S. V., & Nikolenko, O. I. (2022). Global trends in the education system of high-ranking countries according to PISA-2018. *Perspectives of Science and Education*, 55(1), 10–24. DOI:10.32744/pse.2022.1.1

Trade India. (2023). *DC Regulated Power Supply*. Trade India. https://www.tradeindia.com/products/d-c-regulated-power-supply-3271627.html

Triberti, S., Villani, D., & Riva, G. (2016). Unconscious goal pursuit primes attitudes towards technology usage: A virtual reality experiment. *Computers in Human Behavior*, 64, 163–172. DOI:10.1016/j.chb.2016.06.044

Tuomi, I. Cachia, Romina., Villar-Onrubia, Daniel. & European Commission. Joint Research Centre. (2023). *On the futures of technology in education : emerging trends and policy implications*. Research Gate. https://www.researchgate.net/publication/374163715_On_the_futures_of_technology_in_education_Emerging_trends_and_policy_challenges

Udeozor, C., Toyoda, R., Russo Abegão, F., & Glassey, J. (2023). Digital games in engineering education: systematic review and future trends. In *European Journal of Engineering Education* (Vol. 48, Issue 2, pp. 321–339). Taylor and Francis Ltd. DOI:10.1080/03043797.2022.2093168

Udeozor, C., Chan, P., Russo Abegão, F., & Glassey, J. (2023). Game-based assessment framework for virtual reality, augmented reality and digital game-based learning. *International Journal of Educational Technology in Higher Education*, 20(1), 36. DOI:10.1186/s41239-023-00405-6 PMID:36644670

Ullrich, S., Rausch, D., & Kuhlen, T. W. (2011). *Bimanual Haptic Simulator for Medical Training: System Architecture and Performance Measurements*. Paper presented at the EGVE/EuroVR.

Ummihusna, A., Zairul, M., Ab Jalil, H., & Sulaiman, P. S. (2024). Immersive virtual reality in experiential learning for architecture design education: An action research. *Journal of Applied Research in Higher Education*. https://www.emerald.com/insight/content/doi/10.1108/JARHE-06-2023-0266/full/html

Urech, A., Krieger, T., Chesham, A., Mast, F. W., & Berger, T. (2015). Virtual reality-based attention bias modification training for social anxiety: A feasibility and proof of concept study. *Frontiers in Psychiatry*, 6, 154. DOI:10.3389/fpsyt.2015.00154 PMID:26578986

Uzza, A. A., Hamdan, A., & Singh, A. D. (2022). Improving Equity and Inclusion in Education using Virtual and Augmented Reality in Open Distance Learning. *Tenth Pan-Commonwealth Forum Open Learn*. Research Gate. https://www.researchgate.net/profile/Aisyamariam_Abdul_Uzza2/publication/363189882_Improving_Equity_and_Inclusion_in_Education_using_Virtual_and_Augmented_Reality_in_Open_Distance_Learning/links/64490de37b3bca311ca3be3c/Improving-Equity-and-Inclusion-in-Education-using-Virtual-and-Augmented-Reality-in-Open-Distance-Learning.pdf

Valerio, J. E., Ramirez-Velandia, F., Fernandez-Gomez, M. P., Rea, N. S., & Alvarez-Pinzon, A. M. (2024). Bridging the Global Technology Gap in Neurosurgery: Disparities in Access to Advanced Tools for Brain Tumor Resection. *Neurosurgery Practice*, 5(2), e00090.

van Eck, N. J., & Waltman, L. (2017). Citation-based clustering of publications using CitNetExplorer and VOSviewer. *Scientometrics*, 111(2), 1053–1070. DOI:10.1007/s11192-017-2300-7 PMID:28490825

Vardaman, S. A., Logan, L., Davis, S. P., Sciarra, E., Doria, J. B., Baker, J., Feeney, S., Pajarillo, E. J. Y., Seibold-Simpson, S., & Bajwa, M. (2024). Addressing the Shortage of Academic Nurse Educators: Recommendations for Educational Institutions Based on Nominal Group Technique Research. *Nursing Education Perspectives*, 10(4), 1097. DOI:10.1097/01.NEP.0000000000001264 PMID:38602384

Vázquez-Calatayud, M., García-García, R., Regaira-Martínez, E., & Gómez-Urquiza, J. (2024). Real-world and game-based learning to enhance decision-making. *Nurse Education Today*, 140, 106276. DOI:10.1016/j.nedt.2024.106276 PMID:38851020

Veit, M., Capobianco, A., & Bechmann, D. (2009, November). Influence of degrees of freedom's manipulation on performances during orientation tasks in virtual reality environments. In *Proceedings of the 16th ACM Symposium on Virtual Reality Software and Technology* (pp. 51-58). ACM. DOI:10.1145/1643928.1643942

Venkatesan, M., Mohan, H., Ryan, J. R., Schürch, C. M., Nolan, G. P., Frakes, D. H., & Coskun, A. F. (2021). Virtual and augmented reality for biomedical applications. *Cell Reports Medicine*, 2(7), 100348. DOI:10.1016/j.xcrm.2021.100348 PMID:34337564

Vermooten, N., & Malan, J. (2021). Relational dynamics amongst personal resources: Consequences for employee engagement. *Sajhrm.Co.Za*, 19(0), 1–12. DOI:10.4102/sajhrm

Vetrivel, S., & Mohanasundaram, T. (2024). Breaking down walls: The influence of virtual reality on accessible healthcare delivery. *Digital Transformation in Healthcare 5.0: Volume 1: IoT, AI and Digital Twin*, 129.

Volkova, E. N. (2022). Personal characteristics of a 21st-century teacher: An analysis of empirical studies of the problem. *The Education and Science Journal*, 24(3), 126–157. DOI:10.17853/1994-5639-2022-3-126-157

Vygotsky, L. S., & Cole, M. (1978). *Mind in society: Development of higher psychological processes*. Harvard university press.

Wakefield, M., Williams, D. R., & Le Menestrel, S. (2021). *The future of nursing 2020-2030: Charting a path to achieve health equity*. National Academy of Sciences. DOI:10.17226/25982

Walsh, J., Boyle, F., Moriarty, P., Locke, A., McMahon, D., Katamreddy, S., & Riordan, D. (2019). *The development of VR expeditions for primary school learning*. Edu Learn. DOI:10.21125/edulearn.2019.2118

Walton-Roberts, M. (2023). *Global Health Worker Migration: Problems and Solutions*. Cambridge University Press. DOI:10.1017/9781009217781

Wang, , F. (2017). F., Sun, W., Yu, W., & Li, Y. (2017). A meta-analysis of the impacts of virtual reality on learning effectiveness. *World Transactions on Engineering and Technology Education*, 15(4), 261–266.

Wang, Y., Siau, K. L., & Wang, L. (2022). Metaverse and human-computer interaction: A technology framework for 3D virtual worlds. Paper presented at the *International Conference on Human-Computer Interaction*. Springer. DOI:10.1007/978-3-031-21707-4_16

Wang, P., Wu, P., Wang, J., Chi, H.-L., & Wang, X. (2018). A Critical Review of the Use of Virtual Reality in Construction Engineering Education and Training. *International Journal of Environmental Research and Public Health*, 15(6), 1204. DOI:10.3390/ijerph15061204 PMID:29890627

Wang, W.-S., Lin, C.-J., Lee, H.-Y., Wu, T.-T., & Huang, Y.-M. (2023). Feedback Mechanism in Immersive Virtual Reality Influences Physical Hands-on Task Performance and Cognitive Load. *International Journal of Human-Computer Interaction*, 1–13. DOI:10.1080/10447318.2023.2209837

Wang, Z., He, R., & Chen, K. (2020). Thermal comfort and virtual reality headsets. *Applied Ergonomics*, 85, 103066. DOI:10.1016/j.apergo.2020.103066 PMID:32174354

Wani, T. A., & Ali, S. W. (2015). Innovation Diffusion Theory: Review & Scope in the Study of Adoption of Smartphones in India. *Journal of General Management Research*, 2(2), 98–115.

Weber, S., Weibel, D., & Mast, F. W. (2021). How to get there when you are there already? Defining presence in virtual reality and the importance of perceived realism. *Frontiers in Psychology*, 12, 628298. DOI:10.3389/fpsyg.2021.628298 PMID:34025504

Webster, R. (2016). Declarative knowledge acquisition in immersive virtual learning environments. *Interactive Learning Environments*, 24(6), 1319–1333. DOI:10.1080/10494820.2014.994533

Weeks, K., Herron, E., & Buchanan, H. (2024). Aligning Simulation-Based Education With Didactic Learning in Prelicensure Baccalaureate Nursing Education. *Nurse Educator*, 49(3), 125–129. PMID:37851404

Wehrmann, F., & Zender, R. (2023). Inclusive Virtual Reality Learning: Review and Best-Fit Framework for Universal Learning. *Electronic Journal of E-Learning*, 00–00.

Wei, Z., & Yuan, M. (2023). Research on the current situation and future development trend of immersive virtual reality in the field of education. *Sustainability (Basel)*, 15(9), 7531. DOI:10.3390/su15097531

Williams, I. (2020). Contemporary application of ANT: An introduction. *Contemporary applications of actor network theory*, 1-13.

Wohlgenannt, I., Simons, A., & Stieglitz, S. (2020). Virtual Reality. *Business & Information Systems Engineering*, 62(5), 455–461. DOI:10.1007/s12599-020-00658-9

WOHM. (2023). *Benefit of early childhood education.* WOHM. https://wohum.org/the-benefits-of-early-childhood-education-and-its-effect-on-future-success/?gad_source=1&gclid=CjwKCAjwko21BhAPEiwAwfaQCIwWOmK2Kp27qFw7sAAjUItKVsCIS2XwjzgnDQNbtNJ3bLbE1H6MChoC8h4QAvD_BwE

Wu, , Lee, S. W.-Y., Chang, H.-Y., & Liang, J.-C. (2019). Current status, opportunities and challenges of augmented reality in education. *Computers & Education*, 62, 41–49. DOI:10.1016/j.compedu.2012.10.024

Xiao, J., Li, X., Qiao, H., & Liang, X. (2020). Assessing the effectiveness of virtual reality courseware for experiential learning. *2020 International Symposium on Educational Technology (ISET)*. IEEE. DOI:10.1109/ISET49818.2020.00025

Xie, H. (2023). The Applications of Interface Design and User Experience in Virtual Reality. *Highlights in Science. Engineering and Technology*, 44, 189–198.

Yadav, S. (2024). *Empowering Educators With Augmented and Virtual Reality: Integrating AR and VR for Enhanced Interactive Learning Environment Reshaping Learning with Next Generation Educational Technologies*. IGI Global. DOI:10.4018/979-8-3693-1310-7.ch005

Yager, R. R. (2013b, June) Pythagorean fuzzy subsets. In *2013 joint IFSA world congress and NAFIPS annual meeting (IFSA/NAFIPS)* (pp. 57-61). IEEE. DOI:10.1109/IFSA-NAFIPS.2013.6608375

Yager, R. R. (2013a). Pythagorean membership grades in multicriteria decision making. *IEEE Transactions on Fuzzy Systems*, 22(4), 958–965. DOI:10.1109/TFUZZ.2013.2278989

Yang, J. C., Chen, C. H., & Jeng, M. C. (2010). Integrating video-capture virtual reality technology into a physically interactive learning environment for English learning. *Computers & Education*, 55(3), 1346–1356. DOI:10.1016/j.compedu.2010.06.005

Yang, T., & Zeng, Q. (2022). Study on the design and optimization of learning environment based on artificial intelligence and virtual reality technology. *Computational Intelligence and Neuroscience*, 2022(1), 1–9. DOI:10.1155/2022/8259909 PMID:35685146

Yang, X., Cheng, P.-Y., Liu, X., & Shih, S.-P. (2022). The impact of immersive virtual reality on art education: A study of flow state, cognitive load, brain state, and motivation. *Education and Information Technologies*, 29(5), 6087–6106. DOI:10.1007/s10639-023-12041-8

Yieh, K., Chen, J.-S., & Wei, M. B. (2012). The effects of technology readiness on customer perceived value: An empirical analysis. *Journal of Family and Economic Issues*, 33(2), 177–183. DOI:10.1007/s10834-012-9314-3

Yildirim, B., Sahin-Topalcengiz, E., Arikan, G., & Timur, S. (2020). Using virtual reality in the classroom: Reflections of STEM teachers on the use of teaching and learning tools. *Journal of Education in Science, Environment and Health*, 6(3), 231–245. DOI:10.21891/jeseh.711779

Yoo, J., & Brownlee, E. A. (2020). *The past, present, and future of virtual reality in higher education Handbook of Research on Adult Learning in Higher Education*. IGI Global.

Young, B., Ellobody, E., & Hu, T. W. C. (2012). 3D Visualization of Structures Using Finite-Element Analysis in Teaching. *Journal of Professional Issues in Engineering Education and Practice*, 138(2), 131–138. DOI:10.1061/(ASCE)EI.1943-5541.0000093

Youvalari, G. Ramin. (2016). *360-Degree Panoramic Video Coding*. Research Gate. DOI:10.13140/RG.2.2.21662.25921

Yu, Y., Hao, T., Zhang, H., & Liang, Z. (2022). Informatization growth model of artificial intelligence virtual reality technology fusion education. *2022 International Conference on Artificial Intelligence of Things and Crowdsensing (AIoTCs)*. IEEE. DOI:10.1109/AIoTCs58181.2022.00060

Żammit, J. (2024). Could virtual reality be the next approach for international students learning Maltese? *Educational Technology Research and Development*. DOI:10.1007/s11423-024-10375-9

Zenva. (2023). *What is Unity? – A Top Game Engine for Video Games*. Game Dev Academy. https://gamedevacademy.org/what-is-unity/

Zhang, H., & Spiegel, B. (2024). *Introducing the Journal of Medical Extended Reality* (*Vol. 1*, pp. 1-3): Mary Ann Liebert, Inc.

Zhang, L., & Liu, G. (2023). A review of factors affecting cognitive load in immersive virtual learning environment. *2023 IEEE 12th International Conference on Educational and Information Technology (ICEIT)*, (pp. 48–52). IEEE. https://ieeexplore.ieee.org/abstract/document/10107848/

Zhang, X., Chen, Y., Hu, L., & Wang, Y. (2022). The metaverse in education: Definition, framework, features, potential applications, challenges, and future research topics. In *Frontiers in Psychology* (Vol. 13). Frontiers Media S.A., DOI:10.3389/fpsyg.2022.1016300

Zhan, T., Yin, K., Xiong, J., He, Z., & Wu, S. T. (2020). Augmented reality and virtual reality displays: Perspectives and challenges. *iScience*, 23(8), 101397. DOI:10.1016/j.isci.2020.101397 PMID:32759057

Zhou, M., Dzingirai, C., Hove, K., Chitata, T., & Mugandani, R. (2022). Adoption, use and enhancement of virtual learning during COVID-19. *Education and Information Technologies*, 27(7), 8939–8959. DOI:10.1007/s10639-022-10985-x PMID:35340535

Zigunovs, M., Mamchur, D., & Kolodinskis, A. (2023). The Use of Virtual Reality Solutions to Improve Educational Experience for IT Students. *ENVIRONMENT. TECHNOLOGIES. RESOURCES. Proceedings of the International Scientific and Practical Conference, 2*, 214–218. https://journals23.rta.lv/index.php/ETR/article/view/7219

About the Contributors

Shaik Mazhar Hussain is a member of the Faculty in the Department of Computing and Electronics Engineering at Middle East College, Muscat, Oman. He also serves as the Research Coordinator at the Centre for Research and Consultancy (CRC) at Middle East College. Dr. Hussain is a distinguished academician and researcher with a strong background in Electrical Engineering. Dr. Hussain earned his PhD in Electrical Engineering in the year 2023 from the Department of Communications Engineering, specializing in Advanced Telecommunication Technology (ATT) at the school of Electrical Engineering, Faculty of Engineering, Universiti Teknologi Malaysia (UTM), Johor Bahru, Malaysia. His doctoral research showcases his deep expertise and significant contributions to the field. Dr. Hussain's educational journey is marked by notable achievements, including being a college topper in both his undergraduate and postgraduate studies. He commenced his academic pursuit with a bachelor's degree in Electronics and Communication Engineering from Jawaharlal Nehru Technological University (JNTU), Hyderabad, in 2008. Continuing his academic excellence, he earned a master's degree in Embedded Systems from JNTU, Hyderabad, in 2012. Furthering his education, Dr. Hussain acquired a Postgraduate Certificate (PGCert) from Coventry University, United Kingdom, in 2017. His consistent academic excellence throughout his educational journey is a testament to his dedication and expertise in his field. Dr. Hussain has 15 years of teaching and research experience in his field. He has authored and published more than 30+ papers in reputable journals and more than 20+ papers in various conference proceedings . His research endeavors have been supported by numerous internal and external grants, underlining the significance and impact of his work. Dr. Shaik Mazhar Hussain has actively promoted innovation and practical applications of knowledge, exemplified by the fact that he registered four patents in collaboration with his students, two of which are currently in the final stages of examination, the remaining two patents are under review, which shows his commitment to progress the development of technology and the participation of students in real-world research. Dr. Shaik Mazhar Hussain further expanded his expertise by receiving the Professional Certificate of Competency in Fundamentals of Electric Vehicles from the Engineering Institute of Technology (EIT), West Perth, Australia. In addition to his academic and research achievements, Dr. Hussain is an active member of several professional bodies: Sr.Member IEEE, LM Network IP Austria, MISTE, FHEA-UK, MIEI, AAAI, LMISOP, MIAENG,MTSDIW, MIEOM,LMSBAO, MIACA, MAERA, LMTERA.

Vishnu Achutha Menon is an independent journalist, writer, researcher, and an Indian percussionist. He is a recipient of the Junior Scholarship the Ministry of Culture awarded. His research interests are film studies, verbal & nonverbal communication, south Asian performances, Natyasastra, media studies, media analysis techniques, Laban Movement Analysis, and Ethnomusicology.

Edidiong Elijah Akpan is a versatile professional with a wide range of specialized and academic experiences. He obtained a bachelor's degree in Biochemistry, an MBA in Business Administration, and a master's degree in Information Technology. These established a strong basis for scientific investigation and analysis. Edidiong had a prosperous career for himself in the banking industry, gaining ten years of experience there. His work in banking helped him hone his managerial, strategic planning, and operational efficiency skills, which highlights his ability to work with complicated data sets, draw conclusions, and use technology to address challenging issues. Edidiong is a researcher on artificial intelligence, machine learning, and Bioinformatics. His goal of expanding his knowledge of cutting-edge technology and positively impacting the quickly developing field of artificial intelligence is consistent with this endeavor. Edidiong is in a unique position to bridge the gap between scientific research, commercial strategy, technology innovation, and medicine because of his multidisciplinary skills and experience. He is a member of the Chartered Institute of Bankers of Nigeria (CIBN), the National Society of Black Engineers (NSBE), and the Nigeria Society of Biochemistry and Molecular Biology (NSBMB).

Bah Esseme Alain Claude is a seasoned Developer and Architect with a focus on optimizing business processes through Salesforce CRM and various other web frameworks such as Angular, React, and Node.js.. My expertise extends to mentoring aspiring tech professionals, equipping them with essential skills for a successful career. Originally trained as a medical doctor, my passion for technology led me to pursue a full-time career in the tech industry post-graduation. Since then, I have helped numerous businesses achieve significant improvements in efficiency by developing web applications and increasing their customer engagement through automation. As co-founder of PathwayToSalesforce.com, I am dedicated to delivering high-quality training programs that enhance technical capabilities. My proficiency in JavaScript, Java, HTML, and APEX, combined with my Salesforce CRM expertise, helps organizations build robust customer relationships. I am committed to professional excellence and social responsibility, blending technical expertise with mentorship and philanthropy. Additionally, I actively share knowledge through my personal blog and research articles, believing in the collective advancement of our global community.

Sreya Barik is a Diploma CSE student at Brainware University. Her research interests include AI, ML and Social Networking, contributing significantly to advancements in her field.

Elif Çaloğlu Büyükselçuk graduated from Yıldız Technical University in 1999. She took her master degree from Boğaziçi Univeristy in 2003. Her PhD degree is from Marmara University. She has working in Fenerbahçe University since 2019 as the head of the Industrial Engineering Department. Her research areas are decision making problems, supply chain management, supplier selection, water footprint, sustainability and circular economy activities.

Khalid Haruna received his B.Sc. and M.Sc. degrees in computer science from Bayero University, Kano, Nigeria, in 2011 and 2015, respectively, and the PhD degree in information systems from the University of Malaya, Malaysia, in 2018. He is currently the Deputy Dean, Faculty of Computer Science and Information Technology, Bayero University, Kano, Nigeria. He has published several journal articles and presented his research findings in many conferences. His research interests include recommender systems, Internet of Things, semantic web, big data analytics, sentiment analysis, soft set, and e-learning systems.

Shaik Asif Hussain has served Middle East College in various roles since 2015. Presently, he is a Technology Transfer officer and Assistant Professor in the Department of Electronics and Communication Engineering from January 2020 to the present. Shaik has received his PhD, M. Tech in Embedded Systems, and B. Tech degrees in Electronics and Communication Engineering from Jawaharlal Nehru Technological University, Hyderabad, respectively. In addition, he earned his post-graduation certification (PGCERT) in Academic Practices of Higher Education and Pedagogy in Teaching and Learning Mechanism from Coventry University, UK, from 2016-2017. He is currently an IEEE member. His research interests include Robotics, Biomedical Engineering, Artificial Intelligence, RFID systems, Digital signal and Image processing, wireless sensor networks, IPV6 and video communications, Blockchain technology in the healthcare industry, big data Analytics, and decision-making techniques. Shaik received two research grants in 2018 and two research grants in 2022 from The Research Council (TRC) of Oman under the block funding program. Shaik was also awarded one prestigious scholarship for his doctoral studies (2011-2013) from the All-India Council of Technical Education (A.I.C.T.E), India, under the Research Promotion Scheme for $ 16000 thanks to his highest level of achievement. During his academic career, he has supervised 16 postgraduate students and published two books, 32 journals, and 30 conference papers in renowned international journals and conferences.

Jazuli Sanusi Kazaure is an Electrical Engineer and IT Professional. He is a registered Engineer with Nigerian professional bodies. He is an expert on electrical circuit and project designs. He is a consultant who designs and supervises electrical projects in Nigeria. Jazuli is a certified Network Cabling Specialist in copper and fiber optic based systems and a certified instructor in Integrated System Voice and Messaging certified by C-Tech Inc. at Sparta, New Jersey, USA. Jazuli attended Technical School and read electrical installation as a trade; he obtained National Diploma, Higher National Diploma, Post Graduate Diploma and Master's Degree all in electrical engineering. Jazuli was awarded with a Degree of Doctor of Philosophy in Management Information Technology specialized on ICT Management Frameworks. Dr. Jazuli is an academician teaching in Polytechnic and University in Nigeria as well other Universities in West Africa. He started his teaching career from the lowest rank of Assistant Lecturer to the highest rank of Chief lecturer in Hussaini Adamu Federal Polytechnic Kazaure. He was a visiting lecturer at Jigawa State Informatics Institute, a visiting Senior Lecturer with Sule Lamido University Jigawa State, a visiting Senior Lecturer with Maryam Abacha American University of Niger Republic, an External Examiner National Open University and Digital Bridge Institute of Nigeria. Dr. Jazuli held many academic positions in Hussaini Adamu Federal Polytechnic, among others are Head of Electrical Engineering Department, Director Center for Information Technology, Director College of Engineering, Deputy Dean Student Affairs and currently Director Academic Planning and Research Development.Dr. Jazuli published 20 journal articles, presented 20 conference papers and coauthored in 23 books. He supervised many National Diploma, Higher National Diploma and Degree projects as well Master's thesis. Dr. Jazuli is happily married with children.

Narendra Kumar earned his Ph. D. from JS University, Shikohabad, India and currently working as Assistant Professor at Amity Institute of Travel & Tourism, Amity University, Noida. With 23 years of experience in travel & tourism, he has made significant contributions to the area of tourism education. Dr. Kumar has a strong interest in Business travel, tourist behaviour and visitor experiences in the field of tourism and has published extensively on related topics. In addition to his academic pursuits, Dr. Kumar is actively involved in helping young graduates of tourism and hospitality domain to help them in establishing their start-ups. He has been invited to speak at numerous conferences and seminars on tourism and related fields and his current research focuses on student mentoring. Dr. Kumar's previous works include one edited book on "Tourist Behaviour" published by Apple Academic Press, USA; one book on "Digital Marketing" and one on "Ethical Aspects of Business in Tourism".

Mohsen Mahmoudi-Dehaki is an Assistant Professor of TEFL at the Islamic Azad University of Najafabad, Iran. With over a decade of experience teaching undergraduate and postgraduate students, he has established himself as a respected educator and scholar. His research has been widely published in national and international journals, solidifying his reputation as a prominent voice in the field. Dr. Mahmoudi-Dehaki serves as a peer reviewer for several esteemed scientific journals, including RELP, ensuring the highest standards of academic rigor and integrity. His academic achievements include winning the prestigious first place in the English Writing Award in Iran, a distinction earned among all university students from state universities and institutes of higher education. His paper "COVID-19 Lingo or Covidipedia" has garnered significant attention, with over 70,000 visits, making it the most visited paper in Iranian scientific journals. This remarkable achievement underscores his significant impact on the academic community. Dr. Mahmoudi-Dehaki's research and teaching interests span a diverse range of novel branches in applied linguistics, including psycho/cognitive/neurocognitive/forensic/jury/sociocultural/ecological, and clinical linguistics. He is also well-versed in educational technology, educational psychology, and psychometrics, demonstrating his versatility and breadth of expertise in the interdisciplinary fields of education and linguistics.

Asit K. Mantry is a Professor and Head of the Department of Educational Studies, at Central Univerity of Jammu (J&K). He has more than fifteen years of teaching and administrative experience. Prof. Mantry has published more than thirty-five research papers, articles, and book chapters in various journals of national and international repute which includes peer-reviewed, UGC Care and Scopus. His areas of research interest are integral education, educational perspectives of Indian philosophy, policy analysis and educational leadership.

Ugochukwu O. Matthew, presently is an Academic scholar with Hussaini Adamu Federal Polytechnic, Nigeria, in the Department of Computer Science with specialty in AI, Big Data Science, Cloud Computing, Internet of Things, Data Mining, Multimedia and E-Learning Education. A Member of Nigeria Computer Society (NCS), Nigeria Institute of Management (NIM), International Association of Computer Science & Information Technology (IACSIT), European Alliance for Innovation(EAI) and also a member of Teaching & Education Research Association (TERA). Ugochukwu O. Matthew hold Masters in Computer Applications from Bayero University Kano, Nigeria. Ugochukwu O. Matthew had reviewed several Journals and a member of Review Board Committee of Journals Indexed by Scopus and Web of Science including IEEE Access, SN Computer Science (Springer), International Journal of Information Communication Technologies & Human Development(IJICTHD), International Journal of Business Data Communications and Networking (IJBDCN), International Journal of Cloud Applications and Computing (IJCAC). Ugochukwu O. Matthew is a cofounder of U&J Digital Consult Limited, an IT and Educational Consulting Firm in Nigeria.

Ether Emarobebh Muojekwu, (FRSPH), is a seasoned Public Health Nurse, lecturer, and researcher with a passion for improving health outcomes. Specializes in occupational health, work psychology, and health informatics, with a strong focus on integrating technology into healthcare. She holds an MSc in Public Health from the University of Bedfordshire, Luton, England, and a BNSc, in Nursing Sciences, RN,RM,& RPHN from Niger Delta University, Bayelsa State,. A PhD Candidate and a Fellow of the Royal Society for Public Health England UK, She brings a wealth of expertise to her work. She enjoys networking, music, reading, and traveling in her free time. She's enthusiastic about collaborating with tech professionals to drive innovation in health informatics, data analysis, and program management.

Nasim Nasr-Esfahani, PhD, is an Assistant Professor of TEFL at the Islamic Azad University of Isfahan (Khorasgan), Iran. She earned her PhD in TEFL at the Islamic Azad University of Isfahan, Khorasgan. She has over two decades of experience teaching undergraduate and postgraduate students in Iran. Her publications have appeared in leading international journals, such as the Australian Journal of Teacher Education. She serves as a reviewer and article editor of RELP Journal. Her areas of research and teaching interests are dynamic and evolving and span language education, generative artificial intelligence (GenAI) in education, critical thinking skills, oral and written communication skills, student engagement, advancing equity in education, brain-based teaching and learning, neurolinguistics, psycholinguistics as well as teaching and research methodologies.

Matthew Abiola Oladipupo is the Lead Data Analyst at Perch Group Ltd in Manchester, United Kingdom. He earned his Master of Science in Data Science from The University of Salford and holds a Bachelor of Technology in Electronics and Electrical Engineering, as well as a Postgraduate Diploma, from Ladoke Akintola University of Technology. As a passionate scholar in Artificial Intelligence, he brings years of experience in researching machine learning and boasts a distinguished academic profile. His expertise spans across applied statistics and data mining techniques, enabling him to develop decision-making systems for business organizations. This involves collecting extensive datasets and transforming them into actionable insights and reports, aiding organizations in strategic decision-making, business improvement, and future trend prediction

Ajibola Olaosebikan has a background in Industrial Engineering— where he honed his business, engineering and management skills. Understanding that challenges are local, and that solving them requires sustainable tailored solutions, Ajibola has three goals: to research local problems, develop globally acknowledged solution and make societal impactful by mainstreaming technical skills through teaching. Through his job exposure at Nestle and his master's degree in Applied AI and Data Science at Southampton Solent University—where he was also a Junior Data Scientist and worked collaboratively to deliver an AI-powered decision support system, he has developed capabilities in data analytics and engineering, applied artificial intelligence in business, software engineering and research in other to actualize these goals. Currently, he is pursuing the Food Market Vision (FMV) project. This project, that span areas such as route optimization, data acquisition and storage, process automation, cloud computing etc. is aimed at enhancing the core retailing processes in the Sub-Saharan Africa (Nigeria) informal food markets. Among others, this project's major objective is to ensure verified and real-time primary data and information needed to shape food policies are obtainable the source—the informal food markets. Ajibola's research interests spans across application of AI in Business, big data, data strategy, cloud computing. Ajibola's hobby is teaching and to further showcase this, he is building LearniT—a Learning Management System to educate interested users on developing end-to-end data and software projects.

Ononiwu, Chamberlyn Chisom is currently undergoing his Ph.D programme in Computer Science at Anambra State University, Uli. He holds M.Sc in Computer Science from Nnamdi Azikiwe University, Awka, B.Sc(Second Class Upper Division) in Computer Science from Michael Okpara University of Agriculture, Umudike, and a Higher National Diploma (Upper Credit) in Computer Science from Federal Polytechnic Nekede, Owerri. Ononiwu C.C lectures with Imo State Polytechnic, Omuma, in the department of Computer Science

Victoria Enemona Oseni is a passionate data scientist who just completed an MSc in Data Science from the university of Salford, Manchester United Kingdom. I have extensive experience in researching data analytics, Statistics and possess excellent communication skills in English. Having expertise in data collection, data analysis, and interpretation, I specialize in programming, data science, and Statistics. My aim is to develop detection and decision-making software for organizations that enables them to make informed business decisions, predict market trends, and improve their operations. My expertise includes analytical softwares, and proficiency in utilizing tools such as Python, SQL, R programming, Databricks and PySpark to deploy machine learning algorithms, data visualization, and business analytics to deliver value and solve business problems.

Satyabrata Pandit is a Diploma CSE student at Brainware University. Her research interests include AI, ML and Social Networking, contributing significantly to advancements in her field.

S. Suresh obtained doctoral degree in Mechanical Engineering from Anna University, Chennai, India, in 2020. Currently, he holds the position of Associate Professor in the Department of Mechanical Engineering at Erode Sengunthar Engineering College, Tamil Nadu, India. He has 12 years of teaching experience and 2 years of industry expertise in his role. His research focuses on friction stir welding of lightweight alloys and additive manufacturing.

Sutapa Shau is a Diploma CSE student at Brainware University. Her research interests include AI, ML and Social Networking, contributing significantly to advancements in her field.

Saptarshi Kumar Sarkar is an Assistant Professor at Brainware University. With a dedication to academic excellence, he brings a wealth of knowledge and experience to his students. His research interests include AI, ML and Social Networking, contributing significantly to advancements in his field.

Index

A

C

D

E

F

G

I

L

M

N

P

S

T

V

Printed in the USA
CPSIA information can be obtained
at www.ICGtesting.com
CBHW081739280924
15048CB00003B/23

9 798369 364079